Jak P Mallmann Showell, naval historian and author, has written over twenty books on the naval operations of the Second World War. He is a respected authority on the U-Boat war and has researched extensively on original documents both here and in Germany.

# FUEHRER CONFERENCES
## ON
# NAVAL AFFAIRS
## *1939–1945*

Foreword by
**Jak P Mallmann Showell**

CHATHAM PUBLISHING

LONDON

STACKPOLE BOOKS

PENNSYLVANIA

Foreword © Jak P Mallmann Showell 1990

This paperback edition first published in Great Britain in 2005 by
Chatham Publishing
Lionel Leventhal Ltd,
Park House, 1 Russell Gardens,
London NW11 9NN

And in North America by
Stackpole Books,
5067 Ritter Road, Mechanicsburg,
PA 17055-6921

First published 1947 by the Admiralty for limited circulation in a series of
typewritten, cyclostyled volumes. Published 1948 as part of *Brassey's Naval Annual*.
New edition published 1990 by Greenhill Books. The original pagination has
been retained.

*British Library Cataloguing in Publication Data*
Fuehrer conferences on naval affairs, 1939–1945
1. Hitler, Adolf, 1889–1945   2. Raeder, Erich, 1876–1960
3. Dönitz, Karl, 1891–   4. Germany. Kriegsmarine – History –
4. World War, 1939–1945   5. World War, 1939–1945 – naval
5. operations, German   6. Naval Strategy
6. 940.5′ 45′ 943

ISBN 1 86176 255 0

Printed and bound in Great Britain by CPD (Wales) Ebbw Vale

# CONTENTS

# CONTENTS

## LIST OF PLANS AND CHARTS

# FOREWORD

On 7 SEPTEMBER 1939, GRAND ADMIRAL DR ERICH RAEDER, COMMANDER-IN-Chief of the German Navy, met with Hitler to discuss the war at sea. It was the first of a long series of meetings between Hitler, who was the Supreme Commander-in-Chief of all Armed Forces, and the head of the Navy. This book is a record of those Fuehrer Conferences on Naval Affairs. The Germans called the meetings 'Situation Reports' and it must be emphasised that they only focussed on topics which Hitler had requested information about or which Raeder considered of sufficient importance to bring to his attention.

Tactical details, urgent requests and news were transmitted from various naval bases and ships at sea to the Supreme Naval Command in Berlin, where the information was filtered before being passed on via telex, radio, telephone or personal messenger to the Supreme Command of the Armed Forces (OKW – Oberkommando der Wehrmacht). Although the distance between the Naval High Command and the Fuehrer's Headquarters increased at certain times during the war, this flow of essential information continued unabated. Admiral Gerhard Wagner, editor of the German edition of this book and a contributor to it, has emphasised the efficiency of this network, pointing out that it was more than a simple information transmission service. Both sides frequently asked for clarification if things were unclear, or for further details. An insight into these messages can be gleaned from the war diaries of the Supreme Naval Command, many of which are available on microfilm from the National Archives and Records Administration of the United States.

A knowledge of the careers and experiences of Hitler's two naval commanders-in-chief as well as the other leading naval officers might add some perspective to the accounts of the conferences. Erich Raeder, Hitler's first naval commander-in-chief, was born on 24 April 1876 in what is now part of Hamburg. After joining the Imperial Navy in April 1894, he sailed to the Far East in the armoured frigate SMS *Deutschland* and afterwards served aboard a number of other ships. The high point of his sea-going duties was a spell as navigation officer of the Imperial Yacht SMS *Hohenzollern*. During the pre-war years he was also a spokesman at the Navy's Information and Press Department, which gave him the opportunity of working closely with Grand Admiral Alfred von Tirpitz as well as with the national and international press. For most of the First World War, Raeder served as Admiralty Staff Officer for the battlecruiser commander Admiral Ritter Franz von Hipper (Commander-in-Chief of Reconnaissance Forces). Shortly before the end of the war, he gained his own command, the light cruiser SMS *Cöln*.

In 1920, Raeder's career suffered a minor set-back when he was wrongly accused of having been connected with the leaders of the Kapp Putsch. During this time, he worked on a study of the role of cruisers in the First

World War, which eventually earned him an honours doctorate from the University of Kiel. From 1922 to 1928 Raeder held the post of Commander-in-Chief of the Baltic Naval Station and, at the same time, he was able to make a positive contribution to the Navy's future as Chief of Staff for naval training and educational establishments. From these positions, Raeder was promoted to Commander-in-Chief of the Navy. He served in this capacity until his resignation in January 1943. His two predecessors, Admiral Paul Behncke (1920–24) and Admiral Hans Zenker (1924–28) were both 54 years old when they were appointed, each serving for four years. On his appointment, Raeder was two years younger and he remained in the office for some fourteen years.

On offering his resignation towards the end of December 1942, during an argument with Hitler regarding a battle off the North Cape, Raeder was asked by Hitler to name two possible successors. He put forward Admiral Rolf Carls as the most suitable candidate, but also suggested Admiral Karl Dönitz, should the Fuehrer wish to emphasise the importance of the U-boat war. The Führer chose Dönitz. Although historians have accepted Dönitz's promotion as the logical course of events, it was quite an extraordinary move. He had very little day-to-day contact with the Supreme Naval Command and lacked the staff experience usually associated with candidates for such high office.

Dönitz was born on 16 September 1891 at Grünau, which is now part of Berlin, and he joined the Imperial Navy in April 1910. He was signals officer aboard the light cruiser *Breslau* when she and the battlecruiser *Goeben* were ordered into the Mediterranean to form the core of Germany's first naval squadron there. During this part of his career, Dönitz was entrusted with some special duties by Admiral Wilhelm Souchon (Commander-in-Chief of the German Mediterranean Naval Squadron). After his return to Germany in 1916, Dönitz went on a crash course for submariners before being thrown into action as first watch officer in *U39*, under the ace commander Walter Forstmann. Later, he was given his own command, the small *UC25*, and from there moved on to the larger *UB68*. He survived its sinking in the Mediterranean, spending the rest of the war in British prisoner-of-war camps.

In 1919, Dönitz was allowed to return to Germany, and served in a number of sea-going and land-based positions, including a brief spell at the War Ministry in Berlin. His most notable achievements, as far as influencing his promotion to U-boat chief in 1936 was concerned, were the commissioning of two new units. First, he brought a torpedo boat half-flotilla into service and then he re-commissioned the light cruiser *Emden*. Her crew had transferred to the pocket battleship *Deutschland* shortly before she went into dock for an extensive refit. Afterwards she was re-commissioned with a new crew.

The growth of the small submarine flotilla under Dönitz, together with his subsequent promotion to Supreme Commander-in-Chief of the Navy, has led many authors to over-estimate his power and influence at the beginning of the Second World War. In my book *U-boat Command and the Battle of the Atlantic* (Conway Maritime Press, London 1989 and Vanwell Publishing Ltd, St Catherines, Ontario, Lewistown and New York 1989) I made the following points:

Karl Dönitz ranks as one of the most misunderstood men of World War II. At the start of the war, he was at the bottom of a long command chain and in what many people considered to have been an undesirable and unimportant position. As Flag Officer for U-boats (Führer der Unterseeboote), he held the rank of Captain and Commodore and was responsible for running a small operational control department. This carried approximately the same authority as a cruiser captain. The real power in submarine command was wielded by the U-boat Division of the Supreme Naval Command in Berlin, with which Dönitz had virtually no contact. The U-boat Division did not seek his opinions and Dönitz did not influence submarine development, construction programmes or naval policies. His isolation can be illustrated by the position of the submarine training flotilla which came under the jurisdiction of the Torpedo Inspectorate, and not under the Flag Officer for U-boats.

Dönitz's promotion to Commander-in-Chief of the Navy brought a fresh approach to naval representation at Hitler's headquarters. Raeder had gone there only when summoned or when urgent matters required him to meet with Hitler, and even then he would usually only attend the Naval Conference. Dönitz, however, felt it was important to keep a finger on the everchanging pulse of war and made considerably greater use of his access to Fuehrer Headquarters, frequently attending other meetings and briefings in addition to the Naval Conferences. This became more difficult as mounting Allied pressure increased the Commander-in-Chief's workload. Therefore, in June 1944, around the time of the Allied landings in Normandy, Rear-Admiral Gerhard Wagner (Chief of the Operations Department with the Naval War Staff) was seconded to represent the Commander-in-Chief of the Navy at a variety of meetings as Admiral on Special Duty. Later, Wagner was part of Admiral Hans-Georg von Friedeburg's delegation which signed the surrender with Field Marshal Montgomery.

Three other officers whose names appear frequently in this book need to be mentioned. First, Karl-Jesko von Puttkamer, the ex-destroyer commander who became liaison officer with the Naval War Staff and then, in October 1939, went on to act as Hitler's Naval Adjutant until the end in 1945. Unfortunately, his private diary was destroyed shortly before the Russian Army occupied Berlin. Then, in order to improve contacts between Hitler and the naval command, in January 1942 a Permanent Naval Representative was appointed to Fuehrer Headquarters. This position was first held by Vice-Admiral Theodor Krancke, who had earlier been Chief of Staff of the Commander of North Sea Security and then became captain of the pocket battleship (later re-classed as a heavy cruiser) *Admiral Scheer* in October 1939. In March 1943, he was succeeded by Vice-Admiral Hans-Erich Voss, who had held a variety of staff appointments and then commanded the heavy cruiser *Prinz Eugen*, from which he moved to Berlin as Krancke's successor. In addition to these three, a number of other naval officers appear regularly throughout this book. These were either adjutants or staff officers who assisted the Commander-in-Chief.

People attending the meetings were usually limited to those listed at the beginning of each section. Even secretaries were excluded. Therefore, this book is not the result of shorthand notes made when people were speaking. Most of the matters discussed were recorded by the Commander-in-Chief on his way back from the conferences, when the notes were either written personally in longhand or dictated before being typed. Considerable importance was attached to the accuracy of the records. Both Raeder and Dönitz studied the finished typescripts, often adding corrections and annotations before signing them. Admiral Gerhard Wagner, in the German edition of this book, makes the point that despite having been written after the meetings, these accounts can still be taken as an accurate record of the Fuehrer Conferences. He also points out that the fact that a topic does not appear in the account does not mean that it was not discussed. Much tactical information was transmitted directly, as has already been discussed, and this information can be found in the war diaries mentioned previously.

When the Allied armies made their final assault on Germany, Hitler ordered all documents to be destroyed and consequently much important material was burned. However, Dönitz took the view that, having conducted a fair war, the German Navy had nothing to hide. So he ordered documents to be preserved. Many log books and vast piles of documents were stored at Tambach Castle near Coburg, where they fell into British and American hands. The material in this book was first sorted, translated and then edited by Anthony Martienssen before being circulated by the British Admiralty in a series of cyclostyled typescript volumes. Later, in 1948, it appeared as part of *Brassey's Naval Annual*. Incidentally, Martienssen also wrote the absorbing book *Hitler and his Admirals* (Secker and Warburg, London 1948).

Following publication of the Fuehrer Conferences in *Brassey's Naval Annual*, the material in this book disappeared into obscurity until the late 1960s when Gerhard Wagner worked on a German edition, published by J F Lehmanns Verlag (Munich) in 1972. It is important to add that the Germans still did not have access to most of their wartime records at this time; thus the German edition is based on Anthony Martienssen's translation rather than German originals. One drawback of Martienssen having produced this book so soon after the war is that the meanings of some German technical terms were still obscure. It might therefore be helpful to give details of the various headquarters and their code-names. When the Naval High Command's headquarters at Tirpitzufer next to the Landwehr Canal in Berlin were bombed out in November 1942, it moved to a new purpose-built bunker, code-named *Bismarck*, at Eberswalde a few kilometres from the city. Shortly after this, the U-boat Staff moved to a similar command bunker, *Koralle*, at Bernau, also a few kilometres outside Berlin. Dönitz commuted between these two and the Fuehrer's Headquarters at the Reichs Chancellery until 22 April 1945, when he evacuated *Koralle* only a few minutes before the first Russian troops arrived. Hitler's southern headquarters were at his house, the Berghof, on the Obersalzberg near Berchtesgaden in Bavaria. *Wolfsschanze* was the code-name for Hitler's headquarters near Rastenburg in East Prussia, *Wolfsschlucht I*, used during June 1940, was located to the north of Charleville in the Ardennes, and *Wolfsschlucht II*, which was used only for a few days in June 1944, was at

Margival near Soissons. Zopport, mentioned at the beginning of the book, is a town to the northwest of Danzig (Gdansk).

Postwar research, especially into such areas as 'Ultra', code-name for information obtained from British deciphering of German top-secret signals via the Enigma coding machine, has produced new insights into the war at sea. This book is therefore useful inasmuch as it was written without hindsight, giving a good impression of what people were thinking at the time the events took place. By providing a unique insight into the heart of German strategy and tactics, *Fuehrer Conferences on Naval Affairs* is an essential work for everyone with a serious interest in the naval side of the Second World War.

JAK P MALLMANN SHOWELL (1990)

# *Preparations*

SHORTLY BEFORE dawn on September 1, 1939, German forces invaded Poland. Preparations for the invasion were begun six months previously, in April—immediately after the occupation of Czechoslovakia and the Anglo-French guarantees to Poland

The operation was called *Fall Weiss* (Case White) and was linked with the general preparations for war—*Grenzsicherung* (Frontier Defence)—and the seizure of Danzig. Keitel issued the directive to each branch of the home Forces on April 3, 1939:

Top Secret
Officer Only

The High Command of the Armed Forces *             Berlin, April 3, 1939

SUBJECT: Directive for the Armed Forces 1939/40         5 Copies
                                                      2nd Copy

The Directive for the Uniform Preparation of War by the Armed Forces for 1939/40 is being re-issued.

Part I (*Grenzsicherung*) and Part III (*Danzig*) will be issued in the middle of April. Their basic principles remain unchanged.

Part II *Fall Weiss* is attached herewith. The signature of the Fuehrer will be appended later.

The Fuehrer has added the following Directives to *Fall Weiss*.

(1) Preparations must be made in such a way that the operation can be carried out at any time from 1.9.39 onwards.

(2) The O.K.W. has been directed to draw up a precise time-table for *Fall Weiss* and to arrange by conferences the synchronised timings between the 3 branches of the Armed Forces.

(3) The plans of the branches of the Armed Forces and the details for the time-table must be submitted to the O.K.W. by 1.5.39.

                                   The Chief of the O.K.W.
                                      (signed) KEITEL

       *         *         *         *         *         *

Hitler's confirmation followed on April 11:

Top Secret
Officer Only

The Supreme Commander of the Armed Forces        Berlin, April 11, 1939

                                                        5 Copies
                                                        2nd Copy

Directive for the Uniform Preparation of War by the Armed Forces 1939/40

I shall lay down in a later directive the future tasks of the Armed Forces and the preparations to be made in accordance with these for the conduct of war.

Until that directive comes into force, the Armed Forces must be prepared for the following eventualities:

I. Safeguarding of the frontiers of the German Reich and protection against surprise air attacks.

II. *Fall Weiss*.

III. The Annexation of Danzig.

Appendix IV contains regulations for the exercise of military authority in East Prussia in the event of a warlike development.

                                   (signed) ADOLF HITLER

* Hereafter referred to by the initials "O.K.W." (Ober Kommando Wehrmacht).

Appendices to the directive amplify the general instructions for *Fall Weiss*: there was to be no declaration of war, and the aim of the operation was "to destroy Polish military strength and to create a situation in the East which satisfies the requirements of defence." Hitler also outlined his policy: "Policy aims at limiting the war to Poland, and this is considered possible in view of the internal crisis in France and consequent British restraint. Should Russia intervene this would imply Poland's destruction by Bolshevism. German military exigencies will determine the attitude of the Baltic States. Hungary is not a certain ally. Italy's attitude is determined by the Berlin-Rome Axis." In spite of much that has been said to the contrary Hitler undoubtedly expected interference from the Western Democracies. On May 10, 1939, he issued another directive to the armed forces:

Top Secret
Officer Only

The Supreme Commander of the Armed Forces          Berlin, May 10, 1939

7 Copies
2nd Copy

SUBJECT: Directive for the Uniform Preparation of War by the Armed Forces, 1939/40

Herewith, as Part VI of the Directive, instructions for the economic war and the protection of our own economy.

The Commanders-in-Chief of the three branches of the Armed Forces will report to the O.K.W. on the measures taken in consequence of these instructions by August 1, 1939.

(signed) ADOLF HITLER.

\*          \*          \*          \*          \*          \*

The enclosure to this directive stated that the Germany Navy and *Luftwaffe* in particular were to make preparations for the immediate opening of economic warfare against Britain, and, as a second priority, against France. These operations were to be started as soon as *Grenzsicherung* (Frontier Defence) was ordered. Special instructions to the Navy followed:

"The Navy is to make its own preparations for the war against British and French merchant shipping. In co-operation with the Foreign Office, the legal and military aspects of the intended form of the war against merchant shipping are to be regularly examined, and co-ordinated with the expected developments. The problems involved are to be tackled in accordance with the existing peace-time political situation, and with regard to possible war-time coalitions of the enemy. The operation areas for the war against merchant shipping, are to be fixed and regularly revised by the C.-in-C., Navy and C.-in-C., *Luftwaffe*. . . . In the event of war with England, apart from single blockade-runners, we cannot count on trade with foreign countries, so that in this case, the tasks of protecting merchant shipping will be limited mainly to the Baltic, and the inshore waters of the North Sea."

Nor were Raeder and his staff blind to the dangers involved in the invasion of Poland and the real nature of Hitler's preparations, but, following Hitler's lead, they hoped that the Polish "incident" would be isolated and that they would have more time before the war against Britain and France began. On May 16, Raeder, in a memorandum to his staff, stated:

"The major aims in building up the German Army continue to be determined by the hostility of the Western democracies. *Fall Weiss* constitutes merely a completion of precautionary preparations, and should on no account be regarded as the fore-runner of a settlement by force of arms with our opponents in the West. The isolation of Poland will be maintained the more readily, even after the outbreak of war, if we succeed in opening the war with heavy blows struck by surprise and followed up by rapid successes."

Hitler knew well the risks he was taking, and the preparations of the *Wehrmacht* were carried out with meticulous care. Every possibility was examined, and as far as their resources would allow, provided against. The final preparation, however, astounded the World. On August 21 Hitler announced a non-aggression pact with Russia to be signed in Moscow on August 23. Thus secured, Hitler was ready to defy Britain and France. He gathered his commanders together at the Obersalzberg on August 22 and outlined his intentions.

Hitler's speech at the Obersalzberg has been variously reported. Some said that he asserted definitely that England and France would not go to war, while others said that Hitler's opinion was that there was no reason for England to defend Poland, that therefore it was probable she would not go to war, but that it was a possibility to be borne in mind. But whatever Hitler's opinion, the danger was all too clear to Raeder and his staff. On August 21 and 24, respectively, the pocket battleships Graf Spee and Deutschland with their attendant supply ships Altmark and Westerwald were sent to waiting positions in the Atlantic. Between August 19 and 21, twenty-one U-boats were also despatched to offensive positions round the British Isles. These may have been precautionary dispositions, but they were also positive indications of the expected war with England. No such dispositions were made during the Munich crisis in September, 1938.

\*      \*      \*      \*      \*      \*

On August 31, 1939, Hitler issued his first order for War:

Top Secret
Officer Only
The Supreme Commander of the Armed Forces          Berlin, August 31, 1939
8 Copies
2nd Copy

### Directive No. 1 for the Conduct of the War

1. Now that all the *political possibilities* of disposing by peaceful means of a situation on the Eastern Frontier which is intolerable for Germany *are exhausted*, I have determined on a *solution by force*.

2. The *attack on Poland* is to be carried out in accordance with the preparations made for *Fall Weiss*, with the alterations which result, where the Army is concerned, from the fact that it has in the meantime almost completed its dispositions. Allotment of tasks and the operational target remain unchanged.

Date of attack—1.9.39.
Time of attack—4.45. (Inserted in red pencil.)

This time also applies to the operations at Gdynia, Bay of Danzig, and the Dirschau Bridge.

3. In the West it is important that the responsibility for the opening of hostilities should rest unequivocally with England and France. At first purely local action should be taken against insignificant frontier violations.

The neutrality assured by us to Holland, Belgium, Luxembourg, and Switzerland should be scrupulously observed. The German *land* frontier in the West is not to be crossed at any point without my express consent. The same applies to warlike actions *at sea* or any which may be so interpreted. *Pencil note: According to this Atlantic U-boats must remain in their waiting positions for the time being.*

Defensive measures on the part of the *Luftwaffe* should at first be confined exclusively to the warding-off of enemy air attacks on the frontier of the Reich. In doing so the frontier of the neutral states should be observed as long as possible when dealing with single aircraft and smaller units. Defensive operations should only be permitted over this neutral territory when, where French and English attacking squadrons are operating over neutral states against German territory in considerable force, air defence in the West is no longer assured. It is of especial importance that the O.K.W. should be informed with the least possible delay of any violation of the neutrality of third States on the part of our opponents in the West.

4. *If England and France open hostilities* against Germany, the task of those sections of the Armed Forces which are operating in the West is to uphold, while conserving their strength as far as possible, those conditions necessary for the successful conclusion of the operations against Poland. Within the scope of this

duty, damage should be done to enemy forces and their economic sources of supply as far as resources allow. *Green Pencil: Warfare against merchant shipping.* In any case I reserve to myself the order to commence *attack* operations.

The Army is holding the West Wall and is making preparations to prevent its being turned—the Western Powers violating Belgian or Dutch territory in doing so. If French forces move into Luxembourg, the frontier bridges may be blown up.

In its warfare on merchant shipping the Navy is to concentrate on England. To intensify the effect of this, a declaration of danger zones is to be expected. The Supreme Command of the Navy is to announce in which sea areas and within what limits danger zones are considered expedient. The wording of a public declaration should be prepared in conjunction with the Foreign Office and should be submitted to me for approval through the Supreme Command of the Navy. The Baltic should be secured against penetration by the enemy. The C.-in-C. of the Navy is to decide whether the approaches to the Baltic should be mined for this purpose.

The primary task of the *Luftwaffe* is to prevent the French and English Air Force operating against the German Army and German *Lebensraum*.

*Red pencil note : General warning.*

In waging war against England preparations should be made for the use of the *Luftwaffe* in causing damage to sea transport, the armament industry and troop transports to France. Full use should be made of favourable opportunities to make an effective attack on massed English naval units, especially on battleships and aircraft carriers. The decision regarding attacks on London rests with me. Attacks on the English motherland should be prepared, bearing in mind that whatever happens inadequate success with part forces is to be avoided.

(signed) A. HITLER.

\*        \*        \*        \*        \*        \*

Three days later the British and French ultimatums expired and war was declared against Germany. At 9 o'clock on the evening of the same day the liner Athenia was torpedoed and sunk without warning some 200 miles due west of the Hebrides. The war at sea had begun.

\*        \*        \*        \*        \*        \*

The development of the German Navy under the Nazi regime was governed by the amount of ship-building German yards could undertake and the type of warfare to be waged. The first factor limited German naval expansion far more than anything else. The London Treaty of 1935 allowed Germany to have a navy of 35 per cent. of British surface warships and 100 per cent. of British submarines, but in spite of this the limitations of the German shipbuilding yards did not permit a navy of such a size to be completed before 1944/45. The beginning of British naval rearmament on December 31, 1936, caused Hitler to issue an order for German naval construction to be speeded up with particular emphasis on U-boats, but though this order did improve matters slightly, the physical difficulties of insufficient yards and factories could not be quickly overcome.

The type of naval warfare that Germany should wage was the subject of considerable controversy. Goering believed implicitly in the *Luftwaffe*, which he boasted would be more than a match for any ship, and Hitler was to some extent swayed by his opinion. The High Command was also "land-minded" and was ignorant of the importance of sea power. Nevertheless, Hitler supported Raeder's plans during the pre-war years and encouraged the building of a surface fleet as well as the development of the U-boat arm. In deciding what ships to build Raeder was guided by Hitler's early contentions that war would not take place with England until at least 1944 or 1945, though trouble with France, Poland, or Russia might be expected sooner. Raeder therefore decided that he had time to build a small balanced fleet which, though not as big as the British fleet, would still be big enough to wage a successful war against Britain's long sea communications. This plan was based on the practical capabilities of German shipbuilding firms, and was modified from time to time in the pre-war years.

In February, 1939, the plan—known as the Z plan—was as follows:

$$8\begin{cases} \text{6 Battleships} & \text{by the end of 1944} \\ \text{4 Heavy cruisers} & ,, \quad ,, \quad 1943 \\ \text{4} \quad ,, \quad ,, & ,, \quad ,, \quad 1945 \end{cases}$$

$$17\begin{cases} \text{4 Light cruisers} & ,, \quad ,, \quad 1944 \\ \text{13} \quad ,, \quad ,, & ,, \quad ,, \quad 1948 \end{cases}$$

$$4\begin{cases} \text{2 Aircraft carriers} & ,, \quad ,, \quad 1941 \\ \text{2} \quad ,, \quad ,, & ,, \quad ,, \quad 1947 \end{cases}$$

$$221\begin{cases} \text{126 U-boats (all types)} & ,, \quad ,, \quad 1943 \\ \text{95} \quad ,, \quad ,, & ,, \quad ,, \quad 1947 \end{cases}$$

(Destroyers, etc., not included.)

---

To these figures should be added the fleet already in being:

$$7\begin{cases} \text{3 Pocket-battleships (Duetschland, Scheer, Graf Spee).} \\ \text{2 Battleships (Gneisenau and Scharnhorst).} \\ \text{2 Battleships completing (Bismarck and Tirpitz).} \end{cases}$$

$$8\begin{cases} \text{7 Cruisers (Hipper, Bluecher, Nuernberg, Leipzig, Koeln,} \\ \qquad \text{Karlsruhe, Koenigsberg).} \\ \text{1 Cruiser completing (Prinz Eugen).} \end{cases}$$

46 U-boats.

---

Eventually the completed Fleet would therefore have been:

  13 Battleships.
  33 Cruisers.
   4 Aircraft carriers.
267 U-boats.
    And a large number of destroyers, auxiliaries, etc.

But the increasing tension in 1939 made it clear that war with England would take place much earlier than the previous forecasts of 1944/45.   Hitler appreciated the unprepared state of the *Wehrmacht*, but fearing the rearmament of other nations he had decided to strike in 1939 rather than later.   This meant a complete revision of the Z plan, and Raeder was forced to postpone all schemes for a balanced fleet. Instead he had to build, and build quickly, a fleet which would be capable of dealing sharp offensive blows against British sea communications, but which would be unsuitable either for major fleet actions or for normal defensive duties (i.e. convoy escort, contraband control, invasion protection, etc.).   For the type of warfare he envisaged U-boats, battleships acting independently as merchant raiders, and armed merchant cruisers would be required.

In the spring of 1939 a priority list was drawn up for the ship construction programme:

(1)  Battleships and U-boats.
(2)  Heavy cruisers.
(3)  Aircraft carriers.
(4)  Light reconnaissance cruisers.
(5)  Destroyers and torpedo boats.
(6)  Minesweepers.
(7)  Auxiliaries.
(8)  Supply ships.

To avoid arousing suspicion the conversion of selected merchant vessels to armed merchant cruisers was to be left until the actual outbreak of war.

By September 1, 1939, the German Fleet consisted of:

2 Battleships (Scharnhorst and Gneisenau).
2 Battleships nearing completion (Bismarck and Tirpitz).
3 Pocket battleships (Graf Spee, Scheer, and Deutschland—later renamed Luetzow).
3 Heavy cruisers (Hipper, Bluecher, and Prinz Eugen completing).
5 Light cruisers (Koenigsberg, Nuernberg, Leipzig, Koeln, Karlsruhe).
57 U-boats.

Training Flotilla:

2 Old battleships (Schlesien and Schleswig-Holstein).
1 Cruiser (Emden).
2 Sailing vessels (Horst Wessel and Gorch Fock).

\*        \*        \*        \*        \*        \*

There were also a fair number of destroyers, motor torpedo boats, minesweepers, etc.
Twenty-six merchant vessels were to be converted to armed merchant cruisers.

\*        \*        \*        \*        \*        \*

With the means at his disposal, therefore, Raeder had to concentrate on the war against British merchant shipping. There was no question of first seeking out and destroying the British Navy and any fleet actions were to be avoided. For the war against merchant shipping the U-boat was an obvious choice of weapon, and on September 3 at a conference with the Naval Staff, Raeder ordered U-boat production to be increased to 20–30 per month. Work on new battleships was to be postponed.

Raeder nevertheless appreciated as well the value of powerful surface ships acting independently against lightly-defended convoys. Their presence would mean a tremendous strain on the British Fleet who would have to increase the convoy escorts accordingly with a consequent decrease in the actual number of convoys. This in itself would considerably affect the flow of supplies to England, and would be almost as efficacious as actual attacks on the convoys.

One other weapon remained—the mine. Here Germany had an initial advantage in the magnetic mine, but only partial success was achieved.

\*        \*        \*        \*        \*        \*

With these limitations Raeder's war plans were:

for *Fall Weiss*:

(a) to blockade Poland;
(b) to mine the approaches to the Baltic;
(c) to destroy the bridge at Dirschau.

for *Grenzsicherung* (i.e. war against Britain and France):

(a) to make dispositions ready for an attack on merchant shipping;
(b) to mine the approaches to the principal English ports.

The dispositions in the Atlantic have already been briefly mentioned. On August 21, the Graf Spee was sent north about the British Isles to her operational area off South America. Her supply ship, the Altmark, was sent a few days earlier. On August 24, the Deutschland was sent to her operational area in the North Atlantic with her supply ship, the Westerwald. Both battleships were to be prepared for a prolonged period at sea. Twenty-one U-boats put to sea between August 19 and 21. Three were kept in the Baltic, while the remaining 18 took up waiting positions to the north and north-west of the British Isles. All ships were ordered to wage war, in the beginning at least, according to the Hague Convention, and particular care was to be taken by U-boat commanders of causing any incidents which might allow a charge of unrestricted submarine warfare being preferred against Germany.

The operational orders to the Deutschland and Graf Spee consisted of several pages of detailed instructions.　The first and third sections are given below:

Top Secret
Officer Only
C.-in-C., Navy. Berlin, August 4, 1939
　(Operations Division, Naval War Staff)

7 Copies

Operational Orders for Deutschland and Admiral Graf Spee

A. *Political Situation.*

(1) The political situation makes it appear possible that, in the event of a conflict with Poland, the Guarantor Powers (England and France) will intervene.　In the event of this, Italy will probably be on our side.

(2) Russia's attitude is uncertain, though at first, it can be assumed that she will remain neutral, but with a definite one-sided leaning towards the Western Powers and Poland.

(3) With the exception of Spain and Japan, no benevolent attitude will be expected from any neutral Power.

(4) We can count on support for our commerce-raiding forces, only from these Powers, and in their harbours.

(5) The neutrality of all neutral States is to be fully respected, if restrictions (e.g. declaration of danger zones) are not specifically laid down by the Naval War Staff.

\*　　　\*　　　\*　　　\*　　　\*　　　\*

C. *Task in the Event of War.*

(7) "Disruption and destruction of enemy merchant shipping by all possible means."

For this the following is ordered:

(*a*) Merchant warfare is, in the beginning, to be waged according to Prize Law.

(*b*) If in the beginning or during the course of the war Germany declares "danger zones" then unrestricted warfare is permitted in these areas.　To avoid attacks from our own U-boats due to mistaken identity, pocket-battleships are to keep out of "danger zones" unless special areas are named.

(*c*) Enemy naval forces, even if inferior, are only to be engaged if it should further the principal task (i.e. war on merchant shipping).

(*d*) Frequent changes of position in the operational areas will create uncertainty and will restrict enemy merchant shipping, even without tangible results.　A temporary departure into distant areas will also add to the uncertainty of the enemy.

(*e*) If the enemy should protect his shipping with superior forces so that direct successes cannot be obtained, then the mere fact that his shipping is so restricted means that we have greatly impaired his supply situation.　Valuable results will also be obtained if the pocket-battleships continue to remain in the convoy area.

(*f*) The enemy is not in a position to carry his complete import requirements in escorted convoys.　Independent ships can therefore be expected.

\*　　　\*　　　\*　　　\*　　　\*　　　\*

Thus, by September 1, 1939, units of the German Navy were at sea and ready to strike at British sea communications.　It was not a large striking force, but it was still big enough to inflict serious damage on British merchant shipping which was at that stage unprepared and unorganised for war.　Doenitz, then Flag Officer commanding U-boats, was pessimistic, however, and sent the following memorandum to Raeder and the Naval Staff on September 1, 1939:

(The memorandum is too long to quote in full, but all the points Doenitz mentioned have been included.)

MEMORANDUM BY ADMIRAL DOENITZ, F.O. U-BOATS.   DATE 1.9.39

## THE BUILDING-UP OF THE U-BOAT ARM

The state of the U-boat arm at the present time of tension, and the impossibility of producing the desired results with the numbers of U-boats now available, make it my duty to express my views on the relevant questions, and draw the necessary inferences.

I. The task of the U-boat arm.—The Navy's principal task in the war, is the struggle with England. The focal point of warfare against England, and the one and only possibility of bringing England to her knees with the forces of our Navy, lies in attacking her sea communications, in the Atlantic. So long as we do not have sufficient numbers of surface forces which are suitable for this task, it will fall chiefly to the U-boat arm.

Even if our surface forces are equal to the task, the U-boat has the decisive advantage that it can reach and remain in operational areas in the Atlantic without support, and does not have to undergo the same dangers as surface forces. I therefore believe that the U-boat will always be the backbone of warfare against England, and of the political pressure on her.

II. Forces required.—The main weapon in the U-boat war against merchant shipping is the torpedo-carrying U-boat. About 90 are required simultaneously in the most important operational area, i.e. in the Atlantic, north of the Equator. In all, about 300 operational U-boats are necessary. (There follows a technical description of the different types of U-boats required.) How do these requirements compare with :

III. The present situation.—Of the 57 U-boats now in commission :

18 U-boats are in the Atlantic.
21    „    are in the North Sea or are intended for use in the North Sea.
10    „    are in the Baltic.
3    „    are not ready for active duties.
4    „    are still undergoing trials.
1    „    U-boat is set aside for A/S experiments.

———

57 U-boats.

———

From a total of 26 U-boats suitable for operational duties in the Atlantic, 18 are in the Atlantic, 3 in the Baltic, 3 still not ready for active duties, and 2 still undergoing trials. . . . At this time all available U-boats were sent out immediately, and no reserves were held back as replacements. In the event of a war, it would therefore very soon become obligatory to reduce greatly the numbers of U-boats on operation, and later increase that number gradually to about one third of the available U-boats. The number of U-boats for the Atlantic would thus be reduced to about 8 or 9. We cannot expect the number of U-boats now on operation to be more than a petty annoyance to British commerce, and we can expect still less from those numbers which will continue to be available. This means that : *At the present moment we are not in the position to play anything like an important part in the war against Britain's commerce.* Can we expect an alteration in this situation in the next few years on the basis of the existing plans?

IV. The development of the situation in the next few years.—I have been informed that in the coming years we shall have the following numbers of U-boats suitable for Atlantic operations :

| | | Type VII b and c, IX | Type XI, XII | |
|---|---|---|---|---|
| Beginning 1940 | .. | 31 | — | |
| „         1941 | .. | 49 | — | |
| „         1942 | .. | 65 | 3 | |
| „         1943 | .. | 81 | 7 | |
| „         1944 | .. | 106 | 10 ⎤ numbers |
| „         1945 | .. | 131 | 13 ⎬ based on |
| End of   1946 | .. | 160 | 18 ⎦ 1944 |

This means that if the required strength as shown in "II" is acknowledged and, if the present building programme is retained, it will be quite impossible for our U-boats to exercise anything approaching an effective pressure on Britain or her commerce within a reasonable space of time.

V. Inferences.—Measures must be taken even beyond the normal planning and existing Naval problems must be put aside, so that the U-boat arm can be brought as soon as possible to such a condition as will enable it to carry out its main task; that is, to defeat England in war.   I nevertheless believe that such decisive measures can be carried out only under suitable conditions.   I am therefore of the opinion that a central control office, with far-reaching powers and directly responsible to the C.-in-C., must be created to deal with all questions relating to the building of the U-boat arm.   I fully realise that the existing development of the U-boat arm after such a long break in U-boat building is an excellent performance, but incisive measures will be necessary in many departments if, in future conflicts with England, we want to stand forth with a really effective U-boat arm.

(signed) DOENITZ.

\*     \*     \*     \*     \*     \*

Doenitz was not alone in his pessimism.   His C.-in-C., Raeder, also viewed the prospect of naval warfare against England with gloomy forebodings, and, on the outbreak of war with England on September 3, 1939, recorded his view of the situation :

Berlin, September 3, 1939

## REFLECTIONS OF THE C.-IN-C., NAVY, ON THE OUTBREAK OF WAR, SEPTEMBER 3, 1939

Today the war against France and England broke out, the war which, according to the Fuehrer's previous assertions, we had no need to expect before about 1944. The Fuehrer believed up to the last minute that it could be avoided, even if this meant postponing a final settlement of the Polish question.   (The Fuehrer made a statement to this effect in the presence of the Cs.-in-C. of the Armed Forces on the Obersalzberg on August 22.)   At the turn of the year 1944–1945, by when, according to the Fuehrer's instructions, the Navy's "Z Plan" would have been completed, Germany could have begun a war against Great Britain with the Navy at the following strength :

For merchant warfare on the high seas :

   3 fast battleships.
   3 converted pocket-battleships.
   5 heavy cruisers.
   Several mine-laying and reconnaissance cruisers.
   2 aircraft carriers.
   About 190 submarines, including about 6 gun submarines, 6 fleet submarines,
      and 6 mine-laying submarines.

Two groups, each consisting of three of the heaviest type Diesel-powered battle-ships equipped with 40-cm. guns, would have had the task of intercepting and destroying the heavy British forces which, more or less dispersed, would pursue the German forces engaged in merchant warfare.   Two ships of the Scharnhorst and two of the Tirpitz class would have remained available in home waters to hold down some of the heavy British ships.   In this way, especially with the co-operation of Japan and Italy, who would have held down a section of the British Fleet, the prospect of defeating the British Fleet and cutting off supplies, in other words of settling the British question conclusively, would have been good.

On September 3, 1939, Germany entered into a war with Great Britain, as the latter—contrary to the Fuehrer's assumption that "England did not *need* to fight on account of the Polish question"—thought it expedient to fight now with the Polish question as a pretext.   Sooner or later, as she saw it she would *have* to fight Germany, and then probably under unfavourable military conditions, i.e. against an expanded German Fleet.   As far as the Navy is concerned, obviously it is in no way very adequately equipped for the great struggle with Great Britain by autumn 1939.   It is true that in the short period since 1935, the date of the Fleet Treaty, it has built up a well-trained, suitably organised submarine arm, of which at the moment about twenty-six boats are capable of operations in the Atlantic; the submarine arm is still much too weak, however, to have any decisive effect on the war.   The surface forces, moreover, are so inferior in number and strength to those of the British Fleet that, even at full strength, they can do no more than show that they know how to die gallantly and thus are willing to create the foundations for later reconstruction.   The pocket battleships—with the outbreak of war only the Deutschland and the Graf Spee are ready for operations in the Atlantic—if skilfully used, should be able to carry out cruiser warfare on the high seas for some time.   The Scharnhorst and the Gneisenau, which are still by no means ready for action or reliable in operation, will have to attempt to hold down enemy battle cruisers in home waters and keep them away from the pocket battleships.   The pocket battleships, however, cannot be decisive for the outcome of the war, either.

(signed)        RAEDER.
(countersigned) ASSMANN.

# *War*

## THE SINKING OF S.S. ATHENIA

IN SPITE of all the precautions of the German Naval Staff to maintain at least the appearance of adhering to the Hague Convention, the passenger liner S.S. Athenia was torpedoed without warning on the night of September 3, 1939. The Athenia was attacked about 200 miles west of the Hebrides. She was unescorted and was sailing from Liverpool to Montreal with passengers and general cargo. H.M.Ss. Electra and Escort, the Norwegian S.S. Knupe Nelson, and the yacht S.S. Southern Cross answered the Athenia's S.O.S. signals and rescued about 1,300 survivors before the Athenia finally sank by the stern at 10.40 on the following day. There were about 100 fatal casualties.

At first the German Naval Staff did not believe the British reports of the sinking. U-boats at that time maintained radio silence and there were no means of immediately checking what had happened. Orders to the U-boat commanders had been quite clear and it was thought that such a breach of discipline was impossible. Doenitz's staff, however, were less certain, and thought that a U-boat might after all have been responsible. The matter was reported to Hitler who, on the advice of the Naval Staff, decided to deny German responsibility, and instead accused Mr. Churchill—then First Lord of the Admiralty—of attempting to engineer atrocity stories against Germany.

The affair was finally solved when the U-boats returned to harbour. It was ascertained that U.30 (Lieutenant Lemp) had sunk the Athenia. Lemp was aware that he had disobeyed instructions, but he pleaded that he was over excited by the sudden declaration of war—he had opened his sealed orders only a few hours before the torpedoing and it was his first act of war. He was severely reprimanded and he and his ship's company were ordered to observe the strictest secrecy. Very few officers were informed of the truth, and even the Naval Staff were kept in ignorance for some time after the event. The information given here was obtained from Admiral Godt who was Chief of Staff to Doenitz at the time. U.30 was paid off in the autumn of 1940, her officers and some of her ratings subsequently commissioning U.110. This U-boat was sunk on May 9, 1941. Lemp did not survive. On September 4 the following signal was sent to all U-boats: "By order of the Fuehrer, on no account are operations to be carried out against passenger steamers, even when under escort." These orders were gradually modified until eventually unrestricted submarine warfare was permitted.

\*　　\*　　\*　　\*　　\*　　\*

In his first war conference with Hitler, Raeder was principally concerned with the political situation. Hitler decided that as soon as he had conquered Poland he would try once more to make peace with the Western democracies, and it was therefore important that hasty action at sea should be avoided.

## CONFERENCE OF THE C.-IN-C., NAVY, WITH THE FUEHRER ON SEPTEMBER 7, 1939

On September 7 the C.-in-C., Navy, had a conference with the Fuehrer on the following problems:

1. In view of the political and military restraint shown by France and the still hesitant conduct of British warfare, the pocket battleships should for the time being withdraw from their operational areas. Furthermore, it seems that British trade is being stopped and British naval forces

are being sent on planned attacks against German merchant raiders.    The risk is thus out of proportion with the chances for success.

2. In view of the political situation, the waiting attitude of France, the generally impartial attitude of the neutral countries, and the fact that the United States, at least outwardly, claims strictest neutrality, the following restrictions should be observed in submarine warfare:

(a) No offensive action should be taken against the French.

(b) Passenger ships should be spared even in convoys.

(c) A part of the submarines should be withdrawn from operations at present to be available later as relief.

3. The views of *the C.-in-C., Navy*, on the political situation:

(a) Great Britain is unable to draw France into the war unconditionally.

(b) France fails to see any war aim and is therefore trying to stay out of the war.

(c) After the collapse of Poland, which can be expected soon, it is possible that France, and perhaps afterwards Great Britain, might be ready to accept to a certain extent the situation which has been created in the East.

(d) Therefore an attack should not be forced and our strength should be saved for the time being.

*The Fuehrer* agrees with the views and measures of the C.-in-C., Navy, and makes the following decisions in addition:

(a) No attempt shall be made to solve the Athenia affair until the submarines return home.

(b) Submarines in the Atlantic are to spare passenger ships and French ships.

(c) The Graf Spee and the Deutschland are to hold back and to withdraw for the present.

General policy: Exercise restraint until the political situation in the West has become clearer, which will take about a week.

\*        \*        \*        \*        \*        \*

As a result of this conference the pocket-battleships were sent to their "waiting" areas—the Deutschland off Greenland in the Denmark Straits, and the Graf Spee off Pernambuco in the South Atlantic—while the U-boats were tightly controlled. French shipping was left severely alone, and French ports were deliberately not mined.    The Polish campaign proceeded according to plan, and on September 17, Russian troops invaded Eastern Poland.    On the same day the aircraft carrier, H.M.S. Courageous, was torpedoed by a U-boat off south-west Ireland.    At this stage of the war Raeder and his staff were chafing at the restrictions Hitler had imposed on naval warfare.    While appreciating the political importance of the "phoney" war, they realised that valuable opportunities were being lost.    The British had already instituted and organised the convoy system and the measures for blockading Germany were quickly gathering momentum.    The commencement of the Northern Patrol and submarine mine barrages added to the German difficulties.    On September 23 Raeder reported to Hitler and endeavoured to modify his views.

## CONFERENCE BETWEEN THE CHIEF, NAVAL STAFF, AND THE FUEHRER ON SEPTEMBER 23, 1939, IN ZOPPOT

Present: General Keitel

After a report on the situation in the Baltic, North Sea, and Atlantic, *the Chief, Naval Staff*, reported the following:

1. The first phase of the submarine war in the Atlantic and the Channel is over. When war broke out, numerous submarines were at sea; a great stream of ships was returning home to England and France; as yet there were no armed merchantmen; defences were not yet fully organised. It is true the submarines sank 232,000 tons of shipping so far, but they are hampered by political restrictions, e.g. no attacks on passenger vessels and no action against French naval and merchant shipping. The later restriction prevents submarine action against the French battleships Dunkerque and Strasbourg, the chief opponents of our pocket battleships; it hampers our operations against the large convoys from North Africa to France, and interferes with effectively harassing British troop transports to France, especially by mining French ports.

The Navy considers the disruption of British transport traffic a special duty. Mines have been laid in the approaches of some of the many possible British ports of departure, such as Weymouth and Dover, but we cannot be sure they are the ones being used. The number of French ports of arrival is smaller, however, and thus easier to deal with—but it is doubtful whether this is true at the *present* stage. At present, moreover, three submarines are operating against the British troop transport traffic, two from the east and one from the west, and they should not be handicapped in their already tremendously difficult task by having to give consideration to possible French ships which may have to be spared.

On the basis of these arguments, *the Fuehrer*, with the agreement of General Keitel, approved lifting the restrictions on the following eight points:

(*a*) Treatment of French battleships and operational aircraft.

(*b*) Attitude toward French warships sailing in convoy or mixed convoy.

(*c*) Attitude toward French merchant ships sailing in convoy, troop transports, etc.

(*d*) Treatment of French merchant ships.

(*e*) Procedure with regard to French goods.

(*f*) Neutral goods (contraband) destined for France.

(*g*) The use of mines off the coast of France.

(*h*) Action against vessels sailing without lights along the English and French coasts, including the Channel and its approaches.

2. The intensification of anti-submarine measures by aircraft and armed merchant vessels will apparently make it impossible to search British merchantmen in the future. *The Fuehrer* approved the proposal that action should be taken without previous warning against enemy merchant ships definitely identified as such (with the exception of unmistakable passenger vessels), since it may be assumed that they are armed. To offset this, a neutral ship should occasionally be treated especially well in order to show that the system has not been fundamentally altered.

3. *The Chief, Naval Staff*, then broached the question of the measures to be adopted *if* the war against France and England has to be fought out to the finish.

(*The Fuehrer* still hopes to drive a wedge between France and England. He intends to make a statement on the political situation to the Commanders-in-Chief within the next two weeks.)

Among the measures discussed are the following:

The expression "submarine warfare" is to be replaced by the expression "war against merchant shipping." The notorious expression "unrestricted submarine warfare" is to be avoided. Instead of this, the proclamation of the "siege of England" is under consideration; such a military system would free us from having to observe any restrictions whatsoever on account of objections based on International Law. It would be up to the Navy and the Air Force to put the siege into effect. If necessary both branches of the Armed Forces could participate, but the Air Force alone may be sufficient. In about two weeks, after discussions with the Foreign Office, there will be more detailed information as a basis for a decision by the Fuehrer.

4. It will be necessary to commit the pocket battleships by about the beginning of October so that their supplies will not be exhausted or their morale undermined. The second large wave of submarines will also be committed at the beginning of October, presumably against convoys west of Spain, coming from the Mediterranean or from around Africa. The protection of merchant shipping by means of convoys is from now on of primary importance to the enemy.

*The Fuehrer* agrees.

5. According to aerial reconnaissance, the Scharnhorst and the Gneisenau have at the moment no opposition even in the northern North Sea (Shetland Islands–Norway); it would be incorrect, therefore, to send them out on a wild goose chase, whereby they would be unnecessarily exposed to submarine attacks while putting in and out of the Belts and the German Bight. They are still greatly in need of training, and this can be carried out in the Baltic Sea. The Hipper has not had sufficient trial runs. These ships are to be committed when enemy resistance by surface forces in the North Sea is strengthened due to our intensive war on merchant shipping in those waters, which is to begin next week, and which will be directed against the steamers sailing between Great Britain and Scandinavia. At the same time they are to divert the attention of the enemy from the operations of the pocket battleships.

6. The submarine construction programme set up within the framework of the Mobilisation Plan, as ordered by the Fuehrer in the conference on September 7, 1939, gives figures which, in the long run, will not keep pace with the anticipated losses. The planned increases are approximately as follows:

> 1939— 7 submarines.
> 1940—46 submarines.
> 1941—10 submarines per month.

In 1918 the Scheer Programme provided for approximately thirty submarines per month. Thus in about two weeks at the latest, when the aforementioned political decision is made, the number of submarines to be constructed must be increased to at least twenty to thirty per month.   This may have to be done at the expense of other branches of the Armed Forces and by cutting construction of everything not absolutely essential to the Navy, e.g. small torpedo boats.

In connection with the Ju88 programme it was revealed in a discussion with *Field Marshal Goering* that the Air Force would not be able to carry out large-scale attacks until the beginning of 1940 at the earliest, and in all probability—and this coincides with the view of the Chief, Naval Staff—not until the autumn of 1940.   It is probable that the defences will then be so strong that any successes against ports and naval craft in port will be almost out of the question.   It will perhaps be possible to lay mines at night, and during the day under smoke cover.   At all events, the entire burden of the war against England during the whole of the first year will rest on the Navy alone, which means on the submarines.

*The Fuehrer* recognises that air attacks on England have more prospects of success at the present stage, even with fewer aircraft, than later with a larger number of planes, as the defences will then be too strong.   The Fuehrer declared that for these reasons, which he fully appreciates, the submarine construction programme must be promoted in every way, even at the expense of the Ju88 programme.

The C.-in-C., Navy, received instructions to investigate the following:

(*a*) What else could be shelved in the Navy (Bismarck, Tirpitz, and the two 10,000-ton cruisers will not yield very much).

(*b*) What the Navy needs in the way of labour and material in order to realise a monthly increase of from 20 to 30 submarines (problem of engines and periscopes).

7. *The Chief, Naval Staff*, raises the question of Russian and Italian co-operation on the following points:

(*a*) Cession of submarines to the German Navy.
(*b*) Equipment of auxiliary cruisers (Murmansk).
(*c*) Permission for German warships to use Russian ports.

*The Fuehrer* will ask the Foreign Minister to clarify these questions on his next visit to Moscow.   The Italians will certainly be very cautious. Japan will presumably keep her promises regarding permission to use Japanese ports and equipment of German ships.

(Handwritten note: *seen by Chief, Naval Staff*.)

\*   \*   \*   \*   \*   \*

The permission to commit the pocket-battleships and to intensify submarine warfare was welcomed by the German Naval Staff.   On September 26, the Deutschland and Graf Spee were ordered to leave their waiting areas and com-mence hostilities against British merchant shipping.

The Deutschland operated in the area between the Azores and the North American coast and by October 15 had sunk 3 merchant ships.   Requiring repairs and a general refit, she then returned to Germany, arriving at Gotenhafen on November 13.

The Graf Spee operated in the South Atlantic between St. Helena and the Brazilian coast, and by October 22 had sunk 5 merchant ships.   Hunted by British cruisers, she headed towards South African waters, rounded the Cape of Good Hope on November 3, and entered the Indian Ocean.   She sank a small British tanker off Portuguese East Africa on November 15, and then returned once more to her

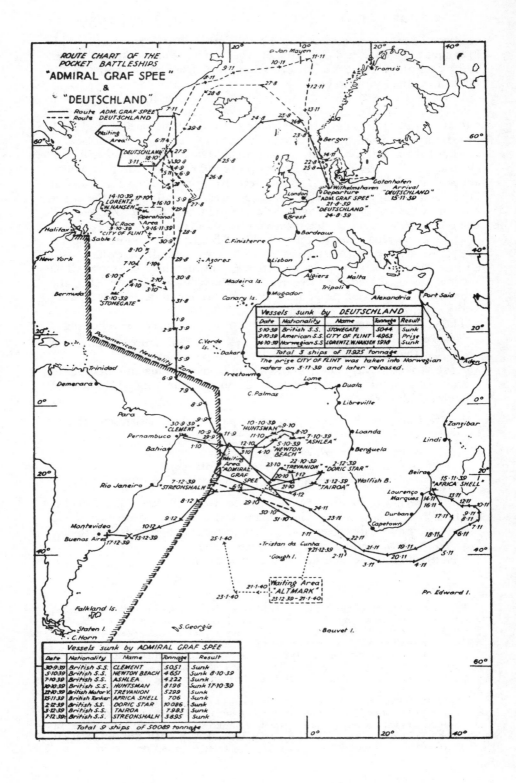

ROUTE CHART OF THE
POCKET BATTLESHIPS
"ADMIRAL GRAF SPEE"
&
"DEUTSCHLAND"

— — — Route ADM. GRAF SPEE
————— Route DEUTSCHLAND

| Vessels sunk by DEUTSCHLAND | | | | |
|---|---|---|---|---|
| Date | Nationality | Name | Tonnage | Result |
| 5·10·39 | British S.S. | STONEGATE | 5044 | Sunk |
| 9·10·39 | American S.S. | CITY OF FLINT | 4963 | Prize |
| 14·10·39 | Norwegian S.S. | LORENTZ W.HANSEN | 1918 | Sunk |
| Total 3 ships of 11,925 tonnage | | | | |

The prize CITY OF FLINT was taken into Norwegian
waters on 3·11·39 and later released.

| Vessels sunk by ADMIRAL GRAF SPEE | | | | |
|---|---|---|---|---|
| Date | Nationality | Name | Tonnage | Result |
| 30·9·39 | British S.S. | CLEMENT | 5051 | Sunk |
| 5·10·39 | British S.S. | NEWTON BEACH | 4651 | Sunk 8·10·39 |
| 7·10·39 | British S.S. | ASHLEA | 4222 | Sunk |
| 10·10·39 | British S.S. | HUNTSMAN | 8196 | Sunk 17·10·39 |
| 22·10·39 | British Motor V. | TREVANION | 5299 | Sunk |
| 15·11·39 | British Tanker | AFRICA SHELL | 706 | Sunk |
| 2·12·39 | British S.S. | DORIC STAR | 10086 | Sunk |
| 3·12·39 | British S.S. | TAIROA | 7983 | Sunk |
| 7·12·39 | British S.S. | STREONSHALH | 3895 | Sunk |
| Total 9 ships of 50,089 tonnage | | | | |

former operating area in the South Atlantic, meeting her supply ship, the Altmark, en route.   The Graf Spee then transferred prisoners, refuelled, and carried out minor repairs.   She began hostilities again on December 2, and sank 3 more merchant ships before she was finally caught and trapped at Montevideo, after 84 days of continuous sea service.   In all she sank 9 merchant ships of 50,000 tons.

\*     \*     \*     \*     \*     \*

On September 27 Warsaw surrendered.   Hitler continued his plan of trying to isolate the Polish "incident" and to declare a temporary peace, or, alternatively, of trying to divide Britain and France.   On October 6 he made overtures for peace with the Western democracies.   Meanwhile Reader had been reviewing German war strategy.   He had no great hopes of England accepting Hitler's offer and was anxious to secure all the advantages possible at this early stage of the war. Appreciating Hitler's policy of maintaining peaceful relations with the neutrals, Raeder realised the importance of partially restricting submarine warfare, but at the same time felt that such restrictions limited the blockade of England.   He therefore evolved the policy of gradually removing these restrictions, but without proclamations or undue excitement.   This policy was accepted.   At his next conference with Hitler, Raeder requested that as the next step in his policy, the remaining restrictions on warfare against British merchant shipping should be lifted ; that special efforts should be made to increase the output of U-boats ; and that bases should be obtained on the Norwegian coast.

The question of Norwegian bases was, at this stage of the war, governed principally by defensive considerations.   If England were to obtain the free use of Norwegian ports, she would be in a position to block the Baltic and the North Sea and thus prevent the movement of German ships into the Atlantic.   The valuable iron ore traffic from Narvik would be stopped, and there was also the possibility of a Swedish alliance with the Allies.   In the event of any of these operations German traffic in the Baltic would be brought to a standstill and the German homeland would become more vulnerable from Allied air attacks.   On the other hand the defence of the long Norwegian coastline was beyond the capabilities of the German Navy and, when previously discussing the problem, Raeder and his staff had decided that it would be best to maintain the status quo— Norway to remain neutral and to guard her own territorial waters.   It was then decided that nothing should be done unless Allied attacks on Norway were imminent.   (A similar decision was made by the Allies when they, too, regarded the strategic position of Norway.   No moves were to be made until there were definite indications that a German attack was to be launched.)   Towards the end of September, however, Raeder became more anxious about Norway.   He feared that the friendliness between Norway and Britain might lead to an offer to Britain to use Norwegian ports, and he decided that Germany would probably have to act.   On October 10 Raeder informed Hitler of the situation, but no decision was made as, in view of the approaching winter, no military operations would be possible for some months.

## REPORT OF THE C.-IN-C., NAVY, TO THE FUEHRER ON OCTOBER 10, 1939, AT 1700

Situation in the Baltic Sea.—War against merchant shipping: The most important factor is to prevent future penetration by British submarines.   It is therefore planned to simplify administration by combining Group East with the Commanding Admiral.

Situation in the North Sea.—During the last few weeks there has been considerable activity by surface forces against merchant shipping in the Kattegat and Skagerrak.   From October 7 to 9 the Gneisenau took part. (The Scharnhorst will not be ready until next week owing to leakage of salt water into the lubricating oil and damage to bearings.)   The Gneisenau moved to Utsire for the purpose of keeping British battle cruisers in the

North Sea and freeing the pocket battleships; she was also to draw British naval forces within the reach of German submarines and aircraft. The latter effect was achieved. *The C.-in-C., Navy*, pointed out that the Gneisenau and the Scharnhorst, operating together, have nothing to fear from the three British battle cruisers, especially as they can withdraw from them if necessary. All-out operations by them, however, are restricted by the fact that they are the only battleships available for protection of the Baltic Sea and the German Bight until the Bismarck and the Tirpitz are ready. *The Fuehrer* definitely agreed with these views.

British cables within reach should be cut. Submarines are no longer to operate against merchant shipping off the Scandinavian coast, in order to prevent sinking Scandinavian merchant ships. The small submarines are to conduct mine warfare off the English east and Scottish west coasts instead, in which direction heavy forces evade us. Mine warfare off Weymouth and the Bristol Channel has achieved successes; evidently the British have no mine-sweeping facilities. Convoys are now the rule. U.35 torpedoed two vessels out of a convoy and U.31 one, operating separately. Eight submarines will operate against convoys next week off the west coast of Spain.

The Deutschland and the Graf Spee, in the Middle and South Atlantic, have reported sinking one British vessel each. Apparently 10,000-ton cruisers were sent against them.

Auxiliary cruisers are being equipped, one in Murmansk. Most of them will go to the Indian Ocean. They will carry mines. The Russians have offered the bay east of Murmansk as a base; this will be investigated.

2. SIEGE OF ENGLAND.—If the war continues this must be carried out at once and with the *greatest intensity*. The Foreign Office, the Ministry of Economics, and the Ministry of Food will be previously notified regarding developments. All objections *must* be overruled. Even the threat of America's entry into the war, which appears certain if the war continues, must *not* give rise to any restrictions. The earlier and the more ruthlessly we commence, the sooner the effect and the shorter the duration of the war. Any restrictions will lengthen the war.

*The Chief of Staff, O.K.W.*, and *the Fuehrer* agree entirely with this.

*The C.-in-C., Navy*, will submit a manifesto.

3. *The C.-in-C., Navy*, reports on the extent of submarine construction within the framework of the mobilisation plan and the large-scale submarine construction plan.

*The Fuehrer* inquires whether it is necessary to complete the Graf Zeppelin. The answer is in the affirmative, as she might be needed to escort the 10,000-ton cruisers out into sea and operate with them, and since trial of *one* such ship is necessary. *The Fuehrer* agrees.

*The C.-in-C., Navy*, emphasises that the submarine construction programme, which is indispensable and of decisive importance for the war against Britain, can be carried out with certainty only by giving it priority over all other programmes. He enumerates the requirements in material, labour, and factory facilities and requests a definite order from the Fuehrer. A draft is submitted. Responsibility is not to fall upon factories, which were completely upset owing to previous procedure. The C.-in-C., Navy, is to submit exact information regarding requirements to the Chief of Staff, O.K.W., and also a breakdown of the output of the various factories to the Fuehrer, who wishes to make suggestions.

*The C.-in-C., Navy*, once again emphasises the necessity of definite concentration on submarines. He declares it necessary to stop the large Krupp expansion, perhaps even to give two assembly lines to Russia. *The Fuehrer* orders that the O.K.W. investigate whether this expansion is not necessary for the Army mortar programme. The consequences for the Navy will be that we cannot lay the keels for all battleships immediately after the end of the war. *The Fuehrer* considers that it would be sufficient in this case, to lay the keels of two battleships.

4. *The Fuehrer* rejects, for political reasons, the proposal to construct submarines in Russia or to buy them from her.

5. *The C.-in-C., Navy*, explains that conquest of the Belgian coast would be of no advantage for submarine warfare. *The Fuehrer* agrees, but emphasises its value for the Air Force. *The C.-in-C., Navy*, points out how important it would be for submarine warfare to obtain bases on the Norwegian coast, e.g. Trondheim, with the help of Russian pressure. *The Fuehrer* will consider this matter.

(signed)      RAEDER.
(countersigned) ASSMANN.

# *"Restricted"* *Submarine* *Warfare*

### (Sinking of H.M.S. Royal Oak.)

ON OCTOBER 12, Mr. Chamberlain rejected Hitler's peace proposals in terms which made it clear that Britain would fight on to the end. German naval expansion was accelerated forthwith, and Raeder began to investigate the possibility of invading Norway. Hitler, even while he was offering peace, had already begun preparations for the invasion of Holland and Belgium—*Fall Gelb* (Case Yellow)— and had issued his first directive on the subject on October 9.

Meanwhile an immediate assault on the British Fleet was planned, and, on October 14, U.47, under the command of Lieutenant Prien, penetrated the defences of Scapa Flow and sank the battleship H.M.S. Royal Oak. The operation was personally planned by Doenitz who selected Prien for the task. A careful survey of Scapa Flow had revealed a weakness in the defences of Holm Sound which was then protected only by three block ships. With careful navigation it would be possible either to pass between the blockships or on either side of them, close to the shore. In his preliminary statement Doenitz wrote: "I hold that a penetration at this point on the surface at the turn of the tide would be possible without further ceremony." The attack was to be made on the night of October 13/14.

The following somewhat dramatic account of the operation is taken from the log of U.47:

*Extract from Log of U.47 (Lieutenant Prien), October 12–October 17, 1939*

12.10.39  Wind SE 7–6, overcast.

During day lay submerged off Orkneys. Surfaced in the evening and came in to the coast in order to fix exact position of ship. From 2200 to 2230 the English are kind enough to switch on all the coastal lights so that I can obtain the most exact fix. . . .

13.10.39.  E. of Orkney Islands.
    Wind NNE 3–4, light clouds, very clear night, Northern Lights on
    entire horizon.

At 0437 lying submerged in 90 metres of water. Rest period for crew. At 1600 general stand-to. After breakfast at 1700, preparations for attack on Scapa Flow. Two torpedoes are placed in rapid loading position before tubes 1 and 2. Explosives brought out in case of necessity of scuttling. Crew's morale splendid. Surfaced at 1915. After warm supper for entire crew, set course for Holm Sound. Everything goes according to plan until 2307, when it is necessary to submerge on sighting a merchant ship just before Rose Ness. I cannot make out the ship in either of the periscopes, in spite of the very clear night and the bright lights. At 2331, surfaced again and entered Holm Sound. Following tide. On nearer approach, the sunken blockship in Skerry Sound is clearly visible, so that at first I believe myself to be already in Kirk Sound, and prepare for work. But the navigator, by means of dead-reckoning, states that the preparations are premature, while I at the same time realise the mistake, for there is only one sunken ship in the straits. By altering course hard to starboard, the imminent danger is averted. A few minutes later, Kirk Sound is clearly visible.

It is a very eerie sight. On land everything is dark, high in the sky are the flickering Northern Lights, so that the bay, surrounded by highish mountains, is directly lit up from above. The blockships lie in the sound, ghostly as the wings of a theatre.

I am now repaid for having learnt the chart beforehand, for the penetration proceeds with unbelievable speed. In the meantime I had decided to pass the blockships on the northern side. On a course of 270 I pass the two-masted schooner, which is lying on a bearing of 315, metres to spare. In the next minute

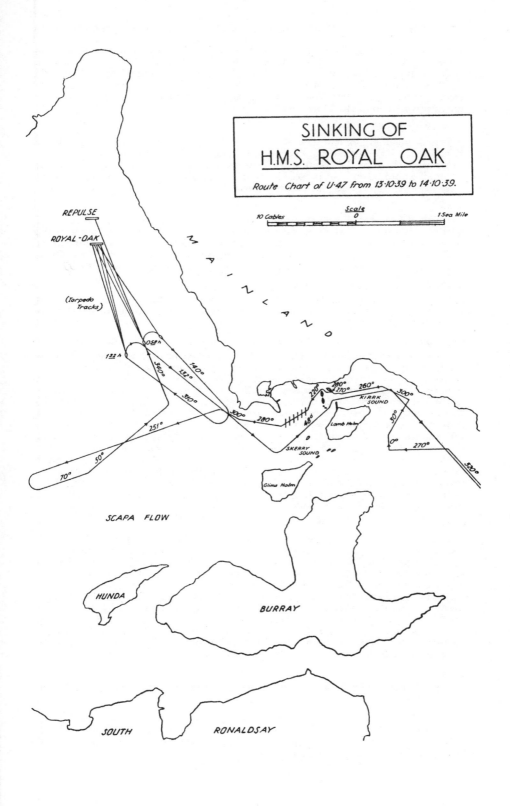

the boat is turned by the current to starboard.   At the same time I recognise the cable of the northern blockship at an angle of 45 degrees ahead.   Port engine stopped, starboard engine slow ahead, and rudder hard to port, the boat slowly touches bottom.   The stern still touches the cable, the boat becomes free, it is pulled round to port, and brought on to course again with difficult rapid manœuvring, but we are in Scapa Flow.

14.10.39.   0027.

It is disgustingly light.   The whole bay is lit up.   To the south of Cava there is nothing.   I go farther in.   To port, I recognise the Hoxa Sound coastguard, to which in the next few minutes the boat must present itself as a target.   In that event all would be lost; at present south of Cava no ships are to be seen, although visibility is extremely good.   Hence decisions:

0055.

South of Cava there is no shipping; so before staking everything on success, all possible precautions must be taken.   Therefore, turn to port is made.   We proceed north by the coast.   Two battleships are lying there at anchor, and further inshore, destroyers.   Cruisers not visible, therefore attack on the big fellows.   Distance apart, 3,000 metres.   Estimated depth, 7·5 metres.   Impact firing.

0116 (*time queried in pencil*, 0058 *suggested*).

One torpedo fixed on the northern ship, two on southern.   After a good 3½ minutes, a torpedo detonates on the northern ship; of the other two nothing is to be seen.   About!

0121 (*queried to* 0102) (*time* 0123 *suggested in pencil*).

Torpedo fired from stern; in the bow two tubes are loaded; *three torpedoes from the bow*.   After three tense minutes comes the detonations on the nearer ship.   There is a loud explosion, roar, and rumbling.   Then come columns of water, followed by columns of fire, and splinters fly through the air.   The harbour springs to life.   Destroyers are lit up, signalling starts on every side, and on land 200 metres away from me cars roar along the roads.   A battleship has been sunk, a second damaged, and the other three torpedoes have gone to blazes.   All the tubes are empty.   I decide to withdraw, because: (1) With my periscopes I cannot conduct night attacks while submerged.   (See experience on entering.)

(2) On a bright night I cannot manœuvre unobserved in a calm sea.   (3) I must assume that I was observed by the driver of a car which stopped opposite us, turned around, and drove off towards Scapa at top speed.   (4) Nor can I go farther north, for there, well hidden from my sight, lie the destroyers which were previously dimly distinguishable.

0128.

At high speed both engines we withdraw.   Everything is simple until we reach Skildaenoy Point.   Then we have more trouble.   It is now low tide, the current is against us.   Engines at slow and dead slow, I attempt to get away.   I must leave by the south through the narrows, because of the depth of the water.   Things are again difficult.   Course, 058, slow—10 knots.   I make no progress.   At high I pass the southern blockship with nothing to spare.   The helmsman does magnificently.   High speed ahead both, finally ¾ speed and full ahead all out.   Free of the blockships—ahead a mole!   Hard over and again about, and at 0215 we are once more outside.   A pity that only one was destroyed.   The torpedo misses I explain as due to faults of course, speed, and drift.   In tube 4, a misfire.   The crew behaved splendidly throughout the operation. . . .

0215.

Set SE course for base.   I still have 5 torpedoes for possible attacks on merchantmen.

0630   57° 58′ N.
       01° 03′ W.

Lay submerged.   The glow from Scapa is still visible for a long time.   Apparently they are still dropping depth charges.

1935   ENE 3–4, light clouds, occasional rain, visibility bad towards land, otherwise good.

Off again, course 180°.   This course was chosen in the hope that we might perhaps catch a ship inshore, and to avoid U.20.

15.10.39   0600   56° 20′ N.
            0° 40′ W.

Submerged and lay at 72 metres.   From 1000 onwards, depth charges were dropped from time to time in the distance.   Thirty-two depth charges were definitely counted.   So I lie low, submerged, until dusk.

1823   Wind NE 5, sea 4, swell from E, cloudy, visibility good.

Surfaced.   On surfacing, Norwegian steamer Meteor lies ahead.   W/T traffic from the steamer is reported in error from the W/T office; I therefore fire a salvo far ahead of the steamer which is already stopped.   The steamer is destined for Newcastle-on-Tyne, with 238 passengers.   Steamer immediately allowed to proceed.   It is reported later by the W/T office that the steamer did not make any signals.

16.10.39   0702   54° 57′ N.
            2° 58′ E.
            Wind NNW 2–2, visibility good.

General course, 180°.   Submerged on the Dogger Bank.   Three drifting mines sighted, 54° 58′ N, 2° 56′ E.   No measures taken, owing to the proximity of fishing vessels.   Proceeded submerged throughout the day.

1856   54° 51′ N.
       3° 21′ E.
       Wind NW 2, light clouds, visibility good.

Surfaced.   Course 128°.   Steered course of 128° into Channel 1.

17.10.39   0404.

Channel 1 passed.   From 0404 to 0447 chased fishing vessel escort ship No. 808 ; gave recognition signal eight times—no reply received.   This fool did not react until V/S was used at a distance of 500–600 metres.   With such guardships, an incident such as my operation could occur in our waters also.

1100   Entered port Wilhelmshaven III.

1144   Made fast.

1530   Crew flown to Kiel and Berlin.

The success of this operation considerably enhanced Hitler's opinion of the German Navy.   Raeder reported on the operation on October 16, and at the same time obtained virtual permission for unrestricted naval warfare against British and French merchant shipping.

## REPORT OF THE C.-IN-C., NAVY, TO THE FUEHRER ON OCTOBER 16, 1939

Also present: General Jodl.

1. A report is made regarding the operation by U.47 in Scapa Flow. The Commander of Submarines is promoted to Admiral Commanding Submarines.   The commanding officer is to come to Berlin to report and to receive the Knight's Cross.

2. The Fuehrer is given a memorandum, following which a report is made regarding the intensification of naval warfare.   *The Fuehrer* grants permission for the following measures:

(*a*) All merchant ships definitely recognised as enemy (British or French) can be torpedoed without warning.

(b) Passenger ships in convoy can be torpedoed a short while after notice has been given of the intention to do so. (*The C.-in-C., Navy,* points out that passenger steamers are already being torpedoed when they are proceeding without lights.)

(c) The Italian, Russian, Spanish, and Japanese Governments should be requested to declare that they will carry no contraband goods, otherwise they will be treated as other neutral nations. (Proceedings to this effect are under way.)

3. *The C.-in-C., Navy* reports that the Russians have placed at our disposal a well-situated base west of Murmansk A repair ship is to be stationed there.

(signed)        RAEDER.
(countersigned) ASSMANN.

*     *     *     *     *     *

In his efforts to intensify the war against Britain, Raeder lacked adequate support both from the civil administration and from the other two Services. He was more aware of Britain's power and resources than other members of the High Command who had been somewhat lulled by the "phoney" war. Raeder thought that as soon as Britain had mustered her strength she would wage war ruthlessly and must inevitably overwhelm Germany's sea power. Under the guise of "Economic Warfare," therefore, Raeder endeavoured to organise a more effective assault on Britain, and at his next conference with Hitler read a lengthy memorandum on the subject. This memorandum outlined three "mainstays" of economic warfare:

"(a) Politics (and propaganda).
(b) Economy (and finance).
(c) Armed Forces (and sabotage)."

To exert political pressure Germany should weaken the enemy economy, promote their own economy, create a united front of neutrals against the enemy, cause the financial isolation and cultural boycott of the enemy and cripple enemy production by the support of strike movements. Purely economic measures should be to prevent entirely all commercial traffic of neutrals or allies with Britain and France, and to reorganise German trade relations in Europe in order to establish a German war economy which would be capable of supporting war indefinitely. Military measures should consist of the proper co-ordination of all three branches of the *Wehrmacht*—particularly between the *Luftwaffe* and the Navy—for the destruction of enemy industries, commercial centres, bases, and trade communications by land and sea. The memorandum stated: "It (i.e. Economic warfare) will result in a completely New Order in European trade relations and this must serve to bring the German and neutral interests of the entire European area into harmony. This New Order should not be considered as an emergency measure for the duration of the war only, but as a permanent institution." The memorandum was in fact a summary of Hitler's own ideas, but Raeder used it to drive home to Hitler the necessity for intensifying the war at sea and for closer co-operation between the Services, if his (Hitler's), ideas were to be carried out.

Raeder's efforts were successful, and Hitler's order directing the formation of an inter-service and departmental committee for "Economic Warfare" is given as an appendix to the conference.

**REPORT OF THE C.-IN-C., NAVY, TO THE FUEHRER ON OCTOBER 23, 1939**

Also present: General Keitel.

1. On October 16 the C.-in-C., Navy, gave a report on the methods used by the Navy in carrying out economic warfare, and showed how it

would be possible to intensify the war against merchant shipping. As the Navy is the branch of the Armed Forces most closely connected with economic warfare, *the C.-in-C., Navy*, begged leave to report on the opinion of the Naval Staff on the significance of economic warfare and the necessity that it be organised under strict control. *The Fuehrer* is in agreement and fully appreciates the significance of economic warfare apart from purely military warfare. British pressure is decisive in Belgium and Holland; Germany cannot exert pressure on these countries unless she occupies them. Pressure on the northern countries is easier to exert. The Fuehrer will give his full authority for carrying out the necessary measures.

2. *The C.-in-C., Navy*, requests that the Deutschland be left in the Atlantic, contrary to the wish recently expressed by the Fuehrer that owing to her name she should be recalled as her possible loss might be taken as a bad omen by the people. The return voyage would be more dangerous than staying in the Atlantic. If worth-while results have been achieved, she might return when the nights are long.

*The Fuehrer* agrees.

3. The Fuehrer has been informed of the plan to allow as many neutral ships as possible to pass through the Kiel Canal in order to have better control over them. *The Fuehrer* warns against sabotage. Steamers carrying cement are not to be allowed passage.

4. The attack by He115's in the coastal waters off southern England resulted in the loss of four aircraft; this area therefore appears unsuitable for attacks. *The C.-in-C., Navy*, declares that conclusions have already been drawn from this experience, namely, that the anti-aircraft defences are apparently very strong along the southern part of the coast of England. The C.-in-C., Navy, asks that no measures be taken as rumoured—for instance, that combined operations over the sea are being considered—for it is absolutely necessary to train and operate naval aircraft in closest co-operation with naval forces. *The Fuehrer* declares that there is no question of such measures.

> (signed)      RAEDER.
> (countersigned) ASSMANN.

### APPENDIX: ECONOMIC WARFARE

Berlin, October 23, 1939

The Fuehrer,
    Supreme Commander of the Armed Forces.

The war against merchant shipping and all other measures for attacking the economic installations, resources, and trade connections of the enemy nations are to be directed uniformly by the O.K.W. according to my orders. The Chief of Staff, O.K.W., will appoint a staff for the comprehensive treatment of the problems arising therefrom and for preparation of my decisions. The Deputy for the Four Years' Plan, the Foreign Minister, the Deputy for the German Economy, and the Commanders-in-Chief of the branches of the Armed Forces will be represented on this staff. The Chief of Staff, O.K.W., will issue the necessary orders for carrying out these plans.

> (signed) ADOLF HITLER.

*Handwritten note.*—On the basis of this order of the Fuehrer, Admiral Schuster is appointed Chief of the Special Staff for Economic Warfare in the O.K.W.   Captain von Weichold is to be Chief of Staff.

*       *       *       *       *       *

Raeder now began to press for the relaxation of restrictions on the sinking of neutral vessels trading with Britain and France.   He had previously put forward the legal quibble that a declaration of the "Siege of England" would enable measures against neutral shipping to be taken without violating International Law.   Hitler was adamant, however, and insisted that there should be no incidents with neutrals until he was ready to strike on land.   The operations of the Deutschland worried Hitler, as, due to her name, the loss of the ship would have serious repercussions in Germany.   As soon as she arrived back her name was to be changed to Luetzow.   These two questions and the problem of the submarine construction programme were discussed at the next conference with Hitler.

(Only Raeder's rough notes are available for this conference.)

Berlin, November 1, 1939

Commander-in-Chief of the Navy.

### Conference Notes

1. The Scharnhorst and the Gneisenau are to be ready for action throughout November and then from January 1, 1940, on; in the intervening period they will be docked for repairs.   The pocket battleship Graf Spee has reported her intention to break through into home waters in January 1940 for engine overhaul.

*The Fuehrer* has repeatedly emphasised the fact that the Deutschland should be recalled because of her name.   In the North Atlantic the pressure from British forces is increasing, and in the long run evasion is far more difficult there than in the South Atlantic, the Indian Ocean, or the Pacific.   It appears correct, therefore, to recall the Deutschland in November, while the nights are dark and the battleships are ready for action (November 12 to 19).   It would be wrong, though, to undertake any offensive action with the battleships during the time of the breakthrough, as this would merely lead to a concentration of British forces in the northern North Sea.   It is important, on the other hand, for air reconnaissance to operate as far out to sea as possible; the Deutschland must pass through the main channels by night and unexpectedly.   Submarine escort must be sent out at the last moment.   The battleships, cruisers, and destroyers must remain in full readiness.   Submarines are to provide protection in a flanking position.   The return of the Deutschland must be kept secret as long as possible; the impression must be given rather that the pocket battleship is continuing operations in the North Atlantic to relieve the Graf Spee.

In accordance with the wishes of the Fuehrer, the Deutschland is to be named Luetzow on her return.   (The Luetzow is to be placed at the disposal of the Russians.)

So as not to complicate matters, the Westerwald is not to return with the Deutschland.   She will receive instructions later.

On October 22 the Graf Spee was told to consider proceeding unexpectedly far into the Indian Ocean, should enemy pressure in the South Atlantic become stronger.   In my opinion renewed operations by pocket battleships are possible only if Italy enters the war and British Mediterranean forces, at present operating on the high seas, are held down in the Mediterranean.

2. At present, submarine warfare against enemy shipping has been intensified as much as possible.   Even passenger vessels proceeding without lights and in convoy may be torpedoed without warning.   All that is lacking now is the declaration of a state of siege against England, in which case neutral ships could also be torpedoed without previous warning once the neutral states have been notified.   As a result of consultations, the C.-in-C., Air, will give orders for action to be taken without warning by the Air Force against merchant ships sailing in convoy.   This is entirely in accordance with international law.   The moment for the declaration of a state of siege will depend on the political developments in the near future and on the time and nature of Army operations.   Should these violate the neutrality of neutral states, then the appropriate moment for the most drastic measures on the part of the Navy has also come.

3. The submarine construction programme has not yet been given priority by the Fuehrer, as the replenishment of Army equipment and ammunition supplies is of prime concern at the moment.   The extensive construction programme is not possible with the present allocation of steel, metals, and labour.   The question will be reconsidered in December.   In order to carry out the large-scale submarine programme, continuous pressure will be necessary.

(signed)         RAEDER.<br>(countersigned) ASSMANN.

\*         \*         \*         \*         \*

Raeder again presented arguments for increasing the war on merchant shipping.

### REPORT OF THE C.-IN-C., NAVY, TO THE FUEHRER ON NOVEMBER 10, 1939

Also present:  General Keitel.
              Lt.-Commander von Puttkamer.

1. The situation in the Baltic Sea and the North Sea; negotiations with Sweden on the question of the three-mile limit; the plan to close the southern part of the Belts in friendly agreement with Denmark.

2. Mine-laying operations off the English Coast.—Charts showing the main barriers and the successes so far are examined.   Further plans are discussed.

3. Submarine warfare.—Recent developments.   Six submarines are known to have been lost up to now.   That means that the replacements which should still be delivered in 1939 have already been exhausted.   New instructions from the Admiral Commanding Submarines and lessons from previous experience give rise to the hope that losses will decrease.   The question is raised whether the proclamation concerning the intensification of submarine warfare should be made to the neutral countries simultaneously with the beginning of a land offensive, so that any protests will coincide with other and possibly sharper protests on the part of the neutrals, thus attracting less attention in the world.   *The C.-in-C., Navy,* suggests putting off the proclamation for the time being, and instead continuing

gradual intensification step by step. Such a statement is at the present time all the more unnecessary as the Americans have of their own accord declared a closed area around England and France for their ships, and thus clashes with the strongest neutral are eliminated. As the next step the C.-in-C., Navy, suggests sinking enemy passenger ships without previous warning. These are often heavily armed, transport troops, and carry valuable contraband. These vessels are known to be armed; there are photographs proving it. *The Fuehrer* agrees, provided that the names of the large ships concerned are made known previously and it is stated that they were being used as auxiliary cruisers and troop transport vessels.

As a later step *the C.-in-C., Navy*, suggests sinking without warning neutral ships which we definitely know are loaded with contraband, and whose points of departure, times of sailing, and routes are known to us, e.g. Greek ships. The proposal of the C.-in-C.; Navy, will be brought up for consideration as soon as there is any change in the attitude of neutral countries, for example, in the event of an offensive. The policy of not molesting ships belonging to friendly nations, i.e. Italy, Japan, Russia, and Spain, is to be continued in the future. Intelligence and control organisations are to be set up in neutral ports.

4. *Political items.*

*Italy.*—If it is taken for granted that Italy will enter the war reasonably soon, should the most important military secrets (torpedoes and mines) be surrendered to them? The C.-in-C., Navy, suggests not until Italy actually enters the war.

*The Fuehrer* is of the same opinion.

*Russia.*—Negotiations are proceeding satisfactorily; however, deliveries of ship's equipment cannot be made at the expense of Armed Forces quotas. *The Fuehrer* and *Chief of Staff, O.K.W.*, state that such deliveries are to be made only from export quotas.

*Japan.*—In answer to the statement of the C.-in-C., Navy, the Japanese Naval Attaché has reported the following from the Japanese Admiralty: Japan will not enter the European war, but the Japanese Navy will support the German Navy in accordance with the negotiations of 1938. Germany is asked to make definite requests soon. *The C.-in-C., Navy*, suggests requesting that German auxiliary cruisers and submarines be permitted to put into Japanese bases, and also that Japan cede to Germany several submarines for warfare against Great Britain in Eastern Asia. *The Fuehrer* agrees.

*The United States.*—The City of Flint case has been mismanaged, as the result of the behaviour of the boarding officer who put into port at Tromsoe and Murmansk, but above all owing to the fact that the Vice-Consul stopped the prize at Haugesund. As matters stand at present, it appears advisable to allow the City of Flint to return to the United States unmolested, as the United States desires to avoid entanglements by declaring its own closed areas, and nothing is to be gained by reconfiscation. Submarines are deployed as required in case confiscation is desired. *The Fuehrer* agrees with the C.-in-C., Navy; no further action is to be taken against the City of Flint.

5. The situation regarding the Deutschland and the Graf Spee and future plans for these ships are discussed.

6. *The Fuehrer* asks the C.-in-C., Navy, whether the Navy has any particular wishes in connection with bases on the Dutch-Belgian coast.

*The C.-in-C., Navy*, replies in the negative, as the bases lie too close to the coast of England and are therefore impracticable as submarine bases. If Den Helder were occupied it could be of occasional use as a base for light forces, although this would shorten the route to the English coast but little as compared with that from Borkum and Emden. The occupation of the Belgian and northern French ports is of importance only if British troop transports were thereby diverted farther to the south and so more exposed to German countermeasures at sea such as submarines and mines.

*General Keitel* points out that it might be necessary to safeguard Belgian ports by means of coastal batteries.

### REPORT OF THE C.-IN-C., NAVY, TO THE FUEHRER ON NOVEMBER 22, 1939, AT 1500

Also present: General Keitel.
Lt.-Commander von Puttkamer.

1. *Baltic.*—Agreement with Denmark and Sweden concerning the closing of territorial waters in the southern approaches of the Belts and the Sound. Attacks by Swedish patrol forces on German naval forces engaged in the war against merchant shipping in the Sound and the Aland Sea. *The Fuehrer* is in favour of drastic measures.

2. *North Sea.*—Mining operations by destroyers; good results. Destroyers laid 540 mines off the Thames and the Humber. Submarines laid mines on the east and the west coasts. Up to now submarines have laid 150 mines. In three nights planes laid 17 mines in the Thames, 24 off Harwich, and 36 in the Humber. Direct and indirect effects of mine barrages are discussed: they are a strong deterrent to neutrals, and incoming traffic is delayed and diverted. Freight rates and insurance premiums are going up.

3. Losses of enemy and neutral merchant shipping from November 8 to 21, 1939, are reported as follows:

| | | | |
|---|---|---|---|
| As a result of submarines .. | 16 ships | (9 British) | 48,195 tons. |
| ,, ,, ,, mines .. | 18 ,, | (8 British) | 66,150 ,, |
| ,, ,, ,, pocket battleship | 1 ,, | (1 British) | 780 ,, |
| | 35 ,, | (18 British) | 115,125 ,, |
| As a result of submarines or mines, not yet confirmed .. | 10 ,, | | 52,626 ,, |
| Total .. | 45 ,, | | 167,751 ,, |

4. The suggestion is made to declare a mine area on the north-west coast of Britain on December 1, 1939. *The Fuehrer* agrees.

5. The C.-in-C., Navy, inquires about future political and military developments to justify a further intensification of submarine warfare. *The Fuehrer* remarks that the coming offensive will give rise to protests from the enemy and neutrals alike; nevertheless it is to be carried out with the utmost intensity as soon as the weather permits. It must be decided after the beginning of the offensive whether the naval war is then to be intensified.

6. The return of the Deutschland and the Graf Spee are discussed. The Luetzow (ex-Deutschland) is to be sent out again in January. Auxiliary cruisers are to be sent out.

7. Operations of the Gneisenau and the Scharnhorst are detailed for November 21 to 27, 1939.*

8. Economic warfare.—It will probably be necessary to call off the German-Danish agreement, because Denmark is supplying food-stuffs to Britain; further, if Britain takes action against German exports in neutral ships, appropriate action will be taken against British exports, for example, export of coal to Scandinavia and Denmark. In this way our export of coal to these countries would be promoted, which would, to some extent, counterbalance Britain's action. *The Fuehrer* agrees to this. If necessary, these steps may be taken without further consultations with him. The Chief of Staff, O.K.W., asks that this question be referred to Admiral Schuster for investigation. The C.-in-C., Navy, concurs.

9. A survey of the planned submarine construction programme is given by the C.-in-C., Navy, who points out, however, that this programme can be carried out on the scale necessary only if the demands for material, facilities, and labour are fulfilled. The O.K.W. agreed to renew inquiry into this matter in December.

10. *The C.-in-C., Navy*, remarks that owing to their great inferiority, the naval forces are dependent to an enormous degree on adequate expansion of the naval air forces. Up to now this has not been approved to the extent agreed upon by the C.-in-C., Air, as regards the numbers of units and types. Negotiations are still in progress. The C.-in-C., Navy, requests the Fuehrer's support now, in case justified demands are not fulfilled.

11. It may be expected that Japan will agree to let Germany have submarines and to permit using Japanese bases. Italy will be asked for submarines once more as soon as her attitude is clarified. It seems to be crystallising by degrees, as witnessed by the note to Britain concerning the molesting of Italian merchant ships. Esthonia and Latvia cannot be asked for submarines, as Russia could easily take this to be an encroachment on her sphere of interest. The Chief of Staff, O.K.W., again advocates getting submarines from Russia. *The Fuehrer* once again refuses, as he is convinced that the Russian ships are in poor condition and that the Russians, who, moreover, must not be allowed to see any of our weaknesses, would in no case consent to give us submarines.

12. *The Fuehrer* gives permission for a press release on mine warfare.

(signed)      RAEDER<br>(countersigned) ASSMANN.

## APPENDIX I

### DECLARATION OF A MINED AREA OFF SCOTLAND

I. Plan.—For the purpose of effectively paralysing traffic proceeding to the east coast of Britain, it is intended to declare a mined area off the Scottish coast. In this area our own submarines will be able to sink

---

* These operations involved on short sortie into the North Atlantic in which the armed merchant cruiser, H.M.S. Rawalpindi, was sunk after a gallant and spirited action against overwhelming odds on November 23.

ships without warning, and it will appear that they struck a mine. The declaration of this mined area is ostensibly purely a preliminary measure for the purpose of combatting enemy military operations, and not of disrupting neutral shipping. It is planned to extend the area southwards up to the British declared area soon after our first announcement.

II. Execution of the plan.—On December 1, 1939, the following announcement will be made by radio as a warning for shipping: "The German Government hereby gives warning that, in the course of operations against British forces and bases on the east coast of Britain, mines have been laid in an area bounded on the north by the latitude of Kinnaird's Head up to 0° 30′ W, on the south by the latitude of St. Abb's Head up to 1° 30′ W, and on the east by the line connecting the above points." Mines will not actually be laid there at present. The Admiral Commanding Submarines will be given permission to operate accordingly beginning December 2, 1939. The submarines are to keep out of sight in accordance with the principle of the plan.

### APPENDIX II

### SURVEY OF THE PLANNED SUBMARINE CONSTRUCTION PROGRAMME

| Date | Additional submarines | Total submarines at beginning of month | Submarines withdrawn for training purposes | Boats at disposal of Com. Admiral Submarines | Boats operating against enemy | 10 per cent. loss | Total submarines at end of month |
|------|------|------|------|------|------|------|------|
| Nov. 39 | 1 | 57 | 12 | 45 | 15 | 5 | 52 |
| Jan. 40 | 2 | 52 | 18 | 34 | 11 | 3 | 49 |
| April 40 | 3 | 51 | 24 | 27 | 9 | 3 | 48 |
| July 40 | 5 | 51 | 37 | 14 | 5 | 1 | 50 |
| Oct. 40 | 6 | 63 | 42 | 21 | 7 | 2 | 61 |
| Jan. 41 | 13 | 88 | 55 | 33 | 11 | 3 | 85 |
| April 41 | 18 | 113 | 55 | 58 | 19 | 6 | 107 |
| Oct. 41 | 26 | 191 | 75 | 116 | 39 | 12 | 179 |
| Mar. 42 | 27 | 253 | 75 | 191 | 64 | 19 | 245 |
| Oct. 42 | 29 | 312 | 75 | 237 | 79 | 24 | 288 |
| Mar. 43 | 29 | 334 | 75 | 259 | 86 | 26 | 308 |
| July 43 | 29 | 347 | 75 | 277 | 91 | 27 | 320 |

# *"The Siege of England"*

THE POLITICAL situation in Europe by the end of November was still relatively fluid. Neutrals were uneasy but determined to remain neutral as long as possible, while the belligerents appeared unwilling to proceed with "total" war. In reality feverish preparations were being made by both sides, and as Hitler was completing his plans for the invasion of the Low Countries, so were the Allies busily building up their armaments and gearing their large industrial resources to the requirements of war. On November 25 Raeder presented the following survey of political developments to senior officers of his staff:

## OUTLINE FOR THE CONFERENCE OF DEPARTMENT HEADS ON NOVEMBER 25, 1939

Information about the most important developments in the international situation. Evaluation of the military strength of our western enemies and the Fuehrer's decisions in view of the over-all situation. This information is only for present company. It may not be communicated to lower departments.

1. *Russia.*—She is at present not capable of action and, as long as Stalin is in power, it is certain that she will adhere strictly to the pact made. It is not expected that there will be any great activity against Britain, Turkey, etc. Extension of her zone of interest in Persia (Persian Gulf) is possible, and will be supported by German foreign policy. Her political attitude may change after years of building up her internal strength, particularly if Stalin is overthrown or dies.

2. *Italy.*—The Duce is adhering to his plan of building up a large Roman Empire. As soon as Germany's military situation appears more favourable, it is expected that Italy will come in actively on the side of Germany. The only followers of this policy are the Duce and his Fascists. The royal family with their followers are opposed. If the Duce should die, a change in policy and an anti-German attitude may be expected.

3. *Scandinavian Countries.*—They are at present neutral under German-Russian pressure. The socialistic parliamentary governments in these countries are in themselves enemies of National Socialism. If Germany's situation deteriorates, their attitude may be expected to alter.

4. *Countries in the South-eastern Area.*—They are neutral under Russian pressure, and are also willing to co-operate economically to a large extent. The attitude of Yugoslavia is determined by that of Italy.

5. *Holland-Belgium.*—With the exception of the Flemish section of the population, there are strong sympathies for the Western Powers. They are at present strictly neutral under German pressure. If the military strength of Britain and France increases and if Germany's position deteriorates, their neutral attitude can definitely be expected to change in favour of the Western Powers.

6. *Great Britain.*—She is determined on a war of extermination against Germany. At present she is not sufficiently armed. The Army is not yet appreciable in numbers, is insufficiently trained, and has no modern

equipment. The Navy is capable only to a limited extent of maintaining supply routes from overseas, since it was disarmed considerably after the last war. Expansion of the fleet is not practically possible until 1941. The Air Force, including the French Air Force, is at present inferior to the German Air Force offensively as well as defensively.

7. *France.*—She has a fairly well-trained army (nine month's training), but it is not equipped for modern warfare. Guns and ammunition are for the most part still from supplies of the last war. The Navy has been built up to a fair strength for the protection of overseas possessions. Both Western Powers may be expected to increase their strength soon with equipment from overseas. In one to two years they will be equal to Germany in armament.

8. Conclusions.—At present there is definite military superiority on the part of Germany. Germany has no military obligations in the East. For the first time in fifty years a war on one front is possible. If Germany takes a defensive attitude, her situation will gradually deteriorate not only from the military point of view, but also in foreign policy. Victory can be achieved by offensive action alone.

9. Decision.—By means of offensive action in the west and an advance into the area of the French Channel coast, we must seek to obtain favourable strategic bases for an offensive war against Britain by submarines, mines, and aircraft. By extending the north German front to the west, the Ruhr—the "Achilles heel" of the armament industry, can be defended. Neutrality questions are irrelevant in case of victory.

10. The Fuehrer expresses his special appreciation of German naval warfare.

*       *       *       *       *       *

Meanwhile, as a reprisal for the German use of magnetic mines (first laid on November 18) Britain decided to confiscate all German exports, which were henceforward to be treated as contraband. (Formerly only imports were subject to contraband restrictions.) An Order in Council was issued on November 27, followed by a French Decree on November 28. Protests were made by Japan, Holland, Belgium, Denmark, and Sweden, and Germany proceeded to exploit the political situation thus created. Raeder took it as an opportunity to declare his long-cherished "Siege of England," but Hitler still refused. He was not yet ready to execute *Fall Gelb* (the invasion of the Low Countries) and while the British and French action served to bring the neutrals closer to him, he did not want his work undone by unnecessary attacks on neutral shipping.

On November 30 Russia invaded Finland. It was of little concern to Germany at that time, serving only to sap the Allies of some of their military supplies and troops. On December 8 Raeder reviewed naval activities at a conference with Hitler.

### REPORT OF THE C.-IN-C., NAVY, TO THE FUEHRER ON DECEMBER 8, 1939

Also present: General Keitel.
Lt.-Commander von Puttkamer.

1. *Situation in the Baltic Sea.*—A protest is being made by the Foreign Office about the Swedish-Finnish minefield in the Aland Sea, as it interferes with the war on merchant shipping. Patrol boats have been lost in the Belt minefields.

2. *Situation in the North Sea.*—Destroyer operations took place off Cromer on the night of December 6. One British destroyer was torpedoed. Further plans are discussed. Aircraft operated on the nights of December 6 and 7 over the Thames, the Humber, and the Downs. Losses sustained were reported.

British counteraction.—Attacks were made on Borkum and Heligoland.

Submarine operations.—Minefields have been laid along the east, south-east, and west coasts. Further plans are discussed.

*War against merchant shipping.*—U.26 is en route to the Mediterranean. There is pronounced activity along the northeast coast; therefore it is not yet necessary to declare a danger zone off Kinnaird's Head. Convoys from Norway to the Shetlands are under attack. Attacks on the Halifax and Freetown convoys are planned for later. The voyages of the U.47, U.37, U.34, and U.49 are reported on. TMC mines and new firing devices are discussed.

3. Operation of the battleships November 21 to 27.—A report is made on the execution and result of these operations. Pressure on the Graf Spee has eased due to the uncertainty of the whereabouts of the Deutschland, leading to extensive measures in the North Atlantic. Plans for January are discussed.

4. Plans for operations of the Graf Spee are discussed.

5. Return of merchant ships. Losses and danger of internment in Dutch ports. The return of the Bremen is discussed. No ships are to be sold.

6. *Economic warfare.*—(a) The British "Order in Council" of November 28, 1939, is a violation of the Paris declaration of 1856 and a threefold violation of international law. Counteraction will be necessary as soon as neutral protests, combined with German propaganda, have had time to take effect—not too late, about the middle of December  If intensive economic warfare (a siege) is planned only in conjunction with general intensification of warfare (an offensive), as the Fuehrer has confirmed, a law altering the prize regulations to correspond with the "order in council" will have to be considered. A suggestion will be made after the report of the Special Staff, Commercial and Economic Warfare.

(b) The British intend to buy ships from neutral powers. A note from the Foreign Office is planned to the effect that if any neutral sells her ships to Britain, all ships of that power will be treated as enemy ships.

(c) Danish deliveries of foodstuffs to Britain must cease; the agreement must be broken off. (Negotiations are planned.) A concentrated effort must be made to cut off Britain, so that the war will be shortened. In this way the difficulties of the Ministry of Food will also be indirectly decreased.

(d) Transport via Sweden and Norway over Trondheim to England is extremely active. Points of departure from the Norwegian coast are very numerous and therefore difficult to control. It is important to occupy Norway. The northern countries should route their exports to Germany, among others.

(e) The urgent need for the Air Force to concentrate its attacks on convoys is discussed. The Fuehrer will work in this direction.

7. Operation *Gelb* (invasion of Holland and Belgium).—Destroyer operations can begin during the first night. Naval plans for defence of the coast are reported on.

8. The effect of the Finnish war on Italy and Spain is discussed.

9. The Japanese have replied that no submarines will be available; further conferences are to be held with regard to supply and communication service. The relations between America and Japan are discussed.

10. *The Fuehrer* advises somewhat delaying the embarkation of Italian officers aboard submarines, but he has no fundamental objections.

11. The question of a temporary delay in the production of heavy naval ammunition. A four month's delay could just be accepted, but no more. The Chief of Staff, O.K.W., says a longer delay is not intended. In three months the C.-in-C., Navy, will make inquiry.

12. The submarine construction programme will be delayed, since for the first quarter of 1940 only 140,000 tons of iron are available instead of 170,000 tons, and there is a substantial decrease in other metals.

The Chief of Staff, O.K.W., says the iron situation will probably improve beginning the second quarter of 1940; the quota for other metals has now been substantially increased.

13. Sales to the Russians.—*The Fuehrer* decides that sale of the Seydlitz and the Prinz Eugen is to be refused, also sale of the turrets of ships "H" and "I." Sale of 20-cm. guns intended for the Luetzow is to be put off (they must be returned by the Army first). If after the offensive a war of position ensues, though we hope this will not be the case, 20-cm. guns will be needed by the Army; otherwise they can be sold. Plans for the Bismarck are discussed. What is the price? The Fuehrer will then make a decision. The C.-in-C., Navy, agrees, as only two ships are being built and the Russians need at least six years to copy them.

(signed)        RAEDER.<br>(countersigned) ASSMANN.

*        *        *        *        *        *

NORWAY.

Between October and December no further progress was made in planning the invasion of Norway, but at the beginning of December Raeder began again to consider the operation. There seemed to be a reasonable chance that the occupation could be carried out by political (5th Column) methods, and to this end, Rosenberg—the "philosopher" of the Nazi Party—had sounded influential pro-Nazi Norwegians. Rosenberg reported favourably on his investigations and named Quisling and Hagelin as the two leaders most likely to assist Germany.

## MEMORANDUM

Re: Visit of Hr. Quisling from Norway.

Supplementary to earlier information, I wish to report that Quisling is one of the best known Norwegian general staff officers. He was Military Attaché in Finland, and from 1927 to 1930, before diplomatic relations between the Soviet Union and Great Britain were broken off, he represented British interests in Moscow. From 1931 to 1933 he was Norwegian War Minister, representing the Norwegian Peasant Party he then resigned and formed a radical national and socialist party called the National Unity Party. This party had, and still has, anti-semitic views, and it recommends closest co-operation with Germany. It has 15,000 registered members, and Quisling estimates the number of his direct followers at two to three hundred thousand; this comprises that 10 per cent. of the population which is in favour of co-operation with Germany even at the present time, when the general attitude in Norway and Sweden is definitely anti-German.   His party also did not participate in voting for the Storthing.

The Storthing, contrary to the constitution, has decided to extend its own period of office from January 12.   Quisling suggests that this fact could be used as pretext for action.   Quisling, as an experienced officer and a former War Minister, still maintains very close relations with the Norwegian Army.   He showed me the original of a letter which he had recently received from the commanding officer in Narvik, Colonel Sunlo. In this letter Colonel Sunlo openly stresses the following: If present conditions continue, Norway will be destroyed.   He only hopes that enough will be left of the nation to form a people which can rebuild Norway on a sound basis.   The present generation is doomed, and rightly so; it must be admitted that they deserve nothing better, for, as he sees it, the Norwegians have violated the unalterable laws of the world.   These laws call for work and idealism, and stupidity has never been considered a legitimate excuse.   "I will do nothing for that old soak Madsen (Minister of Commerce), for that pacifist Monsen (War Minister), it can be good and useful to risk your bones for the national uprising."   Signed: Konrad Sunlo.

Amtsleiter Scheidt, who has been in Norway several times and has a number of acquaintances there, has stated that the commanding officer of the largest troop training grounds, Hroslev, has expressed himself in a similar manner, likewise the Senior Officer of the War Academy in Halden, Captain Fritzner.

Quisling knows the King very well from the time when he was in office, and he believes that the King holds him in esteem, even though the latter is on the whole pro-British.   The Jew Hambro, who is President of the Storthing, and at the same time President of the Committee for Foreign Affairs, is regarded as the greatest enemy of Germany and as perhaps the most powerful political personality.   For all practical purposes the politics of Scandinavia rest in his hands at the present time.   At the same time he is leader of the delegation to the League of Nations and leader of the strongest political party, the so-called "Conservatives," who control the fate of the present minority government.   Hambro also controls the press in Norway.   It is to be feared that the anti-Russian feeling which is fanned by the Russo-Finnish conflict will very soon result increasingly in greater sympathy for Britain and greater antipathy against Germany.

A plan for possible procedure has been suggested.   According to this plan a number of picked Norwegians will be given training in Germany for this particular task.   They will be told exactly what to do, and will be assisted by seasoned National Socialists who are experienced in such matters.   These trained men are then to be sent back to Norway as quickly as possible, where details will be discussed.   Several focal points in Oslo will have to be occupied with lightning speed, and simultaneously the German Navy with contingents of the German Army will have to put in an appearance at a pre-arranged bay outside Oslo in answer to a special summons from the new Norwegian Government.   Quisling has no doubt that such a coup, achieved instantaneously, would at once meet with the approval of those sections of the Army with which he now has connections. Of course he has never discussed political action with them. As regards the King, he believes that he would accept such a *fait accompli.*

Quisling's estimate of the number of German troops needed for the operation coincides with the German estimates.

(signed) A. ROSENBERG.

\*       \*       \*       \*       \*       \*

Raeder was satisfied and a meeting was arranged. Quisling and Hagelin were summoned to Berlin on December 11.

## MINUTES OF A CONFERENCE ON DECEMBER 11, 1939, AT 1200

Hr. H. and Hr. Q. (in writing: Director Hagelin and Quisling) called on the C.-in-C., Navy.

Q. stated that England has not made the desired declaration of neutrality to Norway, as she has to the other Scandinavian countries, and judging by available information and observations, England has no intention of respecting Norway's neutrality for the duration of the war. Only after considerable pressure on the part of Quisling in the Storthing did the British government make the desired declaration. Nevertheless, the present Norwegian government has signed a secret treaty with Britain to the effect that if Norway becomes involved in war with one of the great powers, an invasion by Britain may be carried out with Norwegian consent. A landing is planned in the vicinity of Stavanger, and Christiansand is proposed as a possible British base. The present Norwegian government as well as the Storthing and the whole foreign policy is controlled by the well-known Jew, Hambro, a great friend of Hore-Belisha. For some time the sympathies of the Norwegian people have been consciously driven in a pro-British, anti-German direction, and the whole Norwegian press is under British control. Hambro is misusing his position, and with the help of numerous British agents is trying to bring Norway under British influence or into complete dependence. The influence of Norwegian policy has been sharply felt in the other Scandinavian countries (Sweden, Denmark, and Finland). These countries are also fully aware of the fact that the one who occupies Norway has the key position for all trade in the Baltic Sea and the North Sea. The dangers to Germany arising from a British occupation of Norway were depicted in great detail (example: the Rhine and Elbe estuaries are flanked by the Western Powers). The Baltic Sea is developing into a theatre of war in which Germany can no longer carry on her trade undisturbed.

Great anxiety is felt by all Norwegian patriots over the Russian advance into Finland. Further pressure on the Scandinavian countries is expected. It is understood that at present Germany can do nothing to counter the Russian advance, but it is desired nevertheless to prevent Russia from gaining further influence in Scandinavia. Hambro and his followers believe they can do this with the help of Britain. The National Party, however, does not wish to come to blows with Germany because of Britain's gaining a foothold in Norway. Therefore the National Party desires to anticipate any possible British step in this direction by placing the necessary bases at the disposal of the German Armed Forces.    In the whole coastal area men in important positions (railway, post office, communications) have already been bought for this purpose.    But a change in the German attitude toward Norway's policy is absolutely necessary.    Months of negotiations with *Reichsleiter* Rosenberg have not produced the desired results.    (Incompetency of accredited diplomats.)

Q. and H. stated that this visit to Germany is for the purpose of establishing clear-cut relations with Germany for the future.    From January 10 the present government and the Storthing will no longer be legal.    There is the possibility of a political revolution, in which the National Party would probably not remain passive.    Conferences are desired for discussion of combined action, transfer of troops to Oslo, etc., and the possible laying of protective minefields.    *Amtsleiter* Scheidt was requested as a confidential agent.

*The C.-in-C., Navy,* agreed to confer with the Fuehrer on the matter and to inform Q. and H. of the results of the conference.

\*      \*      \*      \*      \*      \*

The satisfactory outcome of this meeting was reported to Hitler at the noon situation conference on the following day, December 12.

### REPORT OF THE C.-IN-C., NAVY, TO THE FUEHRER ON DECEMBER 12, 1939, AT 1200

Also present:  General Keitel.
              Brig.-General Jodl.
              Lt.-Commander von Puttkamer.

1. Norway.—The C.-in-C., Navy, received Mr. Q. and Mr. H. (Quisling and Hagelin).    Q., former Minister of War and leader of the National Party, made a reliable impression.    He reported the following: Public opinion in Norway is very hostile to Germany, as a result of the conflict between Russia and Finland even more so than formerly.    England's influence is very great, above all through the President of the Storthing, Hambro, a Jew and a friend of Hore-Belisha, who is at present all-powerful in Norway.    Sweden would then also turn against Germany.    There is a very real danger that Norway may be occupied by Britain, possibly soon. The Storthing, and with it the Government of Norway, will no longer be legal from January 11, 1940, since it decided to extend itself for a year, contrary to the constitution.    This would provide an opportunity for a political coup.    Q. has good connections with officers in the Norwegian army and has followers in important places (e.g. railways).    Should the occasion arise, Q. is prepared to take over the government and to ask Germany for aid.    In addition, Q. is ready to discuss preparations of a military nature with the Germany Armed Forces.

*The C.-in-C., Navy,* points out that it is impossible to know with such offers how much the people concerned wish to further their own party schemes and how important German interests are to them.    Caution is therefore advisable.    It must be made impossible for Norway to fall into British hands, as this could be decisive for the outcome of the war; Sweden would then be entirely under British influence and the war would be carried into the Baltic Sea, thereby completely disrupting German naval warfare in the Atlantic and in the North Sea.

*The Fuehrer* also regards the occupation of Norway by Britain as unacceptable. *The C.-in-C., Navy*, points out that German occupation of Norwegian coastal bases would naturally occasion strong British countermeasures for the purpose of interrupting the transport of ore from Narvik. Severe surface warfare off the Norwegian coast would be the result, and the German Navy is not yet prepared to cope with this for any length of time. In the event of occupation this is a weak spot.

*The Fuehrer* considers whether he should speak to Q. personally, in order to form an impression of him; he would like to hear *Reichsleiter* Rosenberg's opinion first, as the latter has known Q. for some time.

*The C.-in-C., Navy*, suggests that if the Fuehrer is favourably impressed, the O.K.W. be permitted to make plans with Q. for preparing and executing the occupation either: (*a*) by friendly methods, i.e. the German Armed Forces are called upon by Norway; or (*b*) by force.

2. *The C.-in-C., Navy*, recommends keeping a clear policy with regard to the Russo-Finnish conflict. No armament is to be sent in support of Finland (via unreliable Sweden). The Chief of Staff, O.K.W., declares that the Foreign Office has been informed that arms would be delivered to Sweden only if the Swedish Government guarantees in writing that they are to be used solely by the Swedish Army. On the other hand, the C.-in-C., Navy, recommends accommodating Russia, for example in the matter of oil supply for submarines, as Russia also offers us practical advantages, e.g. holding foreign ships in Murmansk for three days after the departure of the Bremen. *The Fuehrer* agrees on both points.

(signed)        RAEDER.
(countersigned) ASSMANN.

\*      \*      \*      \*      \*      \*

Raeder's arguments and the conference with Quisling and Hagelin convinced Hitler of the necessity for the operation and of a possible easy solution. He gave the order to start preparations immediately.

Two plans were prepared simultaneously. The first depended on the political success of Quisling who was to be encouraged with coal supplies, propaganda, and the infiltration of a number of Germans without recourse to major military assistance. The second plan was prepared in the event of the failure of the first. This plan was purely military and envisaged a joint naval, air, and land assault on Norway with probable interference from both Norwegians and the Allies. It was given the code-word of *Weser-Uebung* (Weser exercise).

\*      \*      \*      \*      \*      \*

On December 13 the pocket battleship Graf Spee was found and attacked by three British cruisers, H.M.S. Ajax, Achilles, and Exeter, under the command of Rear Admiral Harwood. The Captain of the Graf Spee, Captain Langsdorff, thought at first that he had been sighted by one cruiser and two destroyers only, and hence turned immediately to the attack. He then realised the identity of the British force, but it was too late to break off the action. The battle continued throughout the day and Graf Spee was unable to shake off the three British cruisers. Damaged, and a considerable distance from his home bases, Langsdorff decided to make for a neutral port where he could carry out temporary repairs before attempting to break through once more into the North Atlantic and so back to Germany. He shaped course for Montevideo.

The Graf Spee reached Montevideo on the evening of the same day, December 13, and there followed a prolonged diplomatic argument as to whether the ship should be allowed to remain in port beyond the legal 72 hours.   Meanwhile skilful British propaganda created the impression of a large fleet in the vicinity of the La Plata estuary waiting to annihilate the Graf Spee.   H.M.Ss. Ark Royal and Renown were reported to be at Rio de Janeiro, while in reality they were many thousands of miles away.   The cruiser force had in fact been reinforced by only one more ship, another cruiser, H.M.S. Cumberland.   Langsdorff signalled his appreciation of the situation and his intentions to Berlin.   On December 16 Raeder consulted Hitler.

## REPORT OF THE C.-IN-C., NAVY, TO THE FUEHRER ON DECEMBER 16, 1939, AT 1300

Also present:  Brig.-General Jodl.
              Commander von Puttkamer.

*The C.-in-C., Navy*, reports that at least two weeks are needed to make the Graf Spee seaworthy, and that the Government of Uruguay has granted only 72 hours.   The Foreign Office is requested to continue efforts to obtain an extension of the time allowed; this appears hopeless, however, as Britain and France are exerting great pressure, and Uruguay will conform to their wishes.   Uruguay is unreliable as a neutral, and is not able to defend her neutrality.   Internment in Montevideo is therefore out of the question.   A break-through to Argentina, which is stronger, could be considered, since this would permit us to retain greater freedom of action.   The Captain of the Graf Spee has proposed a break-through to Buenos Aires, and he requests a decision as to whether, if the prospect is hopeless, he should choose internment in Montevideo or scuttle the ship in the fairly shallow waters of the La Plata River.

The Captain's telegram of December 16 follows:

"1. Strategic position off Montevideo: Besides the cruisers and destroyers, Ark Royal and Renown.   Close blockade at night.   Escape into open sea and break-through to home waters hopeless.

"2. Propose putting out as far as neutral boundary.   If it is possible to fight our way through to Buenos Aires, using remaining ammunition, this will be attempted.

"3. If a break-through would result in certain destruction of Graf Spee without opportunity of damaging enemy, request decision on whether the ship should be scuttled in spite of insufficient depth in the estuary of the La Plata, or whether internment is to be preferred.

"4. Decision requested by radiogram.

(signed) Captain, GRAF SPEE."

The C.-in-C., Navy, cannot recommend internment in Uruguay, and he considers the right course to be an attempt to break through, or, if necessary, to scuttle the ship in the La Plata River.   *The Fuehrer* is also opposed to internment, especially since there is a possibility that the Graf Spee might score a success against the British ships in the break-through.   The Fuehrer entirely approves of the instructions the C.-in-C., Navy, proposes to send to the Captain of the Graf Spee.

The text of the instructions follows (sent as radiogram 1347/16 to Graf Spee at 1707):

"1. Attempt by all means to extend the time in neutral waters in order to guarantee freedom of action as long as possible.

"2. With reference to No. 2: Approved.

"3. With reference to No. 3: *No* internment in Uruguay. Attempt effective destruction if ship is scuttled.

(signed) RAEDER."

Note.—The envoy in Montevideo reports in the afternoon, that further attempts to extend the time limit were without result. Confirmation was therefore sent by radiogram to the Captain of the Graf Spee that the instructions in radiogram 1347 with reference to No. 2 and No. 3 remain in force.

The text of the radiogram is as follows: "December 16, radiogram 2239/16 to Captain, Graf Spee. As envoy reported impossibility of extending time limit, instructions according to radiogram 1347/16 Nos. 2 and 3 remain in force." Sent at 0040 on December 17.

*     *     *     *     *     *

On the following morning, watched by a vast crowd of sightseers, the Graf Spee put to sea. The British ships cleared for action, but, before they could engage the enemy, their spotting aircraft reported that the Graf Spee had been scuttled and blown up by her own crew. Three days later, on December 20, Captain Langsdorff committed suicide, leaving this letter addressed to the German Ambassador and meant for onward transmission to Germany and his Fuehrer.

To the Ambassador, Buenos Aires.                        19.12.39

Your Excellency,

After a long struggle I have reached the grave decision to scuttle the pocket battleship "Admiral Graf Spee," in order to prevent her from falling into enemy hands. I am still convinced that under the circumstances, this decision was the only one left, once I had taken my ship into the trap of Montevideo. For with the ammunition remaining any attempt to fight my way back to open and deep water was bound to fail. And yet only in deep water could I have scuttled the ship, after having used the remaining ammunition, thus avoiding her falling to the enemy.

Sooner than exposing my ship to the danger that after a brave fight she would fall partly or completely into enemy hands, I have decided not to fight, but to destroy the equipment and then scuttle the ship. It was clear to me that this decision might be consciously or unwittingly misconstrued by persons ignorant of my motives, as being attributable entirely or partly to personal considerations. Therefore I decided from the beginning to bear the consequences involved in this decision. For a Captain with a sense of honour, it goes without saying that his personal fate cannot be separated from that of his ship.

I postponed my intention as long as I still bore responsibility for decisions concerning the welfare of the crew under my command. After today's decision of the Argentine Government, I can do no more for my ship's company. Neither will I be able to take an active part in the present struggle of my country. I can now only prove by my death that the fighting services of the Third Reich are ready to die for the honour of the flag.

I alone bear the responsibility for scuttling the pocket battleship Admiral Graf Spee. I am happy to pay with my life for any possible reflection on the honour of the flag. I shall face my fate with firm faith in the cause and the future of the nation and of my Fuehrer.

I am writing this letter to Your Excellency in the quiet of the evening, after calm deliberation, in order that you may be able to inform my superior officers, and to counter public rumours if this should become necessary.

(signed) LANGSDORFF,<br>Captain.<br>Commanding Officer of the sunk<br>pocket battleship "Admiral Graf Spee."

By the end of December both the political and strategical position of Germany was becoming clearer. The loss of the Graf Spee had seriously upset the balance of sea power, but it was hoped that it would not be long before Italy entered the war. Submarine warfare was still partially restricted pending the coming attack on the Low Countries and Norway, but, by declaring mined zones without actually laying mines, it was hoped to camouflage U-boat attacks on neutral shipping as legitimate losses due to mines. During the last conference of the year all political and strategical questions were reviewed.

### REPORT OF THE C.-IN-C., NAVY, TO THE FUEHRER ON DECEMBER 30, 1939

Also present: General Keitel.
Commander von Puttkamer.

1. Baltic Sea.—The sinking of a number of German merchant ships, which occurred in the course of Russian naval warfare against Finland, is brought up. The Russians now respect the German flag. An agreement is being discussed with regard to German ore steamers from Lulea. German naval warfare is greatly impeded by the extensive traffic of neutral ships to Britain through Swedish territorial waters, e.g. Falsterbo Channel. Firm pressure should be brought to bear on Sweden with the object of getting her to mine her own territorial waters; all traffic at the southern entrance of the Sound would then pass through the gap in the German minefield, which would be under a combined patrol.

2. Scandinavia.—It is essential that Norway does not fall into British hands. There is danger that volunteers from Britain, in disguise, will carry out an unobtrusive occupation of Norway. Therefore it is necessary to be prepared and ready. Serious resistance in Norway, and probably also in Sweden, is not to be expected. Opinion in higher military circles in Norway is divided: one section believes that Russia will not occupy Tromsoe, as the difficulties would be too great; the other section believes that the partition of Norway between Russia and Germany has already been arranged.

3. Northern sea route.—Negotiations are in progress through the Naval Attaché in Moscow for the use of the northern sea route by returning German ships, i.e. auxiliary cruisers and pocket battleships. Perhaps political pressure from a higher source will be necessary, as subordinate departments do not take the responsibility.

4. Warfare in the North Sea.—The mine belt along the east coast of Britain was extended by destroyers and submarines in December; submarines are carrying out further extension along the west coast. The British now dim their outer beacons at night, and have declared the whole east coast a danger zone; this is a purely defensive measure. At the northern and southern entrances a heavy concentration of traffic will occur, and opportunities for submarine torpedo attacks in the north will therefore continue to be good. In the south it will be necessary to disrupt traffic by laying aerial mines. In view of the new situation the following steps are being taken:

(a) In the coastal waters off the east coast protected by minefields, the C.-in-C., Air, is making bombing attacks on merchant ships sailing unescorted as well as on convoys.

(b) The C.-in-C., Navy, has suggested to the C.-in-C., Air, that neutral ships proceeding through or anchoring in the Downs should also be attacked by bombers, after previous warning to neutral governments. These ships are proceeding under the orders and supervision of the British Navy, and are thus in a way being convoyed.

The C.-in-C., Air, will ask a decision to be made in due course.

*The Fuehrer* also considers a warning necessary; perhaps a favourable moment would be the commencement of a general intensification of warfare. (*Note in writing: Who will do this?*)

The overall effect of the minefields is as follows: British and neutral merchant shipping are suffering severe losses, and neutral shipping is discouraged. On the other hand, the British are constantly able to create gaps in the minefields by taking advantage of the removal of individual mines caused by ships which have been sunk. Traffic is continuing by day at least, though at great risk on account of the great number of wrecks, as many of the neutral captains have stated. Aerial mines must continually be laid to fill the gaps.

In January a large number of submarines will be ready for torpedo attacks and for co-operation with the surface forces. The surface forces will be ready for operations by the second half of January. Operations will be made more difficult in the future by the absence of the strategic effect of the Graf Spee and the Deutschland in the Atlantic. There is a greater concentration of heavy British naval forces in the north (2 to 3 battle cruisers, 5 to 6 battleships, 3 to 4 heavy cruisers). Repairs to Luetzow (ex-Deutschland) and the first auxiliary cruisers will be completed by the end of January, and ready to sail by the middle of February. Italian participation in the war would relieve the situation in the Atlantic, as then a part of the British naval forces would be withdrawn to the Mediterranean.

Air activity.—The enemy is very active in the North Sea; the Navy is dependent to a great extent on good air reconnaissance; modern types of aircraft for the Navy in sufficient numbers are therefore necessary. Negotiations are in progress. Radar equipment has proved very satisfactory and is the only method of warning coastal defence of the approach of enemy aircraft.

5. Intensification of submarine warfare.—Previous experience has shown that gradual intensification without special proclamation is the best method. If a proclamation is planned in conjunction with general intensification of warfare, as advocated by the Fuehrer, only a *general* statement concerning intensified naval warfare should be made, without specific details; moreover it is requested that the Naval Staff be authorized to introduce intensification according to the general situation and the state of preparedness of the forces, subject always to fundamental agreement previously obtained from the Fuehrer. The same procedure is recommended in case no proclamation is made.

*The Fuehrer* agrees to the following:

(a) Merchant ships of all nations which sell or lease ships to Britain, primarily Greek ships, can be torpedoed without warning in the American declared zone by any or all submarines, depending on the situation, possibly with limitations to certain defined areas.

(b) Any or all submarines may fire without warning on neutral ships in those parts of the American declared war zone in which sinkings can be blamed on mines, for instance in the Bristol Channel. Ships of friendly nations are excepted.

(c) The Fuehrer is withholding publication of the ruling in reply to the "Order in Council" until the general intensification of warfare, or, in the case of a long delay in the offensive, until substitute measures are introduced in place of the offensive.

Friendly nations will be handled with consideration as before.

The Italians sent a note requesting designation of a safe harbour. *The C.-in-C., Navy,* suggests replying that this is unfortunately impossible, since all habours concerned have already been mined. It is impossible to establish the exact position of mines laid by submarines and planes, and the German Government therefore can give no guarantee. Italian ships would have to rely on data from British pilots. (Note: *The Fuehrer* agrees.)

6. Sinking of the Graf Spee.—On account of insufficient details, no final judgment can yet be made concerning tactical conduct during the battle, why the Exeter could not be disposed of, and the necessity for entering Montevideo harbour. After the ship entered port and no extension of time for repairs was obtained, the decision of the commanding officer to use all remaining ammunition for effective destruction of the ship was justified, seeing there was no guarantee that after an attempt at a break-through and expenditure of the remaining ammunition the ship could be scuttled effectively in the shallow waters of the La Plata River estuary by merely opening the sea cocks. The defenceless, only partially submerged ship would have been in danger of being captured by the British. *The Fuehrer* reiterated the fact that the Exeter should have been completely destroyed.

8. Submarine construction programme.—Negotiations are in progress with the Chief of Staff, O.K.W., about a submarine construction programme which by January 1, 1942, would provide us with 316 more submarines than we have at present. This would be done by drawing on metal, particularly tin, reserved for the Navy for later years. The Chief of Staff, O.K.W., confirms this and intends to investigate the industry thoroughly to see if any more tin can be obtained. A final decision as to whether this programme can be carried out or whether further reductions must be made can be deferred until May or June 1940.

*    *    *    *    *    *

Whatever Hitler's political machinations might have been aiming at, the Naval Staff was in no doubt as to its real enemy, and, during the last few days of the year, drew up the following proclamation which they desired Hitler to issue. (This proclamation was never, in fact, made.)

### Suggestion for Fuehrer Proclamation

England is our deadly enemy. Her object is the destruction of the German Reich and the German people. Her methods are not open warfare but vile and brutal starvation, in fact extermination of the weak and defenceless not only in Germany but in the whole of Europe. History proves this. The head of the

British Government adhered to this historic attitude when, on September 26, 1939, he declared before the House of Commons that the naval blockade of Germany now being carried out by Britain does not differ in any way from a siege on land, and that it has always been customary to cut the besieged off from all supplies.

We Germans will not allow ourselves to be starved out, nor will we capitulate. Returning like for like, we will make Britain herself feel what it means to be besieged, in order to free the world once and for all from the base and insufferable tyranny of the British.

The Head of the British Government announced in his speech on October 12, 1939, that Britain will use all her resources in this war, i.e. that the war will be waged with every legal and, as has happened already, also illegal means at her disposal.   Likewise we too, while observing the rules of military conduct, will use our weapons ruthlessly in this fight into which we have been forced in the defence of our existence and our rights.

The German Government will take every step to cut off Great Britain and France completely from any supplies, as is done in any siege according to the British Prime Minister.

Any ship encountered in the combat area around Britain and France, regardless of its flag, fully exposes itself to the dangers of warfare.

# *Preparations for Attack*

AT THE beginning of 1940 the German attack on British and French sea communications was the only form of warfare being carried out against the Western Powers. Other plans were well in hand, however, and two major operations were being prepared—the invasion of the Low Countries, and the invasion of Norway and Denmark. Hitler had issued his order for *Fall Gelb* (Case Yellow)—the invasion of Holland and Belgium—on October 9, 1939.

| | |
|---|---|
| The Supreme Commander of the Armed Forces | Berlin, October 9, 1939 |
| Top Secret | 8 Copies |
| | 2nd Copy |

(Stamp) S.O. Only
Access only through
an Officer

### DIRECTIVE NO. 6 FOR THE CONDUCT OF THE WAR

1. If it becomes evident in the near future that England, and France acting under her leadership, are not disposed to put an end to the war, I am determined to take active and offensive action without letting much time elapse.

2. A long waiting period results not only in the ending, to the advantage of the Western Powers, of Belgian, and perhaps also of Dutch neutrality, but also strengthens the military power of our enemies to an increasing degree, causes confidence of the neutrals in German final victory to wane; and does not help to bring Italy to our aid as a brother in arms.

3. I therefore issue the following orders for the further conduct of military operations :

(*a*) Preparation should be made for offensive action on the northern flank of the western front crossing the area of Luxembourg, Belgium, and Holland. This attack must be carried out as soon and as forcefully as possible.

(*b*) The object of this attack is to defeat as strong sections of the French Fighting Army as possible, and her ally and partner in the fighting, and at the same time to acquire as great an area of Holland, Belgium, and Northern France as possible, to use as a base offering good prospects for waging aerial and sea warfare against England and to provide ample coverage for the vital district of the Ruhr.

(*c*) The time of the attack is dependent on the operational readiness of the armoured and motorised units, which should be expedited with the utmost effort, and on the state of the weather at the time and the weather forecast.

4. The *Luftwaffe* is to prevent the combined French and British Air Force from interfering with the Army, and, where necessary, to give direct support to its activities. In this connection, it will be very important to prevent the combined French and British Air Force gaining a hold, and also British troops from landing in Holland.

(*Note in pencil.—The cutting of the routes supplying the English troops once they have landed will be the task of the* Luftwaffe, *for U-boats will soon have to cease operating in the Channel on account of great losses.*)

5. The conduct of the war at sea must concentrate entirely on being able to give direct or indirect support to the Army and Air Force operations throughout this attack.

6. In addition to making these preparations for the start of the offensive in the West according to plan, the Army and the *Luftwaffe* must be ready at any time and in increasing strength, to be able to make an immediate stand against a combined

French and British entry into Belgium, and this in as advanced a position as possible on Belgian territory—also to be able to occupy Holland as extensively as possible while pushing towards the West Coast.

(Margin note.)    Something like this would be more worth striving for in every respect.

7. The disguising of preparations must take the line that nothing more than precautionary measures against the threatening concentration of French and British forces on the Franco-Luxembourg and Belgian frontier are being taken.

8. I request the Commanders-in-Chief, acting on this order, to submit reports on their intentions to me individually as soon as possible, and to keep me informed through the Supreme Command of the Armed Forces of the state of their preparations.                                                    (signed) A. HITLER.

Further instructions were issued by Keitel on December 30, 1939.

O.K.W.                                              Berlin, December 30, 1939
Top Secret                                                          10 Copies
                                                                    5th Copy

SUBJECT:  Intensified Measures for Sea and Air Warfare in connection with
          *Fall Gelb*

In addition to the instructions directly concerned with *Fall Gelb* which have already been issued for the Navy and Air Force, the following intensified measures for the conduct of sea and air warfare come into force with the start of operations in the West:

(1) The Navy will approve the sinking without warning of *all* ships by U-boats, in sea areas off the enemy coasts *where it is possible to use mines*.  (*Red pencil note.— This would be an undesirable limitation.*)    In this case outward appearances should create the impressions that mines have been used. (*Note in green pencil.—Not intended to be.*)    U-boats should bear this in mind when taking action and using arms.

The C.-in-C., Navy, is to decide on the exact limits of these areas, and to give notification of them via the O.K.W.

(2) As long as Army operations in the West are in progress the Air Force will have the following tasks:

(*a*) To give direct support to these operations (Directive No. 6, Section 4). In doing so it is important to attack, outside the actual theatre of operations, troop transports from England to France, Belgium or Holland, including ports of embarkation and disembarkation, as well as British Air Force ground installations in the home country itself, which are used as bases for operations against the Continent.

(*b*) To tie up as strong forces as possible of fighter aircraft in the British Homeland.

It is not in keeping with the whole conduct of the war, however, to unleash the full force of aerial warfare on our own initiative, before we have created for ourselves favourable conditions for it, and before there are strong forces available suitable for operations against Britain.

For this reason, attacks also, which imperil to any great extent the civilian population, are to be reserved for cases which demand reprisals.

                                              Chief of the O.K.W.
                                              (signed) KIETEL.

From this order it will be seen that the Navy's share in *Fall Gelb* was not much more than the continuation of their war against merchant shipping.    There was no question of using the High Seas Fleet, nor of attempting to cut off the Royal Navy.    This was partly because the German Supreme Command could not see how the British and French Fleets could effect what was a purely land offensive, and partly because practically the whole of the German Navy was intended for the other major operation—*Weseruebung* (Weser exercise)—the invasion of Norway and Denmark.

Hitler had ordered this operation to be prepared following the meeting and discussion with Quisling in Berlin on December 11 and 12, 1939.    There it had been decided that the occupation of Norway would be attempted by political methods first.   Quisling and Hagelin, the leaders of the "National" party, were to be encouraged in their efforts to secure control of the Norwegian government, and, when this had been achieved, Quisling was to offer Germany the use of Norwegian ports and bases.   If these political measures failed, force was to be used and preparations for the occupation by force were to be made.   As the occupation of Norway was almost entirely a naval matter, both from the point of view of strategical advantage and of execution, Raeder and his staff were given the principal task of planning and organising the invasion.

*       *       *       *       *       *

While these various plans were being completed, the gradual development of unrestricted warfare against merchant shipping was continued.   Neutral ships were still exempt, except where attacks could be camouflaged as though they were caused by mines, but even the attacks against British and French merchant shipping were still considered inadequate.   The *Luftwaffe* and the Army were not co-operating satisfactorily with the Navy, and on January 26 Raeder reported to Hitler.

### REPORT OF THE C.-IN-C., NAVY, TO THE FUEHRER IN THE AFTERNOON OF JANUARY 26, 1940

Also present:  Chief of Staff, O.K.W.
              General Jodl.
              Commander von Puttkamer.

1. Baltic Sea.—Ice conditions are discussed.   The note from the Foreign Office to the Swedish Government regarding laying of mines in Swedish territorial waters in the Sound by Sweden herself was answered in the negative.

This matter is being considered, since England might easily demand similar steps from Norway if it were known that Germany is exercising pressure on Sweden.   War against merchant shipping in the eastern Baltic Sea is continuing.

2. Northern passage.—Political difficulties will not arise, according to a report by the Naval Attaché.   Practical details are now being worked out.

3. North Sea.—The situation is unchanged.   There is a considerable flow of naval forces back from the Atlantic into home waters.   A large number of ships is under repair at shipyards, among others the Barham, hit by submarine torpedo, and the Nelson, probably hit by a mine off the Scottish coast.   Therefore the situation is favourable for an offensive by our heavy forces against convoys proceeding from Bergen to the Shetlands, regarding which information is continually coming in.   In connection with this, operations by submarines against the heavy British forces proceeding from the bases are to take place probably at the end of the month.   In the German Bight three successes were achieved in anti-submarine operations.   The first British minefield has been located in the British declared area off Terschelling.

Further plans are to send out the Luetzow (ex-Deutschland) at the beginning of March.   Five auxiliary cruisers are to be sent into the South Atlantic and Indian Ocean between the beginning of February and the middle of April.   Mines are to be laid off Halifax and in the Persian Gulf.   The purpose is not so much to sink merchant ships on a large scale as to disturb British merchant shipping continuously over a long period of time and to divert strong defence forces to the high seas, thereby relieving the home theatre.

4. Submarine warfare and mine warfare.—Two operations by destroyers in the Thames and Newcastle areas in the last new moon period have been successful. Submarines laid mines off the east and south-east coasts. On the west coast it is still going on. Here the defences are very strong in view of the importance of the western ports. Minefields have been laid in the Bristol Channel, off Liverpool (very difficult), and off the Clyde, as well as on the south coast off Falmouth. It is intended to lay mines off Plymouth and Portsmouth. Two to three boats are to be sent to Halifax in order to lay mines and carry out submarine warfare, using torpedoes. Questions regarding the American safety zone will be settled beforehand with the Foreign Office. Submarine warfare in the North Sea and the Atlantic is at present being conducted again with greater intensity, after having produced fewer results in December owing to extensive repairs. On January 25 two successes were achieved against a convoy off the Spanish coast by U.44.

5. Intensification of war against merchant shipping.—Gradual intensification continues to justify itself. Political difficulties have been entirely avoided in this manner. Since the Fuehrer has agreed in principle to defining areas off the British coast in which also neutrals—exclusive of friendly neutrals—may be sunk without warning, so long as in the area in question it is possible to put the blame on mines, the following measures are planned:

(a) To extend the area off the north-east coast of Scotland eastward to 2° E.

(b) To extend the area off the Bristol Channel westward to about 10° 3′ W (up to the 200 metre line) and to include the Irish Sea.

(c) To add a new area (approximately from Dover to Flamborough Head) to the northern approaches of the English Channel. It is not planned to block the Channel to the west until the question of operation *Gelb* is settled. Preferential treatment of friendly neutrals is still considered necessary.

*The Fuehrer* agrees to (a), (b), and (c).

6. Effect of the naval war against merchant shipping.—The effect as a whole of warfare against merchant shipping up to now has been quite satisfactory, as is shown by statements in Parliament and in the press. The Navy has shown that, in spite of its limited means, it can achieve considerable success in the economic strangulation of Britain. However, the Navy alone is not at present in a position to produce a decisive effect. (For months the Navy has been carrying on this war practically single-handed.) In order to gain a complete success it will be necessary to have strong support from the Air Force with attacks on convoys in the North Sea and with mine warfare on the west coast.

Above all it is necessary to concentrate on naval and air warfare against Britain. The C.-in-C., Navy, has recently gathered the impression through various orders of the O.K.W. that the general conduct of the war is at present strongly influenced by "continental ideas," as witnessed by the following:

(a) The order of January 17, 1940, regarding transfer of younger personnel (officers, non-commissioned officers, and men) of the coastal defence services, etc., to the Army for the formation of new divisions. Over against this the greatest difficulty on the part of the Navy is that of obtaining personnel for the submarines, without detriment to the discipline on board ships, etc.    It will be necessary to transfer personnel of naval artillery units with the guns to the Channel coast.    Therefore there is no possibility of releasing further personnel for the Army.

(b) The order by the O.K.W. of January 18, 1940, to the C.-in-C., Army. (This was not submitted to the Navy, and it became known only through a lower office of the Army which was instructed to find out from the Naval Ordnance Division the number of naval guns becoming available.)    The order states that if the war lasts a long time, the disarmament of large units of the Navy could be considered.    In this case the Army plans to use all guns of 20 cm. calibre upwards as long-range artillery.    Therefore railway mountings are to be ordered for mobile use of these naval guns, even if their delivery would take considerable time.    The C.-in-C., Navy, emphasises the demoralising effect of this order on the Navy, and points out the false conception that we would ever do with less than a minimum of four battleships in the war against Britain, for the following reasons:

(1) When mines are laid by the enemy in the German Bight, mine-sweeping units will have to search and sweep routes to an increasing extent; for this purpose escort by heavy ships (as in the World War) is absolutely indispensable.

(2) The presence of heavy German ships prevents the British from launching attacks with light forces against our ore traffic from Narvik.

(3) The operations of the heavy ships force the British to keep heavy units in home waters, for whose protection numerous destroyers are necessary.    Attacks by our heavy ships force the heavy British forces to expose themselves to our submarines and aircraft.    It is possible to threaten the eastern part of the North Atlantic sea routes and the patrol lines in the north only by means of heavy ships.

(4) In the Baltic Sea the heavy ships are indispensable for the protection of the whole area, since without them even Sweden, quite apart from Russia, would be a threat to German sea communications and the German coast.

(c) The Army munitions programme, which will adversely affect the submarine construction programme in regard to:

(1) Factory facilities and machine tools.
(2) The question of workers.
(3) The question of iron and other metals.

The Fuehrer declares that he considers increased production of the Ruhr essential for any type of warfare and that it is important for the war against Britain to broaden the territory from which to launch an attack; these measures will have to be taken care of first.    France must be beaten and the British deprived of their base on the Continent.    For the rest, the order under (b) was occasioned by the fact that the Army, in contrast to earlier occasions, is supposed to procure mountings, etc., in good time.

7. Italian requests.—The Italian Navy has for a long time desired the delivery of certain materials.    The High Command, Navy, wishes to

comply with several of these requests if Italy agrees to deliver a few sub-marines.  Delivery of a warhead pistol, or plans for such, is out of the question.  If submarines are offered in exchange for electrical torpedoes, the Navy is willing to agree to the following without any objections :

(*a*) Cession of two electrical torpedoes.

(*b*) Drawings of a submarine fire control system (but no working blue-prints and no equipment).

(*c*) Information regarding accelerated construction of present sub-marine types; possibly plans of the 500-ton class.

(*d*) Information regarding weight distribution and synchronous couplings of the Bismarck class.

(*e*) Continuation of limited exchange of intelligence.

*The Fuehrer* agrees on this condition.

8. Political questions.—*The Fuehrer* desires to delay as long as possible giving plans of the Bismarck class as well as the hull of the Luetzow to Russia, since he hopes to avoid this altogether if the war develops favourably.

*The Fuehrer* believes that Italy will enter the war only in the event of great German successes, and preferably only against France; he sees no great advantage for Germany in Italy's participation in view of the fact that Germany would probably then be burdened with the obligation to make more deliveries to Italy.

Sweden and Norway are at present determined to maintain strict neutrality.

9. Award for Baurat Techel.—A Goethe medal or a picture of the Fuehrer.

Creation of an award is discussed which would be between the Iron Cross First Class and the Knight's Cross of the Iron Cross, corresponding to the Knight's Cross of the Order of the House of Hohenzollern.  It would be awarded to submarine commanders who have sunk 100,000 tons.

(signed) RAEDER.

*       *       *       *       *       *

On February 15 the German supply ship, Altmark, was sighted in Norwegian territorial waters by units of the Royal Navy.  As she was known to be carrying British prisoners from ships sunk by the Graf Spee, the British Government gave permission to H.M.S. Cossack, who was in the vicinity, to board the German vessel and rescue the prisoners.  The boarding operation was entirely successful, and Germany complained loudly about the violation of Norwegian neutrality.

One effect of the "Altmark" incident, however, was to hasten German prepara-tions for occupying Norway.  From the German point of view it was thought that if the British were prepared to violate territorial waters to rescue a few hundred prisoners, how much more would they be prepared to take the same measures to cut off vital Norwegian ore supplies to Germany.

Expected iron ore supplies from Scandinavia to Germany in 1940 were :

| | | |
|---|---|---|
| From Sweden | .. | 10,000,000 tons (of which 2–3,000,000 tons were to be sent via Narvik). |
| From Norway | .. | 1,200,000 tons via Kirkeness and Narvik, and 350,000 tons of other metals. |
| Total | .. | 11,550,000 tons, of which one third was to be sent down the Norwegian coast. |

The expected total German consumption of iron ore in 1940 was 15,000,000 tons. The Scandinavian supplies were therefore of supreme importance to Germany.

These matters and the extension of submarine warfare to the United States neutrality zone were discussed at the next conference. (Hitler forbade U-boat attacks off America.)

## REPORT OF THE C.-IN-C., NAVY, TO THE FUEHRER ON FEBRUARY 23, 1940, AT 1030

Also present: General Keitel.
General Jodl.
Commander von Puttkamer.

1. Baltic Sea.—Due to the ice situation there has been no activity by naval forces. The Naval Staff considers the present time—after the conclusion of the economic pact with Russia—suitable for reviewing the agreements with Russia regarding the boundary line for warfare against merchant shipping (20° E) and for effecting an alteration. We cannot forego control of merchant traffic in the eastern Baltic. The Naval Staff is contacting the Foreign Office.

2. North Sea.—(a) At the present time British naval vessels are being overhauled in large numbers after having been at sea for a long time, so that there are only a few heavy ships entirely ready for action in home waters. Therefore this is an opportunity for operations by our battleships and the Hipper against convoy traffic. The first operation of February 18 to 20 along the line from the Shetlands to Norway was not successful, but is soon to be repeated.

During an operation by a destroyer flotilla off the Dogger Bank on the evening of February 22 for the purpose of bringing in British steam trawlers, two destroyers were lost. The cause has not yet been discovered, but German aircraft may be responsible.

(b) Submarines and destroyers are continuing to lay mines off the east coast of Britain; U.9 operated in Cromarty Firth; two new minefields were laid off Cromer and off North Thames-Shipwash Light Vessel. On the south coast a new minefield has been laid off Portland by U.48. On the west coast U.33 was sent into the Firth of Clyde, an extremely difficult task. The boat was sunk after a surface engagement with a minesweeper. It is to be hoped that the minefield was laid beforehand. U.32 was sent for further mine-laying off Liverpool, U.28 for mine-laying off Portsmouth.

(c) Submarine warfare.—About six submarines are continuously operating in the Atlantic and eight in the North Sea. Results in the Atlantic are increasing: 27,800 tons (six ships), 38,000 tons (eight ships), 43,000 tons (eight ships). Successes also against convoys. In the North Sea the small boats have sunk on an average two steamers, about 3,000 to 4,000 tons, with four to five torpedoes; eleven ships were sunk by one boat during three operations. On February 18 U.23 sank the destroyer Daring out of a convoy.

Losses.—U.15, U.55, U.33; this makes a total of twelve boats, i.e. about two per month.

(d) Intensification of submarine warfare.—So far all ships proceeding without lights, even passenger steamers, may be fired on in the American closed area. It has now been established that British ships proceeding without lights have of late generally carried dimmed running lights, apparently owing to the danger of collision. Neutral ships are instructed to light up their flags and neutral markings also, so that they may be clearly recognised.

*The C.-in-C., Navy*, requests that in the future passenger steamers proceeding without lights but carrying running lights may be fired on without warning, since they are British. The British are using passenger steamers in many cases for freight and troop transport owing to lack of freighters. *The Fuehrer* agrees.

(*e*) The Admiral Commanding Submarines, requests permission to exchange two German submarine commanders for the two British commanders. *The Fuehrer* agrees.

3. Operations by submarines off Halifax.—The C.-in-C., Navy, advances considerations for operations by two submarines with mines and torpedoes off Halifax. He recommends operations within territorial waters with mines, and outside the safety zone with torpedoes. The Foreign Office has no objections. *The Fuehrer* refuses to sanction these operations in view of the psychological effect on the U.S.A.

4. Operations by submarines in the Mediterranean.—*The C.-in-C., Navy*, requests a decision on whether these are permissible from the political point of view. *The Fuehrer* raises the question as to whether such operations are "decisive for the war."

*The C.-in-C., Navy*, states that the net result of all these operations is decisive for the war, and that all those points at which operations are carried out by surprise, and therefore at first without strong enemy counteraction, are especially significant, since they could have a very important effect.

Remark by the C.-in-C., Navy.—The refusal to sanction these two possible operations at particularly favourable points constitutes a real setback to the effectiveness of submarine warfare.

5. Operation *Weseruebung* (Invasion of Norway).—*The C.-in-C., Navy*, when asked by the Fuehrer about the possibility of maintaining the ore traffic from Narvik following the occupation of Norway, replies as follows:

(*a*) The best thing for maintaining this traffic as well as for the situation in general is the maintenance of Norwegian neutrality.

(*b*) What must not be permitted, as stated earlier, is the occupation of Norway by Britain. That could not be undone; it would entail increased pressure on Sweden, perhaps extension of the war to the Baltic, and cessation of all ore supplies from Sweden.

(*c*) The occupation of Norway by us would cause the ore traffic from Narvik to be completely suspended at least for a time, since the protection of sea traffic is very difficult even along the inter-island route on a large portion of the 800-mile passage. Extensive use of submarines and aircraft squadrons would be necessary along a great part of the route. It is possible that enemy submarines would penetrate through the many approaches and the ships would be fired on from the sea. However, only about 2,500,000 to 3,500,000 tons per year would be lost, while if the British occupied Norway, all supplies would be cut off. If Germany occupies Norway, she can also exert heavy pressure on Sweden, which would then be obliged to meet all our demands.

(*d*) Questions on carrying out the occupation are then discussed: The C.-in-C., Navy, points out the difficulty of synchronising occupation in the south by Air Force transports and in the north by naval transports.  Transport would be by ships of the Scharnhorst * class (about 20 knots) or naval store ships (also about 20 knots).  Transports carrying material, perhaps also troop transports, should proceed first of all to "Basis Nord," † since from there the approach route is shorter. The O.K.W. will be instructed to investigate these questions.

6. Purchase of Estonian submarines.—According to a private discussion with the assistant of the Military Attaché, Estonia appears to be ready to transfer her two submarines to Germany, provided that Russia agrees. Estonia herself would have to obtain this agreement from Russia and offer the submarines on her own initiative.   Then the acquisition would be most desirable.   *The Fuehrer* agrees with this procedure.

7. Russian agreement.—During the discussions in Moscow, Stalin indicated that the desired 38-cm. and 28-cm. turrets are intended for ships under construction; he inquired whether installation would still be possible.   The Naval Staff replied that this can be decided only after examining the plans.

(signed)         RAEDER.
(countersigned)  ASSMANN.

* The passenger ship, not the battleship.—Ed.
† "Basis Nord" was the German naval base near Murmansk ceded by the Russians in August 1939.—Ed.

# The Invasion of Norway

REPORTS FROM Hagelin in January and February indicated that Quisling's party was not being as successful as expected. Instead, a new wave of sympathy with, and friendliness towards England was sweeping the country, and the chances of Quisling's accession to power were dwindling. German help had not been forthcoming in spite of Rosenberg's promises, and the coal, money, and selected Germans had not been sent. The German Foreign Office had further bungled the matter by encouraging people who, whatever their feelings towards Germany, were strongly opposed to Quisling, and thus, instead of building up a strong party which would have made German victory easy, the Foreign Office were themselves dividing Germany's supporters. Hagelin appealed for encouragement for Quisling alone, and for stronger German action.

Reports from England were also disturbing. A mine-laying operation has been planned off Norway, and though this was not known to the Germans, it was known that something was brewing. The Allies feared that the mine-laying operation would precipitate German action against Norway, and they were accordingly preparing troops and transports so that immediate steps could be taken if Germany struck.

On March 1 Hitler finally decided that Norway must be occupied by force, and issued the following directive:

The Fuehrer and Supreme Commander of the        Berlin, March 1, 1940
Armed Forces

                                             9 Copies
Top Secret                                        3rd Copy

Directive for *Fall Weseruebung*

(1) The development of the situation in Scandinavia requires the making of all preparations for the occupation of Denmark and Norway by a part of the German Armed Forces (*Fall Weseruebung*). This operation should prevent British encroachment on Scandinavia and the Baltic, further it should guarantee our ore base in Sweden and give our Navy and Air Force a wider start-line against Britain. The part which the Navy and the Air Force will have to play, within the limits of their capabilities, is to protect the operation against the interference of British naval and air striking forces.

In view of our military and political power in comparison with that of the Scandinavian States, the force to be employed in the *Fall Weseruebung* will be kept as small as possible. The numerical weakness will be balanced by daring actions and surprise execution. On principle we will do our utmost to make the operation appear as a peaceful occupation, the object of which is the military protection of the neutrality of the Scandinavian States. Corresponding demands will be transmitted to the Governments at the beginning of the occupation. If necessary, demonstrations by the Navy and the Air Force will provide the necessary emphasis. If, in spite of this, resistance should be met with, all military means will be used to crush it.

(2) I put in charge of the preparations and the conduct of the operation against Denmark and Norway the Commanding General of the XXI Army Corps, General von Falkenhorst (Commander of "Group XXI"). In questions of the conduct of operations the above-named is directly under my orders. The Staff is to be completed from all the three branches of the Armed Forces.

The force which will be selected for the purpose of *Fall Weseruebung* will be under separate command. They will not be allocated for other operational theatres. The part of the Air Force detailed for the purpose of the *Weseruebung* will be tactically under the orders of Group XXI. After the completion of their task they will revert to the command of C.-in-C., Air.

The employment of the forces which are under direct Naval and Air Force command will take place in agreement with the Commander of Group XXI. The administration and supply of the forces posted to Group XXI will be ensured by the branches of the Armed Forces themselves according to the demands of the Commander.

(3) The crossing of the Danish border and the landings in Norway must take place simultaneously. I emphasise that the operations must be prepared as quickly as possible. In case the enemy seizes the iniative against Norway, we must be able to apply immediately our own counter-measures. It is most important that the Scandinavian States as well as the Western opponents should be taken by surprise by our measures. All preparations, particularly those of transport and of readiness, drafting and embarkation of the troops, must be made with this factor in mind. In case the preparations for embarkation can no longer be kept secret, the leaders and the troops will be deceived with fictitious objectives. The troops may be acquainted with the actual objectives only after putting to sea.

(4) Occupation of Denmark (*Weseruebung Sud*).—The Task of Group XXI. Occupation by surprise of Jutland and of Fuenen immediately after occupation of Seeland. Added to this, having secured the most important places, the Group will break through as quickly as possible from Fuenen to Skagen and to the east coast. In Seeland bases will be captured early on. These will serve as starting points for later occupation. The Navy will provide forces for the securing of the connection Nyborg-Korsor and for swift capture of the Kleine-Belt-Bridge as well as for landing of troops should the necessity arise. They will also prepare the defence of the coast. The Air Force will provide squadrons of which the primary object will be demonstrations and dropping of leaflets. Full use of the existing Danish ground defences and air defence must be ensured.

(5) Occupation of Norway (*Weseruebung Nord*).—The task of the Group XXI. Capture by surprise of the most important places on the coast by sea and airborne operations. The Navy will take over the preparation and carrying out of the transport by sea of the landing troops as well as the transport of the forces which will have to be brought to Oslo in a later stage of the operation. They will escort supplies and reserves on the way over by sea. Preparations must be made for speedy completion of coastal defence in Norway. The Air Force, after the occupation has been completed, will ensure air defence and will make use of Norwegian bases for air warfare against Britain.

(6) Group XXI will make regular reports to the Supreme Command concerning the state of preparations and will submit a chronological summary of the progress of preparations. The shortest necessary space of time between the issue of the order for *Weseruebung* and its execution must be reported.

Intended Battle Headquarters will be reported.

(signed) A. HITLER.

The plans of the German Navy were by then almost complete. The attack was to be launched on six main areas, ranging from Oslo to Narvik; transports were to be heavily escorted; and the High Seas Fleet, in two groups, was to cover the flank of the long Norwegian coastline and was to give all its attention to warding off attacks of the British Fleet. No support was to be given to the Army, once the troops had been landed, as the entire German Navy would be needed to defend the invasion areas from sea attack. Raeder appreciated fully the risk of such an operation in waters where they did not have control of the sea, but he relied on tactical surprise and speed to defeat Allied counter-attacks.

On March 9 Raeder informed Hitler of the naval plans and strengthened Hitler's determination to attack. (This conference is also noteworthy because it gives the first indication of Hitler's renewed anti-Russian fears).

### REPORT OF THE C.-IN-C., NAVY, TO THE FUEHRER ON MARCH 9, 1940, AT 1200

Also present: General Keitel.

Operation *Weseruebung*.—1. *The C.-in-C., Navy*, states that he has always been, and still is today, of the opinion that the occupation of Norway

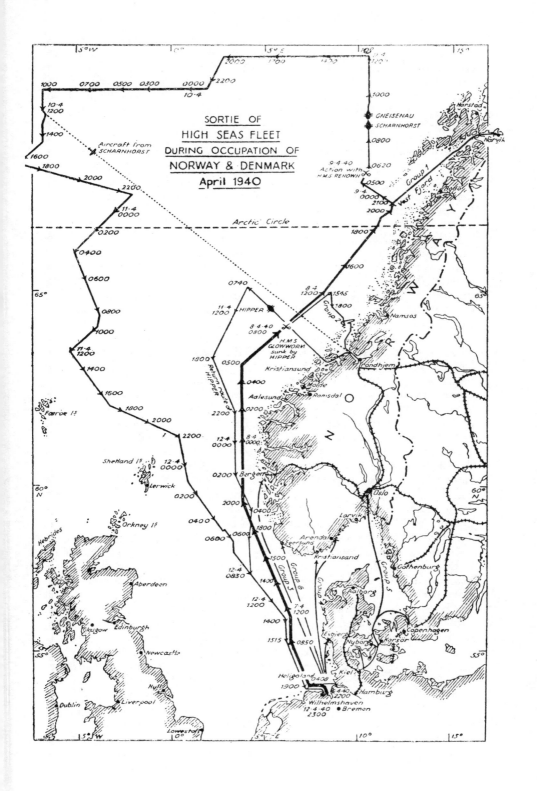

SORTIE OF
HIGH SEAS FLEET
DURING OCCUPATION OF
NORWAY & DENMARK
April 1940

by the British would have a decisive effect against Germany, since then Sweden might also be drawn into the war against Germany and all the ore supplies from Sweden would cease.   The British now have the desired opportunity, under pretext of supporting the Finns, to send troop transports through Norway and Sweden and therefore to occupy these countries if they wish.   Therefore operation *Weseruebung* is urgent. The C.-in-C., Navy, feels it his duty, however, to present to the Fuehrer a clear picture regarding the character of the naval operation.

The operation in itself is contrary to all principles in the theory of naval warfare.   According to this theory, it could be carried out by us only if we had naval supremacy.   We do *not* have this; on the contrary, we are carrying out the operation in face of the vastly superior British Fleet. In spite of this the C.-in-C., Navy, believes that, provided surprise is complete, our troops can and will successfully be transported to Norway. On many occasions in the history of war those very operations have been successful which went against all the principles of warfare, provided they were carried out by surprise.   The critical moment is the penetration of the harbours while passing the coastal fortifications.   It is to be expected that this will succeed if carried out by surprise, and that the Norwegians will not make the decision to fire quickly enough, if they decide to do so at all.

The most difficult operation for the ships is the return voyage, which entails breaking through the British naval forces.   The main British force has lately been stationed in Scapa Flow again; at present there are two battle cruisers, three battleships, and at least three or four heavy cruisers there.   Light naval units will shadow our forces and attempt to direct the main British force to them.   All modern naval forces must combine for this break-through, i.e. battleships, the Hipper, and all destroyers from Narvik and Trondheim.   The forces at and south of Bergen (small cruisers and special service ships) must break through along the coast with the support of the Luetzow.   Not one destroyer may be left behind, let alone a cruiser (the Hipper) either in Narvik or in Trondheim, at a time when the fate of the German Fleet is hanging in the balance.   Strongest co-operation on the part of the Air Force is necessary.   Four large submarines will be stationed in Narvik and two probably in the other bases; a number will be disposed along the advance routes of the British Fleet.

In the period immediately following occupation, escort of transports to Oslo will be of primary importance, as well as the establishment of safe bases for naval forces in the harbours on the south-west and west coasts. Subsequently operations can be carried out from these.   The transport of ore from Narvik will be interrupted until further notice, because the problem of whether and in what manner the extensive coastal waters can be defended against British attacks must be clarified first.

2. The C.-in-C., Navy, suggests that the Russians be informed, following the occupation, that Tromsoe has not been occupied by the Germans. This could be interpreted by the Russians as constituting some consideration for their interests.   It is better to have the Russians in Tromsoe than the British.   *The Fuehrer* does not wish to have the Russians so near, and is of the opinion that Tromsoe will also have to be occupied by us.

3. *The C.-in-C., Navy,* requests permission for the Naval Air Force to lay about six aerial mines in Scapa Flow, in order to inflict damage on the

British capital ships, which might subsequently withdraw to the Faroes. *The Fuehrer* gives his full consent, and considers an agreement with the Air Force necessary, since the latter is planning bombing attacks soon.

4. *The C.-in-C., Navy*, gives a survey on the execution of the naval operation by the various groups.

(signed)      RAEDER.

(countersigned) ASSMANN.

\*     \*     \*     \*     \*     \*

Preparations continued steadily, both for *Weseruebung* and *Fall Gelb*. The German war machine was working more smoothly than it was ever to do again. The planning and preparation of two major operations was continued with the minimum amount of friction between the services, and with the efficiency of well-trained staffs. At the conference on March 26, the date for the invasion of Norway was provisionally settled.

### REPORT OF THE C.-IN-C., NAVY, TO THE FUEHRER IN THE AFTERNOON OF MARCH 26, 1940

Also present: General Keitel.
General Jodl.
Commander von Puttkamer.

1. Operation *Weseruebung*.—Occupation of Norway by the British was quite imminent, according to the following information received at the High Command, Navy: Submarines were concentrated off the Skagerrak on March 13; a radio telegraph message gave March 14 as the time-limit for preparedness of transport groups; numerous French officers arrived in Bergen on March 15. These are all sure indications that an operation was being prepared before the Russo-Finnish peace treaty. Beginning March 10, the Navy stationed submarines outside the main bases in order to combat a British operation. In my opinion the danger of a British landing in Norway is no longer acute at present.

The question of what the British will do in the north in the near future can be answered as follows: they will make further attempts to disrupt German trade in neutral waters and to cause incidents, in order perhaps to create a pretext for action against Norway. One object has been, and still is, to cut off Germany's imports from Narvik. These will be cut off at least for a time, however, even if operation *Weseruebung* is carried out.

Sooner or later Germany will be faced with the necessity of carrying out operation *Weseruebung*. Therefore it is advisable to do so as soon as possible, by April 15 at the latest, since after that date the nights are too short; there will be a new moon on April 7. The operational possibilities of the Navy will be restricted too much if *Weseruebung* is postponed any longer. The submarines can remain in position only for two to three weeks more.

Weather of the type favourable for operation *Gelb* is not to be waited for in the case of operation *Weseruebung*; overcast, foggy weather is more satisfactory for the latter. The general state of preparedness of the naval forces and ships is at present good.

As regards the possibility of getting past the fortifications, the Norwegians have perhaps become somewhat firmer in their desire to preserve their neutrality; however, it is improbable that they will decide to fire quickly enough.

The British Fleet is at present well prepared for action. Five of the battleships attacked in Scapa Flow by the Air Force are reported at sea; it is therefore to be assumed that only large cruisers were damaged.

U.47 sighted three battleships proceeding at high speed on a northerly course off the Orkneys.

*The Fuehrer* agrees to operation *Weseruebung* on D-day about the time of the new moon.

2. North Sea.—Five large submarines are in position off the Orkneys for the purpose of intercepting heavy ships; six small ones are off the southwest coast of Norway, and two each off Narvik and Trondheim.

The Altmark has arrived in the southern part of the Great Belt, and will be brought in on March 27. U.31 was sunk in the Schillig roadstead by a bomber, but has been raised again. The steamer Stinnes was probably sunk in Danish territorial waters by a British submarine. Two auxiliary cruisers are to depart soon.

3. Use of Aerial Mines.—It is particularly necessary to resume aerial-mine warfare since in the meantime one of our mines has come into the possession of the British, and they will introduce countermeasures.

*The Chief of Staff, O.K.W.*, wishes to resume mine warfare with operation *Gelb*. *The C.-in-C., Navy*, proposes that it be resumed at once, at least off the Thames, the Humber, and French ports, since the blockade has become too lax owing to the present lull in submarine warfare. A mine-laying attack on Scapa Flow and the Scheldt estuary was previously approved in any case. *The Fuehrer* believes that resumption of mine warfare would effect a desirable diversion of the British from the north, and he will settle the matter in one or two days.

*The C.-in-C., Navy*, points out that the position of the minefields and the type of mines to be used (depending on counter-measures) would have to be settled in detail between Group West and the Commander of the mine-laying units. There must be closest co-operation between them.

*The Fuehrer* agrees entirely. The Chief of Staff, O.K.W., supports this view.

4. Submarine warfare in the Mediterranean.—*The C.-in-C., Navy*, asks whether this question has been discussed with the Duce. *The Fuehrer* replies in the negative, since no details regarding conduct of the war were discussed. The Fuehrer, however, is of the opinion that submarines could operate in the Mediterranean, but only against British and French ships.

\*    \*    \*    \*    \*    \*

Friction between Goering and Raeder flared up temporarily on the following day over Goering's cancellation of an important mine-laying operation off British ports, and over Goering's demand for naval fuel supplies. Raeder reacted strongly and demanded that the mine-laying operation should be carried out. He also explained scathingly how it was that the Navy was well supplied with oil.

### REPORT OF THE C.-IN-C., NAVY, TO THE FUEHRER IN THE AFTERNOON OF MARCH 29, 1940

Also present: General Keitel.
General Jodl.
Commander von Puttkamer.

1. *Aerial* mines.—*The C.-in-C., Navy*, asks for a decision on the question raised by him at the last conference regarding resumption of aerial mine warfare. Operations with aerial mines against Scapa Flow, agreed upon with the C.-in-C., Air, were planned for March 28; however, on the evening of March 27 they were cancelled by the C.-in-C., Air, without any reason being given, and any further operation was prohibited. Mine-laying in Scapa Flow is essential for operation *Weseruebung*; it is necessary to lay mines in the Thames, Humber, etc., in order to carry out the blockade. The C.-in-C., Navy, proposes that the C.-in-C., Air, carry out the operation in Scapa Flow as soon as possible. The C.-in-C., Navy, will continue mine warfare in the areas of the Thames, the Humber, the Downs, and French harbours. Speed is necessary in view of the waning moon. As soon as the C.-in-C., Air, has sufficient squadrons available, mine warfare will be taken over by him, but with closest co-operation between Group West and the 9th Air Division, as recently discussed.

*The Fuehrer* and *the Chief of Staff, O.K.W.*, fully agree, and will take the matter up with the C.-in-C., Air.

2. Operation *Weseruebung*.—According to a report from the Naval Attaché, anti-aircraft units have been given permission to fire without consulting Oslo; it is probable (but not certain) that such a permission was likewise given to crews of coastal fortifications. It is to be expected that the attitude of the Norwegians is becoming more determined, therefore it is desirable to accelerate operation *Weseruebung*.

Regarding U.21, there are as yet no reports from the commanding officer which would give a clear picture of the incident. At the present moment it is not to our political advantage to put Norway in an unfavourable position as regards Britain by exercising too great pressure, since Britain must not be given any pretext now for action against Norway.

3. Oil supplies.—*Reichsmarshal Goering* made the following statement during a conference in the presence of *Ministerialrat* Fetzer, who informed the C.-in-C., Navy: "Army and non-military supplies will be at an end by May, and those of the Air Force by July. The Navy must help to ease the situation from its large supplies of Diesel oil." The Navy is ready to do so, but it will surrender oil only on special orders from the Fuehrer, so that it cannot be accused later of not having built up sufficient stocks.

*The C.-in-C., Navy*, reports on the incorrect procedure followed by the Ministry of Economics. In peacetime they permitted themselves to become completely dependent on Shell and Standard and, under pressure from these, continually attempted to prevent the Navy from purchasing oil in Mexico. The result is that the Ministry of Economics has neglected to provide oil supplies for industry, and the Navy is now called upon to ease the situation with the supplies accumulated against the wishes of the Ministry, so that industry will not come to a standstill.

Naval Supplies

March 16, 1940—
| | | | |
|---|---|---|---|
| Fuel oil | .. | .. | .. 300,000 tons. |
| Gas oil | .. | .. | .. 570,800 tons. |

October 1, 1940—
| | | | |
|---|---|---|---|
| Fuel oil | .. | .. | .. 290,000 tons. |
| Gas oil | .. | .. | .. 517,500 tons. |

4. Shipping Office.—The C.-in-C., Air, will recommend establishing the Shipping Office in the Ministry of Transport. This has been requested by the C.-in-C., Navy, and is urgently necessary. The importance of shipping is still not being recognised by the Ministry of Transport.

5. Private conference between the Fuehrer and the C.-in-C., Navy.— *The Fuehrer* once again declares that he considers it necessary to leave naval forces behind in Narvik and Trondheim in order to reinforce and support the troops which will have landed (e.g. in setting up the guns). *The C.-in-C., Navy*, enumerates the reasons against this, which have already been set forth repeatedly. In Narvik destroyers are helpless, since they are exposed to the danger of being destroyed by superior forces. Troops on land can, on the other hand, take cover. Steamers for the transport of the guns are available there. Anchorages that are safe from submarines are also not available in Trondheim. Damaged vessels have orders to make for Trondheim and Bergen. *The Fuehrer* gives up the idea of leaving ships behind in Narvik; as regards Trondheim, the C.-in-C., Navy, will investigate the matter once more.

(signed) RAEDER.

\*     \*     \*     \*     \*     \*     \*

On April 1, all plans for the invasion of Norway were completed. The date was settled in Hitler's final order—April 9, at 5.15 a.m.

Naval Officers received an additional exhortation from Raeder.

C.-in-C., Navy                                             Berlin, April 1, 1940

### Decree for Execution of *Weseruebung*

The Fuehrer and Supreme Commander, in order to ensure vital German interests, has imposed upon the *Wehrmacht* a task, the success of which, is of decisive importance to the war.

\*     \*     \*     \*     \*     \*

The execution and protection of the landing operations by the Navy will take place mainly in an area in which not Germany, but England with her superior naval forces is able to exercise control of the sea. In spite of this we must succeed, and we will, if every leader is conscious of the greatness of his task and makes a supreme effort to reach the objective assigned to him.

It is impossible to anticipate the course of events and the situations which may arise locally. Experience shows that luck and success are on the side of him who is eager to discharge his responsibilities with boldness, tenacity and skill.

The pre-requisites for the success of the operation are surprise and rapid action. I expect the Senior Officer of every Group and every Commanding Officer to be governed by an inflexible determination to reach the port assigned to him in the face of any difficulty that may arise : I expect them to enter the ports of disembarkation with the utmost resolution, not allowing themselves to be deterred by the holding and defence measures of the local commanders, nor by guard ships and coastal fortifications.

Any attempt to check or hinder the advance of our forces must be repulsed. Resistance is to be broken ruthlessly in accordance with the Directives in the operational orders.

The Navy has a large part to play in the operation which has been ordered; the greater therefore must be the will to master every obstacle to its successful execution.

Faith in the justice of our cause and implicit trust in our Fuehrer and Supreme Commander give us the assurance that in this task, as always, victory will be on our side.

This Decree is to be promulgated to the entire Officers Corps when under way for the operation.

(signed) RAEDER.<br>Commander-in-Chief of the Navy.

\*    \*    \*    \*    \*    \*

On April 5 the Allies sent strong Notes to the Norwegian and Swedish Governments declaring that they could not allow the present advantages to Germany (i.e. ore traffic) even under pressure, and that they were determined to defend their vital interests.   Two days later British and French naval units sailed for Norway to lay mines off Bud, Stadlandet, and West Fiord.   At dawn, on April 8, the Allies broadcast throughout the world their actions, and the reasons for mining territorial waters.

On the same day (April 8) in the afternoon and evening the German invasion fleet sailed, the advance units—Gneisenau, Scharnhorst, and Hipper—having previously put to sea at about the same time as the Allied fleets.   The German Battle Fleet was intercepted early on the morning of April 8, by the destroyer, H.M.S. Glowworm, who rammed the Hipper, tearing a 120-ft. hole in the German cruiser's bows and forcing her to put in to Trondheim.   H.M.S. Glowworm was destroyed, but the alarm was given and British ships raced to intercept the German Fleet.

The invasion of Norway and Denmark began shortly after 5 a.m. on April 9. After sporadic resistance Denmark surrendered.   The Norwegians opened fire on the German ships advancing on Oslo, sank the cruiser Bluecher, and damaged another cruiser, the Emden, while the submarine, H.M.S. Truant, sank yet another German cruiser, the Karlsruhe.   Fleet Air Arm and R.A.F. aircraft attacked and sank a third German cruiser, the Koenigsberg, at Bergen.

Meanwhile the British Home Fleet was disposed in the North Atlantic to intercept the German Fleet.   Before dawn, on April 9, H.M.S. Renown engaged the Gneisenau and Scharnhorst, but after a short exchange of salvos, the German battleships escaped in the bad weather and mist.   British destroyers were more successful, and at Narvik intercepted and sank nine merchant ships (including one ammunition ship), two destroyers, and damaged another destroyer.   Four days later additional British destroyers, now supported by the battleship, H.M.S. Warspite, again entered Vest Fiord (Narvik) and sank seven more German destroyers and one U-boat, thus clearing Narvik of enemy shipping and making it possible for the Allies to land troops in Norway.

In all, German naval casualties during the first few days of the Norwegian invasion were:

3 cruisers sunk,
2 cruisers severely damaged,
9 destroyers sunk,
1 destroyer severely damaged,
and about 12 merchant ships sunk or damaged.

These losses were severe, but they were approximately what Raeder had expected, and indicated what might be in store for Germany if they also tried to invade England.

\*    \*    \*    \*    \*    \*

Betrayed by the treachery of Quisling's party, however, Norwegian resistance was crippled and by the end of the day of the invasion most of Southern Norway was in German hands.

The German Naval Attaché recorded in his official diary what happened in Oslo:

April 9, 1940

0400.—I am in harbour, ready to receive the German warships. Lt. Kempf is in a German ship out in the bay, to serve as pilot. Berths have been arranged so as to be able to carry out the action in Oslo as quickly as possible. Everything that I can do here has been considered and prepared down to the smallest detail. English and French leave the town of Oslo in the morning hours. The Ambassadors of England, France, and Poland will follow. Secret papers are being burnt in the garden of the English Embassy.

0445.—The German Ambassador presents the Memorandum.

0800.—Shortly after 0800 the first German aircraft fly over the harbour. The Norwegian Flak opens fire.

0923.—The airfield Fornebu—Oslo is in German hands.

0930.—The Royal Standard is taken down from the Castle. German air attack on fortresses Akershus and Hovedoeya. Paratroops are fetched from Fornebo under Flak and machine-gun fire by the Naval and Air Attachés. The arrival of German fleet units is awaited in vain. Berlin gives no reply to W/T. Panic in the town in consequence of flak defence and the appearance of German aircraft. In the office of the Naval Attaché, the top secret papers are partly destroyed, because the position has become tense owing to the delay in the arrival of the German warships. It is possible that Norwegian soldiers, police, or English defence groups will thrust their way into the house. Pistols have been distributed. The house is secured. I drive unmolested through the town in a German car, my uniform under a civilian overcoat.

1200.—About 1200 the first German soldiers land in Fornebo, occupy the Embassy and the most important points of the town. The leader of the action is Colonel Pohlmann of Group XXI. Telephone communications cut off in the town. The telephone connection between the Naval Attaché Office and the German Embassy is in order. In the late afternoon an aircraft report announces German ship has grounded at the entrance at Oscarsburg. Lt. Pusback in the office of the Naval Attaché receives orders to sail to Oscarsburg. On his arrival the task had already been carried out and the survivors brought to German ships. The crew of the torpedoed German steamer assemble in great numbers in the offices of the Naval Attaché. Instead of the Norwegian Government which is in flight, there is a new Government formed towards evening by Quisling.

1700.—The position in the town has become clear. There are no Norwegian officers at their posts in the Defence Ministry. I help the advancing troops by giving them plans of the town and so on.

\*       \*       \*       \*       \*       \*

My conviction that the Norwegian operation would have gone through without a shot had the surprise remained secret has not changed during the process of fighting. Until the late afternoon of the 8th April nothing was known to the Government or the Admiralty staff of the operation. I was continually in communication with authoritative powers under the understandable guise of wishing to hear something of the English operation. I should certainly have obtained an impression if the Government at this time had been ready to defend a German action had they seriously believed one was meditated. No, it was not expected. As, however, the torpedoing of German special ships mounted, and as the survivors of the Rio de Janeiro gave evidence that they had come to protect Norway, the incidents of Posidonia (tanker) and U.21 stood in a new light. During the night of the 8–9 April, the Norwegian Government made its weighty decision. The King left the town on the 9th, during the morning.

\*       \*       \*       \*       \*       \*

On April 10, Raeder reviewed the situation at Hitler's noon situation conference.

## REPORT OF THE C.-IN-C., NAVY, TO THE FUEHRER ON APRIL 10, 1940, AT NOON

Also present: Chief of Staff, O.K.W.
General Jodl.
Commander von Puttkamer.
C.-in-C., Air.
General Bodenschatz.

1. *The C.-in-C., Navy*, refers to his views on operation *Weseruebung* expressed in recent conferences. He had said that passage to Norway would with some degree of luck be successful, provided the element of surprise were maintained; the break-through and landing would probably also be successful if a determined thrust were made through the fortification zones, even though a certain stiffening in the attitude of the Norwegians was observed in the last few days; the return passage would be the most difficult part of the operation, and would call for all-out co-operation by the whole German Navy. The first two parts of the operation, the approach and the penetration and landing, were carried out on the whole successfully as anticipated. The losses (Bluecher and Karlsruhe) are quite in proportion to the risks run, and can definitely not be considered high. The third part of the operation is in progress and will probably entail further losses.

2. The situation was made more difficult than anticipated by the fact that the British were also just conducting an operation involving minelaying on April 8, to be followed by occupation of Norwegian bases. This was confirmed by the presence of transports with the British Home Fleet, which were sighted on the afternoon of April 9 in the northern North Sea by attacking aircraft. Numerous British and French naval forces were thus at sea in the northern North Sea as far north as the Lofoten Islands.

3. Details. (*a*) Battleships.—Yesterday morning there was an engagement with heavy British forces in the Lofoten Islands area. The Repulse and another battleship were probably involved. Further details are not known. In the evening the Fleet Commander reported: Only 25 knots; two heavy turrets out of action. Further inquiries have not yet been answered. Losses by the enemy are probable. Radio telegraph communication with the Lofoten Islands is very uncertain.

Plan.—Both battleships are to force their way into home waters as soon as possible.

If a battleship is put out of action or is not ready for action, the question will arise whether to send the damaged battleship to Narvik for protection against further attacks, which are sure to come. Putting into Narvik means that the ship is eliminated from future operations. She will also be in great danger from aircraft carriers, without the compensation of any promise of effective operation.

Enemy battleships.—Their situation and position this morning was not yet known. The aircraft carrier Furious put out of Scapa Flow yesterday evening, apparently to join the C.-in-C., Home Fleet.

Note.—According to later reports, three British and two German destroyers were sunk; several German destroyers have been partially paralyzed and are serving as barrage batteries.

(*b*) Situation in Narvik.—According to a garbled radio message (not in code) received at 0604 today, destroyers were attacked this morning in Narvik by enemy forces, probably destroyers and several cruisers. The situation is not clear. At 0830 one destroyer reported a severe destroyer engagement off Narvik. The situation must be regarded as serious, since the troops on land are without artillery. The most urgent matters are the defence of Narvik and the question of supplies. No supply vessels have arrived as yet. It is requested that reinforcements and material be sent immediately on Swedish railways via northern Sweden. It is planned to increase the number of submarines in order to take effective measures against British operations.

(*c*) Situation in Trondheim.—The situation regarding the coastal batteries is still obscure; according to information from the O.K.W., fortifications are safe in German hands and the airfield is out of service. The vessels of the supply group have not arrived, and it is uncertain whether they will arrive. Increased submarine protection is also planned here. Cruiser Hipper and two, later three, destroyers will put out this evening, carrying only a small amount of fuel. They are to refuel at sea, but it is questionable whether this can be accomplished.

(*d*) Situation in Bergen.—The cruiser Koenigsberg (damaged), the Bremse (damaged), the Carl Peters, and the PT boat flotilla remain in the harbour. A ship arrived with mines. Three batteries are partially ready for firing this evening. The Admiral Commanding, Scouting Forces, plans to put out this evening with the Koeln and torpedo boats. The situation in Bergen appears to be assured. This base is very exposed to air attacks, however.

(*e*) Situation in Christiansand.—The Tsingtau and the PT boat flotilla remain in the harbour. The Karlsruhe was torpedoed yesterday while putting out and was later sunk. The crew was taken on board torpedo boats.

(*f*) Situation in Oslo.—The Luetzow and the Emden have not put in because the mine situation is not yet clarified. The Bluecher sank yesterday after hitting a mine. It is planned to withdraw the Luetzow this evening.

(*g*) Urgent missions.—Reinforcement of the Skagerrak minefield. Submarine chase is to be carried on in the Kattegat and the Skagerrak with all available means. Sea transports must be escorted. Supplies to western ports cannot be shipped by sea. At the beginning and at the conclusion of the conference, *the Fuehrer* expressed his full appreciation to the C.-in-C., Navy, for the great achievement of the Navy.

(signed) RAEDER.

And again, three days later:

### REPORT OF THE C.-IN-C., NAVY, TO THE FUEHRER ON APRIL 13, 1940, IN THE AFTERNOON

Berlin, April 14, 1940

(The Chief of Staff, O.K.W., was not present.)

1. Battleship operation.—Up to now there has been no report on the course of yesterday's engagement. The aircraft (piloted by Lt. Quaet-Faslem) was catapulted from the Scharnhorst in order to take a radio message, which the Fleet Commander sent to the Hipper, to Trondheim

for transmission to Group West. It returned from Trondheim to Wilhelmshaven, where Lt. Quaet-Faslem merely reported his impressions of the engagement off the Lofoten Islands. Today, April 13, at 1000 the Fleet Commander gave a short report to the C.-in-C., Navy, by telephone, on the tactical situation during the engagement, and his views regarding the break-through. The C.-in-C., Navy, fully endorses the conduct of the Fleet Commander. It would have been wrong to have all-out battleship operations off the Lofoten Islands; the tactical situation was very unfavourable, with the enemy disposed along the dark western horizon, our ships along the clear eastern horizon, and the wind force 10.

2. Our own measures.—The minefield in the Skagerrak was reinforced to the north and south during the night of April 12.

Beginning today, submarines will be distributed as follows:

3 boats in Vaags Fiord.
5 boats in Vest Fiord.
3 boats with supplies en route to Narvik in about three to five days.
1 boat en route to Namsen Fiord.
2 additional boats for Namsen and Folden Fiords were ordered today.
3 off Trondheim.
1 boat is ordered to Romsdals Fiord (Aandalsnes).
5 boats off Bergen.
2 boats off Stavanger.

3. All available defence forces have been detailed for escort and transport of supplies to Oslo. The present units will be reinforced by the assignment of Norwegian torpedo boats and steam trawlers. Troops will be transported only in fast vessels, since there is great danger from submarines in the Kattegat and Skagerrak. Up to now one British submarine has been destroyed.

4. The Luetzow was ordered to Kiel to be prepared as quickly as possible for Atlantic operations. Her presence in the Atlantic would have diverted naval forces from the North Sea, among others aircraft carriers and large cruisers. It is hoped that the two auxiliary cruisers "16" and "36" will have this effect; they have probably just broken through into the Atlantic.

5. Political questions.—(a) May use of Danish naval forces be requested? *The Fuehrer* decides in the affirmative. Payment is to be offered.

(b) The Swedes have extinguished all beacon lights, even the large outer lights. May pressure be brought to bear to leave the beacons lit? *Fuehrer:* Yes; through the Foreign Office.

6. Recognition signals between ships and aircraft.—*The Fuehrer* desires maximum security of the ships. At the proposal of the C.-in-C., Navy, light signals are to be made at night only if the aircraft opens fire, when the ship has been detected. Our rulings will be submitted; they were agreed upon by the C.-in-C., Air, and are very carefully thought through.

7. Role of the Navy in landing operations.—There are doubts regarding the accuracy of the reports on hits made by the Air Force, although submitted in good faith. The greater proportion of the large ships reported hit are still operating in the North Sea. The operations of our two battleships have to be planned with this in view. They will be made ready as quickly as possible.

8. Landing operations were begun two days too late; the C.-in-C., Navy, always insisted on April 7 as being the bext X-day.  Since the British got ahead of us by laying mines, and the Norwegian attitude stiffened (pilots, etc.), it was impossible to bring supply vessels north in time.

(signed) RAEDER.

*      *      *      *      *      *

Resistance was still possible in Northern Norway, however, and from April 15 various Allied landings were made at Narvik, Bodo, Harstad, Namsos, and Aandalsnes.  But the positions could not be held, and some six weeks later the evacuation of Allied troops began.

Hitler discussed the situation in Norway on April 22, 26, and 29.

### REPORT OF THE C.-IN-C., NAVY, TO THE FUEHRER ON APRIL 22, 1940, AT 1500

Also present:  Chief of Staff, O.K.W.
General Jodl.
Commander von Puttkamer.

1. Submarine transports.—The following can transport aviation spirit:

| U.101.. | .. | 36 tons. |
|---------|----|----------|
| U.122.. | .. | 90 tons. |
| U.A .. | .. | 170 tons. |

These boats will proceed in the next few days to Trondheim; they will bring 8·8-cm. anti-aircraft guns.  *The Fuehrer* and *the Chief of Staff, O.K.W.*, are of the opinion that this quantity of spirit will suffice for the present; after that the transport of mountain guns and ammunition is the most important factor.

2. On the morning of April 22 two ships with one 15-cm. gun each arrived in Stavanger, escorted by motor boats; in about five days two additional ones will follow.   10·5-cm. field howitzers are to be brought to Trondheim by vessels of the defence group.

3. Transport to Oslo has been requested from the Navy for the following:

Up to April 24, daily 2,000 men.
On April 25, 1,000 men.
From April 26 on, transport of supplies only.

In addition, according to the O.K.W., transport will have to be provided for the motorised rifle brigade from Denmark.  The Navy is at present fully occupied with these transports and has exhausted its resources.  Fewer demands must be made on it for some time.

4. Transports for Trondheim.—The Bremen and the Europa cannot be used for transports to Trondheim in the present situation.  They would have to be escorted by the whole fleet and by numerous escort forces which would have to be diverted from the Kattegat transports.  Such operations would entail certain loss of the transports and of the whole

fleet. As a result it would also become impossible to escort transports to Oslo. Sufficient escort forces would be lacking; British naval forces would probably penetrate into the Kattegat after our battleships have been eliminated.

*The operation cannot be carried out.*

The following would be possible: Gneisenau * and Potsdam * each could transport approximately 3,000 men with limited equipment to Stavanger escorted by naval forces; four banana ships (15 knots) might transport 350 men and equipment each. The large ships would have to be provided with bow protection gear. *The Fuehrer* decides that the Potsdam and Gneisenau are to be made ready. If possible they should proceed as far as Bergen.

5. Battleships will be ready with three destroyers on April 23; the Hipper not until May 1 because she has a hole of 40 metres in the bow. (Caused by H.M.S. Glowworm.—Ed.)

6. The danger of submarines in the Kattegat-Skagerrak is at present somewhat less, since the boats have to be relieved occasionally here too.

7. The attacks made with aerial mines off the Thames and in the Downs were successful in the last few nights (sinkings reported). A very urgent matter is the laying of mines in Scapa Flow, and if possible also in the Clyde. *The Fuehrer* states that the C.-in-C., Air, does not consider the air units sufficiently experienced yet to lay mines in Scapa Flow.

*The C.-in-C., Navy,* says that the 9th Air Division has already participated in mining the Thames, and they are therefore sufficiently experienced for Scapa Flow action. This request is urgent.

8. British, and possibly French, aerial mines must be expected in the future, as indicated by damage done to the ferry at Korsoer and to a vessel in the Elbe. At present the charges seem to be small, since damage has been slight.

9. *The C.-in-C., Navy,* recommends that the request for use of Danish naval vessels by the German Navy should not be made for a while, in order to spare the self-respect of the Danish Navy. The matter could be taken up later to see whether the Danes themselves wish to undertake certain police and escort services. *The Fuehrer* agrees.

10. *The C.-in-C., Navy,* recommends that Terboven co-operate with Quisling and that the areas in which there is no longer any fighting should be appeased. Quisling warns against the danger of causing a general national resistance by highhanded measures. *The Fuehrer* replies that Terboven has instructions to co-operate with Quisling.

11. Report to the Fuehrer regarding submarines.—Magnetic firing has failed in northern waters as a result of the magnetic conditions prevailing there; it could be that counter-measures by British ships against the magnetic fuses have something to do with the failure. In addition torpedoes with percussion fuses often pass under the target, since untested torpedoes have had to be taken on board because of prevailing ice conditions. This last difficulty has been overcome in the meantime, so that by the end of the week accurate torpedoes will be available. In view of the former shortcoming, the submarines which had been operating very intensively in the north, making attacks on the Warspite, cruisers, destroyers, and transport vessels, were withdrawn from north Norwegian coastal

* Passenger liners, not warships.

waters and sent to the west. The above-mentioned abnormal magnetic conditions will wear off only after a long time (shaking of the boats by storm, demagnetization).

(signed) RAEDER.

On the same day Raeder summarised his opinions of the invasion of Norway.

## SUPPLEMENT TO THE WAR DIARY OF THE C.-IN-C., NAVY

Berlin, April 22, 1940

Operation *Weseruebung.*—1. On October 10, 1939, for the first time the C.-in-C., Navy, called the Fuehrer's attention to the importance of Norway for naval and air warfare.  The Fuehrer stated that he would consider the matter.

On December 12, 1939, Quisling and Hagelin were received by the Fuehrer.  As a result, instructions were given to the O.K.W. to make preparations.  The C.-in-C., Navy, had a survey made, which was completed in January.  Following this survey, Captain Krancke worked in the O.K.W. on operation *Weseruebung.*

Hagelin meanwhile maintained contact with the Chief of Staff, Naval Staff.  His objects were to develop the Quisling Party so that it would become capable of action, and to inform the Naval High Command on political developments in Norway and on Military matters.  In general he urged speeding up the preparations, but he considered it necessary first to expand the Quisling organisation.  The support promised him in money and coal was very slow in coming, and he complained about this repeatedly.  It was not until the end of March that Quisling considered the operation so urgent that expansion of his organisation could not wait. The military advice given by Hagelin was forwarded to the O.K.W.

2. The attitude of the western powers at the end of the Finnish War made the operation urgent, but its commencement was delayed at first by ice conditions in the Baltic.  As soon as these became more favourable the C.-in-C., Navy, in a conference with the Fuehrer, urged the selection of April 7 as X-day, regardless of whether the weather were already suitable also for operation *Gelb.*  The Fuehrer decided on April 2 that April 9 should be X-day.

3. On April 4 there was a conference in K. between Quisling and a G.S.O. of the O.K.W.  Hagelin, on behalf of Quisling, repeatedly urged that Quisling should be given an assault group in good time, with the aid of which he could at once seize power and install a new government with the consent of the King.  This request unfortunately could not be met, since Quisling and Hagelin, according to orders, could not be informed of the imminence and the time of the operation.

4. On April 8 the British laid mines in Norwegian territorial waters. At the same time a stiffening in the Norwegian attitude had been noticed during the preceding days, indicating possible difficulties in the operation.  For example, the coastal fortifications were alerted; troop movements took place—250 Norwegian soldiers were stationed at the pilot station at Kopperwik; there was delay in providing pilots for the supply vessels, delaying their passsage to the north.

An engagement took place between the German and British forces on April 8. Actually, destroyer Glowworm ran into the Hipper group and was destroyed; later at the time of landing an encounter took place between the German battleships and heavy British naval forces off the Lofoten Islands. As far as the Norwegians were concerned, the harbour defences in the various ports to be occupied were on the alert, and losses on the German side resulted. In spite of this, the Navy was able to land in all the harbours chosen for this purpose. The views which the C.-in-C., Navy, expressed to the Fuehrer, and which he held to the very last, that it was wrong to leave destroyers behind in the northern ports as a support for the occupying forces on land, proved to be correct. When, on the first day, the destroyers in Narvik did not finish refueling, since the second tanker had not arrived in Narvik owing to delays caused by the Norwegians their fate was sealed. They were cut off by superior forces and were obliged to fight these in the fiord. The absence of the coastal battery assumed to be at the entrance to Narvik rendered the situation particularly unfavourable.

5. The Navy fulfilled the tasks assigned by transporting the troops, and penetrating into the harbours in order to land the troops. The C.-in-C., Navy, emphasised from the start that it would not be possible to break through to Narvik and Trondheim once more with naval forces for the purpose of supply, since the British would certainly be in control of the seas by that time. Consequently the C.-in-C., Navy, has categorically refused further transport operations by the Bremen and the Europa, etc., since this would mean the complete destruction of these ships as well as of the naval forces escorting them.

6. Seizure of the Norwegian Government and political action in general failed completely. One factor which contributed to this was undoubtedly the delay in the arrival of air-borne troops owing to fog. However, the main reason was the fact that the situation was handled extremely badly on the political side (Minister Braeuer). In such cases the main objective must be to arrest the government at all cost. If energetic steps had been taken it would have been quite possible to do this and also to bring pressure to bear on the King to form a new government. A minister (diplomat) who previously had very correct relations with the King and the Government is the most unsuitable person for such a task. Before the commencement of the operation I expressed my concern to the Chief of Staff, O.K.W., and to General von Falkenhorst at not knowing how the political side was being handled. Both assured me that the matter was being dealt with by the Fuehrer and that the Services were not to be bothered with it. When I mentioned Quisling to General von Falkenhorst, I learned to my astonishment, that the latter considered the Minister of Foreign Affairs (Koht!) also a very sound man who could be used. After this statement I feared the worst regarding the settlement of political questions.

The situation developed accordingly: Quisling did not obtain the necessary support from General von Falkenhorst and from Minister Braeuer. The Norwegian Government escaped. The re-organisation of the government in agreement with the King failed. Quisling was suspected of high treason. An "Administrative Committee," which, however, did not constitute a government, was the result. The Norwegian population was split into two camps. It remains to be seen whether the appointment of Terboven as Reich Commissioner and the recall of Minister Braeuer will bring any changes.

(signed) RAEDER.

### REPORT OF THE C.-IN-C., NAVY, TO THE FUEHRER ON APRIL 26, 1940, AT 1500

Also present: Chief of Staff, O.K.W.
General Jodl.
Commander von Puttkamer.

1. Raid by French destroyers on the night of April 23 in the Skagerrak. Such raids by small destroyer units are always possible, but have little prospect of success.

*Defensive measures.*—(*a*) Air reconnaissance in the evening, which will generally detect large-scale operations.

(*b*) Minefields only discourage destroyers, but do not always prevent their passage, since the destroyers may quite possibly pass them by using bow protection gear and by taking advantage of the dipping of the mines in the current.

(*c*) Defence of the gap in the minefield by the 17-cm. battery at Hanstholm and the 21-cm. battery at Christiansand.

(*d*) Radar gear is being set up in Denmark by the Navy and in Norway by the Air Force. British destroyers have not ventured on such raids either in the German Bight or in the Skagerrak; French destroyers rely on their high continuous speed. The French destroyers encountered patrol boats which fired on them; our torpedo boats were sent after them; naval aircraft squadrons and, finally, three planes of the operational Air Forces were sent into action, so that the destroyers met real opposition. The fact that we are carrying out heavy transport operations practically unmolested, in spite of not having naval supremacy, is to be attributed to geographical conditions and strong escort by naval forces and aircraft. This escort service calls for the most intense and exacting operations of practically the whole Navy.

Orders issued via the C.-in-C., Air, regarding use of a mine-laying squadron and of the He59's for defence of the Skagerrak were unnecessary. Mine-layers are to be used offensively against Britain. Laying of mines in Scapa Flow and the Clyde is as urgent as ever.

2. Submarine warfare.—Small submarines must be withdrawn for training purposes; large ones must be used as soon as possible for submarine warfare against merchant shipping, which just now offers good prospects since large numbers of destroyers are operating in the north and the convoys are left unprotected. Successes against fast, heavily-escorted naval vessels on the Norwegian coast will be achieved only on rare occasions in spite of very large numbers of boats in operation. Some submarines will remain in Norwegian waters (transport submarines). *The Fuehrer* agrees.

3. Defence of bases in Norway.—Fortification of Trondheim is of primary importance for the Navy. Batteries, torpedo batteries, and nets are necessary. Anti-aircraft guns are urgently needed.

Oslo, Trondheim, and Bergen have torpedo batteries; make-shift batteries should now be provided for Hardanger Fiord and Sogne Fiord (later Christiansand, Nord Fiord, and Aandalsnes).

*The Fuehrer* urges use of 38-cm. guns for closing the Skagerrak; these will not be ready until later. The suggestion will be investigated. The Fuehrer urges use of the guns of the two coastal fortifications for the defence of the fiords, e.g. Sogne Fiord.

4. Anti-mine measures are at present of great importance. A British aerial mine with acoustic firing has been found. Therefore it is to be assumed that torpedoes used by submarines in the Skagerrak also have acoustic warheads; this is indicated by propellor hits.

The polarity of some of our mines has been reversed; a combination of both kinds is laid in order to insure their effect.

5. Cargo space.—Of 2,400,000 tons, 1,000,000 tons have been taken over by the Navy; the rest comprises many large ships which cannot be used. Therefore attempts should be made to use Danish and Norwegian ships. There is a great demand for ore and coal transports. The Russians, Swedes, and Danes will have to transport coal with their own vessels.

6. Decision regarding transport to Bergen.—The five vessels carrying 1,800 men with equipment need not be sent; they should proceed via Oslo, since the situation around Bergen has been cleared up. It is not necessary to use battleships for this purpose.

(signed) RAEDER.

## REPORT OF THE C.-IN-C., NAVY, TO THE FUEHRER ON APRIL 29, 1940, AT 1530

Also present: Chief of Staff, O.K.W.
General Jodl.
Commander von Puttkamer.

1. Further construction on the Aircraft Carrier Graf Zeppelin.—The C.-in-C., Navy, proposes cessation of further construction work, since the ship will not be ready for commissioning until the end of 1940, and the artillery will not be installed for about another ten months (the anti-aircraft guns are now already being used elsewhere; fire control of naval artillery has been delayed by transactions with Russia, etc.). Including the necessary trials, the carrier will therefore not be entirely ready before the end of 1941. *The Fuehrer* is of the opinion that, considering the probable developments in aircraft, carriers with planes with internal combustion engines will not be useable anymore in this war. The artillery of the Graf Zeppelin must be used for Norway to protect coastal waters (defence of fishing vessels and coastal traffic).

2. *The Fuehrer* requests that the Emden be left in Oslo for another two weeks for anti-aircraft defence of the harbour, which is quite inadequate. The Emden will be unnecessary as soon as three heavy anti-aircraft batteries are available in Oslo harbour (to protect oil tanks). The C.-in-C., Navy, explains the reasons why the return of the Emden is at present desirable.

3. Troop transports to Norway.—*The C.-in-C., Navy,* explains that the amount transported is not dependent on the number of vessels available, but on the number of escort forces, which are operating uninter-

ruptedly and under greatest pressure. Experience has shown that medium-sized, fast steamers are most suitable for transport purposes, also fast transport by means of torpedo boats, etc. There were no losses recently. The Fuehrer is anxious for speedy transfer of the 2nd Mountain Division, which has been in progress since April 29. *Question:* Can a large part of this division be transported by the Potsdam and Gneisenau?

Answer.—Each ship can take about 3,000 men with limited equipment (no horses). However, there is the danger that large ships are more likely to be sunk by submarines and that a great number of soldiers might thus be lost. In addition, a large number of fast escort forces would be needed, which would then not be available for other transports. The question will be investigated as to when and where these two vessels could be ready and what equipment they could carry—whether, therefore, the transfer of the Mountain Division would actually be accelerated.

(signed) RAEDER.

By the middle of June the occupation was completed, and Norway was in German hands.

# The Invasion of Holland, Belgium and France

PREPARATIONS FOR *Fall Gelb* did not involve much assistance from the German Navy, as the operation was planned almost entirely as a combined land and air offensive. The use of almost all ships for Norwegian operations precluded any great naval effort in support of the invasion of the Low Countries, and naval measures were confined to mining operations, the use of motor-boats in the canals, the seizure of certain strategic islands, and U-boat attacks in the Channel.

At the beginning of March, Admiral Fricke (Raeder's Staff Officer, Operations), sent the following appreciation to the Supreme Command:

Naval War Staff                                          Berlin, March 6, 1940

To the Supreme Command (Air),
and Air Command Staff,
and Group West.

Concerning: Readiness of Sea and Air Forces

1. If *Weseruebung* and *Fall Gelb* are carried out at about the same time, it will not be possible to prepare naval surface forces for *Fall Gelb*.

2. U-boats and aircraft will have to carry out these duties, but, because of *Weseruebung*, only limited numbers will be available.

3. (Summary.) Aircraft from Coastal Air Groups will have to undertake mining operations, and it is requested that Group 9 be placed under the command of Naval Group Command, West.

(Signed) FRICKE.

This policy was maintained in spite of requests from local Admirals to take a more active part, and mining operations were given to the *Luftwaffe*. The final decision was to mine Dutch harbours, to occupy some of the West Friesian islands, and to send three U-boats into the Channel.

On May 7, Raeder conferred with Hitler, but the forthcoming offensive in the West was not discussed.

## REPORT OF THE C.-IN-C., NAVY, TO THE FUEHRER ON MAY 7, 1940, AT 1500

Also present: Chief of Staff, O.K.W.
General Jodl.
Commander von Puttkamer.

1. Submarine transports.—Up to now, seven submarines have been in operation for transport purposes, and they have brought or are bringing all required material to Trondheim. It is proposed to release from transport duties the small boats having little cargo space, and to continue using the remainder until the railway to Trondheim is again in operation (about four weeks). Further, it is suggested that of the six boats which are not yet ready, only the first, namely U.123, be prepared for transport duty; the remaining five, which are very important as communications boats for submarine warfare, should not be converted at present. In an emergency they can be made ready for use within a few days. *The Fuehrer* agrees under these conditions.

2. Of primary importance in home waters is the danger of British aerial mines. These are of the magnetic type, against which our counter-measures are effective, however. It will be necessary to organise the patrol of coastal waters and of river mouths and entrances, and to decide on routes for merchant shipping, etc. Attacks on enemy airfields are the best counter-measures; the British are resorting to this to combat our aerial mines. The Gneisenau hit a mine in the mouth of the Elbe; this only caused buckling and cracks so that lengthy repairs will not be necessary.

3. *The C.-in-C., Navy,* repeatedly stresses the great and decisive importance of laying aerial mines. If the Air Force had shown more interset, the Thames could have been mined during the past few weeks. Mine warfare is a naval matter. The Navy determines where the mines are to be laid, and of what type they are to be; the Navy develops mines; former naval officers train the units. Therefore, in order to conduct mine warfare with the greatest possible effect, the Navy should also carry out operations. The C.-in-C., Air, will have great demands made on his forces by operation *Gelb*, and he will not have sufficient time and interest for mine warfare. *The Fuehrer* states that recently in a memorandum of the C.-in-C., Air, the opposite view was presented, i.e. need for unification of all air units, only one reconnaissance, etc., in order to economise on personnel and material. *The C.-in-C., Navy,* on the other hand, emphasises the necessity of closest co-operation between the naval air units and the Navy.

4. A report is made regarding the seizure of the submarine Seal.*

5. *The Fuehrer* approves the dispatch of a letter from the C.-in-C., Navy, to Admiral Rechnitzer concerning Denmark's attitude.

6. Propaganda is discussed regarding the effectiveness of aircraft against battleships. *The Fuehrer* is considering this from the point of view of the effect on the construction plans of other countries, especially the U.S.A.

(signed) RAEDER.

\*        \*        \*        \*        \*        \*

At dawn, on May 10, German troops invaded Holland, Belgium, and Luxembourg. Air supremacy, the 5th Column, and the use of paratroops in Dutch uniform enabled the invading armies to gain rapid control of key positions. Ships of the Royal Navy went immediately to the aid of the Dutch, and small detachments of Royal Marines and the Guards were rushed across the Channel, but were too few to stop the German onslaught. German naval forces put up no opposition, but the *Luftwaffe* attacked continuously and furiously.

During the next three days the Queen of the Netherlands, members of the Royal Family, and the Dutch Government were evacuated to England, and, on May 14, Rotterdam was savagely bombed and destroyed.

Hostilities ceased on May 15, but the majority of the Dutch Home Fleet made good their withdrawal to England and, together with the bulk of the Fleet which was stationed in the East Indies, became an invaluable and powerful Ally for the rest of the war.

\*        \*        \*        \*        \*        \*

Antwerp fell on May 18, and the subsequent advance of the German Army was rapid. Within a week they broke through the Allied front and reached Boulogne. The question of using the Channel ports was discussed at the next conference on May 21. At this same conference the possible invasion of England was mentioned to Hitler for the first time, but no decisions were made.

\* H.M.S. Seal was damaged by a mine in the Skagerrak on May 5 and later captured by the Germans while attempting to reach Goteborg.

### REPORT OF THE C.-IN-C., NAVY, TO THE FUEHRER ON MAY 21, 1940, AT 1200

Also present: Chief of Staff, O.K.W.
General Jodl.
Commander von Puttkamer.

1. Naval operations. (a) Battleships.—The Scharnhorst, Hipper, and three destroyers will be ready for further operations on about May 27. The Gneisenau will probably be ready for action about the beginning of June. Plan.—The ships are to operate in the northern North Sea and the Arctic Ocean to relieve our land operations in northern Norway, and to defend the Skagerrak and southern Norway by threatening enemy communications between the British Isles and northern Norway. Operations from Trondheim will be conducted later.

(b) Both motor-boat flotillas moved from Norway to the German Bight for operations in the Hoofden-Channel area.

(c) Submarine warfare.

(1) Atlantic.—So far two boats have departed. An additional six boats will be ready for operations by the end of May.

(2) Hoofden.—Four boats are operating there now; another three boats will be ready by the end of May to act as reliefs.

(d) Auxiliary cruisers.

(1) Ship "16" (commanded by Rogge) is to lay mines off Cape Agulhas and to carry out warfare against merchant shipping in the Indian Ocean.

(2) Ship "36" (commanded by Weyher) has sunk one ship in the North Atlantic. She is proceeding through the Pacific for mine-laying duties off Australia and warfare against merchant shipping in the Indian Ocean.

(3) Ship "21" (commanded by von Ruckteschell) is on her way to attack merchant ships in the North Atlantic.

Is it permissible to bombard the French-occupied island of Aruba? The oil installations belong to Standard Oil, an American company. *The Fuehrer* decides this should not be done for the time being.

(e) Mine warfare.—Two minefields were laid to extend the Westwall, and a third one will be laid. Koeln, Grille, destroyers, and mine-laying trawlers participated in the operation. The Skagerrak barrage is to be reinforced against submarines.

2. Holland and Belgium.—(a) At first Den Helder is to be used as a base of operations, later mainly the Scheldt.

(b) Coastal defence.—*The C.-in-C., Navy,* considers that only a few heavy and medium batteries are necessary, as we need not reckon with landing operations in view of our air superiority. *The Fuehrer* agrees. He believes that the batteries will need protection against aerial bombs. This cannot be provided *quickly*.

3. *The C.-in-C., Navy,* asks how long the Fuehrer believes the war will last. Would we be justified in sending all training submarines out on operations now, in the hope that the war will be decided quickly, or would it be better to assume that the war will last some time, and therefore to organise a long-term programme for submarine training and construction?

*The Fuehrer* decides on the second course, which is also recommended by the C.-in-C., Navy. When the main operations in France are over, the Fuehrer will concentrate on the submarine and Ju88 production programmes.

4. The political situation in Norway is discussed.

5. *The Fuehrer* and *the C.-in-C., Navy,* discuss in private details concerning the invasion of England, which the Naval Staff has been working on since November.

(signed) RAEDER.

\*　　\*　　\*　　\*　　\*　　\*

## DUNKIRK

On May 25 King Leopold of Belgium surrendered, and it became clear that if the war was to be continued, the British Expeditionary Force would have to be evacuated. The only ports available were Ostend and Dunkirk. Ostend was captured on May 29, leaving the harbours and beaches of Dunkirk as the sole evacuation port of the British Army.

The German Naval Staff did not think that they would be able to do much to stop an evacuation, and in a memorandum to the Supreme Command, Admiral Schniewind, Raeder's Chief of Staff, stated on May 26 that:

(To the Supreme Command (Air), Fuehrer Headquarters)

" 5. A regular and orderly transport of large numbers of troops with equipment cannot take place in the hurried and difficult conditions prevailing. Larger ships with considerable capacity cannot be used on account of the depth of water, and the harbour conditions in those harbours which the enemy still posses. (*Pencil note.—Transport has certainly been going on for some time.*)

Evacuation of troops without equipment, however, is conceivable by means of large numbers of smaller vessels, coastal and ferry steamers, fishing trawlers, drifters, and other small craft, in good weather, even from the open coast. The Navy, however, is not in a position to take part successfully in this with the means at its disposal. There are no signs yet of such transport being carried out or prepared.

If it should be started, the Navy considers the best counter-attack to be the use of aircraft on moonless nights with flares.

The Motor Torpedo Boat units have received orders to declare whether any signs of troop movements are to be seen.

Special instructions are to be given in connection with the last paragraph.

(signed) SCHNIEWIND.

On the same day (May 26) the British Admiralty gave the order for operation "Dynamo" to begin, and the evacuation of troops from Dunkirk started.

By May 30 the German Naval Staff conceded that the impossible was taking place. The War Diary entry for May 30 stated:

"The evacuation of English and French troops from the Franco-Belgian coast continues during the day. It is favoured by the extremely bad weather—fog and rain—which does not allow the German Air forces to attack. Small steamers, trawlers, and fishing vessels are strongly overloaded on their voyage towards the Downs. The tough resistance of English and French troops makes it possible to hold the Dunkirk area, the defence of which has been rendered more difficult. The operations of the French Navy in defence of Dunkirk are under the command of Vice-Admiral Abrial. The Admiral received from General Weygand a message from the President of the Republic to the Commander of the land army, in which the troops are thanked by the Fatherland for their energetic resistance.

"The great massing of evacuation vessels made it necessary to give an order in the evening that fire should only be opened when certain recognition of the enemy was possible. In the area of the Downs by North Foreland, warnings of magnetic mines were issued.  All merchant traffic from the Downs to the south was stopped.

"The embarkation itself is taking place mostly on the open shore near Dunkirk.  The great lack of motor transport increases the difficulties.  Thousands of troops wait on the shore for embarkation.  Air attacks in the night of May 30 caused several of the transports to be lost."

and in the entry of the following day there was a hint of admiration for the achievement:

"The embarkation of troops on the Franco-Belgian coasts between Nieuport and Dunkirk continues its progress under strong attacks by aircraft, and artillery fire from the land.  The steady laying of mines from the air, and the nightly successful appearance of German speed-boats, heighten the extremely great difficulties of this retreat.  The impression remains, nevertheless, that the Western Powers, under a ruthless use of naval forces and transport vessels, will succeed in getting a considerable part of their troops over to England, even though in complete disorder and without heavy arms or equipment.  The losses, however, must be enormous.  The naval forces and command posts have been encouraged to further efforts by the Dover High Command."

The evacuation from Dunkirk ended at dawn on June 4.  More than 335,000 troops had been saved.

\* \* \* \* \* \*

During the campaigns in Western Europe, the German Navy was strengthening its position in Norway.  The British Home Fleet, besides covering the evacuation of Allied troops, was harassing German sea communications.  Two carriers, H.M.S. Ark Royal and H.M.S. Glorious, provided air support and did considerable damage.  Raeder accordingly planned to send the German Battle Fleet out once more, and the operation — *Juno* — was carefully prepared.  The Gneisenau and Scharnhorst sailed from Germany on June 4, and on the same day Raeder reported to Hitler.

## REPORT OF THE C.-IN-C., NAVY, TO THE FUEHRER ON JUNE 4, 1940, AT 1200

Also present:  Chief of Staff, O.K.W.
            General Jodl.
            Commander von Puttkamer.

1. *The C.-in-C., Navy*, elaborates on the operation of the battleships which began early on 4 June:

(*a*) The situation is favourable on the whole, as so many British ships are undergoing repairs.

(*b*) It is possible to use Trondheim as a base; tankers, mine-sweepers, motor mine-sweepers, a repair ship, ammunition reserves, and anti-aircraft batteries are available there.  Sea reconnaissance could be increased.  There is danger from submarines.

(*c*) Situation at Narvik.—Large supplies of material and food-stuffs are necessary both for us and the Norwegians; consequently considerable convoy traffic is necessary.  An aircraft carrier is at sea about 200 miles from the coast, or off Tromsoe.  One to two battleships as well as cruisers and destroyers are off Harstad or in Ofoten Fiord.

(*d*) It will therefore be possible to relieve Narvik as follows:

(1) By operating against the British naval forces and transports en route to Narvik.

(2) By attacks to be made on bases by suitable forces if no contacts are made at sea and if air reconnaissance indicates a favourable situation in the fiords.

(e) The following plans have been made for later execution with Trondheim serving as a base. Light enemy forces in the coastal waters near Trondheim and Bodoe are to be eliminated; the supply lines for the *Feuerstein* group are to be secured; the coastal artillery defences are to be extended as far as Bodoe. The Nuernberg, with torpedo boats, is to proceed to Trondheim. Consequently the Riedel will be withdrawn.

2. Plans for a landing in Lyngen Fiord have already been discussed with the Air Force. So far the following has been established: 3,000 men with limited equipment can be transported in the Bremen. No heavy cargo can be loaded, however, as the capacity of the cranes is limited to 5 tons. An investigation is being made whether a stronger crane can be installed. The Bremen and the Europa can be ready in about five days, and will have a speed of 26·5 knots. It will be necessary to install anti-aircraft guns and to take barges on board to unload material.

Necessary preparations.—Army and naval officers must carry out air reconnaissance of Lyngen Fiord to investigate landing points, jetties, etc. Air superiority must be established to cover the time of approach and landing. A mountain troop is to be held in readiness, and engineers as well as material must be taken along. After the landing, ships are to proceed to "Basis Nord," as supplies of fuel are limited. The Navy cannot provide further supplies in the north.

*The Fuehrer* considers it necessary to take tanks of approximately 13 tons (Czech) and 8·8-cm. batteries which can if necessary be set up at crossroads. This however depends on the cranes, on the size of the barges, and on the landing conditions. As the preparations will probably take some time (the *Feuerstein* group will arrive before these transports), they are to get under way now.

*The C.-in-C., Navy*, points out that this transport operation cannot change the difficult situation existing at present; transports by air are necessary. The C.-in-C., Navy, suggests that it might be much quicker and easier to land troops by means of freight-carrying gliders instead, for the purpose of seizing the airfield at Bardufoss; further troops could then follow in transport planes. *The Fuehrer* states that this will take place simultaneously with the transport operation.

3. *The C.-in-C., Navy*, reports that the Navy is detailing four anti-aircraft units to Norway and the west, in the face of considerable difficulties, but the anti-aircraft defences of Wilhelmshaven and Kiel or of the Kiel Canal cannot be weakened any further as long as the R.A.F. remains unbeaten. *The Fuehrer* is in complete agreement, as Wilhelmshaven and Kiel are the bases for all naval warfare.

4. *The C.-in-C., Navy*, draws attention to the fact that the curtailed submarine construction programme, which was to be completed January 1, 1942, is being delayed through lack of workmen, iron, and other metals. Already construction has been held up on submarine pens in Kiel, Wilhelmshaven, and Hamburg, and on submarine harbours and repair workshops. *The Fuehrer* explains that he intends to decrease the size of

the Army when France has been overthrown and to release all older men and skilled workmen; the Air Force and Navy will have top priority.

5. Agreements have been reached with the Italian Navy concerning areas for submarine warfare, etc.

(signed) RAEDER.

\* \* \* \* \* \*

On June 8, the German battleships surprised and sank H.M.S. Glorious, her two attendant destroyers, Acasta and Ardent, two merchant ships, and the trawler Juniper. No news of the action was received by the British Fleet until 24 hours later, by which time the German Fleet had already reached Trondheim and were safe under the protection of the *Luftwaffe*.

\* \* \* \* \* \*

During the next two weeks events moved swiftly to a crisis. Italy declared war on June 10; Paris was occupied on June 14; and on June 17 France asked for armistice terms. Four days later the armistice was signed, and Great Britain was left alone to face the full weight of the German *Wehrmacht*.

# Operation "Sea Lion"

## PLAN FOR THE INVASION OF ENGLAND

PLANNING FOR a landing in England began on November 15, 1939, when Raeder issued an order to his staff to investigate and prepare the operation. This was an order to the Naval Staff only, and neither Hitler nor the other two Services were informed or consulted. The plans were apparently prepared not so much because Raeder considered the invasion of England necessary, but because he did not want to be confronted with a sudden directive from Hitler ordering the invasion at short notice. (The Army preparations for the occupation of Western Europe had omitted all mention of a subsequent landing in England). Though Raeder appreciated Hitler's policy of subduing England by "siege" tactics rather than by an actual invasion, he foresaw that invasion would probably be necessary, and instructed his staff accordingly.

\*　　　\*　　　\*　　　\*　　　\*　　　\*

On June 18, the day following the French request for armistice terms, Mr. Churchill damped Hitler's hopes of a speedy capitulation of Britain, when, speaking in the House of Commons, he said:

> "What General Weygand called the Battle of France is over. I expect that the Battle of Britain is about to begin. Upon this battle depends the survival of Christian civilisation. . . . The whole fury and might of the enemy must very soon be turned on us. Hitler knows that he will have to break us in this island or lose the war. . . . Let us therefore brace ourselves to our duty, and so bear ourselves that if the British Commonwealth and Empire lasts for a thousand years men will still say, 'This was their finest hour'."

Two days later, on June 20, Hitler summoned his Cs.-in-C. to a conference to discuss the armistice terms for France. The question of what to do about England was brought up by Raeder—he had first mentioned the plans of the Naval Staff in a previous conference (May 21)—but Hitler, jubilant over his victory in France, paid scant attention. He did not consider that invasion would be necessary, and thought that air attacks and a naval blockade would quickly bring England to defeat. For this reason he was more concerned with the occupation of Iceland—operation *Ikarus*—which Raeder squashed because of the impossibility of maintaining the long sea communications.

## CONFERENCE OF THE C.-IN-C., NAVY, WITH THE FUEHRER ON JUNE 20, 1940, AT WOLFSSCHLUCHT.

Also present: Chief of Staff, O.K.W.
General Jodl.
Commander von Puttkamer.

1. France. The Armistice.—The Fuehrer wishes to refrain from taking any measures which would affect French honour. The fleet is therefore to be interned at Brest and Toulon according to peacetime disposition. The ships are to be put out of action in accordance with special instructions. Some naval units must be available for the defence of Indo-China. Bases on the Atlantic coast with all their resources must be completely at the disposal of the German Navy for warfare against Britain. Demands for mine-sweepers and vessels to defend the harbours and channels are to be made during the negotiations.

*The C.-in-C., Navy*, points out that the Navy can man only the coastal defences and is not in a position to carry out any land defence. The Army will have to hold troops ready inland. *The Fuehrer* is quite aware of this fact. Mechanised forces will be kept in readiness for immediate action at suitable points inland. The Air Force is to take over the air defence. The Navy can provide only two anti-aircraft units. Brest will probably be the main base for submarine warfare, Boulogne and Cherbourg for motor-boats.

*The C.-in-C., Navy*, draws attention to the importance of bases on the Atlantic coast, e.g. Dakar. *The Fuehrer* intends to use Madagascar for settling Jews under French supervision. However, he realises the importance of the proposal made by the C.-in-C., Navy, to exchange Madagascar for the northern part of Portuguese Angola, and he will consider the suggestion.

2. Britain.—(*a*) *The C.-in-C., Navy*, calls attention to the necessity of starting vigorous air attacks on British bases in order to destroy ships under construction and repair. *The Fuehrer* contemplates taking such action soon.

(*b*) The C.-in-C., Navy, reports on negotiations with the Foreign Office concerning a state of siege.

(*c*) The C.-in-C., Navy, makes a report on the preparations for an invasion of England. This report deals with the locality chosen for landing, the question of mines, and shipping available now and in the future. Special craft (of the type proposed by Von Schell and Feder) are discussed. The C.-in-C., Navy, requests that the Navy alone should make and carry out decisions with regard to the construction of special craft. The O.K.W. will receive instructions to insure this. The C.-in-C., Navy, states that air supremacy is necessary for an invasion. The Army must check the composition of the divisions required for this purpose, and all superfluous material must be left behind.

3. Norway.—Trondheim is to be the base for naval warfare. Coastal traffic to Narvik–Tromsoe is to be escorted. Tromsoe and Narvik are to be fortified with 15-cm. batteries. The northern area is to be consolidated first of all, and the southern area afterwards. There is a possibility of getting ore transport from Narvik moving by winter if Sweden helps in preparing railways and in sending supplies to northern Norway and to the troops. A sharp note has been sent. The British will try to upset coastal traffic by raids, mines, and submarines; thus the struggle in Norway is not at an end for the Navy.

The Navy is in urgent need of air support:

(*a*) The Navy has asked the C.-in-C., Air, to leave certain air forces in Trondheim and in the Narvik area. The C.-in-C., Air, sent a rude telegram to the C.-in-C., Navy. The C.-in-C., Navy, reads the telegram and parts of the teletype message and the letter of the Naval Staff.* *The Fuehrer* requests that in the future his decision on such questions be sought through the O.K.W.

(*b*) The C.-in-C., Navy, gives a report on the progress made in returning the squadrons which Group West had voluntarily placed at the disposal of the C.-in-C., Air. *The Fuehrer* replies as in (*a*). The

---

* In connection with this telegram see letters at end of the 1940 Section.

Fuehrer orders that the O.K.W. prepare both these cases for his final decision. The Chief of Staff, O.K.W., will receive the necessary data from the C.-in-C., Navy.

4. Operation *Ikarus*.—The C.-in-C., Navy, reports on the preparations made, the most suitable season, and the most favourable landing place; it is impossible to maintain continuous supplies. The entire Navy will have to be used for operation *Ikarus*.

5. Submarine construction and the war economy.—The C.-in-C., Navy, made a report on the construction programme and the necessity for the immediate allocation of the required material and men if even the restricted programme (January 1, 1942) is to be carried out without further delay. The Chief of Staff, O.K.W., explains that the demands made by the Navy have been approved at this very moment.

6. The C.-in-C., Navy, emphasizes the necessity of increasing and accelerating allocation of ammunition for the Scharnhorst and the Gneisenau. The Chief of Staff, O.K.W., announces that this has likewise been approved.

(signed) RAEDER.

\*　　\*　　\*　　\*　　\*　　\*

In the last days of June, however, Raeder's suggestion was taken up by the Supreme Command, who, on July 2, issued the first directive for operation "Sea Lion."

Supreme Command        Fuehrer's Headquarters, July 7, 1940

Top Secret        5 Copies
2nd Copy

### THE WAR AGAINST ENGLAND

The Fuehrer and Supreme Commander has decided:

(1) That a landing in England is possible, providing that air superiority can be attained and certain other necessary conditions fulfilled. The date of commencement is still undecided. All preparations to be begun immediately.

(2) The Commands of the three Services are to supply the following information:

(a) *Army*

    (1) Estimates of the strength of the British forces, of losses, and of the extent to which the British Army will have been re-equipped a month or so hence.

    (2) An appreciation of the operational strength of our coastal batteries, and their capacity to provide additional protection for our shipping against British naval forces.

(b) *Navy*

    (1) Survey of possible landing points for strong Army forces (25–40 divisions), and estimate of strength of English coastal defences.

    (2) Indication of sea routes over which our forces can be transported with the maximum safety. In selecting landing areas, it must be remembered that landings on a broad front will facilitate subsequent deep penetration.

    (3) Data of shipping available, with probable date on which this could be ready.

(c) *Air Force*

    (1) An estimate of the chances of attaining air supremacy, and figures showing the relative strengths of the *Luftwaffe* and R.A.F.

(2) To what extent can the landing be supported by a parachute attack?
(Highest priority to be given to the production of transport aircraft.)

(3) The Commands of the three Services should co-operate in evolving a plan for the transport of the maximum number of troops with the minimum of shipping and aircraft space.

The invading forces must be highly mechanised and numerically superior to the opposing armies.

(4) All preparations must be undertaken on the basis that the invasion is still only a plan, and has not yet been decided upon.   Knowledge of preparations must be restricted to those immediately concerned.

(signed) KEITEL.

*   *   *   *   *   *

This sudden decision created the very situation which Raeder had sought to avoid.   Although the date was left open there was every indication that Hitler expected the landing to take place shortly.

There now began a series of inter-service arguments as to the details of the operation.   On July 9 the Naval Staff requested the Army and the *Luftwaffe* to state their operational intentions.   At the same time the German Navy emphasised that the undertaking was essentially a matter of transport, and that therefore the landing must take place in an area where naval and air protection could be guaranteed.   They named the Dover Straits as the only area where these conditions could be fulfilled.

The operation, however, was not yet considered necessary and, at the next conference with Hitler on July 11, Raeder, keenly aware of British sea power, pointed out the extreme difficulties of executing "Sea Lion."   Hitler was sympathetic, and more interested in the development of Norway.

### REPORT OF THE C.-IN-C., NAVY, TO THE FUEHRER ON JULY 11, 1940, AT THE OBERSALZBERG

Also present: Chief of Staff, O.K.W.
Commander von Puttkamer.

1. Norway.—The following are reported on: Naval activity in northern Norway; transport operations for the Army; patrol of the sea area Narvik–Tromsoe. The Hipper and the Nuernberg will provide support for destroyers, mine-sweepers, etc. Repairs of the Gneisenau are expected to be finished by July 25. *Question:* Is it still necessary to revive shipments of ore from Narvik by sea for such a short period, in view of the increasing supplies of iron ore from Lorraine, etc.? The Chief of Staff, O.K.W., will investigate and report.

2. Development of Trondheim.—The Navy has begun planning the naval base; it requests to be put in charge of base installations, since the over-all plan will have to be co-ordinated. *The Fuehrer* wishes to make Trondheim a base with extensive defences against both land and sea attack. The occupation force is to be made up of one division of Army, Air Force, and naval personnel. There must be facilities for constructing the largest ships without regard to draught. A beautiful German city is to be built on the fiord, separate from Trondheim; it does not need to be directly connected with the harbour and the shipyards. The Fuehrer agrees that private firms may be commissioned with building the shipyard. A super-highway is to be built via Luebech, Fehmarn Belt bridge, Zealand, Helsingoer bridge, Sweden, Trondheim. Possibly the railway to Narvik could be given to Sweden in exchange for the extra-territorial use of Swedish soil. The Trondheim–Kirkenes road will be widened and improved;

parts of it will have to be blasted out of rock, entailing ten to fifteen years' work.

At the request of the C.-in-C., Navy, the Chief of Staff, O.K.W., will select persons capable of planning the city, etc., with whom the Navy can discuss plans.

3. Situation with regard to submarine warfare.—An effort will be made to use Brest and Lorient as bases for repairs also, so as to make it possible to intensify submarine warfare soon.

4. Six auxiliary cruisers are at sea.—Their crews might be used to effect the occupation of the colonies.

5. The C.-in-C., Navy, points out the total absence of guns and anti-aircraft defences in Baltic bases; he requests prompt information concerning developments in the east, so that bases can be protected against raids. He plans to use captured guns as substitutes.   The Naval High Command is to report the number of such such guns needed to the O.K.W., as the Fuehrer considers re-armament necessary.

6. Siege.—*The C.-in-C., Navy,* considers a declaration of siege practicable when the war against Britain is intensified.   Advantages and disadvantages are discussed; the advantages predominate.   *The Fuehrer* intends to make a declaration.   The Naval High Command has discussed details with the O.K.W. and the Foreign Office.

7. *The Fuehrer* plans to make a speech before the Reichstag and asks whether the C.-in-C., Navy, considers this would be effective.   *The C.-in-C., Navy,* thinks it would, because the contents would become known to the British public.   The C.-in-C., Navy, is of the opinion that for a speedy termination of the war with Britain the impact of war must be forcibly brought home to the British public itself.   This could be done as follows:

(*a*) By cutting off their imports.

(*b*) By heavy air attacks on the main centres.   The present attacks on a number of objectives of lesser importance are only pin-pricks, making no impression on the public, and of more inconvenience to ourselves than to them.   Our own large bases of Wilhelmshaven, Hamburg, and Kiel are continually being attacked and damaged, and all damage affects our naval armament, e.g. the Prinz Eugen, the Luetzow, piers, etc.   An early concentrated attack on Britain is necessary, on Liverpool, for example, so that the whole nation will feel the effect.   The question is whether such an attack would be more useful before or after the Reichstag speech.   The C.-in-C., Navy, is in favour of its being made before the speech.   He also points out the importance of London and its suburbs for the whole life of the British nation.   The great mass of people who cannot be evacuated, difficulties of food supply, and the fact that 40 per cent. of the imports come through the port of London. Therefore continued mining of the Thames is of decisive importance.

8. Invasion.—*The C.-in-C., Navy,* considers that an invasion should be used only as a last resort to force Britain to sue for peace.   He is convinced that Britain can be made to ask for peace simply by cutting off her import trade by means of submarine warfare, air attacks on convoys, and heavy air attacks on her main centres, as Liverpool, for instance.   The C.-in-C., Navy, cannot for his part, therefore, advocate an invasion of Britain as he

did in the case of Norway. Prerequisites are complete air superiority and creation of a mine-free area for transports and disembarkation. It is impossible to tell how long it would take to clear such an area and whether it could be extended right up to the enemy coast. Furthermore, it would be necessary to enclose the transport area by flanking minefields. Lengthy preparation of transport facilities would be necessary, and deep inroads would be made into German economic and armament programmes (submarine construction, withdrawal of transport facilities, etc.). Orders for these preparations should therefore not be issued until the decision to invade has been made. Trials with landing equipment are in progress in co-operation with the Army Ordnance Department, engineers, etc.

*The Fuehrer* also views invasion as a last resort, and also considers air superiority a prerequisite; he expresses his views on installing heavy army guns, which have the advantages of permanent implacement and better camouflage against aircraft.

9. *The Fuehrer* asks whether France should be allowed to take part in warfare against Britain, for instance in the submarine war in the Atlantic. The C.-in-C., Navy, replies that this should be permitted in the Mediterranean if the Italians desire it. They should also be permitted to defend their bases, such as Dakar and Casablanca, but apart from this they should *not* be allowed to operate in the Atlantic. *The Fuehrer* agrees.

10. Bases.—*The C.-in-C., Navy*, points out the importance of Dakar for warfare in the Atlantic. *The Fuehrer* would like to acquire one of the Canary Islands from Spain in exchange for French Morocco. The Navy is to establish which of the islands is the most suitable, aside from the two main islands. The C.-in-C., Navy, declares Madagascar to be of less importance, as the Atlantic remains the main theatre of war.

11. *The C.-in-C., Navy*, reports on a plan for expansion of the fleet. *The Fuehrer* agrees to immediate continuation of construction on H * and J,* unless the war lasts so long that entirely new plans can be worked out. Work on such plans is to be commenced. On the big ships the upper deck must be the strongest in order to be bomb-proof, and everything on the upper deck must be at least splinter-proof; everything else must be eliminated. *The Fuehrer* agrees to continue construction of O,* P,* and Q,* with reinforced upper decks. The C.-in-C., Navy, does *not* discuss the improved type of pocket battleship.

*The Fuehrer* considers cruisers equipped with flight decks necessary for warfare against merchant shipping on the high seas. The C.-in-C., Navy, agrees. The Graf Zeppelin is to be completed and sent on trials, and a cruiser with a flight deck is under construction.

*The Fuehrer* agrees that immediate work on expansion of the submarine fleet is necessary on termination of the war.

12. A war merit pennant is approved by the Fuehrer.

(signed) RAEDER.

*        *        *        *        *        *

In the next few days Hitler changed his mind. On July 15 the Supreme Command informed the Naval Staff that Hitler required the operation to be so prepared that it could be launched at any time from August 15. On the following day, July 16, Hitler issued his directive for the invasion of England.

* New battleships.

The Fuehrer and Supreme Commander of the                    Fuehrer's Headquarters,
*Wehrmacht*                                                          July 16, 1940

Top Secret
## Directive No. 16

### PREPARATIONS FOR THE INVASION OF ENGLAND

As England, in spite of the hopelessness of her military position, has so far shown herself unwilling to come to any compromise, I have therefore decided to begin to prepare for, and if necessary to carry out, an invasion of England.   This operation is dictated by the necessity of eliminating Great Britain as a basis from which the war against Germany can be fought, and if necessary, the island will be occupied.

I therefore issue the following orders :

1. The landing operation must be a surprise crossing on a broad front extending approximately from Ramsgate to a point West of the Isle of Wight.   Elements of the Air Force will do the work of the artillery and elements of the Navy the work of engineers.   I ask each of the fighting services to consider the advantage from their respective point of view of preliminary operations such as the occupation of the Isle of Wight or the Duchy of Cornwall prior to the full-scale invasion, and to inform me of the result of their deliberations.   I shall be responsible for the final decision.   The preparations for the large-scale invasion must be concluded by the middle of August.

2. The following preparations must be undertaken to make a landing in England possible :

(*a*) The British Air Force must be eliminated to such an extent that it will be incapable of putting up any substantial opposition to the invading troops.

(*b*) The sea routes must be cleared of mines.

(*c*) Both flanks of the Straits of Dover and the Western approaches to the Channel, approximately on a line from Alderney to Portland, must be so heavily mined as to be completely inaccessible.

(*d*) Heavy coastal guns must dominate and protect the entire coastal front area.

(*e*) It is desirable that the English fleets both in the North Sea and in the Mediterranean should be pinned down (by the Italians in the latter instance), shortly before the crossing takes place ; with this aim in view, the naval forces at present in British harbours and coastal waters, should be attacked from the air and by torpedoes.

3. Organisation of Commands and of the preparations.—The Cs.-in-C. of  the respective branches of the Armed Forces will lead their forces, under my orders. The Army, Navy, and Air Force General Staffs should be within an area of no more than 50 kms. from my Headquarters (*Ziegenberg*) by the 1st August.   I suggest that the Army and Naval General Staffs establish their Headquarters at Giessen.

The C.-in-C. of the Army will nominate one Army Group to lead the invasion forces.

The invasion will be referred to by the code name "Sea Lion."

During the period of preparation and execution of the landings, the armed forces will carry out the following measures :

(*a*) *Army.*—Will draft a plan for the crossing and operations of the first wave of the invading force.   The necessary flak batteries will remain under the command of the individual army units until such time as their tasks can be divided into the following groups support and protection of the land troops, protection of the disembarkation ports, and protection after their occupation of air bases. The Army will allocate landing craft to the individual units and determine, in conjunction with the Navy, the points at which the embarkation and the landings will take place.

(*b*) *Navy.*—Will provide and safeguard the invasion fleet and direct it to the individual points of embarkation.   As far as possible, ships belonging to defeated nations are to be used.

Together with aircraft patrols, the Navy will provide adequate protection on both flanks during the entire Channel crossing. An order on the allocation of the commands during the crossing will follow in due course. The Navy will further supervise the establishment of coastal batteries, and will be responsible for the organisation of all coastal guns.

The largest possible number of heavy guns must be installed as soon as possible to safeguard the crossing and to cover both flanks against enemy interference from the sea. For this purpose, A.A. guns mounted on railway bogies (supplemented by all available captured guns) with railway turntables will be used. The Todt Organisation will be entrusted with the technical side of the organisation.

(c) *The Air Force.*—Will prevent all enemy air attacks, and will destroy coastal defences covering the landing points, break the initial resistance of the enemy land forces, and annihilate reserves behind the front. The accomplishment of these tasks will require the closest co-operation between all individual units of the Air Force and the invading Army units. In addition, roads used for troop movements will be attacked and approaching enemy naval vessels engaged before they can reach the embarkation and landing points.

I invite suggestions concerning the use of parachute and airborne troops, and in particular as to whether it would be advisable to keep the parachute and airborne troops in reserve for use only in case of necessity.

4. The necessary preparations for the installation of signals communications between France and England are being undertaken by the Signals Corps. The armoured under-sea cables are to be laid in co-operation with the Navy.

5. I hereby order the Cs.-in-C. to provide me with the following information:

(a) The plans drawn up by the Navy and Air Force for providing the above basic conditions necessary for the Channel crossing (see (2)).

(b) A detailed survey of the location of the Naval coastal batteries.

(c) An estimate of the shipping space necessary and of the methods of preparation and equipment. Will civilian authorities be asked to co-operate? (*Navy.*)

(d) The organisation of air defence in the areas in which the invading troops and vehicles are concentrated. (*Air Force.*)

(e) The plan for the Army crossing and operations; the organisation and equipment of the first wave.

(f) Details of measures planned by the Navy and Air Force for the execution of the crossing itself, its protection, and the support of the landing operations.

(g) Suggestions concerning the use of parachute and airborne troops, and the organisation of the flak artillery, once the spearhead troops have advanced sufficiently on English soil to permit their use. (*Air Force.*)

(h) Location of Army and Naval Headquarters.

(i) Are the Army, Navy, and Air Force Commanders of the opinion that the invasion should be preceded by a preliminary small-scale landing?

(signed) HITLER.
(initialled) KEITEL and JODL.

\* \* \* \* \* \*

On July 19 Raeder, through his staff, sent to the Supreme Command a long memorandum explaining the difficulties from the naval point of view.

"The task allotted to the Navy in operation 'Sea Lion' is out of all proportion to the Navy's strength and bears no relation to the tasks that are set to the Army and the Air Force. . . .

"The principal difficulties confronting the Navy are as follows:—

"(a) The transport of Army troops must take place from a coast whose harbour and installations and adjacent inland water-ways have been extensively damaged through the fighting in the campaign against France, or are of limited capacity.

"(b) The transport routes lie in a sea area in which weather, fog, current, tides, and the state of the sea may present the greatest difficulties. . . .

"(c) Owing to the strong defence of the enemy harbours the landing cannot take place there, but the first wave, at least, must land on the open coast. . . . The great navigational difficulties (rise and fall of tide, currents, sea, and swell) are obvious. Alterations to shipping for these special tasks involve extensive and protracted work in the Yards.

"(d) At present there is no information whatever as to the position of mines in the eastern portion of the Channel, through which the transports will have to pass. An adequate safety margin as regards mines will not be obtainable, in spite of the use of all resources. It must be appreciated that the enemy is in a position, at least near his own coast, to lay protective minefields at short notice and at the last moment.

"(e) The gaining of air supremacy is vital to the possibility of assembling the requisite Naval Forces and shipping in the relatively restricted area of embarkation. . . .

"(f) So far the enemy has not needed to use his Fleet fully, as a matter of life and death, but the landing operations on the English Coast will find him resolved to throw in fully and decisively all his Naval forces. It cannot be assumed that the *Luftwaffe* alone will succeed in keeping the enemy Naval forces clear of our shipping, as its operations are very dependent on weather conditions. The task of the German Navy must therefore be to strengthen the effect of *Luftwaffe* operations by the following measures: Minefields, use of light naval forces on the flanks of the transport area, operations for creating diversions. In this connection it must be taken into consideration that the minefields will not afford absolute safe protection in the face of a determined opponent. Thus the possibility must be envisaged that, even if the first wave has been successfully transported, the enemy will still be able to penetrate with resolute Naval forces so as to place himself between the first wave, already landed, and the succeeding transports. . . .

"(g) The great effect of air attacks on defensive installations is undeniable, as shown by the Western campaign. The nature of anti-invasion defences on the enemy coast, however, and the detailed preparations against invasion, which he has been making for a considerable time, cause doubt as to whether the *Luftwaffe* will succeed in eliminating defensive troops on the coast sufficiently to allow a landing to take place, and without any effective artillery support from seawards.

"These reflections cause the Naval Staff to see exceptional difficulties that cannot be assessed individually until a detailed examination of the transport problem has been made."

\*   \*   \*   \*   \*   \*

Meanwhile German Intelligence was trying to estimate the strength of England's defences. On July 17 an extract from the War Diary of the German Admiralty stated:

"The whole foreign Press, in particular the English Press, comments that a major German attack is expected. Thousands of barges and vessels are said to be standing by on the Channel and Atlantic coast. The attack is expected in the Dover area, though the defences here are strongest. Strong air attacks lasting several days will precede the landing."

Two days later a further report was received.

"English defence measures.—Coastal defence by the Army. Defence is based on mobility and concentration of all available fire-power. No fixed defence line with built-in defences. The task of the Fleet and the R.A.F. would be to render impossible the landing of armoured units or surprise landing by troops. The R.A.F. is so organised that strong units can be quickly concentrated at any danger spot, and also to attack the new German bases in Northern France and Holland and to search for indications of German activity, such as the assembly of ships and barges."

These reports, though lacking in definite information, impressed upon the Naval Staff the difficulties of invasion and on July 21 Raeder reported yet again to Hitler.

Only rough notes of this conference are available, but additional information shows that in Hitler's opinion the war was already won, but England had not yet recognised the situation. From being averse to the landing the German Supreme Command had entirely changed its views, and, to the alarm of the Naval Staff, now considered the landing quite a simple operation. Hitler himself was not, however, convinced.

## CONFERENCE ON JULY 21, 1940

*The Fuehrer* raised the following points.—What hopes can Britain have pertaining to the continuation of the war? She may be expecting the following:

1. A change of policy in America. (America lost $10,000,000,000 in the World War, and got back only $1,400,000,000. She is hoping to become the dominant naval power in any case.)

2. Russia's entry into the war, which would be unpleasant for Germany, especially on account of the threat from the air.

Even though Moscow is unenthusiastic about Germany's great successes, she will nevertheless make no effort to enter into the war against Germany of her own accord. Naturally it is our duty to deliberate the American and Russian questions carefully. A speedy termination of the war is in the interest of the German people. There is, however, no urgent need for this, as the situation is far more favourable than it was in the World War. In 1918 the western front was enormously costly. This is not so in the present situation. An abundance of material is available. The fuel problem is the most pressing. This will not become critical as long as Roumania and Russia continue their supplies and the hydrogenation plants can be adequately protected against air attacks. Food supplies are assured for some time, especially if prisoners of war are used to a larger extent as farm hands.

In Britain they may have hopes that the fuel situation in Germany will develop unfavourably. It is necessary to clear up the question of whether a direct operation could bring Britain to her knees, and how long this would take. Also diplomatic steps must be taken in regard to Spain, Russia, and Japan. Such steps are difficult, though, as long as the world awaits a new miracle which has not yet occurred.

The invasion of Britain is an exceptionally daring undertaking, because even if the way is short, this is not just a river crossing, but the crossing of a sea which is dominated by the enemy. This is not a case of a single crossing operation as in Norway; operational surprise cannot be expected; a defensively prepared and utterly determined enemy faces us and dominates the sea area which we must use. For the Army operation 40 divisions will be required; the most difficult part will be the continued reinforcement of material and stores. We cannot count on supplies of any kind being available to us in England. The prerequisites are complete mastery of the air, the operational use of powerful artillery in the Dover Straits, and protection by minefields. The time of year is an important factor, since the weather in the North Sea and in the Channel during the second half of September is very bad and the fogs begin in the middle of October. The main operation would therefore have to be completed by September 15; after this date co-operation between the *Luftwaffe* and the heavy weapons becomes too unreliable. But as air co-operation is decisive, it must be regarded as the principal factor in fixing the date.

The following must be established:

(1) How long does the Navy require for its technical preparations?
(2) How soon can the guns be in place?
(3) To what extent can the Navy safeguard the crossing?

If it is not certain that preparations can be completed by the beginning of September, other plans must be considered.

(signed) RAEDER.

\*     \*     \*     \*     \*     \*

On the following day it was reported to Hitler that the preparations could not be completed by the middle of August, and that the actual date of invasion could only be determined when air supremacy in the Channel had been achieved.

\*     \*     \*     \*     \*     \*

During the next few days the Army sent their theoretical demands to the Naval Staff.

"The General Staff of the Army has given its intentions for carrying out the operation, as follows: about 100,000 men with appropriate equipment, including heavy gear, must be transported in the first wave from the area Dunkirk–Cherbourg to the area between Ramsgate and Lyme Bay. Further waves must follow in quickest succession, so that the formation of a local bridgehead may be followed in the shortest time by a war of movement on the Island. This demands the most rapid turn round of transports after disembarkation of the first echelon."

The amount of shipping required to carry out the Army demands was estimated as follows:

    1,722 barges.
      471 tugs.
    1,161 motorboats.
      155 transports.

The assembly of this armada would impose a severe strain on German economy, and on July 25 Raeder reported to Hitler. (At this same conference the battle of the Atlantic was also discussed.)

C.-in-C., Navy                                      Berlin, July 26, 1940

### CONFERENCE WITH THE FUEHRER ON JULY 25, 1940, AT 1700

Also present: Chief of Staff, O.K.W.
                  General Jodl.
                  Minister Todt.
                  Commander von Puttkamer.
                  Colonel Schmundt.

1. Submarine warfare in the Atlantic; Italian participation.—*The Fuehrer* agrees to Italian participation. As, however, the tactical subordination of Italian submarines under the Admiral Commanding Submarines, might result in a similar demand by the Italians concerning German fliers who might be sent to North Africa, the Fuehrer desires German and Italian submarines to be under completely separate command for the present. *The C.-in-C., Navy*, points out that operations must be co-ordinated; that the Italians must make use of German experiences;

and that moral pressure should be exercised to urge the Italians to strong action. The C.-in-C., Navy, proposes a liaison staff of the Admiral Commanding Submarines with the Italian submarine command. *The Fuehrer* approves this. The Italians are to be responsible for refueling their own submarines.

2. Placement of batteries at the Straits of Dover (report by Captain Voss).—The guns are to be ready by August 15. Only the 38-cm. battery will not be ready until the middle of September. Concrete covers will be built later as a protection against air attack. *The C.-in-C., Navy,* emphasises the necessity for making use of the batteries as soon as they are ready in order to protect minesweepers and to close the Straits of Dover. (The 28-cm. Kurfuerst battery will be ready about August 1.) As British air reconnaissance is obviously closely watching the placing of the guns, firing them will not disclose German plans to any greater degree. *The Fuehrer* agrees.

3. Operation "Sea Lion."—*The C.-in-C., Navy,* describes forcefully once again the effects of these preparations on the German economy: Cessation of inland shipping and a great part of maritime shipping, strain on shipyards, etc. The C.-in-C., Navy, requests that an order be issued that these preparations be given preference over anything else. *The Fuehrer* and *the Chief of Staff, O.K.W.*, agree.

There follows a report on the state of preparations on July 25, 1940. The C.-in-C., Navy, again stresses the necessity of establishing air superiority soon in order to carry out preparations. At the present time, the following can be said. Every effort is being made to complete preparations by the end of August. Provided that there are no special difficulties and that air superiority is established soon, it will be possible to do the following:

(1) Provide and convert barges.
(2) Make available the necessary personnel.
(3) Prepare ports for embarkation.
(4) Reconnoitre the enemy coast.
(5) Clear the invasion area of mines.
(6) Lay protecting minefields.
(7) Set up the organisation.

It is still very uncertain whether a sufficient number of ships can be obtained along the Belgian-French coast and how long it will take to convert them. The C.-in-C., Navy, will try to give a clear picture by the middle of next week. *The Fuehrer* orders a conference for the middle of next week.

(signed) RAEDER.

*      *      *      *      *      *

Preparations for "Sea Lion" now began in earnest. There was intense activity throughout Germany and signals and memoranda passed incessantly between the various commands. An entry in the War Diary for July 29 stated:

"(a) The Army requires the transport of 13 landing divisions (about 260,000 men). In view of their anticipated tasks, the Army High Command regards this as the minimum number, from which no departure can be permitted, even if there are difficulties in transport. This is a considerable reduction compared with the original requirement of the Fuehrer (on July 21) of 40 divisions.

"(b) These 13 divisions must attack the English coast on the widest front (from Ramsgate to Lyme Bay); which means that they must leave the French coast as far as possible simultaneously, and on the widest front.

"(c) The landing divisions must be ready for operations in England within the shortest time, that is, within 2 to 3 days. A period of 10 days for the transport as provided by the timetable for the second wave, is unacceptable to the Army.

"(d) The landing divisions must include sufficient heavy artillery (for own use and for setting up along the English coast) and A.A. batteries (for A.A. protections and for anti-tank defence).

"(e) The Army General Staff requires the landing to take place at dawn."

These demands of the Army began a series of acrimonious disputes with the Navy on the question of landing on a broad or narrow front. From the point of view of the German Navy full security for the landing could only be guaranteed if the landing took place on a narrow strip near Dover and near Beachy Head. The Army demand for a landing area stretching from Ramsgate to Lyme Regis was regarded as quite impracticable by the Navy.

On July 31 Raeder conferred with Hitler and announced that the earliest date for beginning the operation was September 15.

C.-in-C., Navy.                                             Berlin, August 1, 1940

### CONFERENCE WITH THE FUEHRER ON JULY 31, 1940, AT THE BERGHOF

Also present: Chief of Staff, O.K.W.
      General Jodl.
      Commander von Puttkamer.
      C.-in-C., Army.
      Chief of the Army General Staff.

1. Operation "Sea Lion."—*The C.-in-C., Navy*, reports that all preparations are in full swing. It can be concluded from experiences gained during this period that September 15, 1940, is the earliest date which can be fixed for the operation, provided the preparations are not delayed by any unforeseen circumstances due to the weather or the enemy.

Details.—Material has been brought up so far according to plan. Conversion of the barges will be finished by the end of August. The first trial conversion of motor coasters was unsatisfactory and a new one is in progress; these ships should be ready by the beginning of September. Subsequently the barges, etc., will be sent to the operational harbours after they have been manned. They will be ready in the harbours by the middle of September.

The situation with regard to merchant shipping is unfavourable as a result of the heavy ice of the northern winter, losses sustained in the Norwegian operation, and as a result of mines, etc. A comprehensive list has been drawn up. Requisitioning of ships will begin shortly. There will be a period of about four weeks after conversion before the ships can depart for the operational harbours. The personnel problem can be solved by the end of August if large inroads are made on the numbers of men available.

Minesweeping has commenced with exploratory sweeps, but can be carried out according to plan only if we have air superiority. It will take three weeks if the weather is favourable. The fact that three minesweepers were lost off the Hook of Holland shows the difficulty of this undertaking.

Mine-laying will begin at the end of August if we have air superiority, and will last about two weeks.   The C.-in-C., Navy, again draws attention to the effects which operation "Sea Lion" has on the German economy. It will have a very detrimental effect on the situation in Germany in the winter of 1940 to 1941; therefore, the autumn is not a favourable time.

*The Fuehrer.*—What will the weather conditions be at the end of September?   *The C.-in-C., Navy.*—According to experiences of long-standing the weather is generally bad in the North Sea and the Channel around September 20, but good at the end of September and the first half of October; there is light fog during the middle of October, and heavy fog at the end of October.

*The C.-in-C., Navy*, makes the following report on matters concerning the execution of the operation:

(*a*) To assure successful disembarkation as well as safe crossing of the Straits of Dover, the best time for the beginning of the landing is about two hours after high tide.   A landing at low tide has the disadvantage of rising water during the disembarkation, but the advantage that vessels which have run aground will float again.   A landing at high tide has the disadvantage that craft are grounded and immobile for about twelve hours until the next high tide, and if the next high tide does not reach the level of the previous one, it may not even float them.   Rising water is unfavourable in any case at the time of landing, since it causes transport units which are aground to float again and again, thus altering their position and delaying the disembarkation.   The first requirement therefore, is a time when the water is ebbing, about two hours after high tide.

From the point of view of the Army, the best time for the landing is during the early dawn, about one half to one hour before sunrise.   This means that the Channel crossing and the approach would have to take place for the most part in the dark.   The singular composition of the transport fleet will make it very difficult to carry this out in total darkness, i.e. with no moon.   Large numbers of slow, unwieldy transport units concentrated in a small space, mixed with motor boats of the most varied types, and escorted by light units of the Navy and auxiliary vessels make it necessary to have a certain amount of light for navigational reasons, e.g. a half-moon rising at about 2300.

If these three conditions are to be taken into account, the dates can be chosen accordingly.   The following days consequently will be suitable for the operation:

(1) From August 20 to 26.
(2) From September 19 to 26.

The August period is out of the question, as it will be impossible to finish preparations by then.

The early dawn is the most dangerous time for sea operations, as enemy naval forces which were far off, e.g. in Firth of Forth, during the evening may have reached the entrance to the Channel by morning without being noticed by our reconnaissance.   This constitutes a great threat to the operation, should the demand made by the Army for a landing in the early dawn be granted.   If the crossing is made by day, air reconnaissance can locate the position of enemy naval forces. The operation could be stopped if necessary.

Weather conditions are of the utmost importance. The Naval Staff is of the opinion that the transport operation, both as regards the barges to the east as well as the steamers in the centre and to the west, can be carried out only if the sea is calm. The sea must be calm enough for the barges to lie almost motionless when landing, as they would immediately spring leaks by striking the ground or rocks, and this would lead to destruction of their load. In the area used for steamer transports, a heavy sea would make it impossible to transfer the heavy loads into the barges lying alongside.

Even if the first wave crosses successfully under favourable weather conditions, there is no guarantee that the same favourable weather will carry through the second and third waves, etc., as planned, owing to the long intervals between them. As a matter of fact, we must realise that no traffic worth mentioning will be able to cross for several days, until certain harbours can be utilised.

(b) The Army has requested that the landing should cover a wide front, from the Straits of Dover to Lyme Bay. Transports from Le Havre and Cherbourg will proceed virtually unescorted into the immediate vicinity of the main British bases of Portsmouth and Plymouth, from which, even if British naval forces are considerably weakened by air attacks, motor boats and destroyers can come out in great numbers. The unloading of the steamers at the two western landing points will last thirty-six hours, during which time they will be lying off that coast. This is unjustifiable. Full operational readiness of the British Fleet must be reckoned with on this occasion. It would be irresponsible to do otherwise.

The C.-in-C., Navy, is therefore of the opinion that the crossing should be concentrated at first entirely on the Straits of Dover as far as Eastbourne, and that this route should be protected as strongly as possible by guns, mines, and the available naval forces. The demand of the Navy for the most favourable time, i.e. two hours after high tide by day, must also be met. It is clear that the operation will thus be rendered more difficult for the Army. The main thing, however, is to get the Army across in the first place. The Air Force will also not be able to protect the landing effectively at three landing points extending over about 100 kilometers, but will have to concentrate on operating in one area. The C.-in-C., Navy, is of the opinion that the Army and Navy should co-operate in making careful preparations for the operation in this form, and the Straits of Dover route should be prepared accordingly. The best time for the operation, all things considered, would be May, 1941.

*The Fuehrer* decides as follows.—An attempt must be made to prepare the operation for September 15, 1940. The Army should be ready for action by then. The decision as to whether the operation is to take place in September or is to be delayed until May 1941 will be made after the Air Force has made concentrated attacks on southern England for one week. The Air Force is to report at once when these attacks will commence. If the effect of the air attacks is such that the enemy air force, harbours, and naval forces, etc., are heavily damaged, operation "Sea Lion" will be carried out in 1940. Otherwise it is to be postponed until May 1941.

2. The Fuehrer inquires about reinforcements for the Navy during the winter months until May 1941. *Reply.*—Prinze Eugen, Bismarck, and Tirpitz will be available, although training will leave a lot to be desired; possibly eight destroyers, six torpedo boats, and a number of motor boats and submarines will be ready. It is doubtful whether the Seydlitz will be finished, since there have been delays.

3. *The Fuehrer* considers other actions in the meantime. The C.-in-C., Army, advocates supporting the Italian attack on the Suez Canal with two Panzer divisions. The Fuehrer is planning an attack on Gibraltar.

4. *The C.-in-C., Navy*, requests permission for a more extensive submarine programme. More steel and other metals are needed, and in particular the manpower shortage which already hampers the present reduced submarine programme must be relieved. *The Fuehrer* gives his permission.

5. *The C.in-C., Navy*, emphasises the fact that *all* matters having to do with operation "Sea Lion" must be given precedence over the top priority programme. The Chief of Staff, O.K.W., promises an order to this effect.

(signed) RAEDER.

\*  \*  \*  \*  \*  \*

The conference was followed by a directive from Hitler's Headquarters.

Supreme Command                    Fuehrer's Headquarters, August 1, 1940
Top Secret                                             8 Copies
                                                                2nd Copy

OPERATION "SEA LION"

The C.-in-C., Navy, having reported on July 31 that the necessary preparations for "Sea Lion" could not be completed before September 15, the Fuehrer has ordered:

(1) Preparations for "Sea Lion" are to be continued, and completed by the Army and Air Force by September 15.

(2) Eight or fourteen days after the launching of the air offensive against Britain, scheduled to begin on approximately August 5, the Fuehrer will decide whether the invasion will take place this year or not; his decision will depend largely on the outcome of the air offensive.

(3) Should the decision be taken not to attempt the operation in September, preparations are to be continued, but not to the extent of damaging our economy through the tying up of our inland shipping system.

(4) In spite of the Navy's warning that they can only guarantee the defence of a narrow strip of coast (as far west as Eastbourne), preparations are to be continued for the attack on a broad basis as originally planned.

(5) The instructions given in the order of July 16, regarding the location of Headquarters Staffs remain in force, but their move to the proximity of the Fuehrer's Headquarters will not take place until immediately prior to the commencement of the operation.

(signed) KEITEL.

For the next fortnight the "broad" versus "narrow" front controversy raged strongly. There was little appreciation by the Army Command of the transport difficulties involved and they persistently refused to give way to the naval demands. On August 7 there was a meeting between the Chief of the Army General Staff, Colonel-General Halder, and the Chief of the Naval Staff, Admiral Schniewind. There was a strong clash of opinions between the two. Halder dramatically stated: "I utterly reject the Navy's proposal; from the point of view of the Army I regard their proposal as complete suicide. I might just as well put the troops that have been landed straight through the sausage machine!" Schniewind replied as dramatically that it would be equally suicidal; in view of British Naval supremacy, to attempt the transport of the troops over such a wide area. The result was a deadlock between the two services, and on August 13 Hitler was asked to decide.

## REPORT OF THE C.-IN-C., NAVY, TO THE FUEHRER ON AUGUST 13, 1940, AT 1730

Also present:   Chief of Staff, O.K.W.
      General Jodl.
      Commander von Puttkamer.
      Chief of Staff, Naval Staff.

1. Operation "Sea Lion."—The C.-in-C., Navy, requests a prompt decision on whether operation "Sea Lion" is to be carried out on the wide front proposed by the C.-in-C., Army, or on the narrow front proposed by the C.-in-C., Navy, as otherwise preparations will be held back. The C.-in-C., Navy, expresses his opinion on the memorandum of the C.-in-C., Army, dated March 10, 1940. *The C.-in-C., Navy*, sums up as follows: In view of the limited means available for naval warfare and transport, operation "Sea Lion," as emphasized repeatedly, should be attempted only as a last resort, if Britain cannot be made to sue for peace in any other way. *The Fuehrer* agrees completely. Failure on our part would cause the British to gain considerable prestige. We must wait and see what effect our intensive air attacks will have. The Fuehrer will make a decision on August 14 after a conference with the C.-in-C., Army.

2. *The Fuehrer* wants the north Norwegian fiords to be more heavily fortified, particularly at the crossroads, so that Russian attacks there would have no chance of success, and the foundation for occupying Petsamo would be laid. The admiral commanding in the northern area is responsible.

3. The C.-in-C., Navy, requests that production of submarine torpedoes and torpedo tubes be given priority over other top priority items, as otherwise submarine warfare will be jeopardised from October on. The reason is the higher consumption of torpedoes as a result of using Lorient as a base, and the set-back in tube construction due to the fact that the numbers of workmen requested were not provided in spite of all the efforts made by the Ministry of Labour. *The Fuehrer* recognises these demands and gives orders to the Chief of Staff, O.K.W., to settle the question. (The C.-in-C., Air, has also requested that preference be given to certain matters of air equipment.) The C.-in-C., Navy, gives the Chief of Staff, O.K.W., two final copies of a Fuehrer order, together with the draft.

(signed) RAEDER.

On the following day further discussions were held.

August 14, 1940

## APPENDIX

Views of the Naval Staff on the Memorandum of the C.-in-C., Army.

SUBJECT: Operation "Sea Lion."

1. The opinion held by the Naval Staff and the possibilities which it foresees correspond to the facts as they were stated once more at the conference on August 7 between the Chief of Staff, Naval Staff, and the Chief of the General Staff, Army. As regards details, attention is again drawn to the fact that all dates, figures, and other particulars calculated by the

Naval Staff were rather optimistic than otherwise. This applies particularly to the time required for the transfer of the first wave and to the time required by steamers to unload on the open coast; any possible delays owing to unfavourable weather or sea conditions have been disregarded.

2. The Naval Staff recognises very well the reasons for the demands made by the General Staff. Just as the General Staff, from its own point of view, must insist on certain demands which it considers essential for success, the Naval Staff must do likewise with regard to its part in the operation.

The General Staff, Army, has asked for a simultaneous strong landing in the Brighton area, consolidated with sufficient speed. The success of such an undertaking cannot be guaranteed, however. All units cannot land simultaneously because of the difference in the tides and the length of time taken by the steamers to unload, even if we did not take the weather and the enemy into account, which, however, we must do. The necessary strength could not be attained owing to the restricted transport space and again due to the long time required for disembarkation. A quick replenishment of forces and supplies could in no way be guaranteed, mainly because of the lack of transport space, enemy action, and weather conditions. Therefore the conditions necessary for "an additional speedy and successful operation" as desired by the General Staff of the Army cannot be considered as assured.

The same applies to the landing in Lyme Bay. The airborne troops can influence neither the weather nor the sea; they cannot prevent the destruction and incapacitation of the few harbours, nor hold off the enemy fleet or even a small part of it.

3. The Naval Staff comments as follows on the various conclusions of the General Staff:

(*a*) The Army point of view is appreciated. The Naval Staff for its part can see no possibilities for improving the initial operational situation in the narrow landing area.

(*b*) Simultaneous landing operations near Brighton in the west and Deal in the east cannot be carried out. The likelihood that even the first landing will be successful, not to speak of subsequent reinforcements, is so small as to make the attempt unjustifiable.

(*c*) Transport facilities over and above those in the statement by the Naval Staff on August 2, 1940, cannot be provided, nor could they be accommodated in the embarkation ports or area. Consequently it is impossible to meet the demands made by the General Staff for transporting and landing a first wave consisting of ten divisions with appropriate equipment to the area between Ramsgate and the region west of Brighton. It is impossible for the same reasons to follow up more quickly with reinforcements and supplies, all the more so because of the losses in shipping space which we must expect.

(*d*) Additional shipping space for the Lyme Bay landing is even more out of the question in view of these increased demands. The difficulties entailed in landing steamers on the open coast apply here as much as elsewhere.

(signed) SCHNIEWIND.
(Chief of Naval Staff.)

In the end a compromise was reached.

Supreme Command                          Fuehrer's Headquarters, August 16, 1940
Top Secret

### SUBJECT: "Sea Lion"

(1) On August 15 the following decisions were made by the Fuehrer.

(*a*) Preparations for the operation to take place on September 15 are to be continued.   Final orders will not be given until the situation is clear.

(*b*) Preparations for a landing in Lyme Bay are to be abandoned, on account of the inadequate protection available in that area.   Shipping is to be held in readiness along the coast between Ostend and Le Havre, thus avoiding congestion in the ports nearest to the enemy coast, and confusing the enemy as to our exact intentions.

(*c*) Dispositions should be made in such manner as not to exclude the possibility of an attack on a narrow front, should this be ordered at the last minute, and to leave open the possibility of a single landing in the Brighton area.

(2) Suggestions are also invited as to the possible employment of parachute and airborne troops.

(signed) KEITEL.

A further directive followed stating:

"Main crossing to be on narrow front, simultaneous landing of four to five thousand troops at Brighton by motor boats and the same number of airborne troops at Deal–Ramsgate.   In addition on D–1 day, the *Luftwaffe* is to make a strong attack on London, which would cause the population to flee from the city and block the roads."

The question of the landing at Brighton was still not resolved, however, and further discussions followed.   The Naval Staff wanted to make the landing simply a diversionary raid, but the Army on the other hand were determined to make Brighton one of the principal landing areas.   In the end it was decided that four divisions would be landed at Brighton in the first instance and that additional troops would follow if the situation permitted.

On August 27 final decisions were made.   Landings were to take place in four main areas:  Folkestone–Dungeness, Dungeness–Cliff's End, Bexhill–Beachy Head, Brighton–Selsey Bill.   The first operational objective of the Army was a line from Southampton to the mouth of the Thames.

Deception measures were also planned, the principal being a feint landing on the North-east coast.   This operation, under the code word *Herbstreise* (Autumn Journey), involved four transports escorted by four cruisers which, two days before "Sea Lion," were to proceed south from Bergen–Christiansand–the German Bight to the area between Aberdeen and Newcastle, and then to retreat at dusk back to the Kattegat.   Other diversions were to be made towards Iceland, while the pocket battleship Scheer was to make a commerce-raiding sortie into the Atlantic.

Meanwhile the *Luftwaffe* had started their air operations on England.   Their strength at the beginning of August amounted to 2,669 operational aircraft of which 1,015 were bombers, 346 dive-bombers, 933 fighters, and 375 heavy fighters. Attacks were concentrated on the destruction of the R.A.F, and targets were selected which were most likely to force large numbers of R.A.F. aircraft into battle, and only as a secondary consideration were invasion areas "softened."

\*          \*          \*          \*          \*          \*

On September 1, the movement of shipping from German North Sea ports to embarkation ports began.   The *Luftwaffe* had announced at the end of August that the air situation was favourable in spite of the effect of bad weather on their operations.   They estimated R.A.F. losses since August 8 at 1,115 aircraft as opposed to their own losses of 467 aircraft.   Control of the air therefore seemed likely, and on September 3 a directive from Fuehrer Headquarters stated the dates for the landing:

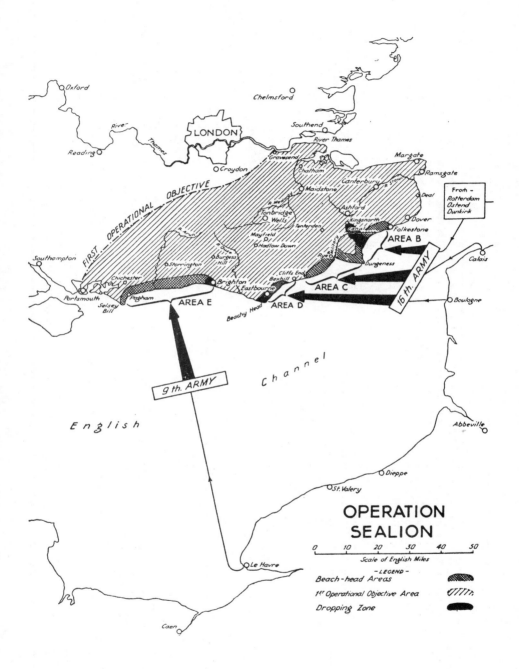

Oxford
Chelmsford
River
Southend
LONDON
Reading
River Thames
Thames
Margate
Gravesend
Croydon
Ramsgate
Chatham
Canterbury
R. Stour
Maidstone
Deal
FIRST OPERATIONAL OBJECTIVE
R. Medway
Ashford
Tonbridge
Kingsnorth
Dover
Wells
Tenterden
Canal
Folkestone
R. Arun
Mayfield
Royal Military
AREA B
Southampton
Hadlow Down
Calais
Storrington
Burgess
Hill
Rye
Dungeness
Chichester
Cliffs End
16th. ARMY
Brighton
Bexhill
AREA C
Portsmouth
Eastbourne
Boulogne
Selsey
Bill
Pagham
AREA E
Beachy Head
AREA D
From –
Rotterdam
Ostend
Dunkirk

English                    C h a n n e l

9th. ARMY

Abbeville

Dieppe

St. Valery

**OPERATION
SEALION**

0        10        20        30        40        50
Scale of English Miles

- LEGEND -

Le Havre

Beach-head Areas

1st Operational Objective Area

Caen

Dropping Zone

| Item | Date | Order | Army | Navy | Luftwaffe | Deception | Remarks |
|---|---|---|---|---|---|---|---|
| 1 | Present time. | Preparation directives and orders. | Movements to ports so that 1st Wave (11 Div.) is ready for embarkation. Further waves can get ready. | (a) Preparation of transports in invasion ports. (b) M/S crossing lanes. (c) Mine-laying in Hoofden. | Air war against England. | The fact that a landing is being prepared is not to be concealed. Through preparations being spread over a wide area enemy can be made uncertain of landing points. Herbstreise in preparation. | — |
| 2 | D–10 (earliest) 11.9. | "Begin operation S." Orders issued. | Embarkation begins (material, etc.), troops to wait. | U-boats proceed (mine barriers to be laid on flanks). | Measures referring to Paratroops will be reported later. | Hipper proceeds on D–9 for Herbstreise. | Operational H.Q. manned. |
| 3 | D–3 (forenoon) (earliest) 18.9. | Decision on D-day and H-hour. | — | Embarkation of troops. | — | Hipper off Iceland. Herbstreise II ships from Norway to S. of North Sea. | (a) H-hour to be 2 hours after high-water a.m. on D-day. (b) C.-in-C., Army gives 72 hour's warning before H-hour. |
| 4 | D–2 (earliest) 19.9. | — | — | Deception. | — | Deception operation from Germany and Norway against English E. coast. | — |
| 5 | D–24 hours. | Last moment for stopping operation. | Maintain present preparations or disperse until a new preparation date. | | — | If the operation is called off the enemy is not to know it. | Preparations can be maintained from day to day until 27.9. After that. . . . |
| 6 | D–1 (earliest) 20.9. | — | — | Transport fleets proceed. | — | Deception orders awaited. | — |
| 7 | D-day. | — | Begin landing. | | Support landings. | — | — |

Supreme Command    Fuehrer's Headquarters, September 3, 1940

Top Secret              8 Copies

                  2nd Copy

      SUBJECT: Operation "Sea Lion."

The following dates for the completion of preparations for operation "Sea Lion" have been decided.

(1) The earliest day for the sailing of the invasion fleet has been fixed as September 20, and that of the landing for September 21.

(2) Orders for the launching of the attack will be given on "D Day minus 10," presumably therefore on September 11.

(3) Final commands will be given at the latest on "D Day minus 3" at mid-day.

(4) All preparations must remain liable to cancellation 24 hours before "zero hour."

               (signed) KEITEL.

\*    \*    \*    \*    \*    \*

German Intelligence, however, continued to give forbidding reports of anti-invasion preparations in England. On September 5 Admiral Canaris' Foreign Intelligence Department sent the following report to the Supreme Command of the Navy:

Foreign Intelligence Department      Berlin, September 5, 1940

To Supreme Command, Navy

  Naval War Staff, Section 3

Re: England. Fortifications on the South coast.

A secret agent reported on September 2:

The Area Tunbridge Wells to Beachy Head, especially the small town of Rye (where there are large sand-hills) and also St. Leonards, is distinguished by a special labyrinth of defences. These defences, however, are so well camouflaged, that a superficial observer on the sand-hills, bathing spots, and fields, would not discover anything extraordinary. This area is extremely well guarded, so that it is almost impossible to reach there without a special pass.

In Hastings, on the other hand, most of the defences can be recognised quite plainly. In the town there are troops of every kind. The presence of numerous small and heavy tanks is most striking. Numerous armoured cars were also seen in St. Leonards and in a small locality where there is a famous golf-course, probably St. Joseph.

*War Organisation (Espionage) Appendix:*

The agent was not able to give a clearer account of the number of armoured cars in the different localities, or of the regiments he saw there.

From the position of Beachy Head (west of Hastings) and Rye (east of Hastings), it can be deduced that the place in question near St. Leonards was the western villa-suburb of Hastings. Tunbridge, which lies on the railway line from Hastings to London, according to the sense of the report, must also lie on the coast, but, as in the case of St. Joseph, this cannot be confirmed from the charts in our possession.

\*    \*    \*    \*    \*    \*

Judging from the standard of this report, it is not surprising to find that the German Intelligence Services miscalculated the size of the British Army.

Intelligence reports in fact assessed the available strength in England as:

      320,000 trained troops

      100,000 reserves

      900,000 recruits

      320,000 others (Home Guard, etc.).

    Total 1,640,000

Unconfirmed reports placed the number of divisions in England as 39, of which 20 were regarded as completely operational, but whose artillery was believed to be at only half the normal strength.

These reports worried the German High Command, and in addition the preparation of barges was behind schedule. It was nevertheless decided to continue with the operation, but there was no longer the same anticipation of easy victory.

\*　　　\*　　　\*　　　\*　　　\*　　　\*

It was about this time (beginning of September) that Hitler began to show his interest in the possibility of attacking Russia. There had been indications throughout the year that he was considering some such move, and on August 27, while ordering the preparations for "Sea Lion," he also decided to reinforce the Eastern Front.

Extract from Supreme Command Directive, September 27, 1940:

(3) The present forces in Poland are to be strengthened immediately. For this:

(a) About ten divisions are to be transferred to the East, but the necessary transport of supplies must not be impaired; and

(b) About two Armoured Divisions from the Homeland are to be transferred to the extreme south-east area of Poland as soon as the material situation permits.

The reinforcement of the new forces is in order to guarantee the protection of the Roumanian oilfields in the event of a sudden demand for intervention.

(signed) KEITEL.

\*　　　\*　　　\*　　　\*　　　\*　　　\*

Hitler was still prepared to invade England, if necessary, but other methods of attacking England had occurred to him and he and his staff began to doubt whether "Sea Lion" was worth the risk. On September 6 the war against England was reviewed, with particular emphasis on the Battle of the Atlantic and the possibility of Mediterranean operations.

C.in-C., Navy                                    Berlin, September 7, 1940
Chief of the Naval Staff

### REPORT OF THE C.-IN-C., NAVY, TO THE FUEHRER IN THE AFTERNOON OF SEPTEMBER 6, 1940

Also present: Chief of Staff, O.K.W.
　　　　　　　General Jodl.
　　　　　　　Commander von Puttkamer.

1. Current naval operations. (a) Home and Channel area.—In preparation for operation "Sea Lion," flank mine barrages were successfully laid in the Hoofden area. Several British destroyers were destroyed there by mines at the beginning of September.

Minesweeping activities have been started in the Channel in preparation for operation "Sea Lion." Owing to weather conditions and the situation in air warfare, the planned operations of the mine-sweeping forces were delayed until now and are still greatly hampered. This is not meant as a criticism of Air Force activities!

(b) Norwegian area.—Extensive transport movements have been carried out as planned to strengthen the Norwegian position. Construction of batteries in northern Norway is in progress. Artillery defences will be completed by the end of the year.

(c) Submarine warfare.—The strategic position of bases at Trondheim, Lorient, and Bordeaux provides extensive operational possibilities. The main operational area at present is the western part of the North Channel and the waters west of Scotland. It is very remunerative! Operations are made from Lorient and from home bases. The results at present are considerable.

A further gradual increase in successes may be expected when the declaration of an operational area around the British Isles and permission to fire without previous warning on all targets have eliminated all restrictions hitherto existing. At the moment anti-submarine defence is provided not so much by naval escort vessels, of which there are few, but by strong air cover.

Losses sustained since the outbreak of war.—Of the 61 operational submarines, 28 boats, or 46 per cent., have been lost! The Fuehrer is asked to acknowledge the contribution of the submarines in his next speech. He promises to do so.

Submarine warfare in the Atlantic is to be supported by Italian submarines. Therefore Bordeaux is to be expanded into a base. Agreements have been concluded with the Italian Navy. The German Navy will equip the base and will be responsible for defence outside of Italian terrain, as well as for the protection of the harbour area and outbound routes. The Italian Navy is to protect its own harbour basin, installations, and docks. Operational command will be in the hands of the German Admiral Commanding Submarines. Liaison officers will be exchanged for the purpose of co-ordination in tactical and operational matters. The first submarine has arrived at Bordeaux. At the moment there are three boats in the Atlantic, and six are en route. Thirty-six boats are to be sent into the Atlantic before the end of October.

(d) Auxiliary cruisers.—Operations, including replenishment of supplies at sea, have progressed surprisingly as planned. The distribution of the ships is as follows: two auxiliary cruisers are in the Indian Ocean, one is in Australian waters, one in the South Atlantic, one in the Middle Atlantic; one is outward bound via the northern route, and is now in the vicinity of the Bering Straits. The successes of all the auxiliary cruisers have exceeded expectations. Ship "16" has sunk 41,000 tons. There are strong indications of concern on the part of the enemy, who is not in a position to carry out extensive search activity.

2. Operation "Sea Lion."—Information is given on transport space, the assembly thereof, clearing of the harbours, fuel supplies, provision of personnel, minesweeping, and minelaying. Relevant charts are shown In summary.—If air supremacy is increasingly established it will be possible to meet the new deadline. The crossing itself will be very difficult. The Army cannot count on keeping the divisions together. The execution of operation "Sea Lion" appears possible, if attended by favourable circumstances regarding air supremacy, weather, etc.

In the north a diversionary manœuvre (a dummy landing) is planned with four large steamers from the German Bight, ten steamers from the Norwegian area, and escort forces. The Hipper is to operate in the Iceland area, in order to relieve the dummy landing operation.

3. What are the Fuehrer's political and military directives if operation "Sea Lion" does not take place? It is hoped that maximum production

in German industry will be re-established through release of the capacity now being used for operation "Sea Lion," the return of personnel and of the steamers, other vessels and barges. At the same time the appearance of an "invasion of Britain" should be kept up. *The Fuehrer* agrees.

4. The Naval Staff's deliberations on further possibilities for warfare against Britain in addition to, or instead of, operation "Sea Lion" are as follows:

Gibraltar and the Suez Canal have decisive strategic significance for German-Italian warfare in the Mediterranean area. Britain should be excluded from the Mediterranean. Control of the Mediterranean area is of vital importance to the position of the Central Powers in south-eastern Europe, Asia Minor, Arabia, Egypt, and the African area. Unlimited sources for raw materials would be guaranteed. New and strategically favourable bases for further operations against the British Empire would be won. The loss of Gibraltar would mean crucial difficulties for British important traffic from the South Atlantic. Preparations for this operation must be begun at once so that they are completed before the U.S.A. steps in. It should not be considered of secondary importance, but as one of the main blows against Britain. *The Fuehrer* gives orders to this effect.

5. The problem of the U.S.A.—In the present significant events, i.e. agreement between the U.S.A., Great Britain, and Canada, the Naval Staff sees the beginnings of a situation which will necessarily lead to closer co-operation between Britain and the U.S.A. The course of events will be accelerated by the dangerous plight in which Britain finds herself. Britain will probably relinquish her leading position in favour of co-operation with the U.S.A. The British Empire is not expected to collapse owing to the peculiar innate force of the political objectives embodied in the conception of the Commonwealth of Nations. The Empire will in all probability have to undergo the most drastic changes, but it will very likely re-emerge as an Anglo-Saxon Empire. Understanding between the U.S.A. and Britain concerning Canada is a prerequisite for this. This understanding has been reached.

The U.S.A.'s resolution to support the British war effort with the delivery of fifty destroyers represents an openly hostile act against Germany. It is not yet clear whether the United States, even in her present policy, is acting selfishly or in Anglo-Saxon interests. The leased islands are of great significance to the U.S.A. They represent a considerable gain in prestige and a decisive step forward in the pursuit of the Pan-American objective. The possibility of exerting influence on the South American countries is increased.

An examination of the possibilities for active participation in the war on the part of the U.S.A. leads to the following thoughts: In the interest of her own position, the United States will hardly support the British motherland with significant amounts of material and personnel. Aircraft may be provided after American needs have been satisfied. The United States may, however, occupy the Spanish and Portuguese Islands in the Atlantic, possibly even the British West African possessions, in an attempt to influence, and if necessary to take over, the French West African colonies. Preparatory U.S. propaganda accuses Germany of action against French West African colonies, and points out that the German Air Force could take off from West Africa and fly across the South Atlantic to attack the United States.

*The C.-in-C., Navy,* stresses once more the extreme importance of Dakar for Germany in this war. The danger of a British or American occupation of the Azores and Canary Islands is particularly great in the event that Spain or Portugal enters the war. *The Fuehrer* therefore considers occupation of the Canary Islands by the Air Force both expedient and feasible. The question of supplies for the Air Force would present the only difficulty, as submarines cannot carry petrol. The C.-in-C., Navy, believes that tankers can reach the Canary Islands from Spain.

6. Treatment of the French Colonies.—In the French possessions in Equatorial Africa there is an open break with Petain's government and a swing over to General de Gaulle. There is danger that unrest and revolt might spread to the French West African colonies. The economic situation in the colonies, particularly as regards foodstuffs, is used by Britain as a means of exerting pressure. An agreement between the colonies and Britain, and revolt against France would jeopardize our own chances of controlling the African area; the danger exists that strategically important West African ports might be used for British convoy activities and that we might lose a most valuable source of supplies for Europe. The danger of an attack on the part of the U.S.A. is not entirely out of the question, in view of the possibilities for such action.

Far-sighted German measures are necessary to counteract any development of this kind. Therefore the Naval Staff agrees in principle to sending French naval forces to the areas threatened; to the resumption of merchant traffic between the colonies and neutral countries by means of French and neutral vessels, in order to alleviate economic difficulties; and to the attempt to re-establish merchant shipping between France and her colonies. A condition is that ships must be scuttled in the event of capture by British forces. Germany and Italy must have the possibility to control the vessels. There must be economic advantages to Germany and German right of recall.

7. Relations to occupied territories and neutral countries.—What are the Fuehrer's plans regarding treatment of the occupied northern areas and of Sweden and Finland? *The Fuehrer* conceives a north Germanic union in which the individual members have a certain sovereignty (diplomatic representation, etc.) and have armed forces trained and equipped by them but organised on the pattern of the German Armed Forces. Otherwise, however, they should be both politically and economically closely connected with Germany. These are the views of Quisling, whose standpoint the Fuehrer recognises to be the correct one as opposed to that of Terboven, the Foreign Office, and von Falkenhorst; the Navy alone, moreover, held these views, quite rightly, from the very first.

8. German merchant shipping.—Since the overthrow of France, the prospects for German maritime shipping have improved considerably. The Ministry of Transport and the Ministry of Economics have been made aware of the existing favourable opportunities for the promotion of maritime shipping; there are certain difficulties to be overcome with these authorities. Apart from the practical advantages to be derived from merchant shipping, as return of German ships and import of goods, one can expect an increase of prestige in neutral countries.

9. The Inter-Allied Investigating Committee's Memorandum of January 1940. Views on German Warfare.—The Allies continually stress the fact that they consider the ruthless submarine warfare for the disruption of merchant shipping in close co-operation with air warfare against facilities and ships in ports of import the greatest danger to Great Britain.

*The C.-in-C., Navy*, is therefore of the opinion that these operations must be continued with tenacity and energy, irrespective of whatever other operations may be undertaken. *The Fuehrer agrees.*

(signed) RAEDER.

\*      \*      \*      \*      \*      \*

On the same day the first heavy air raid was made on London. An entry in the War Diary stated that "the High Command intends to bring about the complete destruction of London's harbours, docks, industries, and supplies by means of continuous air attacks, and so hasten the decision." The next day 300 aircraft raided London. Violent actions with the R.A.F. ensued, and revealed the renewed strength of British fighter defence. The *Luftwaffe* was still elated and confident, but British sea and air attacks on the Channel ports and on minesweeping operations increased. On September 8 the *Luftwaffe* stated : "The attacks will be continued until the destruction of harbours, supplies, and power installations is complete."

On September 10, the day before Hitler was to have given the executive order for "Sea Lion," the Naval Staff reported :

"The weather conditions which for the time of year are completely abnormal and unstable, greatly impair transport movements and mine-sweeping activities for 'Sea Lion.' It is of decisive importance for the judgment of the situation, that no claim can be made to the destruction of the enemy air force over Southern England and the Channel area. The preparatory attacks of the *Luftwaffe* have achieved a perceptible weakening of enemy fighter defence, so that it can be taken for granted that the German forces have a considerable fighter superiority over the English area.

"The English bombers, however, and the minelaying forces of the British Air Force, as the experiences of the last few days show, are still at full operational strength, and it must be confirmed, that the activity of the British forces has undoubtedly been successful, even if no decisive hindrance has yet been caused to German transport movements. In spite of interruptions and delays the timely conclusion of the preparations—the earliest D Day (21.9.40)—is provisionally guaranteed, but is endangered by further difficulties and stoppages resulting from weather conditions and enemy action. The operational state, which the Naval War Staff, as opposed to the High Command, gave as the most important pre-requisite for the operation, has so far not been achieved, i.e. clear air superiority in the Channel area and the extinction of all possibilities of enemy Air Force action in the assembly areas of the Naval Forces, auxiliary vessels, and transports.

"It would be more in the sense of the planned preparation for operation 'Sea Lion,' if the *Luftwaffe* would now concentrate less on London and more on Portsmouth and Dover, and on the naval forces in and near the operation area, in order to wipe out any possible threat from the enemy. The Naval War Staff, however, does not consider it suitable to approach the *Luftwaffe* or the Fuehrer now with such demands, because the Fuehrer looks upon a large-scale attack on London as possibly being decisive, and because a systematic and long drawn-out bombardment of London might produce an attitude in the enemy which will make the "Sea Lion" operation completely unnecessary. The Naval War Staff therefore does not consider it necessary to make such a demand."

\*      \*      \*      \*      \*      \*

Hitler postponed his decision for 3 days, i.e. until September 14. On September 13, the R.A.F. sank 80 barges at Ostend. Ships of the Royal Navy bombarded Calais, Boulogne, Ostend, and Cherbourg, while light coastal forces attacked minesweepers and barges and, on the same day as the R.A.F. attacked Ostend, capital ships of the Home Fleet moved south to Rosyth, in readiness to dash at full speed to the invasion area. The *Luftwaffe* attacks continued, but weather hampered their activities.

On September 14 Hitler called his commanders together. Raeder, before the meeting began, presented a short memorandum.

"(*a*) The present air situation does not provide conditions for carrying out the operation, as the risk is still too great.

"(*b*) If the 'Sea Lion' operation fails, this will mean great gain in prestige for the British; the powerful effect of our attacks will thus be annulled.

"(*c*) Air attacks on England, particularly on London, must continue without interruption. If the weather is favourable attacks should be intensified, without regard to 'Sea Lion.' The attacks may have a decisive outcome.

"(*d*) 'Sea Lion,' however, must not yet be cancelled, as the anxiety of the British must be kept up; if cancellation became known to the outside world, this would be a great relief to the British."

The Conference followed.

## CONFERENCE BETWEEN THE C.-IN-C., NAVY, AND THE FUEHER IN THE AFTERNOON OF SEPTEMBER 14, 1940

*The Fuehrer* has come to the conclusion that it would be wrong after all to call off operation "Sea Lion" as he had apparently planned to do on September 13. The air attacks have been very effective and would have been more so if the weather had been good. The degree of air supremacy necessary to justify executing operation "Sea Lion" has not yet been reached, however. For this reason operation "Sea Lion" is not yet practicable. If the pressure of the imminent landing were added to further air attacks, the total effect would be very strong after all. For not one attack is decisive, but the total effect produced. If operation "Sea Lion" were called off now, British morale would be lifted and our air attacks would be easier to bear.

*The C.-in-C., Navy*, agrees. He has always been of the opinion that operation "Sea Lion" should be the last resort and that the risk is very great. The situation in the air is not yet such as to reduce the risk involved to a minimum. Should operation "Sea Lion" fail, the British would gain a great amount of prestige, and the enormous effect of the air successes would be minimised. In the event of good weather the Air Force must first be given the opportunity to intensify the attacks, especially on London, regardless of operation "Sea Lion." These attacks may decide the outcome of the war. Operation "Sea Lion" must not be abandoned now, however, for the reasons given by the Fuehrer. The air situation can scarcely be expected to change to any great extent between September 24 and 27 as regards the safety of operation "Sea Lion"; for this reason the operation should be postponed until October 8 or 24. If we wish to avoid loss of prestige, it will be permissible to abandon operation "Sea Lion" only at the moment of maximum air successes, on the grounds that it is no longer necessary. *The Fuehrer* agrees, but he wishes to decide on September 17 whether the operation is to take place on September 27 or not.

*The C.-in-C., Army*, declares that the Army no longer attaches such great importance to a landing at dawn, so that the time element involved can be reconsidered. As far as the C.-in-C., Navy, can find out, this sudden change in the Army's initial stubborn demand can be traced to the fact that the front-line generals, like the Navy, are opposed to a night crossing.

In discussing the air attacks on London, the C.-in-C., Navy, supports the view of the Chief of the General Staff, Air, namely, that the attacks on targets of military importance will not suffice to produce mass psychosis and large-scale evacuation, since the residential areas are some distance from the docks, etc. *The Fuehrer*, however, wishes to reserve deliberate attacks on residential areas as a final means of pressure and as a reprisal for British attacks of this nature. *The C.-in-C., Navy*, points out in this connection what a small area the port and dock installations and industrial sections cover in proportion to the gigantic area occupied by the residential part of London.

As soon as the positions of the heavy British coastal batteries have been established, they are to be attacked by dive bombers of the Air Force.

(signed) RAEDER.

\*     \*     \*     \*     \*     \*

The result of this conference was a further postponement of the operation.   A directive was issued from Hitler's Headquarters.

Supreme Command                                    Berlin, September 14, 1940

Top Secret                                                           8 Copies
                                                                            2nd Copy

At the conference of the Cs.-in-C. of the Armed Forces on September 14 the Fuehrer had decided:

(1) "*Sea Lion.*"

(*a*) The start of the operation is again postponed.   A new order follows on September 17.   All preparations are to be continued.

(*b*) As soon as preparations are complete, the *Luftwaffe* is to carry out attacks against the British long-range batteries.

(*c*) The measures planned for the evacuation of the coastal area are not to be set in motion to the full extent.   Counter-espionage and deception measures are, however, to be increased.

(2) Air attacks against London.—The air attacks against London are to be continued and the target area is to be expanded against military and other vital installations (e.g. railway stations).

Terror attacks against purely residential areas are reserved for use as an ultimate means of pressure, and are therefore not to be employed at present.

(signed) KEITEL.

\*     \*     \*     \*     \*     \*

Heavy air attacks by both sides continued for the next two days, and on September 17 an entry in the War Diary stated:

"The enemy Air Force is still by no means defeated; on the contrary it shows increasing activity.   The weather situation as a whole does not permit us to expect a period of calm. . . . The Fuehrer therefore decides to postpone 'Sea Lion' indefinitely."

On September 19 a Supreme Command directive was issued.

Supreme Command of the Armed Forces        Berlin, September 19, 1940

Top Secret                                          8 Copies

                                                           2nd Copy

### SUBJECT : Operation "Sea Lion"

The Fuehrer and Supreme Commander of the Armed Forces has made the following decisions :

(1) The deployment of the Transport Fleet, in so far as it has not yet been finished, is to be held up.

(2) The assembling of ships in the embarkation harbours are so to be thinned out that the loss of shipping space caused by enemy air attacks may be reduced to a minimum. At the same time it should be arranged so that in good weather 8–10 days (from the issue of the warning order) remains sufficient for reassembling the ships in the embarkation harbours at the appointed time.

(3) The 10 steamers intended for the operation *Herbstreise* are to carry on their usual normal employment until further orders. Six further steamers, intended for "Sea Lion," are to be inconspicuously withdrawn, and used for the hastening of supplies to Army Group XXI (Norway).

(4) The Air Command is to strengthen the anti-aircraft defences in the embarkation harbours as much as possible.

                                       (signed) KEITEL.

                                       Head of the O.K.W.

\*      \*      \*      \*      \*      \*

The situation was summed up in the War Diary :

"(i) The preparations for a landing on the Channel coast are extensively known to the enemy, who is taking more counter-measures. Symptoms are, for example, operational use of his aircraft for attacks and reconnaissance over the German operational harbours, frequent appearance of destroyers off the South coast of England, in the Straits of Dover, and on the Franco-Belgian coast, stationing of his patrol vessels off the north coast of France, Churchill's last speech, etc.

"(ii) The main units of the Home Fleet are being held in readiness to repel the landing, though the majority of the units are still in western bases.

"(iii) Already a large number of destroyers (over 30) has been located by air reconnaissance in the southern and south-eastern harbours.

"(iv) All available information indicates that the enemy's naval forces are solely occupied with this theatre of operations."

\*      \*      \*      \*      \*      \*

Although there was still a possibility of invading in October, shipping was dispersed to prevent further losses. By September 21 the state of the invasion armada was :

|  | *Shipping previously available* | *Lost or damaged* |
|---|---|---|
| Transports .. .. | 168 | 21 ( = 12·5 per cent.) |
| Barges .. .. | 1,697 | 214 ( = 12·6 per cent.) |
| Tugs .. .. | 360 | 5 ( = 1·4 per cent.) |

Troops and ships were kept in readiness until October 12, when the operation was postponed until the spring of 1941.

Supreme Command              Fuehrer's Headquarters, October 12, 1940

Top Secret                                        14 Copies

                                                             2nd Copy

(1) The Fuehrer has decided that from now on until the Spring, preparations for "Sea Lion" shall be continued solely for the purpose of maintaining political and military pressure on England. Should the invasion be reconsidered in the

spring or early summer of 1941, orders for a renewal of operational readiness will be issued later.    In the meantime military conditions for a late invasion are to be improved.

(2) All measures taken to reduce present operational readiness must be in conformity with the following principles:

(*a*) The British must continue to believe that we are preparing an attack on a broad front.

(*b*) At the same time, however, our war economy must be relieved of some of the present heavy strain placed upon it by our invasion preparations.

(3) In particular, as regards—

(*a*) The Army.—The formations allocated for "Sea Lion" can now be released for other duties or for employment on other fronts.    We must, however, avoid any noticeable reduction in the forces in coastal areas.

(*b*) The Navy must take all measures to release personnel and shipping space, particularly tugs and fishing craft, for other tasks.    All movements of shipping in connection with the dispersal must be carried out unobtrusively and spread over a considerable period of time.

(signed) KEITEL.

\*        \*        \*        \*        \*        \*

But, by the spring of 1941, Hitler and his staff were deeply involved in the preparations for invading Russia, and operation "Sea Lion" was shelved.

# Other Plans and Invasions

THE VIRTUAL cancellation of operation "Sea Lion" led to a review of other possible war theatres. Italy's entrance into the war had opened up the Mediterranean, and the German High Command saw possibilities of extending their influence throughout Europe and North Africa. The immediate strategic goal was to seize Gibraltar (operation "Felix"), seal off the Mediterranean, and then to advance against Egypt and the Balkans. Hitler himself was becoming increasingly absorbed in the idea of attacking Russia, and in the next few months his Cs.-in-C. did their best to dissuade him, offering instead the tit-bits to be gained from a Mediterranean or African campaign.

## REPORT OF THE C.-IN-C., NAVY, TO THE FUEHRER ON SEPTEMBER 26, 1940, AT 1700

(Without witnesses)

*The C.-in-C., Navy*, begs leave to state to the Fuehrer his views on the progress of the war, including also matters outside his province. The British have always considered the Mediterranean the pivot of their world empire. Even now eight of the thirteen battleships are there; strong positions are held in the Eastern Mediterranean; troop transports from Australia were sent to Egypt and East Africa. While the air and submarine war is being fought out between Germany and Britain, Italy, surrounded by British power, is fast becoming the main target of attack. Britain always attempts to strangle the weaker. The Italians have not yet realised the danger when they refuse our help. Germany, however, must wage war against Great Britain with all the means at her disposal and without delay, before the United States are able to intervene effectively. For this reason the Mediterranean question must be cleared up during the winter months.

(*a*) Gibraltar must be taken. The Canary Islands must be secured beforehand by the Air Force.

The Suez Canal must be taken. It is doubtful whether the Italians can accomplish this alone; support by German troops will be needed. An advance from Suez through Palestine and Syria as far as Turkey is necessary. If we reach that point, Turkey will be in our power. The Russian problem will then appear in a different light. Fundamentally, Russia is afraid of Germany. It is doubtful whether an advance against Russia from the north will be necessary. There is also the question of the Dardanelles. It will be easier to supply Italy and Spain if we control the Mediterranean. Protection of East Africa is assured. The Italians can wage naval warfare in the Indian Ocean. An operation against India could be feigned.

(*b*) The question of North-west Africa is also of decisive importance. All indications are that Britain with the help of Gaullist France, and possibly also of the U.S.A., wants to make this region a centre of resistance and to set up air bases for attack against Italy. Britain will try to prevent us from gaining a foothold in the African colonies. In this way Italy would be defeated.

Therefore action must be taken against Dakar. The U.S.A. already has a consul there, the Italians two representatives, and we are not represented at all. The economic situation will quickly deteriorate, but the attitude toward the British is still hostile. In spite of demobilisation there are still about 25,000 troops left in this area; in the neighbouring British territory on the other hand there are only about six to eight battalions. The possibility of action on the part of France against the British is therefore very promising. It is very desirable that support be given to the French, possibly by permitting the use of the Strasbourg.

It would be expedient to station air forces in Casablanca in the near future. In general, it appears important to co-operate with France in order to protect North-west Africa—after certain concessions have been made to Germany and Italy. The occupation of France makes it possible to compel her to maintain and defend the frontiers advantageous to us.

*The Fuehrer* agrees with the general trend of thought. Upon completion of the alliance with Japan he will immediately confer with the Duce, and possibly also with France. He will have to decide whether co-operation with France or with Spain is more profitable; probably with France, since Spain demands a great deal (French Morocco) but offers little. France must guarantee beforehand to fulfil certain German and Italian demands; an agreement could then be reached regarding the African colonies. Britain and the U.S.A. must be excluded from North-west Africa. If Spain were to co-operate, the Canary Islands, and possibly also the Azores and the Cape Verde Islands would have to be seized beforehand by the Air Force.

An advance through Syria would also depend on the attitude taken by France; it would be quite possible, however. Italy will be against the cession of the Dardanelles to Russia. Russia should be encouraged to advance toward the south, or against Persia and India, in order to gain an outlet to the Indian Ocean which would be more important to Russia than the positions in the Baltic Sea. The Fuehrer is also of the opinion that Russia is afraid of Germany's strength; he believes, for instance, that Russia will not attack Finland this year.

The Fuehrer is obviously hesitant about releasing additional French forces at Toulon; he feels himself bound by previous decisions. He wishes to discuss this matter with the Duce before deciding.

Operation "Sea Lion."—The C.-in-C., Navy, states that the Navy will be unable to maintain readiness for operation "Sea Lion" after the middle of October. The entire Navy has been reorganised on its account; the manning of battleships and the execution of the submarine training programme have been affected, and this cannot be continued after the middle of October. The C.-in-C., Navy, requests a decision by October 15.

Aerial-mine warfare.—At present numerous aerial mines are being dropped on London by the 6th Air Division. They have a decided effect, to be sure; however, the time has come for large-scale mine operations, since the new type of fuse is now available in sufficient quantities (approximately 780; and a weekly increase of 200). If such operations are delayed, there is a danger that this new weapon will become as ineffective as the magnetic mine did some time ago when the C.-in-C., Air, stopped its use off the Thames, etc. *The Fuehrer* is in complete agreement and will give the necessary order.

Russian Navy.—According to a report from our Naval Attaché the Russians are building three battleships in Leningrad, one of which is about 45,000 tons. Several submarines of about 2,800 tons are available.

Further Questions.—*The C.-in-C., Navy*, points out that the probable course of the war, i.e. the entrance of the U.S.A., makes it necessary for Germany to build up her fleet to the highest possible degree now, in order to be prepared for the future. Unfortunately this is impossible today; as Germany's capacity for ship construction is barely sufficient to carry out the submarine programme, to complete the large ships under construction, and to build a few light naval vessels. *The Fuehrer* agrees entirely.

*The C.-in-C., Navy*, remarks that the lack of an adequate fleet will constitute a continual drawback in the case of further extension of warfare, e.g. with regard to the occupation of the Canary Islands, the Cape Verde Islands, the Azores, Dakar, Iceland, etc. *The Fuehrer* agrees that islands taken by the Air Force in surprise attacks can be held only by troops and material transported with the assistance of the Navy.

*The Fuehrer* volunteers the information that the C.-in-C., Air, declared some time ago that he could substitute aircraft for submarines, which would have jeopardised the submarine programme. However, the Fuehrer himself had clearly recognised that the Air Force is partially dependent on the weather, and that its transport facilities are limited. Enemy shipping is best reduced by submarines; harbours can be destroyed by the Air Force. All branches of the Armed Forces must co-operate. It is the combined effect which is decisive.

(signed) RAEDER.

*    *    *    *    *    *

On September 27 the 10-year "Axis" pact between Germany, Italy, and Japan was signed in Berlin, and on October 7 German troops marched into Roumania. Raeder, however, was as always more concerned with the war against England and on October 14 reported to Hitler.

Naval Staff

## CONFERENCE OF THE C.-IN-C., NAVY, WITH THE FUEHRER ON OCTOBER 14, 1940, AT 1600

Also present: Chief of Staff, O.K.W.
General Jodl.
Commander von Puttkamer.

1. Survey of situation. (*a*) North Sea and Baltic Sea.—The situation remains unchanged. As before, lively traffic consisting of patrols, convoys, and single vessels is observed on the east coast of England, including the Thames. The effect of aerial mines is beginning to become evident. It is necessary to increase use of aerial mines, since large convoys are still reaching the Thames and ports on the east and west coasts. Bombing of the harbours alone is obviously not sufficient. The Fuehrer has authorised the C.-in-C., Air, to use the old aerial mines on London again on nights when there is a full moon, but also to drop at least fifty to sixty aerial mines per night off the harbours, first of all on the east coast.

The operation by British destroyers against the Norwegian coast last night led to the loss of two net ships and shows that the enemy is trying to disrupt our traffic in Norwegian waters, making use of the longer nights. Appropriate defence measures have been introduced. In order to eliminate surprise attacks, increased air reconnaissance before dark is urgently necessary during the period of long nights.

(b) Channel.—Continual forays are being made by torpedo boats and motor boats. Successful attack by the 5th Torpedo Boat Flotilla led to the destruction of two enemy anti-submarine vessels and two coastal vessels, as well as probable damage to a destroyer. The enemy is continuing lively air attacks against Channel harbours and the Atlantic coast at Brest and Lorient.

(c) Submarine warfare.—Recent sinkings and their effects have been particularly gratifying in spite of the fact that bad weather is hampering operations. Increasing successes by *Italian* submarines in the Atlantic are expected from operations now scheduled to begin. The complaint by Marshal Badoglio regarding the use of Italian submarines is unjustified since the boats coming from the Mediterranean receive very strict operational orders from the Italian Admiralty. The Admiral Commanding Submarines, has no control over them until they arrive in Bordeaux.

(d) Auxiliary cruisers.—Their operations continue to show very good results. Ship "21," commanded by von Ruckteschell, was particularly successful in the North Atlantic, having sunk over 60,000 tons. She is now no longer fit for operations, as the engines need overhauling, and is therefore returning to the French Atlantic coast.

Ship "10," commanded by Kaehler, has reported regarding an engagement with the Alcantara. The commanding officer handled the situation very correctly. Tanker Rekum has returned after successfully refuelling three auxiliary cruisers in the North and South Atlantic. The achievement of this vessel gives an indication of the possibilities of refueling auxiliary cruisers and the prospects for our merchant shipping in the Atlantic.

2. Relaxation of readiness for Operation "Sea Lion" has been ordered according to instructions by the O.K.W. Orders for improving operational facilities given in these instructions have been taken by the C.-in-C., Navy, to mean that this is to be effected by constant manœuvres, but that new transport vessels in large numbers are not to be ordered, since otherwise the capacity of the shipyards would be occupied to the detriment of the submarine programme, etc. The High Command, Navy, will design an ideal type of motorised ferry and make all necessary preparations so that mass production can be undertaken quickly if operation "Sea Lion" is carried out in 1941. Locomotive engines will be used. *The Fuehrer agrees.*

3. Further plans for naval warfare. (a) Atlantic operations by Scheer. —Departure of the Scheer is planned for October 23, departure of the supply ship Nordmark for October 20. First, the Scheer is to carry out operations against merchant shipping in the North Atlantic. Operations are planned on the North Atlantic convoy route. Their execution will depend on the enemy situation. Subsequent operations against merchant shipping are intended in the southern part of the North Atlantic and in the South Atlantic.

(b) Operations from the French West Coast.—Acquisition of strategic bases on the Atlantic coast would afford facilities for offensive operations and would call for definite concentration of our forces.   From bases along the French West Coast, destroyers are to attack enemy supplies coming from the south.   For this purpose, the full range of the destroyers should be utilised, and emergency refueling stations established in Spanish ports. Operations against ships carrying mine timber from Portugal and ore from Spain are also planned.   Apart from this, destroyers are to lay mines in the St. George's Channel and Bristol Channel, to be supplemented by large-scale aerial mine laying off harbours and river mouths.   Upon arrival of battleships and cruisers on the Atlantic coast in the course of the winter, extensive operations are planned in the North Atlantic against enemy supply lines as well as for the protection of our own blockade-runners and prizes.   It is to be expected that the enemy supply and convoy system will be greatly affected.

(c) In the North Sea and the Channel.—We must continue to disrupt enemy coastal traffic by torpedo boats and motor boats as well as mine-layers, using mines, torpedoes, and guns.   Here also naval operations should be supplemented by the use of aerial mines on a large scale.   *The Fuehrer* agrees.   He asks whether the Navy could help in transporting troops and material in case it should be necessary to occupy the Canary Islands, Azores, or perhaps the Cape Verde Islands.

*The C.-in-C., Navy*, replies in the affirmative, provided that the transport operation to these places gets under way before the occupation by air, etc., takes place.   It would not be possible to occupy the islands first from the air and afterwards bring up reinforcements by ship, for all the approaches to the islands will then be patrolled by the enemy.   The Scheer and other battleships could, if necessary, join in the operations.   8,000 tons of petrol are already on the Azores.

*The Fuehrer* requests that the whole question be investigated and that the necessary preparations be made.

(signed)     RAEDER.<br>(countersigned) ASSMANN.

\*          \*          \*          \*          \*          \*

Meanwhile Britain strengthened her position in the Mediterranean in spite of the apparent continued threat of a German invasion at home.   It was clear now, as it had been in the Napoleonic wars, that the Mediterranean was to be the crucial theatre of the war, but only Raeder and the Naval Staff, possibly because they alone knew the full meaning of sea power, really appreciated the danger.   Hitler paid lip service to their schemes and suggestions, but, as later events showed, his mind was concentrated on land operations—the invasion of Russia.

\*          \*          \*          \*          \*          \*

On October 28 Mussolini invaded Greece and upset all the carefully conceived German plans.   Preparations for capturing Gibraltar were hastened forward, and an effort to seal the western entrance of the Mediterranean was to be made with Franco's assistance.   (Franco's assistance was not certain, but on the day of the next conference, November 4, Spain took over the government of Tangier.   This was probably taken by Hitler as positive evidence of Spanish willingness to co-operate.)

Berlin, November 4, 1940

## CONFERENCE OF THE CHIEF, OPERATIONS DIVISION, NAVAL STAFF WITH THE CHIEF, OPERATIONS STAFF, O.K.W., GENERAL JODL, ON NOVEMBER 4, 1940

1. *The Fuehrer* made a number of decisions today regarding measures to be taken by Germany as a result of the Italian campaign against Greece.

2. Egyptian offensive—the Fuehrer's decision.—No troops (i.e. no *panzer* divisions) are to be sent to Libya, since the second thrust of the Italians against Mersa Matruh will not be possible until the end of December. A necessary third thrust will probably require just as much time for preparation as the second one, so that the actual attack on Alexandria, for which participation of our *panzer* division was planned, cannot be expected until about the middle of summer 1941. The Fuehrer, however, is planning to transfer dive-bomber units to Egypt for the purpose of attacks against the British Fleet in Alexandria after Mersa Matruh has been occupied. He will also send bomber units to mine the Suez Canal.

3. The War in Greece.—This was definitely a regrettable blunder on the part of the Italians. On no occasion was authorisation for such an independent action given to the Duce by the Fuehrer. It seems that Italy has started to attack with entirely inadequate forces, i.e. three divisions. The British have occupied Crete and Lemnos. As a result Britain's strategic position in the eastern Mediterranean has considerably improved. With Lemnos in her possession, she has an advanced position for the purpose of encroaching on the mainland, is able to influence and support Turkey, and also has facilities for launching bomber attacks against Roumania. The Fuehrer considers the Roumania oilfields to be endangered by British forces on Lemnos! Therefore it is necessary to transfer anti-aircraft reinforcements, fighters, and fighter bombers to Roumania immediately.

The support of the Italian offensive against Greece by German troops consisting of two divisions or one corps is being considered. There are two possibilities for operations: To proceed either with or without Bulgaria. An advance against Greece will be attempted through Roumania and Bulgaria in the direction of Salonika-Larissa. The O.K.W. estimates that another four weeks are needed for preparing this operation from Roumania! Details are being investigated by the General Staff. In addition, military support of Bulgaria against Turkey has been ordered to ensure against Turkish attacks.

It is anticipated that Russia will remain neutral. Within the next few days there will be a conference with Molotov in which the problems arising from this neutrality will be discussed. The attitude of Turkey will depend on Russia's future policy.

*The Fuehrer* does not plan to take action against Turkey for the purpose of breaking through to the Suez Canal from the East via Syria. This would be a very lengthy operation and would involve very great difficulties.

4. Gibraltar.—*The Fuehrer* is determined to occupy Gibraltar as soon as possible. Franco is obviously prepared to enter the war on Germany's side within a short time; the Army General Staff has already made

preparations to send the necessary troops. The Fuehrer has given the following orders:

A reconnaissance unit, consisting of about fifty officers, is to be sent to Spain at once.

The transfer of troops to the Franco-Spanish border for the Gibraltar operation must begin at once.

Spain will be requested to make a road available for German troop movements.

It must be assumed that our plans will be revealed by the time German troops reach the Spanish border. The following measures are therefore scheduled to begin when Army troops are ready to cross the Franco-Spanish border:

(a) Commencement of attacks by the German Air Force against the British Fleet in Gibraltar.

(b) Occupation of the Canary Islands. It is planned to strengthen defences of the Canary Islands primarily by Spanish action. Spanish resources will be reinforced by German measures.

(c) Occupation of the Cape Verde Islands.

Regarding the occupation of Gibraltar, certain difficulties will arise due to the fact that the operation and the defence are to be undertaken only with German and Spanish forces. Investigations should therefore be made as to what possibilities are foreseen by the Naval Staff for blockade and defence of the Strait of Gibraltar in view of the limited means available. In this connection Spanish territory and the Ceuta area may have to be utilised. There is no doubt that control of defence in any case must be in German hands.

The possibility of incorporating French forces is to be investigated; it can be assumed that all British defence facilities, i.e. guns, etc., will be put out of action. Therefore the great question is how the Straits of Gibraltar can be closed most effectively, if all British batteries and defence installations are destroyed.

All German vessels assembled in Italy must be made available for transport purposes within the Mediterranean.

5. Cape Verde Islands.—On the question of the occupation of the Cape Verde Islands, the Chief, Naval Staff, Operations Division, expressed fundamental objections; the operation, dependent on support from the French, would be difficult to carry out and we could not be sure of holding the islands in view of the available forces. The islands have no great value for the enemy, but the political disadvantages resulting from our occupation of this Portuguese territory, with possible counteraction by Britain and the U.S.A. against the Azores, Portugal proper, and the Portuguese colonies, must be regarded as very serious.

The Chief, Naval Staff, Operations, Division, points out that the operation against the Cape Verde Islands can be carried out only if Dakar is in our hands. The Chief, Armed Forces Operations Staff, replies that considerable support from France could be counted on. The C.-in-C., Navy, will have to talk to the Fuehrer at some length, since the Fuehrer is apparently very much in favour of an operation against the Cape Verde Islands.

Regarding further action against Portugal, it is planned that, upon occupation of the Cape Verde Islands, three German divisions are to advance to the Portuguese border in order to be able to counteract immediately and effectively any hostile attitude on the part of the Portuguese. The Chief, Operations Division, Naval Staff, is of the opinion that it would be better from a political as well as from a military point of view to desist from occupying the Cape Verdes and from taking immediate military steps against Portugal.    It would be better to use political pressure and the threat of military action to stop Portuguese assistance to Britain.    If the enemy should attempt to land in Portugal it would not be very difficult to drive him out again.    Any German military action against Portugal would, however, afford the British the possibility of occupying the Portuguese colonies of Madeira, the Cape Verdes, and the Azores.

The O.K.W. requests that a report be submitted on the subject of what importance Portugal has for us and for the enemy from the point of view of naval strategy and the war economy.

6. Regarding the transfer of German troops from France to Spain, facilities for protecting troop transports from Bayonne should be investigated, since they are exposed to attacks from the sea. *The Chief, Operations Division, Naval Staff*, replies that it is not possible to use naval forces for protection from the sea.    The possibility of using mines for flank protection is being investigated.    Protection must be effected primarily by motorised Army artillery and by dive-bombers.

7. The Chief, Operations Staff, O.K.W., points out that preparations for an eastern campaign, as well as for execution of operation "Sea Lion" in the spring, have to be continued according to the Fuehrer's decision.

8. Relations with France.—Final clarification has not yet been reached, since the discussions between the Fuehrer and Petain dealt only with basic matters concerning political collaboration and military co-operation. No final agreements have yet been reached.    This week there will be discussions between Laval and Ribbentrop.    In the course of these conferences, the French will submit definite proposals and German demands will be stated.    Co-operation is intended along the following lines:

(*a*) Protection of French colonies by France herself.    She will have an entirely free hand in the colonies for this purpose.

(*b*) Elimination of the threat arising from the De Gaulle movement, and defence against all Anglo-American intentions in the African areas. If possible, the British bases in West Africa are to be attacked.

(*c*) Demilitarisation of continental France is to proceed.

The Chief, Operations Division, Naval Staff, points out that the entire forces of the considerably reduced French Fleet will be necesasry in order to carry out the necessary tasks in the colonies; these can not be handled by a few submarines, fleet tenders, and destroyers.    This fact will necessitate a completely different attitude by the Italians on the question of French disarmament.    It is therefore planned to disarm France, but to leave her freedom of action in the colonies.

9. The meeting at Florence was primarily for the purpose of removing certain objections raised by the Duce, who believed that Germany is

allowing the French too much freedom, and that the Italian requirements are thus receiving no consideration.   The Fuehrer is, in principle, pursuing the definite policy of keeping France weak in order to eliminate any threat to the Axis Powers.   There is no doubt that France will be forced to meet the territorial demands of Germany and Italy!

10.  The following points are therefore to be investigated by the Naval Staff:

(*a*) Facilities for defence of the Straits of Gibraltar.

(*b*) Occupation of the Canary Islands and reinforcement of the defences there.

(*c*) Protection of the coastal road along the southern coast of France for the transfer of German troops to Spain.

(*d*) Occupation of the Cape Verde Islands.

(*e*) The importance of Portugal from the point of view of naval strategy.

(*f*) Release of the French Fleet to take over its tasks within the over-all strategic plan.

(unsigned).

\*     \*     \*     \*     \*     \*

Meanwhile Raeder concentrated on the Battle of the Atlantic.   The pocket battleship Scheer was sent out, and during the night of November 5–6 sank 6 ships of a convoy of 32, after a violent action with the armed merchant cruiser, H.M.S. Jervis Bay, which was also sunk.

Five days later, on the night of November 11–12, the Royal Navy attacked the Italian Fleet at Taranto.   Aircraft of the Fleet Air Arm, operating from the carrier H.M.S. Illustrious, seriously damaged three battleships, two cruisers, and two auxiliaries, thus redressing the balance of naval power in the Mediterranean in Britain's favour.   To the Germans it meant an unwelcome strengthening of Britain's position in the Balkans, but the German High Command was not yet ready to strike.

## CONFERENCE OF THE C.-IN-C., NAVY, WITH THE FUEHRER ON NOVEMBER 14, 1940, AT 1300

Also present:   Colonel Schmundt.
      Commander von Puttkamer.

1. Own situation.   Naval Warfare in Home Waters.—Our operations in the Channel have recently been greatly hampered by the weather. Escort of shipping to the Channel, to Norway, and along the Norwegian coast has been carried out without appreciable losses.   There has been more extensive activity by British destroyers against the Norwegian coast, and also by British submarines which have lately again been appearing in the Skagerrak.   In the night of November 6 operations were conducted by the 1st and 2nd Torpedo Boat Flotillas against the convoy route on the British coast at Firth of Moray.   The *loss of T.*6 due to a mine shows that the enemy has protected the coastal route effectively by flanking minefields.

There is nothing to report on the Atlantic coast.   For the sake of our operations and submarine warfare, and in order to bring in prizes and to enable blockade-runners to operate, it is necessary to extend the defences of our coastal waters.

2. Recent mine warfare and further plans.

I. Naval Forces. (a) Home area.—The Channel area off the British coast has been mined. In the western sector mines were laid by destroyers, in the middle sector by torpedo boats, and on the south-east coast by motor boats.

Plan.—The operations are to be continued with the object of effective mining of British coastal waters. Requirements of operation "Sea Lion" are being taken into consideration.

North Sea.—It is planned to extend to the north the German declared area by laying mines to protect the Skagerrak and the sea routes to Norway. The south-western flanking minefields are to be extended in order to protect the coastal route to the west.

(b) Foreign waters.—Mines are to be laid by auxiliary cruisers in South African, Indian, and Australian waters.

II. Aerial mines.—The use of aerial mines is to be continued on a larger scale. The Thames area is to be mined next. It is possible and very desirable to use still more aerial mines.

Recently there have been clear indications of the increasing effects of the mine-laying offensive. Britain has suffered numerous losses in trawlers, minesweepers, and merchant steamers. The cruiser Galatea struck a mine in the Thames. The effect of the new mine fuse is apparent.

3. Atlantic submarine warfare.—The great successes of our submarines at the end of October are now decreasing. This is unavoidable in view of necessary overhauling and relief. It will be offset somewhat by operations of Italian submarines in the North Atlantic. The Italian successes cannot yet be compared with the achievement of our submarines due to the lack of training and experience of the Italians. But the morale of the crews is good.

Recently there have been appreciable losses in supplies for Britain resulting from the successful warfare waged against merchant shipping by submarines and by the Air Force. Reports from Britain confirm the seriousness of the situation and the anxiety felt there regarding the supply situation. In his last speech Churchill said that the submarine danger is more serious than the continual air attacks, and that large-scale preparations will be necessary in order to meet the very serious dangers from submarines in the coming year.

It is therefore imperative to concentrate all the forces of the Navy and the Air Force for the purpose of interrupting all supply shipments to Britain. This must be our chief operational objective in the war against Britain.

In the course of the last operation, U.31 (commanded by Prellberg) and U.32 (commanded by Jenisch) were lost. Losses up to now have averaged 2·1 per month.

The weakness of British defence and escort forces so far was a great advantage for our submarines. In view of the support given to Britain by the U.S.A. and as the result of new ships built, we must expect a considerable increase in the number of destroyers and anti-submarine vessels. An increase in anti-submarine activity is already perceptible. Therefore the following measures are urgently required:

(*a*) Priority must be given to the submarine programme, which is still handicapped by the fact that too many projects have been awarded special priority. Already the state of affairs is such that at the end of 1940 thirty-seven submarines fewer will have been completed than were planned. Negotiations with the Chief of Staff, O.K.W., have been opened to urge that immediate steps be taken to remedy this situation. If these conversations are not successful the C.-in-C., Navy, will appeal to the Fuehrer!

(*b*) Constant attacks of our Air Force should be aimed at the destruction of British destroyers, escort vessels, and submarine chasers. Every destroyer and defence vessel sunk is of decisive importance for submarine warfare. The air attacks on Britain up to now have not created the conditions necessary for carrying out operation "Sea Lion." Naval vessels are still stationed in harbours like Portsmouth and Plymouth. The situation must change before any new attempt to carry out operation "Sea Lion" is made. In addition, the Clyde shipyards and other shipyards where new battleships are being constructed must now be bombed, too, in order to bring about a more favourable situation at sea in the coming year.

*The Fuehrer* confirms the fact that attacks by the Air Force have not achieved the expected results either on land or in the case of convoys. On land quite often only dummy installations, etc., were destroyed, while at sea it was found difficult to score hits.

4. Cruiser warfare.—(*a*) The Scheer and the supply ship Nordmark succeeded during the second half of October in breaking through the North Sea and Iceland area unobserved by the enemy. On November 5 the Scheer made a surprise attack on a convoy on the Canada route; 85,000 tons were sunk! This was an excellent achievement. Far-reaching strategic effects are to be expected. An immediate reaction on the part of the enemy is evident; the Scapa Group has put out to sea and the Gibraltar Group is in a state of readiness. The enemy will be forced to provide greater protection of convoy traffic. The Scheer is now proceeding south. The withdrawal of British forces from home waters may later result in conditions favourable for renewed attacks by other units of the fleet on the North Atlantic route.

(*b*) Auxiliary cruisers.—Ship "21" has returned. Ship "41" will put out to sea in December, for operations in the Atlantic and the Indian Ocean. Continued successful operations by all our auxiliary cruisers can be reported. The disposition at present is as follows: One auxiliary cruiser is in the South Atlantic, one in the western part of the Indian Ocean, one in the eastern part of the Indian Ocean; two are operating together in the Pacific on the Australian–Panama route. Supplies from non-German sources have up to now been secured with only slight losses, in spite of a very sharp watch maintained by the enemy.

5. The Pan-American safety zone is detrimental to cruiser warfare. It is proposed to change the regulations governing conduct in this zone as soon as the attitude of the U.S.A. becomes more unfriendly, particularly since the British have violated the regulations on numerous occasions.

6. Resumption of merchant shipping. Blockade-runners.—So far three prizes, the catapult ship Ostmark, and the tanker Gedania, successfully reached the Atlantic coast. Likewise the transfer of some ships from Spain

was accomplished. The Gedania carried a valuable cargo of whale oil, which is of special importance for German margarine supplies. Preparations for the return of merchant ships from abroad and for merchant traffic with blockade-runners are being planned in co-operation with the Ministry of Economics and the Ministry of Transport. Supplying the ships, getting them in condition to leave, and contraband control and surveillance by the enemy cause difficulties. A ship is en route to France from Colombia; the escape was well executed. Three ships are ready to sail from Mexico. Four ships are being made ready on the west coast of South and Central America. The return of the motor ships from East Asia is being considered. Four ships are to leave France for South America. The Scheer operation is expected to increase the chances for the blockade-runners. Preparations for merchant traffic in the Mediterranean with Italy and Spain are in progress.

7. For a review of the situation in the Mediterranean see Appendix.

8. Further plans of the Fuehrer:

(a) The views of the Naval Staff regarding occupation of islands in the Atlantic.

(b) An evaluation of the occupation of the Cape Verde and Canary Islands.

(c) An evaluation of the strategic importance of Portugal to Britain and Germany.

(1) Canary Islands.—They are of importance to the British in case Gibraltar is taken, and they are useful to us as a base for submarines, pocket battleships, auxiliary cruisers, and merchant shipping. For this purpose, however, these islands would have to be fully equipped as a base. We must check at once whether sufficient ammunition for coastal fortifications, anti-aircraft guns and ammunition, oil stocks and oil storage space, etc., are available. Spanish troops must be supplemented, in the same manner as the Condor Legion * was used. All this must be done before Spain's entry into the war. Occupation by the British must under all circumstances be prevented in order that they shall have no hold on Spain.

(2) Portuguese possessions.—The neutrality of Portugal is most favourable to us. Portugal will maintain neutrality, since she knows that we could drive the British out of Portugal from Spain. Any breach of Portugal's neutrality by us would have a very unfavourable effect on public opinion in the U.S.A., Brazil, and in South America generally, but above all it would result in the immediate occupation of the Azores, perhaps also of the Cape Verde Islands and of Angola, by Britain or the U.S.A.

The Fuehrer believes that the British would occupy the Azores immediately upon our entry into Spain (the C.-in-C., Navy, has great doubts about this), and that she would later cede the Azores to the U.S.A. The Fuehrer believes that the Azores would afford him the only facility for attacking America, if she should enter the war, with a modern plane of the Messerschmidt type, which has a range of 12,600 km. Thereby America would be forced to build up her own anti-aircraft defence, which is still completely lacking, instead of assisting Britain.

---

* The German Force which supported Franco during the Spanish War.

*The C.-in-C., Navy*, states that the occupation of the Azores would certainly be a very risky operation, but one which, with luck, *could* succeed. On the other hand, it is very doubtful whether we could bring up adequate protection and supplies, and the possibility of holding the Islands is quite unlikely in view of a strong British offensive which would certainly be carried out, perhaps with American help. In addition, German naval forces would for a long time be engaged in defensive tasks of escorting supplies instead of serving the main war aim of offensive operations. Submarines would also have to be used for defence. In this way submarine warfare would be adversely affected, which must not occur under any circumstances. As it is very doubtful whether there are any harbour facilities at all in the Azores for speedy unloading of heavy equipment, or shelters for aircraft and supplies, immediate investigations must be made by both a naval and an air officer. *The Fuehrer* orders this to be done.

*The C.-in-C., Navy*, points out that apart from this Portugal should be influenced at this point to fortify the Azores strongly and to defend them. The C.-in-C., Navy, considers occupation of the Cape Verde Islands and of Madeira unnecessary, since they would offer a useful base neither to us nor to the British.

9. Regarding Russia.—*The Fuehrer* is still inclined towards a demonstration with Russia.

*The C.-in-C., Navy*, recommends postponing this until after victory over Britain, since demands on German forces would be too great, and an end to hostilities could not be foreseen. During the war the area so urgently needed for submarine training in the eastern Baltic would be lost, and submarine warfare thereby very adversely affected. Russia, on her part, will not attempt to attack in the next few years, since she is at present building up her Navy with the assistance of Germany. She attaches great importance to the 38-cm. turrets for battleships; therefore she will remain dependent on German support in the years to come.

10. *The C.-in-C., Navy*, requests permission to buy some Danish torpedo boats to be used as recovery boats at submarine firing exercises; they are urgently needed. *The Fuehrer* agrees.

11. *The C.-in-C., Navy*, reports that construction of submarine shelters in Lorient is proceeding with the help of the Todt Organisation.

12. Construction work for operation "Sea Lion."—The High Command, Navy, has developed a transport barge carrying three tanks at a speed of 13–15 knots. A few samples of this model are being built. The engineers are constructing, with special priority, craft capable of carrying one tank. They have a speed of 5 knots and are less seaworthy. Colonel von Schell is constructing, with special priority, a hydrofoil motor boat in competition with the Navy. The C.-in-C., Navy, requests a new order to the effect that vessels for operation "Sea Lion" are to be constructed only by the Navy. *The Fuehrer* gives instructions to this effect to the O.K.W.

13. *The C.-in-C., Navy*, reports on difficulties in the political administration of Norway, and requests that Quisling and Hagelin be received by Minister Lammers to report. *The Fuehrer* agrees.

*The C.-in-C., Navy*, mentions that the question of Brittany is still being pursued in certain quarters; this is not important in the first place, and besides, in view of the present relations with France, it should not be touched on. *The Fuehrer* gives instructions that the Brittany question is to be dropped. (*Reichsleiter* Bormann.)

14. *The C.-in-C., Navy*, raises the question of money awards which are paid by the Air Force for sinking naval vessels. He considers a general ruling necessary for the Armed Forces but rejects its application as far as the Navy is concerned.

(signed) RAEDER.

The Naval Staff summed up their views on the Mediterranean in a memorandum for the Supreme Command.

Naval Staff                                                            November 14, 1940

### Evaluation of the Mediterranean Situation

1. The consequences of the independent offensive by Italy against Greece, which is not in accordance with the interests of our combined war activities, are as follows:

(*a*) Britain's naval strategic position in the eastern Mediterranean is decidedly improved by the exploitation of naval and air bases on Crete, the Peloponnesus, and Lemnos.

(*b*) Britain has gained in prestige in the Balkan area, Near East, Egypt, and U.S.A., while Italy has lost prestige correspondingly.

(*c*) Conditions for the Italian Libyan offensive against Egypt have deteriorated. The Naval Staff is of the opinion that Italy will never carry out the Egyptian offensive.

There is danger that the situation in the eastern Mediterranean will not develop as Germany had planned, but the enemy will take over the initiative and Italian activities will encounter great difficulties. The Italian offensive against Greece is decidedly a serious strategic blunder; in view of the anticipated British counteractions it may have an adverse effect on further developments in the Eastern Mediterranean and in the African area, and thus on all future warfare. The enemy clearly has supremacy in the eastern Mediterranean at present, and it is possible that his position in the Eastern Mediterranean area will become so consolidated that it will no longer be possible to drive the British Fleet from the Mediterranean.

2. The Naval Staff is convinced that the result of the offensive against the Alexandria-Suez area and the development of the situation in the Mediterranean, with their effects on the African and Middle Eastern areas, is of decisive importance for the outcome of the war.

The Naval Staff is of the opinion that the recognition that Britain and the U.S.A. are constantly moving closer together forces us not only to form a European union, but also to fight for the African area as the foremost strategic objective of German warfare as a whole. If we could secure control of the economic block of Europe and Africa in our hands, it would mean that we would possess the decisive bases for raw materials (cotton, copper, and oil) and foodstuffs. For this purpose the first task is to drive the British Fleet from the Mediterranean Sea in order to gain control of the Mediterranean area.

3. (a) Importance of control of the Eastern Mediterranean.—This has a decisive effect on Italian powers of endurance in Italy proper, as well as in Abyssinia and the East Africa-Libya area. Very important oil supplies for Spain, Italy, and France, would be assured. The necessary supplies of foodstuffs for Spain would be assured, which at present are being sent from Argentina. If Spain enters the war it may be expected that shipments from the West will be greatly reduced. She would therefore be dependent on foodstuffs from the Eastern European (i.e. the Balkan countries and Russia) and the African areas.

The position of the Axis Powers in the Balkans, Asia Minor, Arabia, Egypt, and Sudan would be assured once and for all. Raw materials found in these countries would be included in the German-Italian-Spanish-French economic sphere. A base for attacks against the British Colonial Empire in East Africa would be acquired, and a threat to India would be created.

(b) Importance of control of the Western Mediterranean including elimination of Gibraltar.—The North African area would be under our control and this supply base for Spain and France would be secured. Any attempt at desertion on the part of the French Colonies in North Africa would be prevented. Uninterrupted supplies from the North African area, which are of vital importance for Spain and France and of considerable importance for Germany, would be guaranteed. A base for attack against British West African colonies would be acquired.

4. Deductions.—(a) Occupation of Gibraltar and control of the Western Mediterranean, although very important, are not sufficient in themselves. Domination of the Eastern Mediterranean is also urgently necessary, since this is of decisive importance, both strategically and economically, for further warfare; it is possibly even decisive for the outcome of the war. This is all the more true, if Britain receives little American support. By eliminating British bases and possibilities of operation in the Western and Eastern Mediterranean, the British Fleet would be driven out of the whole Mediterranean area and possibly destroyed.

(b) The Italian armed forces have neither the leadership nor the military efficiency to carry the required operations in the Mediterranean area to a successful conclusion with the necessary speed and decision. A successful attack against Egypt by the Italians alone can also scarcely be expected now. The Italian leadership is wretched. They have no understanding of the situation; above all, they have not yet perceived in what manner their offensive against Greece primarily damages Italy's powers of endurance. Any opposition offered by the Italian Armistice Commission must be overruled. (Recently it requested disarmament of Oran and Bizerta, while Germany wishes to strengthen France in North Africa.)

(c) From the standpoint of the overall conduct of the war, Germany has a decisive interest in solving the Eastern Mediterranean problem according to German-Italian needs. The Naval Staff is of the opinion that Germany should certainly not be a disinterested spectator in the development of the situation in the Eastern Mediterranean, in view of the close connection between victorious German warfare and the Mediterranean-African problem.

The Naval Staff therefore considers the following necessary:

(1) The German leaders responsible for the conduct of the war must in future plans take into account the fact that no special operational activity, or substantial relief or support, can be expected from the Italian armed forces.

(2) The entire Greek peninsula, including the Peloponnesus, must be cleared of the enemy, and all bases occupied. If the Italians have in mind only a restricted operational purpose in Greece, an appropriate change in policy should be suggested to them immediately. The occupation of southern Greece and western Egypt (Mersa Matruh) would considerably reduce the value of Crete for the enemy.

(3) The enemy should be forced out of the Mediterranean by utilising every conceivable possibility. In this connection the demand that Italy carry out the Egyptian offensive must be maintained and should be supported by Germany in every possible way.

An offensive through Turkey can scarcely be avoided in spite of all difficulties.

The Fuehrer expects good results from seizing Gibraltar and closing the Mediterranean in the west; subsequently North-west Africa must be secured. An independent offensive by Germany against Greece— although not until ten to twelve weeks from now, and then with ten to twelve divisions—should secure Greece for us. The Suez Canal should be mined. After taking Mersa Matruh, a German bomber squadron should be stationed there, in order to attack Alexandria and weaken the British Fleet. The Italian bomber squadron should be withdrawn from the north, where it is being used for attacks against the British Isles, and returned to Italy, with the suggestion that the Italian squadrons have as their main objective weakening of the British Fleet in the Mediterranean.

(unsigned).

\*    \*    \*    \*    \*    \*

Hitler now proceeded to bring political pressure to bear on Roumania and Bulgaria. The King of Bulgaria was summoned to Berchtesgaden on November 17, and four days later General Antonescu of Roumania was interviewed in Berlin and announced his adherence to the Axis. On November 27 the Iron Guard struck in Roumania, assassinating, among others, the ex-Prime Minister, Professor Jorga. By these measures Hitler secured his Eastern frontiers and paved the way not only for assistance to the Italians (who were being soundly beaten by the Greeks), but also for his future intention of attacking Russia.

Britain, however, still stood firm, and Hitler began to consider the invasion of Ireland as a possible means of increasing the pressure on the United Kingdom. The Naval Staff was ordered to investigate the problem, and on December 3 Raeder reported to Hitler.

High Command, Navy

## REPORT OF THE C.-IN-C., NAVY, TO THE FUEHRER ON DECEMBER 3, 1940, AT 1630

Also present:  Chief of Staff, O.K.W.
General Jodl.
Commander von Puttkamer.

1. Ireland.—The C.-in-C., Navy, puts forth the views contained in Appendix I, after summarising his general point of view as follows:

It has become increasingly evident, as confirmed repeatedly of late by British and American comments, that the greatest danger which threatens the British is the destruction of their industry and their harbour installations by our Air Force, together with the disruption of supply lines from overseas by submarines supplemented by the Air Force. Therefore these operations must be continued with great intensity; nothing must be allowed to interrupt or weaken them, since they will have a deadly effect in the long run, perhaps even this winter. We must carefully avoid any loss of prestige by operations entailing too great a risk, since this would tend to prolong the war and would, above all, create a strong impression in the U.S.A. Further measures must be taken against Britain for the purpose of relieving Italy and clearing the Mediterranean:

(a) Gibraltar must be seized, which would mean a very heavy loss in prestige for Britain. This would result in control of the western Mediterranean. Later, if it were still necessary, action could be taken in the eastern Mediterranean.

*The Fuehrer* agrees, and makes the following statement regarding Ireland. A landing in Ireland can be attempted only if Ireland requests help. For the present, our envoy must ascertain whether De Valera desires support, and whether he might wish to have his military equipment supplemented by captured British war material (guns and ammunition), which could be sent to him on single steamers. For the C.-in-C., Air, Ireland is important as a base for attacks on the north-west ports of Britain, although weather conditions must still be investigated. The occupation of Ireland might lead to the end of the war. Investigations are to be made.

2. Activities by naval forces.—The Hipper is in the Arctic Ocean ready for a break-through into the Atlantic and to Brest. Battleships and destroyers will follow at the end of December. Submarines sank 160,000 tons on December 2. Two submarines are off Freetown. The auxiliary cruiser "33" has sunk or captured 79,000 tons up to now.

3. Bulgaria.—Bulgarian request must be met. *The Fuehrer* states that the Bulgarian minister has just requested specialists for coastal defence. *The C.-in-C., Navy*, replies that specialists for coastal defence and for mines, as well as expert ship-builders, are ready to leave.

4. Operation "Felix" (Conquest of Gibraltar).—The Navy is prepared for this operation. Fortification of the Canary Islands is being negotiated with the Spaniards. (signed) RAEDER.

### APPENDIX

*The Question of Supporting Ireland against Britain*

I. The first condition necessary for transfer of troops is naval supremacy along the routes to be used. This naval supremacy could never be attained by us in view of the vastly superior British Home Fleet, not even for the duration of one transport operation.

The ratio between the British and German Fleets is as follows:

| | | |
|---|---|---|
| Battleships | .. .. | at least 2 to 1. |
| Cruisers | .. .. | at least 20 to 3. |
| Destroyers | .. .. | about 70 to 6 or 8 at the most. |

The possibility of surprise is ruled out, due to the necessity of starting from the French coast.

II. The geographical position is extremely unfavourable, since the coast of Wales and Cornwall extends like a wedge toward our line of approach; the distance from enemy bases to Ireland is less than that from the ports of embarkation in north-western France. In contrast to the Norway operation, it would not be possible to establish, by means of a surprise attack, a supply line which could be defended. Such a supply line is of decisive importance for the success of the operation.

III. The island has no defended bases or anchorages at all. Although the Irish might willingly open their ports to us, they would also be open to the enemy pursuing us. There would be no time for planned harbour and coastal fortifications, and undisturbed disembarkation of the expeditionary force is unlikely. It would not be possible to send supplies in view of the superior sea power of the enemy and the limited area through which the approach would have to be made.

IV. To a defending force, cut off and left to its own devices, the topography of the country does not afford as much protection against modern weapons as the Narvik region, for example. Without supplies and reinforcements, an expeditionary force would soon feel the increasing pressure of a British expeditionary force brought over under the protection of British naval power; sooner or later our own troops would face a situation similar to Namsos or Dunkirk.

V. Support by the Air Force would depend on the weather. Ireland, the westernmost island of any size in the northern Atlantic, is known to have a heavy rainfall and consequently low clouds and very frequent damp and foggy weather. Air support would have to come primarily from the mainland, since the airfield accommodation in Ireland would not meet our requirements; it would scarcely be possible to expand them because we could not supply equipment. Every attempt at transporting troops by Ju52's would be in great danger from British fighters, which are again increasing in numbers.

VI. It is concluded therefore that it would not be possible to follow up an Irish request for help by sending an expeditionary force and occupying the island, in view of the enemy's superior naval force, the unfavourable geographical conditions and the impossibility of forwarding supplies. Troops landed in Ireland without supplies of foodstuffs, weapons, and ammunition would sooner or later be wiped out by an enemy whose supply routes are difficult to attack.

VII. It will be possible in the winter months to bring occasional blockade-runners with weapons and ammunition into Irish harbours and bays, as long as there is still no state of war between Britain and Ireland, and as long as the Irish co-operate.

*        *        *        *        *        *

Notwithstanding these and other threats against her, Britain proceeded to strike hard at the weakest points of the Axis. On December 9 the first Western Desert offensive began, and with outstanding success the British Army, assisted by the Navy and Air Force, drove the Italians back out of Libya.

*        *        *        *        *        *

In spite of the situation in the Mediterranean, however, Hitler issued his first clear directive for the invasion of Russia on December 18.

The Fuehrer and Supreme Commander of the                    Fuehrer Headquarters,
Armed Forces                                                December 18, 1940

Top Secret                                                              9 Copies
                                                                     Copy No. 2

### Directive No. 21 "Barbarossa"

The German Armed Forces must be prepared, even before the end of the war against England, to overthrow Soviet Russia in a rapid campaign (Operation "Barbarossa").

The Army will have to employ for this all available troops, with the limitation that the occupied territories must be secured against surprise.

For the Air Force it will be a case of releasing for the Eastern campaign sufficient strength for the support of the Army, so that a speedy completion of the land operations can be relied on; and so that the damage by hostile air attacks to the Eastern German areas remains as small as possible. This concentration in the East is limited by the requirements that the whole battle and industrial armament area controlled by us must remain sufficiently protected against enemy air attacks and that the offensive activities against England, particularly her imports, must not be allowed to lapse.

The main employment of the Navy remains, even during an Eastern campaign, clearly directed against England.

I will order the deployment against Soviet Russia, when the case arises, eight weeks before the intended commencement of operations. Preparations, which require longer notice, are, where this has not already been done, to be put in hand at once and are to be completed by 15.5.41. It is, however, of decisive importance that the intention of an attack does not become evident.

The preparation of the High Commands are to be on the following basis:

I. General intentions.—The main body of the Russian Army stationed in Western Russia must be destroyed in both operations by the driving forward of armoured wedges and the withdrawal of combat units into the depth of Russia must be prevented. By rapid pursuit a line is to be reached from which the Russian Air Force can no longer attack Reich territory. The goal of the operation is a screen against Asiatic Russia from the general line Volga–Archangel. Then the last industrial area remaining to Russia in the Urals can in case of need be knocked out by the *Luftwaffe*.

In the course of this operation, the Russian Baltic Fleet will rapidly lose its bases and will therefore no longer be fit for battle.

Effective participation of the Russian Air Force is to be prevented by powerful blows right at the beginning of the operation.

II. Allies envisaged and their tasks. . . .

III. The conduct of operations:

    (a) *Army:* . . .
    (b) *Air Force:* . . .
    (c) *Navy:* . . .

All the arrangements, to be made by Cs.-in-C. as a result of this directive, must show clearly that it is a question of precautions in case Russia should change her previous attitude towards us. The number of officers to be employed from an early date on the preparations is to be kept as small as possible, additional collaborators are to be detailed as late as possible and only to the extent necessary for their duties. Otherwise the danger exists that through a leakage of information about our preparations, the time for the execution of which is by no means fixed, most difficult and military disadvantages might arise.

V. I require reports from the Cs.-in-C. on their wider intentions, based on this directive. Information regarding intended preparations of all branches of the Armed Forces together with the time-table is to be passed to me through the High Command.

                                                        (signed) A. HITLER.

Although this order had been long expected, most of the Cs.-in-C. were horrified, and sought as hard as they dared to change Hitler's decision.   Raeder saw the projected invasion of Russia as an end to his hopes of defeating England.   At the last conference of the year he tried to drive home the importance of the Mediterranean and above all of British sea power, but apart from agreeing to the increased production of U-boats, Hitler was deaf to his arguments.

## REPORT OF THE C.-IN-C., NAVY, TO THE FUEHRER ON DECEMBER 27, 1940, AT 1600

Also present:   Chief of Staff, O.K.W.
              General Jodl.
              Commander von Puttkamer.

1. Review of the situation.—The fears of the Naval Staff regarding unfavourable developments in the situation in the Eastern Mediterranean have proved justified.   The enemy has assumed the initiative at all points, and is everywhere conducting successful offensive actions—in Greece, Albania, Libya, and East Africa; in addition, an imminent and effective attack on the Italian Dodecanese Islands may be expected, all the result of Italy's serious strategic blunder.   The Naval Staff views developments in the Mediterranean area with grave misgivings.   Apart from the considerable prestige gained by Britain, the military and strategic success must not be underestimated.   The threat to Egypt, and thus to Britain's position in the entire Eastern Mediterranean, in the Near East, and in the North African area, has been eliminated with one stroke.

Britain gains are:   strong consolidation of the Eastern Mediterranean position; control of the Mediterranean; the possibility of withdrawing heavy air, army, and naval forces from Egypt to be sent to Greece.   The withdrawal of air units and army formations and their transfer to the Greek zone has already been observed.   The construction of air bases in Greece is in progress.   The fact that naval forces, battleships, and cruisers have been transferred from the Mediterranean to the Atlantic is of great significance for naval warfare.

How does the Fuehrer judge the internal political situation of Italy, Mussolini's position, and the stamina and morale of the Italian people?   Should Germany give support to Italy in order to strengthen Mussolini's position?   *The Fuehrer* answers that there is a complete lack of leadership in Italy.   The royal house is pro-British; it will have to be eliminated if it works against Mussolini.   The Fuehrer is considering where German action would be most effective.   Perhaps in Tripoli, preferably with a thrust from Spanish Morocco, since North Africa could be most easily controlled from there.   For this purpose Gibraltar must be taken.

Results of the latest development in the Mediterranean situation:

(*a*) The Italian position has deteriorated decisively, with serious effect on Italy's power of resistance.

(*b*) It is no longer possible to drive the British Fleet from the Mediterranean as was continually demanded by the Naval Staff, who considered this step vital for the outcome of the war.

(*c*) There is increased danger to German and thus European interests in general in the African area.

The decisive action in the Mediterranean for which we had hoped is therefore no longer possible.

The Gibraltar question.—The significance of German occupation of Gibraltar is increased by the recent developments in the Mediterranean situation. Such occupation would protect Italy; safeguard the western Mediterranean; secure the supply lines from the North African area, important for Spain, France, and Germany; eliminate an important link in the British Atlantic convoy system; close the British sea route through the Mediterranean to Malta and Alexandria; restrict the freedom of the British Mediterranean Fleet; complicate British offensive action in Cyrenaica and Greece; relieve the Italians; and make possible German penetration into the African area via Spanish Morocco. Spanish ports, i.e. Ferrol and Cadiz, are necessary for submarines and battleships, to facilitate attack on convoys.

Conclusion.—Occupation of Gibraltar is of great importance for the continuation of German warfare. The strategic reasons for speedy execution of operation "Felix" still hold good.

*The Fuehrer* answers that he is in full agreement regarding the significance of the occupation of Gibraltar. At the moment, however, Franco is not ready; his decision is delayed by British promises of food supplies. One day these will prove to be a fraud and Spain will find herself without supplies. The Fuehrer will try once more to influence Franco through the Foreign Minister via the Spanish Ambassador.

Singapore.—The present weakness of the British position in East Asia —Singapore indicates the possibility of a Japanese attack on this main base of Britain in East Asia. Japan's interest is very great. She has good prospects of success. The capture of Singapore would mean very serious loss of British prestige in the entire Indian, East Asiatic, and Australian area, as well as in the U.S.A. It is unlikely that the United States would advance against Japan on this occasion. Even if Japan merely threatens Singapore and there is thus constant danger of attack, this would relieve the situation for naval warfare and for our strategic position in the Mediterranean and the Atlantic, and would tie up British forces.

Therefore we make this proposal: Japan's interest in Singapore should be increased, the question of Japanese capture of the city should be examined; possibly measures for attack should be discussed with the Japanese. (Reference is made to the coming arrival of the Japanese Naval Commission as provided by the Tri-Partite Pact.)

*The Fuehrer* believes that Japan will do nothing decisive at the present time, and that Britain will hardly detach heavy battleships for service in the Far East.

2. Britain and the United States.—The entire war economy in Britain has been damaged to a considerable extent by the concentrated air raids and the war against merchant shipping. The armament industry, particularly the air armament industry, is a special weak spot. The question of shipping space is serious, but not yet critical. At present losses in shipping space cannot be replaced by British shipyards; however, this might be done by developing the constructional capacity of the U.S.A. Supply shipments from the U.S.A. are developing favourably for Britain. Iron and steel deliveries have increased tremendously, likewise the number of engines; 350–400 operational aircraft are being delivered per month. The U.S.A. is determined to give still more assistance. The Naval Staff anticipates delivery of merchant ships on a large scale; expansion of

shipyards; increase in ship construction; transfer of additional destroyers and auxiliary vessels; assumption of British patrol duties as in American coastal waters to relieve British forces as much as possible; later possibly, assumption of escort duties in American coastal waters. Very strong support will be forthcoming only by the end of 1941 or the beginning of 1942.

Britain fully realises her dangerous position as the result of German submarine warfare, even though the number of our submarines is small at present. She is determined to do everything in her power to build an effective defence, since it is of decisive importance for Britain to solve the supply problem.

3. Concentration against Britain.—It is absolutely necessary to recognise that the greatest task of the hour is concentration of all our power against Britain. In other words, the means necessary for the defeat of Britain must be produced with the utmost energy and speed. All demands not absolutely essential for warfare against Britain must deliberately be set aside. There are serious doubts as to the advisability of operation "Barbarossa" before the overthrow of Britain. The fight against Britain is carried on primarily by the Air Force and the Navy. There is therefore the greatest need to produce the weapons used by these two services and to concentrate these weapons on the British supply lines, which are taking on increased significance, in view of the fact that the entire armament industry, particularly aircraft and ship construction, is being shifted to America. Britain's ability to maintain her supply lines is definitely the decisive factor for the outcome of the war.

The significance of greatly intensified submarine warfare is emphasised anew. The Naval Staff is firmly convinced that German submarines, as in the World War, are the decisive weapons against Britain. They possess even greater potentialities now, however, owing to the support they receive from the Air Force. The great significance of submarine construction is not yet recognised in the general plan of armament production. Efforts to raise submarine construction capacity are ineffective because the necessary skilled workers are not available. The number of submarines newly constructed or nearing completion is totally inadequate. With the present number of workers the maximum monthly output amounts to eighteen boats at the most, perhaps only to twelve. If such a situation continues, all hope for the decisive effect of this most important weapon against Britain will have to be relinquished. The monthly output of submarines must be increased from twenty to thirty boats as was the case in the World War. Provision of the necessary workers and facilities is one of the most urgent demands submitted by the Naval Staff to the Armed Forces and the Government.

*The Fuehrer* wishes for the greatest possible progress in submarine construction; twelve to eighteen submarines are too few. Generally speaking, however, considering present political developments, i.e. Russia's inclination to interfere in Balkan affairs, it is necessary to eliminate at all cost the last enemy remaining on the continent before he can collaborate with Britain. For this purpose the Army must be made sufficiently strong. After that everything can be concentrated on the needs of the Air Force and the Navy.

*The C.-in-C., Navy*, replies that the situation was the same in July 1940, but that after the Army had reduced its demands for a short time, it took them up again with even greater insistence. *The Fuehrer* attributes this to the new political situation.

*The C.-in-C., Navy,* declares that the fundamental error lies in the fact that workers are assigned who are actually not available, and for this reason all decrees concerning priority grades, etc., can bring no real improvement. The O.K.W. realises that shipyards have special difficulties because of housing conditions, difficult work, etc. *The Fuehrer* suggests that perhaps additional pay would make such jobs more attractive. *The C.-in-C., Navy,* replies that an investigation is in progress, since shipyard workers are generally worse off than other workers in similar trades. Proposals will be submitted.

4. Operation "Sea Lion."—Of great importance for the course of the war as a whole, and especially for submarine warfare, is the fact that the maintenance of constant readiness for operation "Sea Lion"—establishing better facilities, barge construction, etc.—absorbs a considerable amount of labour and material, and greatly decreases the intensity of the current warfare against Britain. It necessarily has an extremely unfavourable effect on submarine training and allocation of needed personnel. The barge construction project cannot help but delay submarine construction. *The Fuehrer* permits the C.-in-C., Navy, to take measures relieving the situation somewhat further without being apparent, since he believes that operation "Sea Lion" will in all probability not take place until midsummer.

5. The Hipper.—It is planned to send the battleship Hipper on a mission. *The Fuehrer* wishes to know the purpose. *The C.-in-C., Navy,* replies that its one and only object is warfare against enemy supply lines, the chief target being the convoys, not the escort forces, which are always to be avoided unless very inferior in strength. *The Fuehrer* agrees.

*The Fuehrer* inquires whether Brest is sufficiently protected by anti-aircraft guns. *The C.-in-C., Navy,* answers that adequate anti-aircraft guns and also a sufficient number of submarine and torpedo nets are available. Mine defences are likewise adequate.

6. Norway defences.—The wish for stronger protection for merchant shipping in Norwegian waters has been expressed by the Reich Commissioner for Norway and the Commanding General, Norway. The utmost is being done in making naval forces available. Nevertheless, it is not possible to protect shipping along the entire coast. It is most important that fighter planes attack enemy aircraft, which are the greatest danger to merchant ships.

7. New influence mines with a combined magnetic and acoustic firing device, are ready. Mass delivery is expected in February.

(signed) RAEDER.

\*　　　\*　　　\*　　　\*　　　\*　　　\*

The following two letters were found in the personal files of Grand Admiral Raeder. They refer to the telegram mentioned in the conference of June 20, 1940.

The *Reichsmarschall*　　　　　　　　　　　　　Berlin August 8, 1940
of the Greater German Reich

Most esteemed Grand Admiral!

Due to special circumstances it was only a few days ago that I read the actual contents of the telegram sent to you some time ago, containing my opinion with regard to your note on matters concerning Norway. I can assure you that I was extremely shocked when I realised that, due to a chain of misunderstandings in my staff, this telegram was delivered to you in this form and with this wording. I alone am of course responsible, for I was in a state of excitement because your proposition was presented to me as so categorical that I saw therein an interference in my own sphere of command. Not for a moment, however, could I assume that my attitude would be so interpreted that such a telegram would be sent to you personally. You can rest assured, my dear Grand Admiral, that I too share the point of view that such a tone in communications between the Cs.-in-C., and especially between two men whom nothing separates but much more unites, is absolutely unthinkable. I regret most deeply that such a thing has happened and I wish to apologise personally and in all due form for having, though quite by mistake, been responsible for such a grave offence. Although the matter in question has been clarified and settled, I beg of you nevertheless to destroy this telegram. The thought of having telegraphed you in such an impossible tone is absolutely unbearable to me. The high esteem which I hold for you would at all times make such a tone toward you seem impossible to me. The only explanation which I can offer you is that the matter was presented to me at a time when other important things were passing through my mind, so that I did not read the telegram myself afterwards. Had I done so, the telegram would of course never have been sent. I would like to assure you once more that really no one ever drew my attention to this telegram up to the moment a few days ago when I myself saw it for the first time in the files. It was clear to me immediately that only a comprehensive apology to you could make amends for it. I would greatly appreciate it if you would not hold the matter against me in the future, although you would certainly be fully entitled to do so. May I also beg that this letter be considered as a purely personal matter?

With comradely greetings and Heil Hitler.

Yours,<br>(signed) GOERING.

*　　*　　*　　*　　*　　*

Commander-in-Chief of the Navy　　　　　　　　　　Berlin August 13, 1940

Most esteemed *Reichsmarschall!*

It was with great satisfaction that I read your letter; I thank you most sincerely. In view of our mutual efforts to co-operate most closely and most effectively, it had depressed me very much of late that it could have appeared as though differences had arisen between us which in turn seemed to have affected the co-operation of the lower echelons. The very comradely form in which you stated your point of view in this matter touched me deeply. The telegram is destroyed. You may rest assured that my personal esteem and respect for you, my dear Reichsmarschall, has at no time undergone a change.

Heil Hitler, yours very respectfully,<br>(signed) RAEDER.

1941: CHAPTER I

# Operational Plans

## FRANCE, GIBRALTAR, THE BALKANS AND RUSSIA

TOWARDS THE end of 1940 and at the beginning of 1941 the O.K.W. was planning four operations. Although the invasion of England had been postponed, three of the operations were directed against British positions or supplies, while the fourth was concerned with the invasion of Russia.

The first operation (which Goering was said to have started) was aimed at excluding Britain from the Mediterranean. Known as operation "Felix," the intention was to capture Gibraltar; to close the Straits of Gibraltar; to occupy the Canaries and Cape Verde; and to obtain the free use of the Atlantic ports of Spain. Spanish co-operation was necessary for the execution of these plans, and at the end of 1940 Hitler felt that Franco would probably assist him, though no firm promise had been given.

The second operation—"Attila"—was the occupation of unoccupied France. This operation was prepared partly to support Hitler's negotiations with the Vichy Government, and partly as a necessary corollary to the intended capture of Gibraltar. The capture of Gibraltar would require extensive troop movements through France and above all the prevention of a possible outbreak of the French Fleet. Hitler moved delicately in his dealings with Vichy as, from the strategical point of view, he did not want useful German divisions tied up in France, yet at the same time he could not afford to have any potentially dangerous forces either cutting across the supply lines to Gibraltar, or threatening his rear during the forthcoming attack on the East.

The third operation—*Marita*—was the invasion of Yugoslavia and Greece. Primarily the operation was planned in order to assist the Italians and to drive British forces out of the Mediterranean. But its secondary purpose was to safeguard the southern flank of the invasion forces in Russia, to protect the vitally important Roumanian oil fields, and eventually to form the base for an assault on Persia.

On November 12 Hitler outlined his intentions in a directive to his Cs.-in-C.:

The Fuehrer and Supreme Commander of the Armed Forces

Top Secret

Fuehrer Headquarters
November 12, 1940

10 copies
2nd Copy

### Directive No. 18

The preparatory measures of the High Command for the future prosecution of the war are to be carried out according to the following terms of reference:

(1) Relations with France.—The object of my policy towards France is to work with this country to continue the war against England with all possible efficiency. For this purpose France will play the role of a "non-belligerent power." They will in their own territory, particularly in the African colonies, permit measures for the prosecution of the war and, if necessary carry out their own defence. The important duty of the French is the defensive and offensive security of their African possessions (West and Equatorial Africa) against England and the De Gaulle movement. From this task the part of France in the war against England may be fully developed. For the time being the Foreign Office, in conjunction with the High Command, will alone conduct the discussions with France which will follow my meeting with Marshall Petain. These discussions will deal with matters outside the present work of the Armistice Commission. Further Directives will follow on the conclusion of this conference.

(2) Spain and Portugal.—Political measures are to be instigated for the early

165

entry into the war of Spain.   The object of German intervention in the Iberian Peninsula (code word " Felix ") is to expel the English from the Western Mediterranean.   For this

(a) Gibraltar will be taken and the Straits closed
(b) and the English will be prevented from gaining a foothold in other parts of the Iberian Peninsula or in the Atlantic islands. . . .

The Atlantic islands (above all the Canaries and Cape Verde) will assume great importance after the occupation of Gibraltar for English naval warfare.   The Cs.-in-C. of the Navy and Air Force are to investigate methods for supporting the Spanish defences of the Canaries and the possibility of occupying Cape Verde. The question of the occupation of Madeira or the Azores I also wish investigated. Results of these investigations are to be placed before me as soon as possible.

(3) The Italian offensive against Egypt.—The intervention by German forces will not be considered until the Italians reach Mersa Matruh.   But even then, operations by German Air Forces will not be instituted until the Italians have set up the necessary air bases.   The preparations of each branch of the Armed Forces for intervention in this or another North African zone will be as follows :

Army :—Preparation of one *Panzer* Division (as previously noted) for intervention in North Africa.
Navy :—To prepare the German ships in Italian harbours as transports to transfer troops to Libya or North-west Africa.
Air Force :—Preparations of attacks on Alexandria and the Suez Canal, in order to prevent the latter from being used by the British.

(4) Balkans.—The C.-in-C., Army, is to make preparations in the event of its becoming necessary, to occupy that part of the Greek mainland in the north of the Aegean operating from Bulgaria, and thereby form a base for the attack of German air units against targets in the Eastern Mediterranean, particularly against English air bases which threaten the Roumanian oil areas.   To make possible all these tasks and to hold Turkey in check one Army Group of approximately 10 divisions is to be formed.   The use of Yugoslavian railways for the transport of these forces is not to be considered.   An early reinforcement of the German Military Mission in Roumania is to be prepared in case of a precipitate demand for this movement. The C.-in-C., Air, is to prepare in conjunction with the Army a sortie of German air units against the South-eastern Balkans.   The German Air Force Mission in Roumania will be reinforced.

(5) Russia.—A political conference will be held in the near future to clarify the Russian attitude.   At the same time, whatever result this conference has, preparations are to be made for the Eastern campaign.   Directives will be issued later as soon as I have seen and approved the fundamental plan of operations of the Army.

(6) Landing in England.—In the event of a change in the general situation the possibility or necessity of reconsidering operation "Sea Lion" might arise in the spring of 1941.   Therefore, each branch of the Armed Forces is to exert itself strenuously to improve its position.

(7) Instructions to the Cs.-in-C.—I should like to have reports from the Cs.-in-C. concerning the measures provided for in this directive.   I will then give orders concerning the method of execution and the co-ordination of the individual actions.
(signed) ADOLF HITLER.

\*     \*     \*     \*     \*     \*

Hitler had not yet committed himself to the invasion of Russia, although his Cs.-in-C. were by now reasonably certain that this was his intention.   On November 16, Molotov, the Soviet Foreign Minister, visited Berlin for the political conferences foreshadowed in the directive above.   But in spite of the apparently successful outcome of these conferences Hitler and his immediate staff continued the preliminary planning for the invasion of Russia.

\*     \*     \*     \*     \*     \*

Meanwhile the war against England was prosecuted with vigour, and preparations for "Felix" were hastened forward.   By November 30 details and a timetable had been worked out.   The actual date of beginning the operation was left open, however, as Franco's co-operation was not yet certain. The task of the German Navy was to have been the defence of Gibraltar after it had been conquered; the control and defence of the Straits; assistance in the invasion and defence of the Canaries; and the occupation of the ports of Vigo, Ferrol, Cadiz and Malaga.

The political situation, however, did not develop as Hitler had anticipated, and on December 11 the operation was cancelled for the time being.

O.K.W.                                              Fuehrer Headquarters
                                                    December 11, 1940

Top Secret                                              12 copies
                                                        2nd Copy
SUBJECT: Operation "Felix"

Operation "Felix" will not be carried out as the political conditions no longer obtain. The investigations now proceeding are to be fully completed. All other intended measures will not take place; preparations which have been started are to be postponed. The German batteries which were to be sent for the reinforcement of the Spanish islands and coast are not to be delivered.

(signed) KEITEL

&ast;         &ast;         &ast;         &ast;         &ast;         &ast;

On December 9 the first British Western Desert offensive opened, forcing the Italians to retreat. Ever since Mussolini had started his campaign against Albania the German High Command had foreseen that German assistance would be required sooner or later; now the British attack in Libya made German assistance urgent. On the next day (December 10) Hitler ordered the *Luftwaffe* into action.

The Fuehrer and Supreme Commander          Berlin, December 10, 1940
    of the Wehrmacht

As a result of agreements made with our Allies, German aircraft formations will operate as soon as possible from the south of Italy in the battle in the Mediterranean (for a limited time). Their most important task is to attack the British Navy particularly in the port of Alexandria but also in the Suez Canal, where attacks are to be made on enemy shipping, and in the Straits between Sicily and the North coast of Africa.

Owing to the critical situation in the Mediterranean however, it may become necessary to operate in the Ionian Sea or the Aegean Sea. For this reason, operations are to be carried out with the entire understanding of the Italian High Command. Since Germany is not at war with Greece it is of prime importance that there shall be no operations directed solely at Greece.

(signed) ADOLF HITLER.

Large-scale German assistance was not yet contemplated, but nevertheless Hitler decided to take precautionary measures in an effort to safeguard the southern shores of Europe and, if possible, to exclude the British from the Mediterranean. Apart from the military operations in the Mediterranean, the greatest potential danger was a rising of the French, and though Hitler hoped by skilful political moves to keep the French quiet, he deemed it necessary to prepare a military operation against Vichy. The following directive was also issued on December 10:

The Supreme Command                        Fuehrer Headquarters
                                           December 10, 1940

Top Secret                                            12 Copies
                                                      2nd Copy

Directive No. 19 Operation "Attila"

(1) In case a movement of revolt should arise in parts of the French Colonial Empire now under the command of General Weygand, preparations must be made for the speedy occupation of the territories of the French Motherland which

are still unoccupied up to the present.  (Operation "Attila")   At the same time, it will be necessary for the French Home Fleet and that part of the French Air Force which is on home airfields to be safeguarded, or at least hindered from going over to the side of the enemy.   Preparations must be camouflaged, in order to avoid alarming the French, in military as well as political interests.

(2) (*a*) The entry, if occasion arises, must take place by heavy motorised groups, to whom sufficient air protection must be guaranteed, proceeding from the Garonne or Rhone; penetrating quickly to the Mediterranean; promptly occupying, if possible, the ports (particularly the important naval port of Toulon); and blockading France from the sea.

(*b*) Companies on the demarcation line on the whole front to march in.   The time between the order to carry out the operation and the entry of the troops must be as short as possible.   For this purpose, single companies must be concentrated, without the purpose of their use being obvious.   A concerted opposition by the French armed forces against the entry is not likely.   Should there be local opposition, it must be ruthlessly broken.   With this in view, as well as a safeguard against possible disturbances, companies of fighter (particularly dive-bomber) aircraft must be provided.

(3) Measures to prevent the French Fleet putting to sea and going over to the enemy must be taken by constantly keeping a watch on anchorages, positions, chance of seizure, and so forth by any unit of the Fleet.   The C.-in-C., Navy, will co-operate with the Foreign Intelligence Department and make arrangements for exploiting the possibilities afforded by the Armistice Commission.   Examination is to be made by the Cs.-in-C., Navy and Air Force as to how the French Fleet can best be put into our power, in co-operation with the military forces marching in.   In particular, it is a question of:

Blockading harbour entrances (especially Toulon).
Air-land operations.
Acts of sabotage.
U-boat and air attacks on ships putting to sea.

The C.-in-C., Navy, is to decide if and to what extent the units of the French Navy are to be withdrawn, in accordance with the provisions of the Armistice Agreement.   Decision as to the method of carrying it through is to be reserved for me.   Orders for the attack will first be promulgated when the French Armed Forces show opposition or a portion of the Fleet, in spite of German counter-orders, puts to sea.

(4) Seizing of the French airfields and any existing portion of the Air Force is to be settled between the Air Force and Army.   Special possibilities (for example: airborne landings) are to be utilised.

(5) The Cs.-in-C. will inform me—this has already been done by the Military—of their views with regard to operation "Attila" (in writing through the Headquarters of the Army).   The necessary period of time between the order and the carrying out of same, and that of the steps involved, is to be estimated.

(6) The preparations for operation "Attila" must be kept strictly secret.   The Italians must not have any knowledge of preparations made or action contemplated.

(signed) ADOLF HITLER.

\*         \*         \*         \*         \*         \*

Hitler's order for the invasion of Russia—"Barbarossa"—was issued on December 18, 1940 (see p. 159).   There is little doubt that Hitler had been considering this operation since at least the middle of 1940, and that the order when it came did not surprise his Cs.-in-C.   Raeder in a private memorandum to the German Naval Historian in 1944 stated that in his opinion Hitler had decided as far back as 1937 to eliminate Russia at least as a Baltic power.   The pact of 1939 was dictated entirely by the political situation then obtaining.   Hitler's staff did their best prior to the issue of the directive to dissuade him from this fatal step, but once the order had been given no further argument was possible and secret preparations were begun at once.   "Barbarossa" was disguised by making the preparations appear to be directed against England.   A "double bluff" was used—troop movements to the Eastern Front were explained as a deception to cover

Germany's real intention of attacking in the West, and popular rumours of invading England in the spring were encouraged.

*       *       *       *       *       *

By the beginning of 1941 preparations for the four operations were well advanced. The military situation in the Mediterranean, however, demanded urgent action by the Axis.   The British Army offensive in Libya had driven the Italians back as far as Bardia (occupied January 5) where the Italians lost 25,000 prisoners, many generals, and much equipment.   In Albania the Greeks, too, were forcing the Italians back, and this, together with the British support in Greece, threatened to become a serious assault on the south-eastern flank of the Axis.   Both the Italian Fleet and the *Regia Aeronautica* had put up little resistance against British attacks. On December 10, 1940, Hitler ordered one squadron of the *Luftwaffe* to go to their assistance and at the same time preparations were to be made to send at least one *panzer* division to Africa.   On January 8 Hitler discussed the situation with his staff.

## C.-in-C. of the Navy

### REPORT ON CONFERENCES WITH THE FUEHRER AND SUPREME COMMANDER OF THE ARMED FORCES AT THE BERGHOF (OBERSALZBERG) ON JANUARY 8 AND 9, 1941

Also present: Rear Admiral Fricke, Chief of the Operations Division, Naval Staff.
Chief of General Staff, Army.
Chief of General Staff, Air.
Minister for Foreign Affairs and others.

1. The main purpose of the conference was discussion of land operations in the Balkans and in Libya.   It was also possible to discuss at some length various questions connected with naval and air warfare, and the Fuehrer gave an evaluation of the general situation.

2. Situation in the Mediterranean.—*The Fuehrer* is of the opinion that it is vital for the outcome of the war that Italy does not collapse, but remains a loyal member of the Axis.   The Duce is emphatically pro-Axis. On the other hand, the military and political leaders are not pro-Axis and reliable to the same extent.   Count Ciano has sharply been attacked by Fascist and military circles.   However, the Fuehrer does not believe that in the present situation Ciano would oppose Germany.   The well-known Italian mentality makes it difficult for the Germans to influence the Italian leaders.   The Fuehrer is of the opinion that if the Italians are to be kept in line he must not go too far in matters of leadership.   We should not make demands; too great demands may cause even Mussolini to change his attitude.   Besides, there is the danger that then the Italians in turn might make undesirable demands.   (For example, the Italians may desire information about German operational plans.   The Fuehrer considers that caution is necessary especially in this connection, and he does not wish to inform the Italians of our plans.   There is great danger that the Royal Family is transmitting intelligence to Britain.)   *The Chief, Naval Staff, Operations Division* expresses the view that the Italian armed forces need to be strictly organized under German leadership.

3. *The Fuehrer* is determined to do everything in his power to prevent Italy from losing North Africa; he fears the very detrimental psychological effect this would have on the Italian people.   It would also mean

a great loss of prestige for the Axis powers. The possibilities for the Germans to bring aid to Africa are small, since the Italians themselves badly need the few available ports for unloading their supplies. The Fuehrer no longer considers it possible for either the Italians or ourselves to re-open the offensive against Alexandria and Egypt with any success. (The Italians themselves go so far as to believe that at best they can attempt defensive actions there; even this appears doubtful to them.)

The Fuehrer is firmly determined to give them support. German formations are to be transferred as soon as possible, equipped with anti-tank guns and mines, heavy tanks, and heavy and light anti-aircraft guns. The Fuehrer, however, wishes on no account to lose these formations. Hence the Italians are to be requested to do all in their power to stop the British offensive. Material is to be shipped by sea, personnel by air. Good results are anticipated from the use of German air units. The German formations should be given air support from bases in Sicily; advance units will be stationed in North Africa (as far as Benghazi). The opportunities are limited, since the Italians are using most of the air-fields. If we succeed in defending the rest of Libya, a large-scale offensive against Alexandria and Egypt would still be possible later, but probably not before winter 1942! According to Italian information, the defence units for Libya cannot be transferred until the middle of February because of Italian transports. The transfer will then take about five more weeks from the time of loading. (Twenty German steamers are available in Italy; a selection must be made from them.)

4. Albania.—The Italian line in Albania must be held. The Greeks must not be allowed to mass against Bulgaria in the region of Salonika, but must be fully engaged in Albania. It is necessary to aid the Italians. *The Fuehrer* orders that sufficient troops be transferred, that is, two and a half divisions, including one mountain division, parts of a *panzer* division, and a motorised infantry division. Conditions for unloading are very difficult. The transport route is from Brindisi to Durazzo. The possibilities for unloading must be very carefully checked (Captain von Pufendorf is at present in Albania). The Fuehrer states that in the near future he will discuss with the Duce the use of these troops and will make certain claims concerning operational control. The transfer of German troops to Albania should begin immediately. The Albanian operation is to take place before the Bulgarian-Greek front is occupied.

The Duce has requested three additional German steamers for Italian transport purposes, besides the three which have already been given him. *The Fuehrer* has ordered the transfer.

5. Operation *Marita*.—In order to be able to carry out the operation according to plan, it is intended to begin at once with the transfer of troops to Bulgaria. After the advance detachments have arrived, the 1st Division is to be moved across the frozen Danube into Bulgaria. (Only one bridge is available, hence use must be made of the frozen river.) Bulgaria should be requested to permit garrisoning of troops in towns. The troops will be self-supporting, and will be no burden to the Bulgarian population. On the contrary, there are prospects of supplying the population with food. No Italian offensive against Greece is expected until March. *The Fuehrer* is determined to do everything in his power to assure a speedy advance in Albania. The troops for operation *Marita* will be assembled and ready

by March 26. Certain troops are reserved for defence against Turkey. The Fuehrer does not believe that any offensive action will be taken by the Turks, however.

6. The question of a possible occupation of Toulon.—If France becomes troublesome she will have to be crushed completely. Under no circumstances must the French Fleet be allowed to get away from us; it must be either captured or destroyed. Hence Toulon must be occupied at the very outset by means of airborne troops and transport gliders. The harbour and coastal batteries must be taken immediately. Naval guns will be brought up in gliders. Toulon harbour is to be mined by an air squadron. After the speedy occupation of Toulon, the troops will push on to Marseilles. The position and the nature of fortifications at Toulon and along the coast must be accurately ascertained as soon as possible.

*The C.-in-C., Army,* reports that in view of the army operations planned, the preparations for operations "Felix" and "Sea Lion" would have to be held up for a time. *The Fuehrer* confirms this view. The operational measures will be carried out in the following sequence: Transports to Albania; transports to North Africa; Toulon (only in the event of operation "Attila").

7. General situation.—*The Fuehrer* states his opinion concerning the strength and importance of Germany's economic potential in the German and European area as over against the limited possibilities found in Britain and America. He is firmly convinced that Europe's armament and economic resources offer far greater possibilities. He stresses the great importance of Norway, where we must be particularly on our guard. Our relations with France are rather obscure. The French were stunned by the course of the war, but are now collecting their wits and beginning to realise what has happened. Those who were not in leading positions have no conception of the situation as a whole. Hence there are many pitfalls for the Petain government. It is not improbable that Petain will still be exposed to much pressure from external sources. General Weygand, well known as a rabid Germanophobe, has demanded the immediate arrest of Laval. The Fuehrer regards Weygand as unreliable and dangerous; he must be watched carefully. At first Petain will adopt a passive attitude, as he is well aware that the Germans intend to occupy the remainder of France if the French prove troublesome.

Spain.—*The Fuehrer* fully recognises the strategic value of Gibraltar, which has so often been emphasised by the Naval Staff. Despite that fact, there is for the time being no prospect of Spain's becoming our ally. She is not willing to do so. This was made perfectly clear by Franco's remark that he will not take part in the war until Britain is at the point of collapse. The Fuehrer has offered Franco a million tons of grain to relieve the acute economic situation. Despite this offer of food, Franco did not feel that he could acquiesce in the Fuehrer's plans.

Yugoslavia is ready to conclude a non-aggression pact, but at present does not wish to become a signatory of the Tri-partite Pact.

Roumania.—The situation is clear; whatever may happen, the oil fields must be protected. The Training Division is being reinforced.

Bulgaria.—Russia's attitude is causing complications here. Russia needs this country in order to assemble her forces against the Bosphorus.

Hence King Boris is very cautious. The King has explained to the Fuehrer that for reasons of foreign policy he cannot officially sign the Tri-partite Pact, but that the Fuehrer should proceed as though this were the case. Russia's attitude in the event of German action in Bulgaria is still not clear.

General observations.—*The Fuehrer* is firmly convinced that the situation in Europe can no longer develop unfavourably for Germany even if we should lose the whole of North Africa. Our position in Europe is so firmly established that the outcome cannot possibly be to our disadvantage. The invasion of Britain is not feasible unless she is crippled to a considerable degree, and Germany has complete air supremacy. The success of an invasion must be absolutely assured; otherwise the Fuehrer considers it a crime to attempt it. The British can hope to win the war only by beating us on the Continent. The Fuehrer is convinced that this is impossible.

Regarding our warfare against Britain, the Fuehrer explains that all attacks must be concentrated on supplies and on the armament industry. Terror raids by our Air Force have small value and accomplish little; the supplies and the ships bringing them must be destroyed. Combined assaults by the Air Force and Navy on imports might lead to victory as early as July or August. Even today the Fuehrer is still ready to negotiate peace with Britain. However, Britain's present leaders will not consider such a peace. Britain is sustained in her struggle by hopes placed in the U.S.A. and Russia. British diplomatic overtures to Russia are apparent. Eden is very pro-Russian.

Stalin must be regarded as a cold-blooded blackmailer; he would, if expedient, repudiate any written treaty at any time. Britain's aim for some time to come will be to set Russian strength in motion against us. If the U.S.A. and Russia should enter the war against Germany, the situation would become very complicated. Hence any possibility for such a threat to develop must be eliminated at the very beginning. If the Russian threat were non-existent, we should wage war on Britain indefinitely. If Russia collapsed, Japan would be greatly relieved; this in turn would mean increased danger to the U.S.A.

Regarding Japanese interest in Singapore, the Fuehrer feels that the Japanese should be given a free hand even if this may entail the risk that the U.S.A. is thus forced to take drastic steps.

\*　　\*　　\*　　\*　　\*　　\*

The conference was followed by a directive setting out in greater detail the assistance to be given to the Italians.

The Fuehrer and Supreme Commander　　　　　　　Berlin, January 11, 1941
　　of the *Wehrmacht*

The situation in the Mediterranean area, where England is using superior forces against our Allies, renders German assistance necessary for strategical, political, and psychological reasons. It is essential to hold out in Tripolitania and to remove the danger of a collapse on the Albanian front. Besides this, Cavallero's Army Group must be enabled, in association with the later operations of Number 12 Army Group, to go over to the attack from Albania.

I therefore order as follows:

(1) The C.-in-C., Army, is to form a regiment designed to combat the British Tank Division and render valuable assistance to our Allies in the defence of

Tripolitania. Basic instructions for its constitution will be given separately. Preparations must be timed to allow this "Anti-tank Regiment" to be taken over at the same time as the Italian tank and motorised divisions are transported to Tripoli (about 20.2).

(2) The *X Flieger Korps* will retain Sicily as an operational base. Its most important task is to attack English naval forces and sea routes between the Western and Eastern Mediterranean. In addition, by using intermediate landing fields in Tripolitania, the necessary conditions are to be created for a direct support of the Army Group under Graziani by attacking the enemy's disembarkation ports and supply bases on the western Egyptian coast and Cyrenaica. The Italian Government has been requested to declare a mined area between Sicily and the North coast of Africa in order to facilitate the task of the *X Flieger Korps* and to eliminate the possibility of incidents with neutral ships.

(3) German units, about one Corps strong, including the 1st Mountain Division and the armoured forces, are to be organised and held in readiness for transfer to Albania. The transport of the 1st Mountain Division should be started as soon as the O.K.W. has received Italy's assent. In the meantime, investigations should be made and the Italian High Command in Albania consulted in order to discover whether further forces could be employed with advantage for an operation in Albania, which forces would be best, and whether they could be kept supplied continuously as well as the Italian divisions. The task of the German forces will be :

(*a*) The immediate task is to act as a rearguard in Albania in case of further crises there.

(*b*) To assist the Italian Army Group to transfer to the attack later, the object being to break up the Greek defensive front at a strategic point for an extensive operation, to open up the pass west of Salonika from the rear and thus support the feint frontal attack to be made by the Army.

(4) The O.K.W. will work out in collaboration with the Italian Armed Forces Staff the general principles for the command of the German troops in North Africa and Albania and the limits of their employment.

(5) Those German transports already in the Mediterranean should be made available for carrying the forces destined for Albania, provided they are suitable and are not already being used on convoy duties to Tripolis. The Ju. 52 group of transport planes based in Foggia should be used for the transport of personnel. Efforts should be made to complete the transport of the main body of German forces to Albania before the transport of the Anti-tank Regiment to Libya begins, since the latter operation will require the bulk of available German shipping.

(signed) ADOLF HITLER.

On January 11 Germany signed the long awaited Economic Treaty with Russia which appeared to settle the outstanding differences between the two countries, but which was in reality merely a cover for Germany's preparations to attack. One week later it was noted in the War Diary of the Naval Staff that Hitler expected relations with Russia to deteriorate due to the forthcoming Balkans operation. His principal concern was the danger of losing the Roumanian oil fields, however, and therefore, in spite of the possibility of alarming Russia, operation *Marita*—the invasion of the Balkans—was still to be carried out.

\*     \*     \*     \*     \*     \*

On January 24 Hitler conferred with Mussolini on the general war situation. He explained that the Russian Note deploring the German advance into Roumania had been rejected, and, without giving away his intention of attacking Russia, Hitler declared that Russia was becoming a great menace and hence considerable German forces were to be held on the Russian frontier. Six days later, on January 30, the draft plans for operation "Barbarossa" were submitted, and as secretly as possible the whole German war machine was directed towards the forthcoming invasion of Russia.

\*     \*     \*     \*     \*     \*

On February 4 Hitler discussed the war situation and his plans with his Cs.-in-C. To the Navy the war against England was still of primary importance, and Raeder described the operations then in progress.

## REPORT OF THE C.-IN-C., NAVY, TO THE FUEHRER IN THE AFTERNOON OF FEBRUARY 4, 1941

Also present: Chief of Staff, O.K.W.
General Jodl.
Commander von Puttkamer.

I. Naval Situation.—1. *The C.-in-C., Navy*, explains with the aid of a map the operations carried out by auxiliary cruisers.

2. The battleships, which are to carry on warfare in the Atlantic in conjunction with cruiser Hipper, are under way. At present the ships are in the Norwegian Sea. The first attempt to break through had to be postponed because enemy forces were sighted. The ships were in contact with a task force consisting of cruisers and destroyers south of Iceland in quadrant AL from 0700 until 1300. After refueling in the Norwegian Sea the ships will make another attempt. The Hipper operation will be launched simultaneously from Brest.

3. It has in the meantime been established that the appearance of enemy forces in the sea area off Stavanger was intended to assist Norwegian steamers in running the blockade from Swedish ports. Our inadequate reconnaissance did not reveal the plans of the enemy in time.

4. The scanty submarine successes are due first to the few boats in operation and second to the hampering effect of the weather. An increase in submarine operations may be expected shortly. Twenty one more submarines will become available for operations in a few weeks due to the fact that ice makes it necessary to discontinue submarine training temporarily.

5. It has not yet been possible to clear the Kaiser Wilhelm Canal completely, since ice complicates the work. At present the passage of the Bismarck and Tirpitz through the Canal is out of the question. It is therefore best that the two ships remain at Hamburg and Wilhelmshaven, where there is a much greater anti-aircraft protection than at Brunsbuettel.

6. Ice conditions in the Baltic Sea are greatly hampering ship movements. The Belts are closed to shipping. Weather also handicaps the training programme.

7. Blockade-running.—After consultation with the Ministry of Transport and the Ministry of Economics, it has been decided to import vital raw materials by sending German and neutral blockade-runners to South America. Blockade-running likewise has great propaganda value.

8. A meeting with Admiral Riccardi at Merano has been planned provisionally for the middle of February in order to discuss naval strategy and to attempt to influence Italian naval warfare through the Naval Liaison Staff at Rome. Escorts for German troop transports are also to be discussed.

II. Operation *Marita*. 1. Roumania.—The Naval Commission under Admiral Fleischer has not yet returned. Thus no complete picture can as yet be formed of the measures to be adopted. The transfer of two coastal batteries, is in progress. By adding German batteries to the defences of Constanza it becomes necessary to obtain control over the whole Roumanian coastal defence system because of its importance as flank protection for the Army. A German admiral is necessary to co-ordinate the use of German and Roumanian forces along the coast. To do this, he must have authority to direct the Roumanian units of the coastal defences: Fleet units, Danube flotillas, coastal batteries, mining vessels, and naval reconnaissance. Liaison officers must be attached to the German Commanding General and to the Roumanian Naval High Command.

2. Bulgaria.—Although there is little or no German naval personnel in Bulgaria, here it is also necessary to have some control over the coastal defences, due to the importance of protecting our flank. However, a liaison staff attached to the Bulgarian Naval High Command will be sufficient, as the matter is on a much smaller scale and the Bulgarian coast is less important than the Roumanian.

3. Greece.—After Greece has been occupied, her coasts will require defences against attacks from the sea, as the British Fleet in the Eastern Mediterranean will still be able to maintain naval supremacy for a time, although threatened by our air forces. Besides, Greek coastal waters will gain particular importance; oil shipments to Greece and Italy from the Black Sea and exports from Turkey must pass through them, since the open sea cannot be used. Fortification and patrol of the rugged coasts of Greece will demand a vast amount of personnel and material, which the German Navy no longer has at its disposal. It is therefore vitally necessary to get Italy and Bulgaria to take over as many of these tasks as possible. Italy should be responsible for the west coast and the Peloponnesus, and Bulgaria for the coast of Macedonia, while the German Navy would be in charge of the east coast, where the main harbours of Salonika, Volos, and Piraeus are situated.

In order to support the Army in occupying and exploiting the ports and to assure immediately at least the most essential protection against attacks from the sea, it is planned to provide a naval shore commander for each of the three harbours named, and to provide crews to man Greek batteries, consisting of one medium battery at Salonika, one at Volos, and two at Piraeus. The means necessary for fortifying the Greek coast, even if limited to the east coast, in a way comparable to the defences along the Norwegian and French coasts cannot be made available without causing extremely vulnerable gaps in the coastline defences of Norway and France. The German personnel and material needed for the task are not available due to commitments made to Roumania and Bulgaria, and for operation "Felix." A naval commander who will be in charge of the naval units stationed in Greece must also be appointed.

4. In order to achieve proper co-ordination between the naval units operating in the entire south-eastern area and to guard all naval interests there, an Admiral (Admiral Commanding Balkans) is required as supreme authority. He would have his headquarters first at Sofia and later in Greece (Salonika or Athens).

*The Fuehrer* sanctions the proposals made in Paragraphs 1 to 4.

III. Operation "Attila."—Lasting success can hardly be expected from the measures planned so far for the purpose of holding French naval vessels at Toulon. It may be possible to limit the operational readiness of the French warships through measures suggested by the Italian Armistice Commission; these include surrender of ammunition and fuel, granting of leave to crews, etc. These measures would, however, cause great ill feeling and might thus have an undesirable political effect. Hence they would serve a useful purpose only if operation "Attila" really takes place within a reasonable length of time.

IV. Operation "Barbarossa".—1. All naval forces in the Atlantic, all destroyers and torpedo boats, and the bulk of the defence forces in the west are being concentrated against Britain as planned. All mine layers and motor boats together with a small part of the anti-submarine and mine-sweeping units are to operate in the Baltic Sea. Finnish harbours are to be used.

The number of submarines operating in the Atlantic will probably increase owing to the curtailment of submarine training; training boats are to be transferred to Trondheim. Several submarines are intended for the Baltic. Nevertheless in the face of the increased British activity which must be expected, operations by the Air Force will be of the utmost importance, particularly in Norway and in the defence of the Skagerrak and Kattegat. In these areas it is only the danger from our planes which restricts British operations.

2. Plan of attack against Russia.—(a) Coastal protection must be provided by coastal artillery, defensive mine barrages, and by declared mined areas from Oeland to Memel and from Sweden to Bornholm to Kolberg.

(b) The entrances to the Baltic Sea will be closed by navigational obstacles and a strong threat from the air, as well as by coastal guns and mine and net barrages. If necessary, use will be made of the floating batteries Schlesien and Schleswig-Holstein: Loaded mine layers are being held in readiness.

(c) It will be necessary to stop all merchant shipping in the Baltic Sea. Especially troops can be transferred to southern Sweden at first only through the Baltic Sea entrances west of Gjedser. If the Russians respect Swedish territorial waters a certain volume of traffic may be possible under Swedish protection. A crossing from Sassnitz to Trelleborg will be possible only if the situation develops in our favour. Perhaps later it may be possible to move gradually farther east.

(d) Offensive measures must be taken in the form of surprise attacks by the Air Force against Russian bases and ships in the Baltic Sea, Arctic Ocean, and Black Sea. The locks of the White Sea Canal must be destroyed in order to prevent the escape of ships to the north. Motor boats, submarines, etc., will be used for mine laying. Mine barrages are to be laid from Finland to block the western entrance to the Gulf of Finland. For this purpose Finnish forces will be used; German mines will be supplied.

(e) The Air Force must operate in the Arctic Ocean against Polyarny and Murmansk; this is very important in order to prevent the British from gaining a foothold there. In the Black Sea support will be given to Roumania and Bulgaria by providing mines and coastal guns.

(f) Vast minesweeping operations will probably be necessary once the Russian fleet is eliminated. Assistance will be rendered by Finland, Sweden, and possibly by captured Russian units.

3. Special proposals: (a) Support by the Air Force:

(1) Immediate surprise attacks on bases and ships in the Baltic Sea, Arctic Ocean, and Black Sea.

(2) Destruction of locks in the White Sea Canal.
(3) Support in warding off British attacks.

(*b*) Preparations for collaboration:

(1) An agreement should be reached with Finland, pertaining to participation of Finnish forces and use of Finnish bases.

(2) The support of Roumania and Bulgaria should be enlisted for the defence of the Danube River and the Black Sea coast.

(3) Sweden.—Inquiries should be made concerning the defence of Swedish territorial waters and of German shipping in those waters. *The Fuehrer* emphasises the necessity of providing a mine-free channel as soon as the bases have been eliminated, in order that supplies can be shipped by sea as far as possible.   *The C.-in-C., Navy* replies that once enemy naval opposition has been overcome this task can be carried out rapidly, possibly with Finnish and Swedish help.   Nevertheless heavy Russian mining and submarine activity must be expected (see "2 f" above).

V. Naval Air Forces.—1. Systematically planned attacks must be made by the Air Force on supply lines, docks, ships, and harbours.   The effective British attacks against the north coast of Germany show the unbroken striking power of the Royal Air Force, which is also operating simultaneously in considerable strength in the Mediterranean.   American airmen are participating.   American Douglas bombers, DB 7, were used for the first time during the night attacks on Bremen on 2 and 3 January. This is an indication of the effective aid already being given to Britain by America, and demonstrates the importance of cutting off as much as possible the supplies of war material to Britain.   Submarine warfare alone is for the time being not in a position to cut off imports effectively because of the small number of submarines available and because of present weather conditions.   Hence the Air Force must attempt to hit Great Britain where it hurts most, by attacking her imports.   To achieve this raids must be made on her main ports of import and lasting damage must be inflicted on naval bases, especially shipyards.

Despite heavy attacks on individual armament manufacturing centres, results have shown that output has not been decisively affected and the morale of the population has remained unshaken.   On the other hand, measures taken by the enemy government and their propaganda reveal that the problems of imports, and this means shipping space, is Britain's most vulnerable spot.   Britain's naval and merchant vessels must be the main target for attack.   Aerial photographs of attacks on Portsmouth, Plymouth, and Cardiff show how ineffective the night attacks were, although some were carried out with considerable forces.   Despite the laying of large numbers of mines by planes, the volume of supplies entering London has not noticeably declined.   So far we have not succeeded in seriously damaging British ports of import from the air, with the exception of Bristol and Southampton and possibly a few of the docks at Liverpool. The enemy has created sufficient auxiliary ports north of the line Liverpool Hull to compensate for losses.   Attacks by the Air Force on enemy shipping will yield better results if production plants and repair ships in Great Britain and ships in the harbours are destroyed than if individual ships at sea are attacked.  Thus attacks on the shipyards in the Tyne and Clyde areas, in Barrow, and, in Chatham and Devonport on the southern coast of England, are especially important.  This elimination of shipyards is not merely of importance for naval warfare; it is absolutely vital for the prosecution of the war as a whole.

The growth of Britain's sea power by the addition of four more battleships, three aircraft carriers, and twelve cruisers requires no comment. In addition, there is the great increase in the number of smaller vessels, such as destroyers, torpedo boats, submarines, escort vessels, gunboats, and mine sweepers, the continuous production of which will have an unfavourable effect on our submarine warfare.  Working in close co-operation, our planes and submarines are capable of exerting a decisive influence in the struggle against Britain and America.  To this end, however, co-ordinated, well-directed operations against enemy shipping are essential. Ships afloat must be the target of the submarines; ships in harbours and shipyards must be the target of the Air Force.  *The Fuehrer* agrees; he is of precisely the same opinion.

2.  *The C.-in-C., Navy*, hands the Fuehrer a copy of the memorandum dealing with coastal air forces and explains it in detail.  The C.-in-C., Navy, emphasises particularly that for reasons of economy of forces the air reconnaissance provided for submarine warfare be likewise utilised for operations carried out by battleships and cruisers; otherwise these operations cannot be justified.  A Commander, Naval Air should be attached to Group West for this purpose.  According to the present arrangment the C.-in-C., Navy, is not authorised to use the planes in this manner.  *The Fuehrer* feels that the C.-in-C., Air, would greatly resent this interpretation, since he is always anxious to assist the Navy.  The Fuehrer thinks it would be better if the C.-in-C., Navy, would attach an officer to the Admiral Commanding Submarines whose duty it would be to direct air reconnaissance to provide information for operations carried out by battleships.  (This would be the Commander, Naval Air.)  When The Fuehrer refers to a new memorandum drawn up by the C.-in-C., Air, the C.-in-C., Navy, requests that General Jodl further clarify and finally decide this matter in conjunction with General Jeschonnek and Admiral Schniewind, with due regard to the two memoranda.

3.  The question of the designation of the naval officers assigned to the Air Force.  *The C.-in-C., Navy*, reports on this matter.  The *Reichsmarschall* has already broached the subject.  *The Fuehrer* therefore points out the effect this would have in practice; a subordinate cannot recognise and correctly address an officer as junior lieutenant or senior lieutenant, etc., if the officer in question is wearing an Air Force uniform.  *The C.-in-C., Navy*, insists that the officers have been deprived of their rights; he declares that he shall continue to address them by their former ranks, and requests that in spite of the fact that for practical reasons the Air Force rank is used while the officers are on duty, their right to use their old rank be confirmed.

VI. Miscellaneous.—1.  Agreement has been reached with the Danish government on the purchase of Danish torpedo boats.  Eight boats will be handed over.  The transfer is to be carried out soon, but is being delayed by the ice conditions.

2.  Despite considerable misgivings regarding security, it has been

decided to accept employment of foreign workers (Danish, Dutch, and French) in the naval shipyards. *The Fuehrer* has grave scruples, and suggests that the French workers might be employed by civilian firms in other towns in order to free Germans for the naval shipyards. *The C.-in-C., Navy*, explains that the enormous shortage of skilled workers has caused this dilemma, which is equally undesirable to the Navy.

3. A certain slackening in the preparations for operation "Sea Lion" was sanctioned during the previous conference. The results are as follows: For as long as operation "Sea Lion" must be maintained as a blind, the measures cannot be further reduced; it is considered essential to continue training activities on their present scale if the deception is to be kept up. Apart from this, everything possible is being done to avoid increasing the preparations if this involves the use of men and material. As things now stand, the Navy needs six months to prepare operation "Sea Lion" if it is to be carried out. This includes the completion of the barge construction programme. If operation "Sea Lion" is to be carried out with present resources, without the barge construction programme, (perhaps merely to police Britain after she has been conquered) two months will be sufficient. *The Fuehrer* states that the deception must be kept up particularly during the spring.

(signed) RAEDER.

\*        \*        \*        \*        \*        \*

On February 6, possibly as a result of this conference, Hitler issued a directive for the prosecution of the war against England.

The Fuehrer and Supreme Commander of                 Berlin, February 6, 1941
the Armed Forces
Top Secret

Directive No. 23 Basic Principles of the Prosecution of War against British
War Economy
(Extracts)
Effects already achieved by our war against England:

(*a*) Contrary to all our previous conceptions, the strongest blow to the British war economy was the high figure for losses in merchant ships as a result of the sea and air war. This effect was further intensified by the destruction of port installations involving the loss of large quantities of goods in storage and also by the limitations imposed on the use of ships by the necessity for travelling in convoy. A further considerable increase in the effects of our war effort can be expected when our U-boat operations are intensified during the course of this year, and this may lead before long to the collapse of British resistance.

(*b*) It is more difficult to assess the effect of air attacks directed specifically against the armaments industry. It can be assumed, however, that as a result of the destruction of many factories and the consequent disorganisation of the industry, output will have been reduced considerably.

(*c*) As far as can be judged from outward appearances, the sphere in which we have achieved the least effect is that of the British nation's morale and capacity to resist.

The object of our future war efforts must therefore be to concentrate every means of waging war by sea and air on enemy supplies from overseas as well as keeping down British aircraft production and inflicting still greater damage on the air armaments industry wherever possible.

(signed) ADOLF HITLER.

\*        \*        \*        \*        \*        \*

Meanwhile in the Mediterranean British forces were advancing rapidly. Benghazi was captured on February 6, and the Italian position became desperate. The German High Command gave instructions that all possible help was to be given to the Italians. The *Panzer* Division and the *Luftwaffe* squadrons were to be reinforced—the *Luftwaffe* in particular to attack British naval forces and Malta, and to endeavour to make the passage through the Straits of Sicily impassable.

In France Admiral Darlan became Vice-Premier to the Vichy Government on February 9, and on February 13 Petain met Franco at Montpellier. On the following day the forces which had been alerted for operations "Attila" and "Felix" were dispersed. German intelligence reports during the preceding period indicated a confused feeling in the French Navy, and may have affected the High Command's decision to abandon the proposed military operations.

The following are two typical agents' reports sent in during this period

Foreign Intelligence Department                    Berlin, February 5, 1941

SUBJECT    France.   Morale of the Navy

Trustworthy secret agent reports as follows
Pronounced feeling against England, but also anti-German. The Germans are always considered to be "Boches." The Navy is loyal to the Government. It would go into action immediately at the order of Petain, even should it be for the support of England. The sailors are in an indifferent state of mind, but they obey, and show good leadership; the discipline is better than in the Army, nevertheless I observed two drunken sailors who brawled without the interference of any officer. Such conditions would have been impossible in former times. The Fleet is not in a state of absolute first degree readiness, but "en ordre," that is, it can sail at any time. During the last days the former spirit of crisis has to a considerable extent calmed down.

Observation time—8 to 16 January.

By Order
(signed).

Foreign Intelligence Department                    Berlin, February 10, 1941

SUBJECT    France.   Report on Naval Morale.

Secret agent reports on February 10, 1941
My personal impression from Toulon
The morale and mood has been raised considerably since last time, especially by the increase of pay in the Navy. Surveillance and protection against espionage, as well as that of information given by sailors, is at present rather pronounced. The Strasbourg and Galissonière who experienced Mers el Kebir are anti-English. The other units which remained in Toulon are not all of one opinion. People hate the English, but hope for an improvement in France's position through the ultimate victory of England. The German war efforts are respected without any friendliness towards Germany being in question. On the whole, however, the average sailor has had a "belly-full" and does not wish to hear any more about this war. To speak of a "good morale" would certainly be going too far. The food on board ship since the Armistice has been very moderate.

By Order
(signed).

\*         \*         \*         \*         \*         \*

The activity in the O.K.W. at this time was intense. The complicated series of operations planned by Hitler involved a considerable amount of both military and political preparations. War on two fronts, which according to the classical German military theorists was to be avoided at all costs, was now being deliberately sought. Hitler tried to minimise the possible consequences of his actions by careful preparations in the West, and by political methods in the Balkans. On February 14 the Yugoslav Prime Minister and Foreign Minister were summoned to Berchtesgaden as a prelude to a Nazi coup-d'etat. On the following day the O.K.W. issued orders for precautions to be taken against a possible British attack on Western Europe or Norway as soon as the invasion of Russia began.   In the Mediterranian the policy was laid down that full-scale operations would not begin until the Autumn of 1941, which was the estimated date for the completion of operation "Barbarossa."   Then Malta *and* Gibraltar were to be conquered and the British were to be finally driven from the Mediterranean.

\*       \*       \*       \*       \*       \*

On February 19 the O.K.W. issued orders to commence the invasion of Bulgaria —the first part of operation *Marita*—on the night of February 28.   The operation met with complete success, and by March 1 German troops held the country and Bulgaria joined the Axis.   Russia sent a strong note of protest which, however, had little effect on either Germany or the Bulgarian Government.

\*       \*       \*       \*       \*       \*

While all these plans were maturing the German Navy had been actively employed in the Atlantic.   Auxiliary raiders, U-boats, and heavy units of the surface fleet, were busy attacking British merchant shipping in an effort to blockade the British Isles.   It was hoped to avoid any question of invading England by cutting off all sources of food supply and munitions of war.   Beginning in December, 1940, heavy ships of the German Fleet embarked on an extensive campaign against British convoys.   The Hipper, the Scheer, and the two powerful battleships Scharnhorst and Gneisenau, operated in the Atlantic and Indian Oceans and sank a total of 187,662 tons (37 ships) in the first three months of 1941.   In the same period auxiliary raiders sank 114,905 tons (25 ships) while U-boats accounted for 554,408 tons (97 ships).   In spite of these severe losses the Royal and Merchant Navies managed to maintain the flow of supplies not only to England but to the Mediterranean as well, and at the same time made possible attacks on Europe such as the raid on the Lofoten Islands.   This raid disturbed the equanimity of the German High Command, as, in spite of the fact that such action by the British had been anticipated, complete success was achieved.   The following is an extract from a German naval report on the raid

The following has been received about the events so far in Svolvaer.   At about 0700 on March 4 the enemy made an assault landing with some 300 men who at once occupied the town and took possession of the ships, blowing up the boilers in some cases.   With assistance from the Norwegians they toured the neighbourhood in buses and lorries and captured every German they could lay hands on.

The patrol vessel Krebs, lying in the harbour, was fired on and casualties, some fatal, were caused on board.   The boat drifted and finally sank off Skraaven.   A British destroyer drew alongside and it is certain that 2 P.O's and 2 ratings were taken prisoner; only one survivor escaped.   The C.O. and 17 ratings were killed.   The German guards withdrew to the hills as far as possible; the Naval Harbour Master and a police sergeant from the Naval Control Service Office were able to escape in this way.   5 Naval ratings from this office were captured.   English reports state that in all 215 Germans and 10 Norwegians (Quisling supporters) were captured.

The following ships were sunk by the enemy:

|  |  |  |
|---|---|---|
| The fish factory ship Hamburg | .. (5,470 t.) | |
| The steamer Eilenau | .. (1,404 t.) | |
| ,,     Gumbinnen | .. (1,381 t.) | |
| ,,     Felix Heumann .. | .. (2,468 t.) | |
| ,,     Bernard Schulte .. | .. (1,058 t.) | |
| The passenger vessel Mira | .. (1,152 t.) | sunk near Brettesnes |
| Total tonnage | (12,933 t.) | |

also the trawler Rissen and the patrol vessel Krebs.   The British announced a total of 18,000 tons sunk.   In Svolvaer, the fish meal factory and the oil factory were burnt down, and the oil tanks destroyed.   In Stamsund the preserves factory and the oil tanks were burnt out.

Warning from the Navy: The Admiral in Command in Norway reported: Consequent upon the transfer to Svolvaer of the refrigerator factory ship Hamburg which had cost 3,500,000, Admiral, Norway, informed the Reich Commissar for Norway on December 7 that the defence of Svolvaer by surface forces or batteries could not be guaranteed. The position was explained fully to the Reich Commissar's expert by a member of Admiral, Norway's staff. When on February 25 a report was received from the Security Service on an important case of espionage involving Svolvaer, Admiral, Norway, brought it to the attention of *Luftlotte* 5 and the Reich Commissar on the same day. On February 28 at a conference between Admiral, Norway, and the Reich Commissar's expert, the danger of having the Hamburg lying in Svolvaer was pointed out once again and attention was drawn to the better protected berths in Narvik or near Tjeldoey.

\*     \*     \*     \*     \*     \*

On March 11 the Lease-lend Bill was approved by the House of Representatives of the U.S.A. and President Roosevelt broadcast to the world that this Bill indicated "the end of compromise with tyranny." Ships, aircraft, food, and munitions were to be sent to the United Kingdom.

On March 18 Raeder reported to Hitler his views on the various theatres of war.

### REPORT BY THE C.-IN-C., NAVY, TO THE FUEHRER ON MARCH 18, 1941, AT 1600

Also present: Chief of Staff, O.K.W.
General Jodl.
Commander von Puttkamer.

1. Warfare in the Atlantic.—(a) The Hipper is due back in home port after March 15. The operations of the Scharnhorst and the Gneisenau and their successes to date are discussed. Submarines are being directed to the Malaya convoy. They are important for relieving pressure in the Mediterranean and Norway. More vigorous action will be taken against the British convoys as soon as four battleships are available.

(b) The Scheer and auxiliary cruisers are discussed. The Scheer is returning after the Hipper. Successes scored by ship "16" and ship "33" are reported. The whalers and the Portland have entered port.

2. Submarine warfare.—The successes from 3 to 17 March have amounted to approximately 200,000 tons.

3. Mine warfare.—Aerial mines equipped with acoustic firing mechanism have brought good results. Harbour entrances, e.g., on the Tyne River, are frequently blocked. However, the enemy is now able to sweep acoustic mines. A new combined type of firing mechanism is ready for operational use. Further progress is expected. A report will be made shortly by the Mining and Barrage Experimental Command.

4. Views on the success of naval and air warfare.—The following reports confirm the correctness of the view always held by the C.-in-C., Navy, namely, that only that naval and air activity which is concentrated on cutting off *supplies* will definitely help to bring about the defeat of Britain, i.e., attacks on merchant ships at sea, on harbour installations and merchant ships in port, on new constructions in the shipyards, on warehouses, on transport facilities for distributing supplies, and on armament factories.

(a) When at the German Embassy in Paris, Jacques Serre, former French Consul at Newcastle, expressed his surprise that Newcastle has not yet been attacked, although the Vickers-Armstrong shipyards there contain an aircraft carrier (to be completed in five to six months), two battleships (to be completed in five to six months), one light cruiser, six or seven destroyers, and three or four submarines under construction. Besides these, about sixty merchant vessels are being built in other shipyards on the Tyne River. Up to the time of his departure not a single bomb had hit Vickers-Armstrong's large ammunition plant in the Newcastle urban area which employs 20,000 workers. He also pointed out the importance of the three large Tyne bridges linking Scotland and England.

(b) The German Naval Attaché in Tokyo has reported that the British Attaché there stated that air warfare alone can never force Britain to give up, especially if it is continued as heretofore with bombs dropped at random on strategic and non-strategic targets alike. Experience has shown that such action merely serves to strengthen the people's will to resist.

The only real danger lies in a concentrated German attack on British shipping by surface, submarine, and air forces. Shipping is Britain's most vulnerable spot. The destroyers available are far from sufficient to protect it. Britain will be done for if the tonnage sunk over a period of little more than six months will approximate the highest amount sunk during the World War, unless Germany in a sort of desperation should stage an invasion. No one doubts today that this would fail under any conditions. The repercussions of such a German catastrophe could not fail to lead to the internal collapse of Germany.

5. The *Westwall* barrage was recently extended to the Shetlands. The last two minefields were laid by mine layers without any escorts, one off the Shetlands on March 7 at a distance of 130 miles from the Norwegian coast, and one on March 11, 120 miles south-west of Egersund.

6. Defence of the coast of Norway by Army coastal artillery was ordered by the Fuehrer after the British raid on Svolvaer. Even these guns will not be able to prevent the enemy's big ships from shooting up such batteries some day, especially during operation "Barbarossa." The presence of air forces along the coast will always remain the greatest deterrent. *The Fuehrer* agrees with this view and states that the C.-in-C., Air, is providing air units composed of various types of planes for southern, central (Trondheim), and northern Norway (Bardufoss). The defence of Narvik is the most important matter, and it is now being organised. *The C.-in-C., Navy*, again points out the need to occupy Murmansk and Polyarnoye by land and if possible also from the air, if operation "Barbarossa" takes place, as the British must be prevented from getting a foothold there.

7. We have information that American convoys, probably escorted by U.S. naval vessels, call at Iceland, where the escort duties are taken over by British naval vessels. The harbour installations at Reykjavik do not permit transhipment. Iceland is not included in the area designated by the U.S.A. as the Western Hemisphere.

*The C.-in-C., Navy*, suggests the following: (a) The closed area should be extended to include Iceland and the Denmark Straits. However, it must be established right from the beginning that in this closed area American ships will be treated in the same way as British and neutral ships in the original closed area, i.e., they can be attacked without warning. The matter is being discussed with the Foreign Office.

(*b*) Germany should refuse to respect the Pan-American neutrality zone or should limit it to a distance of 300 miles from the coast. *The Fuehrer* wonders whether we should extend recognition only to the three mile zone. This matter is to be discussed with the Foreign Office.

(*c*) The present restriction on the treatment of American ships should be lifted, i.e., they should be treated in the same way as all other neutral ships. That means they should be stopped for examination outside the closed area and brought in or sunk according to prize law.

(*d*) The operations against Halifax should be permitted. Points under "c" and "d" are to be discussed with the Foreign Office.

(*e*) *The C.-in-C., Navy*, suggests that propaganda pertaining to the U.S.A. should now lay more emphasis on the extent to which that nation violates neutrality by legislation to render aid to Britain and by her entire conduct; for example it is possible that British naval vessels might be repaired in the U.S.A. *The Fuehrer* agrees. In addition, if British naval vessels are actually undergoing repairs in the U.S., he will try to arrange for repair of German naval vessels in Japan.

8. *The C.-in-C., Navy*, calls attention to the need to secure North-west Africa with the assistance of the French, in order to paralyse British and U.S. control over the eastern Atlantic from there. The C.-in-C., Navy considers that it would be most dangerous if the U.S.A. should later gain a foothold on the coast of West Africa; this would be the best opportunity for the U.S.A. to intervene effectively. Therefore it is necessary to make an agreement with the French. (See Appendix to conference). *The Fuehrer* states that at present there is no possibility of negotiating with France, since she is harbouring new hopes as a result of Italy's weakness. Spain's refusal to co-operate also complicates matters; she is playing an underhanded game due to the dissension caused by Suner.

*The C.-in-C., Navy* suggests that the French problem be clarified after the completion of operation "Barbarossa". *The Fuehrer* agrees. In the autumn he also wishes to force a decision in the Spanish question. It will become more and more difficult to occupy Gibraltar, however, because of British countermeasures.

9. Italy.—(*a*) The conference with Admiral Riccardi in Merano is reported on.

The following points were discussed:

(1) The position of the Chief of the Naval Liaison Staff in Rome.

(2) The war situation in the Mediterranean. Offensive use of Italian naval forces. Use of mines in the Mediterranean, with special reference to the need for closing the Straits of Sicily. Escorts for transports to Libya.

(3) Increase in the freedom of action of the Italian Navy through the occupation of Greece.

(4) Italy's attitude toward France. Preparations for the occupation of Corsica are discussed, of which the Foreign Minister has also been informed through the report from Rintelen. The C.-in-C., Navy, particularly emphasised here that an agreement between the two governments is necessary before such action is taken.

(*b*) The question of transferring mineral oils from German stocks to the Italian Navy is discussed, since otherwise the Italian naval forces cannot take an active part in the war. The Italians have stated that unless they receive assistance the big ships will be immobilised in June of this year and the submarines in February 1942. *The Chief of Staff, O.K.W.*, declares that examination has shown that the Italians admit having 600,000 tons of fuel oil still, hence more than we have ourselves. They claim that they used 35,000 tons for the Genoa operation. It is being. investigated whether we can return the oil that has been used for convoy escort duties. *The C.-in-C., Navy*, asks whether the 600,000 tons actually exist or whether the Italians gave this figure merely because it was the one that had been quoted to the Duce. This would explain the high consumption figures, which may have been given in order to reduce the high total. It is not known whether this is the case.

(c) On the basis of a German report and an offer to deliver German mines, submitted to the Italian Admiralty at the beginning of February, the Italians have ordered mine material for protective barrages off Tripoli. The material has already been sent. Personnel to give tactical and technical advice have also been sent and are already there. 700 explosive floats, 650 cutting floats, 590 UMA, and 560 EMC mines have been delivered. It is expected that mine laying will begin within the next few days.

(d) The question of using German motor boats in the Mediterranean, as requested by General Rommel, has been examined by the Naval Staff on a previous occasion. In view of the tasks anticipated in connection with operation "Barbarossa," motor boats cannot be transferred until this operation has been completed. Until that time Italian motor boats will have to suffice for the tasks in the Mediterranean.

(e) In order to enable the Navy to carry out its tasks in the Mediterranean, it is particularly important to take Malta. In British hands this base represents a strong threat to our troop transports to Africa and later for the supply transports. Besides, it is an undesirable supply base for the shipping plying between the western and the eastern Mediterranean. In the opinion of the Air Force, it appears possible to capture Malta by airborne troops; the Navy is in favour of this as soon as possible. *The Fuehrer* states that more recent reports from the C.-in-C., Air, reveal that the difficulties are greater than anticipated, as the terrain is badly cut up by small walls, making it very difficult for airborne troops to function. Further investigations are being made.

10. Preparations for operation *Marita.*—(a) Material:

(1) The coastal batteries intended for use in Roumania and Bulgaria have been sent.

(2) The Roumanians have requested us to let them have 2,000 explosive floats for the minefields that are to be laid. They have been dispatched from our own stocks along with the requested gear for sweeping British aerial mines.

(3) Examination of the two 600-ton submarines being constructed in Roumania has shown that the boats will be launched at the end of May, will be completed at the end of November, and will be ready for action in March 1942. Delivery of the parts ordered in Germany will cause no great difficulties.

(4) Transport of small German submarines overland to Roumania would take four and one half to five months. Hence the Naval Staff has

decided to give up the idea, especially as the boats cannot well be spared from home waters.

(5) Despite difficulties caused by the state of the German super-highways due to damage from frost, the transport of two Bulgarian motor boats that have been built in Holland has been ordered.

(*b*) Personnel:

(1) The Naval Mission to Roumania (Rear Admiral Fleischer and staff) has taken up its duties.

(2) The barrage expert from the Naval Staff who was requested by Roumania has been in Roumania to advise the Roumanian Navy how to lay the minefields. At his advice the necessary material has been sent and the German specialists required for technical matters are on their way.

(3) The Naval Liaison Staff, Bulgaria has taken up its duties in Sofia.

(4) The Admiral, Greece, left on March 8. The Admiral, South-east, will leave about March 22.

(5) An attempt is to be made to obtain the active co-operation of the available Roumanian and Bulgarian naval forces in the war; for this purpose, besides the operational guidance to be given by the Admiral, South-east, and the liaison staffs, it is intended to intersperse German naval officers and German technical personnel among the crews, as far as the personnel situation permits. About 400 men in all will be required. This personnel must be taken from ships undergoing repairs.

(6) *The C.-in-C., Navy*, requests confirmation of the intention to occupy all Greece, even if a peaceful settlement is reached. *The Fuehrer* assures him that complete occupation is the first requisite for any settlement.

(*c*) Agreement with the Italian Navy for operation *Marita*.—The Italian Navy must be contacted at once in connection with preparations for this operation in the Aegean Sea and the eastern Mediterranean. *The C.-in-C., Navy*, requests the earliest possible indication of the line to be taken and permission to establish contact, as the Italian Navy works very slowly and co-operation must be ensured from the start. The questions to be dealt with in connection with operation *Marita* will have to cover the following points:

(1) Plans for naval operations must be co-ordinated. The operational areas must be defined.

(2) The question of who is to control the naval forces involved must be settled.

(3) Measures to be taken against islands, such as Lemnos, and anchorages in western and southern Greece, particularly measures designed to prevent ships from leaving, must be arranged. The harbours and coastal shipping on the west coast must be organised.

(4) Agreements on communications and recognition signal procedure, etc., must be reached.

(5) An Italian liaison officer must be appointed to the staff of the Admiral, South-east.

*The Fuehrer* promises that the O.K.W. will give the signal for contacting Italy as soon as possible.

11. Operation "Attila."—The units which the Navy is to provide, i.e., a special group of fifty officers and non-commissioned officers and two battery crews for the XI Air Corps, and a special group of twenty men and the Naval Shock Troop Detachment for Army Group D, have been organised so that they can arrive at the points of departure within 72, or in some cases 48 hours.

12. Japan.—Japan must take steps to capture Singapore as soon as possible, since the opportunity is more favourable than it will ever be again. The entire British Fleet is tied down; the U.S.A. is not prepared to wage war on Japan; the U.S. fleet is inferior to the Japanese fleet. Japan is preparing this move, to be sure, but according to all the statements made by Japanese officers she will not carry it out until Germany invades Britain. Hence Germany must make every effort to get Japan to attack at once. If Japan holds Singapore, all other Far Eastern questions in connection with the U.S.A. and Britain will be solved, including Guam, the Philippines, Borneo, and the Dutch East Indies. Japan wants to avoid war with the U.S.A. if possible, and she could do.this if she would take Singapore by a decisive attack as soon as possible. According to a statement made by Admiral Nomura, Minister Matsuoka has grave misgivings with regard to Russia and will raise questions mainly on this point. *The C.-in-C., Navy*, recommends, in a personal discussion with the Fuehrer, that Matsuoka should be informed of plans regarding Russia.

13. General Questions.—(*a*) The manpower situation and problems connected with raw materials are discussed.

(*b*) Result of (*a*): The monthly output of submarines will still remain approximately at eighteen during the second quarter, but after that will drop to fifteen, whereas if the demands for workers, etc., were met, it would rise to twenty by the end of 1941 and twenty-four in 1942. As before, *the Fuehrer* states that he intends to concentrate the greatest efforts on enlarging the Air Force and Navy after operation "Barbarossa" has been completed.

(*c*) Fire in the Bremen.—An investigation is in progress. It is not yet certain whether the fire was caused by sabotage or by a short circuit due to old material. *The Fuehrer* orders investigation to be made as to whether the crane installations on the Europa, the Potsdam, and the Gneisenau could be strengthened to permit the loading of heavy tanks.

(*d*) Dock facilities for the Bismarck and the Tirpitz are.—In Bremerhaven, the Kaiser dock; in Kiel, the floating dock; in Hamburg, the Blohm and Voss dock, but only if the ships are greatly lightened.

(*e*) Readiness of ships.—The Bismarck will be ready for operational use about the middle of May. The Tirpitz should be ready for transfer to Trondheim by the middle of May. She will be able to continue combat training there, and by her presence will discourage British raids on Norway.

(*f*) Displacement.

|  |  | Bismarck. | Richelieu. | Ship "H" |
|---|---|---|---|---|
| (1) | Washington: | 42,343 tons | 38,500 tons | 56,500 tons |
|  | Fully loaded: | 49,947 tons | 46,453 tons | 67,500 tons |

(2) American battleships.—From 1937 to February 1940 the keels of six ships of 35,000 tons were laid. Each has nine 40·6-cm. guns. The speed is 27 knots. In 1940 the keels of two ships of 45,000 tons were laid. In 1941 the keels of two more ships of 45,000 tons were laid. Each of the four has nine 40·6-cm. guns. The speed is 33 knots. The beam of both classes is 32·9 metres. The locks of the Panama Canal are 33·5 metres wide. Our locks, ready in 1946–47, will be 41·5 metres wide.

(signed) RAEDER.

## APPENDIX

The following memorandum was presented at the conference:

France.—France offers the following possibilities for exploitations:
(a) The military power that still remains, primarily the fleet and the forces in Africa, might be used.
(b) The African area with its strategic and economic potentialities is important.

The following paragraphs set forth briefly what would happen if the French, sacrificing the mother country, were to resume the war against the Axis, and on the other hand what the possibilities would be if France became our ally.

I. If France should resume the struggle against Germany on her own initiative it would be impossible to prevent the remaining fleet from escaping from Toulon. Also the parts of the fleet at present in the British sphere would be active within a short time. This would have a detrimental effect on the conduct of the war in the Mediterranean; Italy would be entirely on the defensive; the employment of French forces to carry out escort duties and anti-submarine measures would render it more difficult to disrupt British and supply lines. (However, it would be very difficult to reactivate the fleet for any length of time without the industrial facilities offered by continental France.) Italy's position in Tripoli would become untenable; she would be caught between British and French forces, since the enemy fleets would possess naval supremacy. Every bridgehead in Africa would be lost, so that Africa could not be attacked. This would be particularly grave if it later developed that Germany would have to gain her future colonies by military conquest. At a later date a strong centre of power might be created in North Africa with American assistance. Germany would have to feed continental France as well as herself if she wished to benefit from French industry, as then all imports from Africa would cease. Deliveries of oils, ores, and rubber from French colonies to Germany herself, which are being increased at present, would be stopped. All anti-Axis forces in the world would be given fresh encouragement both politically and propagandistically. France would be missing when it comes to rebuilding Europe.

II. Our aim must be more than merely to prevent this situation from arising; we must win France over to full political action against Britain and we must fully exploit the economy of the African area. The collaboration of France in military tasks and the use of her fleet would also be desirable if France is willing to do this without too great concessions on the part of Germany with regard to the future peace treaty. Thus we must strive to secure the French colonial empire against an Anglo-American attack and against De Gaulle, and to exploit the Franco-African area and its bases for German naval, air, and military forces.   We should then have the following possibilities:

(a) The Air Force based in Morocco could eliminate Gibraltar to a great extent, with all that this implies for British supply lines and the strategic situation in the western Mediterranean.   This would make it easier to restore the situation in Libya.

(b) Sierra Leone could be captured, thus eliminating Freetown. It would not be at all impossible to attack Gambia and Nigeria.   This would relieve the Italians in East Africa, and threaten the Egyptian Sudan. If the situation demanded it, our colonial empire could be acquired through military conquest.

(c) Economically, North and Central Africa are of very great importance in a long war against the Anglo-Americans.   If we control the Mediterranean and have the use of the French, Italian, and German fleets, it would be possible to exploit Africa economically even during the actual course of the war.

(d) All co-operative pro-Axis forces would be encouraged; it would be a great political success with far-reaching effects.   For all practical purposes Europe would be united against the Anglo-Americans.   It is hardly necessary to mention that it might be of the greatest importance if French forces, particularly the fleet, could be induced to go beyond the tasks of defending French interests and to attack British positions, British supply lines, etc.   The possibility of guaranteeing the French retention of at least part of their colonial empire as an inducement for collaboration should be investigated.

\*       \*       \*       \*       \*       \*

Hitler now turned his attention once more to the Balkans.   On March 20 intensive Nazi efforts were made to bring Yugoslavia into the Axis.   Cabinet Ministers resigned, but, by March 25, Yugoslavia had signed the Tri-partite Pact. Germany promised to respect Yugoslav sovereignty and territorial integrity, but Army plans for the invasion were ready, and two days later, on March 27, Hitler gave the order to move.   On the same day, however, there was a sudden revolution in Yugoslavia, and King Peter took over the Government.   The German operation was temporarily postponed.

### EXTRACT FROM DIRECTIVE NO. 25

Fuehrer Headquarters
March 27, 1941

(1) The military *putsch* in Yugoslavia has altered the political situation in the Balkans.   Yugoslavia must, in spite of her protestations of loyalty, for the time being be considered as an enemy and therefore be crushed as speedily as possible.

(2) It is my intention to force my way into Yugoslavia from the area comprising Fiume and Graz on the one hand and the area around Sofia on the other, moving in the general direction of Belgrade and south of this, and to contact and annihilate the Yugoslav Army, also to cut off the extreme southern part of Yugoslavia from the rest of the country, and to take it over as a base for the continuance of the combined German and Italian offensive against Greece.

The approaching opening of the Danube to traffic, and the taking over of the copper mines at Bor are important for reasons of war economy.   An attempt will be made to persuade Hungary and Bulgaria to take part in the operations by hold-ing out the prospect of regaining Banat and Macedonia. The political internal crisis in Yugoslavia will be rendered more acute by the political assurances given to the Croatians.

(signed) A. HITLER.

On the following day the British Mediterranean Fleet engaged the Italian Fleet off Cape Matapan, sinking 4 cruisers and 3 destroyers, and damaging at least 1 batteship and several other vessels. British losses amounted to only 2 aircraft. This action gave British sea-power an overwhelming superiority in the Eastern Mediterranean, and lessened the force of the enemy counter-offensive in North Africa which began on March 30.

One week later the new German plan for the Balkans had been completed, and on April 6 German troops marched into Yugoslavia and Greece. The Germans advanced rapidly. On April 17 the Yugoslav Army capitulated, and King Peter was evacuated by the R.A.F. This new German aggression greatly alarmed Russia, and the Soviet Council of War under Timoshenko ordered military preparations. The German Naval Attaché in Moscow reported on April 24 that the British Ambassador, Sir Stafford Cripps, had prophesied that Germany would attack Russia on June 22. (This statement is true and the prophesy was correct.)

*      *      *      *      *      *

On April 20 Raeder reported on the Battle of the Atlantic and on naval strategy in the Mediterranean.

**REPORT OF THE C.-IN-C., NAVY, TO THE FUEHRER
ON APRIL 20, 1941**

1. German operational situation.—Important points in present naval strategy:

(*a*) Cruiser warfare in foreign waters.

(*b*) Submarine warfare.

(*c*) Protection of all transport and convoy traffic to Norway and in the North Sea and Western Area.

Re (*a*).—Cruiser warfare is still successful, though restricted to a certain extent by necessary overhauling and replenishment of supplies. At present five auxiliary cruisers are still operating. Ship "10" is on return passage in the North Atlantic. Ship "41", operating in the Atlantic, has reported sinking 56,000 tons since the middle of December 1940. Apart from this, one other auxiliary cruiser is in the South Atlantic, two are in the western Indian Ocean, and one is in the eastern Indian Ocean. The numerous supply ships engaged in replenishing the supplies of auxiliary cruisers and submarines in the Indian and South Atlantic Oceans have hitherto been remarkably successful. Only one prize tanker was lost. At the moment three prize ships are en route to Germany.

Re (*b*).—The northern submarine operational area is being shifted from the region just outside the North-Channel to an area farther west, south-west of Iceland, on account of enemy patrols and the short, bright nights. The number of submarines is gradually increasing. At present there are only thirty operational boats. Taking losses into account, the probable number of operational boats will be as follows: On May 1, 37; on June 1, 39; on July 1, 45; and on August 1, 52.

Re (*c*).—In spite of increased enemy efforts to stop or disrupt transport traffic by air attacks, transports to Oslo have continued without interrup-tion. Losses on the west coast of Norway and in the North Sea and the

Channel have been satisfactorily small up to now. This shows the effectiveness of the anti-aircraft guns on board patrol vessels and minesweepers.

The next operation with battleships Bismarck and Prinz Eugen is scheduled for the end of April, when the ships are to leave home waters for the Atlantic. The questions of anti-aircraft defences for the base at Brest, bomb and torpedo hits on the Gneisenau, and bases on the west coast of France are discussed. *The C.-in-C., Navy*, points out that the danger to ships under repair in Kiel and Wilhelmshaven is as great at present as it is in Brest, apart from the fact that a single plane can carry a greater bomb load to Brest. In spite of this, until further notice large ships will put into Brest only in exceptional circumstances. The occupation of Ferrol, which the Fuehrer is determined to carry out in the autumn, is of great importance. If possible the Fuehrer would like to see the Todt Organisation quickly construct a large dry dock in Trondheim. This is being investigated.

2. Intensification of the use of aerial mines.—A new firing device for aerial mines, combining magnetic and acoustic firing, will be ready in May. It is necessary to employ this new firing method at once and as extensively as possible before the enemy discovers the new principle and develops appropriate methods for sweeping the mines. In view of previous firing devices, a conjecture concerning the combination of the new firing device is comparatively easy, even for the enemy. In connection with the mining of the Suez Canal, a new combination of this sort was supposedly already suspected. The mining of the Suez Canal, together with the threat to the British lines of communication through the Straits of Sicily by the X Air Corps, is a classic example of a practical mining operation which has achieved the desired strategic effect by being executed at precisely the right moment. Perseverance in laying the mines and patience in giving them time to take effect are necessary conditions for success. Continual use of aerial mines at the entrance of harbours is the most effective way of supplementing operations by submarines, surface forces, and aircraft against British supply lines.

Considering that our mines present a grave threat to the enemy, while his countermeasures have reached a high degree of efficiency as the result of one and a half years of wartime experience, it is evident that the outcome of the race between offensive mine warfare and anti-mine defence will be of decisive importance. Offensive mine warfare has the advantage at this time, in view of the new firing device with which our mines will be equipped in the near future. However, it is certain that this advantage will prevail for a limited time only. It is therefore imperative that it be exploited at once to the fullest possible extent. Therefore both the Air Force and the Navy must lay aerial mines in large numbers immediately. *The Fuehrer* will see to it that the Air Force acts accordingly.

3. The question of sending German submarines to the Mediterranean.— The present situation in the Mediterranean seems to indicate that operations by German submarines against British transport traffic in the eastern Mediterranean would be particularly desirable and promising. In addition to sinking ships, they would have a strategic effect on Army operations ashore. A detailed examination of the question of sending submarines to the Mediterranean, however, has shown that the

disadvantages of doing this probably outweigh possible advantages. The suggestion is therefore to be disregarded.

Reasons.—(a) The main objective of submarine warfare remains the attack on imports to the British Isles. The concentration of supply ships into convoys demands a similar concentration of the attacking forces, especially as sufficient reconnaissance is lacking owing to the fact that air reconnaissance cannot operate as far out as the submarine operational area. At present only thirty operational boats are available, including those being overhauled. About half of this number are at sea, counting submarines either outward or homeward bound; therefore only one third, or ten, are in the operational area. This small number is sufficient for locating and attacking an occasional convoy in the two main operational areas west of Britain and west of Africa. Any division of forces necessarily reduces the chances for intercepting and destroying convoys.

(b) For operations in the Mediterranean only small boats manned by experienced crews can be considered, in view of the conditions under which they would have to operate. The approach route is very long, and the first boat would not be available in the Aegean or the eastern Mediterranean before May 7 at the earliest; additional boats not until the middle of May.

(c) The effect of single submarines would be very small. At present overhaul and repair is possible only in Italy, which means that boats would have to return to an Italian port after every ten days or two weeks of operations, involving a long voyage to and from the operational area. Really promising operations would therefore be possible only with at least ten boats. This would mean, however, that submarine warfare against the main target, British imports, would be weakened decidedly.

(d) The establishment of an Italian base for our submarines, or a suitable base in Yugoslavia or Greece would require at least four weeks of preparation for installation of necessary workshops, provision of technicians and base personnel, supplies, etc. This would necessarily weaken our submarine bases in Germany and in the Atlantic.

(e) The clear water and the necessity of remaining submerged for prolonged periods make the situation in the Mediterranean unfavourable for submarine warfare. For this reason alone single boats would not accomplish much.

In summary, the Naval Staff considers that the prospects of success for single boats do not compensate for the disadvantages ensuing from removing them from the main theatre of operations in the Atlantic. It is therefore proposed, as already reported, to withdraw Italian submarines from the Atlantic and to concentrate a strong force of Italian submarines in the eastern Mediterranean. The present is a good time for the withdrawal. since the Italians must realise that their submarines are badly needed in the eastern Mediterranean. *The Fuehrer* is in complete agreement with the decision not to send German submarines into the Mediterranean, likewise with the withdrawal of Italian submarines from the Atlantic.

4. Restriction on naval warfare as the result of the Pan-American Safety Zone.—In the presence of the German Foreign Minister *the Fuehrer* decides as follows: In view of America's present undecided attitude resulting from events in the Balkans, the zone as far as 20° N (that part which is off the U.S. coast) will for the present be recognised, but further south only a 300 mile zone. No note is to be sent to the U.S.A., etc.

5. Sanction for warfare against merchant ships of the U.S.A. according to prize regulations: For the same reason as stated under "4," the following procedure is to be used: For from ten days to two weeks there is to be no change; however, the Bismarck and the Prinz Eugen can receive instructions for action, which can be put into force by means of a code word, as soon as the Fuehrer has decided accordingly. The Foreign Minister states that he agree to attacks on neutral ships proceeding alone in the new closed area only providing they are doing escort duty for merchant ships. (According to the definite instructions received from the O.K.W., unrestricted offensive action was sanctioned against all naval and merchant vessels in the blockade area.)

6. Relations with Japan.—What were the results of Matsuoka's visit? Was operation "Barbarossa" mentioned during the conference? What views are held with regard to the Russo-Japanese pact? *The Fuehrer* answers that Matsuoka was informed that Russia will not be attacked as long as she maintains a friendly attitude in accordance with the treaty; if this is not the case, he reserves the right to take suitable action. The Russo-Japanese pact was concluded with Germany's acquiescence. The above stand taken by the Fuehrer has had a salutary effect on the attitude of Russia, who will now conduct herself with great correctness and who expects no attack for the present. The Fuehrer values the Russo-Japanese pact because Japan is now restrained from taking action against Vladivostock and should be induced to attack Singapore instead. Matsuoka and Oshima have assured him that all preparations will be completed by May. The C.-in-C, Navy, draws attention to the extremely vague and non-committal statements of Nomura; he intends to continue to try to influence him.

7. Relations with Russia.—What is the Fuehrer's opinion of the present change in Russia's attitude in an obviously pro-German direction? *The Fuehrer* replies in the same vein as under Paragraph 6. *The C.-in-C., Navy*, points out the need for taking effective steps to mine the White Sea Canal so that submarines and destroyers cannot escape into the Arctic Ocean, and the urgent necessity for heavy air bombardment of the locks in the canal, as it is of little use to mine the Neva. *The Fuehrer* agrees.

8. Conferences between the Army General Staff and the Finnish General Staff have already begun. When can the naval conferences be expected to begin? *The Fuehrer* replies that the conferences so far have been of a very general nature. The time for naval conferences has not yet arrived. Nevertheless the Fuehrer fully realises the importance of this matter.

9. Relations with France.—Does the Fuehrer still consider operation "Attila" necessary? *The Fuehrer* replies that it must be held in readiness for the present, even though he is inclined to believe that Darlan's attitude is trustworthy.

10. Italo-German co-operation in the Aegean Sea.—The following arrangements have been agreed upon:

(*a*) Territorial limits. The east coast of Greece, including the Gulf of Athens, comes under the command of the Admiral, South-east; also the islands off the coast and the islands in the Aegean Sea, as far as they are occupied by German troops. The Peloponnesus and the west coast of Greece come under the command of Italy.

(*b*) Enlistment of Italian naval forces for duty along the German coastal sector for the defence of harbours and inshore waters and as escorts for coastal traffic and island transports.   Request has been made for two torpedo boat or destroyer flotillas of four ships each, three mine-sweeping and three patrol flotillas of six vessels each, two subchaser flotillas, two or three PT boat flotillas of eight boats each, six mine layers, and six submarines, as well as several small transports, tankers, and other supply ships.   The Italian Naval Staff has agreed to provide these vessels, but has pointed out that all available submarines are at present engaged in operations against British transports in the eastern Mediterranean.   Apart from the forces applied for, the Italian Naval Staff plans to put Italian forces stationed permanently or temporarily in the Dodecanese Islands at the disposal of the Admiral, South-east, should he require them.

(*c*) Liaison between Italian naval forces and the Admiral, South-east. An Italian Chief of Staff, who will also be the commander of the above Italian naval forces, will be attached to the Admiral, South-east.   The Admiral, South-east, is permitted to transfer sections of these forces to commanders subordinate to him.   The Dodecanese naval forces temporarily placed at the disposal of the Admiral, South-east, will be operationally and tactically under his command during this time. Captain Count Peccori-Giraldi has been selected as Chief of Staff.

(signed) RAEDER.

\*          \*          \*          \*          \*          \*

In Greece the Allied situation deteriorated and on April 21 the Greek Govern-ment informed Britain of their inability to resist further and asked the British forces to withdraw.   Evacuation began on April 22, and by April 26 the Germans had captured the Isthmus and town of Korinth, entering Athens on the following day.   British forces rallied in Crete, and the Germans began preparing a parachute operation against the island—operation *Merkur*.   Goering was placed in com-mand of the operation, and the naval share was limited to transport operations from Greece as soon as Crete had been taken.

The attack on Crete began on the morning of May 20.   The attack was in the beginning entirely by air, and the air defences of the island which had been previously reduced to 7 serviceable aircraft were overwhelmed.   Ships of the Royal Navy which were disposed for the defence of the island suffered heavily from German air attacks, but managed to destroy the few German transports which attempted to land troops on the island.   Air attacks intensified and prevented ships from operating in the vicinity of Crete by day, but night actions were continued regardless of the opposition.   British troops, when the action began, had only recently been evacuated from Greece.   They were ill-equipped and had little more than rifles and a few light automatics with which to defend the island. Naval vessels had brought in additional supplies, but by May 27 the situation was hopeless, and evacuation began.   It was completed by June 1.

\*          \*          \*          \*          \*          \*

Further exploitation of the situation in the Eastern Mediterranean was envisaged in the following directive from Hitler :

Fuehrer and Supreme Commander of the *Wehrmacht*      Fuehrer Headquarters
                                                        May 25, 1941
Top Secret

### Fuehrer Directive No. 30—Middle East

(1) The Arabian Freedom Movement is our natural ally in the Middle East against England.   In this connection the rebellion in Irak assumes a special

importance.   Its influence extends beyond the boundaries of Irak, and strengthens anti-British forces in the Middle East, it disturbs British communications and ties down British troops and shipping at the expense of other theatres of war.   I have decided therefore, to encourage developments in the Middle East by supporting Irak.   Whether—and if so by what means—it would be possible afterwards to launch an offensive against the Suez Canal and eventually oust the British finally from their position between the Mediterranean and the Persian Gulf cannot be decided until operation "Barbarossa" is complete.

(2)  My decisions for the support of Irak can be summarized as follows :

The sending of a Military Mission
Assistance from the *Luftwaffe*
The supply of arms.

(3)  The Military Mission will be commanded by General der Flieger Felmy. (Its code name will be Special Staff F).   Its tasks are :

(*a*) to advise and support the armed forces of Irak.

(*b*) to establish as far as possible military liaison with anti-British forces, including those outside Irak.

(*c*) to gain experience and information from this area for the German *Wehrmacht*

The composition of the mission in view of these tasks will be in the hands of the Chief of the O.K.W.   The chain of Command is as follows :

(*a*) The Head of the Military Mission is in command of all members of the *Wehrmacht* sent to Irak as well as the Syria Liaison Detachment.

(*b*) The Head of the Military Mission is subordinate to the Chief of the O.K.W. with the proviso that orders and directives for air units shall be issued exclusively by the C.-in-C. of the *Luftwaffe*.

(*c*) The Head of the Military Mission will have dealings with military offices only in Irak.   Matters concerning the Mission which require negotiations with the Irak Government will be handled by the Foreign Office representative in Irak.   Before any military orders are given which may have repercussions on foreign policy the Head of the Military Mission must obtain the consent of the Foreign Office representative in Irak.

(*d*) For the present the members of the Military Mission are to be regarded as Volunteers (after the style of the Condor Legion).   They will wear tropical uniform with Irak badges.   German aircraft also will show Irak markings.

(4) *Luftwaffe* : The numerical force of the *Luftwaffe* which should be employed is to be limited.   Its function is not merely that of an arm of the *Wehrmacht*, but in addition it is that of an agent for prompting greater self-confidence and will to resist among the Irak Armed Forces and civilians.   The nature and extent of German intervention is to be decided by the C.-in-C. of the *Luftwaffe*.

(5)  Supply of Arms :  The necessary orders (deliveries from Syria by virtue of the agreement made with the French for this purpose ;  and from Germany) will be given by the Chief of the O.K.W.

(6)  The Direction of Propaganda in the Middle East is the responsibility of the Foreign Office, working in this instance with the O.K.W.

The Basis of the Propaganda is :  "An Axis victory will bring to the nations of the Middle East freedom from the British yoke and the right of self-determination. All lovers of freedom will therefore join in the fight against England."

Anti-French propaganda in Syria must be suspended for the time being.

(7)  Where members of the Italian Armed Forces are employed in Irak, it will be necessary to co-operate with them in accordance with this directive.   Efforts are being made to bring them within the sphere of authority of the Head of the German Military Mission.

(signed) ADOLF HITLER.

# Sinking of the Bismarck

THE MOST important operation of the German Navy in May, 1941 was operation *Rheinuebung* (Rhine Exercise). This operation was the climax of the series of naval attacks against merchant shipping in the Atlantic. For it the newly completed battleship Bismarck and the new heavy cruiser Prinz Eugen were to make a three months sortie in the Atlantic. Great results were expected and everything possible was done to make the operation a success. Tankers and reconnaissance merchant ships were placed in strategic positions, and an elaborate wireless intelligence organization was set up to track down convoys and independent merchant ships. On May 21 the ships sailed, and on the following day Raeder reported to Hitler. There was, however, little discussion on the forthcoming operation.

C.-in-C., Navy.

## CONFERENCE OF THE C.-IN-C., NAVY, WITH THE FUEHRER AT THE BERGHOF ON MAY 22, 1941

Also present: Chief of Staff, O.K.W.
General Jodl.
Captain von Puttkamer.
The Foreign Minister.

1. Situation. (*a*) Submarine warfare.—Since the beginning of May there has been a further increase in the number of ships sunk by our submarines. Eleven boats are at present in the northern operational area and seven are in the southern area. In the course of the last few days about 85,000 tons were sunk from a convoy. The enemy had adopted a very flexible convoy system, combined with a far-reaching and excellent direction-finding and locator network; the sighting and location reports are evaluated very rapidly for the purpose of convoy control. Enemy defence for convoys has been considerably strengthened; a close watch of the sea area west of Britain is being kept by air reconnaissance, anti-submarine groups, surface forces, and single steamers. The losses incurred by us in March and April made it necessary to move the submarines farther out into the Atlantic. Some of the waiting positions are outside the declared blockade area. Successful submarine operations have been carried out in the area off the West African coast near Freetown. One boat has set out on a minelaying mission in the Takoradi-Lagos area.

(*b*) Cruiser warfare in foreign waters.—Four auxiliary cruisers are still on operations, one in the South Atlantic and three in the Indian Ocean. Ship "10," commanded by Captain Kaehler, returned to Hamburg after nearly eleven months of operations. The ship sank 96,000 tons. Engagements were fought with three superior enemy auxiliary cruisers, one of which was sunk and the other two badly damaged.

Ship "33," commanded by Captain Krueder, sank at noon on May 8 in the Indian Ocean west of Somaliland during an engagement with the heavy British cruiser Cornwall, which has eight 20·3-cm. guns. Only fifty-three survivors were taken prisoner. The enemy himself reported damage to the Cornwall during the engagement. The Commanding Officer's character is a sufficient guarantee that the auxiliary cruiser fought a gallant battle after vainly attempting to escape from the enemy cruiser through use of deception. Ship "33" was the most successful German auxiliary cruiser, which carried out extremely well all the tactical and operational demands made of her. Her successes amounted to 120,000 tons, including several prizes brought to home waters amounting to over 50,000 tons. Three large whale ships from the Antarctic, carrying 22,000 tons of whale oil, were among the prizes; also eight smaller whalers, a valuable tanker, and a steamer carrying wheat. At least two further ships, the names of which are unknown, were captured before the engagement with the Cornwall. Mine-laying missions in Australian waters were brilliantly executed. Apart from sinkings directly caused by the mines (three to four steamers and one minesweeper have been sunk as far as is known at present), these mine operations have great operational effect with extremely far-reaching consequences for enemy shipping. The total success achieved by ship "33" exceeds that of cruiser Emden or auxiliary cruiser Wolf in the World War.

Proposal.—These facts, together with the name of this outstanding commanding officer, should be mentioned and given recognition in one of the next reports of the O.K.W. *The Fuehrer* agrees. He also agrees to announcing the loss of Lt.-Commander Prien at a time when substantial submarine successes are reported.

The prize Speybank put into Bordeaux on May 11 with a very valuable cargo of 1,500 tons of manganese, 300 tons of rubber, jute, and tea. The supply ship Dresden put into a harbour in southern France with 140 Americans, some of them women and children, who were taken aboard auxiliary cruisers during the capture of an Egyptian steamer. It is inexcusable of the U.S. Government to allow American citizens, including women and children, to travel on ships belonging to belligerents. The captain of the Dresden treated the American passengers with great consideration, so that no protests are likely.

(c) Warfare by surface forces against merchant shipping.—The Bismarck–Prinz Eugen task force is en route to its mission in the Atlantic; the ships left Norwegian waters near Bergen on May 21. The purpose of the operation is war against merchant shipping in the North and Middle Atlantic. Fleet Commander Admiral Luetjens is in command of the operation.

(d) German merchant shipping overseas.—Of the four blockade-runners sent to South America, the first is on the return voyage and will arrive at the end of May; the remaining three are discharging and taking on cargo in Brazil. Up to now goods valued at 19,000,000 reichsmarks have been exported. Two German merchant ships, carrying 7,000 tons of rubber in all, are at present en route from Mairen. In a few days a third one will follow with an additional 4,000 tons. The first vessel is to arrive about the end of June; she will proceed by way of Cape Horn. Five vessels put out from Chile for Japan.

2. The enemy's air forces are very active in attacking German convoy and coastal traffic on the Norwegian and German coasts and the occupied Channel coast. Up to now the enemy has achieved no great success, and our defence forces have had good results in shooting down aircraft.

3. Extension of inland waterways in Holland.—The Navy is very much interested in developing the inland waterways from the Ems River and the city of Delfzijl to Amsterdam, Rotterdam and the Rhine River in order to reduce traffic on the sea route, which is exposed to great danger from air attacks, motor-boats, and mines, and in order to economise in the use of our limited escort forces. The Navy has ascertained that it is altogether possible to increase the number of barges on the canals and to utilize them better. Even partial expansion would mean a substantial increase in the amounts transported and would be of advantage to the over-all conduct of the war, not to mention its great importance for peacetime purposes. Up to now the Ministry of Transport has opposed this project. The Naval Staff cannot judge the reasons for this. It is proposed that the Fuehrer should recommend this expansion. *The Chief of Staff, O.K.W.*, will attend to the matter.

4. Continuing use of aerial mines.—In view of the importance of our new mine fuse and the necessity for exploiting it to the fullest possible extent before the enemy counter-measures become effective, the Naval Staff has recommended mine-laying operations on a large scale to the C.-in-C., Air. (A copy of the suggestion was sent to the O.K.W.) As far as is known the Operations Staff of the C.-in-C., Air, agrees in principle with the views of the Naval Staff, but considers that the number of aircraft available would *not* be sufficient for large-scale operations because of the withdrawal of large forces for the Eastern Campaign. *General Jodl* states that the Air Force has agreed to undertake a large-scale mine-laying operation with all available aircraft.

5. Discussion of the present problem of naval warfare in the Atlantic due to the attitude of the U.S.A.

6. Possible exploitation of French bases in West Africa.—*The Chief of Staff, O.K.W.*, states that there are prospects that the French will agree to all our demands. The French have made far-reaching preparations for defending North-west Africa against British and American attacks.

7. Canary Islands. Spanish Navy.—(*a*) *The C.-in-C., Navy*, recommends speedy measures for reinforcing the defences of the Canaries so that the islands can be held at any time against the British and Americans. Such measures would include importing and installing 15-cm. guns and building up supplies of food and ammunition. Enemy occupation of the Canary Islands would endanger our position in West Africa. *The Fuehrer* agrees that the O.K.W. should make preparations for these measures and that they should be carried out.

(*b*) During negotiations between the German and Spanish Navies regarding equipment for Spain, agreement was reached on most points; e.g., German mines are to be delivered. This could be done at once and, would be in the interest of the German Navy. Delivery is being delayed however, by trivial bickering on the part of the Ministry of Economics. *The C.-in-C., Navy*, requests that the Foreign Office clarify the matter. *The Foreign Minister* will attend to the matter.

8. Occupation of the Azores.—This subject was brought up by the Fuehrer. Judging from an earlier summary of the situation, which has not undergone any changes since, it would be possible to carry out the initial occupation of the Azores, using combat forces. It is extremely unlikely, however, that the islands could be held and supplies brought up in

the face of British, possibly also American attacks. Moreover, all our combat forces, including submarines, would be necessary to achieve this, and they would therefore have to be withdrawn from all offensive activities in the Battle of the Atlantic; this is intolerable. The Navy must therefore reject the idea of occupying the Azores. *The Fuehrer* is still in favour of occupying the Azores, in order to be able to operate long-range bombers from there against the U.S.A. The occasion for this may arise by autumn. In reply to the C.-in-C., Navy, the Fuehrer confirms that the Navy's main task in summer 1941 must be the disruption of British supply lines.

9. Plans for operation "Barbarossa."—It is essential that contact and conferences with the Finnish Admiralty be approved soon, at least as regards negotiations on fundamental operational matters, the settlement of which must be considered an essential factor for any operations. Such conferences require lengthy preparation; questions to be discussed include fuel supplies, anti-aircraft defence of bases and anchorages, supplies of foodstuffs, prompt transfer of vessels from the shipyards, etc. *The Chief of Staff, O.K.W.*, states that following the return of Minister Schnurre within the next few days, negotiations will take place between the O.K.W. and the Finns. Subsequently, discussions on the part of the Navy will be possible. Transports to Finland will, as ordered, be carried out in ten instead of twenty-one days. Twenty-five steamers will be withdrawn from merchant shipping for this purpose.

10. Organisation in the south-eastern area.—According to Fuehrer Directive No. 29 it is intended that the Army shall hand over the defence of the whole Greek area, up to Salonika, to the Italian Armed Forces after completion of operation *Merkur*. The directive leaves open for later settlement the question of who is ultimately to provide the occupational forces for Crete. Attention is called to the decisive importance of defending the main strategic points such as Salonika, Lemnos, Piraeus, Melos, and Crete. These points are of decisive importance as strategic bases for any further operations in the Eastern Mediterranean. It is essential that they be adequately protected against all eventualities and be ready to offer determined resistance to any enemy action. This is a necessary condition for successful operations by the X Air Corps. Such protection, however, can be guaranteed only if coastal defence and occupation of the hinterland is in the hands of German forces. The Naval Staff is therefore of the opinion that the bases in question should be firmly held by German forces until the Mediterranean operation as a whole has been concluded, more specifically, until British operations in the Eastern Mediterranean, including Alexandria and the Suez, have been eliminated. This applies especially to Crete, which is essential to the X Air Corps. *The Fuehrer* agrees, and gives the Chief of Staff, O.K.W., appropriate instructions.

11. Italian submarines.—*The C.-in-C., Navy*, once again requests withdrawal of Italian submarines from the Atlantic. The time is propitious, since they are urgently needed in the Eastern Mediterranean. *The Foreign Minister* proposes that he raise this point with Count Ciano or that the Fuehrer discuss it at his next meeting with the Duce, which is to take place soon. *The Fuehrer* agrees.

12. *The C.-in-C., Navy*, asks the Fuehrer for his opinion on Japan's attitude, as he is under the impression that the Japanese are rather cool. (Nomura is negotiating in Washington!) At the present time *the Fuehrer*

has no clear picture of the situation but obviously there are internal political difficulties in Japan. The good friendship policy is to be continued.

*The C.-in-C., Navy*, reports on information received from Admiral Nomura regarding new ships built by the Japanese. *The Fuehrer* emphasises the necessity for complete secrecy.

13. *The C.-in-C., Navy*, stresses the need for deepening navigational channels to accommodate very heavy new vessels after the war. The depth of the Kiel Canal, the Belts, and Jade Bay should be increased to fifteen metres. This work is to be carried out by the Navy, while the Elbe and Weser Rivers should be deepened as a large-scale project of other governmental agencies. *The Fuehrer* agrees entirely, but points out also the urgency of expanding Trondheim.

14. *The C.-in-C., Navy*, states that very careful and detailed preparations have been made for holding back the important materials to be delivered to Russia. The Russian Navy will be informed in the near future that the German Navy is having to draw on some of the things in view of the state of emergency, so that slight delays will occur, but that deliveries as a whole are not jeopardised. *The Fuehrer* agrees. The Foreign Minister has been informed.

15. *The C.-in-C., Navy*, reports that it will take eight months to complete constructing the aircraft carrier, including installations of anti-aircraft guns, if the work is resumed at the conclusion of operation "Barbarossa." An additional year will be needed for trials. As soon as it has definitely been decided to continue work on the carrier, the Fuehrer should order the C.-in-C., Air, to make the necessary planes available in time.

(signed) RAEDER.

*    *    *    *    *    *

The German Fleet was under the command of Admiral Gunther Luetjens flying his flag in the Bismarck. The departure of the German Fleet from Norway was sighted by naval air reconnaissance and reported to the British Home Fleet. Vice Admiral Holland flying his flag in H.M.S. Hood accompanied by H.M.S. Prince of Wales and six destroyers were sent to patrol the Denmark Straits where it was thought that the German ships would probably attempt to break through into the Atlantic. The Bismarck and Prinz Eugen were sighted in the Denmark Straits on the evening of May 23 by H.M.S. Suffolk and H.M.S. Norfolk who were on patrol. The British Battle Fleet altered to an intercepting course and shortly after five o'clock on the morning of May 24 sighted the enemy. H.M.S. Hood opened fire first followed immediately by the Prince of Wales. The Bismarck replied quickly and accurately and hit the Hood with her second or third salvo. Five minutes later the Hood blew up with a tremendous explosion and sank within three or four minutes. Shortly afterwards the Prince of Wales was also hit and temporarily broke off the action.

All possible steps had in the meantime been taken to close the net around the Bismarck. Heavy units of the British Fleet covered every possible avenue of escape. After skilful shadowing by ships and aircraft and a night attack by Fleet Air Arm aircraft from H.M.S. Victorious and later from H.M.S. Ark Royal, the Bismarck was finally brought to bay on the night of May 26/27. On the morning of May 27 after spirited destroyer attacks heavy units of the Home Fleet including H.M.S. King George V. and Rodney attacked the German vessel continuously for one and a half hours. By 10.15 the Bismarck's guns were silenced and she was finally sunk by torpedoes from H.M.S. Dorsetshire.

The German account of this action is given in the following reports and signals taken from the German Naval Archives:

## THE OPERATION OF THE BISMARCK TASK FORCE AGAINST MERCHANT SHIPPING IN THE ATLANTIC

Besides achieving considerable tactical successes, the first operation of battleships Gneisenau and Scharnhorst in the Atlantic from January to March 1941 and the operation of cruiser Hipper, confirmed the fact that such use of surface vessels has far-reaching strategic effects. These effects were not restricted to the waters chosen as the zone of operations, but extended in widely diverging directions to other theatres of war, that is, also to the Mediterranean and the South Atlantic.

Hence naval warfare had to attempt to preserve and intensify the effects of the initial operations by repeating similar operations as frequently as possible, making the most of the experiences gained. In view of the decisive significance which British supplies in the North Atlantic have for the outcome of the war, German naval warfare can most effectively achieve its object only in the North Atlantic.

### 1. MISSION

The mission stipulated by Group West in the operational orders for operation *Rheinuebung* was as follows: Enemy supply traffic in the Atlantic north of the equator was to be attacked. The operation was to last as long as the situation permitted. The route out to the Atlantic was through the Great Belt, the Skagerrak, and the Norwegian Sea. The ships were to attempt to break through unobserved. Even if the break-through into the Atlantic were observed, the mission remained as defined in the operational directive. It was left to the discretion of the Fleet Commander to shorten or break off the operation as the situation developed. According to the Group's directive the main aim throughout the entire operation was the destruction of enemy shipping. As far as possible, they were to shun risks which would jeopardise the operation. Hence they were to avoid encounters with ships of equal strength. If an encounter were inevitable then it should be an *all-out* engagement.

As heretofore, the first portion of the undertaking, that is, the break-through into the Atlantic, if possible unobserved, was regarded as the most difficult part of the operation. Previous experience had shown that enemy forces might appear in the Denmark Straits as well as in the Iceland-Faroes passage. Under suitable weather conditions it was considered certain that there would be enemy air reconnaissance in the Denmark Straits. The lightness of the nights make an unobserved break-through all the more difficult. On the other hand we could expect that air reconnaissance over the northern part of the North Sea would provide an adequate picture of the enemy's disposition, and that in the Denmark Straits, at the ice border, poor visibility would favour the break-through. Since so far it had *not* been established that British ships were equipped with radar, as a matter of fact, observations made so far seemed to indicate that they definitely were *not* so equipped, an unnoticed break-through was feasible.

A certain amount of risk is involved in every break-through into the Atlantic. We had to run that risk, if German naval warfare were not to give up entirely the idea of disrupting British supply lines by means of surface forces.

### 2. COURSE OF THE OPERATION

Originally the beginning of the operation was planned for the end of April, but on account of damage to the coupling in the Prinz Eugen and repairs to the crane in the Bismarck it was postponed twice and finally fixed for May 18. The intention of joint operations with the battleship Gneisenau had to be abandoned because of severe damage inflicted on this ship by bombs and torpedoes in Brest.

The Bismarck and the Prinz Eugen put out from Gdynia on the evening of May 18. Two supply ships and five tankers were waiting at various points in the Norwegian Sea and the North Atlantic to supply the operation. To improve the operational chances of the task force, two scouting vessels were sent out from the Atlantic coast into the Atlantic. All these ships succeeded in breaking out from coastal waters into the open ocean without difficulty. Four submarines were en route to their positions for operating in conjunction with the task force on the North Atlantic convoy routes. In contrast with these extensive preparations for the operation in the Atlantic itself, the possibilities of support during the outward passage through the Norwegian Sea and the Iceland area were very limited, since our naval air forces were numerically few and were inadequately equipped, and since the Air Force has very few powerful long-range reconnaissance aircraft. The chances of carrying out extensive air reconnaissance in the remoter area, such as the Denmark Straits and the area between Iceland and Greenland, were extremely slight. On the other hand, reconnaissance covering the entire central and northern parts of the North Sea and close air cover and fighter escort in coastal waters would give full protection on the first part of the outward voyage.

*May* 19 *and* 20. During May 19 and 20 the task force, protected by mine-sweepers, aircraft, and submarines, proceeded without incident and according to plan through the Great Belt, the Kattegat, and the Skagerrak and on the evening of May 20 lay off Christiansand South.

The enemy situation was deemed favourable. On the morning of May 20 photographic reconnaissance located the main body of the British Home Fleet with two battleships (apparently of the King George class), the battle cruiser Hood, and aircraft carrier (possibly Victorious), six cruisers, and several destroyers in Scapa Flow. No enemy forces were sighted in the North Sea and the Norwegian Sea. Weather conditions handicapped the Focke-Wulf 200 in reconnaissance and in investigation of ice conditions north of Iceland. The drift ice border north of Iceland was about seventy to eighty miles away. The flight was broken off fifty miles north-west of North Cape in low-lying fog.

*May* 21. At 0900 on May 21 the group put into Kors Fiord near Bergen according to plan. There they refueled during the day and kept out of sight of the enemy. From British radio reports it was clear, however, that the enemy had learned that our battleships had put out to the north. Early on May 21 radio intelligence intercepted enemy radio instructions, in which at 0620 aircraft were ordered to keep a look-out for two battleships and three destroyers reported to be proceeding on a northerly course. Group North, in charge of the operation, concurred with the Naval Staff, in the opinion that the enemy received this information from agents in the Great Belt. It was not clear whether the intensified enemy air reconnaissance along the Norwegian coast, caused by this report, had picked up the task force early on May 21 before its entry into Kors Fiord or in the Fiord itself. Our own observations yielded *no* conclusive evidence on this point but the possibility did exist. According to a British Admiralty report of May 27, aircraft of Coastal Command are supposed to have sighted the Bismarck group on the Norwegian coast off Bergen ; however, this announcement might have been a deliberate invention, in order to avoid compromising the agents on the Great Belt and the Norwegian coast.

The report on sighting German battleships led to intense reconnaissance activity by the enemy's 18th Reconnaissance Group during May 21, further inten-sified towards evening and at night. Our own radio reconnaissance located enemy planes over the northern parts of the North Sea, the Norwegian Sea, the Nor-wegian coast, and the Faroe Islands area. On the other hand radio traffic of the British Home Fleet did not point to anything out of the ordinary. Ground and high fog unfortunately prevented planes sent out over Scapa Flow from com-pleting reconnaissance which should have observed any outward movement of the enemy ships. The investigation of the ice situation and reconnaissance in the Denmark Straits also had to be abandoned.

At 2300 the Fleet Commander with his group put out of Hjelte Fiord to con-tinue north. A few hours later several enemy planes flew over the islands near Bergen and dropped flares in their search for the German task force.

In the evening of May 21 it was clear from his air activity that the enemy knew that the Bismarck group had put out to sea, but he was obviously uncertain of its position. There was *no* indication in radio traffic that naval forces were being sent out.

Actually from the British announcements of May 27 it can be deduced that as early as May 21 the British Admiralty took certain measures to strengthen the patrol of the Denmark Straits and of the sea area south of Iceland. It can be assumed that the heavy cruisers Norfolk, commanded by Captain Phillips, with Rear Admiral Wake-Walker on board, and Suffolk, commanded by Captain Ellis, received orders as early as May 21 to take up positions for observation in the Denmark Straits. The orders to the units concerned escaped our notice, as the enemy was able to send them out as early as May 21 by telegraph.

*May* 22. On May 22 the Fleet Commander proceeded according to plan through the Norwegian Sea. The escorting destroyers were dismissed off Trondheim. With the exception of continued brisk enemy air reconnaissance activity over the north and central parts of the North Sea, nothing unusual was observed in enemy radio traffic. Our own reconnaissance did not sight any enemy forces in the North Sea or in the Norwegian Sea. Unfortunately weather conditions made the planned photographic aerial reconnaissance of Scapa Flow impossible; however, a partial visual reconnaissance in the afternoon supposedly located four battleships in Scapa Flow, one of them presumably an aircraft carrier, six cruisers, and several destroyers. On the basis of this reconnaissance report Group North came to the conclusion that there had been no change in the enemy disposition after May 21. Hence this report was a decided relief to the operational control and to the Fleet Commander, who was on the point of undertaking the break-through.

Group North thought that the Bismarck task force would take advantage of the fog and break through into the Atlantic as soon as possible, but as a precaution made preparations for refueling from the tanker waiting in the Norwegian Sea.

In the evening of May 22 the prevailing impression was that in spite of his knowledge that the Bismarck task force had put out, the enemy was still uncertain about the passing of the group through the Shetlands-Norway passage. There was no sign that any naval forces were being sent into operation, and indeed, according to the air reconnaissance over Scapa Flow, such an operation could definitely be ruled out. The Fleet Commander decided, in view of the unusually helpful hazy weather combined with the apparently favourable enemy disposition, to forego refueling in the Norwegian Sea and to wait no longer, but rather to undertake the break through via the Denmark Straits at once. The Fleet Commander was confirmed in his purpose by Group North, who radioed the favourable disposition of the enemy. Group North also called attention to the great successes of the Air Force against the British Forces in Crete, and pointed out that if the fleet were to appear on the Atlantic routes soon, additional severe damage might be inflicted on British sea power.

If the visual reconnaissance in Scapa Flow in the afternoon correctly observed the actual situation, it must be presumed that the British Forces, including the Prince of Wales, the Hood, and the Victorious, left Scapa Flow in the evening of May 22 and proceeded at high speed to take up waiting positions in the area southwest of Iceland.

*May* 23. On May 23 the Fleet Commander proceeded north of Iceland to break through via the Denmark Straits. The weather conditions were extremely favourable for his purpose; East wind, overcast, rain, moderate to poor visibility. At times visibility went down to 200 metres. Cruising speed of the group was 24 to 27 knots. The Fleet Commander considered the enemy disposition favourable. Air reconnaissance over Scapa Flow was impossible because of the weather. Again on May 23 the investigation of ice conditions in the Denmark Straits had to be abandoned.

At first there was nothing unusual to be observed in the enemy radio traffic, with the exception of an operational radiogram through blind transmission intercepted at 1254. This message, however, did not give any direct indication of enemy operations.

At 2015 the evening of May 23, the cruiser Norfolk contacted the Bismarck group at the ice border in the Iceland Straits (square AD 29) and reported it on a south-westerly course. The distance was about 11,100 metres. There was a brief encounter without results. In spite of very poor visibility conditions, due to fog, snow, and hail, the enemy succeeded, obviously by the use of efficient radar sets, in maintaining contact with the Bismarck group. The Fleet Commander reported that the range of British radar sets was 35,000 metres. The task force was unable to shake off the enemy in the fog. Two enemy ships, Norfolk and Suffolk, kept contact throughout the night and reported all movements of the Bismarck group by reconnaissance signals.

In addition, radio interception picked up various urgent operational messages, which pointed to the commitment of heavy enemy forces. The course of the Bismarck group was given by the enemy as varying from 240° to 220°, speed 28 knots.

Considering the general evaluation of the enemy disposition, the encounter with an enemy cruiser patrol in the Denmark Straits to a certain extent came as a surprise to the Fleet Commander, but owing to the complete calm in the enemy radio traffic there was no reason to suppose that any extensive enemy operation was under way to prevent a suspected German advance into the Atlantic. When cruisers Scheer and Hipper made a break-through via the Denmark Straits on their return from the Atlantic, they had also noticed heavy cruisers on patrol and were able to elude the enemy in good time. Hence on sighting the heavy cruiser there was no reason for the Fleet Commander to break off the operation and retire to the east, especially as the very poor visibility made the chances for maintaining contact or for using reconnaissance planes seem very small. But what was most surprising, and of decisive importance for the further course of the operation, was the probability, established for the first time, that the enemy possessed evidently excellently functioning radar equipment. This eliminated entirely the advantage of poor visibility for the break-through of the task force, and prevented a swift escape from the enemy.

*May 24.* At 0543 on May 24 the battle cruiser Hood (Captain Kerr), flying the flag of Vice-Admiral Holland, and the battleship Prince of Wales (Captain Leach) made contact with the Bismarck and the Prinz Eugen. A running fight at a range of between 20,800 and 18,000 metres developed. Of the enemy ships, the Hood was ahead, the Prince of Wales astern. Both ships concentrated fire on the Bismarck. The Bismarck and the Prinz Eugen were proceeding in column. Both ships opened fire on the Hood, which was leading. She received several hits, and five minutes after the engagement began a hit on the stern, probably in the magazine aft, blew her up. Hydrophone observation enabled our ships to avoid several torpedoes from the Hood. After the destruction of the Hood both ships concentrated fire on the Prince of Wales. After certain hits from both ships had been observed she turned off amid clouds of black smoke and then was lost from sight for several hours. The Bismarck received two hits from the Prince of Wales, one of them a low shot beneath the side armour in section 13–14, the other in section 20–21. As a result the Bismarck's speed was reduced; she went down by the bow 1° and the oil tanks were pierced, consequently leaving very strong traces of oil. The maximum speed of the Bismarck was 28 knots. In spite of several near hits, the Prinz Eugen did not suffer any damage.

After the victorious engagement the Fleet Commander continued to proceed south. The position at 1400 was in square AK 11, which is about 240 miles east of the southern tip of Greenland. The Prince of Wales made off for the time being and the cruisers Norfolk and Suffolk maintained contact, which was later resumed by the Prince of Wales also. At noon the Fleet Commander announced his intention of making for St. Nazaire and of releasing the Prinz Eugen to carry on warfare against merchant shipping. If no further engagement ensued, he planned to withdraw during the night.

In the evening Group West sent a radio message (Radiogram 1842) agreeing with the Fleet Commander's proposal to send away the Prinz Eugen to take part in the war against merchant shipping, and expressing the opinion that in case the Fleet Commander is able to elude the enemy, it would seem expedient for the Bismarck to wait for some time in a remote sea area.

The task of shaking off the enemy was obviously made more difficult by the reduced speed, the enemy's long-range radar sets, and the heavy traces of oil resulting from the hit. It is not known whether after the engagement the Fleet Commander considered the possibility of turning back to the north or the east towards Norway, or what was responsible for his decision to put into St. Nazaire. Presumably the Fleet Commander thought that the chances of throwing off the enemy were much better in the south than in the north, and in particular his fear of enemy destroyers and planes, especially planes from the carrier Victorious, probably led him to rate the danger in the southern area as less than in the northern area.

Group West, directing the operations from Germany, intended in agreement with the Naval Staff, to move our forces so as to draw the enemy forces into our submarine operational area. Preparatory orders were given to the submarines and to the Fleet Commander, who himself suggested assembling the submarines that were in the west of square AJ 68 for an attack on the heavy enemy forces at dawn on

May 25.   During May 24 the Fleet Commander did not succeed in throwing off the contact which the enemy, apparently using very good radar sets, very skilfully maintained on the edge of the horizon.   At 1944, in the evening, when visibility was very poor, the Bismarck again advanced to attack the Prince of Wales and the shadowing cruisers and thereby enabled cruiser Prinz Eugen to withdraw to refuel and to carry on warfare against merchant shipping.   The Fleet Commander failed in his subsequent attempt to escape during the fog, since the enemy maintained contact with the Bismarck by radar.   In the evening growing fuel difficulties arising from loss of oil forced the Fleet Commander to decide to make straight for St. Nazaire.   For this reason the plan for the attack by submarines next morning in the rendezvous square unfortunately had to be abandoned.

In the meantime the enemy had succeeded in bringing up additional British naval forces.   Constant reports from the shadowing forces made it possible to send torpedo aircraft from the carrier Victorious (Captain Bovell) to attack the Bismarck.

At 2238 came the first torpedo attack by the carrier planes on the Bismarck, which was evidently unsuccessful.   The attacks were repeated in the course of the evening, and towards midnight, as reported by the Fleet Commander at 0028 there was a torpedo hit on the Bismarck.   It had no effect on the ship's combat readiness, but possibly caused a further reduction in her speed.   According to survivor's statements the torpedo attacks were carried out by twenty-seven carrier planes; of these apparently five were shot down by anti-aircraft gunfire.   Only one plane is supposed to have reached the carrier again, according to information presumably obtained by the ship's radio intelligence service from the carrier's radio traffic.   As according to the Admiralty report the attack was carried out from a great distance, it is highly probable that there were severe aircraft losses, particularly since there were no air attacks on the following days.

As the submarines in the west could no longer contact the enemy on the Bismarck's present course, five submarines which were en route to or from the zone of operation were ordered to take up positions in a line across the course of the Bismarck between B 64 and BF 44.

Preparatory measures were taken for reconnaissance and escort aircraft and light naval forces to meet the Bismarck in the coastal waters of the Atlantic coast. Long-range air reconnaissance far to the west was ordered for May 25.

The Prince of Wales, which since the first encounter early on May 24 had kept at a very great distance from the Bismarck, maintained contact throughout the night, along with Norfolk and Suffolk.

*May* 25.   Radio monitoring fixed the time of the last enemy contact report at 0213, the location, 56° 49′ N.   Enemy radio continued to be busy with urgent operational and tactical messages.   Evidently at this time the enemy had temporarily lost contact.   However, he regained it at dawn and according to the report of the Fleet Commander at 0700 on May 25 the Prince of Wales and the two cruisers were still shadowing the Bismarck in square AK 55.   From the radio traffic it can be gathered that the Bismarck, presumably making use of poorer visibility, succeeded in withdrawing from the enemy at about 1100 in the morning. As before, the enemy radio traffic was extremely busy.   In the course of the day and in the evening and night several urgent operational messages from the British home area and the western part of the Channel were picked up, as well as messages communicating with Force H and with the 3rd Battleship Squadron (Canada), all pointing to comprehensive measures for searching for the Bismarck.   Force H, which with battle cruiser Renown, aircraft carrier Ark Royal, and cruiser Sheffield under the command of Vice-Admiral Sir James Somerville, had already put out from Gibraltar on an unknown course during the night of May 23, was presumed by radio monitoring to be on convoy escort in the eastern Atlantic.   Actually, on May 25 the force was on its way north from Gibraltar.   According to a British Admiralty report of May 27, the enemy, besides bringing up Force H, committed the main strength of the Home Fleet under the command of Admiral Tovey in battleship King George V (Captain Patterson), which advanced from northern Scottish water to the south-west.   At the same time the two battleships Rodney and Ramillies approached from convoy escort duties in the North Atlantic.   The movements of the naval forces were supported and supplemented by comprehensive air reconnaissance by planes of the Coastal Command in Britain and from the Canadian base in Newfoundland.   At noon on May 25 the prevailing impression was that the enemy was concentrating his superior heavy forces for attack on the Bismarck in the sea area between 43° N and 52° N beyond the range of German aircraft, i.e. somewhat west of longitude 15° W. The enemy did not succeed in re-establishing contact in the course of May 25. There could be no doubt about the gravity of the Bismarck's situation at that time, however. There was no possibility of relieving her with our naval or air forces. In view of this situation, the Naval Staff suggested to the Fleet Commander to consider putting in at a harbour in northern Spain, should further developments make such action necessary. It is probable that the Fleet Commander, when he escaped from the enemy on May 25, considered the possibility of withdrawing into the open Atlantic. If he had done so for the purpose of refueling from one of the tankers north of the Azores, the Fleet Commander might have succeeded in preventing the enemy from quickly regaining contact. Even a temporary withdrawal would have forced the enemy to stop his convoys or to resume the protection of convoy routes by means of his fast forces as soon as possible. It must be assumed that owing to the fuel situation the Fleet Commander was unable to push out into the Atlantic in such a manner, and hence was forced to proceed directly to St. Nazaire, in spite of the great risk involved in such a course. Possibly the oil traces influenced his decision also.

The Fleet Commander was confirmed in his decision by a radio message from Group West on the night of May 25, communicating the assumption of the Group that the Bismarck would proceed directly to a harbour in western France, even if there were no longer any contact with the enemy.

*May 26.* The Bismarck, however, did not succeed in evading enemy contact much longer. In spite of the unfavourable weather the determined enemy air reconnaissance succeeded in renewing contact; at 1030 on May 26 the Bismarck was sighted by a Catalina plane of Coastal Command, approximately in square BE 16, 600 miles west of Lands End. Anti-aircraft gunfire from the Bismarck caused the plane to lose contact, but a little later carrier aircraft from the Ark Royal (Captain Maund) finally located the ship and with short interruptions maintained contact throughout the day. The weather was: North-west wind 7 to 8, showers, varying visibility. The task of our reconnaissance aircraft which set out from the Atlantic coast as planned, was rendered much more difficult by these weather conditions.

About 1115 a wheeled plane from the carrier Ark Royal located the Bismarck and thus established contact for Force H coming from the south. This marked the beginning of the unfortunate developments in the withdrawal of the Bismarck.

At 1115 the Fleet Commander reported his position in square BE 27, 600 miles west of Brest. In the afternoon he received instructions to make for Brest, since he would not be able to pass the bar off St. Nazaire if the bad weather in the Bay of Biscay continued. Our Air Force received orders from the *Reichsmarschall* to safeguard the Bismarck's return passage with all forces available in the western area and to insure her protection in coastal waters. In spite of unfavourable weather conditions, four FW 200 reconnaissance planes, exploiting their full range, attempted to cover loosely the sea area between 43° 30′ N and 54° N up to longitude 25° W. Other forces tried to insure an adequate survey of the northern part of the area, as far as about 19° W, and the southern part as far as 14° W. The north-west storms in the Bay of Biscay unfortunately did *not* allow use of the destroyers available on the Atlantic coast to relieve and later meet the Bismarck.

Throughout the day the enemy maintained contact with the Bismarck with carrier planes from the Ark Royal and reconnaissance forces from Coastal Command. At 1620 a British plane reported the position of the Bismarck as 47° 40′ N, 18° 15′ W, course 120°, speed 22 knots.

The Commander of Force H sent the cruiser Sheffield (Captain Larcom) to contact the Bismarck while he himself with the Renown and the Ark Royal kept outside the range of the German Air Force throughout the day.

British reports stated that carrier aircraft from the Ark Royal sent to carry out a torpedo attack on the Bismarck in the afternoon, met with no success. Obviously, due to the prevailing weather conditions, the planes did not get near the Bismarck but passed her.

In the afternoon reconnaissance signals from the aircraft led the cruiser Sheffield to the Bismarck.   At 1824 the Fleet Commander reported the Sheffield's position in square BE 5311, course 115°, speed 24 knots.

The establishment of visual contact with the Bismarck by the cruiser Sheffield was of particular importance for the further course of the action, since the enemy was now in a position to direct the torpedo aircraft in an attack on the Bismarck.

Our Air Force was considerably hampered by the prevailing weather conditions and by the distance involved.   In the afternoon the Bismarck was still outside the effective range of our bomber units.   In spite of this, at 1620 air reconnaissance succeeded in locating an enemy battleship escorted by three destroyers in square BE 2120, 200 miles from the position of the Bismarck, course 170°.   This was the Rodney (Captain Dalrymple Hamilton) who had been diverted from convoy escort in the eastern North Atlantic to the attack against the Bismarck.   No other enemy forces were sighted during the afternoon.   Six of our submarines, four with and two without torpedoes, were sent as a protection north-east of the route to be followed by the Bismarck.   At 1900, U.48, which was in square BF 71, received orders to proceed at top speed to operate against the shadowing cruiser Sheffield.   The submarine did not come to the point of firing however.

In the meantime a report from the Fleet Commander indicated that the fuel supply of the Bismarck had become still worse as a result of oil losses caused by gunfire and torpedo hits; the Fleet Commander requested information as to the possibilities of refueling.   Group West thereupon made plans to send out the supply ship Ermland for refueling during the night of May 26.

During the evening of May 26 the Bismarck, followed as she was by vastly superior forces, was in a very difficult position.   However, there was still reason to hope that, with her guns and engines still unimpaired, she could manage to evade attacks from torpedo aircraft throughout the night and could be afforded substantial relief and support in the morning within easy range of our Air Force.

The decisive turn for the worse came during the evening of May 26.   As a result of successful all-out torpedo attacks by carrier planes from the Ark Royal between 2050 and 2115, the enemy made two torpedo hits on the Bismarck; the first hit the ship astern, the second amidships.   Severe casualties were caused.   Survivors stated that of the thirty-five attacking aircraft, seven were brought down by the ship's anti-aircraft guns.

The torpedo hit astern was the decisive blow; by destroying the steering gear it made the ship incapable of holding a course for our bases.

In the meantime the enemy carried out the final moves necessary to surround the ship, now most severely handicapped in manoeuvring.   At 2000 U 566 (Lieut. Wohlfarth) in square BE 5332 made contact with a battleship of the King George class and the aircraft carrier Ark Royal, which passed unescorted on a straight course quite near the submarine.   It was a tragic accident that just this very submarine, returning from an operation, had no torpedoes left.   After a short time the submarine lost contact in a squall of rain.   At 2015 a German weather ship reported a heavy cruiser of the London class at 45° N 20° W proceeding at high speed on an easterly course.   Urgent operational messages, including some addressed to the Commander, 4th British Destroyer Flotilla (Captain Vian) and some to Force H, ordered the destroyers to attack and gave directions to Force H. At 2325 the Fleet Commander himself reported that he was surrounded by the Renown and light naval forces.

According to reconnaissance and radio intercept reports, the following British vessels were in the battle area around the Bismarck in the evening:

| | |
|---|---|
| Battleships: | King George. |
| | Rodney. |
| | Renown. |
| | possibly also the Prince of Wales. |
| | Ramillies is en route. |
| Aircraft carrier: | Ark Royal. |
| Heavy cruisers: | Norfolk, another cruiser of the London class (probably Dorsetshire). |
| Light cruisers: | Sheffield, and probably another light cruiser. |
| Destroyers: | 4th Destroyer Flotilla with several modern destroyers of the Tribal class (Cossack, Maori, Zulu, Sikh). More destroyers approaching. |

In view of the vast enemy superiority the Bismarck, incapable as she was of manoeuvring, was in a hopeless position. This fact was all the more tragic since, according to a report from the Fleet Command, the ship was perfectly fit for action as regards guns and engines, despite the heavy hits sustained; it was only the damage to the steering gear, which under the very unfavourable weather conditions made her incapable of holding to a course towards the coast.

At 2352 the Fleet Commander reported:

"Ship unmanoeuvreable. We shall fight to the last shell. Long live the Fuehrer."

A further radio message to the Fuehrer of the German Reich, Adolf Hitler, ran as follows:

"We shall fight to the last in our faith in you, my Fuehrer, and in unshakable trust in Germany's victory.

FLEET COMMANDER."

In reply the Fuehrer thanked the Fleet Commander and sent the following message to the crew of the battleship Bismarck:

"All Germany is at your side. Everything still possible will be done. Your exemplary conduct will be an inspiration to our people in their struggle for existence."

ADOLF HITLER.

The appraisal of the situation on the evening of May 26 resulted in the impression that the enemy had obviously not decided to make a strong attack in order to destroy the Bismarck. It was to be expected that he would first attempt to cripple the Bismarck further by additional torpedo attacks by planes and light forces during the night; afterwards he would bring up the heavy forces and force the Bismarck to the final engagement.

A survey of the possibilities of coming to the aid of the Bismarck led to the following conclusions:

The Bismarck was 400 miles distant from Brest. In order to decrease the prospects of attack from enemy torpedo aircraft and possibly from enemy submarines, the ship was forced to keep moving as fast as feasible in the rough sea. This would probably use up the remaining fuel supply, already very low.

The attempt to refuel could be made only if the Bismarck were able to get in the direct vicinity of our coast, where our coastal forces, in particular the air force, could drive off the enemy and make attack by his surface vessels difficult or even impossible. But in view of developments there was no such prospect. It seemed hopeless to try to take the supply ship through the surrounding enemy forces to the rudderless Bismarck.

Tugs were made ready to leave in case there should be a change in the situation or in the weather which would enable the ship to make for a point near the coast after all. From the point of view of seamanship it would be impossible for one or two tugs, together with the ship's engines, to restore the Bismarck's ability to manoeuvre.

The weather conditions still made it impossible for us to send out destroyers. Neither the Gneisenau nor the Scharnhorst could be used, since both ships were under repair and were not ready for operations.

Hence the possibilities of supporting the Bismarck were limited to the determined efforts of the Air Force and the submarines available in the Biscay area. All the submarines in question, with or without torpedoes, were sent to the supposed position of the Bismarck. In the further course of the action they found it impossible to approach the enemy and to effect developments.

*May* 27. According to the available reports, during the night of May 26 there were various encounters between the Bismarck and light enemy forces, whose contact reports were constantly picked up by radio monitoring. The greatly varying accounts of the course of the Bismarck revealed the fact that she was unable to steer and showed that the enemy was also aware of her complete unmanoeuvreability. According to observations by the submarines, which reported gunfire and star shells, and according to the reports from the British Admiralty, light naval forces attacked the Bismarck particularly between midnight and 0100 and between 0400 and 0500. The British Admiralty report that during the night attacks by destroyers of the Tribal class torpedo hits had been scored on the Bismarck, damaging the engines, was not confirmed by statements of the survivors. According to these statements the Bismarck did not receive any torpedo hits during the night, and she succeeded in sinking one of the attacking destroyers with gunfire, and set another one on fire. At 0430 U.74 (Lieut. Kentrat) observed three loud explosions, but was not able to determine any further details.

An enemy attempt to make a dawn attack by torpedo planes from the Ark Royal could not be carried out because of bad visibility. On the morning of May 27 we sent out all available reconnaissance aircraft and bombers to locate and attack the enemy forces surrounding the Bismarck. Besides the long range reconnaissance planes of the 40th Bomber Group and the 406th Coastal Air Group, the available bomber units of the 606th and 100th Bomber groups, as well as Bomber Group 1/28 were brought into action. The planes went to the very limit of their range under unfavourable weather conditions as before. Several times the planes were able to contact the enemy and to attack the cruisers and destroyers with bombs. In spite of all-out efforts they did not succeed in affecting the action around the Bismarck.

We have no precise information about the last engagement of the Bismarck. In his last message at 0625 the Fleet Commander reported the situation unchanged, wind 8 to 9. According to the British Admiralty reports and observations from our own submarines it must be assumed that between 0900 and 1000 the heavy enemy forces engaged the severely damaged Bismarck; at the same time a torpedo attack was made by cruisers and destroyers. One of our reconnaissance planes reported that at 0945 the Bismarck was at 47° 20′ N, 15° 14′ W in an engagement evidently with two heavy and two light cruisers. The British Admiralty reported that the final destruction of the Bismarck was accomplished by a torpedo fired from the heavy cruiser Dorsetshire (Captain Martin).

Fighting a far superior enemy, who had concentrated all his available heavy naval forces for the attack, the battleship Bismarck went down with her flag flying between 1000 and 1100 on May 27.

(signed) ASSMANN

## SIGNALS MADE BY OR TO THE BISMARCK

(Note: H.M.S. Prince of Wales was mistaken for the King George V throughout). *May* 24, 1941.

0552

Am engaging two heavy units.

Fleet Commander.

0632

Battlecruiser probably Hood sunk. Another battleship King George or Renown damaged and turned off. Two heavy cruisers maintaining contact.

Fleet Commander.

0705

Have sunk a battleship in approximate position 63 10N, 32 00W.

Fleet Commander.

0801   To Group North.

(1) Electrical engine room No. 4 broken down.

(2) Port boiler room No. 2 is making water, but can be held. Water in the forecastle.

(3) Maximum speed 28 knots.

(4) Two enemy Radar sets recognised.

(5) Intentions: To put into St. Nazaire. No losses of personnel.

Fleet Commander.

1348   To Naval War Staff and Group West.

1400 approximate position 60 20N, 36 20W. King George with cruiser is maintaining contact. Intention: If no engagement, intend to attempt to shake off enemy during night.

Fleet Commander.

1420   To Prinz Eugen.
Intend to shake off enemy as follows: During rain showers Bismarck will move off on westerly course; Prinz Eugen to maintain course and speed until she is forced to alter course or 3 hours after leaving Bismarck. Following this she is to oil from Belchen or Lothringen and afterwards to engage in cruiser warfare independently. Executive on code word "Hood."

Fleet Commander.

1442   To U-boats.
West boats collect in approx. position 54 10N, 42 10W at dawn. Am approaching from North. Intend to draw heavy units shadowing Bismarck through this area.

Fleet Commander.

1504
(1) English unit K3G made tactical signal at 1223 from appr. position 62 00N, 32 00W.
(2) A/c reports 0825: Sighted 12 merchant ships, 4 destroyers, 030°, 8 knots. Visibility 10 sea miles. Position 56 35N, 14 45W. Position is not exact.

Group West.

1508
Hood annihilated within 5 minutes by gunfire this morning at 0600. King George turned off after being hit. Bismarck's speed limited. Slightly down by bows owing to hit forward.

Fleet Commander.

1511
(1) Air reconnaissance of Scapa has started.
(2) English unit made following to Scapa at 1329: One enemy battleship, 1 enemy cruiser bearing 223°, 8 miles, course 180°. My position is 61° 17′ N, Degrees of longitude were not deciphered, 24 minutes West.

Group West.

(1) Renown, Ark Royal and one Sheffield left Gibraltar on unknown course during night to May 24.
(2) Chief of third battle squadron (Canada) intended to send Royal Sovereign to Norfolk on May 10. Probably into dock.

Group West.

1711
U-boats will be in appr. position 54 10N, 42 10W tomorrow morning.

Group West.

1842
(1) Hearty congratulations.
(2) Preparations being made at St. Nazaire and Brest. Concur with intentions for Prinz Eugen. If possible to shake off enemy withdrawal to remote sea area seems advisable for Bismarck. Assume Bismarck's maximum speed 28 knots. Report when draught is above normal.

Group West.

1914
Short engagement with King George without result. Detached Prinz Eugen to oil. Enemy maintains contact.

Fleet Commander.

1925
(1) 5 U-boats will form patrol line at 0600 between appr. position 54 30 N, 42 40W and 53 50N, 41 30W. One U-boat in appr. position 55 00N, 42 10W. One U-boat in appr. position 54 10N, 40 40W. Attacks only against enemy warships.
(2) Air reconnaissance Scapa today shows 3 battleships. Addition by Group: Dummies are possible.

Group West.

2056
Impossible to shake off enemy owing to Radar. Proceeding directly to Brest owing to fuel situation.

Fleet Commander.

2211

With reference to my 1925 para. 2: In Scapa not 3 battle ships and 3 cruisers as previously reported but only two, probably light cruisers and gunnery training ships.

In the opinion of the Group the enemy is Prince of Wales.

Group West.

2338

Air attack in appr. position 56 50N, 36 20W.

Fleet Commander.

2314

(1) Assume that it is no longer intended to proceed to position 54 10N, 42 10W, but to go directly to St. Nazaire.

(2) Make proposals for development of 5 U-boats in eastern half BE to BF.

(3) Assume earliest E.T.A. is evening of 26th.

Group West.

May 25, 1941

0028

Attack by carrier borne aircraft. Torpedo hit starboard.

Fleet Commander.

0037

Further attacks expected.

Fleet Commander.

0129

(1) Unit "5DL" probably Admiral on King George class battleship repeatedly made three figure tactical signals. Last shadowing report was received at 2234.

(2) Discovery of enemy radar frequency will be valuable for fitting jamming gear later.

Group West.

0153

Torpedo hit of no importance.

Fleet Commander.

0241

West U-boats have been ordered to proceed to the eastward.

Group West.

0252

(1) May 25, afternoon intend to carry out air reconnaissance with FW 200 in area North Spanish coast—Brest—Southern tip of Ireland and as far as possible to the west.

(2) 6 U-boats will form a patrol line between appr. positions 56 10N, 44 00W and 53 30N, 38 10W.

Group West.

0727

0700 appr. position 55 00N, 33 10W. One battleship and 2 heavy cruisers maintaining contact.

Fleet Commander.

0401

Enemy radar gear with a range of at least 35,000 metres interferes with operations in Atlantic to considerable extent. In Denmark Straits ships were located and enemy maintained contact. Not possible to shake off enemy despite most favourable weather conditions. Will be unable to oil unless succeed in shaking off enemy by superior speed. Running engagement at range of 20,800 metres to 18,000 metres. Hood concentrated fire on Bismarck. Hood destroyed through explosion after 5 minutes. After that target shifted to King George which turned off making black smoke after she received some hits and remained out of sight for several hours. Own expenditure of ammunition 93 rounds. After this King George continued action at maximum range. Bismarck received two hits from King George, which reduced the speed and put oil bunkers out of action. Prinz Eugen succeeded in escaping because Bismarck engaged cruisers and battleship in fog. Own radar gear liable to break down, especially when own guns are firing.

Fleet Commander.

0846

Last enemy contact report 0213 from K3G. After that three figure tactical reports but no open position reports. We have impression that contact has been lost. Operational signals are repeated to Bermuda and Halifax but not to Gibraltar or Force H which is suspected to be in Eastern Atlantic.

Group West.

1152

To Fleet Commander.

Heartiest congratulations on your birthday. May you continue to be equally successful in this coming year.

C.-in-C., Navy.

1313

7 U-boats will form patrol line between appr. positions 47 10N, 15 10W and 4500N, 10 50W. One U-boat in appr. position 47 50N, 16 50W.

Group West.

1414

U-boat reports: Appr. position 54 40N, 38 50W. Sighted one destroyer, 050°, high speed.

Group West.

1625

To Fleet Commander.

Best wishes on your birthday.

Adolf Hitler.

1831

With reference to my 0252 reconnaissance carried out to west with gaps. No enemy sighting reports.

Group West.

1932

Strong air forces available for arrival Bismarck. Battle formations up to 14° West. Patrol line in accordance with my 1313 with 5 U-boats in appr. position 47 50N, 16 50W, and 47 50N, 12 20W.

3 destroyers for escort.

Outer channels of Brest and St. Nazaire under control. If necessary possible to put into La Pallice as well. Report when passing 10° West.

Group West.

2344

Assume you will continue directly to French West coast harbour even if no contact with enemy.

Group West.

May 26 1941.

1025

(1) Reconnaissance started according to plan.

(2) Weather situation in Biscay makes extended escort impossible. Therefore only close air cover possible for time being.

Group West.

1154

Enemy aircraft shadowing. Land plane. Appr. position 48 40N, 20 00W.

Fleet Commander.

1156

English aircraft reports to 15th reconnaissance group: 1030—one battleship 140°, speed 20 knots. My appr. position 49 20N, 21 50W.

Group West.

1553

Enemy aircraft reports to Plymouth: Have lost contact with battleship.

Group West.

1713

English aircraft regained contact at 1600.

Group West.

1903

Fuel situation urgent. When can I expect fuel?

Fleet Commander.

**2054.**
Am being attacked by carrier borne aircraft.

Fleet Commander.

**2105**
Ship no longer manoeuvreable.

Fleet Commander.

**2105**
Appr. position 47 40N, 14 50W.   Torpedo hit aft.

Fleet Commander.

**2115**
Torpedo hit amidships.

Fleet Commander.

**2117**
U-boat reports: 2000.   One battleship, one aircraft carrier in appr. position 47 50N, 16 50W.   Course 115°, high speed.

Group West.

**2205**
U-boats ordered to collect in appr. position 47 40N, 14 50W.

Group West.

**2325**
Am surrounded by Renown and light forces.

Fleet Commander.

**2340**
Ship no longer manoeuvreable.   We fight to the last shell.   Long live the Fuehrer.

Fleet Commander.

**2358**
To the Fuehrer of the German Reich Adolf Hitler.   We fight to the last in our belief in you my Fuehrer and in the firm faith in Germany's victory.

Fleet Commander.

**2359**
Armament and engines still intact.   Ship however cannot be steered with engines.

Fleet Commander.

**May 27, 1941.**

**0153**
To Fleet Commander.
I thank you in the name of the German people.

Adolf Hitler.

To the crew of battleship Bismarck:
The whole of Germany is with you.   What can still be done will be done. The performance of your duty will strengthen our people in the struggle for their existence.

Adolf Hitler.

**0221**
To C.-in-C., Navy.
Propose Lt. Cdr. Schneider (Gunnery Officer) be awarded Knight's Cross for sinking Hood.

Fleet Commander.

**0351**
To Lt. Cdr. Schneider.
The Fuehrer has awarded you the Knight's Cross for sinking the battle cruiser Hood.   Heartiest congratulations.

C.-in-C., Navy.

**0710**
Send U-boat to save War Diary.

Fleet Commander.

(This was the last signal made by Bismarck.)

**1322**
To Fleet Commander.
Reuter reports: Bismarck sunk.   Report situation immediately.

Group West.

## SURVIVOR'S REPORT

### (Rescued by U.74)

Statement made by Mtr. Gfr. (Ord. Seaman) Herbert Manthey on the sinking of the battleship Bismarck.

Friday, May 23, 1941 : About 1700 on Friday May 23 a smoke cloud was sighted. At this time I was on my action station No. 5 starboard 2-cm. gun. Immediately afterwards the enemy cruiser opened fire. The cruiser was astern. Bismarck replied with turrets C and D. I do not know how many salvoes were fired. The cruiser thereupon turned off but maintained contact. On the loud speaker system it was announced that the enemy cruiser had made a signal giving Bismarck's position. Half an hour later it was announced that the enemy cruisers were shooting at each other. After that we were relieved. The night was quiet.

Saturday, May 24 : At about 0600 on Saturday, May 24 it was announced over the ship's broadcast that smoke clouds had been sighted. Action stations were sounded. Shortly afterwards the smoke clouds could be seen with the naked eye. At this time I belonged to No. 5 port 2-cm. gun. On action stations the starboard watch came on and I had to change over to No. 5 starboard 2-cm. gun. A few minutes later the first enemy ship opened fire. At this time I did not know which enemy ships were concerned. Shortly afterwards Bismarck and a second enemy ship opened fire. The bridge issued an order concerning the distribution of fire. The two forward turrets fired against the Hood, whilst·the after turrets fired against the King George V. The names of the enemy ships were announced after the action. Three salvoes were fired against the Hood. Whilst this firing was going on the anti-aircraft crews were sent under cover because of the splinter effect and the blast of our own guns. Out of interest in the battle, however, many comrades remained on deck amidships and in the superstructure. During this firing I myself was under cover (deck house). Already after our second salvo had been fired it was announced "enemy is burning," after the third salvo "enemy is exploding." During this engagement with the Hood, the after turrets which were directed from the after control position, had been scoring hits. King George V thereupon turned off. Hood was sunk about the same time. The general enthusiasm was great. It became still greater when it was announced from the bridge that the enemy were the largest British battleships. At the same time it was announced that Hood had been sunk and that King George V had turned off. Only now I heard that yet another enemy cruiser was firing on us. The engagement lasted for about another 10 minutes. At the end of the action we learned that Bismarck had received three hits. In my opinion these three hits were caused by the last enemy heavy cruiser. One hit in the ship's side (at the bows). The second hit went through the starboard picket boat and detonated in the water. Comrades told me that the third hit had gone into the port oil bunker, compartment XV to XVII. I went there myself and saw that oil was pouring out and was also spilled on the upper deck. The damage itself was under water and could not be seen. This was about 2 hours later. At this time it could be noticed that the forecastle lay deeper in the water and that the ship had a very slight list to port. I also heard at this time that the electrical engine room No. IV had broken down owing to penetration of water. A little later it was said that the damage had been repaired by divers and damage control parties. A gunner's mate who belonged to my gun said that only the ship's side had been torn open ; others maintained that the shell had gone through but had not detonated.

At this time the sea was calm and visibility was good. The ship reduced speed and a collision mat was got out on the forecastle and divers were sent down into the ship to find out the damage. I heard that it had been very difficult to get into the compartments full of water. The divers however succeeded in making a pipe connection to the oil bunkers, so that the oil could be pumped aft. In the meantime they succeeded in stopping the leak. As far as I can remember the outboard work took about 2 hours. The ship then increased speed again. During this time pumping was continued below deck. It was continued the whole day as well as the night May 24/25. During Saturday morning I noticed that the forecastle was slowly rising again. On Saturday about noon one flying boat appeared. From the type it was first thought to be a Do 18. From talk I heard I know that a recognition signal was demanded and that the aircraft made the correct answer.

This was announced through the telephone. When the aircraft approached to within 4,000 metres, the anti-aircraft officer Lt. Cdr. Gellert recognised it as an aircraft of American build. Thereupon the 10.5 cm. guns opened fire on the aircraft. The aircraft turned off and tried a few more times to approach again but was forced to turn off every time. The aircraft remained then outside the range but maintained contact.

About 2300 three flights (27 aircraft), bi-planes appeared to attack. First of all they tried to attack together from port. When they could not succeed in this, they attacked singly from starboard, ahead and astern. All available guns including the 38-cm. guns participated in the defence. The attack lasted about an hour and altogether 5 aircraft (according to statements made by my comrades) were shot down. This was confirmed on the order transmission system. I do not know how many aircraft were actually shot down. On my request my anti-aircraft officer Lt. Doelker told me that two flights of torpedo carrying aircraft and one flight of bombers had been involved in the attack. Owing to the continuous zig-zagging (avoiding torpedoes) the anti-aircraft defence was particularly difficult. The aircraft only scored one torpedo hit, starboard amidships, below the aircraft catapult. The torpedo detonated on the ship's side and left merely scratches in the paintwork. Ldg. Seaman Kirchberg who was standing on the starboard 10·5-cm. gun was thrown up by the blast against the hangar and was killed. This was the first fatal casualty on board. I do not know if other comrades were injured.

Shortly after the end of the engagement with the aircraft King George V opened fire on us. Bismarck returned the fire with one or two salvoes. As far as I know no hits were scored on either side. As far as I can remember the night from May 24 to May 25 was quiet. On the telephone it was announced that the enemy was maintaining contact. On May 24 I was on watch on the gun from 2000–2400.

Prinz Eugen I saw for the last time on the morning of May 24 about 0600, when the action with the Hood was in progress. At noon nothing could be seen of her.

Sunday, May 25 : About 0300 on May 15 it was announced through the telephone that of the 27 enemy aircraft which had attacked us only one had returned to the aircraft carrier. At this time the forecastle was again low in the water. Owing to the violent manoeuvres during the air attack the collision mats had broken and water had again penetrated into the forecastle. Speed was reduced, the sea was fairly rough. The damage control parties worked during the whole of Sunday until the next engagement which was on Monday evening May 26. I do not know if the damage control parties continued to work after this engagement on the evening of May 26.

On Sunday May 25 about 1200 the Fleet Commander spoke to the crew. As far as I can remember the Fleet Commander said amongst other things the following : "We were not intended to fight enemy warships but wanted to wage merchant warfare. Through treachery the enemy had managed to find us in the Denmark Straits. We took up the fight. The crew have behaved magnificently. We shall win or die." After the speech of the Fleet Commander the situation became clear to the crew and the mood became serious. On Sunday afternoon a second funnel was built. On this occasion the spirits of the crew rose again. It was piped that the non-duty watch was to go into the second funnel to smoke. Otherwise nothing special occurred on Sunday, May 25.

Monday, May 26 : After the air attack on May 24 both watches ate and slept on their stations. The stations were not left again until the sinking. Enemy shadowing aircraft (2) maintained contact from Monday morning (1000–1100) onwards. Sometimes they tried to approach closer but were each time forced to turn off by the anti-aircraft defence. As far as I know no recognition signals were exchanged. They were two bi-planes. In the evening between 2100–2200 the anti-aircraft control station reported 16 enemy aircraft at great height over the ship. Repel aircraft stations were sounded. They did not try to attack but flew off again. We did not open fire. About 10 minutes later I saw three enemy aircraft (bi-planes) bearing approximately 200°, approach our ship from the clouds. Immediately afterwards aircraft approached us from all sides. It was fairly cloudy. I do not know the exact number of aircraft. All anti-aircraft weapons opened fire. At this time I felt two heavy shakings in the ship, one shortly after the other.

According to statements of my comrades three depth charges lying on the quarterdeck were thrown overboard by the blast of the 38-cm. guns which were firing on a torpedo track. I do not know whether the shakings originated from the depth charges. The attack was broken off after about 30 minutes owing to the heavy anti-aircraft fire.

The attacks were dive-bombing attacks coming from the clouds down to about 10–20 metres above the water. Generally speaking we had the impression that the attacks were made very pluckily. 7 aircraft were shot down. From the main anti-aircraft control position it was announced: "Rudder jamming hard to starboard. Ship goes in circles." I do not know how many torpedoes hit. In my opinion one torpedo hit went aft into the steering compartment and another hit near compartments VII–VIII. Some men were injured on port gun No. 4. Through the telephone I heard that the divers were trying to couple in the hand rudder. After 20–30 minutes we heard again through the ship's telephone that the hand rudder had been coupled in. Shortly afterwards a second report: Rudder absolutely clear again. Whilst the rudder was out of action it was tried to steer the ship with the screws. As far as I can remember the ship after the hit reduced right down from her cruising speed of 24 knots. She was going in circles. By going astern with the screws the ship was put against the sea. When the hand rudder was coupled in, the ship went first of all 13 knots and later increased to 24 knots. When cruising at 24 knots enemy destroyers made an attack (from memory 2400). Action stations were sounded. First of all I did not know whether the attack came from starboard or port, however, I remembered afterwards that it started on the port quarter and a little later shifted to the starboard side. I did not notice that Bismarck made an alteration of course. At this time it was announced over the ship's telephone that one destroyer was sinking and two more burning.

I myself did not see anything of this. During action stations which lasted until about 0700 on Tuesday May 27 the enemy continuously fired starshells. Occasionally it became clear as day. On Monday night various congratulatory telegrams arrived, amongst them one from the Fuehrer awarding the Knight's Cross of the Iron Cross to the Senior Gunnery Officer. The Captain read these telegrams to the crew. Furthermore 81 aircraft were promised for the next day. One U-boat was supposed to be very near to us and all U-boats had been warned. One tanker and two tugs were also on the way to help us. These announcements lifted the morale of the crew again. Many sang. Otherwise nothing on Monday.

Tuesday, May 27: About 0200 more enemy destroyers had approached to within 3,000 metres. The 38-cm., 15-cm., and 10·5-cm. guns were firing. The 3·7-cm. and 2-cm. guns had orders to wait for special permission to open fire. Of these destroyers one was set on fire; this I observed myself as she was on the starboard beam. Before the attack of the destroyers, i.e., before 0200 an aircraft made a dive-bombing attack from the clouds. Anti-aircraft fire forced the aircraft to turn off. The action with the destroyers lasted until about 0600. No torpedo or gunnery hits were scored. Bismarck was making way until this time (0600) I do not know the speed. About 0600 a stand-easy was ordered. I do not know for what reason. She had a slight list to port. Heavy seas. The waves came up to the upper deck. During the night an attempt was made to start the ship's aircraft, but did not succeed. Reason: No compressed air and too much pitching. One aircraft was thrown overboard. It drifted in the water with the floats on top.

During the stand-easy it was piped: All non-duty officers into the charthouse. Immediately afterwards action stations were sounded. Nothing could be seen of the enemy. It was said that smoke clouds had been sighted. Before our own guns fired, enemy shells dropped close to the ship. After about one hour the first hits were scored on our ship. I myself was wearing the telephone. The connection broke off. I took off the telephone. From this time onwards no orders were given by the anti-aircraft control to my gun. As the hits increased the anti-aircraft crews went under cover. We had the impression that we were fired at from all sides. First I was with a group of 20 men in the after gunnery position. After a few hits close by we fled behind the turrets C and D on the upper deck. Before that we threw about 5–6 rafts on the deck below and went with the rafts behind the turrets. Through a hit all rafts except one or two were destroyed. We had now several injured. At this time turret D was still firing. At this time my comrade Herzog came to me. We saw a carley float between turret C and D.

With the help of several others we released it.   This carley float we pulled behind turret D.   There several comrades left us.   Through a hit which went into the water, i.e., the wave, the carley float and we three were thrown overboard.   Nobody was actually on the float.   We all three swam towards the float.   We only succeeded in reaching it after about 15 minutes as hit after hit landed in the water.   Near-by another raft was drifting with one injured and 5–6 other comrades.   In the carley float we drifted astern.   The ship herself we only saw when we were on top of a wave.   Once I saw the Bismarck was getting a list to port.   It appeared that the ship had made a little way to port.   Shortly afterwards I could see Bismarck no longer, but only a smoke cloud.   I did not hear an explosion.   Not far from us I saw two cruisers making towards the place where Bismarck was.   These cruisers were firing.   We had nothing to eat or drink in the raft.   The raft which in the beginning had been near us had gone out of sight.   I do not know what time we were washed overboard.   When the sun was directly over us and we had practically given up all hope of being rescued, we sighted a "Kondor" or FW 200.   We waved to it but could not ascertain whether we had been seen.

We felt tired.   My comrade Herzog had been injured in the foot.   In the evening shortly before 1900 a U-boat suddenly surfaced close to us.   We were taken on board and immediately packed into bunks and fed.   The U-boat—she was U.74—searched for two days for survivors. Only corpses and wreckage were sighted.

I do not know about the radar gear.   I did not hear anything about it on board.

I do not know anything about damage to the W/T station.   Neither did I see whether the aerials had been shot away.

(signed) HERBERT MANTHEY.

*     *     *     *     *     *

The operation was reported to Hitler on June 6.


Naval Staff.

### REPORT OF THE C.-IN-C., NAVY, TO THE FUEHRER ON JUNE 6, 1941, AT THE BERGHOF

Also present: Chief of Staff, O.K.W.
Colonel Schmundt.
Captain von Puttkamer.

1. The course of the Bismarck operation is discussed.—*The Fuehrer* inquires why the Fleet Commander did not return to port after the engagement with the Hood.   *The C.-in-C., Navy*, replies that a break through the northern straits would have been a far more dangerous undertaking than a withdrawal to the Atlantic.   The Fleet Commander was doubtless trying to achieve this as long as his fuel supplies permitted, in the hope of shaking off shadowers and finally making for St. Nazaire.   Tankers were available in the Atlantic.   A return break-through to the north would have incurred great risk of attack from numerous aircraft and light naval forces.   The Fleet Commander's original intention of making a big detour before setting course for St. Nazaire is indicated by the fact that he hoped to draw the enemy across the line of submarines established by Group West and the Admiral Commanding Submarines on May 25.   This plan had to be given up when it became clear that the loss of oil was too great to permit such a detour.   Even the suggestion from Group West to lie low for some time in a remote area after shaking off the enemy could not be followed.

*The Fuehrer* inquires further why the Bismarck did not rely on her fighting strength and attack the Prince of Wales again in order to destroy her after the Hood had been sunk, even if it meant an all-out fight.   Even if this had led to the loss of the Bismarck, the final score would have been two British losses against one German one. *The C.-in-C., Navy*, replies that the Bismarck re-engaged the Prince of Wales on May 24 in order to make the withdrawal of the Prinz Eugen possible. After the Hood sank, however, the Prince of Wales carefully retired out of effective firing range, just as the other heavy enemy ships evidently did later. (The Bismarck's speed is only 28 knots.) Furthermore, the Fleet Commander had to keep his main object in view, that of "damaging enemy merchant shipping," as long as the Bismarck and Prinz Eugen were in a position to do so. Had he forced an action with the Prince of Wales, he would have had to count on severe damage even if he were successful, which would have interfered with operations against merchant shipping. His task was to fight only when the enemy prevented him from attacking merchant shipping. If it had not been for the fatal hit in the steering gear in all probability the Bismarck would have reached the area in which the German Air Force could have provided effective support and could have carried out repairs in St. Nazaire. Seen in retrospect a defeat of the Prince of Wales would naturally have been a greater achievement than the Bismarck's heroic sinking without having accounted for a second enemy ship.

2. Permission to wage warfare against U.S. merchant shipping according to prize regulations is discussed. *The Fuehrer* is of the opinion that for the time being no change should be made in the present situation. The question of searching American merchant ships is to be postponed until units of the fleet are sent to operate in the Atlantic.

3. Considerations with reference to the strategic situation in the Eastern Mediterranean and the further conduct of the war in this area are discussed. *The C.-in-C., Navy*, requests that the Italian Naval Staff should be pressed to intensify attacks on British supply routes with light naval forces, and to improve protection of Italo-German supply lines. The transport of supplies in fast vessels via Greece and Crete to Benghazi and Derna should be organised. *The Fuehrer* approves a meeting between the C.-in-C., Navy, and Admiral Riccardi on this matter. He will write to the Duce to facilitate this. He suggests that old torpedo boats, etc., be converted for fast transport of ammunition, etc. They would have only anti-aircraft armament; the transport would take place during the day with good air support and reconnaissance. The Chief of Staff, O.K.W. has discussed the withdrawal of Italian submarines from the Atlantic with the Chief of the Italian Armed Forces. Both reasons necessitating this were given: Our own need of Bordeaux, and the need for Italian submarines in the Mediterranean.

4. Special items.—*The Fuehrer* sanctions release of an official report concerning the Bismarck operation.

5. *The Fuehrer* permits that Admiral Feige be informed of the general plan for operation "Barbarossa" so that he can take the necessary measures for withdrawing valuable personnel.

(signed) RAEDER.

# 1941: CHAPTER III

# Russia and the Mediterranean

ON JUNE 22 the *Wehrmacht* invaded Russia. The operation had been originally planned to begin some five weeks earlier but had been delayed by the events in the Balkans. It was the opinion of German historians that had Hitler not been forced to support the Italians against the British and Greek forces in Greece, it is possible that the Eastern campaign would have followed a very different course. Beginning rather late in the campaign season Hitler allowed insufficient time to consolidate the German advance before the onslaught of winter.

\*       \*       \*       \*       \*       \*

On the day before the invasion of Russia Raeder conferred with Hitler on the Battle of the Atlantic.

Naval Staff.                                                                    Berlin, June 24, 1941

CONFERENCE OF THE C.-IN-C., NAVY, WITH THE
FUEHRER IN THE AFTERNOON OF JUNE 21, 1941

Also present: Chief of Staff, O.K.W.
General Jodl.
Captain von Puttkamer.
also Professor Speer during discussion of point 1.

1. *The C.-in-C., Navy*, reports on a plan for a large shipyard at Trondheim on the Gulosen Fiord. *The Fuehrer* agrees and instructs Professor Speer to investigate the surrounding country with a view to building a German city.

2. *The C.-in-C., Navy*, using a map, shows the encounter of U 203 with the U.S. battleship Texas and a U.S. destroyer in the closed area. The ships were sighted about ten miles inside the boundary of the closed area; U 203 chased and attempted to attack them as far as about 140 miles to the north-east and back within the closed area; then the ships left the area on a south-west course. No opportunity to attack occurred on account of zig-zag courses and unfavourable weather. The C.-in-C., Navy, is of the opinion that this incident as well as that of the Robin Moor is welcome, because the character of the proceedings make it quite clear to the U.S.A. that the warning was meant in earnest. He states that where the U.S.A. is concerned firm measures are always more effective than apparent yielding. In the case of the Robin Moor, the C.-in-C., Navy, had already given instructions that, for the present, the Fuehrer wishes to avoid incidents with U.S.A. warships and merchant ships outside the closed area under all circumstances. For the closed area, clearly defined orders will be necessary which will not involve submarines in confused and dangerous situations, and which can be carried out. By day under normal conditions a submarine can recognise U.S. battleships and cruisers and avoid attack. By night, on the other hand, no such guarantee can be given. An appropriate order is therefore not possible. The C.-in-C., Navy, proposes a 50 or 100 mile strip inside the boundary of the closed area, inside which attacks on U.S. warships should be avoided.

*The Fuehrer* declares in detail that until operation "Barbarossa" is well under way he wishes to avoid any incident with the U.S.A. After a few weeks the situation will become clearer, and can be expected to have a favourable effect on the U.S.A. and Japan; America will have less inclination to enter the war, due to the threat from Japan which will then increase. If possible, therefore, in the next weeks all attacks on naval vessels in the closed area should cease, especially since in the past few months such attacks have been exceptions in any case. *The C.-in-C., Navy*, agrees that such an order could be given; all the same, at night naval vessels, e.g., those escorting a convoy, might be hit unintentionally, like in the Malaya case. Such a ruling would therefore provide no guarantee either. *The Fuehrer* decides that this order must be issued nevertheless, so that incidents are eliminated as far as possible. *The C.-in-C., Navy*, issues the following order to the Admiral Commanding Submarines, with instructions to inform the submarines of the reason for this order:

Berlin, June 21, 1941

To: 1. Submarine Division of the Naval Staff.

2. O.K.W., National Defence.

Subject: Offensive operations against naval vessels.

I. Today the C.-in-C., Navy, conferred with the Fuehrer on this subject.
II. Result.—The Fuehrer desires absolutely to avoid any possibility of incidents with the U.S.A. until the development of operation "Barbarossa" becomes clearer, i.e., for a few weeks.
III. The following is therefore ordered:

1. For the time being no attacks on naval vessels are to take place either inside or outside the closed area.
2. The only exceptions to this are ships definitely recognised as enemy ones, from cruisers upwards (cruisers, battleships, and aircraft carriers).

IV. (Addition for the Admiral Commanding Submarines, only):

The C.-in-C., Navy, desires that the explanation of these orders as under Paragraph II be included when the order is transmitted to the submarines, in order to acquaint the commanders with the reason for these restrictive orders.
(Addition for the O.K.W. only, omitting Paragraph IV):
Attention is drawn to the necessity for similar orders to the Air Force also.

It seemed expedient to add a paragraph concerning permission to attack any ships definitely recognised as British (battleships, aircraft carriers, and cruisers), a measure likewise endorsed by General Jodl. Also necessary were the instructions concerning the Air Force, as it might find itself in even more difficult situations than the Navy.

(signed) RAEDER.

\*        \*        \*        \*        \*        \*

The importance of the Mediterranean was partly recognised by the O.K.W., and towards the end of June directives and orders were issued for the further prosecution of the war after the invasion of Russia had ended. Briefly these plans were to attack British positions in the Mediterranean and Asia Minor. Three separate operations were envisaged: the first an attack against Egypt from Libya, the second an attack against Asia Minor from Bulgaria through Turkey, and the third an attack against Iran from positions which were to be won in the Transcaucasus. Pending the success of operation "Barbarossa" and to maintain the situation in the Mediterranean the *Afrika Korps* and the *Luftwaffe* were reinforced, while the German Navy was ordered to co-operate with the Italians and to prepare the necessary sea transport.

*      *      *      *      *      *

The United States of America now began to take a more active part in the war, and on July 7 President Roosevelt announced that U.S. Naval forces were to be sent to Iceland. The effect on Germany was immediate and on July 9 Raeder sought a decision from Hitler as to whether the German Navy could now attack American ships.

C.-in-C., Navy.                                    Berlin, July 10, 1941

## CONFERENCE OF THE C.-IN-C., NAVY, WITH THE FUEHRER AT HEADQUARTERS WOLFSSCHANZE IN THE AFTER-NOON OF JULY 9, 1941

Also present:   Chief of Staff, O.K.W.
                C.-in-C., Air.
                Minister of Foreign Affairs.
                General Jodl.
                Chief of the Air Force General Staff.
                Captain von Puttkamer.

1. The Occupation of Iceland by the U.S.A.—*The C.-in-C., Navy,* reports on the situation. He requests a decision on the question of whether from the political viewpoint the occupation of Iceland by the U.S.A. is to be considered as an entry into the war, or as an act of provocation which should be ignored. *The Fuehrer* explains in detail that he is most anxious to postpone the United States entry into the war for another one or two months. On the one hand the Eastern Campaign must be carried on with the entire Air Force, which is ready for this task and which he does not wish to divert even in part; on the other hand, a victorious campaign on the Eastern Front will have a tremendous effect on the whole situation and probably also on the attitude of the U.S.A. Therefore for the time being he does not wish the existing instructions changed, but rather wants to be sure that incidents will be avoided. It is thus permissible to attack merchant ships in the closed area without warning; American merchant ships, however, are to be spared as far as possible, when they are definitely recognised as such. *The C.-in-C., Navy,* states in this connection that no guarantee can be given, and that a commander cannot be held responsible for a mistake. *The Fuehrer* agrees.

Warships are, as before, not to be attacked in the closed area, unless they are definitely established as enemy ships from cruisers up, or it is unmistakable that they are attacking.

2. North-west Africa.—*The C.-in-C., Navy,* points out emphatically how important it is for the outcome of the war that France keep a firm hold on North-west Africa. If the U.S.A. or Britain were to gain posession of Dakar and the rest of the coast, it would be a severe threat to our ability to carry on the war in the Atlantic; the position of the Axis forces in North

Africa would also be severely menaced. Therefore France must receive all the help necessary to hold North-west Africa. *The Chief of Staff, O.K.W.*, states that all the military requirements of France in connection with Dakar will be met. *The Fuehrer* is very distrustful of France and considers her counter-demands excessive. *The C.-in-C., Navy*, once again emphasises the decisive strategic significance of keeping a firm hold on North-west Africa in view of probable plans of the U.S.A. and Britain to drive the French out of that area.

3. The Internment of Russian Warships in Sweden.—*The C.-in-C., Navy*, refers to the possibility that Russian ships may be interned in Sweden. The Naval Staff will try by every possible means to prevent Russian naval forces from breaking out of the Gulf of Finland. If single vessels should be interned in Sweden, pressure must be brought to bear at once on that country to hand over the ships to Germany until Russia has been defeated. *The Fuehrer* instructs the Minister of Foreign Affairs to consider what steps to take.

(signed) RAEDER.

*     *     *     *     *     *

Although the campaign against Russia was proceeding well Hitler was anxious about possible British attacks on his Western Front. On July 19 he ordered that: "In the West and the North all three branches of the Armed Forces must bear in mind the question of possible English attacks against the Channel Islands and against the Norwegian coast. Preparations must be made for a quick transfer of aircraft from the West to all parts of Norway."

It was the duty of the German Navy during the invasion of Russia to be the principal bulwark against an attack on the Western Front, and on July 25 Raeder reported to Hitler.

C.-in-C., Navy.

### CONFERENCE OF THE C.-IN-C., NAVY, WITH THE FUEHRER IN WOLFSSCHANZE IN THE AFTERNOON OF JULY 25, 1941

(The Chief of Staff, O.K.W. was not present.) A verbal report on the conference was subsequently made to General Jodl.

1. A report is made on the general situation in naval warfare against Britain.

(*a*) *The Fuehrer* declares that there is absolutely no reason for the concern of the C.-in-C., Navy, that he has changed his view as to the great importance of the blockade against Britain by submarines and the Air Force. His original view has undergone no changes whatsoever. He would, however, like to avoid having the U.S.A. declare war while the Eastern Campaign is still in progress, also out of consideration for the Army which is involved in heavy combat. But he will never call a submarine commander to account if he torpedoes an American ship by mistake. After the Eastern Campaign he reserves the right to take severe action against the U.S.A. as well.

With regard to our attitude towards France, the Fuehrer declares that France's attitude toward us has changed since the withdrawal of our *panzer* divisions. France's political demands have been increasing since that time. He will therefore probably move the two *panzer* divisions, which have just recently been formed in Germany, to the west in the near future. Then France will become more amenable. He can under no circumstances prejudice our relations with Italy by making concessions to France. He cannot allow our relations with Italy to deteriorate.

As soon as the U.S.A. occupies Portuguese or Spanish islands, he will march into Spain; he will send *panzer* and infantry divisions to North Africa from there, in order to defend North Africa.

(*b*) Surface Ships.—Their effectiveness is limited by their small numbers and by the lack of a naval air arm. In spite of that, they are carrying out decisive offensive warfare against merchant ships, which is the *only* way to conquer Britain. The growing superiority of the British naturally increases the risk involved. (The incorrect use of the Air Force is now having its effect. In spite of constant requests by the Naval Staff, the Air Force did not attack aircraft carriers and battleships under construction, or the forces lying in Scapa Flow. This would have improved the situation at sea a great deal). It is possible that the surface forces will gradually be destroyed. This possibility, however, must not be allowed to keep surface ships from continuing to operate in the war against merchant ships. The fact that they are operating, or even just the possibility that they will appear in the Atlantic, supports submarine warfare to a great degree. The British are obliged to protect their convoys with strong forces. If these forces were free, they could operate with a very disturbing effect at other places, for instance, in the Mediterranean and in the Far East, i.e., Singapore. Moreover, the British would be able to strengthen their anti-submarine defences at the expense of the escort forces, as in the World War, when our fleet ceased offensive operations and the British fleet became inactive accordingly. For these reasons it is urgently necessary to maintain and operate the small German surface fleet. Naturally, favourable circumstances should be fully exploited; bases in Spain, as at Ferrol and places farther south, are most useful. The fact that the British are making great sacrifices in order to keep the battleships from leaving port shows how much they fear the appearance of battleships on the ocean. (In the attack on the Scharnhorst in La Pallice on July 24, 1941, twelve four-engined bombers out of fifteen were shot down). *The Fuehrer* agrees with this view.

(*c*) *The C.-in-C., Navy,* points out that the Air Force considers reconnaissance an inferior task, since it does not show immediate results. *The Fuehrer* states that he will see to it that decorations are given to reconnaissance pilots.

(*d*) *The C.-in-C., Navy,* brought up the question of the use of smoke screens in Brest. *The Fuehrer* will settle the question according to the wishes of the Navy, since the Navy is entirely right.

2. Naval situation in the Eastern Campaign.

(*a*) Situation in the Arctic Ocean.—The importance of capturing Murmansk has been emphasised repeatedly by the Navy. The longer the capture of this harbour is deferred, the more incentive is offered to Britain to gain a foothold there; she has been interested in this Russian port of access to the Atlantic for a long time. The left wing of the Army group under Dietl is brought to a standstill indirectly by the flanking position of the Ribachi Peninsula, and directly by the troops in the strip of land 10 kilometres long between Titovka Bay and Litsa Bay. Only the innermost tip of the latter is in German hands.    Consequently it is possible for the destroyer flotilla to enter Motovski Bay only if a motor mine sweeper flotilla is provided and moreover if there is adequate fighter protection in view of the air situation.    Two submarines are in the operational area off the Ribachi Peninsula, and two more are to leave Trondheim on or after July 24 to be at the disposal of the Admiral Commanding, Norway.    *The Fuehrer* agrees.

(b) Situation in the Gulf of Finland.—The Army's thrust along the eastern edge of Lake Peipus towards Narva to the north and Leningrad to the north-east, during which the left wing weakened and fell back, afforded the enemy sufficient time to sweep enough mines to be able to operate in the area between Reval (Tallinn) and the Baltic islands with disturbing effect, and to attack our supply lines by sea and our right wing.    At the present time the enemy feels the pressure against the Bay of Kronstadt more strongly than against the western sector of the Gulf of Finland; instead of our tying up the bag, so to speak, he is being squeezed out of it from beneath.    This may result in an undesirable transfer of enemy forces to the west, and, if he loses his last base, he may make a desperate attempt to break through to Swedish territorial waters. While a break-through out of the Bay of Kronstadt must seem pretty hopeless even to the enemy if the coast of Estonia is in our hands, if we hold only the Baltic islands and Hangoe, such a break-through can be made more difficult by the use of more submarines and motor boats, but it cannot be prevented entirely.

3. Situation in the Mediterranean.—Transport of supplies is the main problem.    The C.-in-C., Navy, in a letter to Admiral Riccardi, strongly urged active warfare and increased protection for transports.    Preparations are being made to transfer a motor boat and motor minesweeper flotilla at the end of the Eastern Campaign.    In answer to a question by the Fuehrer, *the C.-in-C., Navy*, replies that it is not possible to send submarines into the Mediterranean, as this would handicap operations in the Atlantic.    Moreover, British submarines and aircraft are the forces used in the Mediterranean to attack transports, and these cannot be combatted with submarines.    Italian anti-submarine defence must be properly organised for this purpose.

4. *The C.-in-C., Navy*, reports on the necessity of speeding up the construction of submarines as much as possible.    He defines the nature of the submarine programme, and points out above all the destruction and loss of material suffered by the Navy while escorting merchant ships. This task is being performed daily, under heavy losses, for the sake of the war economy and to maintain the flow of supplies.    Showing graphs, he explains how necessary it is that the monthly output of submarines not be allowed to fall below twenty-five.    If we have 300 operational submarines —a figure which, however, will not be reached until July 1, 1943, at a monthly rate of increase of only twenty-one boats and 5 per cent. losses— —fifteen boats would be lost a month on the basis of 5 per cent. losses. The gain would thus be only six submarines.    If there were 10 per cent. losses per month, thirty boats would be lost, and there would be a deficit

of nine boats.   Our losses of forty-two boats at present amount to about 6 per cent. on an average.   From the end of 1941 on, however, the monthly output of submarines will amount to only about fourteen.   The need for workers for the submarine programme is therefore still very great; there is a shortage at present of about 25,000 men.   It is impossible to make up for lost time now.   The C.-in-C., Navy, therefore requests that Dr. Todt be instructed that after the Eastern Campaign is over, the Navy should also receive the necessary number of workers.   *The Fuehrer* promises this and demands moreover, in reply to an inquiry by the C-in-C., Navy, that construction of the Seydlitz and the Graf Zeppelin is to be continued after the end of the Eastern Campaign.

*The C.-in-C., Navy,* reports that it is not justifiable to use the British submarine Seal even in the transport service, on account of its great technical defects.   The boat is to be used for salvage.

*The C.-in-C., Navy,* reports the necessity for asking for officers, non-commissioned officers, and men from the Army after the Eastern Campaign, in order to provide crews for submarines for a long time ahead. *The Fuehrer* agrees.

5. *The C.-in-C., Navy,* asks whether operation "Sea Lion" is now only going to serve as a camouflage, or whether it is actually to be carried out. *The Fuehrer* explains that this question cannot be answered definitely. It is certain, however, that the operation cannot be carried out before Spring 1942.   The Fuehrer believes that Britain will not continue to fight if she sees that there is no longer a chance of winning.   Britain is already beginning to have misgivings, in view of the U.S. occupation of Iceland.   *The C.-in-C., Navy,* declares that means of transport cannot be provided at the expense of naval raw materials and construction facilities.   The High Command, Navy, will make appropriate representations to the O.K.W.

6. *The C.-in-C., Navy,* reports that the person chiefly responsible for the loss of the three mine layers was unaccountably acquitted at the court-martial.   The C.-in-C., Navy, did not endorse the decision, but ordered another trial.

(signed) RAEDER.

*   *   *   *   *   *

The situation in the Mediterranean was again deteriorating from the Axis point of view and a meeting was arranged between Hitler and Mussolini for August 25.

C.-in-C., Navy.                                        Berlin, August, 26, 1941

**REPORT OF THE C.-IN-C., NAVY, TO THE FUEHRER AT WOLFSSCHANZE IN THE AFTERNOON OF AUGUST 22, 1941**

Also present:  Chief of Staff, O.K.W.
                    General Jodl.
                    Captain von Puttkamer.

I. Points suggested for the conference between the Fuehrer and the Duce.—1. The transport situation in the Mediterranean:

(*a*) By the middle of September, shipping space ready for use, including German ships, ships chartered from Spain, and Danish and Belgian ships taken over from the French, will amount in all to:

| | |
|---|---|
| 16 sea-going ships totalling  ..    .. | 54,100 tons |
| 13 coastal ships totalling ..    ..    .. | 11,600 tons |
| 29 | 65,700 tons |

This shipping is adequate for the time being for transports to Africa.

German shipping reserves in the Mediterranean are low; they are as follows: Eleven ships totalling 31,000 tons used for ore transport; commandeering these would involve economic disadvantages. Seven ships totalling 15,000 tons used for operations in the Aegean and the Black Seas; they are indispensable there. Losses in German shipping up to July 31 amount to 73 per cent. Further losses must be expected.

(*b*) The transport situation could be improved by using the French merchant marine or non-French ships lying in French ports, and later by capturing Gibraltar, making it possible to bring German ships into the Mediterranean.

(*c*) Demands to be presented to Italy:

(1) Increased use should be made of Italian shipping. The following ships are available in Italy:

| | |
|---|---|
| 120 freighters over 2,000 tons, totalling | 552,000 tons |
| 114 freighters under 2,000 tons, totalling | 122,000 tons |
| 46 passenger ships } 19 tankers } | 445,954 tons |
| 299 | 1,119,954 tons |

Previous experiences have shown that the Italians are very reluctant to use their shipping. Their intention to retain their shipping for commercial use during the period after the war when there is a shortage of shipping is obvious. Very strong pressure by the Government is necessary here. In order to carry out German transports most effectively it is necessary that the Italians surrender ships to the German Commanding Officer, Supply and Transports for purely German use.

(2) Malta should be attacked and the escort service should be improved, in order to keep losses within reasonable limits. For this purpose search receivers delivered from Germany should be put to appropriate use by installing them in ships really suitable for anti-submarine warfare, making use of German proposals and experiences.

(3) Italian facilities and workmen should be used for construction of German transport ships according to German plans and under German supervision. German aid in materials should be afforded by the Ministry of Economics. (It is intended to use similar measures in other coastal areas, for example in France, Russia, Roumania, etc.) The construction of these ships (using simplest design and mass production techniques) is important because of constant losses in ships, the impending large transport tasks, and also in order to relieve

and improve merchant shipping. Construction of tankers is particularly urgent. It is planned to construct approximately the following ships, all with "top" priority:

> Thirty troop transports of 5,000 tons.
> Twenty troop transports of 3,000 tons.
> Twenty tankers of 3,000 tons.

2. Capacity of African harbours:

(a) The capacity of Tripoli and Benghazi is barely adequate to handle current supply traffic. A large number of transports could be managed only by considerably increasing transloading performance and by expanding all Libyan ports. Measures of great urgency, such as removal of wrecks and improvement of clearance facilities at the landing stages, are not being carried out with the necessary vigour. The Commanding Officer, Supply and Transports in Italy, on instructions from the Naval Staff, has already repeatedly offered German assistance in expanding the Libyan ports, both verbally and in writing. So far, the Italians have not accepted the offer.

(b) Italy should be requested to make use of the German offer of assistance in material and personnel for expanding African ports.

3. Italian transport ships used in Libyan traffic since the beginning of the German crossings:

(a) Freighters:

| | | |
|---|---|---|
| Troop and cargo transports .. | .. | 22 ships=127,735 tons |
| In addition, from Albanian traffic | .. | 2 ships= 11,711 tons |
| New addition .. .. .. | .. | 1 ship = 6,300 tons |
| Total shipping used for Libya .. | .. | 25 ships=145,746 tons |
| Completely lost .. .. .. | .. | 6 ships= 30,822 tons |
| In operation at the present time .. | .. | 19 ships=114,924 tons |

(b) Passenger ships (purely for transporting men without material or equipment, therefore of no practical use to us):

| | | |
|---|---|---|
| Put in operation .. .. .. | .. | 6 ships= 93,529 tons |
| Lost .. .. .. .. | .. | 1 ship = 17,779 tons |
| In operation at the present time .. | .. | 5 ships= 75,750 tons |
| German ships in operation at the same time: | | |
| Total put in operation .. .. | .. | 38 ships=152,237 tons |
| Damaged .. .. .. | .. | 7 ships= 38,565 tons |
| Completely lost .. .. .. | .. | 18 ships= 83,597 tons |
| Ready for operation .. | .. | 13 ships=29,975 tons* |

The Fuehrer notes and approves the foregoing points, which are given in writing at the same time to the Chief of Staff, O.K.W. He will discuss them with the Duce.

II. Development of relations with France.—The fundamental views of the Naval Staff as expressed in the memorandum on the Battle of the

---

\* Apparent error in original.

Atlantic are stated.   The demands made in this report can be also met step by step rather than all at once, e.g., first of all the question of transport shipping can be solved, then West Africa can be secured, and finally there can be unlimited co-operation.   So far, the French have handed over to us five Belgian and three Danish steamers totalling 15,300 tons.   Our demand for nineteen ships totalling 74,000 tons has not been met as yet.   The following demand should be made:

(a) Suitable ships should be sold or chartered to us.
(b) Certain transport tasks from Toulon and Marseilles to Bizerta should be taken over by French shipping under French escort.

*The Chief of Staff, O.K.W.*, replies with regard to point (a) that negotiations are in progress; and with regard to point (b) that this question can be solved only in conjunction with the whole Bizerta problem.

III. The importance of Gibraltar and co-operation with Spain.—As long as relations with France are not completely cleared up, and co-operation with her is not effectively established, the occupation of Gibraltar continues to be of decisive importance.   If we occupied Gibraltar we would rule the Western Mediterranean, and even the importance of Malta would be reduced to a certain degree.   Co-operation with Spain is not only a necessary condition for the attack on Gibraltar, but also offers very valuable bases on the Atlantic coast to the German Navy, e.g., El Ferrol and Cadiz, which are situated nearer to the operational areas and further away from enemy bases and airports.   Co-operation with Spain and control of the Straits of Gibraltar would enable us to bring naval forces and transport vessels into the Mediterranean.   This might be of decisive importance for the transport situation in the central Mediterranean. *The Fuehrer* fully appreciates the importance of Gibraltar.

IV. Change in the American Neutrality Zone.—In view of the increasingly unfavourable political attitude which the South American countries are adopting towards us, the Naval Staff has asked the Foreign Office to consider whether it might not be warranted to disregard the Pan-American Safety Zone which we still respect as far as 300 miles off the coast of South America.   The Naval Staff suggests that the boundary should be pushed back to 20 miles off the coast.   The opinion of the Foreign Minister is requested on this point.   (All South Atlantic shipping has been transferred into the neutrality zone).   *The Fuehrer* will await a statement from the Foreign Minister.

V. Concentration of submarines in the Atlantic.—*The Fuehrer* touches on the question of transferring submarines to the Mediterranean.   *The C.-in-C., Navy*, states that in view of the fact that enemy convoys are more and more heavily escorted, successes can be achieved only if they are attacked, not by just a few, but by a large number of submarines simultaneously.   The transfer of enemy traffic to more distant and remote areas also necessitates use of a very large number of submarines merely to locate the enemy convoys.   Even with the gradual increase in the numbers of submarines, therefore, all available boats will have to be concentrated in the Atlantic.   Only in this way can we expect to achieve decisive successes.   Submarines should be transferred to other theatres of operations and to other tasks only in cases of great emergency.   The C.-in-C., Navy, has ordered the withdrawal of the four submarines from Finland and the our submarines from the outlets of the Belts and the Sound, in order that the numbers of Atlantic submarines should not be reduced further; he believes that no submarines should be transferred from the Atlantic to the Mediterranean until there are forty operational submarines in position in the Atlantic. The C.-in-C., Navy, also points out the differences between methods of submarine warfare in the Mediterranean and in the Atlantic, as well as the different nature of the anti-submarine defences.

*The Fuehrer* elaborates on the following points: The British will probably undertake an attack on Sollum and Tobruk to relieve the Russians; the surrender of North Africa would mean a great loss both to us and to the Italians; the British are very dependent on supplies by sea in the Eastern Mediterranean; the Italians have achieved nothing with their submarines. It is very desirable to relieve the *Afrika Korps* with a few German submarines, and he proposes sending three groups of two vessels each, totalling six in all. *The C.-in-C., Navy*, recommends a conference with the Duce first and a request for a suitable base, which would then be equipped by us. *The Fuehrer agrees*. The C.-in-C., Navy, does not believe that the Duce will agree.

VI. The question of eliminating Hangoe.—Speedy elimination of Hangoe is necessary. The Naval Staff brought up the question in a letter to the O.K.W., proposing that Hangoe be occupied soon. *General Jodl* states that the Finns will be able to take steps to occupy Hangoe only when operations on Lake Ladoga are over. Heavy artillery can be transported to the vicinity soon.

VII. To what extent will the Baltic countries belong to the Greater German Reich after the war, making it possible for such ports as Libau, Tallinn, and Baltic Port to be used as shipyards and bases? *The Fuehrer* states that the bases can definitely be counted on; he will not surrender the Baltic countries.

VIII. What are the Fuehrer's intentions with regard to the future status of the Channel Islands?—Are they to belong to the Greater German Reich even if the French coast near them is not in our possession? *The Fuehrer* wishes to retain the Channel Islands; he would like to fortify them as strategic bases.

IX. What is the Fuehrer's opinion of Japan's political attitude?—*The Fuehrer* is convinced that Japan will carry out the attack on Vladivostok as soon as forces have been assembled. The present aloofness can be explained by the fact that the assembling of forces is to be accomplished undisturbed, and the attack is to come as a surprise move. The Fuehrer assumes that the positions in Indo-China are being secured at the same time, and that Thailand has special agreements with Japan.

X. Operation "Sea Lion"—*The C.-in-C., Navy*, requests a decision on the proposal made by the Naval Staff with regard to operation "Sea Lion." *The Chief of Staff, O.K.W.*, states that the matter was presented to the Fuehrer; a decision about determining the exact facilities available will be forthcoming within a few days. *The Fuehrer* anxious that the threat to Britain should never quite cease so that as many British forces as possible will be tied down.

XI. Norwegian ships in Sweden.—*The C.-in-C., Navy*, explains the situation with regard to Norwegian ships in Sweden. Sweden has declared that she guarantees none will escape in the immediate future; that Germany should, however, arrange with the Norwegian Shipping Union for the ships to be handed over to Germany. This company is under pro-British management and recognises the old Norwegian Government. This company will work in our interests only if it comes under the control of the National Socialists. Quisling should be commissioned to arrange this. *The Fuehrer* orders an investigation to be made.

(The C.-in-C., Navy, gives General Jodl a copy of the notes made by Professor Aal on these questions).

(signed) RAEDER.

*   *   *   *   *   *

On September 11 President Roosevelt in a broadcast announced that "From now on, if German or Italian vessels of war enter these waters (i.e., Iceland and similar areas under U.S. protection) they do so at their peril." The German Navy saw in this speech an excuse for intensifying the war against merchant shipping and for removing the last restrictions on U-boat warfare.

On September 12 the Naval Staff sent the following memorandum to the Foreign Office:

Naval High Command                                 Berlín, September 12, 1941

To the Foreign Office
Attention : Minister Eisenlohr

Re : Incidents with American ships.   Reference is made to the telephone conversation between Minister Eisenlohr and Count Stauffenberg on September 12, 1941.

With regard to the incidents mentioned by Roosevelt, the following statements can be made, based on evidence available from reports received by the Naval Staff :

1. Greer.—According to a report from a foreign radio station, i.e., Reykjavik, the American destroyer Greer transmitted to all American naval vessels the following message :

"A surfaced submarine sighted at 1121 (German Summer Time) at 62° 48′ N, 27° 30′ W."

According to a message from U.652 she was attacked with three depth charges and further harassed by a destroyer, flag unrecognised, at 1230 on September 4 at 62° 31′ N, 27° 06′ W.   At 1439 the submarine fired a spread of two in defence, which missed and was observed.   She was further pursued with depth charges until 2330.   The submarine suffered no damage.   The weather was good.   So far, no further messages have been received.

2. Robin Moor.—According to a message from a submarine the steamer was sighted at 0430 on May 21, 1941 at about 5° N, 27° W.   She carried no illuminated neutrality markings.   The flag could not be recognised.   The vessel had an unusually high deck cargo, and the submarine commander suspected a submarine trap.

At 0535 the steamer was requested to stop and send over her papers by the captain.   The first officer came alongside in the ship's boat, but without papers, and stated that the ship was American and on her way to South Africa.   Her cargo consisted of engines, engine parts, automobile parts, and general piece goods. The first officer was then informed that the ship was carrying absolute contraband for a power at war with Germany and must therefore be sunk.   The first officer requested half an hour to prepare the boats ; this was granted.   When requested the captain came alongside at 0815 with bills of lading.   The cargo was definitely established as contraband.   The captain accepted the information that the ship must be sunk without raising any objections.   Bread, butter, a bottle of brandy, and first-aid material were given to the captain who accepted them with many thanks.   When the boats had cast off the crew shouted "Heil Hitler" with raised hands.   After the ship had been sunk the upper deck cargo came to the surface and aluminium parts were recognized, which were obviously plane parts.

3. Pursuit of an American battleship in July, 1941 : According to a report from a submarine at 1307 on June 20, she had sighted the American battleship Texas and a destroyer near the boundary line of the zone of operations at about 53° N,

31° W.  The submarine followed them for 150 miles in a north-easterly direction and back again to the boundary line of the zone of operations.  The submarine did not attack.  According to this report the pursuit must have commenced on June 19. At this time the submarines within the zone of operations still had permission to attack all warships.

4.  Sessa.—According to foreign reports the vessel was sunk on August 17, 1941, some 300 miles southwest of Iceland.  She was sailing under the Panama flag. Hence she must have been sunk in the zone of operations, and as she was flying the Panama flag she was legitimate prey for submarines.  At that time there were German submarines in the sea area in question.  No message has yet been received reporting the sinking of the Sessa, however.  The submarines in question have not yet returned.

5.  Steel Seafarer.—This vessel was sunk by the Air Force in the Red Sea area of operations.  No restrictions for attacks on American vessels have been issued for this area.  The Naval Staff has no details of the attack.

\*       \*       \*       \*       \*       \*

Three days later this telegram from Washington was received by Raeder:

Washington, September 15, 1941 at 2011
Received: September 16, 1941 at 0900

After Senator Connally and Pepper, who are supporters of the administration, had already tried in press interviews—evidently on instructions and in order to calm public apprehension—to limit the term "defensive waters," in which the American Navy can fire, to waters of the Western Hemisphere which are patrolled by the American Navy, Secretary of the Navy, Knox, today defined the expression definitely in a talk to the American Legion Convention at Milwaukee: "From September 16 the American Navy will protect ships sailing under all flags carrying lend-lease war material between the American continent and the waters of Iceland 'as completely as lies in our power'."

Thus it is evident that the definition of the term in Roosevelt's speech was deliberately left vague for the present, primarily in order to comply outwardly with Churchill's wishes for active American aid in the war and in order to intimidate us and Japan; it is also evident that the American Navy is not capable of patrolling effectively the entire Atlantic including the route around Africa to Suez, but it can certainly take over entirely convoy escort between the American continent and Iceland.  Knox's statement shows clearly that the President is well aware of the lack of operational capacity of American forces beyond this limited sphere because of commitments in the Pacific.

Am telegraphing appropriate extracts from this speech by Knox along with this message uncoded under reference No. 3194.

(signed) Thomsen.

\*       \*       \*       \*       \*       \*

On September 17 Raeder reported to Hitler.

High Command, Navy.

## REPORT BY THE C.-IN-C., NAVY, TO THE FUEHRER AT WOLFSSCHANZE IN THE AFTERNOON OF SEPTEMBER 17, 1941

Also present:  Foreign Minister.
               Ambassador Ritter.
               Chief of Staff, O.K.W.
               General Jodl.
               Admiral Commanding, Submarines.
               Captain von Puttkamer.

1.  Roosevelt's speech (of September 11).—The strategic and political situation created by the speech of the President of the U.S.A. can be

evaluated as follows: Roosevelt stated that the "time for active defence" has come. The U.S. patrol vessels and aircraft will protect all merchant ships, not only United States ones, within the "American defence waters," and in so doing they will "no longer wait" until the warships of the Axis attack. The mere fact of their presence in these waters "is equivalent to an attack." From now on they will sail in these waters only "at their own risk." Thus the situation has become considerably clearer. In the future American forces will no longer be employed merely for reconnaissance but also for convoy duty, including escort of British ships. German forces must expect offensive war measures by these U.S. forces in every case of an encounter. There is no longer any difference between British and American ships.

In view of this evaluation of the strategic and political aspects, it is suggested that our own orders should be amended as follows

A. Naval vessels.—(1) Naval vessels sailing alone.

(*a*) Within the extended blockade area attack is sanctioned on any warship unless she is definitely recognised as a U.S. vessel. If the action of an American vessel can be construed to constitute an attack or pursuit, attack on the ship in question is also sanctioned.

(*b*) Outside the extended blockade area attack is sanctioned on any warship recognised as an enemy vessel. At night attack is sanctioned on any warship proceeding without lights, unless she is recognised as American.

(2) Escorting forces.—Attacks on escorting forces are permitted in any operational area at any time without regard to the blockade area.

B. Merchant vessels.—(1) Within the extended blockade area attacks without warning are permitted on any merchant vessels (with the exception of the special arrangement with Sweden).

(2) Outside the extended blockade area:

(*a*) Attack without warning is permitted if the ships are in convoy.

(*b*) Against ships sailing alone. Enemy ships can be attacked without warning. American and other neutral ships must be dealt with according to prize regulations. They can be attacked without warning only when they are helping the enemy, use radio, or are proceeding without lights.

C. U.S.A. neutrality zone.—As the President himself no longer mentions the U.S.A. zone, but extends the U.S.A. defence waters (Western Hemisphere) indefinitely to the east according to the whim of the U.S.A., the following is suggested:

(1) Only a 20-mile neutrality zone should henceforth be respected off the coast of the U.S.A. If this measure is too drastic, the neutrality zone off the coast of the U.S.A. should be retained as far as 60° W.

(2) Only a 20-mile neutrality zone should be respected off the coast of South America.

On the basis of a detailed discussion of the situation as a whole, in which it appears that the end of September will bring the great decision in the Russian campaign, *the Fuehrer* requests that care should be taken to avoid any incidents in the war on merchant shipping before about the middle of October. Therefore *the C.-in-C., Navy,* and *the Admiral Commanding Submarines* withdraw their suggestions. Submarines are to be informed of the reason for temporarily keeping to the old orders.

2. Summary of the situation on September 15:

(*a*) The Baltic Sea and the Gulf of Finland.—Following the elimination of Oesel and Dagoe, the Russian naval forces and merchant vessels will still have the use of Kronstadt. Our motor boats and motor mine sweepers are in the process of blocking Kronstadt Bay by means of minefields. Army coastal batteries are scheduled to take part in the blockade. In addition there are Russian minefields which have evidently been laid during the past few days by cruisers and destroyers; they are probably mainly anti-submarine barrages with gaps. At present the Russians are apparently still maintaining a mineswept channel through the German-Finnish barrages to Hangoe. However, no major movements of Russian forces in the Gulf of Finland have been observed recently. Their freedom of movement will be further reduced by German-Finnish mining operations.

The Naval Staff considers it highly improbable that Russian warships and merchant vessels will break out of Kronstadt Bay to Sweden. The whole attitude of the Russian so far speaks against such intent on their part, particularly since they have laid a barrage themselves to close Kronstadt Bay and are using numerous ships crews in land fighting. If they do try to break out, heavy losses can be anticipated from mines, motor boats, and aircraft. If a determined, desperate attempt is made to break out, however, the German Navy cannot completely prevent fast, light units from slipping through. The same applies to Hangoe. On the other hand, once all Russian bases have been eliminated, it will be impossible for Russian forces to attack German sea communications in the Baltic Sea, or to break through the Baltic Sea approaches to the British Isles.

(*b*) Northern Norway.—The British realise the vital importance of the sea route off the Arctic coast for supplies of the German Armed Forces, and they are operating in the northern area with several cruisers, destroyers, one or two aircraft carriers, and submarines. Our own naval and air resources are slight. At present troop transports are unable to proceed east of North Cape. Supply steamers can do so only at very great risk. As the activities of the Air Force are reduced by approaching winter, the threat from surface forces increases. The submarine danger is being reduced as far as possible by the addition of more subchasers and escort vessels. The threat from surface vessels remains, however, since the British, with bases at Murmansk and Archangel, can always commit stronger forces than we. Occupation of Murmansk continues to be an important prerequisite for the protection of our supplies. Even after Murmansk is captured, however, enemy operations in the Arctic Ocean will continue to harass our supply lines.

In a personal talk with the Fuehrer, *the C.-in-C., Navy,* points out the importance of occupying Archangel as well, in order to deprive the

British of every base for attack in the north.   *The Fuehrer* replies that at least the railway to Archangel will be cut.

(*c*) The Channel and the Western Area.—Increased enemy activity by means of new motor boats and by brisk air attacks on our convoys have caused some regrettable losses in material and personnel, and a number of escort vessels were damaged.   Further attacks must be expected, as the enemy will want to profit from the present German concentration of forces on the Eastern Front and the more favourable seasonal conditions.   In early October our own motor boat activity will be intensified after the motor boats used in the Russian area have been overhauled.   Patrolling of the Atlantic coast has been successful.   It is gratifying to report that, through good co-operation between the coastal defences, air reconnaissance, and submarines, the auxiliary cruiser ship "36" and the Anneliese Essberger, coming from East Asia, were successfully brought in.   The cargo included 4,000 tons of rubber!

(*d*) The heavy surface forces are still undergoing repairs, overhaul, or trials.   Operations in the Atlantic with battleships or cruisers will not be possible before the beginning of 1942.   *The Fuehrer* discusses the question of whether it would not be better to station the battleships along the Norwegian coast, in order to defend the northern area.   They cannot be protected from air attacks in Brest.   *The C.-in-C., Navy,* answers that basically the idea of using these ships to wage war against merchant shipping in the Atlantic is the correct one.   Originally the battleships were not supposed to remain in Brest very long, since at that time it was definitely hoped that they would be able to use the Spanish bases, from which the Battle of the Atlantic could have been fought very advantageously.   The heavy vessels will not be ready for important operations before the beginning of 1942.

(*e*) Cruiser warfare in foreign waters.—Despite enemy counter-measures and strategy, the auxiliary cruisers have been able to achieve further successes.   At the present the zones of operations of the auxiliary cruisers are as follows :

Ship "16" is in the West Pacific; at the end of the year she will proceed around Cape Horn to the Atlantic and make for the French coast.

Ship "45" is in the East Pacific, with the valuable prize Kota Nopang loaded with rubber and tin.   She will also return home via the Atlantic in the near future.

Ship "41" is in the Indian Ocean.

Two new auxiliary cruisers will leave port at the end of October and the end of November, and two more in the spring.   As for blockade-runners, one is still en route from East Asia carrying rubber.   Two more ships will be ready to leave shortly.   The steamer Windhuk is to leave South America and make for the Atlantic coast of France.   The outlook for blockade-runners may be considered favourable.

(*f*) Submarine warfare.—The Admiral Commanding Submarines discusses the main aspects of submarine warfare.   Execution of operations, effectiveness, countermeasures, measures against radar, new type of torpedo, etc.   The latest successes should not be allowed to obscure the great difficulties caused by the very strong Anglo-American escorts and the extensive enemy air patrol.    In order to be as successful as last year, three to four times as many submarines are needed in view of the heavily escorted convoys.    Reconnaissance to locate enemy convoys is still the main problem.    However, the number of submarines becoming available by the end of October permits us to anticipate increased successes, especially if the number of planes available for reconnaissance will increase likewise.

(g) Situation in the Mediterranean.—As the Fuehrer knows, our North African supply shipments have recently suffered additional heavy losses of ships, material, and personnel as the result of enemy air attacks by means of bombs and torpedoes, and through submarine attacks. Evidently the appeal for help made by the German General attached to the Italian Armed Forces was responsible for the order from the Fuehrer to concentrate our own air forces on escorting supply shipments, to dispatch immediately six submarines without taking Italian operations into consideration, and to speed up the transfer of motor minesweepers and motor boats.    Submarines for the Mediterranean.    Two boats are en route, two will leave at the end of the week, and the remaining boats will be ready on September 22 and 27.

The Fuehrer sanctions the publication of an article in "Nauticus" on the achievements of Admiral Luetjens and the Bismarck.

3. The C.-in-C., Navy, reports that Captain Bruening has been court-martialled for the loss of the mine layers, and that proceedings have been initiated against an officer of the staff of the Admiral Commanding Cruisers.

4. The C.-in-C., Navy, reports the contents of a communication from Lieut. Witting on the treatment of his wife by the Gestapo.    The communication has been transmitted to the Chief of Staff, O.K.W., by the C.-in-C., Navy, with a request for an investigation.

(signed) RAEDER.

\*         \*         \*         \*         \*         \*

No conference on Naval Affairs was held during the next two months.    On November 13 the war at sea was reviewed.

C.-in-C. of the Navy.

## REPORT OF THE C.-IN-C., NAVY, TO THE FUEHRER AT WOLFSSCHANZE IN THE AFTERNOON OF NOVEMBER 13, 1941

Also present:  Chief of Staff, O.K.W.
General Jodl.
Captain von Puttkamer.

1. Situation in home waters.    (a) Norwegian area.—The most important task is that of bringing up supplies and strengthening coastal defences in the arctic area.    Attacks by enemy submarines and aircraft harass supply traffic; lately the enemy has resorted to mine laying, from which it may be inferred that he no longer intends to take offensive action with surface forces off the fiords.    In view of the length of the sea routes, the number of our own defence forces is very limited, taxing them heavily.

The air forces at present available can protect normal convoy traffic only when the weather and visibility are favourable. So far, losses of transports have been slight because enemy activity has on the whole been less than expected. The long nights are favourable for convoys, as there is less danger of submarine attack.

Submarine operations in the Arctic Ocean.—The arctic night is unfavourable for submarines as it renders it difficult to locate the targets. Winter weather, with blizzards, storms, and fog, has an adverse effect. Air reconnaissance is lacking. It is difficult to attack the ships assembled in Iokanga Bay because of the powerful defences and the prevailing currents. It is impossible to penetrate the west channel because of navigational difficulties, currents and depths, defences, and the aerial mine situation. Coastal traffic is carried on with very small vessels, making attack more difficult. In view of our experiences so far and the difficult conditions, the operational possibilities of submarines in the Arctic Ocean should not be overestimated. At present two submarines are operating; another is en route to the area, and a fourth is homeward bound. Present plans call for three boats to be in the operational area at all times.

(b) Baltic Sea.—The situation is unchanged. Mine sweeping is of primary importance in view of the extensive supply shipments. Traffic from Tallinn to Finland is proceeding as planned. The supply line for Tallinn is threatened by the enemy, who still occupies the island of Odensholm. Up to ten Russian submarines are still at sea, but have achieved no successes so far, unless it was a submarine torpedo which hit U.144. As winter sets in more and more, the possibility that the ships still able to operate might break through diminishes. Battleships are still heard in radio traffic, but are no longer able to operate. The cruiser Marti and some destroyers are evidently still fully capable of operating. A few days ago a Russian group ventured as far as west of the Juminda barrage, where they suffered losses. The purpose of the operation is not known; possibly it was to prepare for the evacuation of Odensholm and Hangoe. We have further reinforced the Juminda barrage. Now that ice is starting to form it is necessary to withdraw motor boats.

(c) North Sea. The situation is unchanged.

(d) Channel and Western Area.—The decided enemy air superiority in the Western Area has made the sea transport situation and the mounting threat to our defence forces more acute. In addition to attacks by aircraft and motor torpedo boats, the enemy is laying mines on a larger scale. (Recently minefields were laid again off Boulogne and Lorient.) Utmost demands are made on the material and personnel of our inadequate escort forces; the physical and nervous strain on the men is very great. By using all available forces it has so far been possible to escort convoys and keep the routes open despite most difficult conditions. In the Western Area 139 convoys consisting of 542 vessels totalling 1,200,000 tons were escorted during October. Eighteen aircraft were shot down during air attacks. Losses include two steamers and one dredger sunk, and sixteen minesweepers, motor mine sweepers, and patrol boats damaged, some severely. We cannot afford such losses. The construction of motor minesweepers is urgent for locating and sweeping mines and for anti-aircraft duties. The engine situation is causing difficulties.

There has recently been a sharp increase in air attacks on submarines entering and leaving port on the Atlantic coast. The only way to relieve the situation at sea is to reinforce the fighter units of the Air Force, an urgently needed step. According to information from the Air Force, this is not possible for the time being.

2. Operations by surface forces. (a) Tirpitz.—It is intended to transfer the Tirpitz to Trondheim in December as previously planned after she has been made ready for combat. A delay was caused by final repairs and additional installations to fit her for use in the Arctic Ocean. She will operate off the Norwegian coast as the situation may warrant. The Tirpitz cannot be sent into the Atlantic as previously intended because of the general oil situation, the enemy situation, and the need for her presence in the Northern Area.

(b) Battleships at Brest.—They will be ready for operations in February, 1942. Careful review of the situation shows that fairly short operations and movements in the Atlantic are still practicable; there are good chances for success and for strategic effect, especially with regard to the Gibraltar convoys. The main difficulties are: providing adequate training for the operations; bringing the ships safely in and out of the coastal waters; and assuring replenishment of supplies out in the Atlantic. To break through in the Iceland area is difficult and dangerous, but it appears feasible if it can be done as a surprise move and under favourable weather conditions. In view of the existing danger of air attacks it is not advisable to keep the ships at Brest after they are ready for combat, even though anti-aircraft defences have become more effective since the introduction of smoke screens; the mere presence of the ships on the Atlantic coast forces the enemy to give his convoys stronger escort. We will not be able to use Spanish harbours in the near future.

In full consideration of the very difficult oil situation, the Naval Staff has arrived at the following conclusions:

(1) No lengthy operations against merchant vessels are to be undertaken in the Atlantic.

(2) Prior to any operations, the battle readiness of the ships must be fully restored and adequate training provided.

(3) When these conditions have been fulfilled, it can be decided whether the ships should operate off the French Atlantic coast in westerly or south-westerly direction against enemy north-south convoys, or whether steps should be taken to transfer the vessels to home waters or to the Norwegian area. The decision will depend on the enemy situation and the oil situation. The concentration of heavy surface forces in the Northern Area would force the enemy to maintain considerable naval forces in the North Scotland region, and would make it possible to attack sea communications to northern Russia and enemy patrols in the Iceland-Faroes area.

(4) It may be possible to bring the cruiser Prinz Eugen through the Channel.

(5) It is proposed to make a final decision in January, as the situation keeps changing constantly: Japan may enter the war; the Spanish attitude may be changed by further successes in Russia.

*The Fuehrer* agrees. He would like to use the ships for an operation against the Azores if this should become necessary—although at present such action is hardly likely. He inquires what the chances are for a surprise withdrawal of the ships through the Channel. *The C.-in-C., Navy*, replies that such a break-through by the Prinz Eugen is thought possible, but so far not for the battleships; the matter is to be further studied.

(c) The pocket-battleship Scheer is ready for operations. The Naval Staff requests permission for the ship to leave port in order to carry out cruiser warfare in the Atlantic and the Indian Ocean. While fully realising the difficulties involved in navigating the Iceland-Faroes Straits on her outward voyage, both the Naval Staff and the Group Commanders recommend that the operation against merchant shipping should be carried out as planned; preparations are under way. The ship should leave port at the end of the week. Particularly in the present situation a powerful ship appearing in remote sea areas, especially the Indian Ocean, should have a very strong strategic effect. It would affect the supplies for the Middle East and the lively British transport traffic in the Indian Ocean; it would tie down British forces, have repercussions in the Mediterranean, and affect the British position in the Indian area. If we wait for and utilise favourable weather conditions when there is no enemy air reconnaissance in the North Sea and off the coast of Norway, and if submarines and aircraft assist by making detailed reconnaissance and by reporting weather conditions, there is a very good chance of a successful break-through into the Atlantic. Prospect for the actual raiding operations must be considered good. Hence it is recommended to carry out the operation as planned. The risk of breaking through is great, of course; the ship has orders to turn back immediately if she thinks she has been detected.

As *the Fuehrer* considers that the possible loss of the ship at present would be a heavy blow to prestige, and that the vital point at present is in the Norwegian Sea, he would rather see the Scheer transferred to the Norwegian coast, i.e., Narvik or Trondheim. *The C.-in-C., Navy*, declares that the Scheer is at a disadvantage because of her low speed as compared to that of the enemy's fast, powerful ships. Therefore she has to rely to a great extent on the bases.

(d) Auxiliary cruisers.—In view of the far-reaching effect of operations by auxiliary cruisers, the Naval Staff still believes in using the vessels for warfare outside home waters despite the fact that operations are being made more difficult by enemy countermeasures and able direction of enemy shipping. as long as auxiliary cruisers are successful in sinking and capturing ships, it is justifiable and necessary to use them. This is still the case today as proved by recent gratifying results; among others two prize ships with rubber and other cargo are now en route to Germany.

Situation of Auxiliary Cruisers.—Auxiliary cruiser ship "45" is at present in the North Atlantic. She will return to the Atlantic coast at the end of November.

Ship "16" is at present in the South Atlantic. First of all she will replenish the supplies of our submarines there. She will return at the end of December.

Ship "41" is at present in the Indian Ocean. She will return in Spring 1942.

Plans.—Ship "10" will be ready to leave port on November 17; her area of operations will be the South Atlantic and the Indian Ocean.

Ship "28" will be ready to leave January or February 1942.
Ship "23" will not be ready until February 1942.
Ship "14" will not be ready until Spring 1942.
The ships leave and return through the English Channel.

3. Directives for conduct of surface forces on encountering American forces.—The aim of these directives is on the one hand to lessen the possibilities of incidents with American forces, and on the other to give the commanders clear guidance for their conduct when meeting U.S. naval forces; guidance which is in keeping with strategic necessity and which upholds the prestige and honour of the German flag. The directives represent the minimum required by the present naval situation. (Reference is made to the fact that the probability of encountering U.S. forces is very slight in any case, considering the choice of the zones of operation and the mission). *The Fuehrer* approves these directives.

In reply to a question from the C.-in-C., Navy, regarding the Fuehrer's intention in case Congress repeals the Neutrality Law, *the Fuehrer* stated that he would let the order stand that all merchant ships, including American ones, may be torpedoed without warning in the old blockade area. Further orders will depend on how the situation develops.

4. Merchant shipping overseas on November 13, 1941.

(*a*) Rubber transport:

(1) Homeward bound:

| | | Approx. position on November 13, 1941 | Arrival Bordeaux |
|---|---|---|---|
| | | Three ships | |
| Burgenland | .. | .. off Bahia | early Dec. 1941 |
| Elsa Essberger | | .. in the southeast Pacific | middle of Jan. 1942 |
| Spreewald | .. | .. in the southeast Pacific | end of Jan. 1942 |

Note.—So far two ships carrying rubber have arrived from Japan; two have been lost.

Special Remarks.—The rubber transport Odenwald was stopped on November 6 by American naval forces in mid-Atlantic; she was scuttled by her own crew. According to orders the ship was flying the *American* flag, as this camouflage was the most suitable in view of the situation so far. It has been arranged with the Foreign Minister that in view of this fact no official protest shall be lodged with the U.S.A. The Naval Staff has ordered other camouflage immediately for the ships in the sea area in question.

(2) Outward bound:

| | Approx. position on November 13, 1941 | Arriving in Japan |
|---|---|---|
| Rio Grande .. | .. Pacific, near the Cook Islands | early December 1941. |
| Portland | Atlantic, off Rio | middle of Jan. 1942. |

(*b*) Plans:

(1) The following will leave Japan for Bordeaux:
1 ship in November 1941.
1 ship in December 1941.
2 ships in January 1942.

In addition two Italian ships under Italian command will leave with a cargo for Germany and Italy. The length of the voyage will be two to three months in each case.

(2) One ship will leave Bordeaux for Japan in January 1942.

5. Submarine warfare.—Submarine warfare on British imports in the Atlantic will be greatly reduced for a time after the boats now at sea have completed their missions, as tasks in the Arctic Ocean and the Mediterranean Sea are more urgent. The Naval Staff is endeavouring to commit all remaining boats wholly for war on merchant shipping. Forces are tied down, however, by urgent escort and defence assignments in connection with returning prizes and blockade-runners. In addition there are delays in carrying out repairs because of labour shortage, so that returning boats need a very long time before they are ready for operations once more. Thus it is inevitable that fewer ships will be sunk, and the enemy supply lines are thus relieved. At present all submarines in the Eastern Mediterranean are at Salamis and are in need of repair. Necessary overhaul is being delayed and made more difficult because the shipyards, repair facilities, and labour are inadequate. (One boat is now ready for operations). No additional boats can be assigned to the Eastern Mediterranean until the base at Salamis has been appropriately prepared. La Spezia will be the main supply base for boats in the Western Mediterranean. Also Palermo and Maddalena can be used as emergency operational harbours. The necessary steps have been taken to build up the submarine base at La Spezia. Four boats have either passed Gibraltar or are getting ready to break through.

Plan.—Later all Mediterranean submarines are to come under the German Admiral in Rome. An operational control organisation is now being set up.

6. Conduct of the war in the Mediterranean.—As feared by the Naval Staff since July, the situation regarding transports to North Africa has grown progressively worse, and has now reached the critical stage. It is pointed out that the Naval Staff has always fully recognised the dangerous situation caused by British naval superiority in the Mediterranean, and constantly emphasized the need for speedy introduction of the proper German measures. (This point was raised in a personal conversation). Today the enemy has complete naval and air supremacy in the area of the German transport routes; he is operating totally undisturbed in all parts of the Mediterranean. Malta is constantly being reinforced. Patrols in the Straits of Gibraltar have been intensified, evidently as the result of German submarine operations. The Italians are not able to bring about any major improvements in the situation, due to the oil situation and to their own operational and tactical impotence. (When the British attacked the 51st Transport Squadron during the night of November 8 with only two light cruisers and two destroyers 140 miles east of Sicily, the enemy was not driven off and destroyed, in spite of an escort of six destroyers and the presence of two heavy Italian cruisers and another four destroyers; these were evidently too far off at the decisive moment). The Naval Staff is deliberating what additional steps might be taken to aid the Italians immediately, such as sending them officers.

Recently the transport situation in the Aegean Sea has also greatly deteriorated. Enemy submarines definitely have the upper hand. German and Italian naval and air forces for patrol and escort duties and for planned anti-submarine measures are inadequate both in numbers and equipment, especially for the additional transport of men on leave, which is evidently considerable. There are constant shipping losses. The number of British submarines must be expected to increase, and thus the situation will become even more critical.

*The Fuehrer* wants to have ships of about 1,000 tons with a speed of 15 to 16 knots built in mass production in the Black Sea and Danube harbours, to be used as transports in the Mediterranean. They should be able to carry three to four heavy vehicles with personnel. These transports would proceed by day with adequate air cover; at night they could anchor behind nets in intermediate harbours or islands. In this way the risk would be divided.

*The C.-in-C., Navy,* reports on construction of merchant ships in Italy, Germany, and the occupied territories; merchant ships are needed everywhere because of the large amount of convoy traffic and the losses incurred. Collapse of our convoy traffic would be disastrous for the outcome of the war. There is a shortage of iron everywhere. The Ministry of Transport cannot procure any; despite strong recommendations by the Naval High Command, allocation has not been granted. This transport programme must have priority equal to the Army's transport programme, which is also very important. *The Fuehrer* acknowledges this and instructed the O.K.W. accordingly; he is also of the opinion that a certain amount of iron should be obtainable in the occupied Russian area in shipyards and ironworks. He recommends that an industrial expert should be appointed to examine the whole matter. *The C.-in-C., Navy,* will have this done. He reports on the possibility of building motor boats and motor minesweepers also in the Black Sea area. *The Fuehrer* sanctions a meeting between the C.-in-C., Navy, and Admiral Riccardi to discuss the problems connected with warfare in the Mediterranean.

7. The state of armament production for the Navy, and the labour situation.—Due to the escort and patrol tasks which are far in excess of the Navy's capacity, the strain on its forces has almost reached the breaking point. In view of the growing importance of the Navy on all fronts, including the Mediterranean and Black Sea, it is essential to give the Navy an opportunity to build up considerably larger forces of men and material as soon as the situation in the east permits. Submarine repairs must be speeded up, motor boat and motor minesweeper construction must be increased, engines must be made available, and damaged escort vessels must be repaired. The question of shipyard workers for submarine overhaul is especially pressing, as there are constant long delays in construction and repairs. It is urgently necessary that a special quota of German skilled workers be allocated to the Navy in addition to the foreign workers; at least 20,000 should be provided at once to relieve the most pressing need. It is requested that instructions be given to Minister Dr. Todt. *The Fuehrer* is aware of the Navy's critical position.

8. Oil situation:

(1) Fuel oil:

| | |
|---|---|
| Total stock of the German Navy | 380,000 tons, distributed in 70 bases. |
| | Of this about 220,000 tons are ready for use; the remainder must be thinned, mainly by the addition of lignite fuel oil (monthly output 12,000 tons) and Roumanian fuel oil. |
| Total stock of the Italian Navy .. | 30,000 tons at 30 bases. |
| total .. | 410,000 tons. |
| Requirements in November .. | 90,000 tons. |
| Monthly requirements of German Navy .. .. .. .. | 100,000 tons from December onwards. |
| Monthly requirements of Italian Navy .. .. .. .. | 100,000 tons. |
| Total monthly requirements .. | 200,000 tons. |
| Additional monthly supplies for the German Navy beginning November 1 | |
| (a) German home production .. | 50,000 tons. |
| (b) Roumanian imports.. .. | 7,000 tons. |
| (c) Roumanian imports for the Italian Navy .. .. .. | 27,000 tons. |
| Total monthly supplies .. .. | 84,000 tons. |

Hence the shortage in November is 116,000 tons.

In view of the decision of the Chief of Staff, O.K.W., with regard to handing over another 30,000 tons of fuel oil to the Italian Navy, the following steps have been taken:

(a) 10,000 tons of fuel oil have been ordered to be transferred from the Gdynia area to La Spezia.

(b) 20,000 tons of fuel oil have been ordered to be transferred from the area of western France to La Spezia.

(2) Diesel oil.—No requests for Diesel oil have been received from the Italian Navy.

| | |
|---|---|
| Available stock of the German Navy | 106,000 tons, at 70 bases. |
| Imports in November .. .. | 45,000 tons. |
| Imports from December onwards | 40,000 tons. |

With a monthly consumption of about 14,000 tons for submarines, which will rise to 20,000 tons by January and then continue to increase by 2,000 tons each month, requirements of Diesel oil can at present be covered by imports. Additional requirements for surface forces and supply vessels amount to the following:

25,000 tons in November.

15,000 tons in December.

15,000 tons in January.

9. Continued construction of the aircraft carrier.—The Naval Staff still attaches great importance to continuing construction of the aircraft carrier. The first essential, however, is that the workers needed to finish the work and the aircraft required for carrier operations should be provided. The development of carrier aircraft would tie up considerable production facilities and involve great expense. According to a report from the Air Force, the new types of aircraft cannot be expected before the end of 1944 even under the most favourable circumstances. In view of the effects on the Air Force programme the Naval Staff thinks that their demands for continuing work on the aircraft carrier will have to depend on whether the Fuehrer decides to make available the necessary manpower for the shipyards and to tolerate certain disadvantages for the current air armament programme. *The Fuehrer* wants work on the aircraft carrier to be continued; he feels sure that the Air Force will be able to help with adapted aircraft at first.

10. *The C.-in-C., Navy*, reports on the special ships designed by Engelmann and Walter.

11. In a private talk *the C.-in-C., Navy*, reports on the importance and prospects of mine warfare. He also recommends the posthumous award of the Oak leaf Cluster of the Knight's Cross to Captain Krueder, the commander of the auxiliary cruiser Pinguin, for outstanding services in cruiser warfare. *The Fuehrer* agrees.

(signed)        RAEDER.
(countersigned) ASSMANN.

\* \* \* \* \* \*

On November 18 the second Western Desert offensive of the 8th Army in Libya began. The British advance was rapid, and by November 29 British patrols had reached a position south of Benghazi. The Axis retreat caused Hitler to issue the following directive:

The Fuehrer and Supreme Commander of the      Fuehrer Headquarters
Armed Forces.                           December 2, 1941
Top Secret.

Fuehrer Directive No. 38

(1) As a foundation for securing and extending our own position in the Mediterranean, and for the creation of a focus of Axis power in the Central Mediterranean, I have come to an agreement with the Duce, and now command that sections of the *Luftwaffe* now released from the East, to the strength of about one *Fliegerkorps* and the necessary air defence forces, be transferred to the South Italian and North African area. Apart from its immediate effect on the conduct of the war in the Mediterranean and North Africa this measure is designed to exert a considerable influence on all further development in the Mediterranean area.

(2) I put Field Marshal Kesselring in command of all the forces to be used in this task, at the same time appointing him as C.-in-C., Southern Area. His tasks are:

To achieve air and sea mastery in the area between Southern Italy and North Africa and thus ensure safe lines of communication with Libya and Cyrenaica; the suppression of Malta is particularly important in this connection.

To co-operate with the German forces operating in North Africa and with the forces of her Allies.

To paralyse enemy traffic through the Mediterranean and to stop British supplies reaching Tobruk and Malta; this is to be effected by close co-operation with German and Italian naval forces which may be available.

(3) The C.-in-C., Southern Area, is subordinate to the Duce from whom he will receive instructions for the task as a whole via the (Italian) Supreme Command.

In all matters concerning the *Luftwaffe* the C.-in-C. of the *Luftwaffe* will deal directly with the C.-in-C., Southern Area; if the matter is particularly important the O.K.W. must be informed at the same time.

(4) The following are subordinate to the C.-in-C.:

All German *Luftwaffe* forces operating in the Mediterranean area and North Africa; the air force and anti-aircraft units which have been placed at the C.-in-C.'s disposal for this task by the Italian *Wehrmacht*.

(5) The German naval forces employed in the Central Mediterranean area remain under the command of the C.-in-C. of the Navy.

The C.-in-C., Southern Area, is empowered, for the purpose of carrying out tasks assigned to him to issue orders to the German Admiral with the Italian Naval High Command and if necessary also to Naval Group South (for the Eastern Mediterranean). Operational orders will be given by the Naval authorities in agreement with the C.-in-C., Southern Area. The wishes of the C.-in-C., Southern Area, regarding the manner in which the combined naval forces shall be employed are to be communicated exclusively to the German Admiral with the Italian Naval High Command.

(6) The tasks of the *Wehrmacht* Commander for the South-eastern Area and of the German General at Italian Armed Forces Headquarters remain unaltered.

(signed) ADOLF HITLER.

\*        \*        \*        \*        \*        \*

But a new war theatre was in the process of being opened in the Far East. The Japanese Fleet was reported at sea, and on December 7 they attacked the American Fleet at Pearl Harbour. The immediate intervention of America into the war, which this attack caused, altered the whole strategy of the war.

On December 12 the strategic consequences were discussed.

C.-in-C., Navy.                                                    December 12, 1941

### REPORT OF THE C.-IN-C., NAVY, TO THE FUEHRER IN BERLIN ON DECEMBER 12, 1941

Also present: Chief of Staff, O.K.W.
                      General Jodl.
                      Captain von Puttkamer.

1. General situation.—The situation in the Atlantic will be eased by Japan's successful intervention. Reports have already been received of the transfer of some battleships from the Atlantic to the Pacific. It is certain that light forces, especially destroyers, will be required in increased numbers in the Pacific. The need for transport ships will be very great, so that a withdrawal of American merchant vessels from the Atlantic can be expected; the strain on British merchant shipping will increase. This calls for intensified submarine warfare on the British supplies. Likewise the situation with regard to surface warfare by auxiliary cruisers and armoured cruisers will probably change in our favour. Stationing the Scharnhorst and Gneisenau in the Atlantic is a step in the right direction; the situation could be improved considerably if Dakar were available as a base, and for this reason the Naval Staff now, as always, is in favour of consolidating the French position in north-west Africa. The danger of major operations against the west coast will also decrease for the present, so that it will be possible to slow up reinforcement of the defences along the west coast; in view of the scarcity of material, transport facilities, petrol, etc., such a respite would be very welcome. *The Fuehrer* does not wish

to postpone the speedy reinforcement of the fortifications, especially as he does not feel that a great deal of material will be required.

Questions put by the Fuehrer:

(a) Does the C.-in-C., Navy, believe that the enemy will in the near future take steps to occupy the Azores, the Cape Verdes, and perhaps even to attack Dakar, in order to win back prestige lost as the result of the setbacks in the Pacific?

(b) Is there any possibility that the U.S.A. and Britain will abandon East Asia for a time in order to crush Germany and Italy first?

As regards (a), *the C.-in-C., Navy*, does not believe that such steps are imminent. The U.S. will have to concentrate all her strength in the Pacific during the next few months. Britain will not want to run any risks after her severe losses of big ships. It is hardly likely that transport tonnage is available for such occupation tasks or for bringing up supplies. However, a firm consolidation of Dakar is desirable for the reasons given above. As regards (b) it is improbable that the enemy will give up East Asia even temporarily; by so doing Britain would endanger India very seriously, and the U.S. cannot withdraw her fleet from the Pacific as the Japanese fleet has the upper hand.

2. Submarine warfare.—A report is made on the disposition of the submarines with the help of a map. At present thirty-six submarines are in or en route to the Mediterranean. It is proposed to station fifty submarines in the Mediterranean, twenty in the eastern area, and thirty in the western and Gibraltar areas. This leaves thirty-six boats at present, three of which are in northern Norway, and five in the south; the latter are transporting the crew of ship "16". Six large submarines are to proceed as quickly as possible to the east coast of America.

In January there will be a large increase in the number of submarines. Up to now there have been long delays due to shortage of labour, the Eastern Campaign, etc. New orders for the conduct of submarine warfare have been issued in accordance with instructions.

3. Transport of submarines to the Black Sea.—Ten months are necessary to transfer boats weighing 250 tons. *The Fuehrer* therefore gives up the idea of such transfers; he inquires whether it is possible to transfer motor boats. *The C.-in-C., Navy*, states that this is possible, but he requests that for the time being only the boats intended for delivery to Roumania and Bulgaria should be transferred, as the new German boats are urgently needed in the Channel. If necessary, the question can be re-opened in the Spring. *The Fuehrer* agrees.

4. Shipping space in the Mediterranean.—The order given to the C.-in-C., Navy, at the last conference for the speedy construction of transport vessels of about 1,000 tons each in Black Sea and Italian shipyards is being carried out with the utmost dispatch. Plans have been drawn up for forty ships of 1,200 tons each; engines have been provided from minesweeper stocks. For the present, eight building slips are available in Italy. Detailed plans are being drawn up at a German shipyard so that production of the plates can commence as soon as the material and the quota permits are available. This is the only cause for delay. *The Fuehrer* instructs the Chief of Staff, O.K.W., to adjust this matter. Work cannot be recommenced at Nikolayev until oil and coal supplies can be brought up. Iron

is available there; probably the plates can be rolled there to the necessary degree of thickness.

5. Oil situation.—The situation is very critical. The Navy's requirements have been cut by fifty per cent.; this has caused an intolerable restriction on the mobility of our vessels. By January 1, 1942, 90,000 tons will have been handed over to the Italians. Supplies by inland routes are inadequate. Roumanian exports to us and to Italy have ceased entirely. The reason is incorrect financial treatment of Roumania, who is demanding gold from us to back her currency. *The Fuehrer* states that the Minister of Economics will give the gold to Roumania as demanded, and discusses other measures to improve the Roumanian situation. He recommends limiting the personnel of our supply organisations there to the utmost. Once the gold has been paid we can rely on renewed supplies of oil from Roumania.

6. Through the Admiral Commanding France, Admiral Darlan has offered to give the German Navy information which he possesses concerning the disposition of British naval forces due to his knowledge of British intelligence methods in the past. *The Fuehrer* sanctions the exchange of intelligence on the British Navy between Admiral Darlan and the German naval office.

7. In private conference.—*The C.-in-C., Navy*, requests and obtains permission for a talk with Admiral Darlan, who has suggested such a talk both through Ambassador Abetz and Admiral Schultze. *The Fuehrer* agrees very readily and explains his views on relations with France.

(signed) RAEDER.

*    *    *    *    *    *

During the last conference of the year the fears of an attack on Norway, which had slowly been developing in Hitler's mind, were openly stated. These fears coloured his strategy for the whole of the following year.

C.-in-C., Navy.

### REPORT OF THE C.-IN-C., NAVY TO THE FUEHRER IN THE EVENING OF DECEMBER 29, 1941, AT WOLFSSCHANZE

Also present: Chief of Staff, O.K.W.
Vice Admiral Fricke.
Captain von Puttkamer.

1. Situation in Norway. Appraisal.—An enemy surprise undertaking of considerable proportions is being carried out against focal points on the trade route off Narvik and near Bergen with the following objectives:

(*a*) To destroy outposts and batteries.
(*b*) To harass and disrupt merchant shipping with incidental successes.
(*c*) For propaganda and prestige purposes.
(*d*) To reconnoitre the terrain and the defences with a view to the later establishment of bridgeheads for the purpose of disrupting and blocking supply routes.

No connected large-scale operation is as yet apparent. Our own shortage in operational naval forces again proves the necessity of having a strong air force ready for operation in the Norwegian area to repulse enemy actions.

2. The question of transferring the Tirpitz to Trondheim is discussed

in this connection, and also the question of where she is to be committed. Up to the present time it has been intended to move her to Trondheim on January 10. She was to operate from Trondheim as the enemy situation, operational requirements, and the situation of our defence, naval, and air forces required.

Strategic function of the Tirpitz:

(*a*) To protect our position in the Norwegian and arctic areas by threatening the flank of enemy operations against the northern Norwegian area and by attacking White Sea convoys.

(*b*) To tie down heavy enemy forces in the Atlantic so that they cannot operate in the Mediterranean, the Indian Ocean, or the Pacific.

(This function will be fulfilled to some extent merely by keeping the Tirpitz ready for action in Trondheim. The operational objective can be attained fully only by actual operations.)

Operational possibilities:

(*a*) Attacks against the convoy route Britain-Iceland-White Sea.
(*b*) Attacks on enemy shipping in the Arctic Ocean.
(*c*) Bombarding of points of military importance.
(*d*) Interference with enemy operations.

*The Fuehrer* will decide this question shortly, when the whole situation in Norway becomes clearer.

3. The question of sending the Scheer out into the Atlantic and Indian Oceans is discussed. Conditions for doing so have improved. There are no more political scruples as regards the U.S.A., and there is the possibility of withdrawing to Japanese bases. The biggest risk is in breaking through. *The Fuehrer* will decide this question shortly.

4. The Scharnhorst, Gneisenau, and Prinz Eugen.—Ready for operations as far as material is concerned, the Gneisenau and Scharnhorst probably on January 10 and 5, 1942, the Prinz Eugen probably on December 31, 1941. Until the ships are ready to that extent only theoretical training and limited practical training at the various battle stations can be carried out. Training in the roadstead and at sea for regular and combat duty, which is necessary to prepare vessel and crew for operations, aims to accomplish the following:

(*a*) To familiarise the crew with the ship and give them some practical training and experience.

(*b*) To give the crew a feeling of belonging together and develop esprit de corps.

This aim can on no account be achieved in dock and with stationary ships. Therefore the battleships will have to undergo at least several weeks training in the waters off the French Atlantic coast before being sent on operations. All necessary security measures should be taken during this time. Training should be carried on first in the harbour and in the roadsteads off Brest, later in Brest Bay, and then at sea off the west coast of France. It is out of the question to send the ships on operations before March 1942. The nature of the operations will depend on an appraisal of the enemy situation and on the oil situation. A final decision as to the nature of the operations is thus not possible at the moment, as the situation is continually changing. Possibilities are attacks on British north-south convoy traffic, or transfer to the northern area. In the opinion of the Naval Staff, the beginnings of these operations must not be delayed beyond March or April at the latest, since operational conditions later in the year will become much more unfavourable, and in summer such operations will *no longer* be possible. Practical training to get the ships ready for operations must therefore begin at once. Otherwise they will lie idle until next winter and be exposed to enemy air attacks on the French Atlantic coast without any action on their part.

The training described above would also be necessary if the breakthrough to home waters through the Channel were to be carried out. This step is impossible, however, according to information to date. The risk, not counting dangers arising from light naval and air forces and from mines, especially the navigational difficulties, is tremendous, and the venture would tax the capacity of both crews and vessels to the limit. It is impossible to safeguard the route sufficiently with our inadequate minesweeping and escort forces; for some time now the route for large ships has been abandoned. It is impossible to evade air attacks in the narrow channels swept clear of mines. It is necessary to reduce speed when following minesweepers and mine-detonating vessels.

*The Fuehrer*: If the British go about things properly they will attack northern Norway at several points. By means of an all-out attack with their fleet and landing troops, they will try to displace us there, take Narvik if possible, and thus exert pressure on Sweden and Finland. This might be of decisive importance for the outcome of the war. The German Fleet must therefore use all its forces for the defence of Norway. It would be expedient to transfer all battleships and pocket battleships there for this purpose; the latter could be used, for instance, for attacking convoys in the north although the Naval Staff does not consider them suitable for this task in this area. (*Marginal note: How come? In winter perhaps?*) The return of the Brest ships is therefore most desirable. This could be accomplished best if the vessels were to break through the Channel taking the enemy completely by surprise, i.e., without previous training movements and during bad weather which makes air operations impossible. (*Naval Staff: Navigational difficulties will also be greatest then*). Any movement for training purposes, especially since the British are kept so well informed by their intelligence service, would lead to intensified British torpedo and bomb attacks, which would sooner or later damage the ships; thereafter, assuming the most favourable circumstances, renewed repairs would be necessary. The only possibility is a surprise breakthrough with no previous indications that it is to take place; even then the chance that it could be executed successfully through the Iceland Straits is very small in view of the presence of aircraft carriers.

If the surprise break through the Channel is impossible, therefore, it would be best to decommission the ships and to use the guns and crews for reinforcements in Norway. In this connection the value of torpedo aircraft is discussed. These are rated very high. The question of the value of battleships in future warfare is also brought up; their value was denied. This statement met with sharp and detailed opposition from the Chief, Naval Staff.

*The Chief, Naval Staff*, points out that the presence of battleships in Brest, even if under repairs, forces the British to protect their convoys with heavy forces which are then not available for other purposes; it would be impossible to justify the decommissioning to the Italians and especially to the Japanese.   The Chief, Naval Staff, further elaborated these points. The training plans should be adhered to so that the battleships could be used at the decisive moment if the situation should change quickly, e.g., if France should come in on our side.   *The Fuehrer* emphasises again and again the importance of defending Norway, and will reserve his decision until the situation there is clear.   After learning of the Fuehrer's new viewpoint, the Chief, Naval Staff, requests permission to go into the whole question once more before a decision is made.   *The Fuehrer* agrees.

(signed) RAEDER.

## APPENDIX

Naval relations with France during the critical years of 1941 and 1942 are best shown in the series of naval conferences with Admiral Darlan which took place in December, 1941 and January, 1942.

The position and use of the French Navy was of supreme importance to both Great Britain and Germany.   The German Naval Staff had appreciated from the beginning of the planning for operation "Attila" that it would be difficult if not impossible to prevent the French Fleet from escaping, unless the ships were put out of action under the orders of the Armistice Commission.   Such a move, however, would have created hostility in France which Hitler, occupied as he was on the Eastern Front, could not afford.   Collaborators were thus encouraged and the traditional rivalry between British and French navies was fostered to the point of creating hatred.

The Admiral Commanding in France.                         Paris, December 4, 1941
To Grand Admiral Raeder.

Sir,
    Attached I am forwarding to you a report on my meeting with Admiral Darlan which only includes the most important points.

    I am checking once more the question of going into the locks of St. Nazaire. Admiral Darlan however insisted very forcefully on his point of view.   The most important item for the Naval War Staff, however, will be his proposal to forward French information of British Fleet movements.   I immediately told Admiral Darlan that I would forward this proposal to you as quickly as possible.

    In case you should want to hear further details of the conversation I request that you name a date when I and my Adjutant who sat next to Admiral Darlan at the table, can come to Berlin to make our reports.

I am, Sir,
Your obedient Servant,
(signed) OTTO SCHULTZE.

   *      *      *      *      *      *

Report on the dinner on December 3, 1941:

Host: Mr. Francois Dupre and wife.

Guests: Admiral Schultze.
        Lt.-Cdt. Fischer.
        Lt. Fudikar.
        Admiral Darlan.
        Mr. Monneraye.   (Commissaire General de la Marine)
        Capt. Fontaine.
        His Excellency Ambassador de Brinon.
        Madame Darlan.
        Countess La Rochefoucauld.
        Madame Mittre.

    Coming from Vichy, Darlan had arrived in Paris on the evening of December 3, 1941.   At the table he very quickly lost his initial reserve and related a number of personal experiences from the China War and the World War.   He also described the coronation ceremonies in London.   He mentioned several times the fact that generally speaking he was not treated very politely in London.   When the British Admiralty had had to look after him, he had been received cordially, but when he had been the guest of the British Government, as one of the three representatives of the French Government, the reception had not been in accordance with his position.

At the beginning of the war he had laid special stress to the proposal that the Admiralty should leave Paris and its political atmosphere, although in case of war he was no longer subordinate to the minister.   He therefore made his head-quarters at the castle of Maintenon and had moved his whole staff there and had been very comfortable.

He commented very unfavourably on the co-operation with the British Admiralty.   He said that the organisation of the whole British Warfare in the sphere of the Navy was suffering from a lack of personalities and a lack of responsi-bility amongst the leading officers.   He mentioned that whilst preparing the Norway operation he had tried to get in touch with the British Commander, responsible for this operation.   He had not succeeded in this but had finally been referred to a Committee.   He had fared similarly on numerous other occasions. The British Admiralty lacked all offensive spirit.   He had proposed in December, 1938 to occupy Narvik and Trondheim which at that time would have been possible with weak forces.   This proposal however, had been refused.

After dinner the conversation was continued amongst the gentlemen.   Admiral Darlan as well as his companions were very open, nearly comradely.   Moreover he proposed to me to install a direct teleprint line between the French Naval Command, in Vichy and a German Naval Authority in Paris.   Based on his co-operation with the British Admiralty he had a very well informed intelligence service, and was in a position and willing to supply the German Naval War Staff with valuable information on British ships' movements and intentions.   So for example in the case of the Bismarck he had had knowledge of the positions and intentions of the British forces at the time when it would have been possible for Bismarck to avoid destruction by escaping to the North-east.   A few similar cases had occurred in the Mediterranean.

Admiral Darlan warned us not to take 35,000-ton warships into the dock of St. Nazaire.   If it was at all possible to get these ships in when fully equipped— slack water and $\frac{1}{4}$ hour before to $\frac{1}{4}$ hour after high tide—it would not be possible to get them out again in time, because, despite dredging, the water depth and local conditions were exceedingly unfavourable.   He was one of the most experienced French seamen and probably one of the greatest experts of the French Atlantic Coast and he described the attempt to take a battleship into St. Nazaire docks as the certain loss of this ship for at least a year.

To the question of further training and a possible active participation of the French Fleet, Admiral Darlan mentioned that this was mainly a question of oil as well as a question of manufacturing ammunition.   In case of action he had sufficient oil stocks to supply the French Fleet for one month.   In an action like the one off Dakar his ships had fired off all their ammunition.   He said about the battleship Dunkerque that it was ready to go to sea, but as she had only been repaired provisionally, she could only proceed at 9 to 10 knots.   Owing to the good English Intelligence Service he could not risk moving her to Toulon as he would have to reckon with attacks from British forces.

Furthermore he spoke of the difficulties in victualling the Fleet and obviously was anxious to obtain French sailors from the occupied areas and to extend the recruiting in the occupied areas, especially in Brittany.   He furthermore mentioned that apart from the French Naval Liaison Officer in Paris, he intended to appoint Liaison Officers also in Cherbourg and Bordeaux.

Admiral Darlan violently criticised Italian Naval warfare in the Mediterranean. He described the Italian attitude as incomprehensible and did not hide his con-tempt.   Also here he mentioned again his knowledge of English ships' movements in the Mediterranean which he thought would be exceedingly valuable to German-Italian warfare.   He particularly pointed out that it was impossible to forward such information through the German Armistice Commission in Wiesbaden to the German Naval War Staff, because the time delay of several days would make it impossible in many cases to evaluate this information.   For example this had been shown during the French campaign in Syria.   Darlan also mentioned the five merchant ships which the British had seized at the Cape of Good Hope and he related that as a reprisal he had ordered two French submarines to sink British merchant steamers in the area around Madagascar.   One of these submarines had put into Madagascar the day before yesterday and reported the sinking of one merchant ship.   This had been confirmed by British reports.

He spoke then of the successes of the French Fleet off Dakar. . . .   He obviously wished that the British Fleet should be driven out of the Mediterranean as soon as possible.   On the possibility of a participation of France to attain this goal he said that the French Fleet was united in its dislike of England.   There was however not the necessary response among the people and that it was impossible to act alone in such questions.   Added to this was Italy's suspicion of France.   Italy seemed to fear that he, Darlan, would one day attack them in the rear with his Fleet.   He said that nothing was further from his mind and he intended no such action.

Finally, Admiral Darlan repeatedly expressed his pleasure at meeting for the first time in this war German Naval Officers at a private dinner party.   He expressed a hope to meet the C.-in-C., Navy, Grand Admiral Raeder at a future date.

(signed) OTTO SCHULTZE.

From the C.-in-C., Navy.                                                            December 18, 1941
To the Admiral Commanding in France.

Admiral Schultze,
    Paris.

Dear Schultze,
    Many thanks for your letter and report of December 4.   I have informed the Fuehrer about the remarks made by Admiral Darlan concerning information he could supply on the movements of the British Fleet as well as his wish to meet me.   The Fuehrer has agreed to both proposals.   I would therefore be very grateful to you, if you would inform Admiral Darlan in a suitable manner that the Navy would gladly accept his proposal.   For this purpose a direct teleprint connection would be installed between him and the Admiral Commanding France.   At the same time I would ask you to inform Admiral Darlan that I shall gladly accept his offer for a meeting and that I hope to be able to name a date very shortly.   I have instructed the Chief of Naval Communications to make the necessary arrangement to install a teleprint line between Vichy and Paris, and I expect that he will get in touch with your authorities.   With the best greetings and Heil Hitler,
                                                                Yours,
                                                    (signed) RAEDER.
                                                    Grand Admiral.

*          *          *          *          *          *

Conversation between Grand Admiral Raeder and Admiral of the Fleet, Darlan at Evry-le-Bourg on January 28, 1942 at 1130.

(1) Greeting.   Mutual satisfaction on the bringing about of the meeting is expressed.

(2) The Grand Admiral expresses his thanks to the French Government for the permission granted by them to take E-boats and minesweepers through unoccupied France.   He further expresses his thanks for the help given when minor repairs became necessary.

(3) The Grand Admiral assumes that the British deciphered the French code during the operations off Madagascar and that they could be in possession of the most recent codes.   The Admiral of the Fleet admits the first possibility, but is of the opinion that in contrast to the present Army and Air Force code which are probably both accessible to the enemy, this is not so in the case of the naval code.

(4) The Grand Admiral states that the Navy has shown understanding for the necessity of defending French West Africa.   The Admiral of the Fleet is of the

opinion that West Africa is sufficiently strong as far as naval and air defences are concerned, there is however a considerable lack of tanks and anti-tank defences. The causes of this lack were not only the limitations imposed by the armistice treaty, but must be ascribed to the insufficient French equipment before the war.

(5) With reference to the French warships lying at Alexandria, the Admiral of the Fleet mentions that they were only there because the British at the time had demanded that French heavy ships had to unite with the British forces to force the Straits of Sicily, as the British Naval Forces were not strong enough to carry out this operation alone. In this connection the Admiral of the Fleet stated that Admiral Cunningham was the only British Admiral with whom he was prepared to shake hands.

(6) The Admiral of the Fleet gives further instances of the Franco-British relations during the campaign 1939/40. He mentioned Winston Churchill's visit to Briar sur Loire on June 12, 1940, where he asked the French to move the French Fleet to Britain. To this the Admiral of the Fleet replied as follows:

"We will not surrender the Fleet to the Germans neither will we surrender it to you, the British."

He then mentioned the visit of the British First Sea Lord, Sir Dudley Pound to Bordeaux immediately before the armistice, when he made again the demand to send the French ships to British instead of African harbours. The Admiral of the Fleet had replied to this by saying that he considered French ships to be best guarded in French African harbours. At the time the British had agreed to this. The Admiral of the Fleet added: "And then Mers-el-Kebir."

The Admiral of the Fleet gives some information on the attitude of the French Navy towards his person. So far the French Navy have obeyed him implicitly, this was also to be expected for the future as long as the necessary moral and material basis was available. At the moment of the Armistice it was in his hands whether the Navy would follow Marshal Petain or not. By telegram he had made it clear to the Officer Corps that this must be done, and it was done. But it was necessary that the basis was really created.

The Grand Admiral states that this was also the wish of the Navy and that as Darlan knew himself, the Fuehrer was of the same opinion. The Fuehrer, however, reserved to himself the right of choosing the moment when to make a political settlement. The Admiral of the Fleet said that he appreciated this: "I am the loser and I have to wait for the moment which the Fuehrer considers suitable."

(7) The Admiral of the Fleet does not believe that a British attack from West Africa is imminent. Only yesterday Marshal Petain told the American Ambassador Leahy: "If you attack us, or if you come without being called, we will shoot." (Pencil note: The Ambassador replied that America did not want to break off diplomatic relations with France for the time being.)

(8) Concerning a possible British attack against Madagascar, the Admiral of the Fleet states that the mere capture of the Island was of little value. The occupying power must try to capture Nossi-Be and Diego Suarez. The Prime Minister of the Union of South Africa had told the French Consul a few days ago that the British had no reason to occupy Madagascar except if the Japanese reached Ceylon. In this connection the Admiral of the Fleet stresses the fact that the Japanese would be acting wrongly if they invaded India. They would never get out again. As the decisive point for the Japanese offensive against the British, the Admiral of the Fleet mentions Ceylon and the Persian Gulf and adds that if the Japanese wanted to start any offensive activities against India at all, they would have first of all to occupy Ceylon and finally Karachi.

(9) As the decisive point of the German front he mentions the extreme right flank (Caucasus—Persian Gulf) and the extreme left flank (Murmansk—Archangel) and enumerates the three vulnerable points of the German front as far as enemy supplies are concerned, as follows:

(i) Rostow, because of the oil.
(ii) Archangel—Murmansk—Kirkenes, because of the possibilities of bringing supplies overseas.
(iii) Vladivostok.

The Grand Admiral fully agrees with the statement.

(10) The Admiral of the Fleet points out that the Dunkerque will probably be ready to reach Toulon shortly under the escort of the French Fleet which will put to sea for this purpose. As a caisson of about fifteen metres length had been fitted over her leak, she was only able to proceed at 14 knots.

The Richelieu was in a position to use three of her four engines. Jean Bart had one turret ready for firing. 38-cm. barrels were probably available at Ruelle or another place. He believed he knew that one of these barrels had been fitted in a coastal battery, it would be valuable to ascertain this as it could be used for another turret of the Richelieu. It could not be used for the Jean Bart as the turret itself was not yet ready.

The Admiral of the Fleet then discusses the question of stopping the breaking up of the aircraft carrier Joffre. The Grand Admiral replies that he has already ordered that this work be stopped. The Admiral of the Fleet is of the opinion that the Joffre is only suitable as a training ship. As an aircraft carrier the Joffre was too small, as with the modern weapons of attack only larger ships had a chance to survive a torpedo hit. In this connection he makes some remarks on the future organisation of naval forces. The ideal squadron he says would consist of several battleships, one aircraft carrier, several cruisers which are liberally equipped with anti-aircraft guns and the appropriate number of flotilla leaders. The question of whether large warships still justified their existence had in his opinion not yet been decided, because so far all naval battles had taken place so close to the coast that the air force had always been able to join in the battle. The Grand Admiral agrees with this opinion and comments on the contradictory opinions which are at the present time held about this problem.

The Admiral of the Fleet mentions that he has been carefully observing the number of warships which have been sunk in this war. According to this about 230 ships had been sunk. In detail:

60 for unknown reasons, mostly submarines.
48 by aircraft bombs.
44 by gun fire.
20 by torpedoes fired by submarines.
 8 by torpedoes fired by surface vessels.
 4 by torpedoes fired by aircraft.

The Admiral of the Fleet points out that it took three days and a great number of ships of all types to sink the Bismarck and in the end it had only been possible because the steering gear had been damaged at the beginning of the action. The question of large battleships or not, would probably be answered by building far larger battleships than hitherto.

In connection with the request to stop the breaking up of the Joffre the Admiral of the Fleet said as follows: "The European Fleet will need aircraft carriers when France is on Germany's side."

(11) In connection with the treatment of the French Fleet in the Armistice Treaty the Grand Admiral says that the Fuehrer had from the beginning realised the importance of this question and had stressed that we must respect French honour. The Admiral of the Fleet recognises this and adds: "If this had not been the case I would not be here now." He stresses that he insisted that the French Fleet was moved to French Mediterranean harbours trusting in the German assurance that they would not have to be surrendered, because if the ships had been transferred to one of the German occupied harbours on the Atlantic coast, he would not have doubted the German word but would have expected the ships to be attacked by the British. In several of his remarks the Admiral of the Fleet describes the British as hypocrites and liars and gives a detailed description of the Fleet negotiations between the former Allies at which he had participated since 1925. Based on the count of the tonnage of German (Versailles), French and Italian warships, the British had tried to get a tonnage even exceeding this figure, on the other hand they had tried to play out Italian tonnage against French tonnage always resulting in a disadvantage for the latter. On this basis the British had tried since 1935 to play Germany (with whom they had the 35 per cent. agreement) against all the other European sea powers and since 1938 they had become uneasy about Germany.

(12) The possibility of putting into St. Nazaire is discussed. The Admiral

of the Fleet warns not to take large warships into this harbour as the possibilities of getting out of them are doubtful.    At Brest as far as he knew artificial fog had been used against air attacks and he enquires about the results.    Also in the French Navy experiments had been carried out in this direction but without any tangible results.    The possibility of using the Roads at La Pallice is discussed.

(13) The Grand Admiral requests that if possible he would like to know the results obtained by the short wave D/F station at Dakar.    This was to be within the framework of the information which the French Admiralty had promised to supply.    The Admiral of the Fleet promises this if possible.

(14) The Admiral of the Fleet mentions that in his opinion the German U-boats at the beginning of the war had used their W/T too much.    He realised that it was necessary to use W/T.    In the French Navy, however, it had been the custom that the F.O.I.C. U-boats used W/T whilst the submarines only used theirs in extreme emergencies.

(15) The Asdic device is discussed.    There are a few sets in the French Navy. In the opinion of the Admiral of the Fleet the German Air Force had been perfectly justified to attack Portland as the assembly and training installations for this device were situated there.

(16) In this connection the Admiral of the Fleet discusses what is in his opinion the best organisation for the Air Force.    He supports a division into Army and to Navy Air Force.    He had succeeded in having this type of organisation introduced in the French Forces.    In England this had not been the case.    However, disadvantages of other organisations were compensated by using aircraft carriers.

(17) The Grand Admiral requests if possible to put the German Naval Authorities in touch with the Vicomte Henri de France who is an expert in the sphere of *Pendelpeilung*.    The Admiral of the Fleet will try to obtain the address of this gentleman.    He gives some reasons for his sceptical attitude on this subject.

(18) Both Admirals expressed their mutual satisfaction about the meeting.

# Winter Fears

## THE ESCAPE FROM BREST

BY THE beginning of 1942 Germany was deeply involved in the Russian campaign, towards which the major part of her war effort was directed. The West Wall was held as lightly as was deemed safe, and England appeared to the German High Command as a fortress which they had temporarily by-passed. Operation "Sea Lion"—the invasion of England—had been indefinitely postponed, and for the moment Hitler hoped simply to keep England on the defensive.

In spite of the U-boat campaign and the attacks of the *Luftwaffe*, however, supplies from the Empire and the Americas were pouring into the United Kingdom. British troops were fighting hard in Libya and Abyssinia, and numerous small raids were being made on the European coast. In particular British raids on Norway greatly disturbed Hitler. Supplemented by persistent rumours and a complex political situation in Scandinavia, these raids convinced Hitler that a full-scale invasion of Norway was imminent. He believed that Sweden was on the point of joining the Allies, and he saw that a pincer movement on Norway—a British attack by sea and a combined Russian and Swedish attack by land—would enable the Allies to join forces and seriously hinder the German advance on the Eastern Front.

Hitler's fear of an invasion of Norway began towards the end of 1941 and persisted throughout the following year. It coloured his entire strategy against the Western Powers, and even after the Allied landings in North Africa he still insisted that Norway was the danger area in Germany's defences. Germany had three zones of defence against a possible invasion of Norway. She could attack the supply routes to the United Kingdom; she could attack the factories and towns in the United Kingdom; or she could attack the invaders in Norway itself. The supply routes to the United Kingdom and the country itself had already been under attack for two years, so that the only zone that needed strengthening was Norway. Hitler, however, did not want to move troops from the Eastern Front. He therefore decided that the threat to Norway must be met by sea and air forces, and accordingly ordered the bulk of the German Navy to be transferred to Norwegian waters, and the *Luftwaffe* squadrons in Norway to be considerably increased.

The transfer of the German High Seas Fleet presented an extremely difficult problem. Part of the Fleet was at Brest and part was training in the Baltic, so that it was impossible to assemble a sufficiently strong force to meet the British Fleet which was known to consist of at least three battleships and two carriers stationed at Scapa Flow. The ships in the Baltic could be transferred comparatively simply, but those at Brest had either a long voyage round the British Isles in the Atlantic, where they would almost certainly be attacked by the Home Fleet, or a shorter but equally hazardous voyage through the English Channel.

The three major units of the German Fleet at Brest (Scharnhorst, Gneisenau, and Prinz Eugen) had served the useful purpose of containing the British Fleet in Home Waters and of distracting British air attacks from German cities, and Raeder, C.-in-C. of the German Navy, was loth to run the risk of moving them. He disagreed with Hitler that the threat to Norway was serious, and strongly opposed the movement of the Brest Group. The crews were untrained and the ships had had no opportunity of attaining anything like full fighting efficiency, so that a long sea voyage round the British Isles and opposed by the British Fleet was out of the question. If the ships were to be moved at all they would have to go through the Straits of Dover. Hitler, however, insisted that the threat to Norway was extremely serious and that the ships at Brest should be moved. This decision was made at the end of December, 1941, and on January 12, 1942, Raeder submitted his plans for the movement of the Brest Group through the Channel.

High Command, Navy
Naval Staff

## MEMORANDUM CONCERNING THE REPORT THE C.-IN-C., NAVY, MADE TO THE FUEHRER JANUARY 12, 1942, ON THE PLANNED PASSAGE OF THE BREST GROUP THROUGH THE CHANNEL

Also present:
1. O.K.W.:
    Field Marshal Keitel.
    Lt.-General Jodl.
    Colonel Scherf, attached to the General Staff.
    Captain (Navy) von Puttkamer.
    Commander Junge.
    Major Christian.
    Major Below, present part of the time.

2. Navy:
    C.-in-C., Navy.
    Chief of Staff, Naval Staff.
    Admiral Commanding, Battleships.
    Admiral Commanding Defences, West.
    Operations Officer to the Admiral Commanding Battleships.

3. Air Force:
    Lt.-General Jeschonnek.
    Colonel Galland.

1. *The C.-in-C., Navy*, opened the session with something like the following remarks: "The question of the passage of the Brest Group through the Channel has been examined by all agencies concerned. In the light of the Fuehrer's opinion, the German Fleet's primary task is to defend the Norwegian coast and ports and, in so doing, it should use its might unsparingly. All parties concerned therefore have approached this study with an open mind. Even though, on the basis of this study, I do not believe that I should take the initiative in advocating such a break-through operation, plans have been worked out that ought to be followed, should the break through the Channel be decided upon. Since you, my Fuehrer, informed me that you insist upon the return of the heavy units to their home bases, I suggest that Vice-Admiral Ciliax report on the details of how this operation is to be prepared and carried out, and that Commodore Ruge subsequently report on the necessary security measures, minesweeping measures, etc., to enable you, my Fuehrer, to make the final decision afterwards."

2. Following these introductory remarks, *the Fuehrer* expressed himself as follows: "The Naval Force (*Geschwader*) at Brest has, above all, the welcome effect of tying up enemy air forces and diverting them from making attacks upon the German Homeland. This advantage will last exactly as long as the enemy considers himself compelled to attack because the ships are undamaged. With our ships at Brest, enemy sea forces are tied up to no greater extent than would be the case if the ships were stationed in Norway. If he—the Fuehrer—could see any chance that the ships might remain undamaged for four or five months and, thereafter, be

employed in operations in the Atlantic, in consequence of a changed over-all situation, he might be more inclined to consider leaving them at Brest. Since in the opinion of the Fuehrer such a development is not to be expected, however, he is determined to withdraw the ships from Brest, to avoid exposing them to chance hits day after day.  On the basis of incoming reports and in view of the increasingly unfriendly attitude of Sweden, the Fuehrer, furthermore, fears that there will be a large-scale Norwegian-Russian offensive in Norway.  He thinks that if a strong task force of battleships and cruisers, practically the entire German Fleet, were stationed along the Norwegian coast, it could, in conjunction with the German Air Force, make a decisive contribution toward the defence of the area of Norway.  He therefore is determined to have the main strength of the German naval forces shifted to that area."

3. Subsequent to these fundamental observations of the Fuehrer, the *Admiral Commanding Battleships*, reports on necessary preparations and planning.  The following points are given special emphasis in this report:

(*a*) The demand for a minimum of ship movements prior to the operation.  The Fuehrer expresses agreement with the opinions presented by the Admiral Commanding Battleships.

(*b*) The necessity of leaving Brest under cover of darkness, taking maximum advantage of the element of surprise, and of passing through the Straits of Dover in the daytime, thus making the most effective use of the means of defence at our disposal.  The Fuehrer likewise expresses approval, emphasising particularly the surprise to be achieved by having the ships leave after dark.

(*c*) It is stressed very emphatically that a very strong pursuit and fighter cover should be provided on the day of the break-through itself from the beginning of dawn to the end of dusk.  The Fuehrer is aware of the decisive rôle to be played by the Air Force in this enterprise. *Lt.-General Jeschonnek* does not believe that he will be able to provide constant unfailing protection for the ships with the available 250 fighters, which cannot possibly be reinforced.  He then promises to draw on the existing night-fighter formations to provide dawn fighter protection.

4. Subsequent to this report of the Admiral Commanding Battleships, *the Fuehrer* asks for opinions as to the feasibility of using the northern route.  He makes it clear that he does not care which route is selected by the Navy, if only it is successful in getting those ships transferred to Norwegian waters.  *The C.-in-C., Navy*, the *Chief of Staff, Naval Staff*, and the *Admiral Commanding Battleships*, explain that the northern route is not suitable for several reasons.  First of all, due to the training situation at Brest, it has been impossible to train crews for full-scale battle manœuvres.  The present disposition of enemy forces also is against such a move; there are two or three battleships and two aircraft carriers in the Home Fleet.  And lastly, the German air forces would not be able to provide the necessary air cover.

5. *Commodore Ruge* then reports on defence problems and the mine situation, coming to the conclusion that, while the deep-water channel cannot be called absolutely safe from mines, a relative measure of safety none the less does exist.

6. *The Fuehrer* subsequently points out once more that the success or failure of this undertaking will depend on how well the secret of it is kept.

7. *The C.-in-C., Navy*, again emphasises the demands to be made on the Air Force for:

(*a*) a very strong fighter cover;
(*b*) attacks on airfields serving enemy torpedo planes in the early morning of the day of the break-through, and possibly a few days earlier.

*Lt.-General Jeschonnek* replies to this as follows:
In view of the over-all situation, reinforcement of our air forces in the West is impossible; however, in compliance with the Fuehrer's orders, the question will be examined once again. The constant air cover, as demanded by the Admiral Commanding Battleships, will leave insufficient aircraft for the heavy air battles that are sure to develop on the day of the break-through. We may expect our fighter force to become very inferior in strength, at least during the afternoon. Lt.-General Jeschonnek also calls attention to the fact that, in the afternoon, our own anti-aircraft personnel is susceptible to fatigue, as experience has shown.

8. *The Fuehrer* sums up once more:

(*a*) The ships must not leave port in the daytime because we are dependent on the element of surprise.
(*b*) This necessarily means that they will have to pass through the Dover Straits in the daytime.
(*c*) In view of past experience the Fuehrer does not believe the British capable of making and carrying out lightning decisions. This is why he does not believe that they will be as swift as was assumed by the Naval Staff and the Admiral Commanding Battleships, in shifting their bomber and pursuit forces to the south-eastern part of England, for an attack on our ships in the Dover Straits. The Fuehrer illustrates his argument by picturing what would happen if the situation were reversed, i.e. if a surprise report came in that British battleships have appeared in the Thames estuary and are heading for the Straits of Dover. In his opinion even we would hardly be able to bring up air pursuit forces and bomber forces swiftly and methodically. He compares the situation of the Brest Group with that of a patient having cancer, who is doomed unless he submits to an operation. An operation, on the other hand, even though it may have to be a drastic one, will offer at least some hope that the patient's life may yet be saved. Passage of our ships through the Channel would be such an operation. It must therefore be attempted.

9. *Colonel Galland* is of the opinion that the strong Spitfire forces at the disposal of the British will render things difficult for the long-range fighters which we are going to employ.

10. In closing, *the C.-in-C., Navy*, again points out emphatically that success or failure of the enterprise will hinge upon the way in which our air forces are used. He once more asks the Fuehrer for a directive to the Air Force to do everything in its power that might further the security of the ships. *The Fuehrer* directs Lt.-General Jeschonnek to do so. The latter, however, emphasises again that unfailing protection cannot be guaranteed because of the lack of needed reinforcements.

11. Tide and daylight will determine the timing of the operation. That is the reason why the date of the operation cannot be changed. The C.-in-C., Navy, then asks what should be done in case one or several ships are unable to move on the date set. It is decided that, if two battleships are in a position to move, they are to undertake the operation, if necessary without the cruiser. If only one battleship and the cruiser can move, they are to do likewise. But in no case should the Prinz Eugen do so alone.

12. Finally the question of transferring the Tirpitz is raised by the Chief of Staff, Naval Staff, and the Fuehrer decides that the Tirpitz is to be transferred at once.

13. Finally *the Fuehrer* emphasises once more that nothing can be gained by leaving the ships at Brest. Should the Brest Group manage to escape through the Channel, however, there is a chance that it might be employed to good advantage at a later date. If, on the other hand, the ships remain at Brest, their "flypaper effect," i.e. their ability to tie up enemy air forces, may not continue for long. As long as the ships remain in battleworthy condition they will constitute worthwhile targets, which the enemy will feel obliged to attack. But the moment they are seriously damaged—and this may happen any day—the enemy will discontinue his attacks. Such a development will nullify the one and only advantage derived from leaving the ships at Brest. In view of all this *the Fuehrer*, in accordance with the suggestions of the C.-in-C., Navy, finally decides that the operation is to be prepared for as proposed.

(signed)        RAEDER.<br>
(countersigned) Lt.-Comdr. ASSMANN.

*     *     *     *     *     *

Rumours and reports of Allied preparations for an attack on Norway persisted. Hitler became even more convinced that an invasion was imminent, and hastened both military and political measures to meet the threat. Troops were to be moved now as well as ships and aircraft, and, at a conference ten days later, outlined his schemes for the defence of Norway, the "zone of destiny."

### REPORT BY THE CHIEF OF STAFF, NAVAL STAFF (VICE-ADMIRAL FRICKE), ON THE CONFERENCE WITH THE FUEHRER ON JANUARY 22, 1942

I. Norway.—1. Latest reports have thoroughly convinced the Fuehrer that Britain and the United States intend to make every effort to influence the course of the war by an attack on northern Norway. Several places along the coast from Trondheim to Kirkenes will probably be occupied shortly. Sweden's support in a spring offensive is expected, for which she would receive Narvik and ore deposits near Petsamo. Finland would be guaranteed her independence within the old borders. The Fuehrer has proof of Sweden's willingness to participate, and therefore plans the following:

(*a*) To expose the intentions of Britain and the United States as well as Sweden's attitude in the world press.

(*b*) To appoint *Field Marshal von Kesselring* as Commander of the Armed Forces in Norway.

Anglo-Saxon domination of the Swedish area will gradually eliminate all freedom of action in the Baltic Sea. Should German naval units still be in the Baltic under such circumstances, we should immediately disarm them completely. The only ships from which we could salvage any appreciable amount of nickel would be the battleships. The Fuehrer is convinced that Norway is the "zone of destiny" in this war. Therefore he demands unconditional obedience to all his commands and wishes concerning the defence of this area.

2. *The Fuehrer* ordered a considerable reinforcement of Army personnel and material in Norway. The C.-in-C., Air, was instructed to strengthen his forces. The latter foresees certain difficulties; he is short of aircraft; reconnaissance and fighting are limited in bad weather; besides, the Norwegian airfields are inconveniently located and are all too few. *The Fuehrer* desires that the Navy must also do everything in its power to head off the British offensive at the very start. The Navy must take over adequate reconnaissance in weather not fit for flying. It must defend the sea lanes to Norway, and must dislodge with all available forces any enemy troops which have landed, entirely foregoing all other warfare "except for the Mediterranean operations."

3. *The Fuehrer* agrees to let the Brest Group complete its mission, using all light defence forces. E-boats are to remain in the Channel. The Fuehrer demands that every available vessel be employed in Norway. He endorses our plans to use battleships, pocket battleships, heavy cruisers, light naval forces, and E-boats; increases his demand for submarines; is of the same opinion as the Naval Staff concerning the improbability of a landing in western France.

4. *The Fuehrer* orders even more of the heaviest artillery pieces to be mounted in Norway. He demands that all heavy calibre guns available be tested and made ready (reserve barrels of the old battleships, captured French barrels, 25–30·5 barrels in Swinemuende, etc.).

5. It will be necessary to investigate further the possibility of bringing in supplies by submarine.

6. *The Fuehrer* emphasised several times that the greatest speed and efficiency are vitally important. He is deeply concerned about the grave consequences which unfavourable developments in the North Norwegian area could have on the entire course of the war.

II. The Fuehrer had no comments to make on the oil problem which I presented as being very serious, especially in view of the planned operations.

(signed) FRICKE.

*　　*　　*　　*　　*　　*

By the beginning of February plans for the movement of the Brest Group were completed. The naval force was under the command of the Vice-Admiral, Battleships, Vice-Admiral Ciliax, and the *Luftwaffe* squadrons under the command of Colonel Galland. For once the *Luftwaffe* had co-operated fully with the Navy, and, in spite of the objections raised at the earlier conference, Colonel Galland had secured an adequate number of both short-range and long-range fighters to cover the operation. More than 250 aircraft were made available to protect the naval force.

On the evening of February 11 the Scharnhorst, Gneisenau, and Prinz Eugen accompanied by destroyer and E-boat escort, slipped out of Brest and began their dash up the English Channel. They were not sighted until shortly before eleven o'clock on the following morning.

The escape had been foreseen in England, but due to the delay in receiving the sighting report, it was not until 1230 that the first attack by Motor Torpedo Boats was delivered. Naval aircraft attacked a quarter of an hour later under extremely hazardous conditions, but all six aircraft were shot down by the German fighter cover. (The V.C. was posthumously awarded to the leader, Lt.-Commander Esmonde.) At 1545 six destroyers of the Royal Navy also went into action, while during the afternoon R.A.F. bombers attacked repeatedly for two and a half hours, but with no effect. The German operation had succeeded far beyond their hopes. "Vice-Admiral Ciliax," wrote the Times, "has succeeded where the Duke of Medina Sidonia failed. . . . Nothing more mortifying to the pride of sea power has happened in home waters since the 17th century."

\*        \*        \*        \*        \*        \*

Hitler's pleasure at the success of the Channel operation gave Raeder a favourable opportunity to present his suggestions on the conduct of the war. He had a much better understanding of the strategical use of sea power than Hitler, and although he had by now submitted to and agreed with Hitler's appreciation of the threat to Norway, he was at the same time anxious to present the possibilities in other theatres of the war. The Baltic and the Black Sea were both areas where German sea power could achieve complete control without much effort, and where such control would materially assist the Russian campaign.

The present situation in the Mediterranean also favoured Germany. The Battle of the Atlantic, the Japanese attacks in the Far East, and the concentration of the German Fleet in Norway had all helped to weaken the British Mediterranean Fleet. Raeder visualised a quick Mediterranean victory dependent on the capture of Malta, which would lead to the sealing of the Straits of Gibraltar, the capture of Egypt, and eventually of the Persian oilfields. A direct link with Japan would then be possible, and Allied sea power could be broken.

Raeder realised that this threat in the Mediterranean must be equally clear to England and he foresaw that the Allies would do everything possible to strengthen their position in the Mediterranean whatever dangers might arise elsewhere, and that there was little time to be lost if full advantage was to be taken of the situation. He foresaw that unless Germany acted quickly the Allies would either attack the Iberian peninsula or invade North Africa.

On February 13, the day after the break-through of the Brest Group, Raeder had a friendly and receptive conference with Hitler.

The C.-in-C., Navy
and the Chief of the Naval Staff

## REPORT TO THE FUEHRER MADE BY THE C.-IN-C., NAVY, THE AFTERNOON OF FEBRUARY 13, 1942

The Staff of the O.K.W. was not present.

1. Norway.—The reinforcement of our position in Norway makes the utmost demands on our escort forces. Delays in shipping supplies are unavoidable at present, in view of the limited number of convoys. The situation cannot be expected to improve until after operation *Cerberus* has been completed. The critical oil situation in Norway is being relieved by oil imports. Numerous escort vessels have been lost through enemy action and the wear and tear of heavy duty. The naval and coastal defences of Norway are still very weak at present. We have increased the protection of our sea lanes in the northern area by laying flanking minefields in the waters between Harstad and Kirkenes. Additional minefields are being laid. The following measures are now in preparation:

(*a*) The Prinz Eugen and the Scheer are to be transferred at the earliest possible moment, the battleships as soon as repairs, now being

made at increased speed, are completed.    Furthermore, all destroyers
and torpedo boats ready for duty are being assigned to Norway, to be
based at Trondheim and Narvik.

(b) Provisions have been made to reinforce our patrol forces in the
Norwegian area, particularly with vessels withdrawn from the western
area.

(c) Admiral Commanding, Norway, will continue to expand the
coastal minefields.

(d) It is planned to increase mine operations in the Skagerrak, in the
northern part of the North Sea, and the Arctic Ocean; completion expected at the end of February or at the beginning of March.

2. Russia.—The following points are of decisive importance for the
renewal of naval warfare in the Gulf of Finland and for the final expulsion
of the Russians from the Baltic:

(a) Continuous attacks on Russian naval forces in Leningrad and
Kronstadt by Army artillery and the Air Force.

(c) Conquest of the islands in the Gulf of Finland in order to get
operational bases for a tight blockade of Kronstadt Bay.    An agreement
was reached with the Army, whereby Army troops are to seize the islands.
The Navy will then take over and be responsible for holding them.

3. Black Sea.—The main problem in the Black Sea concerns transport
of supplies for the Army.    The Naval Staff is fully aware of the complications involved.    Difficulties are due to the lack of sufficient shipping
space and the absence of escort and striking forces.    Measures are being
taken to improve our position in the Black Sea.    E-boats, Italian anti-
submarine vessels, small submarines, landing craft (MFP), etc., are being
added to our forces; minefields are being laid.    Orders have been issued
to speed up all measures and to make every effort to support the Army by
bringing up supplies.    Russian naval forces in the Black Sea must be
attacked and destroyed.    The degree of success obtained will determine
the outcome of the war in the Black Sea area.    Attention is called to the
fact that eventually it will become necessary to occupy all Russian Black
Sea bases and ports.    *The Fuehrer* concurs in this opinion.

4. Western area.—Due to lack of strength, our naval and air forces are,
at present, largely limited to defensive operations on the Atlantic coast
and in the Channel.    The enemy is hampering our transport operations
by the increased use of mines, by air raids, and E-boat attacks.    This
forces us to confine convoy movements as well as patrolling and mine-
sweeping activities to the hours of night.    Steps are being taken to provide
more effective patrol of coastal waters by increasing the patrol forces.    The
offensive operations of our E-boats and aircraft against the very extensive
enemy convoy traffic along the English coast are of particular importance
in the face of our otherwise purely defensive situation.    We must try
with all our might to intensify these operations as much as possible.    Unfortunately the weather greatly hampers E-boat operations during the
winter months.    Aerial mines must be used more extensively in large-
scale attacks.

5. Atlantic.—Submarine warfare in the Atlantic produces good results
at the present time.    In the war against enemy shipping everything depends
on the number of submarines available.    Time and again Churchill speaks

of shipping tonnage as his greatest worry. Britain and the United States are building 7,000,000 tons in 1942, which means that Germany and Japan will have to sink a monthly total of 600,000 tons to offset this increase. This will become possible once the Japanese war against enemy shipping in the Indian Ocean gets under way. If the number of workmen had remained the same after production was adjusted to the cut in the raw material allotment and after manpower had been redistributed between repair work and new construction, our monthly output of submarines would have dropped to about 19–20. Since, however, many workmen are still being drafted into the Armed Forces, this figure will drop to 16–17 in the course of the year. This is entirely inadequate. No improvement can be expected at this time.

6. Mediterranean.—The most significant factor at this time is that not a single heavy British ship in the Mediterranean is fully seaworthy. The Axis rules both the sea and the air in the Central Mediterranean. However, enemy submarines still menace our shipping, there still is a shortage of transport vessels and escort forces, and the oil situation continues to be critical. The Mediterranean situation is definitely favourable at the moment. In conjunction with events in East Asia, it gives us some indication of the possibilities if we were to launch an attack on Egypt and the Suez Canal as quickly as possible. Except for Singapore, the British position is at present weakest in the North Africa–Suez area. Attention is called to the change of Government in Egypt. The British position in Egypt is precarious because Britain has to depend on the 40,000 Egyptian troops to safeguard her rear communications.

(a) Mediterranean shipping.—An agreement was reached with Italy concerning transport vessels for the Mediterranean whereby we will get ten transports to begin with. The Italian Minister of Transport is still objecting to the transfer of another ten; he claims the need of this tonnage for his own war construction programme. According to the findings of our representative, Dr. Scholz, Director of the German Shipyard Company (Deutsche Werft), however, this tonnage could easily be made available. Likewise difficulties are being encountered concerning the chartering of Italian vessels for war purposes, since the Duce has to be consulted in every instance.

The C.-in-C., Navy, requests that these points be mentioned, should the Fuehrer decide to write to the Duce. He will submit a draft, if desired. The Fuehrer agrees.

7. East Asia.—Rangoon, Singapore, and, most likely, also Port Darwin will be in Japanese hands within a few weeks. Only weak resistance is expected on Sumatra, while Java will be able to hold out longer. Japan plans to protect this front in the Indian Ocean by capturing the key position of Ceylon, and she also plans to gain control of the sea in that area by means of superior naval forces.

Fifteen Japanese submarines are at the moment operating in the Bay of Bengal, in the waters off Ceylon, and in the straits on both sides of Sumatra and Java.

With Rangoon, Sumatra, and Java gone, the last oil wells between Bahrein and the American continent will be lost. Oil supplies for Australia and New Zealand will have to come from either the Persian Gulf or from America.   Once Japanese battleships, aircraft carriers, submarines, and the Japanese naval air force are based on Ceylon, Britain will be forced to resort to heavily-escorted convoys, if she desires to maintain communications with India and the Near East.   Only Alexandria, Durban, and Simonstown will be available as repair bases for large British naval vessels in that part of the world.

The Suez and Basra positions are the western pillars of the British position in the Indian area.   Should these positions collapse under the weight of concerted Axis pressure, the consequences for the British Empire would be disastrous.   An early German-Italian attack on the British key position of Suez would therefore be of utmost strategic importance.

According to reports available, the British themselves are fully aware of the great danger which is threatening them in Egypt.   They fear that the German-Italian forces might establish contact with the Japanese. The Japanese, on their part, are making an honest effort to establish contact with Germany by sea and by air since they realise the decisive significance this would have on the outcome of the war.

8. Request for cancellation of operation "Sea Lion."—A decision is required to what extent the commitments of personnel and material for operation "Sea Lion," which are still very considerable, have to remain in force.   Since the operation cannot possibly be carried out in 1942 it is proposed that all commitments be cancelled if at all permissible from a military point of view.   *The Fuehrer* gives his consent.

(signed)        RAEDER.<br>(countersigned) Lt.-Comdr. ASSMANN.

*     *     *     *     *     *

Allied assistance to Russia, which had begun with a small convoy of seven ships in August 1941, had by January 1942 increased considerably.   Large convoys were now sailing at least twice a month from British ports and Hitler realised that such aid to Russia would seriously affect the war on the Eastern Front. Russian convoys therefore became a priority target for the German Navy and *Luftwaffe*.

The first attack was launched in January 1942 by U-boats, and two ships were sunk.   Two more attacks were made during the next six weeks and, on March 4, the Tirpitz, which had previously been sent to Trondheim to offset the threat to Norway, was also thrown into the battle.   A large convoy had been sighted by the *Luftwaffe* and the Tirpitz was directed to attack.

British reactions were immediate.   The departure of the Tirpitz from Trondheim was reported to the Admiralty, who promptly diverted the convoy from its course and informed the Home Fleet which was cruising in the vicinity.   The Tirpitz was sighted by a British destroyer on March 9, and aircraft from the carrier H.M.S. Victorious, were sent in to torpedo her.   Unfortunately a break in the clouds revealed the aircraft before they had got into a favourable position.   The Tirpitz was able to comb the torpedo tracks and escape at high speed back to Norway.

This minor action showed up sharply both the inadequate size of the striking force in Norway and the need for better air protection.   At a conference with Hitler on March 12 Raeder pointed this out, and pleaded once more for a Fleet Air Arm and more carriers.   Work had even had to be stopped on the only carrier being built, the Graf Zeppelin, because of a shortage of steel.   The allocation of raw materials to the German Navy had been severely cut at the beginning of the year, and at the same conference Raeder endeavoured to convince Hitler of the need for increased supplies.   The steel quota had been reduced from 170,000 to 153,000 tons per month for the first quarter of 1942, and to 150,000 tons per month for the second quarter. The overall effect was to curtail U-boat production from 19 to 17 boats per month, and to cancel all work on cruisers and above.

The effect on naval strategy was not immediate, but would certainly be felt later on. Japan was planning the capture of Ceylon and Madagascar, and if Germany and Italy were successful in the Mediterranean a world-wide chain could be forged between the three Axis partners which would be strong enough to withstand the Allies and allow the Russian campaign to be fought without interference. But this chain would depend above all else on sea power.

C.-in-C. of the Navy  
and Chief of the Naval Staff

Berlin, March 14, 1942

REPORT BY THE C.-IN-C., NAVY, TO THE FUEHRER AT HEADQUARTERS WOLFSSCHANZE THE EVENING OF MARCH 12, 1942

1. Submarine warfare.—We must carry on submarine warfare to the utmost, in order to take advantage of the unpreparedness of the United States, for we can most effectively fight England by reducing available cargo space. Losses of submarines, 2·4 per month.

2. The War in the North.—A. The Tirpitz made a sortie into the Arctic Ocean when aircraft reported a fifteen-ship enemy convoy near Jan Mayen, headed for Russia. The Naval Staff is of the opinion that in such cases all forces available must be used unconditionally for the important task of disrupting the shipment of supplies to Russia or preventing enemy landings. The Tirpitz was unable to intercept the convoy. The latter evidently changed its course when the enemy realised that they had been sighted by German aircraft. A strong enemy task force including an aircraft carrier, was sent out in pursuit of the Tirpitz. In spite of daring attacks by torpedo planes, the enemy was unsuccessful. Skilful defence manœuvres, coupled with good luck, were responsible for the Tirpitz's escape.

Conclusions drawn from this operation.—This operation reveals the weakness of our own naval forces in the northern area. The enemy responds to every German sortie by sending out strong task forces, particularly aircraft carriers, which are the greatest menace to our heavy ships. The extreme weakness of our defences is evidenced by the fact that the enemy dares to advance in the coastal waters of the northern area without being smashed by the German Air Force. Our own defensive forces (destroyers and torpedo boats) are so few in number that our ships are always extremely hard pressed whenever they come in contact with the enemy. The following inferences can be drawn from this:

(a) Strong support from our air units in the Norwegian area is, in the absence of aircraft carriers, an absolute prerequisite to successful operation in the Arctic Ocean. (Air reconnaissance is needed, even if it should be at the expense of the Atlantic Air Forces. Torpedo aircraft must be thrown into the fight.)

(b) In view of the enemy's determined stand, every operation in the Arctic Ocean involves the use of all our naval forces. This will be particularly necessary as long as there are enemy carriers.

(c) Therefore our own naval forces should be held back at first, in order to ensure their availability for repulsing enemy landing attempts. They should be committed only after the enemy's exact position and strength has been accurately and unequivocally ascertained by air reconnaissance, and when there is sufficient support by the Air Force.

(d) The Air Force must be ordered to wage relentless warfare against the enemy carriers. Elimination of the aircraft carriers would basically improve our own chances.

(e) Work on our aircraft carrier must be accelerated. In this connection sufficient numbers of carrier aircraft must be provided.

*The Fuehrer* believes that the aircraft carrier is urgently needed and will direct the C.-in-C., Air, accordingly. Everything must be done toward the early formation of a German task force composed of the Tirpitz, the Scharnhorst, one aircraft carrier, two heavy cruisers and twelve to fourteen destroyers. It would be a serious threat to the enemy in the northern area and could be used very effectively.

*The C.-in-C., Navy*, requests that the C.-in-C., Air, receive instructions to reinforce the Air Force in Norway. At the same time he should be informed of the purpose and the aims of aerial activity in that area. *The Fuehrer* approves.

3. The War in the West. Blockade runners.—The Elsa Essberger made port in France. Five ships homeward bound are: Osorno, expected the middle of March; Rio Grande, beginning of April; Fusijama, end of April; Portland and Muensterland, middle of May. All are carrying rubber.

Departures.—The Tannenfels is about to depart. Later it will be possible to send ships to the Dutch East Indies for oil and tin.

4. The Mediterranean.—A memorandum by the Naval Staff analyzes the situation in the Mediterranean. It urges that for strategic reasons the drive for the Suez Canal, if at all feasible should be carried out this year, because of its far-reaching consequences. The favourable situation in the Mediterranean, so pronounced at the present time will probably never occur again. The problem of shipping space for an attack on the Suez Canal can be solved. The Naval Staff is now attending to the details. The Navy cannot judge whether the Army has the necessary number of troops in readiness. The Naval Staff, however, thinks it desirable on the part of the Fuehrer to issue orders that preparations for an offensive against the Suez Canal be begun. Above all, transports should be prepared. The need for the occupation of Malta is pointed out. Advantage should be taken of the present state of its defences, greatly weakened by German attacks. If Axis troops do not occupy Malta it is imperative that the German Air Force continues its attacks on the island to the same extent as heretofore. Such attacks alone will prevent the enemy from rebuilding Malta's offensive and defensive capacities. If our attacks are not continued, the enemy will immediately and hurriedly begin to rebuild Malta. This would complicate the transport of supplies to northern Africa.

What is the Fuehrer's opinion on:

(a) The part Italy will play in the taking of Malta?

(b) The possibility of support by the German Air Force and Army?

*The Fuehrer* knows the Duce's intention. He is afraid that the operation, evidently scheduled for July, will again be postponed. The German Air Force must give support. The Fuehrer is inclined to undertake an offensive against the Suez Canal if the Air Force can remain intact in the Mediterranean. If it is used elsewhere, the offensive cannot be carried out. If Malta falls soon, it will greatly facilitate a Suez offensive. The Fuehrer will discuss these questions with the Duce at their next meeting.

4a.—Japanese bases on Madagascar.—The Japanese have recognised the great strategic importance of Madagascar for naval warfare. According to reports submitted they are planning to establish bases on Madagascar in addition to Ceylon, in order to be able to cripple sea traffic in the Indian Ocean and the Arabian Sea. From there they could likewise successfully attack shipping around the Cape. Before establishing these bases, Japan will have to get German consent. For military reasons such consent ought to be granted. Attention is called to the fact, however, that this is a matter of great political significance, since it touches on the basic question of France's relation to the Tri-Partite Powers on the one hand, and the Anglo-Saxons on the other. Such action on the part of the Japanese may have repercussions in the French homeland, the African colonies, as well as in Portuguese East Africa. *The Fuehrer* is of the opinion that France will not give her consent.

5. Raw materials.—*The C.-in-C., Navy,* reports on developments pertaining to naval construction. It appears that in 1944 only 15 (possibly only 12–13) submarines, 1 E-boat, and 2 motor minesweepers will be under-construction. The C.in-C., Navy, points out that Minister Speer told him more cubic space is being allotted for commercial use than for military use, and that some of these contingents are assigned on the basis of former allocations without specifying for what purpose. *The Fuehrer* absolutely refuses to consider raising the contingents. He repeats again and again that it is impossible to allocate more space than there is. Available space inadequately utilised by certain agencies must be re-allocated. *The C.-in-C., Navy,* suggests that he might re-examine the details with General Thomas, but *the Chief of Staff, O.K.W.,* explains that this can be done only together with him. He states that the allocations of March 5 are only temporary.

6. Reich Commissioner of Maritime Shipping.—*The C.-in-C., Navy,* cites urgent reasons against the appointment of a Reich Commissioner of Maritime Shipping. *The Fuehrer* is in agreement. He says that the four-year plan is a monstrosity and states that he is definitely opposed to appointing a Reich Commissioner of Maritime Shipping.

(signed) RAEDER.

## APPENDIX

Cargo of the Elsa Essberger (Blockade runner)

|  |  | Tons |
|---|---|---:|
| 1. Rubber.. | .. .. .. .. .. | 4,059·0 |
| 2. Dammar | .. .. .. .. .. | 52·0 |
| 3. Tires .. | .. .. .. .. .. | 266·4 |
| 4. Tin .. | .. .. .. .. .. | 55·6 |
| 5. Tin ore.. | .. .. .. .. .. | 30·2 |
| 6. Tungsten ore .. | .. .. .. .. | 48·2 |
| 7. Wood oil | .. .. .. .. .. | 17·0 |
| 8. Coconut oil | .. .. .. .. .. | 334·6 |
| *Carried forward* .. | .. .. .. | 4,863·0 |

|  |  | Tons |
|---|---|---|
| | *Brought forward* .. .. .. .. | 4,863·0 |
| 9. | Walnut oil .. .. .. .. .. | 57·0 |
| 10. | Shelled peanuts .. .. .. .. | 990·0 |
| 11. | Leather goods .. .. .. .. | 85·9 |
| 12. | Sole leather .. .. .. .. .. | 57·7 |
| 13. | Buffalo hides .. .. .. .. .. | 27·1 |
| 14. | Hemp .. .. .. .. .. .. | 189·7 |
| 15. | Gut .. .. .. .. .. .. | 14·0 |
| 16. | Animal tallow .. .. .. .. | 169·0 |
| 17. | Coffee .. .. .. .. .. .. | 23·9 |
| 18. | Tea .. .. .. .. .. .. | 106·7 |
| 19. | Dried egg yolk .. .. .. .. | 65·0 |
| 20. | Nutmeg .. .. .. .. .. | 7·5 |
| 21. | Miscellaneous (gallnuts, duck feathers, black bristles, kapok, etc.) .. .. .. | 110·9 |
| | Total .. | 6,767·4 |

# 1942: CHAPTER II

# St. Nazaire

ON MARCH 28 British forces raided St. Nazaire. The raid was the biggest yet carried out on the European coast-line, and had as its object the destruction of the large lock which was capable of being used as a dry dock, the only one outside Germany big enough to take the Tirpitz.

The raid was led by Commander R. E. D. Ryder, V.C., R.N., in the ex-American over-age destroyer, H.M.S. Campbeltown. The Campbeltown was disguised as a German destroyer, and by using German recognition signals managed to lead the force to within 1½ miles of St. Nazaire before meeting serious opposition. The operation was entirely successful. The Campbeltown, loaded with high explosive, rammed the lock gates and later blew up exactly according to plan. The attack destroyed the confidence of the German High Command. An inquiry was held, and a fortnight later Raeder reported to Hitler.

Naval Staff                                                  Berlin, April 16, 1942

### REPORT BY THE C.-IN-C., NAVY, TO THE FUEHRER AT WOLFSSCHANZE, APRIL 13, 1942, IN THE EVENING

In the presence of the Chief of Staff, O.K.W., during the discussion of points IX and X, Lt.-General Jodl, Vice-Admiral Krancke, and Captain von Puttkamer were also present.

## I. ATTACK ON ST. NAZAIRE

The situation in the Western Area since Summer 1941.—Enemy strength is increasing. Army and Air Force are weaker due to the situation in the East. Nearly all naval forces have been transferred to Norway. We have no means of repulsing an enemy landing attempt. The situation provokes enemy operations like the one of March 28, 1942. The following statements are taken from a British operations order:

Mission:

(1) Destroy the flood gates of the large dock that can accommodate the Tirpitz.

(2) Destroy small locks and all submarines and other craft in the vicinity.

The enemy knew exactly the strength of our naval forces (five torpedo boats) and could adjust his own strength accordingly. The attack was timed according to moon and tide (March 28 to 31). The route from Falmouth to the objective took 35 hours at a speed of 12 knots. They flew the German flag and used German recognition signals. (*Comment in longhand: "Air Force recognition signals."*) One submarine was used as marker boat. The air attack was co-ordinated with the naval attack.

Mission of the destroyer Campbeltown.—Force a lane through the torpedo net and ram the outer floodgate so that the forecastle extends over the floodgate. Land the troops, then sink the Campbeltown. Remove the crew in motor boats. Campbeltown was loaded with demolition charge with a two-hour time fuse.

Advantages for the enemy:

(*a*) Poor, changing visibility, 200–4,000 m.

(*b*) At high water the sand banks are flooded, making it possible for the enemy to evade mines and other obstacles.

(*c*) Good reconnaissance through air attacks, which probably had the additional purpose of distracting our attention and drowning out engine noises of the E-boats. Nevertheless, shore batteries and anti-aircraft batteries observed the enemy boats as soon as they came into view. A short delay was due to exchange of recognition signals. The artillery fire was very effective.

*The Fuehrer* criticises the exchange of recognition signals under such circumstances and also the delay (6½ minutes) before the alarm order was given. (*Comment added in longhand.—New Regulation: shore station demands recognition signal. If naval forces do not answer immediately with naval recognition signal, open fire. New, uniform alarm signal for the Navy has been ordered.*)

*The C.-in-C., Navy*, states that, considering the available means, the defence had been handled correctly in all essentials. However, it should be impossible for a destroyer to reach the floodgate; besides, due to inexperience, the search for the demolition charge and its subsequent removal were not carried out correctly. In other cases demolition charges in locks, etc., were expertly located and removed at great risk.

Possible Countermeasures Necessary to Prevent Similar Raids.

A. Aerial reconnaissance is a prime requisite for prompt recognition. The British were at sea for 35 hours; they approached during daylight. Even during the World War evening reconnaissance was carried out to protect the coast whenever the weather permitted. It is possible that some airfields at high altitudes (as in Norway) have different visibility conditions than prevail at sea. In such cases seaplanes operating from the harbours must do the reconnoitring, since they can see as long as visibility allows enemy naval forces to enter coastal waters.

*Fuehrer:* Seaplanes are too greatly endangered.

*C.-in-C., Navy.*—No more than patrol boats without proper rear protection. All ship-based planes are seaplanes. Furthermore, to assure the necessary protection, some bombers will have to be used for reconnaissance along the entire West Coast. The Naval Air Force is of great importance.

B. Flotillas for patrolling and for protecting the harbours have been established as far as possible and additional ones are being built. There are not nearly enough of them to protect the bases and the long coast. *The C.-in-C., Navy*, using a chart prepared by the War Economy Section of the Naval Ordnance Division, demonstrates on the one hand the repeated efforts of the High Command, Navy, to obtain the workers and raw materials necessary for reinforcing escort and patrol flotillas; on the other hand, he shows how naval requirements continually had to yield to those of the Air Force and of the Army. If the *Reichsmarschall* is perhaps able to build more aircraft it proves that he has manpower and raw materials at his disposal which, by rights, should belong to the Navy. It is certainly not the fault of the High Command, Navy, that there are so few vessels. The cause lies in the distribution of men and raw materials, no doubt always made in view of the particular war situation—in spite of continual requests made by the High Command, Navy, to the Fuehrer, to Dr. Todt, and to the O.K.W.

*The C.-in-C., Navy*, also points out that patrol boats in coastal areas which do not have the support of light naval forces are gravely endangered. It is not difficult for a few destroyers to sink them, once they have been located by enemy reconnaissance. Even then one or another of the boats would be able to report.

C. Minefields:

(1) Heavy ground mines are to be buried in the sand bars to prevent passage at such places.

(2) A field of ground mines is to be laid which will be electrically detonated from the shore. Their success depends largely on a foolproof detonator cable.

D. Harbour booms have been placed wherever harbour and current conditions permit, for example, Boulogne, Brest, Dunkirk. They have not been approved for St. Nazaire, since neither buoys nor dolphins can be used there. The former cannot hold the booms in place due to the swift current, and the latter cannot be driven into the rocky bottom near the mouth of the harbour. Trellis masts on concrete blocks will be tried out if they prove workable. Experiments will be made with a new type of obstacle consisting of a series of barges connected by iron chains.

E. Location-finding devices.—The number on the West Coast will be increased as more devices become available (two, possibly up to four a month).

F. Alarm signal in case of invasion.—The Navy has such a signal, but all parts of the Armed Forces should know it and use it. All posts which see the signal must repeat it continuously until certain that it has been received everywhere. *The Fuehrer* asks whether it would be possible to illuminate the coastal area with parachute flares. *C.-in-C., Navy:* The coastal artillery has star shells which illuminate the coastal area widely. The searchlights used in conjunction with artillery fire have the advantage of blinding the enemy.

Summary by the C.-in-C., Navy.—Experiences gained as the result of this attack are being utilised to the utmost. Nevertheless, we have to consider the possibility of similar raids whenever the enemy is favoured by good visibility. The danger is particularly great as long as there is neither an effective naval defence nor an adequate air reconnaissance. In the absence of almost all naval forces as well as the Air Force from the home waters, due to the changed war situation, even raids in the German Bight, like Borkum and Wangeroog, greatly exposed by removal of guns to the occupied territories, must be better fortified again (e.g. by placing the Gneisenau's 15-mm. battery on Wangeroog).

*The Fuehrer* stresses the fact that he must demand that at least the most important naval bases, like submarine bases, be so well protected that successful raids would be impossible. In his opinion this was *not* the case at St. Nazaire. *The C.-in-C., Navy*, mentions experiences with British explosives which should not only be brought to the attention of the entire Armed Forces, but also of the civilian population in order to prevent sabotage. He hands a large number of photographs to the Chief of Staff,

O.K.W.  *The C.-in-C., Navy,* reports that the population of St. Nazaire and its vicinity strongly favours De Gaulle.  Two days *before* the attacks a successful police raid was staged.

## II. NAVAL SITUATION IN MARCH 1942

Home Waters and the German sphere of influence.  A. Norway.— The cruiser Admiral Hipper was transferred to Trondheim as planned. Luetzow will presumably follow in mid May.  Prinze Eugen will probably return for repairs at the end of April.  Since there are very few destroyers in the Arctic Sea, future operations of surface forces must depend on the possibility of effective air reconnaissance, so far as fuel permits.  The twenty submarines assigned to the protection of the Northern Area have the following missions:

(1) To paralyse enemy convoy traffic in the Arctic Sea and near the ports.

(2) To recognise and thwart promptly any enemy plans to land in the Norwegian area.

B. The attempt made by Norwegian merchant ships to break out of Swedish harbours, which we have been expecting since the beginning of January, was completely unsuccessful.  Reports have furnished us with the details.

C. Traffic of merchant ships during March.—Traffic between German and German-occupied harbours consisted of 1,274 merchant vessels of 2,566,017 tons.  Of these, 1,011 ships of 2,177,136 tons were convoyed. They were distributed as follows:

|  |  |  |
|---|---|---|
| Norway | .. | 405 ships totalling 1,062,666 tons. |
| North Sea | .. | 519 ships totalling 1,145,351 tons. |
| Western Area | .. | 330 ships totalling 358,000 tons. |

No traffic in the Baltic due to ice.

Foreign waters.  A. Cruiser warfare.—Ship "10" operated without success in the Antarctic.  However, in the South Atlantic five enemy steamers were captured without firing a shot.  These were Pagasitikos, Wellpark, Wellesden, Aust, and one other.  Ship "10" will be supplied by Regensburg and proceed to the western part of the Indian Ocean as planned.  An agreement was reached with the Japanese Navy reserving the area west of 80° E longitude and south of 10° S latitude for ship "10," and possibly permitting Japanese submarines to operate in an area 300 miles wide along the eastern coast of Africa.  We recommended to the Japanese the use of submarines near the entrance to the Persian Gulf.

Ship "28" is en route in the South Atlantic.  Doggerbank successfully fulfilled her minelaying mission off Capetown.  She received new orders to lay mines near Cape Agulhas with the coming new moon.  Meanwhile she is waiting in the South Atlantic.

B. Blockade-runners.—Supply ship Regensburg in the Indian Ocean and Tannenfels in the South Atlantic are both en route to Japan.  The tanker Charlotte Schliemann is in the waiting zone in the south-west part of the South Atlantic.  Of the five blockade-runners returning home, two have already arrived in Bordeaux: the Osorno and the Rio Grande, the latter with 3,700 tons of rubber and 3,800 tons of whale oil.  The

Fusiyama is in the South Atlantic, and the Portland and the Muenster are still west of Cape Horn.

The Mediterranean and the Black Sea.—The Valiant left Alexandria after three and a half months of repairs.  The Queen Elizabeth docked there.  Since no sign of the Valiant has been found in the Mediterranean for several days, it is assumed that she left by way of the Red Sea.  It is not known whether she is ready for action.  The Malaya sailed westward from Gibraltar.  Attacks made by German and Italian submarine and planes have seriously weakened light enemy forces.  In short, the situation in the Mediterranean is extremely favourable right now.  Therefore the 5th and 6th Transport Squadrons were sent to Tripoli as planned.

The 3rd E-boat Flotilla is to be used to lay mines off Malta in connection with the current major operation against that island.  The 6th Motor Minesweeping Flotilla is to be transferred to Tripoli for escort duty.  Four more E-boats, now at Cologne, are being assigned to the Mediterranean.  These could ultimately be sent to the Black Sea through the Dardanelles.  *The Fuehrer* permits that they attempt passage through the Dardanelles camouflaged as merchant vessels without previous political negotiations.

In the Black sea new minefields are being laid off the Roumanian and Bulgarian coast.  The plan to mine the Crimean coast had to be dropped temporarily because the necessary Roumanian naval forces were refused.  *The Fuehrer* orders that none of the German batteries be given to either Bulgaria or Roumania.

C. Submarine warfare.—We had 288 submarines on April 1, 1942, of which 122 are operational units.  Location of the 125 boats in operation areas on April 9 is as follows:

(*a*) Arctic Ocean .. Total 19  5 are at Kirkenes, Narvik, and Trondheim, and 14 at sea.

(*b*) Atlantic    .. Total 81  45 in North Atlantic and U.S. coast; 2 in South Atlantic; 34 in bases on the western coast of France.

(*c*) Mediterranean   Total 20  7 at sea.

(*d*) Home ports  .. Total  5  3 overdue.

Submarines sank these vessels in March (confirmed):

German submarines  ..  89 vessels totalling 524,286 tons.
Italian submarines  ..  19 vessels totalling  82,000 tons.
Japanese submarines ..  19 vessels totalling 101,098 tons.

Total enemy losses for March 1942 in ships sunk or captured (Great Britain, U.S.A., Russia, and the Netherlands): 362 vessels of 1,095,393 tons.

*The Fuehrer* agrees with the C.-in-C., Navy, that victory depends on destroying the greatest amount of Allied tonnage possible.  Thus all offensive operations of the enemy can be slowed down or even stopped entirely.  The Fuehrer believes that attacks on the Murmansk convoys are most important at the moment.  *The C.-in-C., Navy*, states that construction of submarines should be stepped up to the very limit.  He requests permission to get copper on the black market in France and Belgium.  *The Fuehrer* wants confirmation whether this is still actually possible.

### III. Support of the German Offensive in the East by Japanese Naval Warfare in the Indian Ocean

It is of decisive importance that Japanese forces attack British supply lines to the Red Sea and Persia in the northern part of the Indian Ocean. The purpose would be to disrupt Russian supplies and thus aid our eastern offensive. The O.K.W. must therefore point out to the Japanese Liaison Staff that a strong Japanese attack on British supply lines would support German operations most effectively. *The Fuehrer* has already given Ambassador Oshima some general indications of the spring offensive.

### IV. Germany's Relations with France

The Fuehrer is asked for his opinion as regard to further developments.

*The Fuehrer* believes that Marshal Petain plays a very insignificant rôle being very old and easily influenced. He thinks it likely that Laval will replace Petain, but he does not consider the French capable of energetic action of any kind at present. Their whole attitude is weak (witness the Riom trial). According to Ambassador Abetz 5 per cent. of the population is for collaboration and 5 per cent. for De Gaulle; the rest are watching and waiting. The Fuehrer believes that the French will try to repulse attacks on West Africa.

### V. The Fuel Oil Situation in 1942

The C.-in-C., Navy, refers to the report made to the Fuehrer.

[The supply of fuel oil, which had become critical in the last quarter of 1941, was even more serious by April 1942. The Italian Navy was in continual need of supplies, and German stocks were running low. The passage of the Brest Group through the Channel and on to Norway had consumed 20,000 tons of fuel oil alone, and by April 1 the reserve stocks of the German Navy were down to 150,000 tons. Roumanian deliveries fell from 46,000 tons per month to 8,000 tons, and as this had been promised to the Italians, who urgently required it for the Mediterranean campaigns, further withdrawals had to be made from the German reserve stocks. The total allocation to both the German and Italian navies for April 1942 was cut from 97,000 to 61,000 tons. The shortage of fuel oil did not affect submarines and pocket battleships, however, as they operated on diesel oil which was still in plentiful supply.—*Editor.*]

### VI. Completion of the Aircraft Carrier Graf Zeppelin

A. It will take at least until summer 1943 to complete the hull and instal the engines.

B. The total time necessary to complete the carrier does not depend on completing the hull and engines, but on changing the flight installations for the use of aircraft adapted from the Ju87D and BF109F. About two years are required to develop, construct, and test the catapults necessary for these planes. If it is possible to convert the existing catapults the time-limit will be reduced by six months. New winches for the arresting gear are needed. The company producing these winches has not yet announced when they can be delivered. The carrier cannot therefore be completed before the winter of 1943. *The Fuehrer* points out that in general the Armed Forces set their requirements too high.

C. Aircraft.—Only ten converted fighters and twenty-two converted bombers (including reconnaissance planes) will be available. There are no torpedo planes. If a new type of special carrier aircraft is developed, mass production cannot be attained until 1946! The Naval Staff maintains that the results of our efforts so far do not justify continuing work on the carrier. While the technical problems concerning ship construction and plane conversion can evidently be solved, the disadvantages which still remain reduce the carrier's tactical value to a critical point. The C.-in-C., Navy, will approach the Fuehrer again, if the discussions with the C.-in-C., Air, in regard to carrier aircraft do not have satisfactory results. *The Fuehrer* believes that torpedo planes are necessary in any case; it is furthermore important that our own types of aircraft are a match for those of the enemy.

VII. MISCELLANEOUS

A. The steamer Scharnhorst is in Japan and can be sold to the Japanese.

B. Distribution of the Gneisenau's guns: three 280-mm guns. from turret A were installed on coast defence gun mounts near the Hook of Holland. Turrets B and C were mounted whole in Norway (by blasting into solid rock).

VIII. ADMIRAL KRANCKE REPORTS ON MANPOWER OF THE NAVY

Upon information about the composition of the First Naval Brigade, the Fuehrer admits that the Navy is very short of officers (only 15,000 officers for 500,000 men). On the other hand, it is not advisable to use Army divisions which can be employed in combat for occupation of the French islands, for if they should be needed in the East they would then not be available. The division on the Channel Islands, for instance, is practically lost to the Army. The protection of the coastal islands is a part of the Navy's coastal defence assignment, and as such is particularly a naval responsibility. Since the Army is in urgent need of additional forces, he must give this task to the Navy in spite of the shortage of naval officers. The Army has had tremendous losses among its officers; it can transfer officers temporarily, but cannot dispense with them permanently. The Naval Staff, Quartermaster Division proposes that the Navy be given until October to complete this task. The Fuehrer considered October too late.

Additional remarks.—On April 14, 1942, the following telegram was sent confirming the results of the above conference:

To the Fuehrer and Supreme Commander, personal; copy to the O.K.W., Operations Staff.

"Request confirmation of yesterday's conference on naval brigades: Navy entirely responsible for defence of islands in Western Area to be designated by O.K.W. Necessary personnel and material to be determined in collaboration with Commanding General, West, and to be installed as soon as possible. Troops to be trained on the islands. Army ordered to furnish necessary officers temporarily until Navy can train its own. Army and Air Force to provide arms and equipment which Navy lacks. This method of taking over naval defence of the land is seems quicker and more economical than adhering rigidly to previous orders.　　　　　　　　　　　　Grand Admiral RAEDER."

IX. DEFINITION OF AUTHORITY IN THE NETHERLANDS (among the Commanding General, West; the General Commanding, Armed Forces, Netherlands; and the Admiral Commanding, North Sea Station)

Vice-Admiral Krancke reports on organisation.—According to the Fuehrer's order No. 40, the Commanding General, West, is responsible for the conduct of the war along the coast in the French, Belgian, and entire Dutch area, without referring to the Commanding General, Armed Forces, Netherlands. In Holland, therefore, he is responsible not only for the area of the Admiral Commanding, Netherlands, but also for that part of the Dutch area commanded by the Admiral, Coastal Defences, German Bight. The Commanding General, West, is responsible not only for coastal warfare, but also for its preparation as regards tactics, organisation, personnel, and material. The Netherlands belongs to the North Sea area as far as naval organisation is concerned (ship traffic, coastal and anti-aircraft defence, widespread dock and supply systems, and replacement units). The Admiral Commanding, Netherlands, is subordinate to the Admiral, North Sea Station.

This means that both the Admiral Commanding, North Sea Station, and the Commanding General, West, are in charge of the same coastal defence. Their orders overlap. The authority of the Commanding General, West, has to deal continuously with matters coming under the jurisdiction of the Admiral Commanding, North Sea Station. The organisation must therefore be changed. The O.K.W., Operations Staff, is asked to investigate this question and to define clearly the respective spheres of command. *The Fuehrer* will make the decision.

X. THE QUESTION OF A NAVAL REPRESENTATIVE AT THE FUEHRER HEAD-
    QUARTERS

In a private conference *the C.-in-C., Navy*, explains why it is necessary to have a permanent representative of the C.-in-C., Navy, at the Fuehrer Headquarters. He compares the Navy with other branches of the Armed Forces. *The Fuehrer* approves a permanent representative of the C.-in-C., Navy, at the Fuehrer Headquarters. He will be a flag officer authorized to move freely between the Naval Staff and the Headquarters; he has the right to report to the Fuehrer on all matters pertaining to the Navy, and to be present at all conferences dealing with the general conduct of the war.

> (signed)        RAEDER.
> (countersigned) ASSMANN.

# Spring Offensives

DURING THE next conference the concentration on details of men and material for the German Navy rather than on operational plans for the conduct of the war is misleading. Far-reaching schemes were in fact made during the spring of 1942, and the absence of much discussion about these schemes was because they were for the most part based on directives issued by Hitler rather than on the result of conferences with him. Questions of men, materials, and organisation were, on the other hand, of the greatest importance if Hitler's directives were to be carried out, and therefore formed the bulk of the subject matter discussed at the conference. German plans made during the spring of 1942 covered the three principal theatres of the war—Russia, the Mediterranean, and the Atlantic. The naval share was notable for the fact that it was in every case regarded as subsidiary to and dependent upon either the *Luftwaffe* or the *Wehrmacht*.

Russia.—Plans against Russia, other than those dealing with the spring offensive of the *Wehrmacht*, were concentrated on preventing Anglo-American aid to Russia, and assisting the Army by offensives in the Baltic and the Black Sea. Russian convoys, however, were to be the principal target for the German Navy, and operations were worked out for a combined sea and air offensive in June, followed by raider warfare carried out by the Scheer operating independently.

Mediterranean.—Until the spring of 1942 Hitler took little interest in the Mediterranean. The success of the British campaign in November 1940 had caused him to send out Rommel with the *Afrika Korps*, and later, in 1941, when the British Mediterranean Fleet had played havoc with the Italian convoys, he was prevailed upon to order German U-boats into the area. But he still saw the African campaign as nothing more than pulling Italy's chestnuts out of the fire.

During the second half of 1941 German U-boats in the Mediterranean achieved considerable success, but they were nevertheless inadequate for the protection of convoys from British sea and air attacks, and, in December 1941, the *Luftwaffe* was ordered into battle as well. The principal base from which British sea and air attacks originated was Malta, and accordingly Malta became the principal target for the *Luftwaffe*, who began their attacks on December 21, 1941.

Effective as the air raids on Malta were, they could not be maintained indefinitely, and Raeder realised that if, for one reason or another, the *Luftwaffe* reduced its attacks the island could be quickly restored. In March 1942, therefore Raeder represented to Hitler that nothing less than the capture and occupation of Malta would suffice. There was a real danger that the *Luftwaffe* squadrons might be removed to the Eastern Front, and Raeder made his arguments for the capture of Malta as strong as possible. Hitler was dubious about the necessity for the operation—not wanting to spare men from either the Eastern Front or Cyrenaica—but agreed to the extent of ordering increased activity by the *Luftwaffe*. Raeder's arguments, however, were supported by Kesselring in Italy and by the Italians themselves. Accordingly the operation for the capture of Malta— *Hercules*—received Hitler's consent and preparations were begun.

In the first week of April Kesselring visited Cyrenaica and reported his observations to both Hitler and Mussolini.

" Telegram from Rome to the Army High Command at the Fuehrer Headquarters, Wolfsschanze.
" Date : April 12, 1942.

"On April 11 and 12 Field Marshal Kesselring made a report to the Duce and General Cavallero on the success obtained so far by the air attacks on Malta and on the impressions he gained during his flight to Africa on April 7 and 8.

"A. Malta.—The planned air attack on Malta between April 1 and 9 has, in the opinion of the C.-in-C. of the Southern Area (Field Marshal Kesselring), eliminated Malta as a naval base. The shipyards and dock installations have been so badly damaged that there can be no question of using Malta as a base for a long time ; the last surface forces have left Malta, and the British submarine base has been transferred to Alexandria. The airfields and their equipment suffered heavy damage, but it cannot be expected that Malta can be completely disposed of as an air base. Even though at several places delayed action bombs probably destroyed some depots and underground stores, the main installations will be undamaged. Anti-aircraft defence has decreased. C.-in-C., Southern Area, intends to continue the attack, if weather conditions permit, until April 20, and then, by continuous harrassing raids, to prevent the enemy from repairing the damage.

"General Cavallero informed me that as a result of this report he had decided that the preparations for the attack on Malta (surprise attack) should be made with a view to carrying out the attack as from the end of May. As only 2–3 Italian parachute battalions can be ready by this time (Cavallero) wishes to know whether German parachute battalions could be made available then. He would also like to have a staff officer with experience of combined air and sea landing operations (Crete) placed at his disposal for the Malta Planning Staff (*Arbeitsstab*) under the direction of Major General Gandin.

"B. Field Marshal Kesselring was in favour of the proposal for the armoured forces to attack the mobile forces near Tobruk about June ; after consulting General Rommel he thought this was possible if transport ships and planes could be brought over in greater numbers while Malta was *hors de combat*. All possibilities for this were examined during an exhaustive discussion at the Italian Supreme Command.

"C. On April 11 at the Italian Supreme Command, Major General Ramke gave an account of the attack on Crete and his experiences with training parachute troops. The Duce and the high officers of the Italian Armed Forces were present and were very favourably impressed.

"D. In view of the considerably improved situation in the Mediterranean, the successful defence on the Eastern Front and the favourable development of the situation in East Asia, the Duce expressed his great confidence in the further development of the war."

Meanwhile Rommel advanced rapidly against retreating British forces, and his success encouraged Hitler to visualise the advantages to be gained by total victory in the Mediterranean—advantages of which the Allied Command was also fully aware—and at the end of April he met Mussolini at Berghof to discuss his new plans. The following letter written by the German Naval Representative at the meeting records the decisions taken :

Berghof, May 1, 1942

Dear Wangenheim,

Here, in haste, are my latest news of the Mussolini Discussion at the Berghof : General impression : most satisfactory—the atmosphere was especially so (at the last meeting last summer, this was not markedly the case). Agreements were finally reached on the Libya operation and on Malta.

First Libya (end of May—beginning of June) then Malta (mid July), since to attempt both simultaneously would cancel out each, particularly in the sphere of air cover.

Important for Africa.—Use of two German parachute battalions and speedy reinforcement for Rommel. Numbers not necessarily large.

Malta.—Fuehrer agrees to participation to great extent by Germany : parachute division with three reinforced parachute regiments. Besides these, assault pioneers and armoured unit composed of captured Russian tanks (T.34 and 52 tons). Important for the Navy—strongest possible concentration and preparation for action of MFP—(ferry barges) although this will probably weaken other areas (Aegean, possibly even the Black Sea).

In spite of these intentions the *Luftlotte* 2 (Naval Air) will not be kept down there until after the Malta operation, but parts of it will be moved elsewhere before that time. The transfers will be made to benefit the West, principally, (*Luftlotte III*). Kesselring, who took part in the discussions, was of the opinion that these transfers could be made without risk of Britain regaining supremacy. Well, we shall see. He ought to know.

To sum up, I consider the outcome satisfactory. Even though the postponement of the Malta operation is not a welcome move, nevertheless, I am glad to see the increased interest displayed by the Fuehrer in this important area and the consequent intensification of German fighting spirit there. The whole business is now assuming importance after having been regarded hitherto as a subsidiary matter in which victories were looked upon as gifts from Heaven, but in which nobody bothered to do anything seriously for the "Italian theatre of war."

Hearty Greeting,<br>JUNGE.

*   *   *   *   *   *

Supplementary reports show that at the beginning of May, Axis plans were first to complete the conquest of Libya, then to take Malta, and then to continue on land to the Nile Delta.

Later these plans were changed, and the capture of Malta was put after the conquest of Egypt with disastrous results for the Axis.

Atlantic.—In the Atlantic Hitler's intentions were to carry out as effective a blockade of England as possible. The aim was to sink ships faster than they could be built and so eventually cut off all supplies from the United Kingdom.

The declaration of war by the United States had opened up a new field for the U-boats, and in the first half of 1942 widespread attacks were made in the Caribbean and off the Atlantic coast of North America. Allied shipping losses reached the highest level of the war.

C.-in-C., Navy                                                      Berlin, May 16, 1942

## CONFERENCE OF THE C.-IN-C., NAVY, WITH THE FUEHRER AT THE FUEHRER'S HEADQUARTERS, WOLFSSCHANZE, ON MAY 13 AND 14, 1942

### CONFERENCE ON THE AFTERNOON OF MAY 13, 1942

Also present: Chief of Staff, O.K.W.
Minister Speer.
Dorpmueller.
*Reichsstatthalter* Kaufmann.
Reich Commissioner Terboven.
*Staatsrat* Blohm.
*Ministerialdirektor* Waldeck.
Vice-Admiral Krancke.

1. The question of increasing ship traffic to Norway is discussed. The Fuehrer agrees in principle with the general outline. He will determine the organisation and appoint the necessary personnel from among the representatives of the shipping firms themselves. There is general agreement that the shipping firms can work only in closest co-operation with the Navy. Such questions as the utilisation of harbours, unloading, etc., can be decided upon only in consultation with the proper naval authorities.

Ship repairs.—The available facilities must be increased if at all possible. Perhaps certain shipyards should be set aside for this purpose (Blohm, Speer).

Construction of new ships.—A standard type of about 2,000–3,000 tons, with a speed of about 9 knots and simple engines is to be built. *Staatsrat* Blohm submits a design. Motor ships under construction which are not needed by the Navy as blockade-runners and mine-exploding vessels (*Sperrbrecher*) are to be equipped with generators and used for merchant shipping. Field railways are to be used for clearing the docks quickly, and the goods should be stored near the harbours in case they cannot be completely removed at once.

2. Special conference.

Also present: C.-in-C., Navy.
Minister Speer.
Vice-Admiral Krancke.
Rear-Admiral Kleikamp.

Discussion concerning the continuation of destroyer construction.— *The Fuehrer* considers it hazardous to discontinue construction of destroyers. *Minister Speer* holds out the prospect of an additional monthly supply of 1,000 tons of copper, which can be obtained from middle and low tension wires if the Armed Forces will extract the copper themselves and provide the necessary iron at the rate of six to one. *The C.-in-C., Navy*, considers it justified under these circumstances to start work again on all vessels up to the size of destroyers on which construction was stopped. *The Fuehrer* agrees.

3. *The Fuehrer* decides that a dock is to be built in Trondheim in the Gallosen Fiord, even if it will take ten months longer to construct it there.

4. In a subsequent conference with Minister Speer, Vice-Admiral Krancke, Rear-Admiral Kleikamp, *the Fuehrer* decides that the Europa, the Potsdam, and the Gneisenau be converted into auxiliary aircraft carriers. The Military Problems and Shipyards Branch, Naval Construction Division, expects to have the plans ready in three months and the converted ships should be completed about twelve months from the time the necessary material is available. The Fuehrer considers it entirely out of the question for larger surface forces to operate without aircraft protection.

### THE AFTERNOON OF MAY 14, 1942

Also present: Chief of Staff, O.K.W.
Lt.-General Jodl.
Admiral Commanding Submarines.
Vice-Admiral Krancke.
Commander von Puttkamer.

1. The Spitzbergen question.—*The Fuehrer* again suggests establishing a base and mining coal at Spitsbergen. *The C.-in-C., Navy*, proposes that the Commanding General, Fifth Air Force, who supposedly called attention to Spitzbergen's importance, be asked to send a commission, including a naval officer and coal-mining experts, in order to investigate on the spot the possibility of establishing a base and the prospects for mining and transporting the coal. The O.K.W. points out the difficulties of supplying a base of any size.

2. Report of the Admiral Commanding Submarines on all matters pertaining to submarine warfare.

(1) Submarine statistics.—124 submarines were in the operational zones on May 1. Of these, 85 were stationed in the Atlantic, 19 in the

Mediterranean, 20 in the Arctic Ocean. On the other hand, as many as 114 submarines, exclusive of training vessels, were in the Baltic Sea getting ready for duty. A submarine is normally supposed to be ready for operation about 4 months after commissioning. Forty-nine of the 114 submarines mentioned above have been commissioned longer than that, and therefore should have been in the operational zones by May 1. Everything possible must be done to relieve this congestion.

(2) Submarine operations.—Submarine warfare is war against enemy merchant shipping. Since American and British ships are under unified command, they have to be regarded as one. Therefore, we must sink ships wherever the greatest number of them can be sunk at lowest cost to us, i.e. where we lose the least number of submarines. We should not concentrate in one certain area if that means sinking fewer ships. This principle applies unless other military factors enter into consideration, as for instance, in the case of our attacks on the convoys to Murmansk, which served the purpose of relieving pressure on the Army. Naturally, in decisions pertaining to submarine warfare, the operational cost must also be considered.

From the point of view of operational cost, our submarine actions in the American area are justifiable. Sinkings from January 15 to May 10 amounted to 303 ships, or a total of 2,015,252 tons. However, submarine operations in the American area are also justifiable from another point of view. We are attempting to offset the merchant vessel construction programme of the enemy. Shipbuilding and other allied industries depend mostly on oil for fuel, and the most important American oilfields are found near the Gulf of Mexico. Consequently, the greater part of American tankers is used in coastal traffic, transporting oil from the oil region to the industrial area. From January 15 to May 10, 1942, we sank 112 tankers or a total of 927,000 tons. Every tanker we sink not only means one tanker less for carrying oil, but also represents a direct set-back to America's shipbuilding programme. Therefore it seems to me that the destruction of these American oil supply vessels is of greatest importance to us. America will have to depend on transporting her oil by water for at least another year. It will take a long time to lay an additional pipeline overland. Besides, a pipeline will hardly be able to supply as much oil as is being shipped by water on tankers. It is also out of the question to transport the same amount of oil by rail as is now being transported by water. Even if America can reduce its overall oil consumption by restricting its usage, all in all the tanker losses will have an ill effect on American industry in the eastern States, and thus on shipbuilding.

I do not believe that the race between the enemy shipbuilding programme and the submarine sinkings is in any way hopeless. The total tonnage the enemy can build will be about 8,200,000 tons in 1942, and about 10,400,000 tons in 1943. That would mean that we would have to sink approximately 700,000 tons per month in order to offset new constructions; only what is in excess of this amount would constitute a decrease in enemy tonnage. However, we are already sinking these 700,000 tons per month now; "we" meaning Germany, Italy, Japan: submarines, air forces, surface vessels, and mines. Moreover, the construction figures quoted are the maximum amounts ever mentioned by enemy propaganda as the goal of the shipbuilding programme. Our experts doubt that this goal can be reached and consider that the enemy can build only about 5,000,000 tons in 1942. That would mean that only about 400,000 to 500,000 tons would have to be sunk per month in order to prevent any increase. Anything above that number cuts into the basic tonnage of the enemy.

The Admiral Commanding Submarines intends to operate submarines in the American waters as long as it is profitable. He closely watches the monthly results of submarine warfare; it means that the average of ships sunk by each submarine is calculated for every day at sea. This daily average amounted to 209 tons in January, 378 tons in February, 409 tons in March, and 412 tons in April. The figures indicate that the average is still increasing slightly. Therefore we are still justified in operating submarines in the American zone. One of these days the situation in the American zone will change. Even at this time everything points to the fact that the Americans are making strenuous efforts to prevent the large number of sinkings. They have organised a considerable air defence and are likewise using destroyers and patrol craft off the coast. However, all these are manned by inexperienced crews and do not constitute a serious threat at present. In any case, the submarines with their greater experience in warfare are mastering these countermeasures. The American fliers see nothing, the destroyers and patrol vessels are travelling too fast most of the time even to locate the submarines, or they are not persistent enough in their pursuit with depth charges. As such, the shallow American coastal waters make it very easy to safeguard and protect shipping. The Americans could safeguard their shipping later on by organising it in the following ways:

(a) They could establish a so-called War Channel through which to conduct their shipping along the coast, protected on the ocean side by net and mine barrages. I do not believe that the Americans will choose this method, because it is too costly.

(b) The other method would be to organise all shipping into convoys. This method will probably be chosen, and the convoys will be led along the coast in shallow waters. The daily traffic will then become lighter and our chances of success will become fewer. However, as long as their escorts are inexperienced, I believe that we will be able to attack the convoys in the usual manner even in shallow waters. The Admiral Commanding Submarines will then also resort to the use of mines against American shipping. So far mines were not used because it was more economical to equip the submarines with torpedoes as long as the daily traffic was heavy. However, in anticipation of the expected decrease, it is planned to mine Chesapeake Bay, Delaware Bay, and New York Harbour during the new moon period in the middle of June. Submarines equipped with mines will leave on missions within the next few days.

If operations in the American area should prove unprofitable, we shall resume warfare against the convoys in the North Atlantic with a larger number of submarines. Up to this time, locating the enemy was always the most difficult part of this warfare. The Admiral Commanding Submarines believes that the larger numbers of submarines will make this easier in the future. The large number of submarines which we expect to have available in the near future will enable us to attack shipping in additional and more remote areas, which are now brought within our reach through the existence of submarine tankers.

The Admiral Commanding Submarines feels that the outlook in regard to submarine warfare is promising in view of the large number of submarines soon available and the variety of operations possible. The defence situation must also be taken into account when the possibilities of submarine warfare are considered. Our submarine losses are extremely light at this time. There is no doubt that the number of losses will rise again once attacks on convoys are resumed and the defences in some zones become stronger. Therefore we must strive with all means at our disposal to improve submarine weapons in order to keep the submarine abreast of defensive devices of the enemy. The most important thing in this respect is the development of a torpedo equipped with a non-contact pistol (*Abstandspistole*). This device would considerably speed up the sinking of torpedoed ships, and would thus save torpedoes, and the members of the crew of the torpedoed ship will not be able to save themselves due to the rapid sinking of the ship. This increase in personnel losses will no doubt make it more difficult to man the many ships America is building. The submarine forces have faith in their equipment and believe in their fighting ability. Therefore, the first thing to do is to get the submarines out of the Baltic Sea as fast as possible, and in general to have as many submarines as possible out at sea engaged in operations.

(signed) DOENITZ.

3. Present: Only the C.-in-C., Navy.

The C.-in-C., Navy, points out once more the need for closest co-operation of the representative of the shipping firms with the Navy. The C.-in-C., Navy, recommends an order which will authorise the Shipping and Transport Branch of the Naval High Command to make all decisions concerning the use of the merchant marine, since the Maritime Shipping Department of the Ministry of Transport has proved itself unfit for the task.

4. *The C.-in-C., Navy*, thanks the Fuehrer for his instructions concerning auxiliary aircraft carriers, but requests confirmation that the priority ratings of the following will not be affected: submarines and everything pertaining to them (inclusive of torpedo recovery vessels), as well as escort and patrol forces from destroyers down. He requests further that the Fuehrer put pressure on the Air Force in the matter of carrier planes. *The Fuehrer* confirms this. He expresses his opinion that the problem of mass production of suitable types of carrier planes can be solved more easily if there are four carriers than if there is only one.

5. In answer to the letter of the C.-in-C., Navy, *the Fuehrer* expresses his belief that it is impossible to build up a naval air force during this war. He realises the necessity, however, of accelerating construction of aircraft carriers even at this late date. *The C.-in-C., Navy*, points out that a naval air force with excellent personnel and aircraft existed at the time the Air Ministry was established.

(signed) RAEDER.

Brazil.—In February 1942, Brazil had granted facilities to British and American warships using her ports, and during the next few months generally showed herself favourable to the Allies, but without an actual declaration of war.   On June 4, the German High Command decided to take countermeasures against Brazil, and ordered a strong U-boat attack on Brazilian shipping and the Brazilian coast.   The operational plans show that roughly 40 U-boats were to be used.   At the next conference, on June 15, these plans were given Hitler's approval, but were not to be put into operation until August.

Russian convoys.—At the same conference the schemes which had been roughed out during the Spring were presented in greater detail.   The next Russian convoy (PQ.17) was selected as the target for the first big Arctic offensive.   U-boats, battleships, and the *Luftwaffe* were all involved in a carefully thought out operation, details of which are given as an appendix to the conference.

Malta.—In the Mediterranean Rommel was advancing at such speed that Hitler once more delayed the assault on Malta.   Raeder tried hard to convince him of the mistake he was making, but Hitler believed instead that the air attacks on the island and on the convoys supplying the island would be sufficient to neutralise it as a base.


C.-in-C., Navy                                            Berlin, June 17, 1942

**REPORT ON A CONFERENCE BETWEEN THE C.-IN.C., NAVY, AND THE FUEHRER AT THE BERGHOF THE AFTERNOON OF JUNE 15, 1942**

Also present:  Chief of Staff, O.K.W.
              Lt.-General Jodl.
              Vice-Admiral Krancke.
              Captain von Puttkamer.

1. (*a*) Submarine attack on Brazilian shipping and ports.—Permission was granted to execute the mission in the beginning of August.   The political situation should be reviewed once more before operations get under way.

(*b*) *The Fuehrer* proposes that an operational group of submarines be held in readiness for the purpose of quick interference in case the enemy should suddenly strike at such points as the Azores, Madeira, or Cape Verde.   *The C.-in-C., Navy*, points out that at this time we cannot afford to divert a considerable number of submarines for such a purpose alone. At the present time, all available submarines must be used in the war against enemy merchant shipping.   It may be possible, however, to form such a group within the framework of our present submarine warfare.   For instance, the Admiral Commanding Submarines has had eight submarines patrol the convoy lanes to and from the U.S. via the Azores.   In an emergency, these submarines could be used as suggested.   The Naval Staff, Quartermaster Division, declares that it might likewise be possible to solve the problem by stationing several submarines for a certain length of time in the vicinity of the endangered area.

2. Attack of the Norway Forces on Convoy PQ.17 in June.—*The Fuehrer* considers aircraft carriers a great threat to the large vessels.   The aircraft carriers must be located before the attack, and they must be rendered harmless by our Ju88 planes before the attack gets under way. Upon the request of the C.-in-C., Navy, our naval forces may be sent to their stations in the North in good time.   There they must await the order to attack.   This is subject to the Fuehrer's approval.

3. Precarious situation of Northern Jutland.—*The C.in-C., Navy*, emphasises that northern Jutland is particularly vulnerable to enemy landings because of its flat coast and the gigantic air base at Aalborg.   If the enemy lands in force, he will be in a position to capture the 38-cm. battery, and the Lim Fiord will provide him with a strong bulwark toward the south. The troops stationed in northern Jutland should therefore be sufficiently strong to be able to keep an invading enemy from digging himself in. *The Fuehrer* as well as the *Reichsmarschall* are of the same opinion

4. Operation *Herkules* (capture of Malta).—*The Fuehrer* recognises how important it is to capture Malta.   However, he does not believe that this can be done while the offensive on the Eastern Front is in progress, and especially not with Italian troops.   During that time the Air Force cannot spare any transport planes.   Once Tobruk is taken, most shipments will be routed to Tobruk via Crete.   On the other hand, the British efforts to get convoys through to Malta from the east and from the west testify the plight of the island.   These convoys, by the way, give us an opportunity to inflict much damage on the enemy.   Once Malta has been bled white by the continuous air raids and the total blockade, we could risk the attack.

5. Auxiliary aircraft carriers.—The plans for the auxiliary aircraft carriers will be submitted within a week.   Four weeks later the construction will reach the stage where the materials can be ordered.
    Number of aircraft:

|           |    |    |    |    |                            |
|-----------|----|----|----|----|----------------------------|
| Europa    | .. | .. | .. | .. | 18 bombers.<br>24 fighters. |
| Potsdam   | .. | .. | .. | .. | 8 bombers.<br>12 fighters. |
| Seydlitz  | .. | .. | .. | .. | 12 bombers.<br>6 fighters. |
| Gneisenau .. | .. | .. | .. | 8 bombers.<br>12 fighters. |

It will not pay to convert the Seydlitz, now 90 per cent. completed, since the superstructure of the vessel would have to be removed to the level of the armour deck.

6. Manpower problem.—*The C.-in-C., Navy*, points out that repairs are taking an excessively long time due to the manpower shortage.   For example, it will take from eight weeks to three and a half months to repair the Prinz Eugen.   Therefore he urgently requests the allocation of a few thousand extra workmen.   The C.-in-C., Navy, asks specifically that no worker engaged in submarine construction or repair be drafted into the Armed Forces, since the submarine war is of decisive importance, and affects all land operations.   *The Fuehrer* recognises the fact that the submarine war will in the end decide the outcome of the war.   Therefore he considers these requests justified.   He directs the Chief of Staff, O.K.W., to see to it that Minister Speer attends to the matter.   In any event, there will be no more reductions from July onwards.

7. Italian requests for fuel oil.—The Naval Staff, Quartermaster Division, submits the latest requests for fuel oil made by the *Commando Supremo*.   He shows that it is impossible to supply the Italians with additional oil.   *The C.-in-C., Navy*, asks that this request be denied, thus confirming the negative reply he already made to Admiral Riccardi.   *The Fuehrer* agrees.                                      (signed) RAEDER.

## APPENDIX

### Operation *Roesselsprung*

1. Task.—Attack on Convoy PQ.17.
2. Task forces

Trondheim Group:

Tirpitz with the Fleet Commander on board, Hipper.
6 destroyers (Ihn, Lody, Galster, Riedel, Eckoldt, and Steinbrink).

Narvik Group:

Luetzow with the Admiral Commanding Cruisers on board;
Scheer.
6 destroyers (Z.24, Z.27, Z.28, Z.29, Z.30, and Beitzen).
Submarines
Three submarines will be stationed north-east of Iceland beginning
June 10. They have the task of locating the convoy. Other available
submarines, probably three or four, will be in attack position between
Jan Mayen and Bear Island. Submarines becoming available at a
later date will be stationed off Bear Island in attack position.

Note.—There are at this time only two destroyers in Trondheim (Ihn
and Lody). The other four destroyers will be transferred from Germany
to Norway within the next few days. Besides these, there are two or three
torpedo boats in Trondheim, which are to serve as escorts to the Trondheim Group.

3. Command

Operational Command for the entire mission: Group North, with
headquarters in Kiel.

Tactical Command:

Trondheim Group and all other forces: Fleet Commander on
board the Tirpitz.
Narvik Group: Admiral Commanding Cruisers on board the
Luetzow.

The submarines will be under the command of Group North through
Admiral, Arctic Ocean, at Narvik, by means of radio relaying station. It
is not intended to place the submarines directly under the command of the
Fleet Commander.

4. Execution.—As soon as Convoy PQ.17 has been located, the task
forces will take their stations. This is to be done as late as possible. The
Trondheim Group will proceed to the northern exit of Alta Fiord. There
they will refuel. They will depart for the operation on receipt of the
code word from Group North. The Fleet Commander will head for the
convoy at full speed. The Admiral Commanding Cruisers is to join
forces with the Fleet Commander.

Main task.—Rapid destruction of the enemy merchant ships. If necessary these should only be crippled and the sinking left to the submarines
and the Air Force. The escort forces should be engaged only if this is
indispensable for accomplishing the main task. In such an event it is

primarily the task of the Tirpitz and Hipper to fight the escort forces, while the Luetzow and Scheer dispose of the convoy during that time.

An engagement with superior enemy forces is to be avoided. The operation should be executed quickly; and should be completed before an enemy security unit composed of battleships and carriers—presumably stationed in the Faroe–Iceland area—has a chance to intervene. The operation can be cancelled by the Fleet Commander or by order of Group North.

5. Aerial reconnaissance.—Extensive aerial reconnaissance is prerequisite for the execution of the operation and especially for the participation of Tirpitz and Hipper. The Air Force has the following assignment:

(*a*) After the convoy has been located, continuous contact should be maintained. The composition of the convoy and the strength of the escort forces should be reported as quickly as possible.

(*b*) An attempt should be made to locate a heavy enemy naval force in the Shetland–Faroe–Iceland–Jan Mayen area, scouting Reykjavik, Scapa, Firth of Forth, and Moray Firth in the process. Once the enemy force has been located, continuous contact should be maintained.

(*c*) As long as the heavy enemy force has not been located, the area within a 250-mile radius of the convoy is to be carefully patrolled and all enemy forces sighted are to be reported.

6. Battle operations of the Air Force.—The Air Force has been requested to order the planes to attack only aircraft carriers and merchant vessels once our forces have engaged the enemy, unless the identity of the ships is unmistakable, or Group North has issued special orders.

Remarks :

(1) This once we shall probably have twelve destroyers available for the operation.

(2) The fuel oil situation permits an operation of this scope at this time.

(3) The weather is especially favourable in June. The period of spring storms is over. Heavy summer fogs do not occur until July.

(4) The ice situation likewise is especially favourable in June. The ice had receded very little to the north, so that it will be impossible for the convoy to evade us to the north. As a matter of fact, beginning about 150 nautical miles west of Bear Island, the enemy convoy has to sail east within 250 to 200 nautical miles off the Norwegian coast. This area is completely dominated by our own Air Forces. Therefore no heavy enemy vessels have sallied into this area so far.

(5) The operation will be executed only if reconnaissance has established with certainty that there is no risk of becoming involved with superior enemy forces.

(6) It is particularly important that the Air Force fulfil the request of the Navy in regard to aerial reconnaissance, if necessary at the expense of participating in battle. The Navy's request would appear to be justified in view of the total success it seems possible to achieve with the aid of our heavy naval forces.

For the next two and a half months no conference on naval affairs was held by Hitler.   The war was progressing well for Germany.

The attack on the Russian convoy (PQ.17) in July was entirely successful, and out of a total of 34 merchant ships 23 were sunk.   The returning convoy from Russia was also attacked and 16 more merchant ships were sunk.   The result of these heavy attacks was to cause the Allies temporarily to postpone convoys to Russia, though fast ships, sailing independently, still contrived to get through.   One convoy was sailed in September, but convoys on the former scale were not resumed until December 1942.

In the Atlantic Doenitz's U-boats sank 145 ships in June, 96 in July, and 108 in August.   The June losses were the heaviest in numbers for any one month of the war.   Merchant raiders were also active, and captured or sank 16 ships in the three months June, July, and August.

In the Mediterranean Rommel captured Tobruk (June 21), Bardia (June 22), Sollum (June 23), Mersa Matruh (June 28), and by June 30 halted opposite the defensive lines of the British Army at El Alamein.   Heavy ships of the British Fleet were withdrawn from Alexandria to Suez, and the situation was ripe for the capture of Malta.   At this point, however, Axis plans were changed with results which altered the whole course of the war in the Mediterranean.   Without reference either to the Italians, or to his own naval command Hitler postponed the capture of Malta until the conquest of Egypt was completed.   In making this decision Hitler was swayed by Rommel's confidence of easy victory over the 8th Army.   Though Rommel realised that by postponing the capture of Malta his communications would still be exposed to attack, he believed that the *Afrika Korps* would be able to live off the country once they got into the Nile Delta, and also be able to use the equipment he hoped to capture from the 8th Army.   Kesselring and Raeder deplored the decision to abandon the capture of Malta, realising the odds against which Rommel was gambling.

The 8th Army stood firm at El Alamein ; the British Fleet returned to Alexandria; and in the beginning of August the siege of Malta was temporarily lifted by the resolute delivery of supplies and aircraft in a heavily defended convoy.   The convoy ran the gauntlet of severe U-boat and air attacks for four days.   One carrier, H.M.S. Eagle, was sunk, and only 5 out of 15 merchant ships got through.   But this was sufficient to break the siege.   Reinforced with supplies, Malta made a rapid recovery, and by the end of August was once more an effective operational base for submarines, cruisers, and aircraft.   Rommel's sea communications were once more vulnerable and the 8th Army's counter-offensive at El Alamein became a real possibility.

At the next conference on August 26 the war at sea was reviewed.   Little was said about the Mediterranean, and the discussion concentrated on means by which the German Navy could aid the Russian campaign and the Battle of the Atlantic.

C.-in-C., Navy                                         Berlin, August 29, 1942

### CONFERENCE OF THE C.-IN-C., NAVY, WITH THE FUEHRER AT WEHRWOLF ON AUGUST 26, 1942

Also present :  Vice-Admiral Krancke.
              Captain von Puttkamer.

I. War situation at the end of August 1942.—The war situation continues to be determined by the following factors :

(1) It is urgently necessary to defeat Russia and thus create a *lebensraum* which is blockade-proof and easy to defend.   Thus we could continue to fight for years.

2. The fight against the Anglo-Saxon sea powers will decide both the length and the outcome of the war, and could bring England and America to the point of discussing peace terms.

*The Fuehrer* agrees explicitly.

A. Use of the Navy in the war against Russia. (*a*) The Arctic Ocean.—
Evidently convoy PQ.18 did not sail. We can thus assume that our
submarines and aircraft, which totally destroyed convoy PQ.17, have
forced the enemy to give up this route temporarily or even fundamentally
to change his whole system of supply lines. Supplies to northern ports of
Russia remain decisive for the whole conduct of the war waged by the
Anglo-Saxons. They must preserve Russia's strength in order to keep
German forces occupied. The enemy will most probably continue to
ship supplies to northern Russia, and the Naval Staff must therefore
maintain submarines along the same routes. The greater part of the
Fleet will also be stationed in northern Norway. The reason for this,
besides making attacks on convoys possible, is the constant threat of an
enemy invasion. Only by keeping the Fleet in Norwegian waters can we
hope to meet this danger successfully. Besides, it is especially important
in view of the whole Axis strategy that the German "fleet in being" tie
down the British Home Fleet, especially after the heavy Anglo-American
losses in the Mediterranean and the Pacific. The Japanese are likewise
aware of the importance of this measure. In addition, the danger of
enemy mines in home waters has constantly increased, so that the naval
forces should be shifted only for repairs and training purposes. *The
Fuehrer* expresses agreement and stresses the danger from mines to ship
traffic to and from Norway.

(*b*) The Baltic Sea.—The particular type of warfare in the Gulf of Finland permits only the use of very small vessels. The most effective weapon
for this region has proved to be the mines. Actions of the Russian Fleet,
which were expected on a larger scale, did not materialise due to mines.
Only two or three submarines broke through into the Baltic, compared to
at least twenty which were destroyed in trying to reach it. The conquest
of Leningrad would terminate naval warfare in that region. This would
improve the situation greatly for the Naval Staff, and it would free forces
for sea and coastal defence. To be sure, the number of Baltic forces which
would become available is small; nevertheless, it is of importance considering the growing lack of manpower on the one hand and the constant
expansion of our sphere of influence on the other hand. Furthermore,
if we could eliminate the mines in those regions where a blockade would no
longer be needed, we could greatly expand the training area in the Baltic
Sea in summer 1943. This is especially important, since the western
part of the Baltic can hardly be used at all for training purposes because of
mines. *The C.-in-C., Navy*, requests a directive that the shipyards in
Leningrad be spared shelling and air attacks and not be destroyed with
the city for obvious reasons. *The Fuehrer* declares that such systematic
sparing of the shipyards is possible in the case of artillery, but not in connection with air raids; however, air raids never achieve complete destruction of docks in any case. The Fuehrer will take the Navy's request into
account, although he is of the opinion that the Russians will destroy the
docks themselves.

(*c*) The Black Sea.—We are still handicapped by lack of forces so that
the main share of sea fighting has to be done by the Air Force. We intend
to strengthen our forces with additional submarines, even though we
hope that the Russian Black Sea Fleet will be put out of action by October
or November. Submarines will remain important in the future when the

Black Sea is used as a training area. Considerable losses in the Sea of Azov were caused especially by Russian mines. Further losses will be incurred in trying to put the ports acquired into navigable condition, always keeping in mind the fighting tenacity of the Russians. The Naval Staff therefore stresses the importance of great caution in the use of the small number of steamers still available, which for the present cannot be replaced. In the opinion of the Naval Staff the only risks that should be taken are in using landing barges (MFP) in cases where Army operations depend on reinforcements by sea. Landing barges are replaceable.

The Italian submarines and submarine chasers (MAS) proved their worth in the Black Sea. Unit and boat commanders showed great daring. The only vessels which can be sent to the Caspian Sea at the moment are coastal mine-layers (*KM-Boot*) and Italian units of the type used in the Black Sea. No final conclusions on how to transport the vessels have been reached. In the Caspian Sea we will be confronted with an enormous Russian superiority, since all our equipment must be brought by land. Our three submarines for the Black Sea will not be ready until October, when they may be used for training purposes. *The Fuehrer* considers the submarines in the Black Sea important because they will have a very favourable political influence on Turkey. He suggests that six submarines for this reason be transferred there. *The C.-in-C., Navy*, agrees.

B. The war against England and the United States.—When our aim in the East, namely the creation of a blockade-proof *lebensraum*, is achieved we must still fight the naval war against the Anglo-Saxons to an end. The only way to bring them to terms is by constant successful attacks on their sea routes.

1. Submarine warfare. (*a*) The enemy transport system in American waters underwent great changes, as the Naval Staff predicted and expected even sooner. The Americans abandoned individual ship movements off their eastern coast and adopted convoy formation. They have considerably strengthened their defences, particularly in the air. Accordingly submarine attacks in these areas must be focused on points where the largest number of ships, not sailing in convoys, has been observed; and where ships are expected to sail alone.

(*b*) Recent submarine attacks were determined by the change in the enemy's transport system and the increasing difficulty of operating along the American coast. At the same time, the satisfactory increase in delivery of new operational submarines from home (twenty-two in July and twenty-six in August) enables us to resume convoy attacks by stationing one or two submarine groups in the northern and middle parts of the North Atlantic. The favourable results of these operations indicated that opportunities for attack are not much worse than before as long as the convoy remains beyond the range of aircraft protection.

*The C.-in-C., Navy*, points out on the map the range within which British aircraft bases at home can protect their convoys. Recently our submarines have suffered heavy losses because of the superior location finding devices on English aircraft (four submarines sunk in the Bay of Biscay, three damaged, four more damaged in contact with convoys, some badly). The C.-in-C., Navy, reports that German submarines have been equipped with radar interception sets (FuMB) since August 8, 1942, and this device and the deception devices (*Bolde*) have shown some favourable results. *The Fuehrer* recognises the need for the best possible aircraft to support the submarines, but he makes no definite promises.

(*c*) The Naval Staff considers it particularly effective to launch submarine attacks at several places simultaneously. Besides stationing several submarines in the Natal Passage and off Capetown with four submarines and a submarine tanker. We plan first to send two submarines into the roadstead of Capetown and follow up with four more outside the harbour.

(*d*) Submarine operations in Norway.—In order to attack the expected PQ convoys at the earliest possible opportunity, two submarines were assigned to patrol the Denmark Straits, north of Iceland. Seven other submarines are now involved in operation *Scheer*. As other submarines become available for action, they should be held ready at their bases until the PQ convoy has been located.

(*e*) Submarine operations in the Mediterranean.—In addition to the four submarines operating in the eastern Mediterranean, there should always be two or three others assigned to the western Mediterranean in order to attack the supply lines between Malta and Gibraltar (at present two boats are on duty in this area).

(*f*) Losses.—Recent submarine losses were higher than we expected. We lost three in June and nine in July, and we must count on an additional loss of eight. These losses are partly due to strong enemy air forces in the Bay of Biscay.

2. Cruiser warfare.—Three auxiliary cruisers are in foreign waters as follows :

| | | | |
|---|---|---|---|
| Ship 10 (Gumprich) | .. | .. | Indian Ocean. |
| Sunk to date | .. | .. | 10 ships of 56,000 tons. |
| | | | |
| Ship 28 (Ruckteschell) | .. | .. | Atlantic Ocean. |
| Sunk to date | .. | .. | 9 ships of 60,000 tons. |
| | | | |
| Ship 23 (Gerlach) | .. | .. | Atlantic Ocean. |
| Sunk to date | .. | .. | 4 ships of 22,000 tons. |

The area of Ship 10 was reduced because of the operations planned by the Japanese Navy in the Indian Ocean. We intend to order Ship 10 to Japan for engine overhaul in September. The record of Ship 28 is especially gratifying because her captain previously had unusual success from May to October 1940 as captain of the Widder (Ship 21), when he sank ten ships totalling 58,000 tons. At the beginning of October we plan to send a fourth auxiliary cruiser (Ship 45) into action.

Movements of the Scheer.—*The C.-in-C., Navy*, shows on a map the movements of the Scheer (operation *Wunderland*) in the Arctic Ocean. He also gives the reasons why it is desirable to send her to the South Atlantic in November 1942 for attacking merchant ships. The chances for success are very favourable, and the operation should have important political and psychological effects. Our chief difficulty lies in breaking out of home waters into the Atlantic. *The Fuehrer* expounds at length why he wishes to keep all larger units available for operations in the north until further notice. (They discourage landing attempts; there is limited air reconnaissance in winter; the coast is insufficiently fortified, etc.). He therefore decides not to dispatch the Scheer to the Atlantic this winter.

3. Mediterranean Sea.—The opinion of the Naval Staff regarding the importance of the capture of Malta remains unaltered. The capture of Gibraltar remains a most desirable objective for the future. It is particularly important to seal off the Mediterranean completely in case a long-drawn-out war requires us to secure our European *lebensraum* as thoroughly as possible. We now have fifteen submarines in the area. Heavy damage was again caused by enemy bombers. Our E-boats are to be reinforced by an eight-boat flotilla in October. No further additions are possible, since we have no more boats of the small type that can pass down the Rhône River.

*The C.-in-C., Navy,* continued to regard a possible attempt of the Anglo-Saxons to occupy North-west Africa and get a foothold in North Africa with the aid of the French as a very great danger to the whole German war effort. They would attack Italy from there and endanger our position in North-east Africa. Therefore Germany must maintain a strong position in the Mediterranean and must above all have unquestionable domination over Crete. By the same token, we cannot afford to relinquish Piraeus and Salonika. *The Fuehrer* concurs in this opinion and states that he wants to replace those troops which have been withdrawn from Crete. For the present he has no intention of giving it up. He does not conceal his increasing dissatisfaction with the Italians, and alludes to plans which he is not yet able to discuss.

II. Concentration of our air attacks on destroying the largest possible amount of cargo space.—The C.-in-C., Navy, requests that our air attacks against England be concentrated on ships in port and on the ways. In this way, our attacks would have a real influence on the outcome of the war, which they certainly do not have at present. *The Fuehrer* stresses the strong defences of such harbours, but acknowledges the wisdom of such a procedure. He hopes for an improvement in the situation by the use of high-altitude bombers which are being delivered now. *The C.-in-C., Navy,* again points out how dangerous it is to have large airfields in the vicinity of important objectives on the coast since enemy airborne troops have easy access to them. *The Fuehrer* states that the Air Force reported all fields are now sufficiently protected by 2-cm. guns.

III. *The Fuehrer* inquires about the labour problem. *Minister Speer* said that it is impossible to take the 8,400 workers out of the munitions industry, substituting foreigners. *The Fuehrer* considers this move necessary nevertheless. *The C.-in-C., Navy,* suggests looking into the possibility of obtaining skilled shipyard workers from the Todt Organisation.

IV. Private conversation between the Fuehrer and the C.-in-C., Navy.— *The C.-in-C., Navy,* believes that the decision to build more battleships will have to await the outcome of the naval war between Japan and the Anglo-Saxons, because the battleship has not yet had a chance to prove its worth in action. In any event, it would probably be wise to prepare the design of a battleship equipped with guns of the largest possible calibre, despite the fact that more experience and future developments might require us to design smaller warships with new weapons, such as remote control glide bombers fired from catapults, perfected remote control rockets, etc. We must also work out plans for large aircraft carriers and cruisers with flight decks, better protected than ever before. These are now in progress. *The Fuehrer* agrees with this opinion. He instructs the C.-in-C., Navy, to find out from the Krupp firm which artillery calibre (45 cm., 50 cm., or 53 cm.) would give the best performance technically and tactically for the largest usable ships. This should be the basis for designing the ship.

V. Remarks of the Fuehrer concerning control of planning in port cities by the *Gauleiters.—The C.-in-C., Navy*, assumes that the Navy in Kiel was the cause of this directive. *The Fuehrer* denies this, and traces it back to the efforts of the Army and Air Force to requisition large districts in cities without regard for over-all planning (e.g. without regard to railways). One person must decide these things, and that is the *Gauleiter*. In case of disagreement, the Fuehrer will make the final decision. *The C.-in-C., Navy*, stresses the need of considering the Navy's requirements before planning is undertaken in naval ports. Certain installations, such as docks, etc., can be placed only at certain points and an over-all plan must be guided by this fact. This must be agreed upon by the *Gauleiter* and the Navy before the final plans are completed. *The Fuehrer* concedes this point. *The C.-in-C., Navy*, mentions the disagreement between the city of Kiel and the Navy over the Diedrichsen estate which has now been legally decided in favour of the Navy, as most of the heirs wished. The Navy needs these premises urgently for the 2nd Admiral of U-boats. It is situated on the harbour outside Bellevue near the Wik. The city of Kiel wants it for an official guest house. *The Fuehrer* will look into this question. It has evidently already been brought to his attention, although he does not admit it.

(signed) RAEDER.

*　　*　　*　　*　　*　　*

## SUBMARINE LOSSES UP TO AUGUST 24, 1942

Losses in boats :

Total number of submarines in operation since the
  beginning of war  ..    ..    ..    ..    ..    304
Total number of submarines lost since beginning of war  105
Average monthly loss  ..    ..    ..    ..    ..    2·9
Average monthly loss to the number in operation  ..    4·9 per cent.

Losses in personnel :

| | Officers | Senior non-com. officers * | Other non-com. officers | Ratings | Total |
|---|---|---|---|---|---|
| Killed  .. | 185 | 184 | 515 | 1,075 | 1,959 |
| Captured .. | 112 | 113 | 323 | 600 | 1,148 |
| Missing  .. | 63 | 59 | 192 | 382 | 696 |
| Total  .. | 360 | 356 | 1,030 | 2,057 | 3,803 |

This means a 38 per cent. total loss of operating personnel each year.

* Portepee-Unteroffiziere.

The Battle of the Atlantic was at this time a source of real satisfaction to the German Navy.  U-boats were sinking ships faster than they could be built, and though the organisation of convoys off the American coast had deprived them of a fruitful hunting ground, other "soft" areas still existed,   U-boat losses, however, had begun to increase slowly as Allied counter measures improved.   They were not yet serious, but they indicated that the U-boats would have to keep in step with the Allied technical developments if they were to continue to enjoy their present success.   At a conference on September 28 the strategy and technical development of the U-boat campaign were discussed.

## REPORT OF THE CONFERENCE WITH THE FUEHRER IN THE REICH CHANCELLERY ON MONDAY, SEPTEMBER 28, 1942, FROM 1630 TO 1830

Present: The Fuehrer.
Grand Admiral Raeder, Dr. h.c.
Field Marshal Keitel.
Admiral Doenitz.
Admiral Fuchs.
Vice-Admiral Krancke.
Vice-Admiral Maertens.
Rear-Admiral Lange.
Captain von Puttkamer.
*Baurat* Waas.

*The Fuehrer* opens the conference with the remark that he wishes to be informed about the present state of the submarine war; he likewise desires to form an opinion regarding the degree with which submarine warfare is keeping pace with the further demands of the war.   He continues with expressing his great appreciation for the achievements of the submarines.   He is convinced that the monthly rate of sinkings will continue to be so high that the enemy will not be able to replace his losses by new construction.   He considers it impossible that the increase in production of the enemy shipyards comes anywhere near what propaganda would have us believe.   Even if the enemy should succeed in launching ships relatively fast, he would still not have the necessary engines, auxiliary engines, other equipment and, most of all, crews for these ships.   In regard to the manpower problem, he calls attention to the fact that it is very much to our disadvantage if a large percentage of the crews of sunken ships is able to go to sea again on new ships.   The Fuehrer stresses the necessity of having new technical developments put into practical use promptly; only in this way can full advantage be taken of the new invention.   This was demonstrated in the construction of the heavy tank which would have given us a decided superiority in Africa had it been available earlier.

*Admiral Doenitz* reviews the present state of the Battle of the Atlantic. He says that the submarine conflict has moved back again from the American coast to the Middle Atlantic because fighting off the American coast was no longer sufficiently profitable.   However, there are still a few "soft spots" left along the coasts where the enemy can be attacked successfully.   He points out that we obtained some results by laying mines off the coast.   Operations around the St. Lawrence River continue to be productive to a certain extent.   He then touches upon the prospects for success in the South Atlantic, especially along the African coast. He points out on the map, however, that the chief task of the Navy is attacking convoys in the North Atlantic.

The increased number of submarines which we are now using makes it easier to locate the enemy. Besides, the enemy convoys usually travel the direct route on the Great Circle, permitting us to conclude that they are now avoiding circuitous routes because of ship shortages. The convoys are very strongly protected. Some of the escort vessels closely surround the convoy, while others are stationed among the ships themselves. In addition, the enemy had adopted a system placing destroyers at a distance, making it very difficult for the submarines to approach the convoys. The great menace for the submarines today, however, is aircraft.

Admiral Doenitz shows on a map what range enemy aircraft bases on the British Isles attained in the years 1940, 1941, and 1942, and in which sea regions therefore an effective attack on convoys by submarines had to be abandoned. This illustrates how concentrated attacks against convoys were pushed farther and farther towards the middle of the Atlantic. If the same process should be repeated along the American coast, it would considerably weaken our present tactics of attacking in numbers. This shows clearly the necessity of our own Air Force supporting the submarines to a much greater extent than has been the case up to the present time. The range of the Heinkel 177 exceeds the territory which is so strongly threatened today by enemy planes. Co-operation with aircraft of that type will provide advanced notice of the enemy and reduce air attacks on our submarines.

Attacks on convoys did not cause heavy submarine losses at all. Our losses are distributed rather evenly over the various regions; at times they rose in the Bay of Biscay due to aircraft attacks. After our submarines were equipped with radar interception sets (FuMB) our losses decreased at once. Emphasis is laid on technical improvements of the submarine and its weapons not because our losses have greatly increased, but because we wish to attain the same success as before in spite of improvements in enemy defence. Most important of all is the demand for increasing underwater speed. This is to be accomplished by the new Walter submarine. A submarine with great underwater speed will be able to come within shooting range of the convoy in spite of enemy escort vessels. It will also enable the submarine to elude its pursuers quickly. In this connection it is stated that enemy Asdic has not improved since the beginning of the war.

*The Fuehrer* fully supports these ideas and adds that, in his opinion, the introduction of a submarine with high underwater speed would have a revolutionary effect. It would immediately render ineffective the whole apparatus of enemy escort vessels and the construction programme of the relative slow enemy corvettes. In the fight against the enemy defence it is especially important to obtain a weapon with which one can successfully eliminate the escort vessels that keep the submarine out of shooting range. This could be a weapon for use either under water or on the surface. To the first group belongs the acoustic homing torpedo (*Geraeuschtorpedo*). *The C.-in-C., Navy*, declares that the development of this torpedo has now progressed far enough to consider prospects of its success favourable. The C.in-C., Navy, adds that we have also made good progress with the new non-contact pistol (*Abstandspistole*). This pistol will give the torpedo a tremendous destructive power, and will therefore increase the loss in human life considerably.

The Admiral Commanding Submarines brings to discussion the problem of surface attack on the escort vessels by submarines; he sees a solution in the remote-controlled rocket. *The Fuehrer* warns against becoming too optimistic about such projectiles, with which Army and Air Force are likewise experimenting. Nevertheless, it is felt that further research is justified since it may possibly lead to a revolutionary development for the submarine. The Admiral Commanding Submarines emphasises once more the necessity of evolving such projectiles for the submarine. The Fuehrer on his part suggests continuing experiments with the remote-controlled torpedo, to which he attaches great importance.

*The C.-in-C., Navy*, reports to the Fuehrer that experiments were made lately with shells filled with an explosive (*N-Stoff*). Some trials shots were fired at oil tanks which were filled with the heaviest mazut oil. The high flame which arose at first broke off; this however, may have been due to the unusually heavy kind of oil. In any case, some submarines are now being provided with this ammunition in order to try out their effect on the enemy. *The Fuehrer* personally places great hope in the use of such shells and gives orders to examine at once the possibility of using the explosive (*N-Stoff*) for loading torpedoes in order to send tankers up in flame.

In regard to surface detection by enemy radar (*DT-Geraet*), *the Chief, Naval Communications Division* (MND), reported on the deflective reflection method of applying slanting surfaces to the conning tower and about the use of the radar interception set (FuMB). *The Fuehrer* mentioned the possibility of feigning the destruction of submarines. He referred to numerous reports by fliers who took it for granted that a submarine had been destroyed after sighting a big oil slick. The Fuehrer had in mind some kind of torpedo which would explode on the surface of the water and eject oil blubber, and similar material. An objection was made that the loss of one torpedo tube for actual attack would be unfortunate. (*Marginal note: I believe it would be more practical to have a container on the upper deck from which air and oil can be blown, so that all torpedo tubes will be saved for their real purpose. Possibly oil and air could be ejected from the bilges.*)

In closing, the Walter submarine was discussed. *The C.-in-C., Navy*, reported that Blohm and Voss and Germania have each been commissioned to build two boats of the smaller type. The larger type has been assigned to the Walter firm for a preliminary design. As soon as the engines of the smaller type have been tried out, an order for twenty-four boats is to be placed. We hoped to be able to make a decision within two months regarding mass production of the larger type. In any case, mass production of these submarines is to be started as soon as possible, with corresponding adjustment of the present submarine construction programme. *The Fuehrer* was entirely in harmony with these plans and emphasises once more the need for quick action. The Fuehrer referred once more to his conviction that the submarine plays a decisive rôle in the outcome of the war.

After the meeting was adjourned, the C.-in-C., Navy, reported to the Fuehrer that a Spanish steamer unfortunately had been sunk by one of our submarines.   *The Fuehrer* decided that the sinking is to be admitted, and that Spain will be fully compensated for the loss of the ship, including the cargo of wheat.   He also ordered that a public announcement be made that the guilty commander will be court-martialled.

The Admiral Commanding Submarines had already issued this order.

# CHAPTER IV

# *"The End of the Beginning . . ."*

OCTOBER WAS the last month in which the Axis powers held the initiative; the epic defence of Stalingrad and Malta, and the stubborn resistance at El Alamein had turned the tide. On the night of October 23, the 8th Army began its offensive against Axis positions at El Alamein, and nine days later a breech in the enemy positions was made. Rommel began to retreat as swiftly as he had advanced. British naval forces kept the 8th Army supplied, and by November 22 Axis troops were forced back as far as Benghazi.

Meanwhile, on November 8, a joint Anglo-American force invaded North Africa. The first major invasion by the Allies, the North African landings met with complete success, and Rommel was now fairly caught between the two Allied armies advancing from east and west. The *Afrika Korps* was trapped in Tunisia.

Raeder, a sound strategist, had long foreseen the possibility of an Allied landing on North Africa, and, working on this assumption, foresaw also the importance of Tunisia to the North African campaign. With the failure of the plans so confidently made in the previous spring—Malta uncaptured, Egypt and Cyrenaica lost—Tunisia was the last stronghold of the Axis in Africa. If Germany could hold Tunisia then they could still prevent the Allies from getting a foothold in Southern Europe. Hitler appreciated these arguments, but was still obsessed with the idea of another Allied landing in Norway, and ordered the continued concentration of German sea-power in that area.

Other difficulties in Germany which had slowly increased during their years of success, now became acute. The fuel oil position was such that the fleet in Norway was severely hampered. The shortage of men and material also made itself felt, and the lack of an adequate navy made it impossible to stop the Allied attacks. The idea of defeat was still far from the German mind, however, and at the next conference, on November 19, offensive, operations in the Baltic, Arctic, and Atlantic were discussed.

C.-in-C., Navy                                           Berlin, November 21, 1942

## CONFERENCE BETWEEN THE .C.-IN-C., NAVY, AND THE FUEHRER AT THE BERGHOF THE AFTERNOON OF NOVEMBER 19, 1942

Also present: Chief of Staff, O.K.W.
            Chief, Naval Staff, Quartermaster Division.
            Captain von Puttkamer.

REPORT ON THE SITUATION, NOVEMBER 17, 1942

1. Own situation. Eastern Sector.—Ice will soon put a stop to enemy activity in the Baltic Sea. No submarines have been observed during the last few days. For the conduct of naval warfare next spring, it is important to seal off Leningrad. The result of such an action would be a saving of underwater defence devices and of naval vessels; at the same time it would make the blockade of Leningrad more effective. If it is absolutely impossible to take Leningrad this winter, then the occupation of the coastal strip Schepel–Oranienbaum and the islands of Lavansaari and Seiskari would considerably improve the situation. The British home air fleet is at present engaged in laying aerial mines. Our effort to sweep these mines is taxing our forces to the limit.

Northern Sector.—The activity of our fleet is hampered by lack of fuel oil. The situation will not improve for the time being, since the amounts of fuel oil being handed over in the Mediterranean are increasing. The following German naval forces are stationed in Norway:

Tirpitz is lying in Trondheim. The engines are being overhauled, but the ship can be ready on short notice.

Hipper and Koeln in the Alta Fiord.

Nuernberg in Trondheim.

4 destroyers in the Alta Fiord, 3 destroyers in Trondheim.

Prinz Eugen and Luetzow will be ready for transfer to the north at the beginning of December.

Scharnhorst cannot be in Norway until January 1943 as a result of delays in repairs.

Scheer returned to Germany the beginning of November.

Operations are intended only when we have actual proof that the objectives will be worthwhile. Passing QP convoys may prove to be such worthwhile objectives since it is expected that they will not be heavily guarded; therefore good results may be obtained. Submarines will be less effective during the arctic night because of absence of aerial reconnaissance. At the present time twenty-three submarines are assigned to the Arctic Ocean. Ten of these are in the operational zones—three near Jan Mayen, seven near Bear Island.

*The Fuehrer* decides that in view of the oil situation only Luetzow is to be transferred, while Prinz Eugen will remain in Germany. The decision concerning the transfer of the Scharnhorst is to be made at the beginning of January. The Fuehrer wants light naval forces to be sent to Norway, however, and desires Norway to be heavily stocked with supplies, since all available reports lead him to fear that the enemy will attempt an invasion during the arctic night. The Fuehrer believes that Sweden's attitude cannot be depended upon in case of an enemy landing attempt.

Western Sector.—The situation has not changed to any extent. The enemy is increasing his air activity over the Bay of Biscay and is apparently interested mainly in out-bound tankers which he suspects of being submarine supply ships; e.g. heavy air raids on Spichern. So far, only two of the blockade-runners left port undetected. Three others had to turn back because of damage. Three blockade-runners have so far returned from their mission. Enemy air raids on submarine bases such as La Pallice and St. Nazaire have increased lately.

Southern Sector.—This is the most important sector at present. We are aiding the Italians with whatever means we have. All the fuel oil we can spare is being shipped to Italy. In addition, we are stocking the mines necessary for closing the Straits of Sicily. The importance of closing the Straits of Sicily immediately was emphatically called to the attention of Admiral Riccardi. The reinforcement of Crete is proceeding according to plan.

2. Enemy situation.—The landing in North Africa proves that there is as yet no shortage of ships for strategic purposes. In case of an emergency, the enemy can make available a sufficiently large number of vessels by cutting down on all other shipping operations. The ships used in the North African operation total approximately 1,300,000 tons according to

reports received about ships passing Gibraltar, etc. There are enough troop transports. Most of these ships are at present on the way home. Approximately 300,000 tons are necessary to supply the troops landed in North Africa so far. The enemy can start another operation of greater scope by the middle of December, if he is able to continue the restrictions on other types of shipping.

Tunisia always was and still is the decisive key position in the Mediterranean. The presence of Axis forces in Tunisia compels the enemy to employ considerable forces, which must be supplied over long and vulnerable routes. It is a simple task, however, to supply our Armoured Army, since our lines are short. At the same time the presence of our forces in Tunisia prevents enemy success, since passage through the Mediterranean is denied him. If we are able to hold Tunisia, the enemy will have gained only the advantage of moving his air bases closer to our North African position and to Italy. This is offset, however, by disadvantages due to vulnerable supply lines and the large number of troops needed.

Should the enemy succeed in dislodging us from North Africa altogether, he will have enough ships and troops to start an all-out attack on the southern flank of Europe. This attack might be launched in any one of three directions: the Iberian Peninsula, Italy, or the Balkans. If the enemy has not enough forces available for an operation of such scope, he may possibly occupy the various islands in the Mediterranean, such as the Balearic Islands, Sardinia, and Corsica in the western Mediterranean, and Rhodes and Crete in the eastern Mediterranean.

The following factors cause the C.-in-C., Navy, to fear a sudden powerful attack on the Aegeian from the Suez area: the quiet in the Eastern Mediterranean, the large number of troops landed in South Africa during the last few months, the complete absence of reports from the western * Indian Ocean, and reports of increased commando activity on Cyprus. Paralysis of our oil sources in Roumania will, of course, always be one of the principal enemy goals. *The Fuehrer* repeatedly voices agreement with this opinion. He considers it absolutely necessary that Crete and the troops in the Peloponnesus be reinforced, and that air units be left on Crete. The Fuehrer is convinced that the Bulgarians will live up to their treaty obligations under such circumstances.

3. Submarine warfare. Plans.—The number of submarines in the Arctic Ocean is not to be permitted to fall below 23. There were 24 submarines in the Mediterranean, 5 of which have been lost in the meantime. The number is to be brought up to 24 again. Only 5 or 6 submarines are still in the western Mediterranean zone of operations because of the strong anti-submarine defences and air patrols. It is planned to retain that number of submarines and, if possible, to hold several additional submarines in reserve. Fifty-seven submarines and 2 submarine tankers are in the zone of operations in the Atlantic. Thirty-three are en route to or from the zone of operations. Three submarines are still

---

* Japan has at present only 5 submarines and 4 auxiliary cruisers in the Indian Ocean, since she believes that she will need her forces for the battle near the Solomons. On November 7, 1942, Japan withdrew her naval forces to the treaty line, 70° East. Therefore, unfortunately, she is contributing hardly anything at this time to weakening the enemy and disrupting his transport shipments in the western Indian Ocean, in spite of the fact that she is fully aware of the situation.

operating off the Cape, 4 in the Gulf of Guinea–Freetown area, and 7 off Trinidad. The greater part of the submarines, 25 in all, is west of Gibraltar, waiting to attack enemy supplies headed for the Mediterranean. A group of 14 submarines is in the North Atlantic. This group is reinforced mainly by submarines coming from Germany. Attacks on enemy North Atlantic convoys are especially successful at this time, since the enemy escorts are weak. It has been planned that for the time being a group of 12 submarines is to continue to operate against enemy supply transports in the area between the Azores and the Iberian Peninsula-Strait of Gibraltar. The remaining available submarines will be used in the North Atlantic and current zones of operations in order to exploit the weakness of the enemy escort forces and to inflict the largest possible losses on enemy shipping.

*The Fuehrer* is in agreement concerning the number of submarines to be stationed in the Mediterranean and in the area west of Gibraltar. He feels that the opportunities in the Atlantic, resulting from the reduction in enemy escort forces, should be exploited. Above all, he desires that measures be taken against enemy shipping to Egypt and the Middle East via South Africa, in order to relieve the pressure on our troops in Africa, and to facilitate a later advance to the Near East. Furthermore, it must be possible to reinforce the submarines in Norway immediately in case of an invasion there. *The C.-in-C., Navy*, states that this can be done any time by issuing appropriate orders to submarines out-bound from Germany, and by diverting submarines from the North Atlantic.

*The Fuehrer* also wants transport submarines to be built. The reason he gives is that since the Americans took over Iceland, he has again taken up the idea of a sudden invasion and establishment of an air base there. *The C.-in-C., Navy*, agrees to look into the matter.

4. Of the auxiliary cruisers, only ship "28" is at present operating in the southern Indian Ocean. The C.-in-C., Navy, gives an account of operations of ship "23." The crew of this auxiliary cruiser returned on board Tannenfels after sinking a camouflaged enemy auxiliary cruiser and scuttling their own badly damaged vessel.

5. North Sea West Wall.—*The C.-in-C., Navy*, emphasises the necessity for reinforcing the North Sea coast and the principal islands by means of a West Wall. The conditions which permitted a certain weakness of the fortifications, namely presence of a strong Air Force able to repel the enemy, no longer prevail. Since our Air Force is operating over such a large area, it would not be able to keep the Allies from launching an attack in this area for the purpose of establishing air bases. The C.-in-C., Navy, requests permission to give Minister Speer directions accordingly. *The Fuehrer* has always been of the same opinion and fully agrees.

6. Shipping space in the Mediterranean.—*The C.-in-C., Navy*, points out the necessity of building more transport vessels and landing craft in Italy. According to our information, there is sufficient capacity for this in a number of shipyards. However, pressure will have to be put on the Italians from the highest quarters, since there is still an attempt on the part of the Italians to build with an eye toward peace. *The Fuehrer* agrees.

(signed) RAEDER.

\* \* \* \* \* \*

For the next few months Allied operations in North Africa were the chief concern of the Axis. It was decided to make a stand in Tunisia, and supplies were rushed in by sea and air. Hitler also feared that the French Navy might be encouraged by the Allied successes to break out and join the Allies, and accordingly ordered the military occupation of Toulon. In the early hours of November 27, German land and air forces moved into Toulon, but Admiral De Laborde in command of the French Fleet there, gave orders for the Fleet to be scuttled. French forces gallantly resisted the German entry long enough to ensure the destruction of most of the ships.

At the last conference held during 1942, Raeder put forward schemes for the occupation of Spain and Portugal. He saw in the occupation of the Iberian peninsula the only really effective answer to the Allied moves in North Africa. Hitler agreed with him, but pointed out the political difficulties. He decided, however, to examine the whole question carefully and see what could be done.

C.-in-C., Navy                                                      Berlin, December 24, 1942

**REPORT BY THE C.-IN-C., NAVY, TO THE FUEHRER AT THE FUEHRER'S HEADQUARTERS, DECEMBER 22, 1942**

I. Norway.—Distribution of naval forces:

In the Alta Fiord: Hipper, Luetzow, Koeln, and five destroyers.

In the bay of Narvik: Nuernberg, one destroyer.

In Trondheim: Tirpitz (ready for action again in January), three destroyers.

The Scharnhorst, the Prinz Eugen, and five destroyers are ready for transfer from the Baltic Sea at the beginning of January. The Luetzow is assigned to cruiser warfare in the Arctic Ocean, since supplies are apparently being carried to northern Russia in unescorted vessels at the present time, and submarines are not very effective during the dark months of winter for patrolling the northern supply routes.

The fuel oil situation is going to become more difficult in the near future because the Italians need large additional supplies, due to the reduction in Roumanian deliveries during the winter months. Even now our fuel oil situation is such that the large vessels cannot be refuelled in the main harbours unless the allocations are made far in advance, since we are unable to keep sufficient supplies on hand.

*The Fuehrer* considers that the danger of a possible Allied invasion of northern Norway is greatest in January. Anti-aircraft defences are helpless because of the darkness. Therefore the Fuehrer postpones his decision until the beginning of February.

II. Western Area.—The situation has become worse due to our loses and because British naval forces, including destroyers, have repeatedly appeared along our coast. The enemy has apparently cleared channels through our minefields. Our own forces are not sufficient to repulse such raids or to lay enough mines, particularly in the Channel. Strong enemy air activity continues. The transfer of ship "14" had to be postponed from January to February because adequate mine protection cannot be provided until then. Because of this situation, the first eight vessels converted into artillery barges (*Artillerie-MFP*), which were supposed to be sent to Norway this month, were ordered to remain in the Western Area.

III. Baltic Sea.—Since we have so few escort vessels and these are so heavily taxed, we must review once more the advantages to be gained from an occupation of the islands of Lavansaari and Seiskari and of the Schepel-Oranienbaum strip before the spring of 1943. Only a really effective blockade of the eastern part of the Gulf of Finland, close to the enemy's key bases, could give us hope of saving fighting forces and mines. Even if Leningrad were completely destroyed by artillery fire, the submarine danger would still exist because Kronstadt remains a base. Every submarine, however, that gets through the blockade is a threat to the entire Baltic Sea and endangers our shipping which is already barely sufficient. *The Fuehrer* recognises the importance of this matter. He will keep it in mind and further it as much as possible. The Allies are still using air-laid mines to a large extent. The situation is well in hand, however, in spite of some difficulties and occasional losses.

IV. Submarines. A. Summary:

1. Operational submarines:
   (Fifteen of our submarines were lost during November; this exceeds the number becoming ready for operations (11) by 4.)
   (*a*) Of the above number, the following are in harbours .. .. .. .. .. 100
   (*b*) En route to or from operational area .. 47
   (*c*) In operational area .. .. .. .. 63
2. School submarines (unchanged) .. .. .. 53
3. Submarines being tested and in training.. .. 119

   Grand total of submarines 382

   Losses up to December 18, 1942.. 147 (an average of 3·8 per month).
   Decommissioned .. .. .. 9

During this month for the first time one of our own U-boats, commanded by Lt. Gilardone, was rammed by another while operating against a convoy. The boat and most of the crew were lost. Losses for the last months:

October: 13; November: 15 (new output, 11); December (up to the present); 3 (1 in a convoy).

B. Walter Boats.—Now that the building programme has been successfully met, we can carry out our decision, namely, mass production of the 24 submarines and the construction of 2 large experimental submarines. The dates of completion which the High Command, Navy, required of the shipyards are in some cases earlier. A safety margin has been added to cover unexpected difficulties. The experimental boats will be commissioned after completion of the test runs. *The Fuehrer* suggests that such valuable construction should be carried out in concrete shelters. The C.-in-C., Navy, will check on this.

V. At dinner alone with the Fuehrer, the C.-in-C., Navy, discusses the Iberian question. It is a great temptation for the enemy to get the Iberian Peninsula in his power. Such a step would be the best way to fight the submarines. It would likewise be of utmost strategic importance to us to take over the entire Iberian Peninsula, among other reasons in order to intensify submarine warfare and blockade running and to neutralise or eliminate entirely the Anglo-American occupation of North Africa. However, since we do not want to divert either the military or the economic forces necessary for such action unless it is imperative, we must strive to maintain the neutrality of the Iberian Peninsula. This, however, requires extensive military and political measures immediately.

If the enemy should take over the Iberian Peninsula, we would be confronted by an extremely critical situation from a military point of view. Moreover, the economic problem would be even worse, and almost impossible to cope with. Thus Germany must be ready to seize Spain and Portugal by force and to integrate them into the economic life of Europe at the very moment when the danger of an enemy seizure of the peninsula is imminent, even if such a step should entail great economic sacrifices for the rest of continental Europe. *The Fuehrer* is of the same opinion. He intends to enter into negotiations with Spain and to prepare for an occupation. For the moment he wants to await the results which General Munoz Grande may obtain.

VI. Raw material quotas for the Navy for the first quarter of 1943 and their effect.—*The C.-in-C., Navy*, considers it his duty to state that action on some of the Fuehrer's orders must be delayed, that others cannot be carried out at all. He must insist that future allotments recognise the importance of the Navy and the decisive significance of naval warfare for the whole war effort and reveal proper understanding of the constantly increasing duties of the Navy (ever greater numbers of operational submarines, constantly enlarging combat zones, and war conditions which are becoming more and more difficult). He cannot possibly find such recognition in the steel allotment to the Navy, which with its 127,000 tons represents a mere 5 per cent. of the total of 2,500,000 tons.

*The Fuehrer* understands the Navy's difficulties. He has also had to reduce greatly the quotas of other branches of the Armed Forces, however. He explains in detail how he must first of all prevent a collapse of any front where the enemy could substantially injure home territory. There is still a great deal to be done on this score. The Fuehrer has personally discussed the situation of the Navy with Minister Speer, but he cannot see his way clear to help the Navy at the present time. He hopes that the situation will be better in the second quarter, but he can make no promises. *The C.-in-C., Navy*, proposes that Admiral Schmundt be made a member of the committee for "Central Planning." This would improve matters greatly because the Navy could make it needs known promptly. *The Fuehrer* will look into the matter; he points out, however, that the Army does not have a representative either.

VII. Decree concerning conscription of the German youth for auxiliary war service.—Excerpts from the Regulations concerning auxiliary war service of German youth in the Air Force.

Paragraph 1.—For the performance of auxiliary war service in connection with air defence, the C.-in-C., Air Force, has at his disposal all male students from secondary schools who have completed their fifteenth year, and all female students from secondary schools who have completed their seventeenth year.

Paragraphs 2 to 4 omitted.

Paragraph 5 (last sentence only).—Any diversion of personnel for similar functions within the spheres of the Army and the Navy or of other authorities engaged in vital tasks is to be decided by the Air Minister and C.-in-C., Air, in consultation with the branches of the Armed Forces concerned or with the proper government offices.

Paragraph 6.—The Air Minister and C.-in-C., Air, together with the Reich Youth Leader, will decide how many of the students from secondary schools liable to the auxiliary war service draft are to be deferred so as to guarantee a sufficient number of leaders for the Hitler Youth.

\*       \*       \*       \*       \*       \*

*The C.-in-C., Navy*, briefly explains the main objections of the Navy, as they were stated in the letter of protest which the Naval High Command sent to the O.K.W. He emphasises the problem of naval replacements and the training of the Naval Hitler Youth. The Chief of Staff of the O.K.W. reports that the Fuehrer has already given orders for a new decree to be issued in which the wishes of the Navy are to be respected. *The Fuehrer* himself now orders that the problem of the Naval Hitler Youth be handled as the Navy desires. The question of volunteers has already been taken into consideration.

VIII. New mines (*Acoustic and pressure mines.—Ed.*).—*The C.-in-C., Navy*, briefly states that a report on new types of mines will soon be submitted. They should be very successful as a surprise weapon if they are suddenly used simultaneously by both the Navy and the Air Force· after a sufficient quantity is procured. *The Fuehrer* will issue an order at once. The Chief of Staff of the O.K.W. proposes that a preliminary draft be submitted.

(signed) RAEDER.

\*       \*       \*       \*       \*       \*

The year which had begun so auspiciously for the Axis and which had shown such promise of early victory, ended in gloom. From North Africa the Allies would be in a position to attack at will any part of the "soft underbelly of Europe." On the Eastern Front the *Wehrmacht* had begun to retreat, and in England there were signs of increasing activity. Hitler was by no means defeated, however, and saw in the reverses suffered during the last quarter little more than the sort of reverse every military commander experiences in war. He still believed victory possible.

Raeder, who had repeatedly tried to impress upon Hitler the necessity for sea power, saw the real danger of the Allied victories. They proved conclusively that the sporadic successes of the U-boats and the *Luftwaffe* had been insufficient to wrest control of the sea from the Allies, and without control of the sea the Axis would be unable to prevent the major invasion of Europe which now became inevitable. Against Hitler's conviction that capital ships and carriers were nothing more than "playthings of the decadent Democracies" Raeder had been powerless, and during the years of Germany's preparation for war undue emphasis had been given to U-boats and the *Luftwaffe*. Though both had achieved much, neither could equal the surface warship's ability to sustain an action over a prolonged period. On the other hand, the surface warship without air protection was extremely vulnerable, and it was obvious that a combination of both sea and air forces was essential. The German Navy could have achieved this combination by the use of aircraft carriers and by close co-operation with the *Luftwaffe*, and indeed, Raeder had tried hard to fulfil both these requirements. But, in the face of Hitler's ignorance and Goering's opposition, he failed.

# Crisis in the German Navy

ON DECEMBER 31, 1942, a German Task Force comprising the Hipper, Luetzow, and six destroyers attacked an allied convoy bound for Russia. Spirited defence by the escort, led by Captain R. St. V. Sherbrooke, V.C., in H.M.S. Onslow repulsed the attack and the convoy got through to Murmansk intact. The Hipper was damaged, and the Admiral commanding the task force had mistaken the two British cruisers, Kent and Jamaica, which had come to the assistance of the convoy, as the vanguard of a battle squadron. He had therefore broken off the action and retired in accordance with previous orders. Owing to a breakdown in communications the report of this action was not immediately available at Hitler's Headquarters, and in fact the first news he received was from an English news broadcast. Hitler's anger knew no bounds. His impatience while waiting for the outcome of the action had been fed by Goering who had complained bitterly of "wasting" *Luftwaffe* squadrons on guarding the big ships, suggesting that they should be scrapped.

When news of the action did finally come through, Hitler raged. He condemned the German Navy for not fighting the action through to the finish, and declared that the defeat spelt the end of the German High Seas Fleet. Capital ships were a waste of men and material and served no purpose other than to contain much-needed aircraft and small vessels for their defence. He ordered Grand Admiral Raeder, C.-in-C., Navy, to report immediately. The Naval Staff, however, took steps to delay the conference until Hitler's anger had somewhat subsided, and it was not until January 6 that the conference took place.

C.-in-C., Navy                                                    Berlin, January 11, 1943

**CONFERENCE BETWEEN THE C.-IN-C., NAVY, AND THE FUEHRER ON JANUARY 6, 1943, IN THE EVENING AT WOLFSSCHANZE**

Also present: Chief of Staff, O.K.W.

*The Fuehrer* talks for an hour and a half about the rôle played by the Prussian and German navies since they came into existence. The German Navy was originally patterned after the British Navy, and proved to be unimportant during the wars of 1864, 1866, and 1870–71. The first distinct contribution of the German Navy was the development of the torpedo boats. Special care was taken to perfect this weapon. Submarines constituted the most important branch of the German Navy in the last war and must be considered equally important today. The High Seas Fleet made no notable contribution during the World War. It is customary to blame the Kaiser for this inactivity, but this opinion is unwarranted. The real reason was that the Navy lacked men of action who were determined to fight with or without the support of the Kaiser. As a result of this inactivity a large amount of fighting-power lay idle, while the Army was constantly heavily engaged. The revolution and the scuttling of the fleet at Scapa Flow do not redound to the credit of the German Navy. The Navy has always been careful to consider the number of their own ships and men as compared with the enemy before entering an engagement. The Army does not follow this principle. As a soldier, the

Fuehrer demands that, once forces have been committed to action, the battle be fought to a decision.

Due to the present critical situation, where all fighting power, all personnel, and all material must be brought into action, we cannot permit our large ships to ride idly at anchor for months.  They require constant protection by the Air Force as well as by numerous smaller surface craft. The same situation would hold in case of an invasion of Norway, where the Air Force would be of more value in attacking an invasion fleet than being obliged to protect our own fleet.  For this reason, the fleet would not be of great value in preventing the enemy from establishing a beachhead.

Until now light naval forces have been doing most of the fighting. Whenever the larger ships put out to sea, light forces have to accompany them.  It is not the large ships which protect the small, but rather the reverse is true.

Due to the mining of the Baltic the large ships find it more and more difficult to engage in manœuvres.  The Coast Defence could use the guns from these large ships very effectively.  Heavy naval guns, if mounted where invasions on a large scale would be practical, could possibly prevent such landings.  In this connection consideration should be given to the North Sea area.  It should not be considered a degradation, if the Fuehrer decides to scrap the large ships.  This would be true only if he were removing a fighting unit which had retained its full usefulness.  A parallel to this in the Army would be the removal of all Cavalry Divisions.  The Fuehrer also points out that the Italian Fleet uses the complements of her large ships for duty in the destroyers.

The Navy shall consider the following:

1. Should the three aircraft carriers which were planned, be retained? Should other ships be converted into aircraft carriers (especially in case the De Grasse cannot be used)?  Are the Hipper and the Prinz Eugen, because of their great speed, more suited than the Luetzow and the Scheer, which have a more extensive operating radius?  If the latter were lengthened, could they develop greater speed and could they be given a larger landing deck?

2. Where would the heavy guns of these ships best be mounted on land?

3. In which order should the ships be decommissioned?  Probably the Gneisenau would be the first, since she will not be ready for active duty until the end of 1944.  Next would probably be the ships which are now due for overhauling and repairs.  Personnel of these ships will remain with the Navy.

4. Can the submarine programme be extended and speeded up if the large ships are eliminated?  The C.-in-C., Navy, shall prepare a memorandum giving his views on the above.  These comments will be of historical value.  The Fuehrer will carefully examine the document.

The C.-in-C., Navy, rarely had an opportunity to comment, but his final impression was that the Fuehrer, even though he described his decision as final, would reconsider some of his views if sound arguments were presented.  Concerning the question of the C.-in-C., Navy, whether the the Scharnhorst and Prinz Eugen are to be sent to Norway, *the Fuehrer* replied in the affirmative and said that for the present, Norway is to be defended as strongly as possible.

During a private conversation between the C.-in-C., Navy, and the Fuehrer the *C.-in-C., Navy*, tried to explain the reason for the delay in communications on December 31/January 1. It was explained that the Admiral Commanding Cruisers had expected to obtain reliable information from the radiogram with the date/time group December 31 at 1234, which would report success or failure of the operation and the presence of enemy cruisers. The C.-in-C., Navy, further pointed out the difficulty in compiling a composite report from the two cruisers and six destroyers after they had anchored. Finally he mentioned that the teletype station at Alta greatly delayed the transmission of the final report. The course of the operation itself was only briefly mentioned at the beginning of the discussion with the Fuehrer. At that time the C.-in-C., Navy, explained that the Admiral Commanding Cruisers and the individual commanders had obeyed orders to the letter. The orders of the Naval Staff strictly limited the extent of the operation.

\*       \*       \*       \*       \*       \*

Carrying out Hitler's instructions Raeder produced a memorandum on the decommissioning of big ships on January 15. He presented as well a child's guide on the use of sea power, and strenuously resisted Hitler's intentions—but to no effect. This conflict between Hitler and Raeder brought to an end Raeder's long and unsuccessful attempt to make Hitler appreciate the use of sea power. Raeder was a sound strategist and saw clearly the need for a balanced Navy. He had repeatedly asked for an Air Arm to be formed and for more big ships to be built, but had been continually opposed by the continental thought of the Army Command, and by Goering's belief that the *Luftwaffe* could do as much and more at sea than the Navy. Accordingly on January 30, Raeder resigned his command, which he had held since October 1928.

Hitler appointed Grand Admiral Doenitz, Flag Officer Commanding Submarines, as his successor. In the first conference between Doenitz and Hitler the whole of the war at sea was reviewed. In the Atlantic the Allies were gradually gaining mastery over U-boat attacks; the invasion of North Africa and the advance on Tunisia had thrown a great strain on sea transport and naval protection in the Mediterranean; and blockade runners were finding it increasingly difficult to get through. The German Navy was faced with the problem of insufficient air reconnaissance in all theatres, and the defence of the long European coastline was proving extremely difficult. Frequent Allied raids on Norway lead Hitler to expect a serious landing in the near future. The whole problem was also dominated by shortages of men, material, and fuel. For the solution of all these problems Doenitz, in the beginning, had but one solution—more and yet more U-boats.

On February 8, therefore, Hitler called a conference with Doenitz and Speer, the Minister of Supply and Production, to discuss the situation.

The Naval Staff                                    Berlin, February 13, 1943

**MINUTES OF THE CONFERENCE BETWEEN THE C.-IN-C., NAVY, AND THE FUEHRER. FEBRUARY 8, 1943, AT THE FUEHRER'S HEADQUARTERS, WOLFSSCHANZE**

Also present part of the time: Admiral Krancke.
                              Minister Speer.

1. *The C.-in-C., Navy*, explains with the aid of maps that during this month the enemy, surprisingly enough, found out the locations of our submarines, and, in some cases, even the exact number of ships. It was

confirmed later on that his convoys evaded the known submarine formation. This detailed information can come from two sources:

(*a*) Treason.

(*b*) Undetected reconnaissance planes locating the formations.

The C.-in-C., Navy, reports that in regard to the possibility of treason all necessary steps have been taken. If the enemy located our submarine formations solely by means of reconnaissance our formations will have to be scattered more widely.

The C.-in-C., Navy, explains further that the locating of convoys headed for Gibraltar is largely a matter of chance. However, the spotting and engaging of these convoys would be very simple if there were aerial reconnaissance. Therefore, the weakest point of our conduct of the war is the complete lack of any means of reconnaissance in naval warfare. This weak point can be counteracted only by increasing the number of ships. This increase in the number of ships, however, is dependent on a very short stay in the shipyards and completion of the ships under construction as fast as possible. The C.-in-C., Navy, explains that the question of repair docks is of utmost importance in intensifying submarine warfare. He therefore asks that the submarine branch together with its equipment, as well as all surface vessels engaged in submarine warfare, be exempted completely from transfer to the Army.

*The Fuehrer* consults Minister Speer. *Minister Speer* agrees with the C.-in-C., Navy, providing that additional men will not be demanded from other branches to make up for the loss of Navy men. *The Fuehrer* agrees in principle with the statements made by the C.-in-C., Navy. However, he intended to discuss this matter once more with Field Marshal Keitel. He assures the C.-in-C., Navy, that he will do everything possible for the submarine branch. (A directive, prepared by the C.-in-C., Navy, concerning the exemption referred to above was signed by the Fuehrer at noon on February 9, 1943.)

2. *The C.-in-C., Navy*, submits the proposed plan for placing the large ships out of commission. *The Fuehrer* has no objections. However, he says that, if the molybdenum imports from Portugal should stop, it might become necessary to dismantle several ships in order to get the necessary nickel steel of the armour plate. In that case he would issue the necessary orders.

3. *The C.-in-C., Navy*, submits the situation of the blockade-runners. *The Fuehrer* emphasises how tremendously important it is to get especially those vessels through that carry cargoes of *rubber*. He has already ordered that the Focke Wulf 200 be transferred to do reconnaissance for the blockade-runners. The C.-in-C., Navy, states his intention to build supply submarines. He proposes, as an emergency measure, to use the Italian submarines in the Atlantic as supply ships and, if possible, load them at sea, possibly in the Capetown–Madagascar area, and thus shorten the route. In exchange for these Italian submarines he intends to give Italy German submarines for use against convoys. The Fuehrer considers this a good idea, and orders further investigation of the plan. In case it is worthwhile to convert Italian submarines to supply ships, he will inform the Duce of the impending exchange by letter.

4. *The C.-in-C., Navy*, explains to the Fuehrer in which areas British

submarines in the Mediterranean have sunk our vessels. He shows that there have been no sinkings on the supply route Palermo–Tunis, in spite of the occasional presence of British submarines. He shows further that most sinkings occurred along the Italian coast, frequently right off the harbours. The C.-in-C., Navy, states that these sinkings must be and can be prevented. For this purpose he consulted with Admiral Weichold. After discussing the matter it was decided that the situation would be improved by ordering the 22nd Submarine Chaser Flotilla to follow German tactics and by having German naval officers instruct the Italian Escort Command. In order to safeguard the convoy route between Sicily and Africa it would be necessary to make it a "War Channel."

5. *The C.-in-C., Navy*, informs the Fuehrer of the proposed personnel changes at the highest level of the Naval High Command. *The Fuehrer* also grants the request that Vice-Admiral Krancke be relieved by Captain Voss. He further agrees that Commander Junge will present the naval war situation at the conferences at Headquarters. This is part of a proposed plan of the C.-in-C., Navy, to furnish more complete information regarding the naval war situation.

6. The question of the future commitment of heavy ships is clarified by Vice-Admiral Krancke on February 9 by order of the C.-in-C., Navy, since this question had not been taken up the night before. The C.-in-C. is of the opinion that he has the responsibility to order the heavy ships to battle as soon as a worthwhile target and a chance for success appear. Once ordered to sea, the officer in command would have to act and fight entirely on his own initiative according to the tactical situation without awaiting special instructions from a higher echelon. Under such circumstances one would have to expect loses. *The Fuehrer* expresses his complete and definite approval of this interpretation.

(signed) DOENITZ.

*     *     *     *     *     *

As a result of the conference Doenitz prepared a scheme for stopping new construction and decommissioning most of the big ships. A summary of this scheme shows that only Tirpitz, Luetzow, and Nurnberg would be operationally available in Norwegian waters until August 1943, and only Scharnhorst and Prinz Eugen in the Baltic. The latter ship was to be turned into a training ship in May 1943. Thus Prinz Eugen, Scheer, Leipzig, Emden were only to have as much work done on them in the yards as would enable them to be used as training ships.

Hipper and Koln were to be paid off on 1.3.43.
Schleswig-Holstein was to be paid off on 1.4.43.
Schlesien was to be paid off on 1.5.43.
Scharnhorst was to be paid off on 1.7.43.
Tirpitz was to be paid off in Autumn 1943.

This would release 250 officers, of whom 92 could be used for U-boat service, and 8,000 petty officers and men, who would be used for U-boats, and for coastal and flak batteries, and as replacements in the remaining surface ships. 1,300 dockyard workmen would also become available for work on destroyers, M-boats, and U-boat repairs. (Hitler approved this plan.)

*     *     *     *     *     *

But three weeks later Doenitz, too, appreciated the value of big ships and obtained Hitler's approval for modifying his original instructions. At this conference (February 26) Doenitz also started his campaign for air support for his U-boats. The lack of a naval air arm or of anything approaching R.A.F. Coastal Command was a handicap which was severely felt in view of the steadily improving anti-submarine measures of the Allies.

C.-in-C., Navy                                    Berlin, March 5, 1943

**NOTES TAKEN AT A CONFERENCE OF THE C.-IN-C., NAVY, WITH THE FUEHRER IN HIS HEADQUARTERS AT VINNITSA ON FEBRUARY 26, 1943**

Also present: Admiral Krancke.
Lt.-General Jodl.
Captain von Puttkamer.

1. A brief discussion by the C.-in-C., Navy, concerning the submarine situation.—The month of February may be considered as typical for present submarine warfare. During fourteen days at sea nothing was sunk because nothing was sighted. Three reasons may be advanced: bad weather and poor visibility, possibly the location of the submarines' position by the enemy, but above all, the complete absence of our own reconnaissance. Maps were brought along to illustrate what areas could be covered by various types of long-range reconnaissance planes. It was reported to the Fuehrer that the problem of air reconnaissance had been discussed with the *Reichsmarschall* and that he had promised his support, but said that the construction of long-range air reconnaissance planes would have to be given priority. *The Fuehrer* sharply criticised promises which were readily made regarding the performance and range of certain types of reconnaissance planes, which later proved illusory. He does not believe that much will be gained by rebuilding the He17. At the request of the C.-in-C., Navy, the Fuehrer promised to find out whether the three BV222 could not be made available immediately for submarine reconnaissance in the West.

2. *The C.-in-C., Navy*, reports as follows.—The Fuehrer has previously decided that we cannot afford to let our large ships lie idle, since they are not in a position to engage in combat. As a result of this decision, the following were decommissioned: the Hipper, the Leipzig, and the Koeln. These will be followed shortly by the Schlesien and the Schleswig-Holstein. The C.-in-C., Navy, is however, of the opinion that the Archangel convoys would make excellent targets for the large ships, and he considers it his duty, in view of the heavy fighting on the Eastern Front, to exploit these possibilities to the fullest extent. He therefore considers it essential that the Scharnhorst be sent to Norway to strengthen the forces there. The Tirpitz, the Scharnhorst, and for the present the Luetzow, together with six destroyers, would be a fairly powerful task force. *The Fuehrer*, however, is strongly opposed to any further engagements of the surface ships since, beginning with the Graf Spee, one defeat has followed the other. Large ships are a thing of the past. He would prefer to have the steel and nickel contained in these ships rather than send them into action again.

When the C.-in-C., Navy, mentioned that ships were severely limited by the imposed restriction that they must not be sacrificed, and therefore, commanding officers of ships at sea could not be censured, the Fuehrer replied, that he had never issued an order restricting commanding officers in this manner. If in contact with the enemy, ships must go into action. However, he no longer valued their effectiveness. By way of contrast he explained how bitterly the men fought on the Eastern Front, and how unbearable it was to see the strength of the Russians constantly increased by convoys, like the last one of twenty-five ships, reaching their destinations. Thereupon *the C.-in-C., Navy*, declared that, instead of decommissioning the two heavy ships, he would consider it his duty to send them into action whenever possible and as long as suitable targets could be found. *The Fuehrer* finally agreed to let the Scharnhorst join the task force, as recommended by the C.-in-C., Navy. He asked how long it would be before a suitable target would be found. The C.-in-C., Navy, thought in the next three months. *The Fuehrer* replied: "Even if it should require six months, you will then return and be forced to admit that I was right."

3. Since so little is to be gained by using Italian Atlantic submarines as supply ships, the Fuehrer decided not to ask for them.

4. *The C.-in-C., Navy*, reports that the Japanese Admiral Nomura had mentioned that the Japanese Navy was planning to use submarines against merchant shipping and that he had asked Ambassador Oshima and Foreign Minister von Ribbentrop to request that two German submarines be put at Japan's disposal. The C.-in-C., Navy, explained that nothing would be gained in a military way by turning over the submarines, since he did not believe that they could be produced in large numbers in Japan because they lacked the necessary materials. *The Fuehrer* favoured the idea of releasing one submarine partly to repay the shipments of rubber from Japan. It would be easier for us to give up a submarine than high-grade steel and finished products, such as machine tools. He will not decide the matter until he is asked directly.

5. In order to reduce the loss of ships supplying Tunis, *the C.-in-C., Navy*, considers it necessary to mobilise not only all anti-submarine craft in the area of southern France, but also to obtain similar vessels located in Italian ports. Here there must still be ships, such as private yachts, which could be used for this purpose. Admiral Meendsen-Bohlken has been ordered to take up this question with the Italian Naval Command. It would be best if these vessels were manned by Germans, provided that this can be done without hurting the feelings of the Italians. It must first be ascertained whether such craft are available, then the matter of manning the ships can be taken up. *The Fuehrer* agrees. He will write to the Duce after the facts have been established. The Fuehrer criticises the delay in organising the 22nd Anti-Submarine Flotilla. More German workers should have been assigned to complete its construction in time.

(signed)             DOENITZ
(countersigned) Lt.-Cmdr. PFEIFFER.

# The Tunisian Campaign

DURING THE first quarter of 1943 the Allies made great advances in North Africa. Axis troops were forced into Tunisia and it became clear to the Axis that, unless they held the Allies in Tunisia, Italy would be doomed. Reinforcements and supplies were therefore sent into Tunisia, and were so effective that on January 6 General Eisenhower represented to the Chiefs of Staff that "unless this (i.e. Axis reinforcement) can be materially and immediately reduced, the situation both here and in the 8th Army area will deteriorate without doubt." However, the Mediterranean Fleet, the R.A.F., and U.S.A.A.F. proceeded to take a heavy toll of Axis shipping and to destroy supply ports in the Mediterranean, thus enabling the Allied armies to force the Axis steadily back towards Tunis and Bizerta.

By the beginning of March the situation had become critical for the Axis. More ships were required to transport men and material to Tunisia and these ships required more and more protection. The Italian Navy was available, but seemed to be doing little to help, and so far the onus of naval protection had fallen on the U-boats and the *Luftwaffe*. The loss of Tunisia meant the loss of Italy, and to save Tunisia required control of the sea. Between March 14 and 18 Hitler held two conferences in a determined attempt to find a solution to the problem. He wrote to Mussolini, and at the conference ordered Doenitz to go to Italy and present the situation to the Duce on the lines that he, Hitler, had indicated.

C.-in-C., Navy                                      Berlin, March 19, 1943

## MINUTES TAKEN AT CONFERENCE OF THE C.-IN-C., NAVY, WITH THE FUEHRER ON MARCH 14 AND 18, 1943, AT HEADQUARTERS WOLFSSCHANZE

### CONFERENCE ON MARCH 14, AT 1230

Also present: Field Marshal Keitel.
Field Marshall Kesselring.
General Jeschonnek.
Lt.-General Jodl.
Rear-Admiral Machens.
Rear-Admiral Voss.
Rear-Admiral Wagner.
Captain von Puttkamer.

*The Fuehrer* expressed his views as follows: Tunisia is strategically of prime importance. Conquest of Tunisia means a saving of 4–5 million tons and more to the enemy, so that the submarines have to work 4–5 months to effect equalisation. Retention of Tunisia is a question of supplies. The 80,000 tons per month cited as necessary by the Italian Supreme Command are entirely inadequate; rather 150,000 to 200,000 tons monthly are needed. We estimate for each division about 1 train— 500 tons daily. For the 8 divisions in Tunisia, inclusive of the Italians, this makes a total of 4,000 tons daily. The Fuehrer draws a comparison with Norway and Crete, both of which are supplied much better than

Tunisia.   Norway carries supplies for 8 to 9 months, Crete now has a 72-day supply, and half-year supply by sea.   It is impossible to supply armies by air.   A single 9,000-ton steamer, for example, can carry as much on one voyage as a whole air fleet can carry over a longer period of time.   Protection of convoys by the Air Force alone is not possible; ships continue to be required.   The Straits of Sicily must teem with patrol and escort vessels.   Good organisation is essential.   Only the German Navy can organise this on the basis of its experience and success in this field.   We can reinforce the Armoured Africa Army by sending the 7th Airborne Division, the 999th Brigade, and the remainder of the Goering Division as planned, only if we are successful in increasing the supplies and in transporting them safely.

It is therefore necessary at the present time to confront the Italians boldly with the alternative of either making an all-out effort to get through supplies regardless of personnel considerations, or to lose Tunisia, and with that also Italy.   The C.-in-C., Navy, is authorised to present these views to the Duce and to insist on having his suggestions followed as closely as possible.   *The Fuehrer* reads a few paragraphs from his letter to the Duce, setting forth these same ideas.   Field Marshal Kesselring is to deliver this letter to the Duce even before the arrival of the C.-in-C., Navy.

*Field Marshal Kesselring* calls attention to the fact that it is essential that the transfer of German units from southern France be speeded up and that a considerably greater number of small craft, such as cargo ships, landing craft, and Siebel ferries must be made available in order to get the situation brought about by the present emergency under control. He believes, however, that it is impossible to do this without large ships. He offered the Italians German fire fighters to control fires in ships.   He arranged with *Gauleiter* Saukel that 10,000 to 15,000 Italian workers be sent from Germany to increase the Italian ship repair capacity.   In order to relieve the Italian shipyards, he proposes that mobile repair shops be set up for the repair of landing craft similar to those in existence for Siebel ferries.   *The C.-in-C., Navy,* re-affirms his previous recommendations that the German Command take a strong hand in the convoy conferences.   However, in carrying out the Fuehrer's orders, he will take care lest, due to the Italian mentality, the opposite of what is desired will be accomplished through passive resistance on the part of the Italians.   He does not think it impossible that, even though the Duce should agree, lower officials might sabotage putting the measures planned into effect. *The Fuehrer* emphasises that he prefers the most drastic solution, but that he would agree to a milder one reluctantly.

In a final brief, private conference with the Fuehrer, the C.-in-C., Navy, reports to the Fuehrer the measures planned to increase the output of submarines.   *The Fuehrer* approves.   In addition, the C.-in-C., Navy, reports to the Fuehrer that the reports made by *Gauleiter* Kaufmann are not always accurate.   He will talk with the *Gauleiter* himself later. The Fuehrer stresses that he attaches great importance to these reports since he has to depend on receiving information from as many sources as possible.

CONFERENCE ON MARCH 18, 1943, AT 1530

Also present: Field Marshal Keitel.
Lt.-General Jodl.
Rear-Admiral Voss.
Captain von Puttkamer.

1. *The C.-in-C., Navy*, reports the results of his conference with the Duce, and of the talks with the Italian Naval Staff in Rome. He submits the signed agreement, and gives a step-by-step description of how the agreement was reached. In so doing he calls attention particularly to the Duce's emphatic approval and the cordial tone of the talks. A note of restraint and disapproval was noticeable from the very beginning in his conference with the Italian Naval Staff, which, according to Admiral Riccardi, was due to the fact that he understood very little of what was said during the conference with the Duce, since the conversation was carried on in German. The proper rapport was established only when the C.-in-C., Navy, spoke in stronger terms after the Italian counter-proposals had not provided a basis for understanding. Complete agreement was then reached, since the form adhered to 'by the C.-in-C., Navy, gave the Italians the possibility of saving face. Subsequently the C.-in-C., Navy, briefly gives details about the six war vessels handed over by the Italians. Torpedo boats Pomone, Bombarde, Iphigenie (ready for action), Baliste, Bayonnaise (still to be raised), and gunboat Yser (ready soon in Toulon).

2. The Duce stressed particularly his intention of committing the entire Italian Fleet in case of an Anglo-Saxon landing on Sardinia, but states that he lacks the necessary fuel oil. The C.-in-C., Navy, gave his approval of this plan and agreed to investigate the fuel question immediately upon his return to Berlin, since he is convinced that this operation has possibilities of success against an enemy who is hampered by his landing operations. Furthermore, he feels that it would be better for the Italian ships to get into the fight even at the risk of heavy losses, rather than to fall into the hands of the enemy in the harbours, perhaps even without a fight.

3. *The C.-in-C., Navy*, subsequently calls attention to the fact that the Air Force is indispensable for the protection of supply shipping. It is impossible to fight off present and future air attacks by naval forces alone. *The Fuehrer* agrees as far as high-altitude attacks are concerned, but expresses the hope that measures taken will improve the defence against low-flying planes.

4. The C.-in-C., Navy, stresses the implications of the inadequate shipyard and repair facilities in Italy, as a result of which about two-thirds of the Italian escort vessels are always laid up. Therefore the 15,000 Italian workers to be returned to Italy should be selected in such a way that most of them will be shipyard workers. *The Fuehrer* agrees, since he recognises the importance of keeping the escort vessels in a good state of repair.

5. *The Fuehrer* does not approve of the request made by the C.-in-C., Navy, that the E-boat flotilla based in the Bodo area be released for service in the Mediterranean, unless they are replaced, since the presence of E-boats in Norway is still essential. The Fuehrer orders an investigation to determine whether it would be possible to divert one of the E-boat

flotillas from the English Channel to Norway as replacement; in that event he would approve of sending one E-boat flotilla to the Mediterranean.

5. *The C.-in-C., Navy*, reports that the Italians agree to the use of their Atlantic submarines for transport purposes, with the single exception of submarine Gagni, which is to continue in combat. The Italians accordingly would eventually get nine newly built German submarines. The distribution of rubber is to be made as usual according to the existing trade agreements. Field Marshal Keitel affirms the accuracy of this assumption.

(signed)         DOENITZ.<br>(countersigned) Lieut. SPITSBARTH.

\*        \*        \*        \*        \*        \*

The promised all-out effort by the Italian Fleet did not materialise. Allied sea and air attacks continued to destroy Axis shipping. The Italian cruiser Trieste (10,000 tons) was sunk in Maddalena, Sardinia, and another cruiser the Gorizia, was damaged. Merchant vessels were ruthlessly attacked, and Italian ports were heavily bombed. The Allied control of the sea in the Mediterranean seemed unbreakable. In these circumstances Doenitz turned once more to his U-boats in which he saw the only hope of victory. But here, too, severe losses had occurred, and to keep up the offensive, production would have to be increased still further. New types of U-boats were being designed, but these would not be operational until 1944 at the earliest. At the next conference with Hitler, on April 11, Doenitz stressed these points once more, and produced a lengthy memorandum on the war at sea prepared by the Naval Staff.

The C.-in-C., Navy                                    Berlin, April 21, 1943

### MINUTES OF THE CONFERENCE BETWEEN THE C.-IN-C., NAVY, AND THE FUEHRER ON APRIL 11, 1943, AT THE BERGHOF

Also present: Rear-Admiral Voss.
            Captain von Puttkamer.

1. *The C.-in-C., Navy*, reports.—The submarine losses in February amounted to 19. In March 15 and, so far, in April 16 ships were sunk. These losses are high. Submarine warfare is difficult. However, it is obvious, that the aim of sinking merchant ships must be to sink more than the enemy can build. If we do not reach this objective, the enemy would continue to suffer severely through loss of his material substance, but we would not be successful in bleeding him to death due to diminution of his tonnage. I therefore fear that the submarine war will be a failure if we do not sink more ships than the enemy is able to build. I believe that the enemy could not stand an overall loss of 100,000–200,000 tons per month for any length of time. Both Germany, with her submarines, E-boats, and Air Force, and her allies, Japan and Italy, must exert every possible effort to achieve this objective. A situation must not be allowed to arise where we must blame ourselves for not having defeated the enemy because we did not put forth a little more effort and press home the attack against merchant shipping. In this course, many more submarines are required today to achieve what one U-boat could accomplish in 1940. We must therefore increase our submarine building programme as much as our shipyard capacity permits, so that the proportion between losses and new ships does not become too unfavourable. The C.-in-C., Navy, herewith submits the proposed plan for the increase in our submarine building pro-

gramme.   *The Fuehrer* fully agrees with the C.-in-C., Navy.   An increase in the submarine building programme must be made possible.

2. Supporting his contentions with maps, *the C.-in-C., Navy*, explains that it is a matter of life and death for us to maintain our supply lines and our foreign trade.   The protection of this ocean traffic is very much endangered because it has to be accomplished with comparatively small forces.   The available protection is definitely not able to cope with the increasing attacks of the enemy.   These attacks, however, must be anticipated, because the enemy's material is constantly increasing.   Besides, some day we will have to expect a stronger attack against our shipping lanes by forces which will be released from some other theatre.   When that happens we will no longer be in a position to give this protection with our meagre forces.   We cannot permit our lines of communication to be broken.   Tunis should be a warning to us.   Anticipating this danger, we should do everything possible at this time to speed up the building programme of our defence forces, because the realisation of such a plan will take a long time.   Besides, any extension of our sphere of influence in Europe, as in the case of *Gisela*, (occupation of north coast of Spain) will certainly increase our supply problem.

*The C.-in-C., Navy*, presented a chart, to explain the proposed increase in the building programme.   He emphasises the construction of E-boats, the mission of which is obvious, i.e. force the British to maintain escorts along the English coast, in order to keep them from attacking our convoys and to supplement submarine warfare by sinking the many ships moving in English coastal waters.   He also stressed the need for building large numbers of landing craft (MFP), which are always required everywhere. The chart does not contain any padded figures, but only such as are absolutely essential for conducting the naval war.   *The Fuehrer* completely agrees with the C.-in-C., Navy, and feels that Africa demonstrates the correctness of the latter's contentions in the most convincing manner. The problem remains : Where can the steel be obtained?   To be sure, in a totalitarian state he could order that the required amount be made available, but that would mean exacting it from some other arm.   The pressing needs of the Army for tanks and anti-tank guns, and of the Air Force for A.A. guns, etc., would not permit this over a period of time. He feels that the Army should be equipped with the newest type of weapons in sufficient quantities to prevent excessive loss of life.   In order not to lose the war in the air, the material of our Air Force should be increased enormously.   Finally, the Navy must receive sufficient material not only to prevent the submarine warfare from falling off, but rather to increase its effectiveness.   Something also must be done for the Merchant Marine in order to help solve the supply problem.   To this end Minister Speer and Messrs. Roechling and Duisberg were ordered to take part in a conference with him during the next few days to discuss the question of increasing the steel production from 2·6 to 4 million tons per month.   He is fully aware of the fact that such a programme would presuppose a considerable allocation of steel, both to the construction of new facilities such as blast furnaces, and to improvement of existent steel mills.   He is convinced that this is the only way in which the shortage of iron can definitely be overcome.   *The Fuehrer* again emphasises that he fully agrees with the plan of the C.-in-C., Navy, for the increase of the construction programme of small ships up to and including destroyers, although he disapproves of the construction of heavy ships.

In answer to a question, *the C.-in-C., Navy*, states that both of these construction programmes taken together call for a monthly production of 30,000 tons of steel over and above the present requirements of the Navy. *The Fuehrer* is certain that the Navy will receive these additional 30,000 tons as a result of the increase in steel production, and he states that there is nothing further that the C.-in-C., Navy, needs to do in this matter.

3. *The C.-in-C., Navy*, reports that the first German submarine to be transferred to Japan will be ready in the beginning of May. He has permitted Admiral Nomura and the new Group Leader of the Party's Foreign Division for Japan to make the voyage to Japan on board the submarine. *The Fuehrer* agrees to this.

4. At the suggestion of Minister Speer, *the C.-in-C., Navy*, raises the question of hospital ships and refrigeration vessels in the Norwegian area. *The Fuehrer* points out that, as long as we have such a shortage of shipping space, it would be inexcusable not to make full use of every available ton of shipping. He intends to improve the Narvik railroad because later on he wants to divert some of the supplies to this railroad. At the moment, however, he needs every available vessel in order to furnish the Norwegian area with the necessary shipping space. In addition to normal requirements, he has to transfer two divisions to the south Norwegian area. He asks that the necessity of maintaining hospital ships and refrigeration vessels be re-examined.

(signed) DOENITZ.

(countersigned) Comdr. PFEIFFER.

*     *     *     *     *     *

The memorandum which Doenitz presented to Hitler at this conference dealt first with the advantages to be gained by occupying Spain and Portugal. By such an operation the Naval Staff hoped to be able to close the Straits of Gibraltar, to increase the number of Atlantic ports for use as U-boats bases, to gain additional airfields for air reconnaissance, and to make vailable the natural resources of Spain. The memorandum also states, however, that this operation—*Gisela*—could only be carried out with the consent of Spain, and did not seem possible at the present moment.

The second half of the memorandum presented a strong case for increasing the allocation of iron to the Navy. The iron quota for the Navy was increased by 45,000 tons for the second quarter of 1943. The recognised lowest figure for the iron requirements of the Navy are 181,000 tons per month (not including needs for construction of transport U-boats) which means that there is still a minus quantity of 15,000 tons monthly on the new quota.

A very detailed survey is given, covering all operational areas and commands, stressing that everywhere the German Navy is desperately short of escort vessels (*Sicherungsstreitkrafte*). Owing to its value as an offensive weapon, it is urgently necessary to increase production of E-boats. The figure of six new E-boats per month is proposed as the lowest requirement. Figures for other types of ships:

| | |
|---|---|
| Destroyers .. .. .. | New building must cease from 1945, owing to shortage of *Copper*. |
| Torpedo boats .. .. | 18 T-boats must be built per annum. |
| E-boats .. .. .. | 72 per annum. |
| M-boats .. .. .. | 74 ,, ,, |
| R-boats .. .. .. | 72 ,, ,, |
| Guard and escort ships .. | 300 ,, ,, |
| *Sperrbrecher* .. .. | 35 ,, ,, |
| Transport barges .. .. | 900 ,, ,, |
| Torpedo-recovery craft .. | 15 ,, ,, |

The stepping-up of the U-boat building programme is planned as follows:

| 1943 | 1944 | | 1945 | |
| --- | --- | --- | --- | --- |
| 2nd half of year. | 1st half of year. | 2nd half of year. | 1st half of year. | 2nd half of year. |
| Increasing to 27 per month. | 27 per month despite going over to production of Type VIIC/42. | 27 + 3 Type XX per month. | 27 + 3 Type XX per month. | 30 per month. |

Iron requirements for the above programme:

|  |  |  |  |
| --- | --- | --- | --- |
| For U-boat building per month .. | .. | .. | 4,500 tons. |
| For stepping-up torpedo production | .. | .. | 1,500 tons. |
|  | Total .. | .. | 6,000 tons. |

# The Mediterranean

THE AXIS efforts in North Africa during the Spring of 1943 were no avail. On May 7 Tunis and Bizerta fell simultaneously. Allied command of the seas cut off the retreat of the remaining forces in the Cape Bon peninsula, and they finally surrendered on May 13. The Tunisian campaign had demonstrated forcibly the meaning of sea power to the Axis. They had made a serious mistake which must not be repeated. The Italian battlefleet, however, had not been committed, and there was still a chance that by mustering all their naval resources the Axis might be able to call a halt to the Allied advances.

The immediate problem was where were the Allies going to strike next. Either Sicily or Sardinia seemed the most likely objectives, and it was obviously a matter of the utmost urgency to see that these two islands were adequately fortified and defended. Again control of the sea would be the deciding factor. Hitler therefore sent Doenitz to Italy to find out what the Italians were doing, and to try all in his power to muster the maximum possible resources. Doenitz left Berlin on May 12 and spent four days conferring with the Italians and the German commanders in Italy. His report on these four days shows clearly the serious cleavages in German-Italian co-operation.

Naval High Command

### THE VISIT OF THE C.-IN-C., NAVY, TO ROME, MAY 12, 1943, TO MAY 15, 1943

May 12, 1943
0800 Depature from Berlin. 1300 Arrival in Rome.

CONFERENCE AT HOTEL EXCELSIOR WITH VICE-ADMIRAL RUGE, REAR-ADMIRAL MEENDSEN-BOHLKEN, AND REAR-ADMIRAL LOEWISCH

Both Commanders give a brief summary of the situation. The C.-in-C., Navy, very briefly discusses immediate problems: Which is more important, Sicily or Sardinia? After lunch *the C.-in-C., Navy*, asks the Commanders what they consider the best solution for the present unpleasant situation regarding the two German Commands which, as the representatives of the German Navy, are not effective in dealing with the Italians and do not guarantee a smooth and close collaboration. Both Commanders are convinced that the present dualism will have to end. *Vice-Admiral Ruge* believes that a merger of the two staffs could be effected by transferring the entire Operations Staff of the German Naval Command to the *Supermarina* (Italian Admiralty) and that the influence which was gained by the German Special Staff over the *Supermarina* could still be maintained. *Rear-Admiral Meendsen-Bohlken* does not consider this solution possible for technical reasons, such as space requirements and the communication system. The C.-in-C., reserves his decision for the present; it has already been influenced by the fact that Admiral Riccardi has asked the C.-in-C., Navy, through Commander Sestini, that Vice-Admiral Ruge be appointed sole representative of the German Navy with *Supermarina*.

1630 TO 1930  CONFERENCE AT SUPERMARINA, MAY 12, 1943

*Admiral Riccardi* thanks the C.-in-C., Navy, for his visit, and expresses the hope that this conference will further the common cause of Italy and Germany. He also welcomes the C.-in-C. in the name of the Italian Navy. *The C.-in-C., Navy*, states that the purpose of his visit is to discuss matters personally, and to exchange information, since it is difficult to do this from a distance and by mail. Admiral Riccardi gives a summary of the present situation from the Italian point of view.

It is a fact that the enemy is preparing for further operations in the Algerian coastal harbours; at the same time he is systematically destroying the Italian habours. Since the fall of Tunisia, an attack on the Italian islands is expected any day. There are three ways of meeting the enemy invasion: Air attack on the African embarkation points; attack on the approaching invasion fleet at sea; or local defence at the point of invasion. The enemy will most likely employ forces strong enough to make his first attempt a certain success. It is, therefore, necessary that our own weak forces be consolidated. The invasion can be prevented by complete success of one of the three ways mentioned above. The main weapon is the Air Force.

Air attacks caused severe damage in the Straits of Messina (Messina–Reggio di Calabria). It has become difficult to supply the island of Sicily. Since railroad traffic has come to a complete standstill in Sicily, the island has to be supplied by sea from Naples. The only way to improve transportation facilities on the island itself would be an increased use of lorries. Before the war, Sicily had supplies for 40 days. Today there is enough for only 7 days. The question of supplies is becoming more and more difficult every day, because the enemy Air Force is constantly increasing. The same situation prevails in Sardinia. Most of the piers in Cagliari are destroyed. Porto Torres is of very little use, so only Olbia remains. Railroads in Sardinia are badly crippled, lorries are the only solution.

*Rear-Admiral Sansonetti* now explains the plans of the Italian Navy in greater detail. The Admiralty Staff has investigated two problems: What possibilities the enemy has (a) *before* he occupies Tunisia, and (b) *after* he starts to use the harbours Bizerta and Tunis. These studies showed that, as long as he cannot make use of Bizerta and Tunis, there is no reason to expect an invasion of Sicily. Of course, the enemy knows of the minefields between Sicily and North Africa, but these minefields divide his lines of approach. Since it takes from one to four weeks to sweep these minefields, an invasion of Sardinia is to be considered more likely at this time. An enemy invasion of Spain or southern France is not being considered.

The main objective of the Western Allies is a free line of communications through the Straits of Sicily. To attain this objective, the Balearic Islands and southern France are not essential, however, Sicily and Sardinia are important. The Italian Admiralty therefore believes that Sardinia will be the first to be invaded. An invasion of Sicily may be expected sometime after June 22.

Only three large battleships are actually available in La Spezia, as well as three cruisers and eight destroyers. Fighter escort for the planned operation is ready and is being trained by the fighter-director officer of the battleship Roma.   There are five fighter airfields and two Italian fighter groups on Sardinia; fifty German fighters are expected to be transferred. The area for the operations of the Italian naval forces has been carefully delineated.   It is entirely within the range of our own fighters.

After hearing the views of the German Admirals stationed in Rome, *the C.-in-C., Navy*, states that he believes that the enemy attack will come soon.   He states that our own forces are too weak to foil the enemy's plans by either destroying his embarkation points or the approaching invasion fleet.   He is going to send more German submarines to the Mediterranean although he is convinced that submarines will never be able to stop an invasion; they have only nuisance value.   Consequently, our whole problem is a successful defence on land.   Although preparations for the battle at sea are necessary they are not decisive.   The battle on land alone is decisive.   Therefore, the most important part of the Navy's mission is to make battle on land possible.   That means safeguarding the supply lines across the sea.   Due to our limited means this problem will have to be considered before anything else.   It would be fine if we could inflict damage on the enemy while en route, but this may be done only if it will not affect our supply system.   The problem, which is difficult already, will continue to become worse.   We saw in Tunisia how our difficulties increased immediately when enemy airfields were brought closer to our lines.   Even a small corner on Sardinia, with an enemy air-field, means a serious threat to us.   The North African campaign has taught us the following lesson: As long as conditions are comparatively favourable to us we will have to use the time to bring in supplies.   Supplies depend on: means of transportation, security, and unloading. These are the only decisive factors, and they call for a closely co-ordinated, large-scale organisation.   If the supply system fails the islands cannot be held.   However, a defeat at sea would not be decisive for us.   We must therefore use every available means to get as much material to the islands as possible.   Even small vessels will have to be used for shallow harbours and open bays.   We can worry about distribution later on.   If there are not enough small vessels, submarines will have to be used.

*Admiral Riccardi* interrupts at this point: "To transport supplies?" *The C.-in-C., Navy*, replies: "Yes, because submarines are not decisive in battle."   Cruisers, too, must frequently make fast trips with supplies. He is thoroughly convinced that we must make use of the available time, since the difficulties are constantly increasing.   We must therefore make it a point to concentrate everything on supplies.   Harbour facilities must be exploited to the fullest extent.   The responsible Italian officer must also have the right to draft civilians for this.   It must not happen again, as it did in North Africa, that we are defeated because our supply system failed. He will do everything in his power to help the Italian Navy.   Four auxiliary anti-aircraft vessels, the three torpedo boats, and as many land-ing craft (MFP) and sweepers as possible will be put at the disposal of the Italian Navy to handle supplies.   Although U-boats are necessary to attack the enemy, he is willing to use German submarines as supply vessels, because he considers this the most important problem.   If even the smallest suitable place is made available for unloading it should be possible to hold the islands.   Therefore an Italian general, as a dictator, should investigate all locations suitable for unloading and further distribution on each of the islands.   Even though a naval officer would prefer to fight the enemy at sea we must realise that our forces are too limited, and that maintenance of supplies is our main task.

*Admiral Riccardi* states that he will use all available means to help solve the transport problems.   However, he asks the C.-in-C., Navy, to use his influence in having the Air Force increased.   *The C.-in-C., Navy*, replies that he had, of course, only taken up naval matters.   However, upon his return to Berlin he would stress the absolute necessity of increasing the number of planes.   The very lack of planes must make us take full advantage of the present moment because, once the enemy again has airfields near the front, it might again be too late for many things.   The unique sacrifice of the Italian Fleet might have helped considerably had it come earlier; later on, the effort was dissipated by the increased enemy Air Force.   (At this point a misunderstanding is caused by the faulty translation of the Italian interpreter which makes it obvious that Admiral Riccardi interprets the remarks of the C.-in-C., Navy, to be a reproach of the Italian Navy.   The reaction of the Admiral, as a reflection of Italian opinion, was very enlightening.)

*Admiral Sansonetti* interjects at this point that the Italian Admiral Borone in Sicily had reported yesterday that a month from now nothing would be left on his island unless strongest efforts for the defence against enemy air raids would be made.   *The C.-in-C., Navy*, replies that this is an argument in favour of speed.   *Admiral de Curten* reports that in Messina not even 130 heavy anti-aircraft guns, concentrated in a small area, were able to prevent the air attacks.   Only good fighters can achieve results. On Pantelleria, the anti-aircraft batteries had good results only because the enemy came in at lower altitudes.   *The C.-in-C., Navy*, asks Admiral Riccardi if troops were still being transferred to Sardinia.   *Admiral Riccardi* replies that the transfer itself poses no difficulties.   The real obstacle is the availability of ships for heavy equipment.

*The C.-in-C., Navy*, points out that the main consideration is the cargo space of small craft.   He is willing to place even mine carriers at the disposal of Admiral Riccardi.   Everything shall be done to accommodate Admiral Riccardi.   However, speed is necessary.   He will emphasise that an increase in air power and A.A. batteries are most urgently needed. He asks if Admiral Riccardi has any further requests.   *Admiral Riccardi* replies that the above is already a large large order.   He is convinced that whatever Germany would provide will be most helpful.   As far as he knows the Duce has already wired the Fuehrer regarding the Air Force question.   He is aware that Germany, too, is having great difficulties. *Admiral Sansonetti* regards the chief problem of the Axis for the summer of 1943 to be either maintaining the status quo in the Mediterranean or cleaning the waters of the enemy.

In conclusion, *the C.-in-C., Navy*, commends Captain Grossi for his excellent work in converting Italian submarines into transport vessels for raw rubber.   He promises Captain Grossi every assistance.   In case the Italians want to transfer more large submarines to the Atlantic for carrying supplies, and possibly as a replacement for one large boat which has meanwhile been lost, he would be willing to exchange one German submarine for every one that they transfer.   He would even welcome such an exchange because both countries would benefit thereby and because the rubber supply is of such great importance.

2000 DINNER in the staff quarters of the German Staff with *Supermarina*.

May 13, 1943, in the morning.—Continuation of the conferences with representatives of various German offices; reports by the Commanding Officer of the Hermes (Captain Rechel), the Operations Officer of the Naval Command, Tunisia (Commander Wachsmuth), and other naval officers who returned from North Africa.

### 1100 VISIT OF GENERAL AMBROSIO

General impression.—Polite but formal reception. *The C.-in-C., Navy*, explains that, at the moment, the chief weakness in the defence of the large Italian islands is a lack of reinforcements and supplies. No time should be lost in sending these because the enemy is constantly increasing pressure on our supply lines. Once the enemy has undertaken an operation, pressure at unloading points may be expected to be particularly heavy. He is of the opinion that a large number of unloading points should be established, since adequate air coverage can never be expected. This calls for improvisation, such as collecting small craft and using them as lighters to unload larger ships at temporary unloading points. Transportation to the interior of the islands must be organised by the Military, who have the proper authority. After establishing numerous unloading stations, it may very well be that submarines, cruisers, and other vessels will be pressed into service in order to complete the transportation of men and supplies as quickly as possible. It is more important for the Navy to supply transport than to engage the enemy in battle. *General Ambrosio* did not fully agree with the above; he felt that submarines and cruisers should fight. *The C.-in-C., Navy*, replied that naval forces have already ceased fighting. When the serious need for transport is compared with what may be gained by engaging the enemy, the former takes precedence.

### 1130 INTERVIEW WITH THE DUCE

General impression.—The Duce is well, optimistic, composed, very frank, sincere, and amicable.

*The Duce* states that he is confident about the future. The only result of British air raids on Italy will be that the people will learn to hate the British, which has not always been the case. This helps in carrying on the war. If there is one Italian who hates the British, it is he himself. He is happy that his people are now learning the meaning of the word hate as well. He has answered the Fuehrer's offer of five divisions, by stating he wants only three of them. This refusal came as a surprise to the C.-in-C., Navy. The Duce explains that he had asked that these three divisions should include six armoured battalions with 300 tanks, two of which are detailed for Sardinia, three for Sicily, and one for southern Italy. He believes that Sicily is in the greatest danger, and supports his contention by referring to the British press which had repeatedly stated that free route through the Mediterranean would mean a gain of 2,000,000 tons of cargo space for the Allies. *The C.-in-C., Navy*, gives his opinion of the general situation to the Duce along the same lines as he did during the interview with General Ambrosio. *The Duce* immediately reacts to this by himself stressing the necessity for improvisation and considers this easily possible, particularly because of favourable weather conditions during the summer.

1630 CONFERENCE WITH VICE-ADMIRAL RUGE AND REAR-ADMIRAL MEENDSEN-BOHLKEN

*The C.-in-C., Navy,* announces his decision that Admiral Ruge will take over the German Naval Command and still maintain the Operations Staff with *Supermarina*. Rear-Admiral Meendsen-Bohlken will be recalled for other duty. The C.-in-C., Navy, explains his reasons for the decision to Rear-Admiral Meendsen-Bohlken. Afterwards, drive to Nemi Lake; inspection of the old Roman Ships.

1930 CONFERENCE WITH THE REPRESENTATIVE OF THE GERMAN TRANSPORT MINISTRY (BVM), SENATSSYNDIKUS ESSEN

*The Representative of the German Transport Ministry* briefly describes the situation in regard to cargo space, and repeatedly stresses the smooth co-operation with the Navy. He states that, on the recommendation of the Commanding Officer, Supply and Transports, Italy (*Seetransportchef-Italien*) the Organisation Todt has been ordered to prepare many small harbours and unloading points, including 150 moorings for small vessels, on the mainland as well as on the islands. The Todt organisation is getting under way. He expresses the opinion that the traffic volume of small cargo vessels coming to Italy from Marseilles has declined since the Naval Attaché in Rome relinquished his command. He asks that the convoys of small auxiliary craft be sent without escort in order to increase the volume of traffic. Action was taken in Rome immediately with reference to this request. He asks, furthermore, that any converted auxiliary craft of the type *Seeloewe* be turned over to him by the Navy for use in the Mediterranean and the Aegean rather than to release them for commercial use. It would be foolish to cancel the conversion of these vessels, because the need for them is so great that he would have to initiate such action all over again. *The C.-in-C., Navy,* states that he fully approves of this temporary solution of the transport problem in the Mediterranean, and that the final solution would be to transfer the entire problem of transport and supplies to the Representative of the German Transport Ministry; this would be done some time in the future whenever the situation permits.

2000 DINNER with the German Ambassador.

2200 CONFERENCE WITH FIELD MARSHAL KESSELRING

1. *The Commanding General, South,* states that the Fuehrer is considering the transfer of the Herman Goering Division and the 7th Airborne Division to Italy.

2. The fact that the Italian *Commando Supremo* had partially refused the Fuehrer's offer of five divisions was reported directly to the O.K.W. without informing the Commanding General, South, or General Rintelen. The Commanding General, South, considers this an act of political importance inasmuch as it proves that the Italians want to remain masters in their own house. Relations between him and General Ambrosio are not very cordial. If his person represents an obstacle to better relations

with the *Commando Supremo,* he is going to express his willingness to make way for another German C.-in-C.

3. On his tour of inspection in Sicily the Commanding General, South, has noticed that Italian defence preparations were very incomplete. He had therefore impressed this fact on the Italian C.-in-C., General Roatta. A similar tour of inspection of Sardinia is planned during the next few days.

4. The Commanding General, South, agrees with the Duce that an attack on Sicily is more probable than an attack on Sardinia.

5. The Commanding General, South, states that the joint naval forces are so weak that they are able to play only a minor rôle in reconnaissance and coast defence against an invasion attempt. He would like to have patrol vessels operate along the southern coasts of Sicily and Sardinia to prevent surprise attacks. He will get in touch with the Italian Air Force about increasing their aerial reconnaissance at sea.

6. The Commanding General, South, intends to recommend to the Fuehrer and to the *Reichmarschall* that the 2nd Air Fleet be increased sufficiently to destroy enemy embarkation harbours.

7. He considers an attack on the Iberian Peninsula the best way of bringing relief to the Mediterranean situation, and intends to submit such a plan to the Fuehrer.

*The C.-in-C., Navy,* repeatedly stresses that the crux of the problem is the transport of supplies and that these must be brought to the islands speedily and in large quantities. He believes that there are a sufficient number of harbours, that steps for the extensive improvement of these harbours have been taken and, with the exception of smaller vessels which are beginning to arrive, that there is sufficient shipping to provide adequate cargo space. The one drawback is that the Italians are accustomed to working in a leisurely manner. In a subsequent private conference the C.-in-C., Navy, tells the Commanding General, South, that he had appointed Vice-Admiral Ruge as the sole responsible representative of the Navy in Italy. He asks the Commanding General, South, to refer all questions pertaining to naval warfare in the Mediterranean exclusively to this officer rather than directly to *Supermarina* or other units such as *Dahms* Staff. *The Commanding General, South,* agrees and will place *Dahms* Staff under Admiral Ruge. He declares further that, in future, all problems pertaining to naval warfare will be left to Admiral Ruge as final authority. *The C.-in-C., Navy,* further stresses the necessity of initiating practical methods of improving the collaboration between Air Force and Navy in the Mediterranean, because this is still unsatisfactory. This should be done jointly by Admiral Ruge and *Dahms* Staff.


May 14, 1943

0930   AUDIENCE WITH THE KING

General impression.—Warm reception, agreeable, impressive, a wise experienced person. The King is lively and vivacious and has a good memory.

*The C.-in-C., Navy,* gives his opinion of the general situation to the King as previously discussed with General Ambrosio. He is convinced that Tunisia's fall was due only to the lack of supplies. If we master the supply question, we will defeat the enemy. *The King* points out that unfortunately most of the land routes in Italy are also close to shore and are therefore subject to attack from the sea. The audience was terminated with stories about his travels to Spitzbergen and Norway.

1030  Departure from Rome.

1630  Arrival at Wolfsschanze.

1850  Departure for Berlin.

2045  Arrival at Tempelhof.

The C.-in-C., Navy, was accompanied by: Rear-Admiral Wagner.
Commander Pfeiffer.
Lt.-Comdr. Freiwald.

From Rome to the Fuehrer's Headquarters: Captain Engelhardt.

\*　　\*　　\*　　\*　　\*　　\*

At Wolfsschanze Doenitz reported on his Italian conference to Hitler. The Italians were obviously weakening and Doenitz had little faith in their promises. Hitler, too, began to have doubts about Fascist loyalty to the Axis. There were signs that unless strong action were taken his Italian partner would collapse and go over to the Allies. The military problem of where the Allies would next strike was still unsolved. While Doenitz was in Italy, however, an Allied order had been discovered and shown to Hitler, pointing to Sardinia and the Peloponnesus as the next Allied objective. At the conference between Hitler and Doenitz, Hitler showed that he accepted this information as true and laid his plans accordingly.

### REPORT TO THE FUEHRER AT HEADQUARTERS, WOLFSSCHANZE, MAY 14, 1943, AT 1730

*The C.-in-C., Navy*, reports the progress and outcome of his conference with the Duce. He adds, that while the Duce did not disapprove of concentrating all efforts on the transport of supplies, no action was taken as the result of the C.-in-C.'s report. The Fuehrer believes that the Duce partly rejected the offer of several German divisions under the influence of the Italian High Command, in order to keep a free hand. *The Fuehrer* does not agree with the Duce that the most likely invasion point is Sicily. Furthermore, he believes that the discovered Anglo-Saxon order confirms the assumption that the planned attacks will be directed mainly against Sardinia and the Peloponnesus.

*The C.-in-C., Navy*, then reports on his conference with the *Supermarina* and mentions the places on Sardinia and Sicily where the Italians believe landing attempts will be made. He stresses the fact that the demand of the *Supermarina* for air attacks on enemy embarkation points in North Africa is definitely justified, but that aside from this, all efforts must be concentrated on safeguarding the shipping supplies. Therefore it is not enough merely to say, for example, that Olbia cannot handle more than its present load. On the contrary, every effort must be made to increase transport facilities by opening up smaller harbours, or even by using small craft, such as fishing vessels and utility boats, to unload in open bays. He believes that the *Supermarina* failed to grasp the full import of this point.

*The C.-in-C., Navy*, reports that the Italians listened to his suggestion that, if need be, all serviceable cruisers and submarines should be used for transport purposes, but he believes that nothing will come of it.   A complete understanding was also lacking on this point in his conference with General Ambrosio.   The C.-in-C., Navy, has therefore come away from these conferences with the impression that the Italians will do nothing about the all-important matter of increasing shipping facilities.   He was therefore very much pleased to note that Captain Engelhardt, Commanding Officer, Supply and Transports, Italy, had already begun to make the necessary arrangements in this respect.

*The Commanding Officer, Supply and Transports, Italy,* submits the following for the Fuehrer's consideration :

A. The following supplies are to be transported overseas :

1. 200,000 tons per month to Sicily.
2. 80,000 tons per month to Sardinia.

This includes the needs of both the German and Italian forces.   The following are available for this purpose :

(*a*) German and Italian steamers.
(*b*) German supply ships (KT).
(*c*) German and Italian landing craft (MFP) and Siebel ferries.
(*d*) Small craft and tank lighters from France.

Regarding point (*a*) it should be pointed out that it is improbable that larger steamers can make the passage in any appreciable numbers, since enemy action is too pronounced.   Tunisia may serve as a warning. Vessels as per points (*b*)–(*d*) offer the real solution, and therefore the following proposal is made : to use small craft in great numbers ; to run these ships on a broad front from Sicily to Corsica, from the harbours of Imperia to Taranto along routes which will be changed according to reports of the enemy situation so as not to give him a clear picture.

To achieve the above, the following will be necessary :

1. Direction and disposition of all available German merchantmen and small craft by the Commanding Officer, Supply and Transport, Italy.
2. Utilisation of the Todt Labour Organisation for the construction of slips and temporary landing places in the entire area.
3. Utilisation of four construction battalions for the reconstruction of the destroyed harbours, for construction of bases and bunkers, as well as for help in loading and unloading in harbours.
4. Employment of a sufficient number of lorries for transporting construction materials and cargo.

The Commanding Officer, Supply and Transport, Italy, reports that he has observed that the Italian troops and civilian population are not fitted for this kind of work, since they run away during air raids, their leaders have no initiative, and they actually sabotage our efforts by failure to furnish personnel or lorries.

B. Interference by the Supply and Transport Office of the Armed Forces Overseas (*Heimatstab Uebersee im OKW*) in allocating shipping space is undesirable.   This office may issue general directives, but should not actually allocate space.   Only Commanding Officer, Supply and Transports (Navy), and the Representative of the German Transport

Ministry should direct the details of actual transport operations. *The C.-in-C., Navy*, says to the Fuehrer that he considers this to be a question of finding the most practical solution and that the Commanding Officer, Supply and Transports (Navy), would need all the help he could find. The following requirements would have to be met:

1. A sufficient number of lorries. *The Fuehrer* decides that these should be procured from the Italian area.

2. Four construction battalions. *The Fuehrer* approves. Field Marshal Keitel will contact Minister Speer at once.

3. 50 million lire for the Todt Labour Organisation. *The Fuehrer* sees no complication in this connection. Field Marshal Keitel will make the necessary arrangements.

4. The Supply and Transport Office of the Armed Forces Overseas or other offices must not be given control over shipping space, since this may lead to situations where certain orders cannot be carried out locally for military reasons, or where the entire movement of supplies is seriously impaired. Higher authorities may set up requirements, but only the Commanding Officer, Supply and Transports (Navy), and the Representative of the German Transport Ministry will be responsible for carrying out instructions. *The Fuehrer* repeatedly and emphatically expresses his agreement on this point.

*The Fuehrer* asks the C.-in-C., Navy, whether he thinks that the Duce is determined to carry on to the end. *The C.-in-C., Navy*, answers that he accepts this as certain, but that he cannot be sure, of course. He has gained the impression that the primary failing of the Italians is their lack of initiative. *The Fuehrer* asserts that he does not trust the Italian upper class. He believes that a man like Ambrosio would be happy if Italy could become a British dominion today. *The C.-in-C., Navy*, states that generally speaking, since his return from Rome he has come to the conclusion that the plan to hold the Italian islands will result in a purely defensive operation. It will consume much energy without getting the Axis out of its defensive position. It must furthermore be kept in mind that the Anglo-Saxon powers have gained two million tons in shipping space since the Mediterranean was cleared. *The Fuehrer* interrupts here: "Which our trusty submarines will now have to sink." *The C.-in-C., Navy*, continues: "Yet we are at present facing the greatest crisis in submarine warfare, since the enemy, by means of new location devices, for the first time makes fighting impossible and is causing us heavy losses (15–17 submarines per month)." *The Fuehrer* interjects at this point: "These losses are too high. Something must be done about it." *The C.-in-C., Navy*, continues: Furthermore, at the present time the only outbound route for submarines is a narrow lane in the Bay of Biscay. This passage is so difficult that it now takes a submarine ten days to get through. In view of this situation, the occupation of Spain, including Gibraltar, would be the best strategic solution. This would constitute an attack against the flank of the Anglo-Saxon offensive, the Axis would regain the initiative, a radical change would take place in the Mediterranean, and submarine warfare could be given a much broader basis. In reply *the Fuehrer* states that we are not capable of an operation of this kind, since it would require first class divisions. Occupation of Spain without the consent of the

Spaniards is out of the question, since they are the only tough Latin people, and would carry on guerilla warfare in our rear. In 1940 it might have been possible to get Spain to agree to such a move. However, the Italian attack on Greece in the autumn of 1940 shocked Spain.

The Axis must face the fact that it is saddled with Italy. Therefore the shipping and transport of supplies must be handled in accordance with the suggestions made by the Commanding Officer, Supply and Transports (Navy). In conclusion, *the C.-in-C., Navy*, reports to the Fuehrer that he is working together with Minister Speer in order to speed all possible countermeasures pertaining to submarine location. He believes that developments along these lines are more important than anything else at this point.

# The Battle of the Atlantic

FROM THE Mediterranean Doenitz turned to the Atlantic. Up to 1943 the rate of shipping destroyed in relation to the number of U-boats lost had been very favourable to Germany, but in the first four months of 1943 Allied countermeasures began to make themselves felt and U-boat losses mounted rapidly. R.A.F. Coastal Command and escort carriers of the Royal Navy provided air cover on a scale which could not be matched by the Germans, and in April the Allied Chiefs of Staff initiated a series of combined sea and air offensives directed against U-boats in the Bay of Biscay. Doenitz was to be attacked in his own waters.

The result of these and other Allied operations was that in the month of May 1943, 37 U-boats were sunk, representing approximately 30 per cent. of all U-boats at sea. The situation for Germany was critical. Doenitz was forced to withdraw his U-boats from the North Atlantic, and on June 24, Allied ships of 15 knots or over were able to resume trans-Atlantic passages, independent of convoy protection. Both Hitler and Doenitz considered the U-boat campaign of supreme importance. It was their best weapon against the Allied build-up for the attack on the Continent, and they could not accept the defeat of the last month. On May 31 Hitler ordered Doenitz to report on the U-boat campaign.

C.-in-C., Navy                                   Berlin, June 5, 1943

**MINUTES OF THE CONFERENCE OF THE C.-IN-C., NAVY, WITH THE FUEHRER ON MAY 31, 1943, AT THE BERGHOF**

Also present : Field Marshal Keitel.
               Major-General Warlimont.
               Captain von Puttkamer.

A. *The C.-in-C., Navy*, reports as follows : The substantial increase of the enemy Air Force is the cause of the present crisis in submarine warfare. By means of sound detection it has been determined that as many planes now pass through the narrows between Iceland and the Faroe Islands on one day, as only recently appeared in the course of a week. In addition, aircraft carriers are being used in conjunction with North Atlantic convoys, so that all convoy routes are now under enemy air protection. However, the submarine crisis would not have come about solely as a result of an increase in enemy aircraft. The determining factor is a new location device evidently also used by surface vessels, by means of which planes are now in a position to locate submarines. When the ceiling is low, visibility poor, or at night, they can carry out surprise attacks. Without this device the planes would be unable to locate the submarine at night or in a heavy sea. This is shown too by our losses, the great majority of which were caused by planes. Surface vessels have not been very successful, although a relatively large number of U-boats, five to be exact, were surprised by destroyers during a heavy fog which suddenly set in while a convoy was being attacked on May 8. Without this location device it would have been impossible to surprise the submarines in a fog. Accordingly, approximately 65 per cent. of the losses occur while the submarines are en route or lying in wait ; only about 35 per cent. occur near the convoys themselves. That is to be expected, for a submarine spends most of the six to eight weeks of an operation en route or lying in wait. During this time the danger of sudden attacks from the air, when it is dark or when visibility is poor, by enemy who cannot be detected beforehand, is very great. Our losses have increased during the last month from approximately 14 submarines, or 13 per cent. of the submarines at sea, to 36 or even 37, or approximately 30 per cent. of all submarines at sea. These losses are too high. We must conserve our strength, otherwise we will play into the hands of the enemy. The following measures have been initiated :

1. I have withdrawn from the North Atlantic to the area west of the Azores in the hope of encountering less air reconnaissance there. I am lying in wait there for a convoy headed for Gibraltar. It is very difficult however, to locate this convoy in so large an area. With new submarines now becoming available I shall proceed to more distant areas in the hope that the planes there are not yet as fully equipped with the modern location devices. I intend, however, to resume attacks on convoys in the North Atlantic at the time of the new moon, provided that the submarines will have additional weapons at their disposal by that time.

2. The following equipment is required :

(a) An efficient radar interception set, that is, an apparatus which will show the frequency used by the radar-equipped plane and will warn the submarine of an impending attack. We do not have such a set. We don't even know on what wave length the enemy locates us. Neither do we know whether high frequency or other location devices are being employed. Everything possible is being done to find out what it is. Until such a warning device is made available, I have ordered that our submarines shall operate at night only on one electric motor. Elimination of noise of the Diesel engines will facilitate detection of the plane by sound. This seems to me the only means of warning submarines of an air attack. An investigation is being made whether it is possible to install a sound detection apparatus on the submarine conning tower that will stand up under diving and other conditions at sea.

(b) A second possibility is that of jamming or dispersing the enemy radar waves. We have not got facilities for jamming the enemy's reception, since the range of a jammer on a submarine is too limited. Furthermore, a jammer which does not automatically adjust itself to the wave length of the enemy beacon, can very easily be evaded by changing to a different wave length. Such an automatic device is being experimented with under Minister Ohnesorge, but is still far from being ready for submarine use. Only in regard to dispersion of the enemy radio waves have we anything positive to offer. Beginning this June we are going to equip our submarines with the so-called *Aphrodite*. This device produces the same kind of reflective effect as a conning tower, and can be released by the submarines in order to confuse the enemy. Furthermore, in June large buoys will be planted in the Bay of Biscay, which also produce a reflective effect like the conning tower of a submarine, and are meant to mislead enemy planes. Since we are here dealing with a new weapon, I request permission to introduce it. *The Fuehrer* gives permission.

(c) So far no satisfactory solution has been found which would enable the submarine to detect the searching plane by means of its own radar set. The difficulty lies in the fact that the submarine's location beam is very narrow—comparable to a narrow beam searchlight—and therefore it takes much too long to search the sky with it.

(d) Experimental measures to protect submarine conning towers against radar detection have shown that it is possible to reduce the reflections of the conning tower to 30 per cent. In other words, an enemy who was formerly able to detect the submarine from a distance of 9,000 metres can now do so only from a distance of 3,000 metres. Actual use alone will tell whether this device is effective on all wave lengths. We are still a long way from putting it into actual use.

(e) Four-barrelled machine guns will be installed in increasing numbers beginning this coming July, and the conning towers rebuilt accordingly.

(f) It will not do the submarines much good to fight off the planes with the four-barrelled machine gun unless they have the anti-destroyer torpedo at the same time. Otherwise the destroyer called to the scene by the plane can still force the submarine to submerge. By October we are definitely going to get the so-called *Falke*, an acoustic torpedo which can be used effectively against an enemy not making over 12 knots. This limitation is a great drawback. Therefore everything possible must be done to put the so-called *Zaunkoenig* into use at the front by autumn. This torpedo is effective against an enemy making up to 18 knots. I shall discuss with Minister Speer what steps will be necessary to make *Zaunkoenig* available to the front by autumn. I ask your support in this, since I consider it absolutely necessary that the submarines be supplied with the anti-destroyer torpedo before the favourable winter fighting season. *The Fuehrer* agrees that everything possible must be done to make *Zaunkoenig* available.

(g) It is necessary to concentrate aerial attacks on the Bay of Biscay, where enemy planes are attacking our submarines on departure and return without interference. Support from our Air Force is completely inadequate there at the present time. The Ju88 can fly only in formation, since otherwise it would in turn become the victim. Only when flying in formation are the Ju88 occasionally able to shoot down an enemy plane. In my opinion it is essential that the Me410 be brought to the Bay of Biscay as soon as possible. In this I concur with the request of the 3rd Air Fleet and the Commanding Officer, Naval Air, Atlantic.

*The Fuehrer* is doubtful whether the Me410 is suitable for this purpose, but will look into the matter. He then criticises the faulty production schedule of combat planes. By excessively favouring Stukas and two-motor bombers, the production of four-motor planes with their longer range was neglected. At the moment we lack planes suitable for combat. If we were to attack England with those we have now, we would suffer from 25 to 30 per cent. losses, and we cannot afford that. Our industrial centres are being attacked intensively and systematically, and in the long run we cannot hope to prevent these attacks through defensive measures alone. If long-range bombers were available, the Fuehrer would have to decide whether to use them for naval warfare or to attack England. The ultimate purpose of the latter would be the protection of our cities and industrial centres.

*The C.-in-C., Navy*, is of the opinion that the construction of suitable planes for naval warfare should have been undertaken at the latest moment we began to build a large submarine fleet. *The Fuehrer* agrees with this. Our submarines undoubtedly could have sunk more shipping during the past year if we had had naval planes. These can further submarine warfare by scouting, as well as by affording protection against enemy planes. Many of the planes in the Atlantic area are inferior to our planes. Furthermore, the Air Force would find many targets in the Atlantic, and in that way could increase the tonnage sunk by us. Even now it is not too late to give our naval forces an Air Force. *The Fuehrer* agrees fully with these views.

*The C.-in-C., Navy*, states that it will be necessary in that case to begin the training of the plane crews in time and to allow for an adequate training period, otherwise we shall have to use untrained and inexperienced personnel who know nothing about naval warfare. Therefore a school for naval flyers must be started at once at Gdynia in direct conjunction with the convoy training flotillas directed by the submarine branch, for the naval flyers must be trained just as systematically for four to five months as the submarine personnel. The naval flyers must learn navigation at sea, celestial navigation, drift computation, how to keep contact with a convoy, co-operation with the submarines by means of direction-finder signals, how to be guided to the convoy by other planes, and the necessary communications. In short, they must receive their training in the Baltic Sea together with the submarine personnel so that they will speak the same language and can subsequently fight together. A situation must not arise where co-operation in the Atlantic between submarines and the Air Force breaks down because certain mistakes are made which actually have nothing to do with the fundamentally sound principle of co-operation. Such errors might lead to the false generalisation that co-operation is useless. *The Fuehrer* agrees fully with the views expressed and stresses once more the tasks, prospects, and possibilities which our own Air Force would have in the Atlantic. He then closes with the words: "It seems that long-range bombers should be sent into the Atlantic area."

*The C.-in-C., Navy*, has the following to say about the future prospects of submarine warfare: At the present time our efforts are being frustrated by a technical device against which countermeasures will be found. It is impossible, however, to foretell to what extent submarine warfare will again become effective. The enemy's anti-submarine defence on water and from the air will be improved. That entails many uncertainties and unknown factors. In 1940 a submarine was able to sink an average of 1,000 tons per day at sea; toward the end of 1942, approximately 200 tons. This shows clearly the growing effectiveness of anti-submarine defence, and the diminishing effectiveness of submarines. Nevertheless, I am convinced that submarine warfare must be carried on, even if great successes are no longer possible. The forces tied up through submarine warfare were considerable even during the World War. *The Fuehrer* interrupts at this point with the following remark: "There can be no talk of a let-up in submarine warfare. The Atlantic is my first line of defence in the West, and even if I have to fight a defensive battle there, that is preferable to waiting to defend myself on the coast of Europe. The enemy forces tied up by our submarine warfare are tremendous, even though the actual losses inflicted by us are no longer great. I cannot afford to release these forces by discontinuing submarine warfare." *The C.-in-C., Navy*, continues: "I therefore believe that we must continue the present effort to increase submarine production. As a matter of fact I don't believe that 30 submarines are sufficient. Even in what amounts to purely defensive submarine warfare in the Atlantic we will need great numbers of submarines. In my opinion we should strive for 40 submarines. In agreement with Minister Speer, I have already arranged for the construction of 30 submarines and for building auxiliary vessels as previously mentioned. I now request that this order be signed by the Fuehrer." *The Fuehrer* agrees, changes the number of submarines from 30 to 40 per month, and signs.

B. *The C.-in-C., Navy*, proposes destruction of lines of communications along the North African coast by means of submarine assault troops, so that the enemy will be forced to use considerable resources of material and personnel for coastal defence, and will not have the forces landed in Africa available for offensive operations alone. *The Fuehrer* believes, however, that the British in that case would use the French for such defence operations and therefore would not suffer any curtailment of their own forces. *Field Marshal Keitel* calls attention to the fact that the "Brandenburg" Battalion is already engaged in similar operations. *The C.-in-C., Navy*, says that he will, nevertheless, make corresponding suggestions to the O.K.W., Operations Staff (OKW/*Fuehrungastab*) since he believes that these operations should be carried out in strictly military fashion.

C. *The C.-in-C., Navy*, proposes a surprise attack on Gibraltar with the new weapon of the Air Force, as soon as these have been stock-piled in sufficient numbers; in other words, about the end of June. He thinks that this is preferable to letting the British naval forces get out of Gibraltar and then hunt them down and attack them individually when they have considerable fighter escorts. Gibraltar could readily be reached from the Marseilles area. *The Fuehrer* is of the opinion that he will then run the risk that some of the new weapons might fall on land at Gibraltar, and that the British will find out what they are. Furthermore, he is doubtful about reaching Gibraltar, particularly since it is becoming increasingly difficult from a political point of view, to fly over Spain. The C.-in-C., Navy, stresses once more that it is necessary to concentrate these weapons. *The Fuehrer* remarks that he had intended to make up for the falling-off in submarine warfare, which must be expected during the next few months, by means of some such attacks.

D. *The C.-in-C., Navy*, advocates the mining of Port Said and Alexandria in order to interfere with British movements through the Mediterranean. *The Fuehrer* says that it would be possible to do this by operating from Rhodes, but that planes are not available. In conclusion the Fuehrer states that means must be found to offset the enemy's present advantage over us in regard to technical submarine devices. The C.-in-C., Navy, assures him that any aid, no matter how insignificant, would be welcome, for a number of such measures together might in the end enable the submarines to resume the offensive. The Fuehrer is worried that the new detection device might involve principles with which we are not familiar. The crisis must be overcome by all possible means.

(signed)          DOENITZ.
(countersigned) Comdr. PFEIFFER.

\*          \*          \*          \*          \*          \*

The shortage of manpower was as urgent as the shortage of U-boats. A table of requirements of naval personnel consequent on increasing U-boat production to 40 per month has been discovered among the German naval archives and gives the following figures covering the period from June 1943 to September 1944:

|  |  |  |  |  |
|---|---|---|---|---|
| Personnel allocated | .. | .. | .. | 102,984 |
| Personnel required | .. | .. | .. | 437,822 |
| Shortage |  |  | .. | 334,838 |

About 62,000 of the personnel required were for U-boats, a total of 634 boats requiring to be manned. Doenitz reported the manpower position to Hitler on June 15.

C.-in-C., Navy                                      Berlin, June 29, 1943

### NOTES ON THE REPORT OF THE C.-IN-C., NAVY, TO THE FUEHRER ON JUNE 15, 1943, AT THE BERGHOF

Also present:  Field Marshal Keitel.
                    Major-General Warlimont.
                    Rear-Admiral Voss.
                    Captain von Puttkamer.

*The C.-in-C., Navy*, reports:

1. Since April 1942 the number of men assigned to the Navy has suffered because most personnel were sent to the Army. The situation at this moment is such that the 30,000 men now assigned to the Navy barely cover the losses. Since April 1942 the commissioning of naval vessels, the extension of shore defences and air defences, and the transfer of personnel to the Mediterranean have raised additional personnel problems. The demands could scarcely be met by refusing all replacements for shore and air defences and bringing in women. These sources have now been exhausted. If the present manner of assigning personnel to the Navy is retained, a shortage of 200,000 men is already in evidence. This figure is based on the assumption that submarine construction will be raised merely from 25 to 30 per month, and that anti-aircraft defence, both ashore and afloat, will be extended rapidly to keep up with new tactics developed by the enemy. By increasing the submarine programme to 40, and by building the additional light ships, which have already been ordered, the shortage becomes even greater and will require an immediate change in the assignment of personnel. *The Fuehrer:* "I haven't got this personnel. The anti-aircraft and night-fighter forces must be increased in order to protect the German cities. It is also necessary to strengthen the Eastern Front. The Army needs divisions for the protection of Europe."

*The C.-in-C., Navy*, calls attention to the consequences if submarine warfare ceases, since losses surpass new constructions. He suggests the possibility that the whole material strength of the enemy will be hurled against Europe and that our coastal supply routes will be endangered. If naval warfare ceases, then the war has actually come to an end for the majority of English people, since they would feel that their own lives were no longer endangered. The lowest limit has already been reached in officer complement. The officer candidates who enter in the autumn of 1939 are now becoming submarine commanders. In order to carry out the large submarine programme it will be necessary to transfer officers from the Army and the Air Force to the Navy and to increase considerably the annual number of officer candidates for the Navy. The C.-in-C., Navy, states that it was his duty to point out the consequences of too small an allocation of personnel. If the Navy does not receive the requested personnel then, from January 1944 on, no newly commissioned patrol boats, minesweepers, E-boats, etc., could be manned. By January 1, 1944, the last available soldiers would be transferred to submarine training. The remaining training schools of the Navy would run out of men in the winter 1943–44. *The Fuehrer* declares that a cessation of the submarine warfare is out of the question, that he would have to allocate personnel as they become available, and orders a list of the required personnel with the date when they will be needed drawn up and submitted to him. He will see to it that appropriate action is taken.

2. *The C.-in-C., Navy*, states that a larger submarine construction programme and the increase in the construction of minesweepers, E-boats, etc., make an allocation of workmen and steel to the shipyard industry necessary. Even though a further increase in production by the shipyard industry will, no doubt, be possible through new efficiency measures, only a relatively small saving in the requested number of workmen and the requested increased allocation of steel will be obtained. In such an undertaking of simplification and systematising one must also take into consideration that the present rapid output of the shipyards must not suffer from such a change and that, no doubt, a standardisation of the shipbuilding process, which takes much time and is very complicated, is more difficult than that of arms and equipment. In regard to the question of labour for the shipyards the present situation is such that, instead of the requested increase, there is a further loss of workers caused by the 2nd SE Action which cannot be tolerated. *The Fuehrer* declares that the removal of workmen from naval production is out of the question and orders Field Marshal Keitel to take the necessary steps. The enlarged construction programme must be carried out at all costs. He will discuss the question with Minister Speer and immediately inform the C.-in-C., Navy.

(signed) DOENITZ.
(countersigned) Lt.-Comdr. MEJER.

\* \* \* \* \* \*

Besides increasing the number of U-boat personnel Doenitz had three more ideas for dealing with the U-boat crisis. The first two were purely technical—a development of a new "electro" submarine capable of high underwater speeds, and the improvement of the A.A. armament of U-boats. His third idea, however, was to intensify minelaying operations. He planned to lay 3,000 mines per month off the coasts of Britain, and on July 8 reported his ideas to Hitler.

Naval Staff                                      Berlin, July 31, 1943

## MINUTES OF THE CONFERENCE OF THE C.-IN-C., NAVY, WITH THE FUEHRER ON JULY 8, 1943, AT 1630 AT THE HEADQUARTERS, WOLFSSCHANZE

Also present: Field Marshal Keitel.
Rear-Admiral Voss.
Captain von Puttkamer.

*The C.-in-C., Navy*, reports to the Fuehrer the successful design of the "electro" submarine and enumerates the tactical advantages of such a fast submarine. Entirely new possibilities are introduced by permitting the submarines to approach a convoy quickly and also to take fast evasive action under water instead of being obliged to surface. This will make the present anti-submarine defence of the enemy entirely ineffectual because the construction of escort vessels is based on a low speed of submarines under water. The advantages of an underwater speed of 19 knots would remain effective for a long time, since the convoy speed of roughly 10 knots cannot be increased very much. The design is based on well-known factors of propulsion and retains only the hull of the Walther-submarine which is especially suited for speed under water. Since he is well satisfied with the model, he believes that it should be built with the greatest possible speed.

*The Fuehrer* inquires at length about technical details, such as radius of action, maximum speed, recharging requirements, armament, and depth of submergence. *The C.-in-C., Navy*, clarifies these points and states that the new submarines has important advantages both on the offensive and defensive. The great depth of submergence and the new underwater speed enable it to dive quicker than previous submarines when attacked by escort vessels and planes. Moreover, because of its long cruising radius submerged, the dangerous coastal areas can be passed in a short time. In comparison with the Walther-submarine it has the additional advantage of being able to recharge its batteries and thus extend its sea endurance considerably. In reply to the question of the Fuehrer as to when the first of these submarines could be completed, the C.-in-C., Navy, states that he discusssed this question with Minister Speer and ordered the Naval Construction Division (*K-Amt*) to make an estimate which he is submitting. He considers the date November 1944, as fixed by the Division, much too late, and states that he discussed with Minister Speer ways and means of speeding up construction. It is his conviction that the greatest effort must be made to accomplish this in three shifts, possibly even day and night shift, because this development means a revolutionary change in submarine warfare.

*The Fuehrer* declares that he recently discussed with Minister Speer the possibility of resuming the production of the new Skoda 37-mm. gun. He believes that this weapon may prove very effective in submarine warfare. *The C.-in-C., Navy*, reports that in very many cases the present quadruple 20-mm. gun had failed to bring down attacking aircraft in spite of direct hits, while in other cases the planes were not brought down until after they had succeeded in dropping their bombs.

*The C.-in-C., Navy*, further reports that our efforts to increase the number of submarines in the Mediterranean have met with great diffi-culties.   Of the last four submarines which attempted to pass through the Strait of Gibraltar three were lost.   These losses are too high.   He is planning therefore to ship the small Walther-submarine by way of the Rhône from Germany to the Mediterranean.   Although this U-boat carries only three torpedoes, it has the same advantages as the "electro" submarine except for the difference in propulsion (he submits a sketch). In reply to the question of the Fuehrer whether transport by way of the Rhône is actually feasible, the C.-in-C., Navy, replies that it could be accomplished by transporting the submarine on its side, and that this method had been tried.   The first submarines could be ready in April 1944, since their small size makes a speed construction possible.

*The Fuehrer* expresses his complete agreement with the plan and discusses with the C.-in-C., Navy, the problem of organising the con-struction of the new submarines.   He says that he is firmly convinced that technical changes will continue alternately to favour or impede offensive or defensive warfare.   One must therefore not become dis-couraged but ever be receptive to new ideas.   A man whose mind is closed thereby admits his defeat.   The same is true of the Air Force.   However, one must not make exaggerated demands on the technicians and thereby prevent the quick construction of really useful arms and conveyances. For this reason he had recently personally intervened in the question of using aircraft for reconnaissance at sea and had interviewed the proper authorities of the Air Force.

*The C.-in-C., Navy*, reports that a commission for ship construction has been formed by him with the co-operation of Minister Speer, inventors, technicians, and construction specialists, so that there could be agreement concerning construction details.   *The Fuehrer* comments:   "That is right."   He has proceeded similarly with tank construction.   The Air Force would do well to follow this method.   For reconnaissance in the Atlantic, Professor Messerschmidt has developed a new six-engine aircraft, based on the four-engined plane, with a range of 17,000 km.   This new plane possesses very strong armament and high speed.   These machines will be used later to work in conjunction with submarines.   He will do everything in his power to push their construction and to eliminate exaggerated demands.   He has given up the idea of bombing the U.S.A. because the few aircraft which would get there would be of no significance but would only arouse the will to resist in the population.   The C.-in-C., Navy, expresses his conviction that efficient reconnaissance in the Atlantic will always be needed even after the new submarines are at our disposal.

In regard to the general situation of submarine warfare he reports to the Fuehrer that he has transferred the submarines from the North Atlantic after it had to be abandoned as a result of the lost battle in May.   In the new areas the anti-submarine measures are not yet so strong and efficient. As a result of these changes there were few sinkings during June, but July has begun to show some improvement.   It is now quite evident that the enemy is directing his main efforts against the exit lanes of our submarines, i.e. against the Strait of Shetland and the Bay of Biscay.   Consequently, our losses in these areas are still very high.   Most of these losses were caused by the enemy's Air Force, but of late apparently also by escort groups and naval forces which are co-operating with the Air Force.

Against this combination we have no defence as yet, and for the time being the departure of submarines from home ports has been stopped until all have been equipped with quadruple and twin mounts.

By the end of July he expects again to have an efficient radar interception set, i.e. a warning device against enemy radar location. With the help of Minister Ohnesorge and the technical laboratories of the Post Office Department, two apparatus are being developed, one of which will make possible the simultaneous reception of all radar waves and the second one the recording of flash fix. So far, there is no indication that the enemy is using a new radar system. Our present difficulties may be due to the inability of our old receivers to register the flash fix. After these improvements have been made in our submarines and long nights again give us an advantage, the northern route can be used again.

Little progress has been made with regard to the problem of the "black" submarine. However, Professor Krauch of the I. G. Farben is convinced that he will soon find some material with which a 100 per cent. absorption of radar waves can be obtained. As a result of the dielectric absorption, reflection will be practically nil, and this will effectively nullify radar location. In addition, we are still working on the development of other porous materials (*Schwaemme*) for absorbing high frequencies. Of equal importance to these defensive measures against the enemy Air Force is the anti-destroyer torpedo to combat enemy surface vessels. Until this anti-destroyer torpedo is ready for use, the C.-in-C., Navy, does not intend to resume attacks on convoys in the North Atlantic. He is therefore making every effort to speed up the construction of the anti-destroyer torpedo, but is not sure that he will succeed. Until then he will use the submarines for mining operations except some which will be sent to more distant areas. (He submits a chart.)

In regard to the general use of mines he reports that he is planning to use the new mines in a surprise attack in August, as agreed upon with the Air Force. *The Fuehrer* expresses repeatedly his great misgivings as to the use of these mines by the Air Force because he is afraid that the mines might be dropped on land, and inquires into the details of their employment (depth of water, location, new moon). The C.-in-C., Navy, reports that only 500 mines can be laid per month with the fast layers at his disposal. This is too small a number. At least 3,000 mines ought to be laid, and for such a large operation the co-operation of the Air Force is indispensable.

He explains with the aid of two charts the initial success which was obtained with the magnetic mines, and shows also the extent of traffic around the British Isles. He states that with the destruction of each ship that part of the enemy's war potential is a complete loss. In dropping a bomb on enemy territory one cannot always ascertain the success. But one cannot overestimate the great losses inflicted on the British by mine warfare, even though they are no longer sensational and, as a rule, can be ascertained only later on. Besides, their use is less costly for us, since the Air Force does not have to reckon with such high losses as in the case of an attack on an enemy city. Therefore, as many aircraft as possible should be set aside for minelaying operations because the enemy will be hit at the most vital spot. Enough mines can be accumulated by the end of August. An increase in sinkings through mines would be particularly welcome now in order to tide us over during the period of few submarine sinkings, so that the enemy's gain in tonnage can be held as low as possible during these months.   Our goal must be to maintain sinkings at a rate that will balance the new construction of enemy ships, and this will be possible with the new submarine.

The drawback in this proposed programme is the question of man-power.   According to the last report of the O.K.W., we shall soon face the situation that Minister Speer is in fact producing the submarines but that there will be no men to man them.   For the enlarged programme the Navy needs 262,000 men by the autumn of 1944, and they must be young men.   *The Fuehrer* considers this figure too high but accepts it after a lengthy discussion with the C.-in-C., Navy.   He decides that, in addition to the measures which have already been decided upon by the Chief of Staff, O.K.W., 10,000 technicians of the age group 1925 are to be given to the Navy in exchange for other men.   The C.-in-C., Navy, calls this only a stopgap and presents a summary of the total requirements.

*The Fuehrer* discusses the present availability of men with Field Marshal Keitel.   The Chief of Staff, O.K.W., holds to his proposal.   The Fuehrer ends the discussion by assuring the C.-in-C., Navy, that he would help the Navy and, of course, also the Air Force, as soon as the situation improves.   The C.-in-C., Navy, states that, under these circumstances, he cannot commission certain vessels because he needs the technicians who are to be trained for these vessels and who are to be the future non-commission officers now.   He would have to present a new demand in September, at the latest.   *The Fuehrer* replies: "By September we shall be a little further along."   He says that he is favourably inclined towards the Navy and will do everything possible for it.   He suggests that the C.-in-C., Navy, investigate the possibility of obtaining personnel for the Navy from the occupied territories, as the S.S. has done so successfully. He believes that this offers great possibilities for the Navy, and that some 20,000 to 25,000 men could be recruited.   *The C.-in-C., Navy*, declares that he will try it and will also contact *Reichsfuehrer S.S.* Himmler.

In regard to the Italian submarines carrying raw rubber, the *C.-in-C., Navy*, reports the loss of three boats.   He states that Admiral Riccardi has not complied with his request to put at his disposal the two submarines Romolo and Remo which are especially well suited for transport, giving as the reason for his refusal that the U-boats are needed in the Italian theatre of war.   Admiral Riccardi is guarding his boats jealously and is making the same mistake as in the case of the Italian combat submarines.   The Commander Italian Submarines, Admiral Legnani, has expressed his displeasure with the ineffectual use of the submarines.   Admiral Legnani is also in disagreement with *Supermarina* in regard to the small Italian submarines.   He has therefore submitted the plans of construction for these small submarines to the C.-in-C., Navy, who has found them suitable for the purpose.   He therefore requests the Fuehrer's permission to announce the visit of Admiral Legnani in the papers.   *The Fuehrer* gives his permission and discusses with the C.-in-C., Navy, the employment of the Italian Fleet and submarines.

*The C.-in-C., Navy*, emphasises the importance of the capture of Leningrad.   This would discourage greatly any landing attempt by the British in Norway, for whom the security of Russian Leningrad is a tempting objective. At least the Oranienbaum basin should be taken, since it is of great importance for the protection of the nearby oilfield. *The Fuehrer* explains the present front on a map and states that he has given orders to examine the question of Oranienbaum. However, no Russian submarine has succeeded so far in getting out of Leningrad harbour. The C.-in-C., Navy, admits this. He then requests permission to see the reports of the Foreign Office concerning the enemy. *The Fuehrer* agrees and gives the order, but emphasises that the reports are exclusively for the personal information of the C.-in-C., Navy.

In conclusion the C.-in-C., Navy, again stresses the importance of the speedy construction of the new submarine. *The Fuehrer* agrees heartily, and says to Minister Speer, who enters at this moment: "The construction of this new submarine is of the utmost importance." Minister Speer replies: "There is no doubt about that. I have given top priority to the new submarines."

(signed)          DOENITZ.
(countersigned) Lt. RUDOLPH.

# The Italian Collapse

ON JULY 10 the Allies invaded Sicily. Hitler had accepted the indications he had been given that the landings would take place in Greece or Sardinia with the result that considerable surprise was achieved and Sicily was ill-prepared to meet the Allied assault. In his previous review of the Mediterranean Doenitz had decided that the Axis navies were too weak to achieve anything useful at sea, so he had instead concentrated all naval efforts on supplying the Axis armies on land. The result of this somewhat negative policy was to hasten the deterioration of the Italian Navy and in the week following the Allied landings he received alarming reports from the German naval commanders in Italy. In spite of the fact that the Italians still had well over a hundred warships and more than 200,000 tons of shipping they did practically nothing. Their spirit was broken. As the Allied victory in Tunisia had broken the remnants of the Italian Army, so the invasion of Sicily, which they had been powerless to prevent, broke the Italian Navy. Doenitz was desperate. He had somehow either to boost the morale of the Italian Navy or alternatively to take over the Italian Fleet. On July 17 he reported to Hitler.

C.-in-C., Navy

## MINUTES OF THE CONFERENCE OF THE C.-IN-C., NAVY, WITH THE FUEHRER AT HEADQUARTERS, WOLFS-SCHANZE, JULY 17, 1943

Also present :  Field Marshal Keitel.
      Lt.-General Jodl.
      Rear-Admiral Voss.
      Captain von Puttkamer.
      Colonel Scherff.
      And, temporarily, Field Marshal Rommel.

*The C.-in-C., Navy*, says that he is making this report because he feels that it is his duty to give the Fuehrer his opinion about the situation in Italy. Generally speaking his views are the same as those submitted by Lt.-General Jodl in written form. He happens to know that the younger officers of the Italian Navy, who have really seen action, for example with the Tunisian convoys, and also the young submarine commanders are opposed to the *Supermarina*. Already at the time when the C.-in-C., Navy, first visited Rome, these young officers had expected a change in the high command of the Italian Navy, since it is completely out of touch with what is going on at the front and is therefore not recognised by most of the younger officers. Furthermore, the C.-in-C., Navy, is of the opinion that the Italian Navy would have been of much greater help to us if it had been under German leadership. This holds true today. He believes that there are quite a few Italian officers who sincerely want to fight on our side and have proved their willingness in action, but who at the same time would welcome a change in leadership.

The C.-in-C., Navy, believes that it would be advisable to place a young Italian admiral who has the confidence of the officer in command of the Italian Navy, to be assisted by a German staff. *The Fuehrer* asks whether the C.-in-C., Navy, has an admiral in mind.   The C.-in-C., Navy, mentions Admiral Manfredi as his first choice, and Admiral Legnani as second.   *The Fuehrer* is very happy to learn these names, since he himself does not know any of the persons that would come in question.

*The C.-in-C., Navy,* declares that the attitude of the High Command in the employment of the Italian Fleet at the present time is infamous.   In spite of all his efforts, he was unable to get Admiral Riccardi to use his light forces to drive the enemy from the Straits of Messina, an intolerable situation, since he has the forces available to do so.   Admiral Riccardi is hoarding these light forces in case the battleships should put to sea.   The C.-in-C., Navy, believes that this will never be the case.   However, he, the C.-in-C., Navy, has no way of doing anything about the situation except to send telegrams.   Riccardi replies to these that he will submit them to the Duce.   At this point the Fuehrer exclaims : "The Duce is not getting them."

The C.-in-C., Navy, continues : "Later an answer arrives that for very subtle strategic reasons it is impossible to take the necessary steps.   The situation would be greatly improved if the present *Supermarina* would be done away with and a new command with a good German staff be put in its place.   This presupposes further, however, that we make an effort to win over the young officers in the garrisons, tell them what it is all about, and ask them whether they want to join or not.   The collaboration of the young officers is also needed because, in the event of new landing attempts, it is absolutely necessary to eliminate the enemy forces before they have successfully established a beachhead.   Otherwise, in view of their un-contested supremacy of the sea, they will be in a position to bring more troops to the scene than we.   We must not permit harbours with excellent dock installations to fall into the hands of the British, as was the case in Syracuse and Augusta.   If we want to hold Italy, German troops and German naval coast artillery must take over these harbours.   Otherwise Taranto and Naples may meet the same fate as Augusta."   *The Fuehrer* replies that he himself has been pondering the question how this might best be done.   The greatest problem is the demoralisation of the Italian Army, about which nothing has been done.   Only very severe measures, like those applied by Stalin in 1941 or by the French in 1917, will be of any avail.   If only individual units were affected, we could appeal to their sense of honour by offering medals, etc., but the whole army is in a state of collapse, and only barbaric measures can help to save the nation.

Therefore the Fuehrer believes that a sort of directorate, tribunal, or court-martial should be set up in Italy to remove undesirable elements. Some capable people must be left in Italy, for everything could not suddenly have turned evil.   He has already consulted Ambassador von Mackensen, but the latter could suggest no one capable of taking over the leadership.   The C.-in-C., Navy, expresses his opinion as follows : "I believe, my Fuehrer, that we either have to do without the Italian Army altogether, or we must try to strengthen it with German troops."   *The Fuehrer* replies : "Without the Italian Army we cannot defend the entire peninsula.   In that case we would have to withdraw to a relatively short line."   *Lt.-General Jodl* points out that this would have very serious repercussions in the Balkans.   *The C.-in-C., Navy,* replies : "That is why I believe that we must infiltrate our men into the Italian Army."

At this point Field Marshal Rommel enters, and *the Fuehrer* asks him whether he knows of any really capable persons in the Italian Army who are fully co-operating with Germany.   *Field Marshal Rommel* replies that there is no such person.   Ferrari Orsi would have qualified, but was killed in action.   At the present time Roatta would probably come closest, although he is not to be trusted and is without character.   The C.-in-C., Navy, says that he will again ask in Navy circles to see whether they might know of a suitable Army man.   The Fuehrer declares that everything depends on a radical change in the Italian situation.   If this can be brought about, it will be worth taking the risk.   If not, there is no point in throwing in additional German troops and thus engaging our last reserves.

Then follows a discussion of the measures that must be taken to safeguard the Straits of Messina, particularly the installation of medium and heavy coastal batteries.   In this connection Rear-Admiral Voss reports on the results of his trip to southern Italy and Messina.   *The Fuehrer* asks the C.-in-C., Navy, whether he thinks it would be worthwhile to station more submarines in Sicilian waters.   The C.-in-C., Navy, answers in the negative.   Above all we must keep in mind that at the present time it is impossible for submarines to get through the Straits of Gibraltar. Perhaps this situation may be changed by autumn.   He does not believe that we can radically change the situation at sea with the means at our disposal, in view of the tremendously superior forces of the Anglo-Saxons. Even our E-boats have lost their effectiveness due to a tenfold superiority of enemy gunboat flotillas.   Against light forces we can use only the Italian light forces.   Coastal batteries will be our only means of defence against enemy cruisers and battleships.   After a thorough discussion of the problem, the Fuehrer, C.-in-C., Navy, and Rear-Admiral Voss came to the conclusion that heavy batteries cannot be brought from other areas, since it would take too long to dismantle them and install them anew. Finally the Fuehrer asks Rear-Admiral Voss to look into the question of the 24-cm. guns.

*The C.-in-C., Navy*, expresses the opinion that we ought to give the British something new to worry about.   For this purpose he suggests that we begin laying our new mines in great numbers by the end of August. *The Fuehrer* repeatedly asserts that he is very much worried that the enemy in turn might use these new-type mines if he finds them.   This could easily be the case if the Air Force makes a mistake in dropping them. He is willing to let the Navy lay the new mines at any time, but you can never tell where the Air Force will drop them.   The C.-in-C., Navy, points out that experienced units of the Air Force, for example the IX Corps, were very successful in laying mines, and that with the proper training this could be done successfully even now.   For minelaying the navy must depend on E-boats which can lay 500 mines per month at the most, and that is not enough.   *The Fuehrer* replies to this: "All right, I agree, but I call attention to what can happen if the British should drop these mines in the Baltic Sea.   Then we are through."   He then orders that the possible effects of laying pressure mines in the Gulf of Taranto be explored.

In conclusion, *the C.-in-C., Navy*, reports that work on the antidestroyer torpedo has progressed to the point where it will be possible to equip submarines therewith in the beginning of August.   This torpedo was

completed two to three months earlier than he had expected.    He expects
to resume his attack in the North Atlantic by the end of August.    Following this *the Fuehrer* describes the demonstrations held at the Torpedo
Experimental Establishment in 1938, when the Navy and Air Force,
probably the only time they were ever in full agreement, tried to convince
him that it would not be advisable to develop an aerial torpedo force.
Those cleverly executed demonstrations made him abandon his plan to
build up a strong aerial torpedo force which could have been used as a
surprise measure at the outbreak of war.    He would have gone ahead with
those plans if the utter uselessness of this undertaking had not been proven
to him so expertly at that time by means of these wretched demonstrations.

(signed)        DOENITZ.
(countersigned) Lt. RUDOLPH.

\*        \*        \*        \*        \*        \*

The fears expressed at this conference of the possibility of Italy surrendering
to the Allies were very real, and on July 19 Hitler met Mussolini at Verona in an
effort to prevent the Italian collapse.    On July 25, however, Mussolini quietly
resigned, and Marshal Badoglio issued a proclamation that by the King's order he
had assumed the military government of Italy with full powers.

Hitler refused to accept the situation.    He thought that Fascism in Italy was still
strong enough to prevent a complete collapse and that Mussolini could still be
used as a puppet dictator—provided that German support was strong enough.    To
begin with, therefore, two operations were ordered.    The first—*Eiche*—was
concerned with the rescue of Mussolini, while the second—*Student* laid down
broad measures for the restoration of Fascism, and involved the occupation
of Rome.    Two other operations were also planned in the event of an Italian
armistice—*Achse* and *Schwarz*.    These operations provided for the capture
or destruction of the Italian Fleet, and the seizure by the German army of key
positions on land.    Hitler distrusted Badoglio, and was sure that he was intending
—if he had not already begun—secret negotiations with the Allies.    It was urgent,
therefore, that preparations for the four operations, *Eiche, Student, Achse,* and
*Schwarz* should be started immediately.

He called a conference on July 26.

C.-in-C., Navy                                        Berlin, August 5, 1943

### MINUTES TAKEN WHEN THE C.-IN-C., NAVY, VISITED THE FUEHRER ON JULY 26 TO 28, 1943

Also present: Rear-Admiral Machen (until July 27).
Rear-Admiral Wagner.
Lt.-Commander Freywald.
Lieutenant Hansen-Nootbar (until July 27).

1. Discussion of the war situation at the Headquarters of the Fuehrer,
July 27, 1943, at 1230.—A. It will very likely become necessary to occupy
Rome and to take a hand in the forming of the new Italian government in
order to bring forward those men who are willing to lend us their unquali-
fied support.    Plans have been made for the Army Group B, under the
command of Field Marshal Rommel, to enter Italy.    *The C.-in-C., Navy,*
states it will be necessary to seize the large ships of the Italian Fleet at
the same time or, at least, to prevent their passing into the hands of the
enemy.    He recommends that a naval detachment located at the submarine
base Spezia be placed under the command of a man of action, possibly
Rear-Admiral Meendsen-Bohlken.    The support of both the Army and

the Air Force would be required.   Submarines should guard the harbour entrance.   The possibility of evacuating Sicily and Sardinia at a later date is discussed.

B. *The Chief of the Armed Forces Operations Staff* recommends that Captain Junge be sent to Rome in order to inform Field Marshal Kesselring.   *The Fuehrer* agrees.   *The C.-in-C., Navy*, gives the following oral instructions to Captain Junge to pass on to Vice-Admiral Ruge:

(i) If Rome is occupied, the German Navy will immediately secure the Italian Fleet units in La Spezia, Taranto, and Genoa, as well as the Italian merchantmen in all ports.   While keeping our plans secret, preparations for the above should include a selection of trusted men in the Italian Navy.   Grossi and Sestini can be helpful.   The availability of our own forces must be studied to determine what reinforcements must be supplied by the Commander General, South.

(ii) The Commanding Officer of Submarines, Italy, shall station submarines off La Spezia making sure, however, that the Italians do not become aware of this.   Order.—They will destroy the large ships of the Italian Navy if the latter should leave without our approval.

(iii) The German Naval Command will supply the German troops which are stationed on the islands and will evacuate our troops from Sicily and Sardinia if this should become necessary.

(iv) If there should be a breakdown of communications in Italy, it will be of utmost importance to protect our bases, i.e. loading beaches. If necessary these will have to obtain their supplies and fuel by sea.

Captain Junge left for Rome in the afternoon of July 26.

C. Since the 11th Italian Army has already been placed under the command of the German Commanding General, South-east, the question was discussed whether the west coast of the Balkans should not be occupied exclusively by German troops.

2. In connection with the discussions of the general war situation which were held on the evening of July 26 and at noon and in the evening of July 27, the Fuehrer took up the Italian question with a select few.   The C.-in-C., Navy, took down the following notes:

A. The situation in Italy.—*The C.-in-C., Navy*, expressed his views as follows:   Italy must under no circumstances be abandoned.   No doubt there are a good many people in Italy who feel honour-bound to continue the war on our side.   These people must be aligned with us. It is my conviction that this group, which certainly includes a large number of younger Italian Navy officers, now feels less bound to the Fascist Regime but is loyal rather to the House of Savoy to which it is also bound by oath.   Our measures must therefore be so designed as not to give the impression that they are directed against the Royal House.   These elements do not accept most of the present and former military leaders because they did not pursue the war aggressively enough.

A removal of the present leaders by us might, nevertheless, have an undesirable effect on them if it is not skilfully engineered.   I doubt whether Fascism still means anything either to those who favour continuing the war on our side or to the Italian people themselves.   It is not to be expected that we can superimpose conditions on the Italian people. On the other hand, it is quite clear that the present Italian government will not keep on fighting in spite of its pretence.   We must forestall by all means any surprise action by the Anglo-Saxons.   All will depend on the correct timing of any contemplated action against the present Italian government. I believe there is still time and that it can be used by us for further strengthening our position in the Italian area by bringing in several more divisions.   As the situation develops we may find a better propagandist approach against the present government which, after all, still pretends to be fighting the war on our side, and is trying to maintain order and be considered the King's government.

*Rommel* and *Richthofen* agree with the C.-in-C., Navy, but *Jodl* is very outspoken that Fascism will be revived.   He recommends refraining from any action against the government but merely reinforcing our troops in Italy.   *Goering* and *Ribbentrop* take the same stand as the *Fuehrer*.   *Kesselring* believes that the present government is trustworthy and he is therefore against any interference on our part.   For views of Ruge see the attached report.

Views expressed by *the Fuehrer*: We must act at once.   Otherwise the Anglo-Saxons will steal a march on us by occupying the airports.   The Fascist Party is at the present only stunned and will rise up again behind our lines.   The Fascist Party is the only one that is willed to fight on our side.   We must therefore restore it.   All reasons advocating further delays are wrong; thereby we run the danger of losing Italy to the Anglo-Saxons.   These are matters which a soldier cannot comprehend.   Only a man with political insight can see his way clear.   Decision of *the Fuehrer*: The operation *Student* will be carried out as soon as possible.

B.  The Fuehrer and the C.-in-C., Armed Forces, make plans to evacuate Sicily.   The C.-in-C., Navy, is against it and repeatedly voices his objections.   The reasons given by the C.-in-C., Navy, are:

(i) We are holding our ground in Italy.   The British are making little progress.   Our Air Force must prevent them from bringing up supplies and reinforcements by destroying their ships.   We are engaging considerable forces of the enemy in Sicily.   If we withdraw, these forces and material will be released and become available for new landings.   This ever-present danger is increased through the uncertainty of knowing where such landings will be made.   The best means of preventing such new operations is by tying up the enemy forces in Sicily.

(ii) An easy conquest of Sicily will also be of great psychological value to the enemy, and he will surely make the best of it.

(iii) If we abandon Sicily we expose the route to the Balkans by way of southern Italy.   We must gain time to strengthen our position in the Balkans and in Italy with reinforcements.   Even if we can hold Sicily for only a short period, the time won will be of great strategical value to us.

*The Fuehrer* admits that much can be said for both sides of the question concerning the withdrawal from Sicily and therefore has not given his final decision.

[On July 27 Vice-Admiral Ruge made the following statement in answer to the instructions delivered to him orally that same day by Captain Junge:]

3.  "The resignation of Mussolini without offering any resistance whatsoever has brought about the almost complete collapse of the Fascist Party.

The situation is made worse by an acute food problem and chaotic traffic conditions. The new government is trying to assert itself and has taken positive steps which show its willingness to carry on the war. How long this attitude will prevail is hard to say. The Navy is backing the Royal House of Savoy. The younger officers reject most of the older leaders because the latter did not fight the war with enthusiasm. They are in favour of a more vigorous pursuit of the war, but cannot be counted on to support Fascism, at least not for the present. Fascism has lost its hold on the people completely. The operation *Student* might therefore find some support in scattered places, but will certainly be opposed by the Armed Forces and the majority of the people. This would lead to a complete disruption of communications, which are difficult to maintain as it is. Without the co-operation of the Italians the evacuation of our troops from the islands is entirely out of the question. In brief, I believe that the proposed plans, if carried out now, will alienate the great majority of those Italian forces which are still in existence. Thus Germany will be discredited before history, without having been able to effect a change in the situation."

*The C.-in-C., Navy*, presented this report to the Fuehrer in its entirety. *The Fuehrer* did not agree with Vice-Admiral Ruge's point of view.

4. During the general discussion of the war situation on July 27–28 the following matters which concern the Navy were brought up:

A. The Fuehrer wants the use of the aerial mine with the old primers discontinued until a new ignition is developed, at which time he considers an extensive use of the air mine essential.

B. Minister Speer receives orders to prepare a new position on the *Gotenkopf*.* The Fuehrer is fully aware of the fact that the abandonment of Novorossisk would greatly endanger our position on the Kerch Strait and in the Crimea.

C. The Navy is ordered to scatter the storage of torpedoes which are being kept without concrete shelter near the harbour of Canea, on Crete, so that they will be separated into small lots.

(signed)         DOENITZ.<br>(countersigned) Lt.-Comdr. MEJER.

*     *     *     *     *     *

During the next few days the situation worsened considerably. Mussolini was thrown into prison, the Allies were rapidly advancing in Sicily, and reports from Italy more than ever confirmed Hitler's suspicion of Badoglio. Besides these events, Allied operations in the Bay of Biscay had seriously disrupted the U-boat campaign, while air-raids on Hamburg had wrought havoc among the factories, docks, and civilian population. The situation in Italy posed three distinct problems for Hitler:

(*a*) How to restore Fascism and prevent the Italians from surrendering to the Allies.

(*b*) If Italy surrendered, how to minimise the effect of the surrender.

(*c*) The tactical problem of whether to abandon Sicily or to hold on as long as possible.

Hitler saw that if he could solve the first problem then the other two problems would cease to exist, and to him Mussolini was the key to the whole Italian

---

* Rear position to be constructed by Minister Speer's personnel on the Kuban Peninsula. The positions were designed to protect the Kerch Strait and keep open the sea routes to the Crimea as a result of the fall of Novorossisk to the Russian forces.)

situation.   If Mussolini was rescued and restored as Duce, Hitler was sure he would make short work of Badoglio and the King, and, with German support, would be able to reform the Fascists into a sufficiently effective force to withstand the Allies.   Operation *Eiche*—the rescue of Mussolini—was therefore given top priority.

By August 1 the second problem also became urgent as it was then certain that Badoglio was negotiating with the Allies.   Pending the success of operations *Eiche* and *Student* (Nazi infiltration into Italy) plans had to be made to ensure that as little as possible was lost if the surrender occurred suddenly.   The Italian Fleet was the most important item, and Doenitz was ordered to take all necessary steps to ensure that the ships were either captured or destroyed.   (Operation *Achse*.)   They were not on any account to be allowed to escape to the Allies. The second operation in the event of an Italian surrender, *Schwarz*, was closely linked with *Achse* and involved the military occupation of Italy.   However, the final stages of both operations were to be deferred until the outcome of *Eiche* and *Student* was known.

Meanwhile, as Badoglio was still bargaining with the Allies and co-operation still existed, every opportunity was to be taken to move German troops into Italy. On the question of Sicily, Hitler's staff was divided.   Doenitz and Rommel were in favour of hanging on, while Jodl and Kesselring wanted to retreat up the Italian peninsula to a more easily held position.   Hitler was unable to decide, and the Allies solved the problem for him by completing the capture of Sicily on August 17.

Throughout the first half of August these three problems were discussed endlessly at Hitler's Headquarters.   All depended on the success of *Eiche* and *Student*, and as the progress of these two operations fluctuated so orders were issued and cancelled and issued again, presenting a picture of confusion and indecision.

(The following time-table of events and notes of discussions were written up about six weeks after the events depicted, and relate to the problems as they affected the German Navy.)

C.-in-C., Navy                                    Berlin, September 15, 1943

**MINUTES OF CONFERENCE AT FUEHRER HEADQUARTERS, AUGUST 1 TO 3, 1943**

July 30, 1943.—Word is received from Admiral, Fuehrer's Headquarters, that relations with Italy are becoming more strained, since there are further indications that the Italian government is double-crossing us. Nevertheless, operation *Schwarz* is to be deferred, in order to permit pouring as many troops into Italy as possible while co-operation still continues.

July 31, 1943.—Chief of Operations Section, Naval Staff (Ia), is despatched to Rome with instructions for Ruge covering the following points :

1. Information about the situation.

2. Operation *Schwarz*.   It will be the task of the Navy to seize Italian warships and merchant vessels.

3. Methods for guaranteeing availability of fuel for German naval forces and transport facilities.   Bases.   Supplies from southern France.

4. Measures for instructing and equipping the scattered German marine troops.

5. Transfer of ships to the Aegean.

2230.   A call is received from the Admiral, Fuehrer's Headquarters, that the Fuehrer wishes to see the C.-in-C., Navy, at Headquarters.   The

C.-in-C., Navy, directs the Chief of Operations Division, Naval Staff, to accompany him.

August 1, 1943.—0930. Departure from Tempelhof. 1130. Arrival at Headquarters. 1230. At a conference with the Fuehrer, information is obtained from Engineer Desauer concerning the Duce's possible whereabouts. Thereafter the order is issued to the Navy, under Ruge, and the Air Force, under Student, to proceed with operation *Eiche*. This order is handed to General Student, who leaves August 2 at 0700. A copy of the order goes to Lt.-General Jodl. Movement of German troops into northern Italy continues. The Chief of Operations Section, Naval Staff (Ia), arrives in Berlin in the evening.

August 2, 1943.—1000. The Chief, Operations Section, Naval Staff (Ia), arrives at Headquarters. He reports on his trip to Rome. The main points covered are as follows:

1. Ruge's ill health—kidney trouble. Ruge himself had informed the C.-in-C., Navy, thereof in an official communication.
2. Italian warships can be seized only with the help of strong military forces (about one division each will be needed in Spezia and Taranto). No final decision has as yet been reached by Kesselring.
3. Stationing our submarines off Spezia involves grave risk of compromise.
4. The *Supermarina* is becoming increasingly mistrustful. The transfer of E-boats to Cotrone and Taranto, for example, has made the *Supermarina* suspicious, since this move was evidently not sufficiently justified by Ruge on military grounds.
5. The great risks involved in the passage of steamers through the Straits of Messina.
6. The general impression is that the various German officers understand the task at hand. They are, however, somewhat overwhelmed by the difficulties that must be dealt with and overcome by the weak and widely scattered units of the German Navy in the event of operation *Achse*.

After the conference the C.-in-C., Navy, has breakfast alone with the Fuehrer. The following notes are based on conversations which took place at that time:

1. *The C.-in-C., Navy*, explains that submarine warfare will remain very difficult until the new-type submarines are in operation. This is due to the overwhelming enemy Air Force, which has had another large increase since May and is making itself felt everywhere along the submarine routes and in their operational areas. *The Fuehrer* corroborates this observation. He believes, however, that we must continue submarine warfare in spite of this, otherwise large enemy defensive forces will be freed to undertake the offensive.
2. The terrific destruction in Hamburg and its effect on the war economy are discussed. *The Fuehrer* remarks that, in spite of the many devastating attacks on the Ruhr, production there has been cut by only 8 per cent. The workers in the Ruhr area have helped themselves in a remarkable manner by building shelters for their families. Miners are, of course, particularly tough. The C.-in-C., Navy, asserts: No matter how painful

the destruction is in Hamburg, we must strive to keep the factories going by providing housing for the workers.

3. *The Fuehrer* continues: The pursuit plane and anti-aircraft programme is functioning well. However, defensive operations alone are not enough. We must resume the offensive. However, we cannot do this as long as the resulting losses are too great, as is the case, for example, in submarine warfare at the present time.

4. The present predicament can be overcome only if we bear all hardships and do everything humanly possible to keep armament production going.

5. In connection with the situation in the Bay of Biscay, *the Fuehrer* remarks that Spain was ready to enter the war in 1940, and that only Italy's jealousy kept her from actually doing so.

The conference with the Chief, Operations Section (Ia), continues in the afternoon. The Chief, Operations Section (Ia), departs at 1730 to inform the Chief of Staff, Naval Staff, about the general situation and operation *Eiche*. On the basis of the report by the Chief, Operations Section (Ia), the C.-in-C., Navy, decides to call Rear-Admiral Meendsen-Bohlken to Headquarters at once. He is to be informed of the situation and sent to Rome to be at the disposal of Vice-Admiral Ruge. He is to be prepared to take over in case Ruge's health should make this necessary.

2000. Arrival of Rear-Admiral Meendsen-Bohlken. He receives instructions from the Chief of Operations Divisions, Naval Staff, and then from the C.-in-C., Navy, who tells him to have Vice-Admiral Ruge report at once on the following points:

1. Seizure of the Italian warships in the event of operation *Achse*.
(*a*) What means of his own he has at his disposal.
(*b*) To what extent the Army will have to help.
(*c*) What further provisions must be made by the Naval Staff for this task.
2. Provisions for the seizure of merchant vessels. Extent to which the anti-aircraft units afloat have been informed.
3. Extent to which the naval units on land have been informed.
4. Preparations made to ensure the proper employment of German naval forces. Safeguarding of certain bases. Movement of fuel, provisions, and munitions supplies from southern France.
5. Possibilities and intentions of transferring ships to the Aegean.
6. Preparations made for operation *Eiche*, including provisions for taking over the body, if necessary.
(Rear-Admiral Meendsen-Bohlken is to depart for Berlin on August 3, at 0800, for consultation with the Chief of Staff, Naval Staff, and the Chief, Operations Section (Ia). He has instructions to proceed to Rome by plane early August 4.)

In the afternoon, Aviation-Engineer Dessauer has a conference with the Fuehrer. He reports that a column of cars heavily guarded by Carabinieri, was sighted, but the Duce himself was not seen. During the evening session, the order is given to immediately bring Petty Officer Laurich unobtrusively from Gaeta to Headquarters via Berlin. He was mentioned by Dessauer as an additional witness. Furthermore, it is directed that operation *Eiche* be limited to Ventolene Island [*where reports indicated Mussolini was held.—Ed.*]. Orders are sent out accordingly.

August 3, 1943.—1230.  At the Fuehrer conference *Lt.-General Jodl* reports that the Italians have completely ceased resistance to our measures. During the discussion of the possible reasons for this, *the Fuehrer* advances the theory that they may just be biding their time in order to come to terms with the Anglo-Saxons before an open break with Germany.  Jodl and the C.-in-C., Navy, suggest that the Italians may feel helpless and therefore want to rely more on us again.  It remains to be seen what the actual situation is.  Operations *Achse*, *Eiche*, and *Schwarz* are not to be undertaken yet.

1500.  The C.-in-C., Navy, visits the Fuehrer once more and makes the suggestion that readiness for operation *Eiche* be put on 48 hour's notice.  He requests permission to leave for Berlin.  *The Fuehrer* agrees as far as operation *Eiche* is concerned.  In view of the fact that the C.-in-C., Navy, can be recalled to Headquarters within a few hours, the Fuehrer reluctantly consents to his departure.  1615.  Departure from Fuehrer Headquarters for Berlin.  1835.  Arrival at Tempelhof.  In the afternoon a message is received from Vice-Admiral Ruge that everything will be ready for operation *Eiche* by August 6.  Whether everything can be ready by the 4th will be apparent only by the evening of the 3rd.

August 4, 1943.—Forenoon.  A long-distance call is received from the Admiral at the Fuehrer's Headquarters.  The Fuehrer requests the C.-in-C., Navy, to reduce the time of preparation for the operation *Eiche* to 24 hours, or to as short a period as possible.  A corresponding inquiry is sent by wire to the Admiral, German Naval Command, Italy.

1000.  Captain Bramesfeld, who is the Chief of Staff, German Naval Command, Italy, makes his report to the C.-in-C., Navy.  Rear-Admiral Meendsen-Bohlken is also present.  The following points come up for discussion:

1. The possible evacuation of Sicily and Sardinia.—The evacuation of Sicily will present no difficulties as long as southern Italy remains in German hands.  However, at present only night traffic is possible since fighter bombers are a serious threat by day.  The evacuation of our troops from Sardinia to Corsica will take from 10 to 14 days, provided that the weather is favourable and there is no interference by the enemy.

2. Ships required for these operations.—The C.-in-C., Navy, decides that half of the German tonnage in the Tyrrhenian Sea, exclusive of small vessels, is to be transferred to the Aegean Sea.  Vice-Admiral Ruge is given orders to report which ships are to be released and how their transfer is to be accomplished.

3. Operation *Achse*.

(*a*) The provisioning of our forces seems assured.  If the Naval Staff is called upon to give assistance, such a request should be initiated by the German Naval Command, Italy.

(*b*) The seizure of the Italian ports and warships must be carried out by armed forces, but the Navy will provide "pilots."

(c) It will be the task of the specially assigned anti-aircraft detachments to safeguard the ships. These detachments should therefore be reinforced in so far as possible. Ships stationed in the harbours without such German detachments on board must be seized at the time the respective harbours are taken over.

4. The C.-in-C., Navy, discusses the necessity of having all German naval commands, even the smallest, prepared to take independent action in case the situation in Italy becomes serious, that they must do their utmost in defending the honour of the German flag to the last man.

August 5, 1943.—The Admiral at the Fuehrer's Headquarters reports that, according to additional information from the *Reichsfuehrer S.S.* only the island Ventolene needs to be considered for operation *Eiche*. A wire from Vice-Admiral Ruge states that a minimum of 48 hours is required for the preparation of *Eiche* if armed forces are to carry on their regular assignments to a limited extent.

Afternoon. After reporting this to the Fuehrer, the Admiral at the Fuehrer's Headquarters transmits the former's approval.

August 6, 1943.—1345. The Admiral at the Fuehrer's Headquarters reports that the *Reichsfuehrer S.S.* has sent information that the Italians are holding a destroyer in readiness for removal of the "valuable object" in case of an emergency. The destroyer is said to be stationed at Gaeta. The Fuehrer wishes to have the C.-in-C., Navy, informed at once, asking him to re-examine the distribution of the Italian destroyers. Preventive measures must be taken at once; he suggests the use of submarines. 1400. The Admiral at the Fuehrer's Headquarters telephones that the Fuehrer has no objection to a blockade of Ventolene harbour by submarines.

After consultation, the C.-in-C., Navy, decides to send the following reply: An inconspicuous blockade of the harbour, even by submarines, is impossible since it would have to stand right off the harbour entrance. Likewise, he knows of no inconspicuous means with which to render the destroyer at its present anchorage harmless. The C.-in-C., Navy, therefore advises against a blockade, not because of its impossibility, but in order to prevent our intentions from being recognised prematurely. If the Italians become aware of our plans, they will certainly remove the "valuable object" secretly, e.g. by motor boat, to a different place. The only possible military solution exists in forestalling the Italians, but such a step will have serious consequences. It is not within the province of the C.-in-C., Navy, to make decisions in such matters.

1630. The above report is forwarded to the Admiral at the Fuehrer's Headquarters. 1830. Answer from the Admiral at the Fuehrer's Headquarters: "The Fuehrer will reconsider the matter." A telegraphic message from Admiral de Courten informing us of his intention to take the offensive with his cruisers and to reinforce the troops on the islands off Naples and north of it, is transmitted to the Admiral at the Fuehrer's Headquarters. The C.-in-C., Navy, comments that if Admiral de Courten actually carries out the contemplated offensive, he would interpret this as proof of a sincere desire for co-operation.

August 8, 1943.—Laurich, PO/2c, reports to the C.-in-C., Navy, who decides that Laurich shall fly with him the next day to the Fuehrer's Headquarters. He is put under oath to observe absolute secrecy.

August 9, 1943.—The C.-in-C., Navy, leaves for the Fuehrer's Headquarters accompanied by the Chief of Operations Division, Naval Staff, and the Aide of the C.-in-C., Navy. 1330. A report was made on the general war situation, which was followed by a discussion of the situation in Italy. The entry of our troops into Italy has been marked by an ever increasing number of incidents still of minor importance. Distrust is mounting. The Fuehrer is convinced that both the King of Italy and the Badoglio Government are planning treachery. He is struck by the increased activity of the Italian Navy, e.g. their success at Gibraltar, sorties of their cruisers, and new minelaying operations. The C.-in-C., Navy, believes that the Italian Navy is probably not informed about any political intrigues because an influential group of officers has accused the former High Command of inactivity. *The Fuehrer* gives orders that General Student and Captain von Kamptz be called at once to the Fuehrer's Headquarters.

*The C.-in-C., Navy,* reports to a select few about the situation of the submarine warfare. The C.-in-C., Navy, has breakfast with the Fuehrer and the Ministers Dr. Goebbels and von Ribbentrop. At supper the same group is present.

Afternoon. Conference of the Chief of Operations Division, Naval Staff, with Captain Junge. 2230. After the general war situation has been discussed, *Laurich, PO/2c,* makes his report before a select few. Present are besides the Fuehrer, the C.-in-C., Navy, the Minister of Foreign Affairs, the *Reichsmarschall,* the *Reichsfuehrer S.S.,* Field Marshal Keitel, Ambassador Hevel, the Admiral at the Fuehrer's Headquarters, the Chief of Operations Division, Naval Staff, and Captain von Puttkamer. The Fuehrer dismisses him with the words "Well done, my boy." Then follows a long discussion concerning the operation *Eiche* and Italy.

[Petty Officer Laurich, in a German escort vessel in Italy, had received information from a friendly Italian officer that the Duce had been sent to Ventolene. He had zealously reported this to his Commanding Officer, and Hitler had insisted on interviewing him personally.—*Ed.*]

Result of the conference.—An early execution of the operation *Eiche* appears necessary. The general conviction is that Mussolini is on San Stefano. Therefore the action will be confined to this island. An aerial photograph shows that the only possible access to the island, by means of steps and a road cut into the rocks, can easily be secured. The rest of the coast is practically inaccessible because of cliffs over 150 feet high. The question, whether the use of parachutists is preferable to a landing along the coast, is debated at length. The C.-in-C., Navy, considers a sea landing, at an unguarded spot at night, the only possibility that promises success. An alternative, in case the landing party cannot get through, the use of parachutists and support by the Air Force might be planned. *The Fuehrer* points out the necessity of covering the operation with several submarines. Under given circumstances it may become necessary to deny, at least temporarily, any part played by the Navy and Air Force in order to give the impression that the deed was accomplished by local Fascists.

Thereupon *the Fuehrer* expresses his views on the Italian situation in detail. He calls it shameful the way the Duce has been treated after he had directed the destinies of Italy for twenty years and had been hailed by all of Italy during this time. He especially criticises the attitude of the King, and speaks about the lack of responsibility among many rulers who rely upon unscrupulous historians to touch up their record and who therefore fail to recognise their accountability before history. The Fuehrer feels the predicament of the Duce all the more due to the close ties of friendship which exist between them. The Fuehrer still considers the Italian Government as being extremely unreliable and, on the basis of recent events, believes it capable of almost any kind of treason.

August 10, 1943.—1230. During the discussion of the general war situation, *Lt.-General Jodl* proposes the evacuation of Sicily. He is convinced that it cannot be held because of insufficient manpower and increasing difficulties with supplies. These deficiencies will increase when traffic in Italy comes to a complete standstill as a result of the operations *Eiche* and *Achse*. We can no longer fight on the islands. *The C.-in-C., Navy*, objects very strongly to this proposal because, in doing so, we would voluntarily abandon an extremely important position. We will thereby release strong enemy forces for further thrusts in the direction of the main line of attack: southern Italy–Balkan Peninsula. The southern part of Calabria and Apulia will then likewise become untenable. Furthermore the possibility of being cut off by an enemy landing in central Italy remains, so that little is gained by an evacuation of Sicily, but much would be lost which can never be recovered. Defence of the bridgehead Sicily is still justifiable on the basis of current political events.

*The Fuehrer* is of the opinion that the C.-in-C., Navy, would doubtlessly be right if Italy had a reliable government. However, this is not so. The pro and con are discussed at great length but no decision is reached. The Fuehrer suggests during the evening of August 9 that aerial photographs of St. Stefano should be made. Since it is doubtful whether the Chief, O.K.W., has given the necessary order, Colonel Christian is asked to request the Chief of General Staff of the Air Force High Command to take the necessary steps.

August 11, 1943.—1230. After reviewing the general war situation, the Italian problem is discussed again at great length. *The Fuehrer* states: The Italians will not show their true colours until the presumed trip of Grandi to Lisbon or the meeting of Churchill and Roosevelt in Canada has produced results. The Italians are going ahead with their negotiations at full speed. They will be taken in by any promise of the Anglo-Saxons if only the continued rule of the Royal House is guaranteed. Their negotiations are treasonable. They go along with us in order to gain time. The Italian Army cannot be used in combat against the Allies. In contrast to former occasions, they have not appealed to us for military support in connection with the meeting at Tarvisio, but remained completely inactive. During our last meeting at the station, the Duce suddenly remarked: "I don't know how my generals reason, where they want to defend Italy and why they keep such strong forces in northern Italy!" On the other hand it is quite conceivable that they themselves are becoming frightened since they realise they face two great dangers: capitulation or communism. The one and only point that speaks against treason is the fact that the Crown Prince has sent his children to north-western upper Italy. However, if the Government remains on our side, there exists the danger of an uprising among the people.

*Lt.-General Jodl* still maintains that Sicily must be abandoned because the German forces in southern Italy must concentrated in view of the danger of an attack near Naples. *The C.-in-C., Navy*, is in favour of our holding on to Sicily since we don't know yet:

(*a*) Whether the Italians will commit treason.

(*b*) When they might do it.

(*c*) Whether it would then be possible to return our troops even from southern Italy, in which case it would be better to have our men in Sicily. The evacuation means an irreparable loss of this strategically important position which should not be undertaken while present developments are obscure but only when we have no alternative.

*Field Marshal Rommel* is of the same opinion. *The Fuehrer* believes that the enemy will not attack the Italian mainland if Italy remains loyal, but possibly Sardinia. However, his intuition tells him that Italy is planning treason.

*Field Marshal Rommel* suggests frank negotiations, the removal of German divisions from the Rome area in order to ease the pressure on the Italians, and the proposal of a common defence plan, including Sicily. In this manner they will be forced to commit themselves. *The C.-in-C., Navy*, believes that we ought not to show our hand sooner than necessary in order that we may utilise the time to best advantage before a political decision is reached. *The Fuehrer* replies that everything so far indicates treason. Clarification of the situation now becomes imperative. Rommel shall negotiate.

Subsequently *the Fuehrer* discusses indications which point to growing differences between the Anglo-Saxons and the Russians: the recall of Maisky and Litvinoff; the meeting of Churchill and Roosevelt without Stalin. The Anglo-Saxons do not wish to see Russia in Finland, nor, under any circumstances, to have Russia improve her sea communications with the Atlantic in the North; Poland is to be restored; the Russians shall not come near the Bosphorus and shall be kept out of the Balkans as well as Iran and Iraq. These reasons are enough to nettle Stalin.

1445. The C.-in-C., Navy, has breakfast with the Fuehrer together with von Ribbentrop, Himmler, Rommel, and Jodl. 1300. Captain von Kamptz arrives. During the afternoon he is brought up to date on the discussions concerning the operation *Eiche* and reports on his own preparations which seem to promise success for the operation. Contrary to previous deliberations, he is of the opinion that the removal of the "valuable object" by submarine takes too much time and is therefore dangerous; he proposes transportation by aircraft.

2045. The C.-in-C., Navy, has supper with the Fuehrer. 2130. Discussion of the general war situation:

(*a*) An aerial photograph of St. Stefano is presented. It gives a clear picture of many important details on the island.

(*b*) The Rommel-Jodl defence plan for Italy which is to be used as a basis for discussions with the Italian leaders and which is intended to clarify the situation, is presented.   This plan calls for continued resistance in Sicily, the southern tip of Calabria, and Apulia, as well as in several defensive positions strung across the island.   The northernmost and main defensive position is to be at the southern slope of the Apennine Mountains.   Protection against landings is to be given by motorised reserve troops.   *The Fuehrer* agrees.   In regard to Sicily and the southern tip of Italy he makes no definite decision but wishes to have the various solutions considered as possible choices.   The military discussions shall be started immediately and shall be carried out by Rommel and Jodl.

(c) Following the review of the general war situation details of the operation *Eiche* are discussed.   Present: The Fuehrer, the C.-in-C., Navy, Himmler, Ribbentrop, Jodl, Student, Hevel, Wagner, von Kamptz, von Puttkamer, Scherf.   As a result, the following orders are given:

1. General Student is put in charge of the whole operation.   The command of the naval and army forces remains unchanged, namely, von Kamptz and the commanding officers of the 1st Parachute Regiment.   Further preparations and final instructions will follow later.   The final order will be given by the Fuehrer.

2. The operation is to be limited to St. Stefano:   Only in case M. is not found there and his actual whereabouts have become known, will a new action be undertaken immediately by parachutists against the new site.   Participation of the naval forces will have to be improvised accordingly.   For this purpose special code words are given for Ventolene and Ponza.

3. Regardless of other assignments, one anti-aircraft corvette and possibly more minesweepers and E-boats are to be added to the naval forces already agreed upon in order to have sufficient transportation for parachutists and liberated fascists.

4. From 100 to 200 parachutists are to jump from troop-carrying gliders and small gliders and to land soon after dawn.   These will be followed by additional forces coming in from the sea.   If necessary, the way for the troops landed from the sea must be cleared by the parachutists.

5. The *Wuerzburg* radar station in Ventolene is to be given secret orders not to take radar-bearings of aircraft on this day.   Part of the crew is therefore to be relieved by men who have received the new instructions.   The relieved men shall be questioned about St. Stefano, particularly about cables, wireless station, other observations made, and rumours among the population.   It may be advisable to send the commanding officer of the 1st Parachute Regiment in anti-aircraft uniform to enable him to survey the location.

6. The most important liberated men shall be flown by seaplane to Pratica, near Ostia, and from there to Germany by land-based plane.   Other liberated men are to be brought to southern France by submarine as quickly as possible.

7. In order to make all the facilities of the 2nd Air Force available to General Student without revealing the secret to more persons, he will be charged with the duties of Richthofen who during that time will be called to the Fuehrer's Headquarters for report.

8. The Fuehrer himself will give the necessary orders to the Chief of the General Staff, Air, for the relief of the *Wuerzburg* personnel, the dispatch of seaplanes, and the recall of Richthofen.

Captain von Kamptz is given orders to convey point 3 as an order of the C.-in-C., Navy, to the Admiral, German Naval Command, Italy.

(signed) G. WAGNER

## CONVERSATIONS WITH THE FUEHRER AT THE FUEHRER'S HEADQUARTERS BETWEEN AUGUST 9 AND 11, 1943

*The Fuehrer.*—We shall overcome the air menace by employing new methods of defence and by expanding our anti-aircraft and fighter defences. This we must do, for the people are under a severe strain. Those who are not needed in the cities for war work must get out of the cities. Small houses will be built in very large numbers. They are to have a bedroom for the parents, another one for the children, with double-decker bunks, and a place for cooking. We shall succeed in keeping up our armament programme; the new defensive weapons which technology is providing will make the air raids too costly and will cause them to be discontinued. The present situation is perilous and the coming months will bring hardships; however, there are many instances in history, when an unexpected way out presented itself in the midst of a difficult situation such as ours. As our difficulties mount, the conflicting objectives of the Allies increase and become more evident. Maisky and Litvinov have been recalled unexpectedly. The war aims of Moscow and the German Committee have caused the British to sit up and listen, and they are commented upon uneasily by responsible British newspapers. There is danger of an expansion of Russian power into the heart of Europe. I have no doubt whatsoever that the Anglo-Saxons are still ruthlessly bent upon our annihilation. Actually the British have manœuvred themselves into an awkward position. They entered the war in order to preserve the balance of power in Europe. Meanwhile Russia has awakened and, from the viewpoint of technological and material advancement, developed into a great power, which now constitutes more of a menace than in the past. Only if all of Europe is united under a strong central power, can there be any security for Europe from now on. Small wars cannot be fought without strong air forces. Small countries are in no position to maintain such forces. That means that in the future the challenge of the East can be met only by a Europe united under German leadership. This will be to the advantage of Britain also.

*The C.-in-C., Navy,* is of the opinion that the British must hold themselves in readiness in the eastern Mediterranean against a possible Russian thrust in the direction of the Balkans. In that area the interests of Britain and Russia clash sharply. This war has strongly impressed England with the importance of the Mediterranean to her existence. In the future she will wish to make the sea route through the Mediterranean fully secure; under no conditions will she give up Sicily and North Africa again, and under no conditions will she tolerate that the Russians get a foothold in the Dardanelles. *The Fuehrer* agrees. The Russians are aware of this opposition. Britain, furthermore, is interested in seeing Finland and the Baltic countries restored. All this shows quite clearly the discrepancies between the war aims of Britain and Russia. In North Africa, in turn, Britain and America do not see eye to eye. Britain will want to keep North Africa. America does not approve of that. Even though today the

Anglo-Saxons are still determined to annihilate us, favourable political developments are by no means impossible in the future.

*The C.-in-C., Navy:* As far as we are concerned, everything will depend on our holding out stubbornly. We are much better off with regard to food than we were in 1918. In addition, we have the great psychological asset of the unity of the German people. Being our most precious possession, this unity must be maintained religiously. I believe that there are numerous groups among the German people who lack stamina and easily become critical without being able to improve conditions or even to comprehend them fully. *The Fuehrer:* It is hardly possible for me to speak to the German people now. I am not in a position to express my views on the Italian question. If I should do so in an approving manner, I would lend support to the circles who are even now preparing for treachery. Nor can I speak out against the present Government of Italy, for well-known military reasons. However, I cannot ignore the problem of Italy either, since that would be interpreted as a sign of internal and external weakness. As soon as the Italian question has been clarified one way or the other, I shall be in a much better position to address the German people. As to the food situation, Backe considers it safe to announce to the public even at this early moment that there will be more bread in the future, and perhaps more fat also. Since Backe has always been very conservative in his estimates, I see no reason why I should not publicise that now. *The C.-in-C., Navy:* I do not believe for a moment that the British intend to fight in Europe on a wide front. The British shrink from heavy losses. They will look for strategic bases, possibly Norway, or for air bases. *The Fuehrer:* Yes, and they are still facing the war with Japan. Besides, the war is not very popular in the U.S.A., and heavy losses will not make it any more popular. We just have to gather all our faith and all our strength and act.

*Note by the C.-in-C., Navy:* The enormous strength which the Fuehrer radiates, his unwavering confidence, and his far-sighted appraisal of the Italian situation have made it very clear in these days that we are all very insignificant in comparison with the Fuehrer, and that our knowledge and the picture we get from our limited vantage are fragmentary. Anyone who believes that he can do better than the Fuehrer is silly.

(signed)          DOENITZ.

(countersigned) Lt.-Comdr. MEYER.

\*       \*       \*       \*       \*       \*

During the following week the political situation in Italy remained fluid, and Hitler decided to postpone operation *Eiche*. In any case it was not yet certain where the Italians were holding Mussolini. Reports indicated that he had been moved to Sardinia, but while his whereabouts was still in doubt it meant that an unnecessarily large number of troops and ships would be required to cover all possibilities. The new Italian government, under Marshal Badoglio, were still co-operating with Germany, and Hitler evidently decided that rather than risk forcing them into opposition (which would be the inevitable result of *Eiche*) he would take advantage of the present lull to continue pouring German troops into Italy. Rommel and Jodl had discussed a common defence plan with the Italian Generals Roatta and Rossi, but had achieved little other than securing an assurance of non-intervention and the safety of German supply lines from the Italians.

Meanwhile in other theatres the war continued. Hamburg was now practically a daily target for Allied air forces, and Doenitz became seriously concerned about the morale of its citizens. He reported his views to Hitler on August 19, and suggested that Hitler should make a "blood, toil, tears, and sweat" speech. Doenitz also reported his intention to begin the U-boat campaign again at the end of September.

C.-in-C., Navy

### MINUTES OF CONFERENCES AT THE FUEHRER HEADQUARTERS ON AUGUST 19, 1943

1. *The C.-in-C., Navy*, reports to the Fuehrer privately on visit of the shipyards at Hamburg. The general feeling of the people is one of depression, in spite of their willingness to work. Everybody sees only the many reverses. In view of the impressions I gained from my visit in Hamburg and on the basis of many reports and intelligence, I believe it is very urgent that the Fuehrer speak to the people very soon. I consider this to be absolutely necessary in view of the current difficult war situation; the entire German nation longs for it. *The Fuehrer* says that he intends to speak, but that he must wait until the Italian situation is clarified. The C.-in-C., Navy: The questions which the workers in Hamburg asked were typical. They wanted revenge for the air raids, and asked: "How well are we prepared for defence against further raids?" I believe that the workers are willing to work but they are beginning to ask themselves what there is to be gained if in future air raids all their work is smashed again. I did not tell the workers when we would start to retaliate or that our defences would be improved in the near future, and gave as the reason that I would be working into the hands of the enemy if I were to tell them. I believe it is necessary to tell the German people that they must show patience and fortitude, that they cannot always expect to hear when and how conditions will improve, and that they have no right to give up if they are not told these things. The latter would merely confirm the well-established British opinion that they can bear up under the air raids because they can endure hardships while the Germans, on the other hand, are more like the Italians in this respect. Therefore I believe that we must appeal to German pride and honour without making promises or raising hopes which later cannot be fulfilled.

I believe that the air raids can hardly endanger our essential industries in a material way. I saw machines standing right next to a bomb crater in the machine shops of the Hamburg shipyards. Even though the bomb scored a direct hit on a shop, the machines were absolutely undamaged, since the effect of the explosion seems to act not horizontally but vertically. It seems that steel construction with glass roofs is advantageous because the roofs shatter immediately and thus have no concentrating effect. Thus I believe that it is possible and necessary to maintain ship construction in the large western shipyards, in spite of the air raids, in so far as it is necessary that such facilities be located near the water. Only plants that do not require a location near the water should be moved. I thus believe that it is possible on the whole to preserve our armament programme, but think that the most important thing is to keep up confidence, and with that the will to work, and the spirit of the worker.

Therefore, we do not have to succumb to the air raids, but we might if the morale of the worker suffers from them and in consequence our production decreases.   I am of the opinion that we now have to inspire strength in the people and I keep telling my officers that this now is our solemn duty toward our soldiers as well as toward the entire German people.   In my opinion the greatest danger arises when the intelligentsia starts to utter their opinions in a wise and important manner.   These opinions are false most of the time, since these people see only part of what is going on and do not have an overall picture.   They do untold harm, since they weaken the will to resist.   By senseless chatter these people help to bring about the destruction of the very things which are dear to them.   Everything should be done to correct this state of affairs.

*The Fuehrer* listened very intently to these statements from the C.-in-C., Navy, and agreed with him.   The symptoms of weakness must be eradicated since they strengthen the enemy's will to attack us.   The C.-in-C., Navy, concluded by saying that he considered it his duty to report his very deep concern to the Fuehrer and that he therefore asked to be heard privately.   The Fuehrer thanked him very warmly.

2. *The C.-in-C., Navy*, reports on the *Metox* radiations which may have been responsible for grievous losses.   These radiations may explain all the uncanny and unsolved mysteries of the past, such as the enemy avoiding traps set for him, and losses on the open seas while comparatively few U-boats were destroyed during convoy attacks because the *Metox* was always turned off then.   Future experiences will prove whether the assumption is justified that the *Metox* is responsible for the majority of our losses.   The C.-in-C., Navy, reports that attacks on convoys in the North Atlantic are scheduled again for the end of September.   He hopes that an improvement of the weapons will again enable us to fight, but that the struggle will no doubt continue to be a hard one.   *The Fuehrer* listens with utmost interest to these explanations.   He believes that the theory just advanced does account for many baffling facts, such as the ability of the enemy frequently to determine the exact number of submarines in a patrol.   With this discovery the Fuehrer believes that a great step forward has been made.   [Later on the same day the German Ambassador to Italy gave his views to Doenitz.]

Conference with Ambassador von Mackensen.—Mackensen expresses his views concerning conditions in Italy.   There is dissatisfaction in Fascist circles and confidence in the Duce's direction of the war has vanished.   The Fascist Council voted without realising the consequences. Not even the Duce was aware of conditions.   It remained for the King to make the Duce aware of the state of affairs that even his Fascist Party had lost faith in him.   Following this the Duce offered his resignation and asked for a guarantee of safety for himself and his family.   The King agreed, and the Duce then was allegedly placed in protective custody. Mackensen believes that Badoglio had no previous knowledge of the entire affair.   He says that the longing for peace is widespread among the Italian people, but that the present Government is willing to continue the fight because the impossibility of obtaining peace without making all of Italy a battlefield is realised.   Mackensen states that present conditions do not warrant a pessimistic attitude; that the Fuehrer was seeing matters in a more pessimistic manner than, in his opinion, was justified.   He could, of course, offer no proof that he was right and the Fuehrer wrong.

(signed)          DOENITZ.
(countersigned) Lt.-Comdr. MEJER.

\*         \*         \*         \*         \*         \*

On September 3 Marshal Badoglio signed an Armistice with the Allies, not to be announced until September 8.   On September 9 the Allies landed in strength on the Italian mainland at Salerno.   German plans were ready for all these events, and operations *Achse* and *Schwarz* were immediately started.   Ports and ships were seized, the Italian battleship Roma sunk, and key points on land occupied by the German Army.   Part of the Italian Fleet, however, managed to escape to the Allies as Doenitz had not been able to cover all ports adequately.

Also on September 9 Mussolini was definitely located in the Villa Weber, outside Maddalena in Sardinia.   He was closely guarded by the local Carabinieri.   Operation *Eiche* commenced that evening, and Mussolini was in German hands shortly after midnight.   Following the success of *Eiche*, operation *Student* was ordered, and a puppet Fascist Government of Italy was set up under Mussolini by September 23.   Thus the situation at the end of September was that Central and Northern Italy were nominally under the puppet government but virtually under German martial law.

By ruthless action Hitler had managed to prevent the Italian collapse from becoming a total disaster, and paved the way for what was to become one of the longest and most bitter campaigns of the war.

# The Eastern Front, Denmark, the Atlantic, and the Aegean

WHILE HITLER was busy saving what he could out of the Italian collapse, the Russians began their offensive on the Eastern Front. Retreat was difficult, and naval aid was needed both to evacuate troops across the Sea of Azov, and to assist in building up the Crimea as a key defensive position. At the same time the Underground Movement in Denmark increased its activities to such an extent that an ultimatum was sent to the Danes threatening them with full military occupation if these activities did not stop. A joint naval and military operation—*Safari*—was planned against Denmark, and was actually started, though the disturbances had already calmed down by the time the army moved in.

C.-in-C., Navy

**MINUTES OF THE CONFERENCES OF THE C.-IN-C., NAVY, AND THE CHIEF OF STAFF, NAVAL STAFF, AT FUEHRER HEADQUARTERS, ON AUGUST 28 AND 29, 1943**

I. WAR SITUATION REPORT TO THE FUEHRER. AUGUST 28, 1943, AT 1215

At the outset of the conference *the Fuehrer* orders the C.-in-C., Navy, to send all available naval forces, including naval coastal artillery lighters (MAL), minesweepers, and E-boats into the Sea of Azov to assist the Army in checking a strong penetration along the Mius Front, a move which also threatens the southern wing on the Sea of Azov. (An order to this effect is transmitted by teletype at 1615 by the Chief of Staff, Naval Staff, to the Chief, Operations Division, Naval Staff.) Futhermore, the Fuehrer orders immediate occupation of Toulon by the German Armed Forces, since there is every indication that Italy is making preparation for an uprising against us in Toulon. At 1645 the Chief of Staff, Naval Staff, sends a similar order to the Chief, Operations Division, Naval Staff, by teletype. [Toulon had been occupied by the Italians in November, 1942, and its seizure by the Germans was to forestall any difficulties arising out of the Italian collapse.—*Ed.*]

Following the discussion of the general war situation, *the C.-in-C., Navy,* presents the problems growing out of the plans for an East Wall on Lake Peipus. He calls special attention to probable effects on naval warfare in the Baltic Sea generally, on warfare in the Gulf of Finland, and the menace to the Estonian oil-shale region. *The Fuehrer* fully agrees with the views of the C.-in-C., Navy. Also Lt.-General Jodl supports the demands made by the C.-in-C., Navy. Therefore the Fuehrer declares that the construction of the East Wall on Lake Peipus is meant only as a precautionary measure. He certainly does not intend to withdraw the North Front so far. In this connection *Lt.-General Jodl* advocates the complete destruction of Leningrad by the Air Force, and the elimination of Kronstadt as well.

II. CONFERENCE BETWEEN THE CHIEF OF STAFF, NAVAL STAFF, AND LT.-GENERAL JODL. AUGUST 28, 1943, AT 1900

*The Chief of Staff, Naval Staff*, tells Lt.-General Jodl about the reports that have come in during the late afternoon from the Naval Command, Baltic, about developments in Denmark. According to these reports, the Danish government rejects the ultimatum of the German plenipotentiary, Dr. Best. Therefore the *Safari* measures are being put into effect. In this connection it becomes evident that during the last three days Lt.-General Jodl has received his information about developments in Denmark only through the reports of the Naval Staff. Neither the Ministry of Foreign Affairs nor the Commander, Armed Forces, Denmark, has kept him informed, since they considered the matter purely political. Jodl states that he will take the matter in hand at once in view of the fact that *Safari* has got under way and hopes to have a full report on the situation from the Commander, Armed Forces, Denmark, in the course of the evening.

III. During supper the Chief of the German Press informs a small group of those present that the Bulgarian King died that afternoon.

IV. EVENING WAR SITUATION REPORT TO THE FUEHRER. AUGUST 28, 1943

*The Chief, General Staff, Army*, proposes to the Fuehrer that the Mius Front be pulled back because of strong enemy pressure. *The Fuehrer* agrees. Furthermore, the Fuehrer decides that Toulon is to be occupied on August 29. After this, the Fuehrer is informed of the latest developments in Denmark. Since the situation seems comparatively quiet, the Fuehrer asks: "Why then all this to-do about Denmark?" He addresses the Minister of Foreign Affairs, who sits somewhat apart, as follows: "My dear Foreign Director, what do you have to say about this?" Ribbentrop replies that the whole thing is purely a political question and it would have been better if the Commander, Armed Forces, had kept out of it altogether. This the Fuehrer dismisses with the remark that it was a matter of military concern. Ribbentrop contends that it is still possible to stop operation *Safari* even though the troops are already on the march. The Fuehrer refuses to consider withdrawal from an action once it has begun. We cannot keep changing our orders according to our whims. Upon this, Ribbentrop remarks that sooner or later we would probably have had to resort to these measures anyhow.

V. THE DANISH SITUATION

Late in the evening of August 28 a message is received to the effect that the Danish Fleet has been ordered to be ready for action on 15 minutes' notice. The Fuehrer is afraid that the Danes might make a break for Sweden. The Chief of Staff, Naval Staff, informs Admiral Voss, who is supposed to report to the Fuehrer on our preparations, that if everything goes as planned, the Navy could be ready for operation *Safari* at 2 o'clock that night at the earliest. The Chief of Staff, Naval Staff, calls attention to the fact that the Danish naval forces are widely dispersed.

Furthermore, there has been little time for putting into effect recent changes in the plans for operation *Safari*; the operation will have to be carried out by training units of the Navy; and finally, the weather can do a great deal to interfere with the perfect execution of the plans.   After his conference with the Fuehrer, Admiral Voss reports that the Fuehrer was fully aware of the difficulties involved.   In the meantime the O.K.W. issued orders scheduling the operation for 0400 on August 29.

VI. AFTERNOON WAR SITUATION REPORT TO THE FUEHRER.   AUGUST 29, 1943

The situation on the southern sector of the Eastern Front is described as critical.   The blowing up of bridges is interfering with our retreat along the coast.   The Navy must help out with landing craft (MFP).   As far as southern Italy is concerned it is the consensus of opinion that the enemy has designs on Calabria and Apulia.   Russian newspapers and reports from Roumania imply that Stalin is becoming more insistent in his demands for a second front in western Europe.   If these demands are not complied with, Stalin might reserve the right to act on his own.   *The Fuehrer* takes up the matter of air attacks on Berlin which have threatened anew.   In Denmark, generally speaking, operation *Safari* has been completed. The Fuehrer remarks that we had to expect the present situation in Denmark, and that sooner or later we would have been forced to resort to the measures just undertaken because the Danes were constantly exposed to enemy propaganda which we are not in a position to counteract.

(signed) MEISEL.

\*     \*     \*     \*     \*     \*

Doenitz was now ready to begin another round of the Battle of the Atlantic. He had two new weapons for his U-boats, the acoustic torpedo and improved A.A. guns; and two new types of mines, the D-pressure mine (Oyster) and the A.105 acoustic mine.   For both submarine and mining operations, however, he needed the full support of the *Luftwaffe*, and towards the end of August he had started healing the strained relations between the two services.   At a staff conference, held on August 29 between Doenitz's Chief of Staff and the Chief of Staff of the *Luftwaffe*, full air support had been promised and schemes had been worked out for the training of selected *Luftwaffe* pilots in naval reconnaissance and mine-laying.   In one important respect Doenitz had a great advantage over his predecessor, Raeder, in that he was high in Hitler's favour.   The result was that other Service commanders were somewhat chary of crossing him, and Goering, for example, instead of blustering about the omnipotence of the *Luftwaffe* as he had done to Raeder, showed himself eager to co-operate with Doenitz.

C.-in-C., Navy                                    Berlin, September 15, 1943

**MINUTES OF CONFERENCES AT THE FUEHRER'S HEADQUARTERS FROM SEPTEMBER 10 TO 12, 1943**

Also present: C.-in-C., Navy.
              Chief of Operations Divisions, Naval Staff.
              Chief of Bureau of (MPA), Naval Personnel.
              Aide to the C.-in-C., Navy.

I. SEPTEMBER 10, 1943, AT 1230.   REPORT ON THE SITUATION IN PRESENCE OF THE FUEHRER

In the course of the report: 1. *The C.-in-C., Navy*, reports on the submarine situation and the plans for submarine warfare.   Fewer U-boats have been lost since the *Hagenuk* * device was introduced and the *Metox* * switched off. Conditions for sending out submarines have definitely improved. Operations against convoys in the North Atlantic will begin again with the advent of the new moon in September. An attempt will be made to take the enemy by surprise. Difficulties may be encountered in locating the convoys. It will be a hard fight in spite of our new weapons (anti-aircraft guns, anti-destroyer torpedo). There is no doubt that enemy defence measures will rapidly be brought back to previous strength.

2. *The C.-in-C., Navy*, reports on the defensive use of mines with new fuses. The coastal areas where landings might be attempted are too extensive and the available number of mines is too small to permit the laying of defence barrages. Besides, such minefields are intolerable because our own movements would be severely curtailed. Defensive mine barrages will therefore be laid only when the direction of the enemy thrust is known. An exception will be made in mining the Vergoyer Bank. Until the time is ripe for the laying of defensive minefields it will be wiser to conserve the mines on hand for offensive uses.

3. *The C.-in-C., Navy*, reports that he plans to use the Italian submarine crews under Grossi to man patrol vessels and E-boats.

## II. September 10, 1943. Brief Conference with the Reichsmarschall and the Chief of General Staff, Air

Submarine warfare requires air reconnaissance. The *Reichsmarschall* agrees to order the new Ju290 planes for long-range reconnaissance duty as soon as they are ready for action. *The C.-in-C., Navy*, is anxious that reconnaissance start on September 18. The BV222 planes which are ready for action, will remain on duty to assist in submarine warfare.

## III. September 11, 1943, at 1145. Discussion of Personnel Problems with Field Marshal Keitel

1. *Keitel* promises to investigate the possibility of classifying the Naval *Hitler Jugend* as potential naval personnel. However, he states that allocation of the Naval *Hitler Jugend* to the Navy could only be permitted as part of the personnel contingent already assigned to the Navy.

2. Keitel requests an investigation of the number of Navy personnel in Roumania, Bulgaria (and possibly Greece), where, in his opinion, many German soldiers might be relieved by Bulgarian or Roumanian personnel. Besides that, the necessity of maintaining the "Musicians' Corps in Sofia" and some "500 young men of a Navy motor pool in Holland" should be investigated.

## IV. September 11, 1943

The C.-in-C., Navy, has lunch with the Fuehrer. *The C.-in-C., Navy*, discusses with the German Foreign Minister the problem of how the French Fleet is to be treated after Italy ceases to be a political factor. Subsequently this problem is also taken up with the Fuehrer. *The Fuehrer* is of the opinion that latest events have definitely freed France of her rival in the Mediterranean, i.e. Italy. This might possibly result in an increasingly rigid French attitude. Therefore caution should be

* See Glossary.

exercised in dealing with France. *The German Foreign Minister* emphasised that he is aware of the interest which the C.-in-C., Navy, has in the careful treatment of the French Navy, since their co-operation is of vital importance to Germany. He promises to keep this in mind. He does not consider it appropriate to extend special favours at this time, but he will be careful to avoid cause for friction with the French Navy. *The C.-in-C., Navy,* does not plan for the present to take any steps regarding a declaration of honour to Admiral de Laborde (who was recently arrested by the Gestapo and then released again), or the creation of a *Flotte Symbolique.*

(signed) G. WAGNER.

*      *      *      *      *      *

After the surrender of Italy, a small British force had seized several islands in the Aegean. The islands were not strongly held, but the presence of British troops, sea and air forces was sufficient to cause grave concern among the Germans. German ships were sunk, and sea communications between Italy and Greece were seriously threatened. On September 14 the Germans occupied Rhodes, and later killed or disarmed the Italian garrisons of various small islands in the Ionian Sea. Although they had managed to occupy Rhodes, the key position in the Aegean, the German commanders were still very disturbed by the British threat to their sea communications. A conference was called on September 24.

The C.-in-C., Navy                                  Berlin, September 25, 1943

### CONFERENCE MINUTES OF THE C.-IN-C., NAVY, AT THE FUEHRER'S HEADQUARTERS ON SEPTEMBER 24, 1943

The C.-in-C., Navy, was present when *Field Marshal Baron von Weichs* reported to the Fuehrer on the situation in the south-east and recommended the timely evacuation of our outposts on the islands in the Aegean Sea, including Crete. The C.-in-C., Navy, had intended to make the same proposal, moved by the following considerations:

(*a*) The next strategic moves of the enemy are evidently directed against the Balkans. It is possible that the start of the contemplated operation has been delayed by the German success at Salerno. However, it would be a mistake to conclude from this that the action directed against the Balkans has been given up.

(*b*) Our own position in Greece and the neighbouring areas of the Adriatic and the Aegean Sea is very precarious. Our forces on the peninsula are kept busy with the suppression of partisan activities and are hardly in a position to prevent a landing attempt in force. The naval forces assigned to coastal defence are likewise not of sufficient strength to prevent such a landing; they do not possess any fighting strength to speak of, except in the Aegean area.

(*c*) At sea we have only small vessels which are without military value once the enemy decides to bring his superior naval forces into play.

(*d*) The enemy's air superiority in the whole area is undisputed.

(*e*) The bases on the islands, in particular in Crete, were established at a time when we were still planning offensive operations in the eastern Mediterranean area. Meanwhile, the situation has changed completely. The Italian Armed Forces no longer exist. Our position on the Balkan Peninsula is in danger for lack of sufficient forces; maintenance of security in Balkan rear areas has become a difficult task. The advanced island bases are of no value in a defensive situation such as this, since the enemy will by-pass them and force their surrender, sooner or later, by cutting off their supplies. Thus we shall lose, without a compensating strategic advantage, irreplaceable troops and material which could be of decisive importance for defence of the Continent.

(*f*) A quick decision is imperative because:

(1) The evacuation must be undertaken in time, i.e. before the enemy attacks our sea routes, before he inflicts irreparable losses on our shipping or expands his bases to the point where he can completely disrupt our sea-borne traffic.

(2) The scarcity of shipping space and the weakness of the protective forces at our disposal will make this a relative slow affair.

*The Fuehrer* agrees with the line of argument presented by Field Marshal von Weichs and the C.-in-C., Navy. However, he cannot order the proposed evacuation of the islands, especially the Dodecanese and Crete, on account of the political repercussions which would necessarily follow. The attitude of our allies in the south-east, and likewise Turkey's attitude, is determined exclusively by their confidence in our strength. Abandonment of the islands would create the most unfavourable impression. To avoid such a blow to our prestige we may even have to accept the eventual loss of our troops and material. The supply of the islands must be assured by the Air Force.

*The C.-in-C., Navy*, took the opportunity to present to the Fuehrer his opinion in regard to the present situation in Italy: From a military standpoint, it is clear that Sicily and southern Italy are especially important for the enemy as a bridge to the Balkans. Therefore it is necessary for us to do all in our power to block this route as long as possible. From this point of view Sicily should have been held to the very end. Strategically it was worth every sacrifice. Now another opportunity for determined resistance presents itself in Apulia. To prepare, follow through, and secure a beachhead for a possible assault on the Balkans, the enemy needs the airports near Foggia. This was the pattern followed in Sicily and Salerno. If these airfields remain in our hands, the attack on the Balkans will be effectively delayed. *The Fuehrer* agrees with the C.-in-C., Navy, and will issue directives for the conduct of the war in Italy accordingly.

*The C.-in-C., Navy*, presented an extensive report on the successful submarine campaign in the North Atlantic. In this connection, *the Fuehrer* pointed with unprecedented emphasis to the importance of submarine warfare against shipping which is the only bright spot at present in an otherwise dark war situation. Submarine warfare must therefore be stepped up by all available means.

*The C.-in-C., Navy*, then reported on the attack on the Tirpitz by British midget submarines on September 22, and used charts to explain what protective measures had been taken previously. *The Fuehrer* agreed that the battleship should not be taken to a German shipyard for repairs. In this decision he is guided by vital interests of submarine warfare, as set forth by the C.-in-C., Navy.

(signed)                        DOENITZ.
(countersigned) Lt.-Comdr. MEJER.

The Russian advance on the southern sector of the Eastern Front during the autumn of 1943 forced the German armies steadily back.   Hitler saw his hold over the Ukraine slipping, and the "invincible" *Wehrmacht* fighting a rearguard action.   The Black Sea, however, was perhaps the only area where Germany's sea power was undisputed, and Hitler turned to Doenitz to see how this sea power could be used offensively, or, in the last resort, to secure the safe evacuation of the *Wehrmacht*.   The Crimea was the key position, and at a conference on October 27 plans were discussed for making the Crimea an unassailable stronghold.

Armed Forces High Command                                          October 25, 1943
Operations Staff (Navy)

**MINUTES OF THE CONFERENCE REGARDING THE CRIMEA
HELD AT WOLFSSCHANZE ON OCTOBER 27, 1943**

Also present :  Grand Admiral Doenitz.
The *Reichsmarschall* (Goering).
Chief of O.K.W
Chief of O.K.W., Operations Staff.
Chief of Army General Staff.
Naval Staff, Chief of Operations Section.
O.K.W., Operations Staff (Navy).
Chief of the Air Force General Staff (General Korten).
Chief of Operations Division, Air Force Staff (Colonel Christian).

1. *The Chief of the Army General Staff* reports on the situation along the Southern Front and in the Crimea.   *Grand Admiral Doenitz* comments on the naval coast artillery situation in the Crimea and the use that is being made of our naval forces in the Black Sea.    At present approximately 8 E-boats, 12 motor minesweepers, 60 barges (MFP), and 6 naval artillery lighters (MAL) are in service in the Black Sea.    Three of the submarines are in action, and one will be ready soon.   *The Fuehrer* wants to know whether the submarines can be used in waters south of the Crimea to assist in preventing landings.   Grand Admiral Doenitz answers this question in the affirmative.   Questioned as to the extent to which landings are possible in the Crimea, the C.-in-C., Navy, states that, weather permitting, it is possible to land anywhere on the Kerch peninsula and along the southern coast of the Crimea.   In the long run it would be difficult to bring in supplies if the use of harbours were denied us.   However, small bays could be made to serve the purpose for some time.

2. With a map of the Black Sea on hand, *the C.-in-C., Navy*, explains the present status of the Russian Black Sea Fleet.   He points out that the one battleship is not ready for action and that the cruisers have remained completely inactive thus far.    Then he remarks on our own shipping space in the Black Sea, which amounts to about 9 steamships totalling 21,900 tons, 5 motor ships totalling 6,900 tons.   In addition, there are several trains of barges and a few tankers.   Numerous auxiliary sailing vessels, lighters, and motor boats are available, but can be used only under favourable weather conditions.

Referring to a possible evacuation of the Crimea, *the C.-in-C., Navy*, mentions the following : Approximately 60 landing craft (MFP) are available, each capable of carrying about 200 to 300 men with light equipment. In winter their capacity averages no more than 200 men.   Their capacity is dependent upon the weather. The distance from the west coast of the Crimea to Sulina is about 180 nautical miles. A trip to Sulina takes about one and a half days either way. In other words, about 4 days should be allowed for a round trip. The C.-in-C., Navy, believes that we can count on perhaps 50 landing craft (MFP) in the event of an evacuation. These together can carry a total of approximately 10,000 men on each trip. The weather, above all, will determine whether or not it is feasible to use sea-going lighters, which are towed at reduced speed. About 35 of these are in serviceable condition at this time. *The Fuehrer*, however, does not believe he can count on these lighters. His conservative estimate is that only about 5 steamers and 50 landing craft (MFP) will be available for evacuation purposes. Since the C.-in-C., Navy, believes he can guarantee that 2,000 men will be carried per steamer, each trip of the combined evacuation fleet would make possible the evacuation of 20,000 men with light gear. Thus 10 round trips would be necessary to effect the evacuation of 200,000 men. *The Reichsmarschall* calls attention to the great agricultural importance of the Ukraine, urging strongly that the area be held. *The Fuehrer* himself states that loss of the Crimea would greatly endanger the Roumanian oilfields. It is felt at this time that the arrival of strong reinforcements may yet restore the situation on the Southern Front.

3. *The C.-in-C., Navy*, requests information concerning supply requirements in case the Crimea is cut off and must be treated as an island. *The Fuehrer* expects that supplying the Crimea will follow the same pattern as was formerly used in defence of the Kuban bridgehead. The Chief of the Army General Staff does not consider the supply problem to be crucial at this time. Ammunition on hand will last two or three weeks; food until the middle of December. The Fuehrer believes that available cargo space will assure seaborne supplies in sufficient quantities, i.e. at least 50,000 tons per month. The C.-in-C., Navy, hopes that a somewhat higher figure may be reached. The Chief of the Army General Staff sets forth that a force of 10 divisions needs about 2,000 tons of supplies daily, or 60,000 tons per month. However, there are large stores of food on the island proper which would not require transportation.

*The Fuehrer* believes that it should be possible to restore the Southern Front with the help of the 8 divisions just transferred to that sector. This attempt must be made, since the Crimea is of the utmost strategic importance. But the attempt will be worthwhile only if the Crimea is actually held. The problem is rendered difficult by the fact that there are Roumanian, not German divisions in the Crimea. These troops have demonstrated repeatedly that they are poor fighters, if they fight at all. The Chief of the Army General Staff dwells on this point with particular emphasis, fearing a complete collapse of the Roumanian divisions in the event of a determined Russian landing. The Fuehrer is much more concerned about an airborne landing, which might present greater difficulties and might be harder to repel than a seaborne landing.

Basing his estimate on aerial reconnaissance *the Chief of the Operations Division, Air Force Staff*, believes the following sea-going transportation to be available to the Russians: approximately 43 landing barges in the area north of the Taman Peninsula; approximately 63 landing barges in the area south of the Taman Peninsula, as far down as Gelendshik; in addition about 26 to 30 steamers totalling approximately 90,000 tons in the area north of Tuapse.   It is not known how many of these ships are ready for action.

4. *The Fuehrer* again stresses the fact that an evacuation of the Crimea would most seriously endanger the Roumanian oil refineries and oilfields. For this reason the Crimea must be held as long as possible.   An evacuation by land is out of the question.   Adequate preparations for an evacuation by sea must be made no matter what happens.   In other words all available shipping space, including small craft, must be mobilised to the fullest extent.   *The C.-in-C., Navy*, promises full mobilisation.   He points out, however, that ship losses are possible, hence a system of replacing lost shipping space must get under way.   He further explains that considerable time will be required for evacuation as well as for supplies. If bad weather and winter storms are taken into account, it will take about 80 days to evacuate 200,000 men.   He stresses the fact that it will become very difficult to supply the Crimea once the Russian Air Force is in a position to attack our seaborne traffic from bases west of the Crimea, i.e. in the area east and south-east of Kherson.

The rest of the discussion is concerned with the problem of providing reinforcements both for Field Marshal von Kleist's Army Group and for the Crimea.   The Air Force is directed to attempt destruction of as many enemy landing craft and as much shipping space as possible.   The Fuehrer, in any case, expects the main landing along the Kerch Strait.

Conclusions reached at the conference.—If at all possible, an evacuation of the Crimea is to be avoided as long as there remains any chance of restoring the situation on the Southern Front.   Should an evacuation become unavoidable, it would have to be by sea.   The necessary steps for mobilising cargo space are to be taken regardless of what is going to happen, since this cargo space will be urgently needed either for supplying or for evacuating the peninsula.   The Army and the Air Force are to be reinforced with the greatest possible speed.

O.K.W.
Operations Staff (Navy).

\*　　　\*　　　\*　　　\*　　　\*　　　\*

Throughout the year the manpower position of Germany had been critical. The following discussion was to try to achieve the maximum economy in non-operational personnel of the armed forces.

C.-in-C., Navy

### MINUTES OF THE CONFERENCE OF THE C.-IN-C., NAVY, WITH THE FUEHRER ON NOVEMBER 25 AND 26, 1943, AT THE WOLFSSCHANZE HEADQUARTERS

Also present : *Reichsmarschall* Goering.
Field Marshal Keitel.

*The Fuehrer* has called a meeting of the C.-in-C., Armed Forces, the *Reichsmarschall*, and the C.-in-C., Navy, to impress upon them the urgent necessity of securing more men from the service forces than ever before.   The *Reichsmarschall* declared he was convinced that a large number of front-line soldiers could be obtained from the Service Command of the Air Forces. *The C.-in-C., Navy,* pointed out that the Navy has scarcely 69,000 soldiers assigned to its Service Force. Nevertheless, the Navy would be able to limit administrative activities and further reduce the quota for guard and sentry duty. In that way the C.-in-C., Navy, hopes to make available 30,000 men. Thereupon *the Fuehrer* ordered Field Marshal Keitel to prepare a directive.

(signed) DOENITZ.

*    *    *    *    *    *

At the last conference held during 1943 all theatres of the war were reviewed. In the Atlantic the U-boats had had some success, but were still hampered by lack of air reconnaissance and by out-of-date radar and signalling equipment. The resumption of Allied convoys to Russia—they had been suspended during the summer months—promised additional targets, and an operation had been planned for the battleship Scharnhorst. An Allied invasion of Western Europe was expected, probably in the spring of 1944, and plans were being drawn up to strengthen the West Wall. In the Far East Japan was in uneasy control, pending Allied reinforcement of Burma and the Pacific, while in Eastern Europe the Russian advance was now threatening the Roumanian oilfields.

C.-in-C., Navy                                                    January 8, 1944

**MINUTES OF THE CONFERENCE OF THE C.-IN-C., NAVY, WITH THE FUEHRER ON DECEMBER 19 AND 20, 1943, AT HEADQUARTERS WOLFSSCHANZE**

1. *The C.-in-C., Navy,* reported to the Fuehrer in detail about the present situation in submarine warfare. He pointed out especially the need for very extensive long-range air reconnaissance which is wholly inadequate at present. The tentative building programme of the Air Force for 1944 is such that it will in no way improve the situation during the coming year. Aside from the shortage of planes, insufficient training in navigation and communications has hampered the effective functioning of our aerial reconnaissance during the past few weeks, and has shown the need for a co-ordinated training programme. In spite of the improved U-boat models, submarine warfare in 1944 will be ineffective unless there is adequate reconnaissance; because of the enemy's superiority, our submarines are limited more and more to underwater operations.

[The following paragraph was deleted from the original draft of the conference report:
   The *Reichsmarschall* who was present at this conference, insisted that the Air Force does not bear the sole responsibility for the failures so far. Of course, the C.-in-C., Navy, never made any such assertion.]

Plans for the increase in production of Ju290 aircraft were discussed. In this connection the C.-in-C., Navy, demanded that the whole output of new Ju290 should be used exclusively for long-range reconnaissance and not for bombing. *The Fuehrer* promised to speak with the *Reichsmarschall* in support of this proposal.

*The C.-in-C., Navy,* stressed the need for placing greater emphasis on original research in the high frequency field and said that Minister Speer and he would make a report on this question to the Fuehrer on January 2,

1944. Since the report will recommend the removal of a large amount of research from direct control of the *Reichsmarschall*, who is in charge of the four-year plan, he will be kept fully informed. At present the research facilities are chiefly of value to the Air Force.

2. *The Fuehrer* expressed his intention of utilising the Danube monitors not only on the Danube, but especially in the Black Sea and the Kerch Strait. He therefore ordered the construction of additional monitors. *The C.-in-C., Navy*, declared that the construction of monitors would interfere greatly with the building programme of the Navy. Manpower and equipment vitally needed elsewhere would have to be diverted for this purpose. The Fuehrer requested that an investigation be made nevertheless, to see whether it would be feasible to construct useable monitors by salvaging available hulls, engines, and guns. The C.-in-C., Navy, agreed to do so. Furthermore, he said that the four Danube tugboats would be converted as soon as they have been taken over.

3. *The C.-in-C., Navy*, reported to the Fuehrer that it is intended to have new submarines built in Odessa and requested that the necessary diplomatic steps be taken to have the Roumanians place the Odessa shipyards at our disposal. The Fuehrer gave Lt.-General Jodl orders to this effect.

4. When asked about further plans for an Italian Army, *the Fuehrer* said that he does not believe anything will come of it. Germany is no longer interested in an Italian Army because our relations with Italy are too strained as the result of the events of last September and are bound to remain so. The organising of Italian military units would therefore demand greatest caution and watchfulness. The C.-in-C., Navy, asked that the Italians be forbidden to place any orders for warships with Italian shipyards. The Fuehrer ordered that Ambassador Rahn be instructed accordingly.

5. *The C.-in-C., Navy*, fully discussed the Japanese situation and the question of Timor with the Fuehrer. The latter showed little interest in having Germany step in to settle the Timor dispute even though he admitted that it would be in our interest to strengthen the position of Salazar, and that German intervention would accomplish this.

6. Regarding Turkey's attitude, *the Fuehrer* stated that the Turks are cleverly trying to preserve their neutrality as long as possible.

7. The intention of holding the Crimea as long as possible, if only for political reasons, was reaffirmed.

8. During the discussion of possible plans for an Anglo-Saxon invasion of Western Europe, *the Fuehrer* felt that the British have become somewhat less optimistic as a result of events in Italy. He was therefore not entirely certain where and when the invasion might take place, but expected landings on the Dutch coast and in northern France by the beginning of 1944.

9. *The C.-in-C., Navy*, informs the Fuehrer that the Scharnhorst and destroyers of the task force will attack the next Allied convoy headed from England for Russia via the northern route, if a successful operation seems assured. It would pay to reinforce the submarines in the North if the convoys were to travel the northern route regularly. The C.-in-C., Navy, has already ordered additional U-boats to operate in the Arctic Ocean.

10. In connection with the machine-gunning of shipwrecked survivors by British naval forces in the Aegean Sea, *the Fuehrer* spoke of his intention of retaliating for the mock-trial at Kharkov by holding similar trials in Germany for British and American officers who have violated international law.  He gave orders to draw up appropriate charges.

(signed)        DOENITZ.<br>
(countersigned) Comdr. PFEIFFER.

*    *    *    *    *    *

The year ended, with a major naval disaster.  On the night of December 26 the Scharnhorst was sunk off the North Cape.  Hitler had had one more lesson in the importance of sea power and the need for a strong, balanced fleet.

# Anti-invasion Preparations

IT IS difficult to say exactly when the O.K.W. accepted the fact of Allied superiority, but by the beginning of 1944 they were openly on the defensive, and sought simply to hold the territory they had conquered. Large scale offensive operations were out of the question, and it was evident that the Fatherland itself was in danger. Runstedt's famous answer to Keitel's frenzied appeal for advice—"What shall we do? Make peace, you fools. What else can you do?"—did not occur until June 1944, but it is obvious from later events that it must have been in the first months of 1944 that defeat became a real and unpleasant possibility for Germany's war leaders.

The loss of the Scharnhorst at the end of December, 1943 left Germany with only one operational battleship, the Tirpitz. The remainder of the major warships of the German Navy (2 pocket battleships, 7 cruisers, and 2 old battleships) were all used to train personnel in the Baltic. Germany's U-boat fleet consisted of 419 boats of which 161 were operational, 168 on trial, and 90 used for training. There were besides a large number of minesweepers, E-boats, and patrol vessels. This fleet was clearly too small to oppose effectively the combined Allied fleets which would be used for the invasion of Europe, and other defence measures had to be found.

Ever since the winter of 1941-42, when Hitler was obsessed by the fear of the invasion of Norway, plans had been gradually evolved for meeting a full-scale invasion of France and the Netherlands. A directive by Hitler in February, 1942, (Directive No. 40) had laid down the fundamental organisation between the commands of the three services in the event of an invasion, and thereafter various supplementary orders had been issued for the construction and strengthening of the defences of Western Europe. By the spring of 1944, however, these defences were still paper plans rather than solid obstructions, and Directive No. 40 which had sought to settle once and for all the problems of interservice relationships had, in fact, by its different interpretation by each of the three services, considerably increased the friction between them.

The biggest problem with which the German High Command had to contend was to estimate the most likely point on the long European coastline where the Allies would land. If they could do this with any certainty then they would be able to achieve a greater concentration of their limited forces. But German Intelligence had become increasingly unreliable with the progress of the war and from the many reports which they received they were totally unable to make any sound appreciation of Allied intentions. Hitler's intuition, too, played havoc with the German plans. At different periods Holland, Jutland, the Gironde, Bay of Biscay, and once even Normandy, were named by Hitler as the threatened area. This lack of intelligence made the task of defence almost impossible, and Germany's forces were so dispersed that they would be powerless against the Allies during the first days of an invasion.

The naval share of these defences was both more realistic and better organised than that of the Army, but they too suffered from decreased production of ships and weapons, and much of their planning was dependent upon having the necessary resources available by the time invasion took place. Appreciating the strength of Allied sea power, Doenitz realised that it would be both impractical and suicidal to use the major warships of the German fleet. Of the forces at his disposal two branches of naval warfare appealed to him as being probably the most effective defence in the circumstances. The first of these was the development of midget submarines, one-man torpedoes, and similar "small battle units"; the other was a new type of mine which being extremely simple to construct promised great success in coastal warfare. The planned use of both these defence measures was however entirely governed by the numbers of each which German factories could produce, and therefore Doenitz could not afford to neglect the older forms of shore defence—coastal batteries.

The length of coastline deemed vulnerable made it impossible for coastal batteries to cover every area, and Hitler had solved the problem by declaring certain towns and ports as "fortresses" which simply meant that coastal artillery units were to be concentrated at these particular points which were to be defended to the last. The batteries were manned jointly by naval and army personnel and this dual command later caused much difficulty when they went into action. The whole problem of shore defence was made more difficult by the attempt of Army commands to employ naval personnel in military defence units. Doenitz was adamant in his refusal to allocate naval personnel to the Army, saying that he required them for the U-boat campaign in which he still placed his greatest hopes of victory and in which he was to a certain extent supported by Hitler. The result was a conflict between the Army and Navy which seriously disrupted the coastal defence organisation.

## U-BOAT CAMPAIGN

The U-boat campaign during the pre-invasion era was slowed up, partly in order to have the maximum number of boats available when the invasion actually began, and partly because Allied countermeasures were by now so successful that U-boats had the greatest difficulty in approaching their targets. New types were being produced however, and with these Doenitz hoped to restore the balance in his favour. The first of the two new types of U-boat was the normal U-boat fitted with *Schnorchel*—a device which enabled U-boats to operate their Diesel engines while submerged, thereby increasing their underwater endurance and at the same time making them less liable to detection. The second new type was that sometimes known as the "Walter" submarine. These U-boats with specially designed hulls and engines were capable of higher underwater speed than the older types of U-boat, increasing their manoeuvrability, and designed with the hope of overcoming the Allied countermeasures.

The value of the new U-boats, however, was considerably offset by heavy Allied air attacks on U-boat production centres. Only three ports (Hamburg, Bremen, and Danzig) could be used for the final assembly of the new U-boats, and each of these was subject to extremely heavy "carpet' bombing, with the result that none of the new U-boats was operational by D-day. Secondly, the Baltic, which was the only area left for the training of U-boat crews, was threatened by the Russian advance on the Eastern Front. In spite of these difficulties Doenitz had high hopes for his new U-boat campaign which he proposed beginning in the second half of 1944 against the Russian and Atlantic convoys. So great was his faith in the new U-boats, that there are indications that he believed it would bring about a stalemate in the war and make possible a negotiated peace.

## ANZIO

The Allied landings at Anzio and Nettuno on January 22, 1944, were regarded by the O.K.W. as a preliminary experiment before the main assault on Western Europe and they were therefore particularly anxious, not only for the sake of German morale but also as a possible hindrance to the Allies, that these landings should be defeated. On January 28, 6 days after the landing began, Hitler sent the following message to all the armed forces in Italy:

"Within the next few days the 'battle for Rome' will commence. This will be decisive for the defence of Central Italy, and will also decide the fate of the 10th Army. This battle has a special significance because the landing at Nettuno marks the beginning of the invasion of Europe planned for 1944. Strong German forces are to be tied down in areas as far as possible from the bases in Britain where the majority of the invasion troops are still stationed. The object of the Allies being to gain experience for future operations.

"Every soldier must therefore be aware of the importance of the battle which the 14th Army has to fight. It must be fought with bitter hatred against an enemy who wages a ruthless war of annihilation against the German people and who, without any higher ethical aims, strives only for the destruction of Germany and European culture. As in the battle for Sicily, on the Rapido River and at Ortona, it must be driven home to the enemy that the fighting power of Germany is unbroken and that the invasion of the year 1944 is an undertaking which will be crushed in the blood of British soldiers."

(signed) ADOLF HITLER.

Thus inspired the German Army managed to contain the Allies in their bridge-head for the next four months, and gave the *Wehrmacht* an opportunity to try out some of their anti-invasion measures. Although neither the coastal batteries, nor the mines, nor the midget submarines employed at Anzio were of the standard to be used in Western Europe, the *Wehrmacht* was yet able to hold back a superior force for more than four months, and the experience at Anzio must have seemed to the Germans good proof that similar measures would be as effective against the "Second Front."

## SUMMARY OF ANTI-INVASION MEASURES

On February 19, 1944 Doenitz sent the following appreciation and general policy governing naval anti-invasion measures to all German naval commands:

"General directions for the employment of the forces in the event of a enemy landing:

" Enemy Situation:

" (1) The enemy is making extensive preparations for the opening of a second front. Before long he intends to make a thrust into the heart of the Continent and bring the war to a speedy conclusion. Using bluff and propaganda, he is endeavouring to conceal his real main object and to make full use of the element of surprise.

" (2) The enemy will endeavour to break up German resistance, by means of small operations preceding or simultaneous to the large scale landing. In addition to those areas mentioned in Fuehrer Directive No. 51 as mainly threatened (Channel and Jutland/Skagerrak) and the coast of Southern France and Biscay which have recently come into the picture, almost all areas at present under German domination must now be regarded as endangered.

" (3) The enemy's landing tactics are known to us from experiences in the Mediterranean and from captured information and in future, he will probably also carry out the same procedure. There will be special points of weakness in the following:

" (*a*) In order to guarantee success, the first landing forces must be brought up and the landing of the first waves must be well organised and carried out according to a previously fixed time-plan.

" (*b*) Superiority in strength can only be effective after a strong bridgehead has been formed. In the past this has proved to be a critical time for the enemy.

" (*c*) As the operation progresses, the enemy must carry out an extensive supply programme and keep a continuous watch over large and unwieldy forces, and this will undoubtedly produce snags and weak points."

Doenitz went on to describe the difficulties and requirements for adequate defence. He stated that although the Navy alone could neither prevent nor repulse the enemy landing, yet by delaying actions they could gain time which could be of decisive importance to the Army. He emphasised the need for taking great risks, and ordered the naval commanders to disregard completely the safety of their ships or crews. All available naval forces were to be concentrated in the combat area, and should accept the risk of being bombarded by their own coastal artillery. Operational control in the invasion area was to be maintained by the C.-in-C., as long as communications existed. He ended his message with the following exhortation:

"The importance of the task demands that special attention be paid to the spiritual preparation of the forces. When our enemies begin a decisive attack against our *lebensraum*, their troops will be imbued with a will to destroy with-out mercy, and will be well trained in the arts of brutal warfare. Every crew and every man must know that only stubborn and tenacious struggle brings success and help us to pass through the decisive phase of the war which lies ahead of us.

(signed) DOENITZ."

The anti-invasion measures of the German navy may therefore be summarised as follows:

(a) To attack the landing craft with U-boats, patrol craft, and coastal artillery.

(b) To attack the invasion area with midget submarines and other "small battle units."

(c) To protect the European coast with new mines. (Known as the RMK or KMA mine, it was simply constructed out of concrete and operated by a contact fuse. Doenitz planned to lay these at the rate of 1,200 per month.)

(d) To destroy Allied sea communications by a new campaign against Atlantic convoys with the new U-boats.

During the first half of 1944 all these problems were discussed at the Fuehrer Conferences and the anti-invasion plans consolidated.

C.-in-C., Navy.                                           January 13, 1944

## MINUTES OF THE VISIT OF THE C.-IN-C., NAVY, AT HEADQUARTERS, WOLFSSCHANZE, ON JANUARY 1 to 3, 1944

*The C.-in-C., Navy,* spent January 1 to 3, 1944, at Fuehrer Headquarters. He had many discussions on the current problems of the war with some of the leading personages, as well as with the Fuehrer himself in private. He reported to the Fuehrer on the following matters in particular:

1. The course and the results of the engagement of the Scharnhorst in the Arctic Ocean, explained with the aid of a battle sketch. As Lt.-General Jodl, Chief of the Armed Forces Operations Staff had done previously, *the Fuehrer* fully agreed with the idea that the Navy should make every possible use of its forces. However, the thing that grieves him, besides the unsatisfactory outcome, is the unanswered question of how the task force commander could have made the grave error at 1223 of assuming that he was confronted by heavy ships, when only enemy cruisers were involved. Our battleship, in fact, ran away from the cruisers although it was superior to them both in fighting power and armour. The Fuehrer always suspects that such happenings occur because too much thought is given to the safety of the ships as in the case of Graf Spee. *The C.-in-C., Navy,* explained to the Fuehrer that the engagement had proved that surface ships are no longer able to fight without effective radar equipment. We cannot expect our ships to be very successful in preventing enemy landing attempts, since the enemy has the equipment and is in a position to eliminate our ships beforehand, or to fight them during the approach. Therefore much better results might be achieved by using the fleet for operations against convoys in the North and not as a defence against enemy landings. Moreover, for reasons of strategy, it is important to maintain our strength in the North, because this influences British invasion plans and also has some effect on the situation in the Pacific. Therefore the C.-in-C., Navy, gave orders to look into the possibility of transferring the heavy cruiser Prinz Eugen to the task force in northern Norway.

2. The problem of the Baltic Sea is likewise to be viewed in the light of the new submarine weapon, because the Baltic Sea is the only training area for the new offensive U-boats. *The Fuehrer* was fully aware of the problem. He said that the situation in the South compelled him,

nevertheless, to withdraw troops for the North, and that he was trying to replace them with Latvian and Estonian divisions. Fortunately it so happens at the moment that the Russians are not very strong in the North. Everything depends on checking the Russian offensive on the southern part of the Eastern Front and on holding the Crimea. If the front can be stabilised in the South, forces would become available also for the North. The Fuehrer therefore remains firm in his determination not to yield an inch if he can help it. Nevertheless it should be kept in mind that our forces in the North are so weak that we have to retreat if the Russians attack.

During this visit of the C.-in-C., Navy, Minister Speer reported to the Fuehrer on the new submarine construction programme, i.e. the progress made so far in the prefabrication of "electro" submarines. Finally, the C.-in-C., Navy, took this opportunity to have a far-reaching discussion between Minister Speer and himself on the one hand and the *Reichsmarschall* on the other, for the purpose of bringing about strict concentration of all German facilities and resources in the field of high frequency technique. This discussion was to prepare the way for a later decision to this effect by the Fuehrer. For the same purpose, a demonstration of electrical equipment had been held earlier before the Fuehrer for an hour, with a lecture by Dr. Lueschen, Chairman of the Central Committee for Electrical Engineering in the Ministry of Armaments and War Industry. A report made by Professor Kuepfmueller to the Fuehrer and arranged by the C.-in-C., Navy, and Minister Speer also was in the same vein. It dealt with the problems of location in naval warfare. To bring about this concentration, the Fuehrer is planning to give Dr. Lueschen the necessary full powers over all developments in the field of electrical engineering, in addition to his other duties. Furthermore, this authority is meant to give the "Deputy for Electrical Engineering" as far-reaching an influence on research as possible.

During the discussion with the *Reichsmarschall*, serious differences of opinion occurred at first. These were cleared away mainly because Minister Speer supported the need for concentration and the measures suitable for bringing it about. The C.-in-C., Navy, and the C.-in-C., Air reached complete agreement. When the Fuehrer inquired, they informed him accordingly. Minister Speer and Dr. Lueschen subsequently proceeded to draft the text of the authorisation and to work out details of the organisation.

(signed)                 DOENITZ.
(countersigned) Comdr. PFEIFFER.

High Command, Navy.                                      January 24, 1944

## MINUTES OF THE CONFERENCE OF THE C.-IN-C., NAVY, WITH THE FUEHRER ON JANUARY 18 AND 19, 1944, AT HEADQUARTERS, WOLFSSCHANZE

Accompanied by Rear Admiral Wagner.

1. January 18, 1944, 1300. Situation Conference with the Fuehrer.—
(*a*) During the report on the air situation, *the Fuehrer* brought up the question of the anti-aircraft defences of Pola. He referred to a letter from

*Gauleiter* Greiner who discussed the heavy damage caused by the air raid on Pola with the remark that reconstructing the Pola shipyard would be a hopeless effort if no improvement is made in anti-aircraft artillery and fighters, since the enemy is at present complete master of the situation. The representative of the General Staff of the Air Force, Major Buechs, announced that anti-aircraft batteries had been transferred from Fiume to Pola, and that the whole question of air defences in Istria was now under consideration by the General Staff of the Air Force.

(*b*) The following was announced.—A Croatian Colonel who up to now had been liaison officer to the German liaison staff in Croatia fled with his wife in a Do217 which we gave to Croatia and probably joined the British. He possesses a thorough knowledge of the military situation in Croatia.

*Note.*—This incident throws light upon the reliability of the Croatians, and should be kept in mind when their services are used by the Navy.

2. January 18, 1944. Report to a small group by the C.-in-C., Navy, after the Conference.—(*a*) Supplies to the Crimea. *The C.-in-C., Navy*, believes that the Navy will be able to ship 45,000 tons per month to the Crimea provided enemy interference does not grow appreciably. In the spring, shipments will possibly increase to about 50,000 tons per month. *The Fuehrer* believes that the Army's request for 2,500 tons per month from April onwards is probably too high (cf. Demiansk and Stalingrad). He will have it checked.

(*b*) *The C.-in-C., Navy*, requests the Fuehrer to make a decision concerning the departure of four blockade-runners for Japan, which has been planned for the next new moon phase beginning on January 22, 1944. He reports on all vital points and in concluding expresses his belief that the advantages will outweigh the great risk involved. *The Fuehrer* considers that there is also imminent danger that tungsten shipments from Spain and Portugal might cease. He has therefore given orders to bring in as much tungsten as possible now. He no longer considers the need for rubber decisive enough to the war effort to justify the enterprise; buna tyres, if not driven at speeds over seventy kilometres an hour, last 40,000 kilometres as compared with only 20,000 kilometres in the case of rubber tyres. On the whole he does not consider the economic factors really worth-while. He believes that the plan has so little chance of succeeding that even the importance of supporting Japan plays no part here, since the ships will never reach that country anyway. He decides that no surface blockade-runners are to leave port, and thereby specifically abandons all intentions of importing raw materials from Japan in the future with surface blockade-runners.

(*c*) *The Fuehrer* agrees to the construction of fifty midget submarines as planned, and considers the development of both the mine-carrying and torpedo-carrying types correct.

(*d*) *The Fuehrer* approves the construction of one-man torpedoes which according to the report of the C.-in-C., Navy, are to be used particularly as a defence weapon in case of enemy landings.

(*e*) The development of the concrete coastal defence mine (RMK) and the plans for using it have the Fuehrer's emphatic consent.

(*f*) *The C.-in-C., Navy*, reports on the new explosive for torpedoes developed by *Oberregierungsrat* Dr. Buchmann. *The Fuehrer* expresses full approval. He is convinced that more can be achieved by improving the explosive than by increasing the charge.

(g) *The C.-in-C., Navy*, suggests to the Fuehrer that the solution to the problem of monitors in the Danube and the Black Sea lies in mounting 10·5-cm. guns on each of the next six artillery barges (AMFP), the essential parts of which are to be armoured.  *The Fuehrer* agrees.

(h) *The C.-in-C., Navy*, reports on the plan of using radar spar decoy buoys (*Thetis-Geraete*) in the Bay of Biscay and in the Atlantic.  *The Fuehrer* approves this measure.

(i) *The C.-in-C., Navy*, informs the Fuehrer about the optical improvement of the night vision aiming periscope (*Nachtzielsehrohr*).

(j) *The C.-in-C., Navy*, reports that there is a possibility of attempting an attack on a convoy in the North Atlantic in the near future with submarines equipped with 3·7-c.m. anti-aircraft guns.  We will have to concentrate our weak air reconnaissance at the proper time and place.  On the other hand, there is danger of an Anglo-Saxon landing in Portugal for which our submarines might then be too late.  The submarines would be occupied approximately three weeks by the operation against the convoy, and during this period would require about nine days to reach Portuguese waters.  *The Fuehrer* believes that there will be more obvious signs when the enemy intends to land, and gives his consent for the convoy attack.

3. January 18, 1944.—The C.-in-C., Navy, and Lt.-General Jodl have a brief disucssion concerning the shipyard in Odessa.  *The C.-in-C., Navy*, states that he must build submarines in Odessa and, this is possible only if the shipyard comes under definite German management.  He has the Fuehrer's consent for this, but can get no satisfaction from the above answer of the O.K.W.  *Lt.-General Jodl* believes that the Chief of the German Military Mission in Roumania, Lt.-General Hansen, can put the matter through in our favour only if he is assisted by Navy experts capable of refuting Roumanian counter-arguments.  *The C.-in-C., Navy*, therefore decided to speak with Hr. Merker first and then to send two experts, one for shipyards and one for submarine construction, to Lt.-General Hansen to see that our demands are realised.

4. January 18, 1944.  Noon and evening.  The C.-in-C., Navy, was invited to dinner and supper with the Fuehrer.

5. January 19, 1944, 1100.  Telephone call from Field Marshal Kesselring to the C.-in-C., Navy.—(a) *The Commanding General Armed Forces, South-west*, proposes that the Navy turn over her intended construction projects in the Italian area to the Organisation Todt, as did the Army and the Air Force.  *The C.-in-C., Navy*, agrees to examine the proposal.

(b) The Commanding General Armed Forces, South-west, requests personnel for naval coastal artillery.  The C.-in-C., Navy, replies that the personnel problem is a bottleneck in the Navy and that no promises can be made.  He will have an investigation made, however.

(c) The Commanding General Armed Forces, South-west, requests more submarines for the Mediterranean.  The C.-in-C., Navy, replies that new submarines are being continuously sent there and will be sent there in the future.

6. January 19, 1944.  1300.  Situation conference with the Fuehrer, followed by a report of the C.-in-C., Navy, concerning measures taken by the Navy against an invasion in the Western Area.

*The C.-in-C., Navy*, reviews in general outline the fleet and defence forces available in the Western Area from the Polar coast to Spain, the plans for using them, the mine situation, and the plans for future use of mines. The following particulars are brought out:

(*a*) The C.-in-C., Navy, mentions that he intends to transfer the Prinz Eugen to northern Norway in February. The Fuehrer receives the information without special comment.

(*b*) *The Fuehrer* shares the view that our cruisers cannot be used against enemy landings in the Channel–Holland area. In addition he considers cruiser operations in the Skagerrak hardly possible, especially since a high percentage of the crews are officer candidates for submarines. The loss of such personnel would jeopardise the development of the submarine service.

(*c*) In answer to the report of C.-in-C., Navy, that drafting emergency units also from Group A would cripple part of the training programme and therefore handicap the development of the submarine service, *the Fuehrer* replies that when taking these measures the greatest consideration must be given to submarine requirements. General Jodl later requests that only such units be designated belonging to Group A as can be used without injury to the submarine service. The C.-in-C., Navy, orders that the whole question be re-examined, bearing in mind that decisions on the use of training vessels and emergency units must rest with him, and that a general alarm will take place only in case of a large-scale attack in the Skagerrak–Jutland area.

(*d*) The reinforcement of the Skagerrak minefields planned for spring is in the Fuehrer's opinion particularly important.

(*e*) *The Fuehrer* wishes to be informed about the feasibility of using pressure mines (DM-Minen) as a defence against enemy landings. *The C.-in-C., Navy*, declares that their use for defence directly off our coast is not practical, since small landing craft have too little displacement and larger ones approach the coast at too slow a speed to activate the detonator. The use of the mines for this purpose, in contrast with their use off the enemy coast, is therefore not advisable.

(*f*) *The Fuehrer* inquires about the surface speed of the new submarine types when the electric motors are used. The C.-in-C., Navy, replies that their surface speed is fifteen knots, and thus because of the fish-like shape of the vessels is actually less than their underwater speed. The Fuehrer suggests corresponding tests with the older boat types. The C.-in-C., Navy, intends to come back to this question at the next Fuehrer conference.

(*g*) The Fuehrer expresses particularly anxiety concerning a possible landing in the area south of the Gironde.

8. January 19, 1944. The C.-in-C., Navy, was invited to dinner with the Fuehrer.

(signed)            DOENITZ.
(countersigned) Comdr. PFEIFFER.

C.-in-C., Navy.

## MINUTES OF THE VISIT OF THE C.-IN-C., NAVY, AT FUEHRER HEADQUARTERS, BERGHOF, ON FEBRUARY 26 AND 27, 1944

A. The C.-in-C., Navy, was present at the situation conference February 26, 1944, and reported to the Fuehrer as follows:

1. The submarine operation against convoys on February 18.—Using a map, he explained that our air reconnaissance must be sure to contact

enemy convoys at the exit of the North Channel; later contact is too uncertain because the convoys are likely to scatter, either to the north or all the way around to the south. On the other hand, the submarines cannot take up positions close to land because enemy air patrols are too strong there, even at night. These two circumstances make it necessary for our own reconnaissance to be extended over several days, probably about five. With the limited forces at our disposal it is possible that our own air reconnaissance is lacking on the decisive night preceding the actual night of the attack, just when final dispositions of the submarines must be made. On this account the submarine formation in the operation under discussion did not succeed in moving submerged farther south the day prior to the night of the attack. The result was that the convoy was contacted only by the southern end of the submarine formation on the night of the attack, and only very late, so that the boats were not able to close in before dawn. At dawn, however, the boats had to submerge on account of strong carrier-based aircraft protection. They were immobilised and the operation came to an end.

Nevertheless, this case shows clearly what prospects the submarine type XXI would have had. With this type it would have been possible to shift the location of the boats sufficiently while submerged even on the day preceding the night of the attack. Besides, these boats would not have been immobilised after the attack, but could have continued the operation under water. Our general tendency to change over to underwater tactics is thus correct in every respect. We will always be at a disadvantage on the surface due to the enemy's air superiority and his surface location-finding devices, so we must avoid them by submerging. Taking everything into account, a fundamental defence by the enemy against a submarine operating while submerged is hard to imagine. Of course, it could possibly be detected by listening devices, but their range is not anywhere near so great as that of the high frequency location-finding equipment used in aircraft against submarines operating on the surface. It is still true that a ship is sunk if the submarine is able to close in. The difficulty lies in getting close enough to the target, because this still has to be done on the surface. With the new submarine it is possible under water. Since the new submarine has great chances of success, the intended construction programme must be accelerated in every way possible. *The Fuehrer* agrees wholeheartedly.

Unfortunately, however, construction has already been delayed by two months for type XXIII and one month for type XXI. The main reason is the damage done to the electric motor industry at the Siemens-Schuckert plant by the latest air raids. Nevertheless, everything that is humanly possible is being done in close co-operation between the Bureau of Naval Armament and Minister Speer. The same is true for the rest of the naval construction programme, the realisation of which must be striven for just as fanatically. Already the mine situation at the entrances to the Baltic Sea is a cause of great anxiety to the C.-in-C., Navy. Enemy pressure against our coasts and sea routes will certainly increase greatly during the coming year. For this reason the Navy will go through a critical period until the programme ordered by the Fuehrer in April 1943 for construction of defensive vessels such as minesweepers and motor minesweepers, begins to take effect. This programme has to be completed with all possible speed. All the submarines in the Baltic Sea are of no use if the entrances cannot be kept open, not to speak of the danger to the quite considerable ship traffic, now 1,730,000 freight tons a month, which has to move through the western part of the Baltic. It goes without saying that the enemy intends to blockade us with mines in those waters. In order to realise the naval building programme, the C.-in-C., Navy, will exert himself to the utmost to provide the necessary personnel, to have them trained promptly, and to prevent their possible use for other purposes.

2. Plans for establishing a base for naval forces, involving pier construction, in the Sea of Azov are explained with the help of a map. *The Fuehrer* agrees. He keeps the map to inform Marshal Antonescu personally of this measure. At the same time he stresses his anxiety that the Russians will land in the Crimea by way of the Sea of Azov.

3. The development of a submarine base on Lemnos is out of the question because neither the Balkan railway nor ships in the Aegean Sea can provide adequate transport facilities. The Bay of Mudros, which alone has natural protection, has a flat coast, so that underground galleries are impossible there. We have had to abandon concrete and overground construction for the submarine base intended at Salonika, because it would require 65 per cent. of the 45 vitally important trains allotted the Navy monthly in the Balkans to transport the necessary material. In place of these we now plan underground galleries in Volos. Concrete construction at Mudros is out of the question. In principle the C.-in-C., Navy, is of the opinion, nevertheless, that a well fortified Lemnos directly in front of the Dardanelles would be of the greatest strategic value. *The Fuehrer* agrees in general with the report. He directs, however, that the value of the Mudros Bay be kept in mind, and suggests that it might be used even now as an unprotected base for E-boats.

4. Intended use of Captain Grossi's men.—It is necessary to transfer the men to the Italian theatre; to use an Italian unit in the West seems no longer proper because of the danger of enemy landings, even though this was intended originally. *The Fuehrer* agrees with this and asks about the dependability of Captain Grossi and his men. The C.-in-C., Navy, declares that Captain Grossi proved loyal. Nevertheless, he has relieved him of his submarines, promising him replacements. He is obliged to keep this promise, thereby running the risk of being taken in by Grossi. *The Fuehrer* agrees.

5. Special conditions in the Navy regarding commissioning of officers for Special Troop Service.—The Navy has no civilian paymasters but administrative officers who are regular officers. Therefore the administrative officers of the Navy cannot be made officers for Special Troop Service, as in the case of the Army and the Air Force where the paymasters are officials. On the other hand, the Navy must relieve the high-ranking officials of their character as civilian officials, because they would have a lower status in comparison to high-ranking officials in the Army and the Air Force of the latter are transferred to the Special Troop Service. The C.-in-C., Navy, intends therefore to commission the capable high-ranking officials of the Navy as administrative officers, and thus to regular officers, so that the Navy does not have two different classes of officers in the administrative service. Naturally such an adjustment is only for the

duration of the war and is not meant to impede the transfer in peace-time of all administrative officers to the Special Troop Service.

*The Fuehrer* is inclined to agree with this arrangement. *The Chief of Staff, O.K.W.*, however, fears that this procedure will cause great dissatisfaction in the Army and the Air Force since the high-ranking officials in the Navy would have a considerably better position than those in the other branches of the Armed Forces. He requests permission to examine the matter once more.

6. It would be a mistake to hand over the defence of the Aaland Islands to the Navy if they should be occupied. *The C.-in-C., Navy*, is of the opinion that the Navy possesses neither the forces nor the specific knowledge necessary to cope with such a typical army problem. *General Jodl* expresses a different view. He thinks that in connection with the occupation of the Aaland Islands naval engagements would develop, so that it would seem expedient that the Navy should take over the command. No final decision was reached since the Fuehrer did not consider it necessary yet.

[The manpower situation in Germany had been critical ever since the end of 1942. By 1944 the O.K.W. was becoming desperate in its search for more troops, and attempted to co-opt naval personnel for the Army. The result was the beginning of a struggle between Doenitz and the Army which lasted until the end of the war. The struggle began with a mild attempt by Rundstedt to allocate a few naval troops for guard duty in France.—*Ed.*]

B. Following the conference on the war situation the C.-in-C., Navy, had a short talk with Field Marshal Keitel and General Jodl in regard to the use of naval shore units in the West. He made it clear that these troops are stationed in the West only because there are no longer any barracks to accommodate them at home. He explained that these men have had only two months basic training and could not possibly assume any additional tasks arising in their territory except in the case of a direct threat against the place where they are stationed. To this General Jodl remarked that as far as he knew the Commanding General, France, had only proposed a slight shifting of these units for the protection of railways in case of emergency. The C.-in-C., Navy, made it very clear that it was out of the question for these naval units to take over any tasks which are in the Army's sphere. He does not intend to endanger the shipbuilding programme ordered by the Fuehrer by the possibility of having no crews for the new ships because they have not been trained.

At this point Field Marshal Keitel agreed explicitly with the C.-in-C., Navy. He emphasised the fact that if the naval men really were used on land it would be simply impossible to replace the carefully selected young personnel. For this reason the O.K.W., would have to support the view of the C.-in-C., Navy. The C.-in-C., Navy, concluded the conversation by repeating his former statement that he would under no condition permit the use of a single one of his men for other than naval purposes.

The Fuehrer listened to this discussion in an adjoining room separated only by a curtain.

[The conference ended with a discussion on the re-organisation of the German Secret Service. Before the discussion Himmler had no control over the military intelligence services, and both for political reasons, and because he suspected them of being unfavourable to Hitler, sought to have them all under his orders.

*Organization Kaltenbrunner*, which came into being as a result of the conference, combined all the intelligence services under Dr. Ernst Kaltenbrunner who was also in charge of Himmler's central Reich Security Office, and thus gave Himmler complete control.]

C. The C.-in-C., Navy, discussed with Field Marshal Keitel and Vegelein, the representative of the *Reichsfuehrer S.S.*, the consequences of the re-organisation of the Counter-Intelligence Service. He learned that the *Reichsfuehrer S.S.* in accordance with the wish of the Fuehrer was to build up a sort of German Secret Service. The Chief of Staff, O.K.W., asked the C.-in-C., Navy, for his view on the question and the latter replied that no branch of the Armed Forces should be permitted under any circumstances to maintain or initiate any extra organisation. The greatest effect could only be attained through a unified organisation always ready for action. The counter-intelligence services of the different branches of the Armed Forces, so far as they do not have to be maintained directly among the troops, should in his opinion be turned over to the *Reichsfuehrer S.S.* The branches of the Armed Forces must represent their interests by having their own people in the large organisation of the *Reichsfuehrer S.S. (Organization Kaltenbrunner)* which should absorb the different counter-intelligence services. Deputy Vegelein was convinced that the *Reichsfuehrer S.S.* would approve of this proposal.

D. On February 27, 1944, the C.-in-C., Navy, took part in the conference on the situation and in the discussions with Marshal Antonescu in the guest house Glessheim.

(signed)            DOENITZ.

(countersigned) Lt.-Comdr. von MANTEY.

Naval Staff.

## MINUTES OF THE VISIT OF THE C.-IN-C., NAVY, AT FUEHRER HEADQUARTERS, WOLFSSCHANZE, ON MARCH 20 AND 21, 1944

The C.-in-C., Navy, had several private talks with the Fuehrer. In addition, the C.-in-C., Navy, reported to the Fuehrer on the following points:

1. Only the Navy can determine the use of battle units and weapons of all types at sea. This naturally applies to high speed landing craft. It is planned to use the small battle weapon *Mohr\** at Nettuno. *The Fuehrer* agreed.

2. The effects of the loss of Odessa on shipping and the general situation in the Black Sea, especially on supplies for the Crimea. *The Fuehrer* again emphasised that he wants to hold the Crimea. For that reason he already mentioned the consequences of its loss to the High Command, Army, telling them that Odessa must be held. The Fuehrer asked the C.-in-C., Navy, to write a memorandum explaining the importance of Odessa for holding the Crimea, so that the commanding generals of the Army would hear these things not only from the Fuehrer, but also from someone else.

---

\* The *Mohr* was first used at Anzio on April 21. It consisted of two torpedoes joined together. The pilot occupied one, the "mother," and released the other torpedo in the normal way. They were called "chariots" by the Allies and "*maiales*" (sows) by the Italians. The whole apparatus was of German manufacture and German manned.

3. The disastrous financial situation of Greece and its effects on ship repairs.—The Fuehrer believes that the workers should be paid in terms of board and lodging in order to avoid the problems of inflation.

4. The problem of the alarm units in the West.—The C.-in-C., Navy, explains in detail what the 27,000 men being trained there mean for naval warfare. He wants them to fight only for the protection of their own stations. Field Marshals von Rundstedt and Rommel state that the Navy would get these men back. But the C.-in-C., Navy, replies that this is very uncertain, since no one has control over developments in case of an invasion. *The Fuehrer* believes that, if they are needed, a special decision will have to be made about the disposition of the training units. He instructs the O.K.W. to give corresponding orders to the various branches of the Armed Forces.

5. Attention must be given to the weakness of the anti-invasion and coastal defences in the German Bight, even if an enemy landing there seems unlikely at the moment. *The Fuehrer* promises that something will be done to strengthen this vulnerable spot after projects in the West are completed, i.e. in the spring, by the end of April.

6. Matters pertaining to the arrest of the French admirals.—*The Fuehrer* decides that the following French admirals should not be put under arrest.—(*a*) Those who are co-operating with us; and (*b*) those whom we consider trustworthy. The C.-in-C., Navy, is to furnish the *Reichsfuehrer S.S.* with a corresponding list.

7. Plans to use submarines more sparingly in view of the high losses, except in the event of an invasion. *The Fuehrer* gives his consent.

8. Regrettably high shipping losses in the northern area.—The situation can be expected to improve only when more escort forces are available. Much too little has been built during the last few years. *The Fuehrer* asked when the increase in E-boat construction would take effect.

9. Plans for placing additional available anti-submarine guns south of the Gironde for coastal defence. *The Fuehrer* welcomes this. He demands, however, that the Navy extend the mine barrages in shallow waters and on the beaches in the West.

(signed)     DOENITZ.<br>(countersigned) Lt. j.g. MOMMERT.

\*     \*     \*     \*     \*     \*

The Tirpitz, stationed in Alta Fiord on the north coast of Norway, had been damaged by heavy air attacks launched from aircraft carriers of the Royal Navy. Although the Tirpitz was at this stage of the war little more than a threat, nevertheless her presence in Arctic waters tied down part of the British Fleet which might otherwise have reinforced the Allied Fleets in the Pacific. Damaged, however, the Tirpitz was valueless, and it was therefore urgent that she should be repaired as soon as possible.

Naval Staff.

## MINUTES OF THE CONFERENCE OF THE C.-IN-C., NAVY, AND THE FUEHRER AT HEADQUARTERS, BERGHOF, ON APRIL 12 AND 13, 1947

1. Tirpitz.—*The C.-in-C., Navy*, reports on the plans for the Tirpitz. The ship is to be repaired and to remain stationed in northern Norway.

This course will be followed even if further damage is sustained.   Regardless of how much work and manpower may be involved, the repairs must be made.   After all, the presence of the Tirpitz ties up enemy forces.   The ship will hardly have any further opportunity for action, unless later political developments, such as a falling out between England and Russia, were to bring this about.   In any case, it is impossible to know what will happen.   It is very unlikely that the Tirpitz will be used in the event of an invasion.   Air attacks have shown that a ship is helpless without fighter escort.   Therefore the idea of using the Scharnhorst during the Arctic night was basically correct.   Aside from the fact that the Tirpitz will tie up enemy forces if left in northern Norway, it would be a mistake to recall the ship to Germany, since that would increase the danger of air raids on our German ports.   *The Fuehrer* voices his wholehearted approval. He agrees with the C.-in-C., Navy, on every point.

[Coastal forces of the Royal Navy, based on the Island of Vis in the Adriatic, seriously interrupted German sea traffic to Greece, capturing eight ships and sinking three in the first twelve days of April alone.   A small airfield was also built on the island and greatly increased the opportunities for offensive action by Allied and partisan forces.   Doenitz, therefore, sought to have the island liquidated. It was not strongly held, but the Allies would be able to muster assistance quickly in the event of any German attack.   The help of the *Wehrmacht* and *Luftwaffe* was thus necessary, and Doenitz proposed his schemes to Hitler.]

2. Vis Island (Lissa).—*General Jodl* informs the Fuehrer that the seizure of Vis is purely a naval matter.   There is a difference of opinion between the Navy on the one hand and the Army and the Air Force on the other. The latter believes that the Navy is too weak to carry out the seizure. Moreover, it is doubtful whether Vis is worth the committment of so many valuable forces, since it is a question whether we will be able to supply and hold it afterwards.   The continual interference with German coastal shipping could not be stopped by the seizure of Vis, since the airports in Foggia and the ports on the southern coast of Italy are at the disposal of the British very close by.   *The C.-in-C., Navy*, points out that Vis is a vulnerable spot on the Dalmation coast.   Infiltration of enemy troops and weapons is easier through Vis than straight across the Adriatic from Italy. Therefore it is important to seize Vis.   Our losses of transport vessels in this area are almost always caused by enemy air forces, which attack our ships even while they are lying in the harbour.   Naval escort forces will, of course, be unable to provide sufficient protection, especially in the event of destroyer attacks.   Naturally, the C.-in-C., Navy, is not at all certain that the British will use destroyers.   Surprise is the most important element of the undertaking.   Therefore the approach will have to be well camouflaged.   In addition, the C.-in-C., Navy, considers the support of our air forces as absolutely necessary for the invasion.

The *Reichsmarschall* is against the operation.   First he asserts that the destroyers are too much of a danger.   Then he claims that British aircraft from Foggia would appear during the landing and annihilate everything. *General Jodl* says that he and the Army also consider the risk too great.

*The Fuehrer* tends to agree with the C.-in-C., Navy.   He calls attention to the fact that the British are building an airport on Vis Island, which would make attacks on our supplies still easier.   On the other hand he also agrees with the Chief of the O.K.W. that there is great danger from enemy aircraft and possibly from destroyer attacks, against which our own old torpedo boats would be powerless. It goes without saying that our Air Force would have to support the operation. *The C.-in-C., Navy,* believes the operation could successfully be carried out under proper weather conditions and with the aid of dark nights. An essential condition would be the ability to keep the island supplied afterwards. *The Fuehrer* believes that the latter is possible, if need be with the help of submarines. He reserves the decision on the seizure of Vis until the return of the officer who was sent by the O.K.W. to investigate the above matters.

General impression.—The Fuehrer is inclined to agree with the C.-in-C., Navy, but argues as follows: "If the Army is opposed to begin with, and the inner conviction is lacking, then nothing will come of it anyway."

[Russian convoys continued to cause anxiety to the O.K.W. The supplies that they took to Russia clearly affected the progress of the Red Army on the Eastern Front, and Hitler was adamant in his demands that the convoys should be attacked. But by the use of escort carriers and the co-operation of R.A.F. Coastal Command had made it almost impossible for the old type of U-boats to get within range of the convoys, and, until the new U-boats were ready, the assistance of the *Luftwaffe* was essential for success.]

3. Operation against convoys in the Arctic Ocean.—*The C.-in-C., Navy,* explains the part carrier-based aircraft are playing in the Arctic in connection with convoy operations. He points out that the submarines can no longer get near the convoys, and how close carriers have come to the Norwegian coast. He shows how easily the Air Force could have attacked the carrier by means of search receivers and torpedoes. This would have given our submarines a chance to get closer to the convoy, and thereby provided further opportunity for destroying valuable war materials intended for Russia. The *Reichsmarschall* does not want to undertake this. He doubts that carrier-based aircraft alone prevent submarines from approaching the convoy. He considers the carriers too far from our air bases. *The Fuehrer* supports the C.-in-C., Navy, on all counts, and demands an attack on the aircraft carrier of the next PQ convoy.

The *Reichsmarschall* declares his willingness hereafter to transfer forces to northern Norway for short periods of time. *The C.-in-C., Navy,* points out that convoys are located not more than three days in advance. It is very doubtful that this would be long enough to effect the transfer. The *Reichsmarschall* believes that it would suffice if the ground installations were set up beforehand. He wants to begin work on these immediately, so that only the planes themselves would then have to be transferred. The *Reichsmarschall* gives corresponding orders to the Chief of the General Staff, Air.

4. Submarine warfare.—With the aid of an English monthly report captured by the Japanese and giving data on Allied shipping losses and anti-submarine warfare, *the C.-in-C., Navy,* shows the great extent to which naval forces were tied up by submarine warfare as early as January, 1942. His estimate for the present time is much higher. The *Reichsmarschall* stresses the large number of enemy air forces tied up by submarine warfare. The C.-in-C., Navy, points out that Churchill admitted in his last monthly report on submarine warfare, that an extraordinarily large number of forces is being tied up in this way. The C.-in-C., Navy, therefore believes that submarine warfare must continue in spite of losses.

The C.-in-C., Navy, explains the submarine distribution for April 15 from the following points of view: (a) enemy forces tied up; and (b) submarines in readiness in case of an invasion. *The Fuehrer* agrees on every point.

5. The Walter submarine.—*The C.-in-C., Navy,* reports on the plan to change to the Walter submarine, and mentions the bottleneck encountered in tube manufacture. Special measures may have to be taken. As the result of the priority granted the Air Force, types XXI and XXIII have been delayed, causing other armament to suffer. An example of this occurred in the Augsburg Division of the *Maschinenfabrik Augsburg-Nuernberg*. The engines were not completed because too few construction workers were employed to repair bomb damage. And the ready submarine strakes could not be welded together because the engines were not ready. *The Fuehrer* admits that this is a great disadvantage. However, from a broader point of view, the *Jaegerstab* will have to have this power. Otherwise industry might be destroyed still more, and thus submarine construction completely halted. The *Reichsmarscall* agrees wholeheartedly.

6. Small battle weapons.—The C.-in-C., Navy, indicates which small battle weapons he has now definitely decided upon.

(signed)          DOENITZ.<br>(countersigned) Comdr. PFEIFFER.

Naval Staff.                                           May 17, 1944

## MINUTES OF THE CONFERENCES OF THE C.-IN-C., NAVY, WITH THE FUEHRER AT THE BERGHOF FROM MAY 4 TO 6, 1944

1. Protection of prefabricating and assembly yards for new submarines.—*The C.-in-C., Navy,* showing shipyard plans and the construction programme, points out the completely inadequate protection of submarines under construction. Since thirty to forty parts of one kind are built simultaneously in one shipyard, a loss of thirty to forty submarines may be caused by a single air raid. The same condition exists in the assembly plants. In Hamburg for instance, thirteen submarines are assembled each month. Since it takes more than two months to complete assembly, more than thirty boats are always under construction on the building slips. Assembly in Hamburg and Danzig is entirely unprotected. Shelters are being built for the assembly yards in Bremen which, however, are not to be ready before spring 1945. Excavations are being made in Hamburg for similar shelters. They will be completed at the earliest in 1946. No plans at all have been made for the security of the assembly yards in Danzig. So far the Navy has had no raw material quotas for these shelters. Our own naval quotas for building materials are so very small that they do not even suffice to provide the necessary basic installations for present ship construction. The C.-in-C., Navy, is convinced that the British will wait until construction of the new type submarine is quite advanced and then they will begin systematic bombing of all plants. We are in danger of seeing our new submarines destroyed before they have even been finished.

*The Fuehrer* recognises the demand for protection as absolutely justified and says that it is completely out of the question that completion of the shelter be so long delayed; rather, more of them must be built. The C.-in-C., Navy, reports that his means are absolutely exhausted and that only the Fuehrer can still help. The Fuehrer mentions the fact that he will discuss the question in the next few days with Dorsch and that he will direct him to build the shelters without fail. The C.-in-C., Navy, also points out the weakness of anti-aircraft and smoke screen protection for Hamburg, Danzig, and Bremen. He submits to the Fuehrer, in the presence of the *Reichsmarschall* and the Chief of the Air Force General Staff, the demands for an increase in air protection. The *Reichsmarschall* points out that complete security could not be attained by an increase in anti-aircraft and smoke screen protection. The C.-in-C., Navy, considers an immediate improvement nevertheless necessary since even with the greatest effort it would take too long to build concrete shelters. Smoke screens are better than no protection at all.

*The Fuehrer* agrees that anti-aircraft and smoke screen protection should be increased. The *Reichsmarschall* receives corresponding directives.

2. Lack of workers for submarine construction.—*The C.-in-C., Navy*, reports that submarine construction is continuously being cut down. According to the latest data only 140 submarines are to be completed in 1944 instead of 218, due to a lack of workers in steel construction. The Labour Exchange is not furnishing the promised labour; on the contrary, workers are being withdrawn. The C.-in-C., Navy, recommends that Speer should have authority over Sauckel. *The Fuehrer* refuses. He will however under no condition agree to a decrease in submarine construction; Speer assumed the task and it is up to him to find a way to finish it. Speer must furnish the original number of workers for submarine construction under any circumstances.

3. Latest operation in the North Sea against a QP convoy.—*The C.-in-C., Navy*, using a map, explains that the submarines in the first patrol line, fighting in a stationary position, were close to the convoy and were able to sink several steamers and destroyers. In the days following, however, the farther the convoy proceeded to the south and the stronger the enemy air defence became, the more the submarines were forced away from the convoy. This shows that whenever the submarines are close to a convoy, ships are sunk just as in the past. This operation proves again that submarines of the new type which proceed under water would have been able to change their position and stay with the convoy, making a continuous attack possible. The weakness of our own Air Force prevented us from attacking the aircraft carriers in the convoy. The C.-in-C., Navy, raises the fundamental question whether it would not be more advantageous to use the torpedo-bomber squadrons in the North Sea rather than in the Mediterranean. The *Reichsmarschall* explains that an attack on aircraft carriers could not be made in broad daylight on account of our own weakness in the air. He agrees, however, that attacks on convoys are more important in the North Sea than in the Mediterranean. *The Fuehrer* agrees with the statements of the C.-in-C., Navy.

4. *The Fuehrer*, in a discussion of situation in the south-east, brings up again the question whether it is possible to increase the submarines in the Crete–Peloponnesus area of the Aegean Sea. The existence in Egypt of enemy divisions of battle strength is well established; the Fuehrer is very much afraid that this means the Anglo-Saxons might in the course of an

invasion begin an operation against the Rhodes–Crete–Peloponnesus area. This region, especially the Peloponnesus, has no adequate defences. The Fuehrer anticipates great success from submarines stationed in this region. *The C.-in-C., Navy*, reports as follows:

(*a*) The submarine force in the Mediterranean is weak.

(*b*) If the submarines were consolidated in the region Crete–Peloponnesus, these boats would no longer be available for the war in the Mediterranean and nothing would be sunk during the time of waiting.

(*c*) The British would notice the consolidation very soon and would concentrate all their means for defence in this area.

(*d*) Submarine losses in ports from air attacks have seriously increased in recent weeks due to lack of shelters.

(*e*) Submarines have constantly been sent to the Mediterranean but the new supply just covers the losses.

The Fuehrer appreciates these difficulties and misgivings but replies that he would again approach the C.-in-C., Navy, should the signs of danger increase in this region.

5. The mine situation in the North Sea and the Baltic Sea.—*The C.-in-C., Navy*, showing a mine map of these areas, announces that enemy warfare was intensified in the North Sea and the Baltic Sea in April. The Navy has been able to control this aggravated situation in recent weeks only with difficulty by utilising all school flotillas for mine defence. Naturally as a result training in this important field has suffered greatly. No improvement can be expected before the autumn when the naval building programme of 1943 will begin to show results. The C.-in-C., Navy, points out that this mine war threatens the submarine training regions, the supply service to Norway, and ore imports from Sweden in a very serious way. *The Fuehrer* concurs with the statements of the C.-in-C., Navy.

6. Use of new mines off the English coast.—*The C.-in-C., Navy*, announces his renewed intention to increase minefields off the invasion ports along the southern coast of England with the most varied types of mines. He expresses his doubts concerning the use of pressure mines, since in the recent tests they failed to come up to expectations. Besides, there is the danger that the secret may be discovered, and if this should happen the enemy would have a great advantage in using this mine in the Baltic Sea. *The Fuehrer* agrees and he directs the *Reichsmarschall* to take care that under no condition mines of this type fall into the hands of the enemy in case of an invasion or through careless disposition of them along the coast.

7. Grossi.—*The C.-in-C., Navy*, reports that Captain Grossi had tried to smuggle 3,400,000 francs into Spain at a meeting on the international bridge in Irun with the Italian naval attaché in Madrid. The C.-in-C., Navy, considers it advisable that the case should be investigated by Italy. He reports that he requested the Italian Minister for Naval Affairs to have Grossi transferred to Italy. *The Fuehrer* says that such offences by Italians are a matter of indifference to us. He does not consider an investigation worth while, because nothing would be gained by it. He wants Grossi to be sent back to Italy.

8. Lake Peipus.—During the discussion of the situation in the East, the C.-in-C., Navy, requests information from the Army as to whether the Russians are making any preparations on the east coast of Lake Peipus for using naval vessels. The Army and the Air Force report that nothing of the sort has been observed to date, and they promise to inform the Navy immediately should their reconnaissance reveal any such activity. *The Fuehrer* requests brief reports concerning the strength of the naval forces, the distribution and type of vessels to be used for the intended operation of certain ports. In general the Fuehrer is satisfied.

# Invasion

THE LANDINGS in Normandy besides achieving tactical surprise also found few of the German naval anti-invasion preparations completed. The production of midget submarines and mines was far behind schedule—due to Allied bombing attacks—while the coastal batteries were badly sited and unable to cope with the bombardment of Allied battleships. The artificial harbour at Arromanches, the *Mulberry*, upset what few preparations the German Navy had made in the Seine area. These preparations had all presupposed that a large unloading port would be one of the first objectives of the Allies, and Le Havre had been specified as the most likely port to be attacked. There is no evidence that the German naval staff had any previous intelligence of the size and scope of the *Mulberry*. The next few conferences indicate the progress of the invasion.

Naval Staff.                                                                June 13, 1944

## MINUTES OF THE CONFERENCE OF THE C.-IN-C., NAVY, WITH THE FUEHRER AT BERGHOF HEADQUARTERS ON JUNE 12, 1944

I. At 1300 the C.-in-C., Navy participates in the situation conference with the Fuehrer.

1. It is mentioned that the enemy would gain a suitable debarkation point by seizing the harbour and the very well situated roadstead of St. Vaast. The possibility of mining it by air and naval forces should be investigated.

2. Concerning the emergency units of the Navy, it was briefly stated that 45,000 men have been made available for security duties. At present there is no necessity for any further transfers.

3. *The C.-in-C., Navy*, reports on the supply and delivery of DM 1 mines. It is impossible to lay minefields in all potential landing areas. The C.-in-C., Navy, believes it best to lay first of all as many of these mines as possible in the Seine Bay area, especially off the mouths of the Vire (by air) and the Orne (by air and naval forces) and off Le Havre. Next in importance are Cherbourg, Dieppe, Boulogne and Ostende. *The Fuehrer* agrees.

4. During the report on the Russian attack against the Finnish Front on the Karelian Isthmus *the Fuehrer* decides that the Army is to send several armament shipments to Finland. "So long as the Finn fights, he will receive support; as soon as he begins to negotiate, the deliveries will be stopped." *The C.-in-C., Navy*, considers this a confirmation that it is correct to send them the promised E-boats on time, two at first.

5. Renewed minelaying off Sevastopol is discussed. The Fuehrer proposes that the Navy and the Air Force investigate the possibilities for such action.

6. *The C.-in-C., Navy*, reports on supply shipments to Crete. So far as tonnage is concerned, we can ship 6,000 tons per month at this time. However, the C.-in-C., Navy, cannot guarantee this since the success of the shipments depends entirely on how much enemy interference is

encountered and on the strength of our own fighter defences. The Navy will do its utmost to comply with the demands as far as possible. The Fuehrer states that the figure of fifty tons per day, as supplied by Lt.-General Breuer, cannot be considered a basis for procedure. There is no point in using operational submarines for supply shipments since their capacity is only thirty to forty tons. The C.-in-C., Navy, announces that we cannot count on the first Italian transport submarine before about three months from now.

II. 1500. The C.-in-C., Navy, has lunch with the Fuehrer.

III. 1630. The C.-in-C., Navy, and Rear-Admiral von Puttkamer confer with *Reichsleiter* Bormann.

IV. 1730. The C.-in-C., Navy, Rear-Admiral Voss and the Chief of Operations Division, Naval Staff confer with Field Marshal Keitel and General Jodl. Keitel and Jodl consider the situation very serious, although they still see a chance would lie in an unsuccessful enemy landing attempt at another point. It is doubtful whether the enemy will make such an attempt. The most likely spot for it would be the coast between Dieppe and Boulogne or between Calais and the Scheldt River. It is hoped that the long range bombardment of London, [*with V.1's.* ED.] which will begin during the night from June 12 to 13, will on the one hand divert enemy aircraft and on the other induce the enemy to attempt a second landing in northern France. (This last thought was mentioned during the situation conference with the Fuehrer.) If the enemy succeeds in fighting his way out of the present bridgehead and gains freedom of action for mobile warfare in France, then all of France is lost. Our next line of defence would be the Maginot Line or the old West Wall. Field Marshal Keitel believes that even then there is still a chance to defend Germany. General Jodl does not commit himself in this respect since everything depends on how the situation develops and on how many troops we can save. It was possible to transfer a small reinforcement from the Eastern Front. Air Force units from the Eastern Front are not suited for warfare in the West since they are too inexperienced to oppose the well trained personnel of the western Allies.

V. Conclusions of the C.-in-C., Navy from II and IV.

1. It is still too early to abandon altogether the long range planning policy of the Navy in favour of short range action.

2. It is absolutely necessary to employ all naval forces in any way suitable in the Channel battle area. In this connection it must be investigated how many of the submarines in Group *Wallenstein* are suited for this purpose.

3. The possibility of dissolving Group *Wallenstein* is to be considered in order to continue with training.

4. For the time being no further emergency units are to be formed in the West.

5. The submarines of Group *Landwirt* which are stationed in the Bay of Biscay are to be withdrawn. They risk serious losses in that area while being of no practical value because, to judge by the present situation, there is no likelihood of an enemy landing in the Bay of Biscay.

6. It must be kept in mind that it might become necessary to move all submarines to Norway.           (signed)           DOENITZ.
                                                           (countersigned) Capt. PFEIFFER.

The success of the invasion could not be denied, and though the German soldier had been promised a miracle in the form of "secret weapons" the following message, sent by Keitel on June 14 to the control staffs of all three services, indicates the extent of German disorganisation:

"(1) The large-scale enemy landing in Normandy has shown that coastal batteries set up in the open, and possessing neither the necessary range nor the penetrating power against enemy battleships and heavy cruisers, are put out of action by the guns of the ships, before they can put up even the semblance of a fight. The Fuehrer, cancelling all other existing orders, has ordered the immediate examination of the emplacements of all coastal batteries, and wherever possible, the batteries are to be withdrawn to hidden positions and the emplacements improved. The resulting loss in arc of fire or range, and the difficulty of controlling fire from hidden positions will not be so important as the advantage gained, because then, the batteries will at least be able to take part in the fight against the landing.

"(2) The enemy landed at places where the fortifications were weakest and where the coastal batteries were easily wiped out. Strong reserves must be sent there immediately.

"(3) Considerable forces must be dispatched to that area on a broad front and where the countryside is suitable they must proceed in formations of small mixed battle-groups, keeping away from the main roads and using divers byways. The main thoroughfares are watched day and night by the enemy air force and so traffic in a column could not get through. They can now only be used by single vehicles. Allowance must be made for delays in movements to the front, but this is better than having a unit destroyed or attacked by the enemy air force. If a column, a stationary unit, or a village is attacked by low-flying aircraft, every soldier must open fire with his infantry weapon.

"(4) The ability of the enemy to land very strong forces behind our front by glider or parachute, makes it necessary for every German soldier to be on the alert immediately the alarm is given. There is no longer any division between the front, which does the fighting, and the units at the rear, which do not have to fight; it is all one force which must always be ready for battle. Since it is never possible to tell the exact moment of an enemy attack, every unit, and above all, those units in the rear who are unaccustomed to fighting, must be maintained at the highest state of battle readiness. This is all the more necessary when guerrilla warfare, acts of terror, and sabotage are spreading and often have easy successes because of the inoffensiveness of the unit.

"(5) Accurate and quick reports on the situation in the battle-zone, especially in the first phases of the landing from the sea or air, give the senior control the details for planning countermeasures.

(signed) KEITEL."

Naval Staff.                                                                    July 12, 1944

## MINUTES OF THE CONFERENCES OF THE C.-IN-C., NAVY, AT THE FUEHRER HEADQUARTERS, BERGHOF, FROM JUNE 29 TO JULY 1, 1944

*Accompanied by:* Rear-Admiral Wagner on special duty and Lt-Commander Hansen-Nootbaar, Aide.

I. June 29, 1944. 2000. Conference with the Fuehrer Concerning the Situation in the Invasion Area.—After considerable time spent in private discussions in which only the Field Marshals von Rundstedt, Rommel, and Keitel and General Jodl participated, *the Fuehrer* summed up his conception of the war situation in the following terms: The overpowering aerial superiority of the enemy and his very effective naval artillery limit the possibilities of a large-scale attack on our own part. We cannot fix the time of an attack; it is dependent on when troops and supplies can be brought up, and this cannot be calculated in advance. On the other hand we must not allow mobile warfare to develop, since the enemy surpasses us by far in mobility due to his air superiority and his super-abundance of motor vehicles and fuel. Therefore everything depends on our confining him to his bridgehead by building up a front to block it off and then on fighting a war of attrition to wear him down and force him, back, using every method of guerilla warfare. In attacking enemy supply lines our Air Force must concentrate on mines, torpedoes, and guided missiles (FK); the Navy on mines, torpedoes, and small battle units. Reference is made to the circling torpedo of the Air Force which compels the enemy to abandon the waters he has cleared of mines and forces him back into the minefields. Fighters should be converted into fighter bombers, especially the jet-propelled fighters which can fly over and attack the battle area in short quick sorties in spite of the enemy's superiority in the air. For the safety of our own supply lines he proposes forming several strong anti-aircraft highways which are protected against strafing planes by a large number of anti-aircraft emplacements and are covered by fighter patrols. We will have to concentrate all possible lorries in our supply lines in the West even at the expense of other groups which need them.

The *Reichsmarschall* says: Anti-aircraft artillery must be withdrawn from the airfields of the Reich. The use of mines seems to bring good results. To judge from the latest aerial photographs, the enemy is shifting the centre of his unloading activities from the mouths of the Vire and the Orne rivers, where minefields have been laid up to now, to the area of Port en Bassin. This will be taken into account in our future mining operations. (Note: This shifting of enemy unloading activities has not been confirmed by other sources.) In discussing our fighters, *Field Marshal Sperrle* states that the area of the 3rd Air Force is in need of an additional twelve to fourteen hundred fighters. This would enable us to operate five to six hundred fighters per day.

*The C.-in-C., Navy*, reports.—The means of the Navy for operations in the Seine Bay are very limited. However, all suitable weapons possible will be used. At present twelve E-boats are ready for action in the Channel area. An E-boat flotilla of eight boats (the 6th E-Boat Flotilla) is on its way there and will be followed by another one of six boats (the 10th E-Boat Flotilla) after its training period, in about four weeks. The last torpedo boat left in the English Channel will be withdrawn to the East about the middle of July after necessary repairs have been made, since a single torpedo boat can hardly operate successfully. The transfer of a torpedo boat flotilla is intended later. To be sure, torpedo boats operate under greater difficulties in the Channel than E-boats. All submarines with *Schnorchel*, eight at present, are now operating in the Channel. They will be reinforced in July by fourteen boats, seven from Germany, and seven from the West. Although great losses are anticipated, their use in this area is justified by the results. We will continue to lay DM mines with motor boats. Since the output of these mines has increased at 1,200 per month, the supply has become adequate. The bottleneck at present is the lack of sufficient boats for minelaying. Operations with small battle units (*Neger* midget submarines and remote controlled explosive motor boats) will soon be started. These weapons are subject to weather conditions and their practical value has yet to be established under actual war conditions.  In concluding, the C.-in-C., Navy, makes it clear that minefields should be established in the Seine Bay as soon as possible, since they are the most effective means for eliminating the danger arising from the superior supply facilities of the enemy.

*The Fuehrer.*—We have got to lay more mines and still more mines in the Seine Bay with the tenacity of a bulldog, following the British procedure against our own transport network.  Just as they do, we must concentrate practically everything against the enemy supply lines; it is incomparably more effective to sink a whole cargo than to have to fight the unloaded personnel and material separately on land at a later date. Enemy warships must be attacked, too, especially the battleships.  If the enemy should lose six to eight battleships in the Seine Bay, this would have the greatest strategic consequences.  Just as we succeeded in Norway in forcing the enemy out of the country by harassing his supply lines with aircraft, submarines, and battleships, we must do the same thing here, too, by using every possible weapon.

II. June 30, 1944.  1300.  The C.-in-C., Navy, Participates in the Fuehrer's Situation Conference.

(*a*) *The C.-in-C., Navy,* reports that four naval coast artillery lighters were placed at the disposal of the Finns for use on Lake Ladoga.  The question of transport has been solved.

(*b*) Following a report from Ambassador von Papen concerning renewed difficulties which the Turks are having with the British on account of the passage of German vessels through the straits, the C.-in-C., Navy, declares that no more ships will be sent through for the present until the question is finally settled with the Foreign Office.

III. July 1, 1944.  1300.  The C.-in-C., Navy, Participates in the Fuehrer's Situation Conference.

(*a*) *The C.-in-C., Navy,* announces his intention to send a strong submarine force into the North Atlantic in the near future in order to force the enemy to increase the protection of his convoys by withdrawing destroyers and aircraft from the Seine Bay, thus relieving the situation there.  If this step is taken, the submarine reserve for defence against invasion in the Biscay Bay would be practically dissolved and the North Sea submarine group would be reduced by about ten boats.  The *C.-in-C., Navy,* believes that both consequences are supportable, since we hardly expect enemy action in the Bay of Biscay now, and we have observed no PQ convoys in the Arctic Sea for some time.  *The Fuehrer* agrees.

(*b*) In connection with the general strike in Copenhagen, the Fuehrer expresses the opinion that terror can only be fought with terror.  A court-martial only creates martyrs.  History proves that the whole world talks about those legally tried while no mention is made of the many thousands who lose their lives on similar occasions without a court-martial.

IV.  July 1, 1944.  1700.

The C.-in-C., Navy, is present at the state funeral for General Dietl at Castle Klessheim.  After the ceremony he has a short conversation with the Foreign Minister.

(*a*) The latter asks whether the Navy is in a position to send additional ships through the Bosphorus, since it might be desirable not to give in to the pressure exerted by the British on Turkey.  Incidents such as that with the cargo ship (*KT-Schiff*) Kassel must be avoided, however.

[On June 5, 1944, the German war-transport Kassel entered the Bosphorus from the Black Sea en route to the Aegean.  Turkish authorities stopped her, and as she was a camouflaged warship, forbade her passage through the Straits under the Montreux Convention.  The incident precipitated a political crisis in Turkey, forcing the pro-German Foreign Minister to resign.  If there was another such incident the Germans feared that Turkey might enter the war on the side of the Allies.  *Ed.*]

*The C.-in-C., Navy*, replies that passage of ships through the Bosphorus has been stopped for the time being in order not to aggravate the political situation in regard to Turkey through military measures; a resumption of this shipping is possible, though.  He would, however, wait for the Foreign Office to take the necessary steps.

(*b*) Speaking of Bulgaria, the Foreign Minister says he is not inclined to give in with regard to withdrawal of German naval vessels from Bulgarian ports.  He is trying to steer the discussions into purely military channels, with the aim of bringing the Bulgarians to the point in the negotiations where they themselves will express the wish that the German naval vessels remain where they are.  The Fuehrer has not yet approved this procedure, however.  The C.-in-C., Navy, states that so far Group South had received orders to reduce the number of naval forces in Bulgarian ports to a certain extent, and that further measures would not be taken if the Foreign Office should so desire.

V  JULY 1, 1944.  EVENING.
    Return by plane to *Koralle*.

(signed)                       DOENITZ.
(countersigned)   Capt. PFEIFFER.

Naval Staff.                                                    July 10, 1944

## MINUTES OF THE CONFERENCE OF THE C.-IN-C., NAVY, AT FUEHRER HEADQUARTERS, WOLFSSCHANZE, ON JULY 9, 1944

1. 1200.—A limited group conferred with the Fuehrer on the situation in the East.  The following persons participated: from the Navy only the C.-in-C., Navy; from the Eastern Front: Field Marshal Model, Lt.-General Friesner, and General von Greim.  The conference topic is the problem of clearing up the serious situation on the central sector of the Eastern Front.  In this connection a withdrawal of the Northern Army Group is out of the question.  Experiences with the Fourth Army on the Central Front have shown that we cannot withdraw during the summer without incurring serious losses, because at this time the enemy is able to follow up on an extended front across the open country without depending on roads.  By doing this he can pass through gaps in the retreating armies and cut them off.  Besides, a withdrawal of the Northern Army Group with all its equipment would require at least four weeks; the present crisis is too advanced for such a measure.  A reinforcement of the penetration area by bringing up additional divisions before July 17 is considered to be the solution to the problem.  The commanders of the Eastern Front

believe that it will be possible to intercept the Russian thrust this way without having the Northern Army Group cut off.

On the Fuehrer's request *the C.-in-C., Navy*, points out what consequences a Russian break-through to the open Baltic Sea would entail. He refers to the importance of our control of the Baltic Sea; it is essential to Swedish iron ore imports which are of decisive importance for our war economy, and to the construction of the new submarine force. The most westerly position which still permits the closing of the Gulf of Finland is the position east of Reval, i.e. the Nashorn minefields. The possession of the Baltic islands is likewise important for this purpose. However, should the enemy break through to the Baltic Sea further south, in Lithuania or East Prussia, then our position on the Gulf of Finland including the Baltic islands would be worthless. Enemy bases in the immediate vicinity, would threaten or even completely eliminate the ore shipments and the submarine training areas. The prime objective, therefore, to which everything else must be subordinated, even the possible withdrawal of the Northern Army Group, is the prevention of a Russian break-through to the Baltic Sea. Once the enemy has broken through, the threat to our flank from the Russian air force bases in Lithuania will make it impossible to supply the Northern Army Group and Finland by sea.

Concerning the employment of naval personnel for army purposes *the C.-in-C., Navy*, reports that the Navy has only three battalions which have had some training for land combat. These are the Naval Coastal Artillery Battalion 531, at Tytaersaari; the Naval Special Operations Unit, from the Narva Front, which is to participate in operation *Tanne Ost*; and the Naval Battalion *Hossfeld*, formerly in the Crimea, the remaining troops of which are now stationed in Bulgaria. Eighty per cent. of the entire Navy personnel is directly employed in the defence of Europe. The remaining twenty per cent. are needed until the end of 1944 for the fleet, for the present submarines, for newly commissioned submarines, and for assault and defence units. There is already a lack of personnel for other newly commissioned vessels. Therefore it will be impossible to give up any personnel so long as the Navy is expected to fulfil the duties it has had up to the present time. Aside from that, the Navy has absolutely no equipment for land-based troops. Lt.-General Friesner, Commander of the Northern Army Group, states that he has enough men without equipment (Esthonians) so that such troops are of no interest to him. *The Fuehrer* decides that no Navy personnel will be transferred to land activities.

During the course of the conference *Field Marshal Model* reports that he is constantly conducting training courses for non-commissioned officers behind the front and has thereby achieved a continuous supply of fresh replacements at the front. Wherever this is not done—and it does not seem to be the case in other places—the troops eventually become fatigued and fail when suddenly called upon.

2. 1400.—After the conference the C.-in-C., Navy; the *Reichsfuehrer S.S.*; Field Marshals Keitel and Model; Generals von Greim and Jodl, and Lt.-General Friesner have lunch with the Fuehrer.

3. 1530.—Conference with the Fuehrer concerning other theatres of war:

(*a*) *The C.-in-C., Navy*, reports on the qualities of the long range torpedo (*Langstreckentorpedo*), evolved from the G7e LUT, and the plans for its employment: it is to be fired by E-boats from the area near the Le Havre approach buoys into the landing area in the Orne estuary. The C.-in-C., Navy, emphasises that the idea was developed by an alert employee of the Torpedo Experimental Station. *The Fuehrer* is very pleased and urges investigation into whether this type of torpedo could also be used with a pilot.

(*b*) In the discussion of the attack made by enemy fighters on the one-man torpedo (*Neger*) pilots returning from their mission during the night of July 7 to 8, the Fuehrer raises the question whether one could not help these pilots by laying smoke screens from the air.

(*c*) The Chief of the General Staff, Air, reports that V.1's are to be launched from planes during the coming night of July 9 to 10. This will serve to broaden the area from which they can be launched and will thereby scatter the enemy defences.

(*d*) He also reports that the first four jet-propelled planes (Me262) will be put into action against the beachhead within a week to ten days.

(*e*) Subsequent to the conference on the air situation *the Fuehrer* makes approximately the following statement: The extreme importance of air superiority is apparent on all fronts. The Anglo-Saxons are particularly accustomed to advance only under protection of strong air cover. Everything depends therefore on our fighter aircraft construction programme. It must be kept top secret and we must accumulate ample reserves. Then the enemy will be very much surprised when in about four months the situation will begin to change in regard to air supremacy.

4. *Field Marshal Keitel* asks the C.-in-C., Navy, for naval support for protection of the hydrogenation plants. The continuous destruction of these plants constitutes the greatest handicap to our conduct of the war at this time. The last air raids cut gasoline production again from 2,200 cu.m. per day to 1,100 cu.m. per day. The Air Force has been ordered to double the smoke screen protection of the hydrogenation plants and also to improve their protection in other ways. However the Air Force does not have sufficient equipment at present. The Navy is therefore requested to assist in the emergency by providing the following:

(*a*) The 12·8-cm. anti-aircraft guns which are to be delivered to the Navy in the near future.

(*b*) Smoke troops with equipment from Navy units. Demands for their return after a stipulated period could be considered. The C.-in-C., Navy, promises to investigate this request.

(signed)        DOENITZ.
(countersigned) Capt. PFEIFFER

Naval Staff.                                                July 14, 1944

## MINUTES OF THE CONFERENCE OF THE C.-IN-C., NAVY, AT THE FUEHRER HEADQUARTERS, BERGHOF, ON JULY 11 TO 13, 1944

Participants: Rear-Admiral Wagner, on Special Duty.
              Lt.-Commander Hansen-Nootbaar, Aide.

1. July 11, 1944. 1300. Situation conference with the Fuehrer.—On the basis of this conference and several private conferences, the situa-

tion in the East appears as follows: The situation at the Central and Northern Army Groups, which was so optimistically described by the Commander of these two Army Groups on July 9 at Wolfsschanze, is not developing quite as expected. Even though the measures taken for the purpose of stabilising the front in the area of the Central Army Group may still prove successful, the possibility that things may take a turn for the worse must also be considered. It is therefore necessary to make plans in advance in case there should be a successful Russian penetration into East Prussia. To prepare for such an eventuality a telegram was sent by the C.-in-C., Navy, to the Chief, Naval Staff. After the conference, the C.-in-C., Navy, lunched with the Fuehrer.

2. July 11, 1944. 1530.—The oak-leaf cluster of the Knight's Cross of the Iron Cross is awarded to Captain Petersen, Commander of E-boats; Lt.-Commander Hoffmann, Commander, 5th Torpedo Flotilla; and and Lieutenant von Mirbach, Commander, 9th Motor Boat Flotilla.

3. July 12, 1944. 1300. Situation Conference with the Fuehrer.

(a) During the discussion of further enemy invasion possibilities, *the C.-in-C., Navy*, points out the necessity of air reconnaissance in the Thames area, so that enemy operations originating there may be discovered in time. The transfer of a large part of American troops from the area south of the Thames into the area between the Thames and the Humber suggests a possible enemy surprise attack from the Thames in the direction of Holland–Belgium, the German Bight, or even Jutland–Skager-rak. However, this transfer might be the result of V.1 bombardments.

(b) The Chief of the General Staff of the Air Force is asked to secure aerial photographs of the port of Cherbourg as soon as possible which will reveal to what extent the enemy can use the harbour for supply shipments.

(c) *The Fuehrer* asks whether the Navy could spare 10,000 men to occupy part of the Narva position, so that one division may be released for duty on the front of the Central Army Group. It is a well fortified position, and all the soldiers would need is high morale in order to fulfil their mission there. They would be relieved by September 1 at the latest, because the last divisions that are to be brought up to strength will then be ready for action. *The C.-in-C., Navy*, replies that he believes he can provide 10,000 good soldiers, but that the Navy is absolutely deficient in weapons and is particularly lacking in commanding officers and subordinate commanders who would be capable of handling this situation, which is not within the scope of the Navy. The Chief of Staff, Army, General Buhle, is ordered to investigate the problem of armament. No final decision has been reached on this question for the time being.

4. July 12, 1944. 1500. Conference of the C.-in-C., Navy, with Field Marshal Keitel.

(a) Motor vehicles for the Admiral, Small Battle Units.—*The C.-in-C., Navy*, asks that the motor vehicles needed by the Admiral, Small Battle Units, be made available from the stocks of the O.K.W. at appropriate times. In return, the Navy will forego claiming the equipment of the 2nd Naval Motor Transport Battalion from Army Group E. The O.K.W. will be supplied with the exact list of the motor vehicles required with the dates they are needed. *The Chief of Staff, O.K.W.*, promises to deliver the required motor vehicles in time.

(b) Concerning the question of personnel, *the C.-in-C., Navy*, again emphasises that any naval personnel drafted for other types of duty will henceforth be at the direct expense of the submarine service. The only exception will be those troops already engaged in defence operations in the West.

(c) *The C.-in-C., Navy,* requests the O.K.W. to take steps to free the captured submarine Commanders Luedden and Landfermann.

(d) *The C.-in-C., Navy,* once more stresses the necessity for thorough air reconnaissance in the Thames area and the southern North Sea, so that enemy operations originating in that area may be discovered in time.

5. July 12, 1944. 2000. The C.-in-C., Navy, is the guest of the *Reichsfuehrer S.S.*

6. July 13, 1944. 1300. Situation conference with the Fuehrer.

(a) The situation in the East and questions of Army command are discussed by a very small selected group. The C.-in-C., Navy, is the only representative of the Navy. During these discussions the Fuehrer decides that the 5,000 men to be furnished by the Navy for a blocking unit (*Sperrverband*) are not to be taken from men in training for submarine duty, but from those training units already now engaged in defence operations in the West.

(b) Situation conference concerning the other theatres of war, including naval and air situation, a larger group participating.

1. *The C.-in-C., Navy,* again points out the possible danger to the Skagerrak. The main reason for this is the fact that the enemy, experienced on the sea, chooses coasts protected from the prevailing west wind for landings. This was also the case in the Seine Bay. *The Fuehrer* is more inclined to believe that further attacks will more likely be directed at the Holland–Belgium area or the Pas de Calais.

2. *The C.-in-C., Navy,* expresses the opinion that in the case of an evacuation of the Narva position by the Army, the island of Tytaersaari must be held under all conditions to the bitter end, since it is the key to all the minefields in that region. *The Fuehrer* agrees with this.

7. July 13, 1944. 1620.—Take-off from Salzburg for return flight to *Koralle.*

(signed)                    DOENITZ.
(countersigned) Capt. PFEIFFER.

# The Revolt of July 20

THE FULL history of the one genuine revolt against the Nazis by Germans themselves will probably never be told. The subsequent Nazi purge of the revolutionaries and the machinations of Goebbels destroyed much of the evidence, and what little is left is not sufficient for a comprehensive and accurate account. Goebbels sought to make what was in fact a widespread revolt appear as a dangerous, but restricted act of treachery, and this propaganda distorts the few documents in the German naval archives which refers to the attempted assassination of Hitler. The brief history of the revolt given here is based partly on what was revealed at the Nuremberg Trials, partly on fragments pieced together by Allied intelligence officers, and partly on subsequent German accounts from those who had knowledge of the revolutionary movement.

The revolt properly began in 1938 when General Ludwig Beck who was then Chief of Staff to the O.K.W. resigned as a protest against the intended invasion of Czechoslovakia.

Until then Beck had paid little regard to Hitler's internal politics, but the invasion of Czechoslovakia, and unprovoked attack on a foreign country, meant war. To Beck the occupation of Austria and the Sudenten was possibibly justified on the grounds that both countries did contain a large number of Germans, but this was not true of Czechoslovakia, and it is an indication of the hold which Hitler had over intelligent and responsible Germans that it needed the bloodshed in Czechoslovakia to open their eyes. As Ribbentrop cynically remarked to Ciano; it was not land that Hitler wanted, but war.

Having resigned, Beck set about gathering round him a group of soldiers and civilians with the intention of wresting power from the Nazis and over-throwing Hitler. Beck's difficulties were immense, and for the next few years his movement was driven deeper and deeper underground both by the Gestapo, and by the popularity which Hitler had gained from his early military successes. Nevertheless such men as Count von Moltke; the ex-Mayor of Leipzig, Doctor Karl Goerdeler; the former German Ambassador in Moscow, Count Friedrich von der Schulenberg; the Generals Witzleben, Hoeppner, and Olbricht; and Admiral Canaris, head of the Abwehr (Military Intelligence Service), joined Beck's circle in the early years.

The revolt was essentially a revolt from the top. It was impossible under the regime of Himmler's Gestapo for ordinary people to take part, but an indication of its extent is given by the fact that according to one source, based on names and places, more than 4,980 Germans were exterminated by the Nazis in the purge which followed July 20. In order to succeed, therefore, it was necessary to have the sympathy of most of the Army commanders, who alone would be capable of seizing power. But the one great obstacle to obtaining the sympathy of the Army was the personal oath of loyalty which all officers had taken to Hitler. In England it is difficult to understand how much this personal oath meant. Hitler's crimes alone would seem to have been sufficient reason for breaking such an oath, but to the German officers nothing less than the death of Hitler could absolve them from their obligations. For the success of Beck's movement, therefore, the assassination of Hitler was a *sine qua non*.

The motives which inspired Beck's movement were varied. They were obviously united by a common hatred of Hitler, but undoubtedly some of the other generals, who later joined the movement, were concerned principally for the salvation of the *Wehrmacht*. On the other hand such men as Goerdeler and Beck himself were genuinely determined not only to rescue Germany from the destruction of war, but also to rid themselves forever of those elements within their nation which had made Nazism possible. It was not until the defeat of Germany became certain, however, that sufficient numbers joined Beck to make the revolt feasible.

The realisation of defeat divided Germany into two camps—those who wished to prevent further needless destruction, and those who still followed Hitler. This division gave Beck's movement the status of a full-scale revolt. Many more officers joined him, and success became possible. Among his new supporters was Count von Stauffenberg whose vigorous and dashing personality gave an added impetus to the movement, and plans were accordingly completed.

On the other hand Hitler was fanatically opposed to surrender and determined to defend Germany or drag the whole nation to destruction with him. Not many appreciated Hitler's intentions of national suicide, but the majority of Germans still supported his determination to defend Germany, and many, deluded by promises of secret weapons, even hoped that his skill and luck would bring about a stalemate, and possibly a negotiated peace.

In the Germany Navy a few naval officers had joined Beck's movement, but they were neither sufficiently senior nor numerous enough to have any real effect on the navy as a whole. They were in any case not essential to the revolt as they had little influence on land. Doenitz, himself, remained staunch to Hitler and continued in increasing favour with him; and most of the German Navy, imbued as they were with Nazi doctrine, followed his lead.

This was the political background when on July 20, 1944, Count von Stauffenberg attempted to assassinate Hitler at Rastenberg. Briefly the plan was that as soon as Hitler's death had been established, General Witzleben was to assume command of the *Wehrmacht*, while Fromm, at the head of the Home Army, was to seize Berlin. All Gestapo and *Sicherheitsdienst* (S.D.) Headquarters were to be surrounded, and in particular all communications with the O.K.W. were to be cut. As soon as order had been established Goerdeler and Beck were to form a government and sue for peace with the Allies. They realised that the Allies would only accept unconditional surrender, but they believed that however harsh the terms they would still have saved many lives and prevented the further destruction of Germany.

The plan miscarried, firstly because Stauffenberg did not wait to make sure that Hitler was dead, secondly because the communications were not secured, and thirdly because Fromm, uncertain of Hitler's death, betrayed the movement. Even so other parts of the plan were put into operation. Units of the reserve army began their march against Berlin without Fromm, and Witzleben issued several orders and proclamations before he was caught. Considerable confusion resulted, and, for two days, few in Germany knew what was happening in spite of Hitler's prompt action against the revolutionaries. Most of the Army was suspect, and those at a distance from Berlin did not know which of the many orders to obey. Army Generals like von Kluge, C.-in-C. of the armies in France, and Rommel, had given their tacit support to Beck, and until they knew for certain that Hitler had escaped, did not interfere with his plans. In Paris, for example General Stuelpnagel was able to arrest the local S.D., and imprison its General, General Oberg.

But the failure of the assassination attempt was broadcast rapidly throughout Germany—Hitler himself spoke over the radio—and this together with Fromm's treachery lost Beck those supporters in the Army who needed Hitler's death to absolve them from their oath and give them courage to seize power from the Nazis. The terror which followed was one of the worst that Hitler ever organised against his own people. In the German Navy, however, only three officers were caught and tried, one of them being Stauffenberg's brother.

The following account by Doenitz, though lacking in detail, gives some idea of the confused situation, and shows clearly the attempt to belittle the revolt.


Naval Staff.                                                                July 25, 1944

### MINUTES OF THE CONFERENCE OF THE C.-IN-C., NAVY, WITH THE FUEHRER ON JULY 20 TO 21, 1944

Also present:  Rear-Admiral Wagner, on special duty.
               Lt.-Commander Hansen-Nootbaar, Aide.

*Note.*—The C.-in-C., Navy, had originally intended to spend July 20 and 21 at Fuehrer Headquarters. When the Admiral at Fuehrer

Headquarters telephoned that the Duce was expected there on July 20, the C.-in-C., Navy, decided to postpone his visit until July 21 and to confine it to this one day.   On July 20 about 1315 an urgent call from the Admiral at Fuehrer Headquarters told the C.-in-C., Navy to come to Fuehrer Headquarters at once.   No reason was given.   Consequently the C.-in-C., Navy, departed on July 20 about 1450.

1. July 20, 1944 about 1645.—The C.-in-C., Navy, was met at the airport in Rastenburg by Commander Meyer who was the first to inform him of the attempt on Hitler's life.

2. July 20, 1944, 1730.—After his arrival at Fuehrer Headquarters, the C.-in-C., Navy, was ordered to the Fuehrer who was in conference with the Duce.

3. July 20, 1944.   2000.—Release of a proclamation addressed to the Navy by the C.-in-C., Navy.

"Men of the Navy:
The treacherous attempt to assassinate the Fuehrer fills each and every one of us with holy wrath and bitter rage towards our criminal enemies and their hirelings.   Divine Providence spared the German people and its Armed Forces this inconceivable misfortune.   In the miraculous escape of our Fuehrer we see additional proof of the righteousness of our cause.   Let us now more than ever rally around our Fuehrer and fight with all our strength until victory is ours.
Grand Admiral DOENITZ."

4. July 20, 1944.   2050.—The C.-in-C., Navy, instructs the Chief, Naval Staff by telephone to issue an order to all Naval commands at once containing the following points:

"(a) There has been a military conspiracy by a clique of generals (Fromm, Hoeppner).

(b) Reichsfuehrer S.S. has been made Commander of the Replacement Army.

(c) The Navy is ordered to be in a state of readiness.

(d) Orders issued by Army commands are not to be executed.   Only orders of the C.-in-C., Navy, or of other Senior Naval officers are to be honoured.

(e) Demands of the Reichsfuehrer S.S. must be complied with by the Navy.   Long live the Fuehrer.
C.-in-C., Navy."

5. July 20, 1944.   2140.   The Admiral on Special Assignment called the Chief of Naval Staff concerning the arrest of Assistant Judge Advocate General, Count Stauffenberg, brother of the would-be assassin of the Fuehrer.

6. July 20, 1944.   2200.—The C.-in-C., Navy, is present at the evening war situation conference with the Fuehrer.   Nothing of special interest to the Navy was discussed.

7. July 20, 1944.   2330.—Radio broadcast of the Fuehrer's speech to the German people and of the address by the C.-in-C., Navy.

8. July 21, 1944.   1300.—Situation conference with the Fuehrer. The C.-in-C., Navy, reports to the Fuehrer on the results of submarine operations against the enemy invasion forces.   Of twelve boats which were

sent out, six were lost. The six boats which returned succeeded in sinking eleven destroyers and twelve transports. In addition it may be assumed that the six submarines which were lost also did some damage. Although these losses are severe, nevertheless the submarine operations are worth while.

9. Further conferences of the C.-in-C., Navy.—(a) Conferences with Field Marshal Keitel, concerning the lorries for the Admiral, Small Battle Units. The Chief of Staff, O.K.W. promises to make the requested number available. He also gave the necessary orders in regard to the radio trucks, which, however, are still causing some problems.

(b) Conference with General Jodl and General Warlimont for the purpose of discussing whether coastal batteries should be placed further inland for purposes of camouflage. Both are convinced that greater care than heretofore must be taken to camouflage the batteries on the seaward side. They agree, however, that the seaward effectiveness of the batteries must remain the prime consideration. Thereupon the C.-in-C., Navy, orders that the Naval commands concerned should receive instructions supplementary to the directive from the O.K.W., to the effect that the ordered camouflage measures must not be permitted to affect to any appreciable extent the direct fire or the seaward range of the batteries.

10. July 21, 1944. 1415—The C.-in-C., Navy, instructs the Chief, Naval Staff by phone to rescind the state of readiness order.

11. C.-in-C., Navy, appoints the Admiral on Special Assignment to substitute for the Admiral at Fuehrer Headquarters. He is also to take over reporting to the Fuehrer on the naval war situation.

12. July 22, 1944. 1630.—After visiting the wounded officers at the hospital at Rastenburg, the C.-in-C., Navy flies back to Berlin.

(signed)          DOENITZ.<br>
(countersigned) Capt. PFEIFFER.

\*      \*      \*      \*      \*      \*

As the German Navy was not deeply involved in the revolt little information is available in the Tambach documents, but the following signals from Witzleben, Keitel, Fromm, and Himmler may help to fill in some of the missing details. The signal from Fromm is particularly interesting, in that he himself had been a member of Beck's group. He was later found out and shot in spite of these efforts to regain favour with Hitler.

\*      \*      \*      \*      \*      \*

Extracts from a signal sent by General Field Marshal von Witzleben to the Chief of Staff of the Operations Division of the Naval War Staff. Time: 1928. Date: July 20, 1944.

(1) The Fuehrer Adolf Hitler is dead. An unscrupulous clique of non-combatant party leaders utilising this situation, has attempted to stab our fighting forces in the back and seize power for their own purpose.

(2) In this hour of extreme danger the Government of the Reich, to maintain law and order, has decreed a military state of emergency and placed me in supreme command of the German Armed Forces.

(3) I hereby decree: The *Waffen S.S.* is from now on included in the Army.

(4) Officers with executive power are responsible for maintaining order and public security. In particular they have to look after:

(a) Safeguarding the means of communication.

(b) Elimination of the S.D. Resistance is to be broken ruthlessly.

(5) In this hour of extreme peril for the Fatherland the unity of the armed forces and the maintenance of discipline is of the utmost importance. I therefore make it the duty of all Commanding Officers of the Army, the Navy, and the Air Force to support all officers with executive power and so enable them to carry out their difficult tasks and to ensure that their orders are carried out by subordinate authorities. The German soldier has a momentous task and the safety of Germany depends on his energy and attitude.

C.-in-C., Armed Forces
(signed) von WITZLEBEN
*Feldmarschall*

\* \* \* \* \* \*

Signal to the Chief of the Naval War Staff. Time: 2920. Date: July 20, 1944.

With immediate effect the Fuehrer has appointed *Reichsfuehrer S.S.* Himmler to the command of the Reserve Army and has given him the appropriate authority. Only orders from the *Reichsfuehrer* and from myself are to be obeyed. Any orders issued by von Fromm, von Witzleben or Hoeppner are invalid.

(signed) KEITEL,
*General Feldmarschall.*

\* \* \* \* \* \*

Signal from Rear-Admiral Stummel (Chief of Naval Communications).

I hereby report that about 2300 the false signal bearing the signature of Witzleben, which was received this afternoon by the Naval War Staff, was received as a W/T signal from the Naval W/T station Bologna. I have ordered the cancellation of this signal and also the immediate transmission, on the same wavelength, of the C.-in-C., Navy's message.

(signed) Chief of Naval Communications.

\* \* \* \* \* \*

Signal issued by *Generaloberst* Fromm to Admiral Stummel. Time: 0127 Date: July 21, 1944.

The *putsch* attempted by irresponsible generals has been ruthlessly subdued. All the leaders have been shot. Orders issued by General Field Marshal von Witzleben, *Generaloberst* Hoeppner, General Beck, and General Olbricht are not to be obeyed. I have again assumed command after my temporary arrest by force of arms.

(signed) FROMM,
*Generaloberst.*

Note from the Naval Communications Officer Berlin: This signal was not transmitted. Request instructions.

(signed) Naval Communications Officer, Berlin.

\* \* \* \* \* \*

Signal issued by Himmler to the Naval War Staff. Time: 1540. Date: July 21, 1944.

In my capacity as C.-in-C. of the Reserve Army I appoint S.S. *Obergruppenfuehrer* and General of the S.S. Juettner as my Chief of Staff. The orders and directives issued by him on my behalf are to be obeyed. S.S. *Obergruppen-Fuehrer* and General of the *Waffen S.S.* Juettner has commenced his duties as Chief of Staff. The restrictions ordered by me are hereby cancelled and normal conditions are again in force in the Reserve Army.

(signed) HIMMLER.

\* \* \* \* \* \*

The effect on the German Navy is best shown by the following extract from the War Diary of the Admiral Commanding Group West (France and the western coast of Europe), Admiral Kranke, who gives a graphic description of the confusion which resulted in Paris:

July 20, 1944.—After the report had been made over the radio in the afternoon announcing the unsuccessful attempt on the Fuehrer's life, a secret teleprint message comes in from *Koralle* (Headquarters of C.-in-C., Navy):

2120  The message from Witzleben (quoted on p. 408) is received.

This order, coming from a retired General Field Marshal, and containing an order for the imprisonment of the Security Service, must be false, although it is issued as an "Officers only" teleprint message from *Koralle*. I immediately phone the Grand Admiral who assures me that the Fuehrer is alive, that this order is false, and that only orders from him or from Himmler are to be obeyed.

2135  The proclamation from Grand Admiral Doenitz is received.  (See p. 407).

I try to contact Field Marshal von Kluge by telephone in order to clarify any mistakes which might have arisen.  The Field Marshal answers that he is at present in conference and cannot speak to me.  A short time afterwards I receive a phone call from the Chief of Staff of C.-in-C., West, General Blumentritt.  I inform him that after receiving the signal from Field Marshal von Witzleben, I had a conversation with the C.-in-C., Navy, and that the declarations and orders contained in that signal are false.  C.-in-C., West, has received a similar signal from *Generaloberst* Fromm.  General Blumentritt has also received information on the real situation from General Warlimont of the O.K.W./Ops and informs me that "everything is in order."

2300  The teleprint message comes in from the Grand Admiral. (See p. 407 (4) ).

2315  The Naval officer with the C.-in-C., West, Commander Koenig, phones and states that all the circulating rumours are false and that the Fuehrer has appointed *Reichsfuehrer S.S.* Himmler as C.-in-C., Reserve Army.  He receives the answer that I am well informed of the situation, and that C.-in-C., Navy, has given clear orders.

2340  The following W/T Signal comes in from C.-in-C., O.K.W, General Field Marshal Keitel:

With immediate effect, the Fuehrer has appointed *Reichsfuehrer S.S.* Himmler as C.-in-C., Reserve Army, and has given him full powers over all personnel of the Reserve Army.  Orders are to be taken only from *Reichsfuehrer S.S.* Himmler and from me.  Any orders which might come from von Fromm, von Witzleben, or Hoeppner, are invalid.

(signed) C.-in-C., O.K.W., Keitel,
*Feldmarschall.*

2400  Announcement from Communications Equipment Command:
Increased watchfulness tonight.  Beware of possible plot.  Open fire immediately.

(signed) C.O. Paris.

A telephone message comes in from Naval Communications Division West:
At 2210 today an Army establishment in the middle of Paris was attacked by disguised terrorists.  The terrorists, wearing German uniform, drove up with four heavy lorries and disarmed the guards.  All sentries are to be instructed immediately that no military personnel are to be allowed to enter military establishments and bases without first of all giving an explanation outside the bases.  On the approach of every unknown Army vehicle the guard is to receive a warning. A sharp look-out is to be kept and every one is to remain ready for immediate action.

It later turns out that the "Terrorists" incident was only an assumption of the S.O. of the Naval Communications Division.  Actually, they were only German soldiers whose activity was so unusual that they were believed to be disguised terrorists.

0030

An Army patrol stopped an armoured vehicle outside my Staff Quarters.  The patrol explained to my sentry that they had an order to imprison the S.D. (Security Service).  I immediately phoned Field Marshal von Kluge who was at the H.Q. of Army Group B. outside the city, in order to inform him of this action taken by the usurpers.  He thanked me for the information and assures me that he will have all the necessary steps taken in Paris.

**0040**

In order to obtain reliable information I endeavoured to speak with the G.O.C. Security Police and the Security Service (S.D.), General Oberg. At his quarters, however, the O.C. 1st Security Regiment, *Oberstleutnant* von Krewel, answered instead, and informed my Chief of Staff, who is known to him personally, that General Oberg and all the S.D. (Security Service) have been arrested by the Military C.-in-C., in France.

**0045**

I order B.S.W. (F.O.I.C. Western Defences) and the High Command of Naval Stations in Paris to prepare their troops for immediate action.

**0048**

I try unsuccessfully to reach Field Marshal von Kluge by telephone, to inform him of Oberg's arrest and to let him know that the order for this came from General von Stuelpnagel. He sends me the answer that he is at present unable to speak to me. Is there anything wrong?

**0056**

Notification is received from Chief of Naval War Staff that, after the Fuehrer, the Grand Admiral will speak over the radio to the Navy. A corresponding signal is sent out to all stations.

**0107**

My Chief of Staff has a conversation with the O.C. 1st Security Regiment. He asks him if he has heard the Fuehrer's speech and expresses the opinion, that he has been the victim of a gross misunderstanding. *Oberstleutnant* von Krewel intends to contact his superior the O.C. Paris, General von Boineburg, immediately.

**0111**

After the Grand Admiral's speech my Chief of Staff informs General Blumentritt, that I have been trying in vain to speak to Field Marshal von Kluge, and that von Krewel has arrested General Oberg and all the S.D. (Security Service). General Blumentritt replies: "I have been ordered to relieve the Military Officer in Command, General von Stuelpnagal, of his post, and to set General Oberg free again."

**0132**

Over the telephone I inform the B.S.W. (F.O.I.C. Western Defences), Rear Admiral Breuning, of the events.

**0136**

The Chief of General Staff, C.-in-C., West, General Blumentritt, informs my Chief of Staff that he has suggested to C.-in-C., West, that he be appointed Military Officer Commanding in France. C.-in-C., West, has agreed to this suggestion and he, General Blumentritt, is going to Paris immediately and promises that everything will be settled in an hour.

**0137**

Since I could not manage to reach the O.C. Paris, *General-leutnant* von Boineburg, or his representative, General-major Bremer, I contacted the Chief of Staff of the C.O. Paris, *Oberstleutnant* von Unger. General Oberg and the S.D. are to be released immediately, failing which I shall take steps with my troops to set them free. I inform him that the Military O.C. France, General von Stuelpnagel, has been relieved of his command. I demand to know what is happening. He reports that they can do nothing. General von Stuelpnagel has given orders.

**0140**

I now summon the Chief of Staff of the Military O.C. in France, *Oberst* von Linstow. Oberst von Linstow informs me that the O.C. 1st Security Regiment has just received an order to free General Oberg and the S.D. (Security Service). At the Headquarters of the Military O.C. it was considered to be a *Gestapo-Putsch*.

**0154**

The O.C. Paris phones me and informs me that he was taken by surprise. The Military O.C. has ordered that all measures already taken be rescinded immediately.

0156

I inform the B.SW. (F.O.I.C. Western Defences) and the High Command of Naval Stations in Paris of the developments, and cancel the state of immediate readiness. State of readiness No. 1 remains in force.

0206

General Blumentritt phones my Chief of Staff: "Where can I find General Oberg? Answer: "In Hotel Continental, which is being used by the O.C. Paris as a place of detention." General Blumentritt: "If I should be made prisoner there, can I depend on you to release me again?" Answer: "Yes."

0215

On trying once more to reach General Oberg at his station, I am put in touch with *Standerten Fuehrer* Bickler who informs me that he has been held prisoner at the S.D. Station in Avenue Foch, that he has, however, just been set free and is about to go to the S.D. Station in the Boulevard Lannes to meet General Oberg.

0247

My Chief of Staff speaks with the Chief of Staff of the G.O.C. of the Security Police and Security Service, *Stuermbannfuehrer* Hagen. He learns that General Blumentritt was there and is on his way to the Military O.C. with General Oberg, who has just been set free.

0335 The following W/T signal from C.-in-C., West, comes in:

The following delayed W/T Signal was received by C.-in-C., West, at 0145 on July 21, 1944:

To C.-in-C., West: The *Putsch* attempted by irresponsible Generals has been ruthlessly subdued. All the leaders have been shot. Orders issued by General Field Marshal von Witzleben, *Generaloberst* Hoeppner, General Beck, and General Olbrict are not to be obeyed. I have again taken over command after my temporary arrest by force of arms.

(signed) FROMM,
*General.*

The W/T Signal aroused astonishment. I again order that instructions issued by *Generaloberst* Fromm are not to be carried out.

0655 The following signal is received:

The last sentence of the signal from *Generaloberst* Fromm is invalid. In accordance with the order of the Fuehrer I have taken over the command of the Reserve Army. Only orders issued by me are to be obeyed.

(signed) HIMMLER.

1540

A W/T Signal is received from *Koralle* (German Navy H.Q.): "The State of immediate readiness for the Navy is now cancelled." This order is issued straight away. In the forenoon General Oberg phones and expresses his appreciation of the Navy's energetic behaviour during the previous night.

\*　　\*　　\*　　\*　　\*　　\*

The revolt officially ended on August 7 and 8 when amidst the blare of Goebbel's propaganda those leaders who had not yet been shot or tortured to death were brought before the People's Court and tried for high treason. The verdict and sentence was previously ordered by Hitler, and Goerdeler, Witzleben, Hoeppner, Schulenberg, and von Moltke were either hanged or shot—von Moltke in spite of the fact that alone among the revolutionaries he had refused to countenance the death of Hitler because of his religious scruples against the taking of life.

For the rest, Beck, Stauffenberg, and Olbricht were shot by Fromm who was himself later court-martialled and shot by the Nazis; Admiral Canaris, after suffering some months at the hands of the Gestapo, was either murdered or committed suicide, while the many other members of the movement were gradually hunted down and eliminated by Himmler. Terror raged for the next six months, and guilty and innocent alike were tortured and massacred in this the last and worst outburst of the Nazis against their own people.

# Beginning of the End

THERE ARE no records of Fuehrer Conferences on naval affairs from July 20 until October 13, and it seems likely that none took place, as, during this period, Hitler was recovering from the injuries he received at Rastenburg. Much happened in those three months. The Allied armies advanced steadily from the Normandy bridgehead; further Allied forces landed in southern France; the Channel ports were cleared; coastal "fortresses" surrendered; and France was liberated.

The German naval anti-invasion measures had proved as inadequate as was expected. But they did do some damage, and at one stage of the landing operations the activities of the "small battle units" and *Schnorchel*-fitted U-boats caused the Allies some anxiety about the security of the Arromanche anchorage. U-boats, mines, and "small battle units" sank 60 merchant ships in the invasion area and United Kingdom coastal waters during the second half of 1944, but as there were more than 4,000 Allied ships taking part in the invasion these losses were not serious.

The outstanding problem which the German Navy had to face, however, had little to do with the Allies, but lay in the confusion resulting from the dual command of Army and Navy over naval personnel and equipment. Time and again naval equipment was commandeered by local Army commanders who had little idea of how or where to use it with the result that naval defence measures were hopelessly disorganised. In reports from the Admiral Commanding, Group West, and his subordinate authorities, Doenitz received a sorry story of constant interference with naval defence operations. At Cherbourg, for instance, the fortress commander ordered the naval batteries "Blankenese" and "Bastion-Cherbourge" to be blown up long before they were attacked, either by sea or by land, and later laid up the harbour defence vessels, transferring their guns and crews inland where they were of little use for the defence of the port. Other reports described confused withdrawal orders which paid no regard to naval requirements and rendered any defence or salvage of material impossible. All reports combined to show that naval units should have been under naval and not army command. In one area only did the dual command work effectively, and that was in Holland where the German Navy and Army together managed to ferry some 90,000 troops through the Scheldt and Walcheren to safety. Doenitz took these problems to Hitler and during the conferences held in the last quarter of 1944 secured a certain degree of independence for the Navy.

The Tirpitz which had been the subject of periodical attacks throughout the year was finally sunk by R.A.F. bombers on November 12, thereby reducing the German Navy to little more than a U-boat fleet. Doenitz however still believed that these U-boats, especially the new types which were then undergoing trials, would more than compensate for the loss of his major warships, and in the remaining conferences of the year continues to give encouraging reports of their possibilities.

Naval Staff.                                                        October 16, 1944

**MINUTES OF THE CONFERENCES OF THE C.-IN-C., NAVY, AT FUEHRER HEADQUARTERS, WOLFSSCHANZE, FROM OCTOBER 13 TO 14, 1944**

Participants: Rear Admiral Wagner, on special duty Lieutenant Luedde-Neurath, Aide.

1. OCTOBER 13, 1944.

1100. Conference with Minister Speer. 1200. Report by Rear Admiral Moessel. 1210. Report by Captain von Conrady on the situation in the East. He tells of the plans of the Northern Army Group and the proposals by the Chief of the General Staff, Army, concerning probable higher transport requirements, in reference to the telegram received by the Naval Staff. A copy of the answer from the Naval Staff, Quartermaster Division, Shipping and Transport Branch, on October 14 is given to Major von Freytag-Loringhoven.

2. 1500.—Situation conference within a very small circle with the Fuehrer. Only the C.-in-C., Navy, represents the Navy. This was followed by a private conference of the C.-in-C., Navy, with the Fuehrer. The following questions were discussed:

(*a*) Command of the Armed Forces on the coast and in the coast fortifications on the lower levels. Naval officers are better qualified for such work than army officers. Therefore the present arrangement in the coastal areas at home remains the best solution; that is, naval commands under the Commander of the Replacement Army. *The Fuehrer* confirms this opinion. The C.-in-C., Navy, shows the Fuehrer the reports of the admirals in the West.

(*b*) The importance of Antwerp to the enemy. *The C.-in-C., Navy,* produces a map of the Scheldt River showing the minefields laid by the Navy which are expected to delay the enemy for about three weeks. *The Fuehrer* remarks that even two weeks would help. He grants the recommendation of the C.-in-C., Navy, that the Knight's Cross of the Iron Cross be given to Commander Czyskowitz, commander of the harbour of Antwerp. After the headlong evacuation of the city by the Army he was killed while carrying out demolition work according to orders. A map of the flooded areas at Walcheren is shown.

(*c*) The situation in the eastern Baltic. This is an important training ground for the Navy, and it is necessary to do everything possible to combat enemy attacks from sea and air. Fighter aircraft have been requested from the C.-in-C., Air.

(*d*) Progress in the construction of the new submarine models. The C.-in-C., Navy, hopes to put the first vessels of model XXIII into action in January 1945, and about forty submarines of model XXI in February.

(*e*) The greatest danger to the new submarines lies in the air raids on the harbours according to the C.-in-C., Navy. Therefore extensive construction of submarine pens in the home ports is absolutely necessary. Besides those already completed and those under construction, 196 more pens are planned. Minister Speer urges that as soon as the building facilities, being used at present to provide shelters for fighter aircraft construction, are freed in the course of next spring, they should be released for making submarine pens. *The Fuehrer* is in full agreement with this proposal.

(*f*) *Seehund* midget submarines with a larger range will probably be put into action off the east coast of England starting in December. A map with the distribution of small battle units is shown.

(*g*) The morale of the naval troops is satisfactory.

(*h*) Captain Werner Hartmann is assigned as leader of home defence (*Volkswehr*) in Danzig, West Prussia, on the request of Gauleiter Forster.

(*i*) The oil problem. The supplies of fuel oil are satisfactory. The Diesel oil situation is very strained and the shortage is already affecting operations.

(*j*) A chart showing shipments in connection with prefabrication of submarines is presented.

3. 1830.—The C.-in-C., Navy, has a conference with General Jodl about questions of command of Armed Forces on the coast and in coastal fortifications. The C.-in-C., Navy, gives the Chief of the O.K.W. Operations Staff a copy of the same papers which he had earlier given the Fuehrer. He asks that the interpretation of the Fuehrer's directive No. 40 as recommended by the Naval Staff be issued as an order of the O.K.W.

4. 2000.—Supper in the *Haus der Marine* with *Reichsfuehrer* S.S. Himmler, Major-General (S.S.) Fegelein, *Staatsrat* Johst, and Lt.-Colonel (S.S.) Grothmann as guests of the C.-in-C., Navy.

5. OCTOBER 14, 1944.

1215.—Conference of the C.-in-C., Navy, with Field Marshal Keitel.

(*a*) Command of the Armed Forces on the coast (see 3) is discussed.

(*b*) The O.K.W. requisitioned 300 Navy lorries for the Army which were in repair or being reconverted for use as gas generators. The Chief of the O.K.W. promises that these trucks will be returned.

(*c*) Lt.-General Ziegler's memorandum about combining the supply and administrative services of the three branches of the Armed Forces is mentioned. The Chief of the O.K.W. declares that this question is unimportant and out of date, since the Reichsfuehrer S.S. has been instructed to regulate these departments in the Army, and since the *Reichsfuehrer* S.S. as well as the C.-in-C., Navy, and the C.-in-C., Air, do not agree with Ziegler's suggestions. Zeigler's suggestions are to be submitted.

6. 1415.—Among other things, the C.-in-C., Navy, discusses problems of command within the Air Force with the *Reichsmarschall*.

7. 1500. Situation conference with the Fuehrer attended by a very small group. *The C.-in-C., Navy,* emphasises the necessity of holding the peninsula of Svorbe as long as there is a possibility that we might have to withdraw the northern Army Group by sea. The C.-in-C., Navy, indicates the necessity of substantially reinforcing the fighter units on the polar coast in support of operation *Nordlicht*.

8. 1715.—The C.-in-C., Navy, has tea with the Chief of the O.K.W.

9. 2020.—Return trip on special train of the O.K.W.

(signed)     DOENITZ.<br>(countersigned) PFEIFFER.

Naval Staff.                                           Berlin, November 7, 1944

## MINUTES OF THE CONFERENCE OF THE C.-IN-C., NAVY, AT FUEHRER HEADQUARTERS, WOLFSSCHANZE FROM OCTOBER 31 TO NOVEMBER 2, 1944

Participants: Rear-Admiral Wagner, on special duty Lieutenant Luedde-Neurath, Aide.

1. October 31, 1944. 1200.—Captain von Conrady, Naval Liaison Officer attached to the General Staff, Armed Forces, reports to the C.-in-C., Navy, on the situation on the Eastern Front.

2. October 31, 1944.   1500.—Situation conference with the Fuehrer and a very small group.   Only the C.-in-C., Navy, and the Admiral at Fuehrer Headquarters represent the Navy.

(a) In connection with his report on laying aerial mines around the new anchorage of the Tirpitz and the subsequent discussion on the outcome of operation *Nordlicht, the C.-in-C., Navy,* announces his intention of using the coastal batteries which become available in the polar region for the purpose of strengthening the defences of the Lofoten Islands.   The C.-in-C., is of the opinion that no large-scale landing attempts by the British are to be expected in northern Norway. Since Churchill and Stalin could reach no agreement concerning this region at the Moscow Conference, as is clearly revealed by Churchill's last speech, and since on the other hand Churchill will avoid everything which might cause friction between him and Stalin, we do not expect British action in northern Norway which would obviously be directed against Russia.   *The Fuehrer* does not consider this sound reasoning, since relations between Churchill and Stalin are strained in any case, and since England can only prevent Russia's advance into Norway, e.g. in the region of Narvik, by occupying that territory herself.   The Fuehrer fears that the British might establish themselves in certain places in order to cut off our land and sea connections by penetrating inland.   He makes special mention of the island of Andoy, north-west of Harstad, which, on account of its level topography, permits the construction of airfields.   He considers it necessary to give the island our special attention when we strengthen our defences.

(b) *The Chief of the Operations Staff, O.K.W.*, again suggests using submarines together with aircraft against aircraft carriers appearing along the north coast of Norway.   *The C.-in-C., Navy,* declares that the use of submarines for this purpose is hopeless and should not be attempted. *The Fuehrer* fully supports this view.

(c) In his report on the war situation in the West, *the C.-in-C., Navy,* again points out how important it is to hold Walcheren in order to block the enemy from the Scheldt River and thereby prevent him from utilising the harbour of Antwerp.   *The Fuehrer* and *the Chief of Staff of the O.K.W.,* are in complete agreement with the C.-in-C., Navy.

3. October 31, 1944.   2000.—The Chief of Staff of the O.K.W. is the dinner guest of the C.-in-C., Navy, in the *Haus der Marine.*   Commander Meyer, Major von Schimonsky, Major von John, and Lieutenant Bevermeier were also present.

4. November 1, 1944.   1530.—Situation conference with the Fuehrer. The C.-in-C., Navy, and the Admiral, Fuehrer Headquarters, are the only ones present.

(a) The C.-in-C., Navy, reports that because of the threat of losing Walcheren, he had ordered an increase in small battle units in the Holland area, with special concentration in the Scheldt region.   All available motor boats there will likewise be used.

(b) Following the situation conference, *the C.-in-C., Navy,* and the *Chief of Staff of the O.K.W.* submit to the Fuehrer an outline of a directive for exempting shipyard workers from being drafted in the Fifth Drive and all future drives of a similar nature. *The Fuehrer* gives his consent and signs the directive.

5. November 1, 1944. 1730.—There is a short discussion between the C.-in-C., Navy, and General Jodl, Chief of Staff of the O.K.W.

(*a*) *The C.-in-C., Navy*, rejects the proposal for supplying the fortifications in the West by submarines, because such a measure would be ineffective. Fortifications must in the future acquire their own additional provisions by means of sorties. He suggests simultaneous sorties from Lorient and St. Nazaire in order to occupy and to exploit the area in between. Especially important supplies could, however, in exceptional cases be brought by submarine.

(*b*) *The C.-in-C., Navy*, refers to the proposals of Rear Admiral Hueffmeier, Commander of Coastal Defences, Channel Islands, who suggests prolonging the occupation of the Channel Islands until the end of 1945 by means of drastic confiscation and by severely reducing consumption. The recent assignment of Rear-Admiral Hueffmeier to the additional position of Chief of Staff to the Commanding Officer of the Channel Islands is looked upon by the C.-in-C., Navy, as a happy choice and the proper way to give this energetic personality a voice in the over all command of the Channel Islands.

6. November 1, 1944. 2000.—*Reichsleiter* Bormann is the dinner guest of the C.-in-C., Navy, at the *Haus der Marine*.

(signed) DOENITZ.
(countersigned) PFEIFFER.

Naval Staff. December 1, 1944

MINUTES OF THE CONFERENCE OF THE C.-IN-C., NAVY, WITH THE FUEHRER ON NOVEMBER 28, 1944, AT 1530 AT THE REICH CHANCELLERY

At the situation conference with the Fuehrer, the following questions concerning naval warfare came up for discussion.—1. The effect of the loss of the Svorbe Peninsula on the war situation in Kurland. With Svorbe eliminated as an obstacle, the possibility of Russian landings along the coast of Kurland increases. *The C.-in-C., Navy*, submits a plan to the Fuehrer, showing the disposition of the coastal batteries in Kurland. All work necessary to prepare them for action has just been completed.

2. The C.-in-C., Navy, reports to the Fuehrer that he is somewhat worried about the effectiveness of our own mines since reports of self-detonations of German mines that have torn loose from their moorings are quite frequent. To be sure, the latest aerial photographs and reports of the enemy press seem to indicate that the enemy has not made very much headway in clearing away the mines in the Scheldt region. Thus the mines have held him up longer than the C.-in-C., Navy, anticipated, i.e. since the loss of Walcheren on November 11, 18 days to date. This may be attributable to the use of different combinations and types of mines and firing mechanisms. *The Fuehrer* requests a list of the mines used, indicating type of fuse and setting.

3. During the discussion of the situation in Norway, *the C.-in-C., Navy*,

makes reference to the Navy's proposal to retain a few coastal batteries with the necessary infantry protection in front of the Lyngen position. Their purpose would be to make it more difficult for the enemy to occupy these important fiord regions, especially since only small Norwegian forces have fought there so far, the Russians having withdrawn again behind the Finnish frontier. In the opinion of the Navy, the region of the Altenjord and Hammerfest are well suited for such an enterprise. *The Fuehrer* gives approval to this measure.

4. In regard to the transfer of troops from Norway to Denmark, the C.-in-C., Navy, reports that shipping space is not causing any concern. Enough is available to handle the number of troops as they are brought to the embarkation points by rail. The length of time it will take to transfer the troops is much more dependent on the weather, on enemy interference, and on the limited number of escort vessels.

5. In the discussion of possible enemy landings in Holland, the C.-in-C., Navy, stated that conditions at present are not favourable for a landing in that area. He pointed out, however, that according to the reports on hand, several British divisions are assembling in the area south of the Thames, and that the influx of enemy troops to the Western Front will increase considerably after the Scheldt River becomes navigable. *The Fuehrer* confirms this view.

(signed) DOENITZ.
(countersigned) *Lieutenant* NEUMANN.

Naval Staff. December 1, 1944

## MINUTES OF THE SITUATION CONFERENCE WITH THE FUEHRER, ATTENDED BY THE C.-IN-C., NAVY, ON NOVEMBER 30, 1944, AT 1600

I. During the conference, the following questions concerning naval warfare came up for discussion:

With reference to the situation in the West, *the Fuehrer* stresses the great importance of transferring the 6th S.S. Mountain Division and the 2nd Mountain Division, together approximately 36,000 men, quickly from Oslo to Aalborg. In this connection, *the C.-in-C., Navy*, reports that no congestion has so far occurred in Oslo, except for about 14,000 troops on leave or otherwise returning home, who must wait until these divisions have been shipped. The eleven transports assigned, together approximately 50,000 tons, are adequate to take care of the troops arriving at the rate of six trains per day. In addition, thirty coastal motor ships left Holland a week ago. These will increase the transport facilities and help to reduce the congestion.

2. *The C.-in-C., Navy*, refers once more to the serious threat to German shipping along the Norwegian coast, and to the great losses we incur there, primarily inflicted upon us by the enemy air forces. Unless we can guarantee adequate air reconnaissance against enemy aircraft, aircraft carriers and surface forces, the time will not be far off when ship movements in this region will come to a complete standstill. *The Fuehrer* agrees with this view. He stresses the importance of constructing railways along the northern coast of Norway as substitutes for sea traffic, emphasising their comparative safety from air attacks due to the fact that

one third of the distance is through tunnels, and the remainder mostly along high mountains. Then he discusses the necessity of forceful measures to be taken by the Air Force against attacking aircraft carriers and naval forces.

3. In connection with Churchill's claim, which is unsubstantiated as yet, that the first convoys have arrived in Antwerp, the Chief of Operations Staff, O.K.W., emphasises that the Air Force and the Navy must take all possible measures in order to disrupt these enemy supply shipments, not to mention the bombardment of Antwerp with V.1's and V.2's. *The C.-in-C., Navy*, reports to the Fuehrer that two motor boat flotillas were sent on minelaying missions in the West Scheldt the night before, and another motor boat flotilla on a torpedo mission west of the Scheldt. He again requests that Antwerp and the Scheldt River be photographed from the air, so that he may get a true picture of the situation. Brigadier General Christian, the representative of the Chief of the Air Force General Staff, received orders to that effect.

II. Following the situation conference, *the C.-in-C., Navy*, informs the Fuehrer that he was asked to address the German-Japanese Society at its next meeting and asks the Fuehrer's permission to do so. This is granted.

III. As the result of the overall picture presented at the conference on the situation with the Fuehrer, the Navy at this time should concentrate its efforts on the following tasks:

(1) The fast and safe transfer of the Operational divisions from Norway, which is sufficiently important to justify exposing the escort vessels, i.e. cruisers Emden and Koeln, to greater risk.

(2) The fight against enemy movements on the Scheldt River, which must be carried on with all means that can be made available.

(signed)      DOENITZ.
(countersigned) *Lieutenant* NEUMANN.

Naval Staff.

## MINUTES OF THE CONFERENCE OF THE C.-IN-C., NAVY, WITH THE FUEHRER ON DECEMBER 3, 1944

I. December 3, 1944. 1600.—The C.-in-C., Navy, attends the situation conference with the Fuehrer. He is accompanied by the Admiral on Special Duty.

1. *The C.-in-C., Navy*, reports to the Fuehrer his decision to station seven submarines, the only ones equipped with the *Schnorchel* device available in that region, outside Scapa Flow for attacks on entering carrier task forces. In reply to the Fuehrer's question whether it is correct to assume that Scapa Flow is the base for carrier task forces, the C.-in-C., Navy, states that in all probability such is the case, although he has no definite proof.

2. During the discussion of the possibility of sending the entire equipment of the operational divisions to be evacuated from Norway directly to Denmark by sea, and to transport only the personnel by train to Oslo and from there by boat to Denmark, the C.-in-C., Navy, makes the following comment: Little time would actually be saved in view of the time required for loading, not to mention possible delays due to the weather and

enemy interference. Escort forces are insufficient to afford sufficient protection for these extensive shipping operations in addition to their other tasks, such as escorting supply convoys, anti-submarine warfare, and minesweeping. Great losses must therefore be expected. The C.-in-C., Navy, proposes that twenty ships of the Reich Commissioner of Maritime Shipping be assigned to this task, and that the remaining equipment be transported to Oslo by rail as was previously suggested. *The Fuehrer* agrees with this proposal and directs that the equipment to be transported by sea should be chosen on the following basis: the most bulky goods, which take up the most space on the train, in other words all types of vehicles, should go by water. In view of the risk involved in transport by sea, such vehicles should be chosen which can most easily be replaced, that is, approximately in the following order: horse-drawn vehicles, passenger cars, trucks.

II. December 3, 1944. 1730.—Private conference of the C.-in-C., Navy, with the Fuehrer. Besides certain personal matters, the following points were discussed.

1. *The C.-in-C., Navy*, announces his intention of sending ten to fifteen German naval officers to Japan, giving them the opportunity of becoming acquainted with naval warfare on a large scale by participating in fleet operations there. Their experiences could later be utilised to build up a German fleet. Since German naval warfare, with the exception of submarine warfare, has developed into a purely coastal war, we have no opportunity whatsoever of acquiring experience of this nature in the European theatre. *The Fuehrer* agrees.

2. *The C.-in-C., Navy*, submits to the Fuehrer the report of Lt.-Commander Nollmann, who was in charge of a submarine equipped with a *Schnorchel* in its operations off the east coast of Scotland. Nollmann speaks in the most positive manner about the great possibilities of this ship and states the conviction of his crew that with the introduction of the *Schnorchel* the old effectiveness of the submarine has been re-established.

In view of this very favourable evaluation of the *Schnorchel* submarine, corroborated also in other instances, the C.-in-C., Navy, has no misgivings about the new submarine models, which will be equipped even better for underwater warfare. He believes that the revival of submarine warfare will be chiefly a home and shipyard problem, since the enemy will concentrate all his efforts on the outbound routes of the submarines, their construction and repair yards, as well as their bases, as soon as the first successes of the new submarines become known. While other industries can be moved to less endangered regions, the shipbuilding industry is by its nature confined to the coast and the large ports, and nothing can take its place elsewhere. He fears, however, that *Hauptamtsleiter* Saur of the Ministry of Armaments and War Industries will be under such pressure on account of numerous special programmes of other branches of the Armed Forces ordered by the Fuehrer, that the shipbuilding programme may easily suffer. The C.-in-C., Navy, therefore solicits the aid of the Fuehrer to impress Hr. Saur with the needs of the Navy. *The Fuehrer* agrees with the argument of the C.-in-C., Navy, and indicates that he might approach Hr. Saur regarding the matter.

3. As for the propaganda angle of submarine warfare, *the C.-in-C., Navy*, proposes to lull the enemy into a state of security and not to inform the

public at first of our success, in order not to provoke countermeasures on the part of the enemy prematurely. *The Fuehrer* agrees.

(signed) DOENITZ.

Naval Staff.                                                                December 15, 1944

## CONFERENCE OF THE C.-IN-C., NAVY, WITH THE FUEHRER ON DECEMBER 10, 1944, AT 1500

Also present: Admiral on Special Duty, Rear-Admiral Wagner.

During the situation conference the following problems pertaining to the Navy are brought up:

1. During the discussion of the Army situation in Hungary, *the Chief of the General Staff, Army*, points to the importance of taking defensive measures on Lake Balaton and asks the Navy to help as far as possible. *The C.-in-C., Navy*, reports to the Fuehrer that in addition to the assault boats which are already operating, twenty-four remote-controlled explosive motor boats have been made ready, and the transfer of small vessels from the Danube is under consideration. The Navy is also closely co-operating on this matter with the Hungarian Danube Flotilla, which is at our disposal.

2. *The Chief of the General Staff, Army*, emphasises the importance of destroying the Russian Danube bridges south of Budapest. *The C.-in-C., Navy*, comments that naval shock troops are available for such tasks in the area of the Southern Army Group, and that it is the responsibility of the local authorities to plan and execute the details.

3. The Russians seem to be withdrawing large forces from the sector of the Northern Army Group, but the destination of the troops which are being diverted has not yet been established. There are various indications that the assault army before Memel is being reinforced, among others. *The Fuehrer* asks the C.-in-C., Navy, to "throw everything the Navy has" into the defence of Memel, should the Russians launch a major attack. *The C.-in-C., Navy*, emphasises the importance of Memel to the Navy and states that the loss of the city would endanger still more our bases, training areas, and convoy lanes.

(signed) DOENITZ.
(countersigned) (illegible).

\*      \*      \*      \*      \*      \*

Defeat was now inevitable. Even the U-boats, in which Doenitz had so firmly believed, had suffered such losses in the construction stage that out of 290 boats promised only 65 were delivered, while the number of U-boats in commission fell from 181 in June to 140 in December, 1944. In spite of these serious shortcomings Doenitz decided to continue the U-boat campaign.

As a result of the German evacuation of ports in Western Europe all U-boats had been withdrawn from the Atlantic in the autumn, but in December Doenitz mobilised his dwindling fleet for a final assault against Allied sea communications. Although there was now no hope of making the new campaign big enough to cut off Allied supplies, the success of the *Schnorchel* and the possibilities of the new *Walter* submarines encouraged Doenitz to believe that at least some damage would be done. Accordingly in the last days of December U-boats were sent out to the Bristol Channel, the Irish Sea, the Minches, and off the north-east coast of England, areas where they had not ventured since 1940. In these shallow waters, aided by the *Schnorchel*, the U-boats hoped to evade patrol vessels and convoy escorts, and deliver their final blow against Allied shipping.

# 1945

DURING THE last few months of the war Doenitz attended Hitler's Conferences far more frequently, with the result that the minutes of the conferences give what is almost a day-by-day account of the closing stages of Germany's defeat. The editorial background has therefore been reduced to a bare chronology of events during each month.

\*     \*     \*     \*     \*     \*

A comparison of these last four months with the period immediately preceding the Italian collapse shows how much the O.K.W. had declined. In the summer of 1943, when the collapse of the Italians was imminent, Hitler was able to appreciate the situation as a whole and to draw up both military and political plans to avert disaster: Mussolini was rescued, Fascism was restored, and the military measures which Hitler initiated succeeded in delaying the Allies for more than a year.

By the beginning of 1945, however, Hitler's ability had deteriorated, and he showed himself quite incapable of viewing the war situation as a whole. Where one would expect to find an acceptance of military defeat leading to plans being made for guerilla warfare and for continuing the fight underground, there are instead nothing but a series of tactical schemes for bolstering individual sections of the three fronts, neither related to nor co-ordinated with any general strategy. The Ardennes offensive and the last strike of the *Luftwaffe* in January were linked together, but they, too, were apparently unconnected with any overall plan, and the conferences give a clear picture of Hitler and his staff, desperate in the face of a situation they could no longer control, and so harassed that they could not think beyond the immediate requirements of battle.

Alone among Hitler's staff Doenitz continued to give encouraging reports, promising great successes with his new *Walter* U-boats, offering Naval Brigades to assist the Army, organising the evacuation of troops and refugees from East Prussia, undertaking the distribution of coal, and generally cheering his Fuehrer. In an essay which he later wrote in captivity, Doenitz stated that it was the Allied demand for unconditional surrender which forced the *Wehrmacht* to continue fighting, but he also said that there were real hopes that the new U-boats, V-weapons, etc., might still have brought about a favourable change in the war situation for Germany. How much he himself believed in the new weapons is not clear, but whatever his beliefs were, Doenitz continued to give Hitler hopes of possible successes, and even as late as March 1945 discusses with him particulars of the post-war German Navy. Throughout these last few months Doenitz drew closer and closer to Hitler, and gradually became his principal military adviser, until finally Hitler rewarded his loyalty by appointing him his successor.

\*     \*     \*     \*     \*     \*

As the conferences end on April 18 a selection of signals made during the last few days has been included to bring the history to a close. They illustrate the confusion in Germany and give some particulars of the events immediately preceding the surrender.

From February 9 until April 18 the conference minutes were kept by the Admiral on Special Duty at Hitler's Headquarters, Rear-Admiral Wagner, who served throughout the war on the Operations Staff of the German Admiralty.

\*     \*     \*     \*     \*     \*

At the first conference of 1945, Doenitz used an elaborate multi-coloured pictorial chart—not reproduced here—to convince Hitler of the continued importance of sea communications. The war then appeared to be wholly on land, but Doenitz managed to convince Hitler of the necessity of sea transport for transferring troops from Norway to the Reich, and for evacuating Kurland (Lithuania) and East Prussia. Doenitz also pointed out the use that might be made of German warships supporting the German Army on the Baltic coast, as well as stressing once more the vital importance of the Baltic for U-boat training. The chart also showed the direction of British sea attacks against Norway and the still outstanding "fortresses" on the French coast, of which Doenitz was particularly proud as they were nearly all manned by naval personnel.

# *January*

## U-boat Campaign

The U-boats sent out at the end of December 1944 sank 9 merchant ships, totalling 59,000 tons, for the loss of 7 U-boats in action and 5 through other causes. In January, 11 merchant ships, totalling 57,000 tons, were sunk for the loss of the same number of U-boats as in December. U-boat bases were moved from the Bay of Biscay to Norwegian ports during the last few months of 1944. This change-over added about 1,000 miles to their passage to the operational areas round the English coasts.

## Chronology of Important Events—January 1945

Jan. 1. Beginning of Ardennes offensive—800 *Luftwaffe* aircraft attack Allied airfields, losing 188 machines.

Jan. 3. Turkey breaks off diplomatic and economic relations with Japan.

Jan. 11. Warsaw entered by Russians.

Jan. 12. Red Army launches big offensive in southern Poland.

Jan. 16. British 2nd Army attacks German salient east of the Maas—end of Ardennes offensive.

Jan. 17. Allied troops reach Diekirch.

Jan. 20. Allied 3rd Army enter Brandenburg—Russian armies break through on 50-mile front in East Prussia.
Provisional National Government of Hungary signs armistice with Allies.

Jan. 22. Russians reach the Oder on a 35-mile front.

Jan. 25. Tarpiau, Allenburg in East Prussia taken by Russians—Oder crossed near Breslau and near Steinau.

Jan. 27. Memel captured and Lithuania completely freed—Russians cross Vistula near Thorn.

Jan. 28. Russians enter Pomerania.

## Naval Staff

### VISIT OF THE C.-IN-C., NAVY, AT FUEHRER HEADQUARTERS FROM JANUARY 1 TO 3, 1945

Accompanied by: Admiral on Special Duty, Rear-Admiral Wagner.
Adjutant, Lt.-Commander Luedde-Neurath.

1. January 1, 1500.—The C.-in-C., Navy, attended the Fuehrer's situation conference The following questions of naval warfare are discussed:

(*a*) The C.-in-C., Navy, informs the Fuehrer that six *Biber* midget submarines will be carried by submarines to Kola Bay, and will then proceed on their own against the battleship which has been located there, and against other worth-while targets.

(*b*) With the aid of a map the C.-in-C., Navy, reports to the Fuehrer on planned operations for small battle units in the Scheldt River area during January 1945. He states that on January 1 the first eighteen *Seehund* midget submarines are to start on their first mission. He also present two maps showing submarine successes off Cherbourg and those of E-boats and small battle units off the Scheldt River.

(c) The C.-in-C., Navy, then shows a copy of the magazine "Picture Post" dated October 28, 1944, and calls attention to an article dealing with a film of the Battle of the Atlantic, in which comments are made on the poor construction of the liberty ships. He states that similar statements have also been made elsewhere.

(d) Reporting on the shipping situation between Norway and Denmark, the C.-in-C., Navy, points out that this area is very exposed; at the moment the enemy is making increased use of aerial mines and aircraft, and he may create an even worse situation in the future by using surface forces as well. While the German Skagerrak minefields are no great obstacle in themselves, they evidently greatly discourage the enemy from operating in these waters. It is planned to reinforce them.

2. January 1, 1700.—The Admiral on Special Duty confers with the Deputy Chief of the Armed Forces Operations Staff, General Winter, on the following subjects:

(a) The jurisdiction of the Commanding Admiral, North Sea, as Commander, Armed Forces, in the coastal area. General Winter explains that the O.K.W. did not intend to interfere with the authority of the Naval Command, North Sea. General Winter believes that the O.K.W. need not interfere, since the C.-in-C., Navy, and the *Reichsfuehrer S.S.* are in agreement. Rather, the Naval Staff and the Commander of the Replacement Army or the Naval Command, North Sea, and the Operations Staff, North Norwegian Coast, can best settle directly whatever differences still exist between them. The C.-in-C., Navy, joins them later and gives his approval.

(b) The question is raised as to what action has been taken on the ten demands contained in the memorandum on the "Necessity for Providing Additional Facilities for the Navy and Merchant Shipping"; they had been approved by the Fuehrer. General Winter replies that at first, due to a misunderstanding, the O.K.W. had dealt only with those matters directly concerning them; in the meantime, however, action has been taken on the other matters as well. As for the confiscation of cranes and docks in Denmark, the C.-in-C., Navy, has already discussed this question with the Foreign Minister, who gave his assurance that the proper instructions would immediately be sent to the competent German official in Denmark.

3. January 2, 1700.—The C.-in-C., Navy, attended the Fuehrer's situation conference. During the report on the situation in the Baltic Sea, the C.-in-C., Navy, elaborates on the strained mine situation in the Baltic Sea, and emphasises that German forces are not sufficient to accomplish all tasks simultaneously, in spite of the reinforcements which have been ordered.

4. January 3, 1345 to 1500. Coastal Fortresses.—The Commanding Admiral, West, visits Bad Schwalbach. The Commanding Admiral, West, Admiral Kranke, requests that each month a submarine be dispatched with supplies to German naval fortresses in western France, above all to Lorient and St. Nazaire. It is his opinion that the time the fortresses can hold out can be lengthened considerably if vital supplies, even in small quantities, can be sent to them, and he stresses the effect on morale that such supply missions would also have. Four submarines would be required to carry out these missions. *The C.-in-C., Navy, reserves his decision.*

5. January 3, 1900.   U-boat campaign.—The Fuehrer and the C.-in-C., Navy, have a private discussion.

*The C.-in-C., Navy,* reports to the Fuehrer on the present state of sinkings and likely developments in the near future.   Assuming that out of the eighty *Seehund* midget submarines scheduled to operate per month only fifty are able to attack, then one hundred torpedoes would be fired at the enemy.   If 20 per cent. of the torpedoes hit their targets, about 100,000 tons will be sunk.   Latest reports turned in by submarines with *Schnorchel* equipment and information submitted by radio intelligence prove that these boats, too, can achieve success even in waters where German submarines were forced to cease operations more than three years ago, i.e. the Cherbourg area, the Irish Sea, Scapa Flow, and Peterhead.   However, this success will serve to forewarn the enemy that a new German submarine offensive has begun.   Therefore we will have to be prepared for strong countermeasures in the immediate future, even before the new submarine models are ready for operations.   Since it is difficult to combat these submarines at sea because of their ability to remain submerged, these countermeasures will of necessity be directed against submarine bases and yards, and against the routes used by the submarines in entering and leaving the harbours.   The attack against Hamburg on December 31, 1944, and the increased mine offensive in the western part of the Baltic Sea and the Skagerrak appear to be the beginning of these countermeasures.   Thus the difficulties involved in the new submarine offensive do not lie in operations at sea, but entirely in the threat to home bases by the enemy air force.   The importance of the ten demands contained in the memorandum submitted to the Fuehrer is thus emphasised time and again by every renewed consideration.   In this connection the C.-in-C., Navy, proposes to concentrate the use of smoke screens in areas which cannot be reached by the enemy's boomerang method, since that method cancels the effect of the smoke anyhow.   *The Fuehrer* agrees entirely with the viewpoint expressed by the C.-in-C., Navy, and discusses with him countermeasures in detail.   He stresses particularly the fact that he himself will see to it that the harbours are given anti-aircraft reinforcements.

6. January 3, 2000.—The C.-in-C., Navy, departs from Fuehrer Headquarters.

(signed)          DOENITZ.
(countersigned) Lt. NEUMANN.


Naval Staff                                          January 19, 1945

### CONFERENCE OF THE C.-IN-C., NAVY, WITH THE FUEHRER ON JANUARY 18, 1945, AT 1600

1. Naval brigades.—During the discussion of the situation on the Eastern Front, *the C.-in-C., Navy,* offers the Fuehrer a naval rifle regiment of 3,000 men, to be sent to the Army front.   The regiment has infantry equipment, i.e. hand weapons, light and heavy machine guns, light infantry guns, and medium mortars.   Light mortars and some field kitchens are lacking.   The regiment will be ready for transfer at forty-eight hours' notice.   The North Sea coast will be exposed by the transfer,

to be sure, but this can be borne in view of the emergency in the East, since the North Sea coast is not in acute danger during the winter months. *The Fuehrer* agrees with this opinion and approves the proposal. The C.-in-C., Navy, determiꞇꞇes jointly with the Chief of the General Staff, Army, that the regiment is to be sent to the Tilsit sector.

2. *The Fuehrer* asks if the troop transports from Norway to Denmark cannot be speeded up, but the C.-in-C., Navy, answers in the negative. The delay is due to the weather, and especially to the mine situation.

3. U-boat campaign.—*The C.-in-C., Navy*, gives a short report on possibilities for naval operations against the enemy supply traffic between the Thames and Antwerp. Destroyers and torpedo boats could be used only at the risk of very severe losses and with little positive effect; therefore it cannot be justified—particularly since these vessels cannot be spared from combat and escort duties in other areas. The area is unfavourable for submarine operations. Nevertheless, in the near future a VII C submarine with *Schnorchel* will be despatched to the Channel. An unexpected storm interfered with the success of the first operation by *Seehund* midget submarines. However, valuable experience was gained, and the boats are continuing to operate. Because of the long distances involved, the other small battle weapons can be used only as suicide weapons, and then only if the weather is suitable, as they would otherwise not even reach the area of operations. Despite these liꞇꞇitations, all efforts will be continued to interfere with the enemy supply traffic to Antwerp.

4. During a report on the distribution of the British Fleet, the reasons why the British are keeping such a relatively large number of vessels in home waters are discussed. The C.-in-C., Navy, believes that these vessels might be used to operate against our sea communications along the west coast of Norway and to penetrate into the Skagerrak. He again calls attention to the necessity of protecting the Skagerrak strongly on the western side.

(signed)      DOENITZ.<br>
(countersigned) Lt. NEUMANN.

Naval Staff                                                January 20, 1945

### CONFERENCE OF THE C.-IN-C., NAVY, WITH THE FUEHRER ON JANUARY 19, 1945, AT 1600

1. Sea transport.—*The Fuehrer* decides that in addition to the transfer of three divisions which has already been ordered, two more divisions are to be removed from Kurland to the Reich. *The C.-in-C., Navy*, reports that nine ships are already available for embarkation in Libau. The time required for the transfer is at present determined by the speed with which the Army can bring up its troops overland.

2. *The Chief of the General Staff, Army*, reports that a battalion of Tiger tanks is to be transferred by naval barges from Memel to Pillau. The C.-in-C., Navy, comments that this transport operation depends very much upon the weather. However, steamers cannot be used because there is a wreck in the entrance to Memel which would prevent their passage and, furthermore, there are no steamers available for transporting tanks.

3. Naval brigades.—*The C.-in-C., Navy*, reports that the 3rd Naval Rifle Regiment, which has been made available to the Army for the Eastern Front, will be ready by the morning of January 20.

4. After the situation conference *the C.-in-C., Navy*, directs the Fuehrer's attention to the decisive significance of the East and West Prussian area for naval warfare. Its loss would paralyse naval warfare, especially submarine operations. *The Fuehrer* completely agrees with this opinion.

5. *The C.-in-C., Navy*, asks the Chief of Staff, O.K.W., for the speedy assignment of the light anti-aircraft weapons required to arm the merchant ships, as provided by the memorandum of December 19, 1944, approved by the Fuehrer. General Winter will take the necessary measures.

6. Coal.—After the situation conference, Reich Commissioner Terboven (Norway), General Jodl, and the C.-in-C., Navy, confer about the coal supply of central and northern Norway at Terboven's request. The latter feels that the Norwegian railway should take over coal shipments from the south to the north at the expense of a certain delay to troop transports from the north to the south. The C.-in-C., Navy, and the Chief, Operations Staff, O.K.W., however, think that bulky cargoes like coal should continued to be moved by ship, and that sea transport, despite some losses, can still cope with this task. It is only necessary to get the proper priority rating; otherwise the problem can generally be solved by local authorities.

(signed)      DOENITZ.<br>
(countersigned) Lt. NEUMANN.

Naval Staff

January 23, 1945

## CONFERENCE OF THE C.-IN-C., NAVY, WITH THE FUEHRER ON JANUARY 20, 1945

1. January 20, 1600. Coal.—In a conference requested by Reich Commissioner Terboven (Norway) with the Chief of Staff, O.K.W., the C.-in-C., Navy, the Reich Commissioner for Maritime Shipping, and representatives of the Reich Coal Commission and the transport office, the question of Norway's coal supply is discussed once more. *The C.-in-C., Navy*, is of the opinion that the time has come when it is necessary to establish a strict and uniform control of the entire coal supply within the German area through central agencies, both as regards overall distribution as well as distribution between the Navy and merchant shipping. These agencies must determine how much coal is available, and must decide how it should be distributed. The needs of naval warfare must have top priority, as the transfer of the divisions from Kurland and Norway depends on the Navy. Priorities must be decided in the following order:

(*a*) All ships afloat, both escort forces and transports.
(*b*) Repairs.
(*c*) New construction.

Supplies sent outside the country, e.g. Norway, must be adjusted to the supply situation at home. *The Chief of Staff, O.K.W.*, agrees with the C.-in-C., Navy, with some additional suggestions of his own, e.g. pertaining to railways for troop transports. Appropriate steps are to be taken.

2. January 20, 1645. Situation conference with the Fuehrer. (*a*) Sea transport.—Concerning the troop transports from Libau to Gdynia *the C.-in-C., Navy*, reports that two destroyers and ten ships are waiting in Libau already loaded. The time of their departure depends on the weather situation. Later the Fuehrer receives an additional report that five ships have left Libau.

(*b*) Naval brigades.—In view of the threatening developments in the East, *the C.-in-C., Navy*, puts 20,000 naval troops at the disposal of the land forces. *The Fuehrer* accepts this offer, and after a discussion of the type of troops to be used he decides that the above-mentioned number of men from training units of the Navy are to be transferred to the Danish area, where they are to join the land defences. This would free twenty-two Army replacement battalions from the Danish area for service on the Eastern Front. This solution has the advantage for the Navy that the naval personnel will stay together, and can later be re-assigned to naval operations when the overall situation has changed. The C.-in-C., Navy, further declares that of the four branches of the Navy, i.e. the submarine arm, escort forces, anti-aircraft, and coastal artillery, the first three cannot be touched. Coastal artillery in Holland, Denmark, Norway, and the Eastern Baltic Sea cannot be weakened. Thus there remain only the 7,000 men along the coast of the German Bight; but there too it is inadvisable to expose the key bases of Heligoland, Borkum, and Sylt. *The Fuehrer* decides that coastal artillery is not to be weakened either since this would be of no advantage.

(signed)        DOENITZ.

(countersigned) Lt. NEUMANN.

Naval Staff                                          January 21, 1945

### CONFERENCE OF THE C.-IN-C., NAVY, WITH THE FUEHRER ON JANUARY 21, 1945, AT 1600

1. Naval brigades.—In view of the fact that the situation on the East Prussian land front continues to be extremely strained, *the C.-in-C., Navy*, offers Naval Artillery Units 629, in Gdynia, and 533, in Pillau, for use under Army command. This will mean that all coastal batteries on the Gulf of Danzig will be silenced. The C.-in-C., Navy, feels that this must be done, however, since the sea front does not seem to be endangered, whereas the land front is threatened most seriously. *The Fuehrer* approves the proposal.

2. The evacuation of Memel, which is to be carried out partly by sea and partly by way of the Kurische Nehrung, is discussed. *The Fuehrer* decides in favour of the proposal made by the C.-in-C., Navy, that contrary to previous orders the destruction of the harbour is to be prepared and carried out at the proper time. (As for the German bases in the Gulf of Danzig, *the C.-in-C., Navy*, of his own accord orders that preparations for the destruction of the harbours be organised and the necessary material made ready. No active preparations are to be made as yet. The measures ordered are to be kept secret and should be carried out without attracting attention.)

3. U-boat campaign.—*The C.-in-C., Navy*, using a chart of the central

part of the Baltic Sea indicating all areas free of ground mines, elaborates once again on the great importance of the Gulf of Danzig, the only submarine training area, for the continuation of naval warfare. He emphasises that the loss of this area would paralyse submarine warfare.

4. Reporting on the successes achieved by Submarine Commander Hechler off Gibraltar, the C.-in-C., Navy, points out that they are very impressive proof of the operational possibilities of submarines equipped with the *Schnorchel* device and of the new submarine models.   He reveals that in past break-through attempts in that area our losses have amounted to 60 to 80 per cent.   Now a single boat can operate there for as long as ten days and can achieve considerable results.

5. Coal.—After the situation conference *the Chief of Staff, O.K.W.*, informs the Fuehrer of the difficult coal situation and of the necessity for organising coal distribution very strictly.   *The C.-in-C., Navy*, declares that the present situation is untenable, because everyone is confiscating coal for his own purpose, and the most important tasks of the Armed Forces are therefore being endangered.   Coal must be secured for sea transports and defence forces; otherwise divisions can no longer be sent to the front, and Army Group, Kurland, which can be supplied only by sea, will be cut off entirely from supplies.   The distribution of coal is a task of military nature, and it can be accomplished only by a determined member of the Armed Forces with the necessary authority.   The agencies concerned must keep in constant contact with one another and get the facts on the coal situation; on these findings the coal czar must base his decisions as to the proper distribution according to military needs.   In addition to the Reich Commissioner for Coal as the supplier, all the agencies requiring coal must be represented: the O.K.W., the Navy, the Reich Commissioner of Maritime Shipping, railways, and the *Gauleiters*.   *The Fuehrer* adds war industries to the list.   *The Fuehrer* approves the proposal that a member of the Armed Forces be appointed coal czar.   He also approves the suggestion that the shipment of 40,000 tons of coal en route to Norway be held back, and that one fourth of this amount be diverted to Danzig.

(Following the conference on the situation, *the C.-in-C., Navy*, offers his services as coal czar to the Chief of Staff, O.K.W., who had declared that there is no one with sufficient authority available for this position. The O.K.W. must make the decisions as to where the delivery of coal is most vital from a strategic point of view; the C.-in-C., Navy, would take over the practical execution.   The Chief of Staff, O.K.W., will see to it that the matter is regulated in this way.)

The C.-in-C., Navy, also reports that Rear-Admiral Engelhardt is organising seventy to ninety tugs and a corresponding number of barges on the Rhine to ship coal to the Netherlands.   The Navy is supplying the required number of officers and 1,000 men for this task.   Light anti-air-craft guns are needed.   *The Fuehrer* welcomes this initiative and decides that the anti-aircraft weapons are to be provided.

6. *The C.-in-C., Navy*, calls attention to the serious oil shortage in the Navy, and to the fact that even the submarine arm is now affected by it. The C.-in-C., Navy, reveals that in order to send out the twenty-seven submarines ready for operations in January, he was forced to make use of

the reserves of the Scheer and the Luetzow, and these ships are thereby unable to operate for the present.

(signed)        DOENITZ.
(countersigned) Lt. NEUMANN.

Naval Staff                                     Berlin, January 22, 1945

### CONFERENCE OF THE C.-IN-C., NAVY, WITH THE FUEHRER ON JANUARY 22, 1945, AT 1600

1. Refugees.—*The C.-in-C., Navy*, reports to the Fuehrer with regard to the evacuation of refugees from East Prussia that the Reich Commissioner of Maritime Shipping can provide a total of eighteen ships in home waters for refugee evacuation without interfering with current troop movements.   But there is only a three weeks' supply of coal available for sea transport tasks, e.g. bringing up divisions and supplying Army Group, Kurland, and there is only a ten days' supply for rail transport to take the troops to the front.   Thus the allocations will probably have to be altered in favour of rail transport, because no additional shipments of coal can be expected in the near future.   Thus there is nothing else to be done but to abandon the evacuation of the refugees.   The Navy will do everything possible to evacuate refugees on oil-burning vessels which can temporarily be spared from other operations.   *The Fuehrer* agrees with the view of the C.-in-C., Navy, and decides that coal supplies which are still available must be reserved for military operations alone and must not be used for evacuating refugees.   Afterwards the C.-in-C., Navy, informs *Reichsleiter* Bormann of this situation and of the Fuehrer's decision, and asks him to instruct the *Gaulieter* concerned accordingly.   (The C.-in-C., Navy, issues orders to use cruiser Emden for the evacuation of refugees as soon as she is ready for temporary duty; also other naval vessels which are being transferred to the region west of the Gulf of Danzig are to be used for this purpose.   Under no circumstances, however, is this to interfere with vital strategic operations of the Navy involving the transport of troops and supplies, and the escort services.)

2. Memel.—*The Fuehrer* decides that Memel is to be evacuated.   The bulk of the troops is to retreat by way of the Kurische Nehrung.   Heavy equipment is to be shipped by sea.   *The Chief of the Army General Staff* mentions that local authorities estimate it would take the Navy about two weeks to organise and carry out the demolition of the port;   the Fuehrer decides, upon the proposal of the C.-in-C., Navy, that only as much time as is available be used for demolishing the harbour, but that evacuation should not be delayed.

3. Naval brigades.—*The C.-in-C., Navy*, proposes to the Fuehrer that the submarine training division in Gdynia with about 900 non-commissioned officers and 600 men be used on the land front in the defence of Danzig.   *The Fuehrer* rejects this proposal, pointing out that these 1,500 valuable specialists would be unable to change the situation on land, while every single submarine operating against the enemy is of more value to the war effort than this entire division if used for fighting on land.

4. Instead the Fuehrer inquires whether it would not be possible as a special measure to transfer an infantry regiment with limited heavy equipment to Elbing or Danzig within a very short time, without interfering

with the Kurland transports. The C.-in-C., Navy, replies in the affirmative and issues the necessary instructions at once.

5. Coal.—*The C.-in-C., Navy*, asks the Chief of Staff, O.K.W., to instruct the Commanding General, West, to take measures to protect the coal transports of the Navy on the Rhine near Lobith, between Emmerich and Arnheim, where they are endangered by enemy artillery because they are so near the front. *The Chief of Staff, O.K.W.*, replies that such instructions have already been issued, and that the Army artillery in this area is already being reinforced in order to neutralise the enemy's artillery.

6. *Hauptdienstleiter Sauer* of the Ministry for Armament and War Production reports to the C.-in-C., Navy, that 150 15-mm. triple-barrelled guns are being set aside for the naval tugs and coal barges on the Rhine. Shipment to Duisberg is to begin on January 23, 1945. The exact address of the receiving unit is still to be given.

(signed)        DOENITZ.<br>(countersigned) Lt. NEUMANN.

Naval Staff                                               January 23, 1945

### CONFERENCE OF THE C.-IN-C., NAVY, WITH THE FUEHRER ON JANUARY 23, 1945, AT 1600

1. During the discussion of the situation in the East, *the Fuehrer* points out the vital strategic areas on the Eastern Front. The Hungarian oil lands and the oilfields in the Vienna Basin are of first importance, since without this oil, which is 80 per cent. of production, it will be impossible to continue the war. The Danzig Bay area, which is vital for the continuation of submarine warfare, and the Upper Silesian industrial area, which is the centre of the defence industry and coal production, are next in importance.

2. The Fuehrer points out that Memel will have to be evacuated very suddenly and quickly to prevent the pursuing Russians from causing losses. He asks the C.-in-C., Navy, to allocate naval forces to protect the evacuation.

3. U-boat campaign.—The report about the successes of Submarine-Commander Dobratz off Halifax leads the C.-in-C., Navy, to explain that the new submarine types have even better chances of success than the old VII C *Schnorchel* boats. This proves again that we have gone in the right direction by changing to the new submarine types and by keeping them below the surface. *The Fuehrer* emphasises again the strategic importance of the Bay of Danzig for the whole war, since it is the training area for our submarines.

4. During a report on the air situation, *the C.-in-C., Navy*, stresses the importance of mining the Scheldt River by aircraft, as mine hits in the narrow channels can considerably delay enemy supply shipments to Antwerp.

5. After the situation conference, *the Fuehrer* discusses measures for preventing sabotage in Norway with a small group consisting of the Foreign Minister; the Cs.-in-C., Air and Navy; the Chief of Staff, O.K.W.; Minister Lammers; the Chief, Operations Staff, O.K.W.; and

*Reichsleiter* Bormann.   The Fuehrer decides to resort to severe counter-measures, as advocated by the C.-in-C., Navy.   Detailed orders will follow.

6. Coal.—*The C.-in-C., Navy,* informs the Staff, O.K.W., of the coal situation on the coast as reported to him by Rear-Admiral Engelhardt at a conference in Hamburg.   The present supplies on hand are sufficient to maintain naval transports, escort forces, shipyards, and rail traffic essential to the war for twelve days beginning January 22.   The daily requirements for the above consumers are 5,000 tons.   It is therefore necessary that eleven days from today, i.e. beginning February 3, 5,000 additional tons must be provided daily.   *The Chief of Staff, O.K.W.,* promises to make the necessary arrangements.

(signed)    DOENITZ.<br>(countersigned) Lt. NEUMANN.

Naval Staff                January 25, 1945

### CONFERENCE OF THE C.-IN-C., NAVY, WITH THE FUEHRER ON JANUARY 25, 1945, AT 1600

1. U-boat campaign.—(*a*) Of the ten *Seehund* midget submarines which left Ijmuiden on January 21, 1945, between 1400 and 1600, nine have so far returned.   Partly because of technical defects and partly because of the unfavourable weather, their mission was unsuccessful.   *The C.-in-C., Navy,* comments as follows:

The *Seehund* midget submarines underwent a severe test during their first operation.   Despite negligible successes the operations were of the greatest value.   All the defects which might never have been discovered during further tests in the Baltic Sea showed up under the severe conditions in the Hoofden, and can thus be corrected.   The limitations of this weapon under adverse weather conditions have been established.   The most important discovery made was that enemy aircraft and naval forces can neither see the *Seehund* submarines nor locate them by radar even when they have surfaced.   Furthermore, they are relatively immune to depth charges because they offer so little resistance because of their shape, that they are tossed aside like a cork instead of being damaged.   Thus the *Seehund* submarines have proved relatively immune from enemy defences. Despite the negligible initial successes, the crews have gained considerable confidence in their equipment.   It can be expected that future mass operations by *Seehund* will score considerable successes under favourable weather conditions.

(*b*) *The Chief, Operations Staff, O.K.W.,* relates some of the experiences gained during manoeuvres of the Commanding General, Armed Forces, Denmark.   The C.-in-C., Navy, takes this opportunity to point out the importance of Zealand.   By getting possession of this island the British, with very small land forces, and making use of their naval superiority, could create a very favourable situation for themselves.   Zealand blocks almost completely the approaches to the Baltic, and the loss of Copenhagen would put us at a considerable political disadvantage and would cause us great loss of prestige.   Once the enemy has established himself there, it would be very difficult to drive him off.   If the British Navy were under the leadership of a Nelson or a Lord Fisher it would certainly have recognised the strategic significance of this area and taken daring action accordingly.  Even though the British lack this daring in action at present, and though the situation in the West makes new operations seem unlikely at the moment, this problem must be kept in mind for a later date, and it must not be forgotten when the defences in the Danish area are further reinforced.  Besides, we must attempt to appear stronger in the Skagerrak and Kattegat than we actually are.  The Navy has therefore spread stories to this effect through the foreign news services.  Also the transfer of the small battle units to the Danish area, which cannot be kept secret, will have the same effect.

(signed)              DOENITZ.
(countersigned) Lt. NEUMANN.

Naval Staff                                                       January 28, 1945

### CONFERENCE OF THE C.-IN-C., NAVY, WITH THE FUEHRER ON JANUARY 28, 1945, AT 1600

1. *The Fuehrer* inquires whether it is not possible to replace the 28-cm. gun barrels on the Schlesien in order to increase her firing efficiency against land targets.  *The C.-in-C., Navy*, replies that since the loss of the Schleswig-Holstein the Schlesien is the only ship in the Navy which can be used as a heavy icebreaker.  The Fuehrer replies that after the war the Navy must build heavy icebreakers at once so that the German Reich will not be dependent again on begging icebreakers from Russia for use in German waters as before the war, or will have to use naval vessels for this task in wartime.

2. In reporting the engagement of the 4th Destroyer Flotilla with two cruisers of the "Fiji" class off the west coast of Norway on January 27, *the C.-in-C., Navy*, informs the Fuehrer that he approves the manner in which the commander of the flotilla, Captain von Wangenheim, conducted the action.  He succeeded in scoring hits on the enemy vessels, but he quite correctly withdrew his destroyers from the action while there was still time, since the enemy was superior, and the full moon gave the enemy cruisers the additional advantage of very good visibility.  With the limited forces at our disposal we must avoid unnecessary losses on occasions which promise no particular advantage, so that we may keep our few destroyers for vital tasks.

3. Refugees.—*The C.-in-C., Navy*, informs the Fuehrer that the refugees can be evacuated by sea only in so far as this operation does not affect the transfer of fighting forces from Kurland and Norway.  Besides this, everything possible is being done to move the refugees west.  Up to January 28 a total of 62,000 refugees from East and West Prussia had been evacuated westward by sea.

4. U-boat campaign.—With reference to the report that the last of the ten *Seehund* midget submarines which left on January 21 has now returned, *the C.-in-C., Navy*, calls attention to the fact that this particular *Seehund* remained at sea for six days.  The experience gained on this occasion will be of the greatest value in planning future *Seehund* operations.

5. Captain Assmann reports on the present state of submarine warfare. The C.-in-C., Navy, adds that four submarines which operated in the waters around the British Isles are due to arrive in Norway. It is to be hoped that these boats will arrive; however, even if they are lost, there is no reason for abandoning the current operational areas. Radio intelligence has revealed that quite a number of successes were achieved in these waters. Therefore the allocation of a large number of submarines to this area is justified all the more so because shipping losses so close to the British coast must be particularly disagreeable to the enemy. Judging from present experience, it can be assumed that enemy anti-submarine warfare is concentrated primarily on deep-laid mines, which, however, are troublesome for British shipping too: change of tide causes difficulties; the mines tear loose in heavy seas; control of mines is hampered. German submarines attempt to by-pass this danger by operating close to the coast in British inshore waters or along the enemy's known convoy routes, where they stay very close to the surface. If submarine construction can proceed in the near future without too much interference, it will be possible to launch about sixty submarines for operational use by the end of February. The first submarine of Type XXIII is to leave Oslo on January 29 for operations off the east coast of Britain.

(signed) DOENITZ.

Naval Staff                                                          January 30, 1945

## CONFERENCE OF THE C.-IN-C., NAVY, WITH THE FUEHRER ON JANUARY 30, 1945, AT 1600

1. Naval brigades.—During the discussion of the serious developments in the East, *the C.-in-C., Navy*, emphasises again the importance of Stettin and Swinemuende for the continuation of naval warfare, particularly for the maintenance of all transport operations to and from the Eastern Front. The Navy is constantly examining what naval personnel could be spared for the land defences, and has decided to make available the three remaining regiments of the Naval Rifle Brigade of the Naval Command, North Sea. This constitutes a grave reduction in strength for the Navy, as there are valuable specialists in these regiments who are needed for the new ship construction programme which is to start within the next few months. However, since the threat to Stettin and Swinemuende is already endangering the home bases of naval warfare, the C.-in-C., Navy, considers it best to put up with the considerable disadvantages, and to assign the brigade to the land forces of Army Group, Vistula, under the Reichsfuehrer S.S. *The Fuehrer* agrees to this proposal. The brigade is to be sent to Stettin as quickly as possible, where the necessary weapons and gear are to be provided; it is to be assigned to the Steiner S.S. Corps. Provision is to be made for return of the brigade to the Navy as soon as the situation changes. In view of the great shortage of radio technicians and the long time required to train them, the C.-in-C., Navy, decides to withhold one battalion of the Naval Rifle Brigade from the land forces and to keep it in the Navy, because 70 per cent. of its members are radio techicians.

2. On January 29 the C.-in-C., Navy, informed the Fuehrer via the Admiral at Fuehrer Headquarters that he is considering organising a naval

corps; today *the C.-in-C., Navy*, inquires whether he could not retain a part of the 20,000 men earmarked for Denmark in order to form a naval division. The Chief of Staff, O.K.W., and the Chief, Operations Staff, O.K.W., support this request. *The Fuehrer* decides that all personnel which has not yet been transferred to the Army shall be held back. The *Reichsmarschall* is willing to furnish guns mounted on trucks or trailers in order to provide the division with the necessary artillery.

3. During the report on the bombardment of land targets by the 2nd Task Force in the Cranz area, *the Fuehrer* asked why bombardment of land targets was not carried out near Elbing as planned. *The C.-in-C., Navy*, reports that a task force was made available for this purpose, but that the orders were cancelled by the Army. The Fuehrer orders the Chief of the Operations Division, Army General Staff, General Wenk, to investigate the reason for this action.

4. Sea transport.—During the discussion of the Norway transports, *the C.-in-C., Navy*, points out that the difficulties in the Skagerrak and the Kattegat due to the weather and to enemy mining operations continue to be very great, and therefore it may not be possible to accelerate the transfer of the 163rd Infantry Division and subsequent transport operations.

(signed)      DOENITZ.<br>
(countersigned) Lt. NEUMANN.

Naval Staff                                               February 1, 1945

### CONFERENCE OF THE C.-IN-C., NAVY, WITH THE FUEHRER ON JANUARY 31, 1945, AT 1600

1. Naval brigades.—*The Fuehrer* orders that the Naval Rifle Brigade which is to be assigned to the lower Oder is to be equipped especially well and completely, since first-class soldiers must have first-class weapons. He orders the assignment of thirty-one assault guns, and personally directs the Chief of Staff to the general of the *Panzer* Troops, General Tomale, and the Chief of the Army Staff, General Buhle (Artillery), to speed up the supply of weapons. *The C.-in-C., Navy*, directs the Admiral at Fuehrer Headquarters to push the matter in co-operation with the above-named Army officers.

2. Sea transport.—In connection with the sinking of the passenger steamer Wilhelm Gustloff by submarine torpedoes on the outer route north of the Stolpe Bank, *the C.-in-C., Navy*, declares that with the extensive transports in the Baltic Sea, it was realised from the start that there would be losses. Painful as any loss may be, it is very fortunate that more have not occurred. However, he must point out that Russian submarines are able to operate undisturbed in the Baltic Sea only because there are no German aircraft there to combat them. Because of the shortage of escort forces the Navy must restrict itself to direct protection of convoys. The only practical defence against submarines is the radar-equipped aircraft, the same weapon which enabled the enemy to paralyse our own submarine warfare. *The Chief of the Air Force, Operations Staff*, reports that the Air Force lacks both fuel and sufficiently effective equipment for such operations. *The Fuehrer* underlines the arguments of the C.-in-C., Navy, and orders the Air Force to investigate how the matter can be remedied.

3. U-boat campaign.—A report is made on the *Biber* midget submarine operations in the Scheldt River, during which one tanker was sunk and four other explosions were definitely established. *The C.-in-C., Navy,* points out the great effectiveness of this weapon. Even though only two ships were sunk, it was at the cost of only nine men, which is very low in proportion to the success achieved.

4. Refugees.—*The Fuehrer* orders that the ships evacuating refugees should carry food for the refugees on their return trip to the east. The O.K.W. is to arrange the assignment of the food through *Reichsleiter* Bormann or the Gauleiters.

5. *The C.-in-C., Navy,* reports that there is a congestion of more than 20,000 refugees in Swinemuende. These endanger troop transports from Kurland. Though it is a strategic necessity to evacuate these steadily increasing masses of refugees, only one hospital train left Swinemuende yesterday, and not even one train of refugees. *The Fuehrer* orders that the refugees be dispersed at once among the surrounding villages, and that facilities are to be provided to speed up evacuation. *Reichsleiter* Bormann is responsible for the execution of this order.

(signed)          DOENITZ.
(countersigned) Lt. NEUMANN.

# *February*

U-BOAT CAMPAIGN

Rapid improvements had been made in U-boat production since the decline at the end of 1944. By February 23 there were altogether 437 U-boats. Of these 177 were operational, 237 in training flotillas or undergoing trials, and 23 undergoing repair. A further 114 boats were being built. The use of the *Schnorchel* imposed different tactics on the Allies. Systematic air raids were made on U-boat bases and factories, while large minefields were laid off the German coast and in the Baltic. During February attacks were renewed on the Russian convoys, but only one merchant ship was sunk. In all areas 15 Allied merchant ships, totalling 65,000 tons, were sunk for the loss of 22 U-boats (14 in action, 8 through other causes).

CHRONOLOGY OF IMPORTANT EVENTS—FEBRUARY 1945

Feb. 1. Allied troops cross Moder and capture Oberhoffen.
Feb. 2. British 2nd Army cross Maas.
Ecuador declares war on Germany and Japan.
Feb. 4. Yalta Conference. (Conference ended Feb. 11.)
Feb. 8. Allies launch offensive south-east of Nijmegen.
Paraguay declares war on the Axis.
Feb. 9. Allied forces break through part of Siegfried Line defence zone.
Russians occupy Elbing, East Prussia.
Feb. 10. Russians capture Landau.
Feb. 12. British and Canadians enter Cleves.
Feb. 14. Canadian and British forces reach the Rhine opposite Emmerich.
Feb. 15. Russians take two towns covering approaches to Danzig ; Breslau completely surrounded.
Feb. 21. American reconnaissance troops enter Saarburg.
Feb. 23. Russians capture Poznan.
Turkey declares war on the Axis with effect from March 1.
Uruguay declares war on the Axis.
Feb. 24. Egypt declares war on Germany and Japan.
Feb. 26. Syria declares war on the Axis.
Feb. 27. Canadians capture Kalcar and Undem.
The Lebanon declares war on the Axis.
Feb. 28. Roumanian Government resigns.

Naval Staff                                         February 1, 1945

## CONFERENCE OF THE C.-IN-C., NAVY, WITH THE FUEHRER ON FEBRUARY 1, 1945, AT 1600

1. Eastern Front.—During the discussion of the situation in Pomerania, the C.-in-C., Navy, as well as the Chief of the Army General Staff and the Chief of Staff, O.K.W., emphasise that the Stettin–Swinemuende area is of great strategic importance, due to the harbours, the shipyards, the Poelitz hydrogenation plant, and the connection with Pomerania and West Prussia. *The Fuehrer* agrees with them that everything in any way possible must be done to defend this area. Future developments in this area will depend on how fast the Steiner S.S. *Panzer* Corps can be brought up from Kurland, the 4th Police Division from the west, the 163rd

Infantry Division from Norway, and the Naval Rifle Brigade from the area of the Naval Command, North Sea.

2. The various reports made today concerning ships damaged by mines in the Bay of Swinemuende cause the C.-in-C., Navy, to emphasise that the shipyards must maintain full production at all costs. Due to the extensive mining operations by enemy aircraft, a large number of ships is required for countermeasures. In order to keep sea traffic going at all, therefore, the damaged mine-detonating vessels, minesweepers, and other patrol units must be repaired.

3. As for the troop shipments from Norway, the C.-in-C., Navy, expresses hopes that they can be accelerated with the aid of two mine-detonating vessels just completed and two additional transport ships.

4. *The C.-in-C., Navy*, discusses with Minister Speer the necessity of including minesweepers, motor minesweepers, and mine-detonating vessels in the emergency armament programme as previously requested by telegram. *Minister Speer* promises to take appropriate action.

5. As a result of the situation conference, the C.-in-C., Navy, issues the following instruction:

(*a*) The Stettin shipyards are to continue full force with repairs and new construction. In order to utilise to the fullest extent the repair capacity of these yards, vessels requiring only a few weeks for repair are also to be taken to Stettin.

(*b*) Information is to be obtained at once as to whether or not it will be possible to use naval equipment, i.e. depth charges or mines with special fuses, to break the ice on the Oder River, an operation considered necessary by the Army. Immediate steps for all possible measures are to be taken not later than tonight.

(*c*) Information is to be obtained at once as to how the Navy can contribute to the defence of the Oder River. The necessary measures are to be started immediately.

(signed)        DOENITZ.<br>(countersigned) Lt. NEUMANN.

<br>

Naval Staff                                                February 3, 1945

### CONFERENCE OF THE C.-IN-C., NAVY, WITH THE FUEHRER ON FEBRUARY 2, 1945, AT 1600

1. Naval brigades.—At the proposal of *the C.-in-C., Navy*, it is decided that 5,000 of the 10,000 men promised to the Commander of the Replacement Army several days ago, but afterwards held in reserve for the naval division, are to be made available to him by the Navy after all. They are to be used solely as replacements for *Waffen-S.S.* divisions. The Navy will keep the remaining 5,000 men for the naval division, or for replacements in the Naval Rifle Brigade.

2. *The C.-in-C., Navy*, reports to the Fuehrer that he has reduced the Naval High Command drastically, discontinuing work in many fields which are important under ordinary circumstances but which can now be dispensed with. The original 8,000 have been reduced to 2,800. About 4,000 men have become available for other purposes, chiefly for naval emergency units. An advantage of this reduction is that the Naval High

Command has achieved greater mobility and can thus adapt itself better to the exigencies of the situation. The section of the Naval High Command in Eberswalde and *Koralle* are being transferred to the Sengwarden-Varel area. The C.-in-C., Navy, will remain in *Koralle*. The sections of the Naval High Command in Berlin will remain there. *The Fuehrer* welcomes this measure with great satisfaction and calls it an example for the other branches of the Armed forces and other offices.

(signed)　　　　　　DOENITZ.
(countersigned) Lt. NEUMANN.

Naval Staff　　　　　　　　　　　　　　　　　　February 4, 1945

### CONFERENCE OF THE C.-IN-C., NAVY, WITH THE FUEHRER ON FEBRUARY 3, 1945, AT 1600

1. In connection with today's air attack on the centre of Berlin, *the C.-in-C., Navy*, expresses his concern regarding possible air raids on Stettin and Swinemuende, which would surely have disastrous results because of the heavy concentration in these cities of naval and merchant vessels, refugees, and wounded soldiers. These harbours are of decisive importance, and from a strategic point of view the enemy made a mistake in attacking Berlin rather than these harbours. It can be assumed that political motives determined the target of the raid. Everything possible must be done to protect the seaports.

2. The C.-in-C., Navy, reports that the congestion at Swinemuende has increased. At present there are about 35,000 refugees in Swinemuende and 22,000 more are on the way. It is urgent that the *Gauleiter* alleviate the situation.

3. Ammunition shortage.—*The C.-in-C., Navy*, informs the Chief of the Army General Staff, General Wenck, once more in detail about the critical shortage of ammunition for the heavy guns of the heavy cruisers. The available ammunition for 20·3-cm. guns is sufficient only for one ship for ten missions and the ammunition for 28-cm. guns only for one ship for thirteen missions. It is no longer possible to manufacture new ammunition of this calibre. As the situation can develop in a way which may offer many opportunities for decisive operations by these ships, the C.-in-C., Navy, asks the General Staff to restrict heavy naval gun fire against land targets to cases of extreme urgency.

(signed)　　　　　　DOENITZ.
(countersigned) Lt. NEUMANN.

Naval Staff　　　　　　　　　　　　　　　　　　February 5, 1945

### CONFERENCE OF THE C.-IN-C., NAVY, WITH THE FUEHRER ON FEBRUARY 5, 1945, AT 1600

1. Baltic ports.—During the report on the Northern Army Group, *the Fuehrer* declares that it is the most important task of the Group to clear up and secure the situation around Koenigsberg and Pillau. These ports are the life lines of the East Prussian theatre of war. The fighting for a western passage to Danzig must be subordinated to this task.

2. The Fuehrer again emphasises the significance of Stettin for the whole war situation. Army Group, Vistula, is to conduct its operations accordingly.

3. Oil shortage.—*The C.-in-C., Navy*, again reports to the Fuehrer how vitally important it is to assign adequate amounts of Diesel oil for the continuation of submarine warfare. *The Chief of Staff, O.K.W.*, assures the Fuehrer that he will do his utmost to satisfy the demands of the Navy, so that the sixty submarines which will be ready for operations in February can be equipped in time. *The Fuehrer* agrees with the arguments of the C.-in-C., Navy, and points out that this proves again the correctness of the measures he ordered for the protection of the oil-producing areas in Hungary and in the Vienna Basin, which produce 80 per cent. of our present oil supply. Modern warfare is primarily economic warfare, the requirements of which must have first consideration.

4. Coal.—On orders of the C.-in-C., Navy, *the Admiral at Fuehrer Headquarters* explained to the Chief, O.K.W., Operations Staff, on February 4 how important maintenance of the front west of the Rhine between Emmerich and Arnheim is for the coal transport on the Rhine. The C.-in-C., Navy, discusses this subject again with the Chief, O.K.W., Operations Staff, and emphasises the catastrophic consequences which an interruption in coal transports on the Rhine would have for the supply of German ocean-going shipping and harbours, and for the situation in Holland, where coal keeps the pump works running.

(signed)          DOENITZ.<br>(countersigned) Lt. NEUMANN.

Naval Staff                                           February 6, 1945

### CONFERENCE OF THE C.-IN-C., NAVY, WITH THE FUEHRER ON FEBRUARY 6, 1945, AT 1600

1. During his report on operations by *Seehund* midget submarines and E-boats, *the C.-in-C., Navy*, calls attention to the fact that they are greatly handicapped by the long spell of unusually bad weather, in spite of the great perseverance with which new attempts are constantly being made.

2. Baltic ports.—*The C.-in-Navy*, reports that the anti-aircraft defence of Swinemuende and of Stettin is inadequate compared with that of Poelitz. There are 29 anti-aircraft guns in Swinemuende, plus 8 at the anti-aircraft training school, and 12 en route; in Stettin are 80; in Poelitz, on the other hand, are 329. The situation is serious in view of the vital importance of these ports. *The Fuehrer* orders that the Air Force send sufficient reinforcements from the 10·5-cm. batteries which have been released in the west. The O.K.W. will issue the necessary instructions.

3. Sea transport.—During the discussion on the situation in the area of Army Group, Vistula, *the Fuehrer* approves the decision that the 389th and the 181st Infantry Divisions, now being transferred from Kurland to Gdynia, are not to be employed in the Elbing area but on the Pomeranian front, so as to be sure to prevent a Russian break-through into Pomerania. Should also communications between Eastern Pomerania and the Danzig–West Prussian area and the west be cut off, it would no longer be possible to master the supply situation by sea. *The C.-in-C.*,

*Navy*, reports in this connection that even now all facilities of the Navy and the Reich Commissioner of Maritime Shipping are being taxed to the utmost, so that it would be quite impossible to take on any additional, large-scale tasks.

4. *The Fuehrer* stresses that it is the most important task of the Northern Army Group to safeguard communications between that part of East Prussia which we still control and Pillau and Koenigsberg, as well as to secure land and sea communications between these two ports, since the present method of transporting supplies over the Haff is only an emergency measure which will be inadequate in the long run. The C.-in-C., Navy, confirms the fact that supplies for East Prussia and the Northern Army Group can be guaranteed only if we remain in firm control of the harbours and the Pillau–Koenigsberg area.

(signed)         DOENITZ.
(countersigned) Lt. NEUMANN.


Admiral on Special Duty with C.-in-C., Navy          February 10, 1945

## CONFERENCE OF THE C.-IN-C., NAVY, WITH THE FUEHRER ON FEBRUARY 9, 1945, AT 1600

1. Baltic ports.—In a discussion of the situation at the Northern Army Group sector *the C.-in-C., Navy*, points out that Koenigsberg can at present be supplied only by way of the road on the southern side of the Haff. We shall not be able to use the sea route before the southern coast of Samland is in our hands again. *The Fuehrer* confirms that there are plans to accomplish this as soon as possible.

2. Coal.—The situation in the Cleves–Nijmegen area causes *the C.-in-C., Navy*, to refer once more to the fact that a further enemy advance to the Rhine would paralyse our coal shipments on the Rhine. *The Fuehrer* orders the necessary forefield west of the Rhine to be held under all circumstances.

3. Sea transport.—*The Fuehrer* highly commends the accomplishments of the Navy in transferring the 3rd S.S. *Panzer* Corps from Libau to Stettin, and he remarks that this transfer was effected more rapidly than the land transfer of the western divisions to the East.

4. Air raids.—In connection with the report of the damage done to the E-boat shelters in Ijmuiden by heavy bombs, *the C.-in-C., Navy*, states that he ordered the shelters to be cleared of E-boats whenever weather conditions permit direct target bombing by enemy planes. In such a case the shelters would be nothing but "mousetraps," and would actually help in giving the enemy targets for bombing, without providing protection for our E-boats. The above order proved its worth in this attack; the E-boats were scattered and not one was damaged, in spite of severe damage to the shelters.

5. Concerning the small expenditure of ammunition by the heavy anti-aircraft batteries during the air attack on Poelitz on February 8, *the Fuehrer* pointed out that the concentration of heavy anti-aircraft guns at one location—there were 370 guns in Poelitz—can be advantageous only if they are used for heavy barrage fire and consume large amounts of ammunition. In this connection *the C.-in-C., Navy*, reports that the

Navy had achieved excellent result with barrage fire by destroyers during air attacks on Skagerrak convoys, since it had the effect of dispersing the enemy and preventing accurate bombing.

7. *Lt.-Colonel von Greiff*, Deputy Chief of the Air Forces Operations Staff, reports to the C.-in-C., Navy, that the Air Force has reinforced the anti-aircraft protection of Swinemuende. In addition Lt.-Colonel von Greiff reports that the minesweeper squadrons at Dievenow and Langfuhr, whose activities had been stopped by local command stations because of lack of fuel, were returned to action immediately by the Air Forces Operations Staff.

8. *The Chief, O.K.W.*, asks the C.-in-C., Navy, with the approval of the Fuehrer, whether the Navy could manage with only 20,000 volunteers of the 1928 age-group instead of the 30,000 volunteers and 5,000 conscripts which were originally intended for the Navy. The C.-in-C., Navy, promises an investigation.

9. Naval brigades.—*The C.-in-C., Navy*, asks the Deputy Chief of the Armed Forces Operations Staff to help supply the 2nd Naval Division with equipment and arms, since the Navy can provide almost nothing besides the personnel, and has to depend on the Army for equipment and arms, according to the decision of the Fuehrer.

10. Refugees.—*The Admiral on Special Duty* confers with Colonel (S.S.) Zander, representing *Reichsleiter* Bormann, about sending a representative of the Party chancellery to the Admiral Commanding Baltic Sea, as a deputy for matters dealing with refugees, in order to regulate all problems of a non-military nature concerning the transport and care of refugees, in co-operation with the Party offices concerned—the *Gauleiters* and the National Socialist Organisation for Public Welfare. The C.-in-C., Navy, agrees to this proposal. Colonel (S.S.) Zander considers the next main task to be the transport of as many refugees as possible from East Prussia to West Prussia and Pomerania. Although the transport of refugees farther west is very desirable, it must be subordinated to this more important task.

(signed) ADMIRAL ON SPECIAL DUTY

(Rear-Admiral Wagner).

Admiral on Special duty with C.-in-C., Navy         February 12, 1945

**CONFERENCE OF THE C.-IN-C., NAVY, WITH THE FUEHRER ON FEBRUARY 11, 1945, AT 1700**

1. Coal.—Following the account of the situation at the Western Front in the Cleves Sector, *the C.-in-C., Navy*, reports to the Fuehrer as follows: Since the ice has melted on the Rhine it has been possible to send about twenty vessels with 9,000 tons of coal from Duisburg via the Ijssel to Holland. Twenty additional vessels with another 9,000 tons of coal are lying in the harbour of Lobit. Since the enemy has succeeded in penetrating as far as the Rhine in this region, Lobit is being strafed by enemy machine-gun fire. Twenty tugs and 160 coal barges with a capacity of 38,000 tons that are ready to leave Holland cannot be sent up the Rhine for the same reason. Coal transport on the Rhine has thus come to a standstill for the time being.

2. In connection with the loss of the hospital ship Steuben *the C.-in-C.*, *Navy*, reports that in spite of the regrettable losses, the use of large ships for evacuating the wounded from the Eastern Area cannot be dispensed with. Otherwise the possibility of transporting the wounded would be reduced by about 40,000 men a month; the small ships which are available could carry about 17,000 in all. After all, a total of about 76,000 wounded has been transferred west by water from the Eastern Area up to the present time, and the losses represent only a small percentage in comparison. *The Fuehrer* agrees.

3. U-boat campaign.—*The C.-in-C.*, *Navy*, reports to the Fuehrer details of the submarine operations along the British coast. Our own losses have increased again lately, and the number of submarines lost is probably as high as seven. But in any case 4·4 enemy vessels, mostly steamships, were sunk for each submarine lost, so that the C.-in-C., Navy, feels that the results achieved justify continuing the operations. Up to the present time there is no clear picture as to the reason for these losses; it is to be hoped that they are due to a variety of causes. At least there is as yet no reason to believe that the enemy has found a new defence against submerged submarines. *The Fuehrer* is in full agréement with the C.-in-C., Navy, particularly on the point that the continued use of submarines must still be considered advisable.

4. *The C.-in-C.*, *Navy*, informs the Chief of Staff, O.K.W., that he cannot possibly agree with the proposal of the Reich Defence Commissioner, Minister Dr. Goebbels, to institute commissions with the power to issue orders which are designed to make a systematic search of the branches of the Armed Forces for personnel for the Army. The Navy on its own is doing everything in its power already in order to help the Army. He cannot permit an outside commission to make decisions about the personnel requirements of the Navy. Such a procedure would only be the source of perpetual friction, without having any better results than the C.-in-C., Navy, is already achieving himself. A statement of the position of the C.-in-C., Navy, is en route to the Chief of Staff, O.K.W., by telegram. In addition the C.-in-C., Navy, informs the Chief of Staff, O.K.W., that the Navy is contenting itself with 10,000 volunteers of the 1928 age group.

5. Naval brigades.—*The C.-in-C.*, *Navy*, again confers with the Deputy Chief, Operations Division, Major-General Winter, on the problem of arming and equipping the 2nd Naval Division. The C.-in-C., Navy, cannot consent to arrangements made by subordinate naval representatives with the corresponding Army Headquarters that small arms and motor vehicles are to be furnished by the Navy. The Navy is so short of small arms that the C.-in-C., Navy, has already ordered all arms in naval vessels to be mobilised in order to equip fully at least the anti-aircraft regiment at Gdynia. No section of the Navy has sufficient small arms; therefore it is no longer in any way possible to equip the 2nd Naval Division from the naval stocks. The motor vehicle situation is similar. Major-General Winter agrees to take the necessary steps to secure arms and equipment for the 2nd Naval Division from Army sources.

(signed) ADMIRAL ON SPECIAL DUTY.

Admiral on Special Duty with C.-in-C., Navy          February 15, 1945

## CONFERENCE OF THE C.-IN-C., NAVY, WITH THE FUEHRER ON FEBRUARY 14, 1945, AT 1600

1. A report that a number of Russian submarines were observed in the Baltic Sea causes *the Fuehrer* to bring up the question of whether our anti-submarine aircraft are supplied with adequate radar equipment. *The Chief of Air Force Operations Staff, Brigadier-General Christian,* answers that enough aircraft have been allocated, but that the radar equipment (*Hohentwiel* make) which is provided is not sufficiently effective against submarines.   Until now no satisfactory radar equipment has been produced for this purpose.   *The C.-in-C., Navy,* explains that in the course of the past few years very little progress has been made in radar development, and that it is absolutely necessary to produce an efficient radar device similar to the British Rotterdam (Berlin device) for operational use.

2. Sea transport.—In discussing the situation in the East *the C.-in-C., Navy,* reports that at present the reason the Northern Army Group is receiving only a very small amount of supplies is because sufficient supplies are not being provided by the Army;  naval transports could handle considerably more if supplies were available.   A discussion on this question ensues between the C.-in-C., Navy, and the Chief of Army General Staff, and the latter finally admits that the C.-in-C., Navy, is right.   In explaining the situation, the C.-in-C., Navy, merely desires to point out once more the danger of not sending sufficient supplies to the Northern Army Group;  the danger can be avoided only if the Army provides adequate quantities in time.

3. Naval brigades.—*The C.-in-C., Navy,* reports to the Fuehrer the result of his inspection of the front at the 1st Naval Division on February 12, 1945.   He gained a very good impression of the troops and their readiness for action.   Shortcomings in training are still apparent; however, they can gradually be eliminated.   In equipment there is a need above all for heavy weapons, particularly since the assault gun brigade which was allotted them has temporarily been withdrawn.   The C.-in-C., Navy, believes that the division could well adapt itself to mobile warfare in time. He has his doubts, however, whether the officers in the middle ranks, from battalion commanders upwards, can cope with the demands of modern land warfare.   *The Fuehrer* requests the deputy of the *Reichsfuehrer S.S.* in the Fuehrer Headquarters to urge the *Reichsfuehrer S.S.* to return the assault gun brigade to the 1st Naval Division as soon as possible.   Finally, the Fuehrer remarks that he believes the Naval Division capable of great perseverance regardless of its lack of experience in land warfare.   The Fuehrer remarks in this connection that in the past he has regarded the defence of naval fortifications too much from the land point of view.   He is now convinced that the protection of naval fortresses and shore batteries on the land side, too, should be the responsibility of the Navy.   For this task the Navy requires infantry units of its own in the form of naval corps.

4. Coal.—Captain Assmann reports to the C.-in-C., Navy, that the Dortmund-Ems Canal would presumably be back in operation by February 16.   Thus the shipments of coal from Duisberg, which can no

longer take the Rhine route owing to the British advance in the Cleves area, could be sent north through the Dortmund-Ems Canal.

(signed) ADMIRAL ON SPECIAL DUTY.

Admiral on Special Duty with C.-in-C., Navy        February 16, 1945

## CONFERENCE OF THE C.-IN-C., NAVY, WITH THE FUEHRER ON FEBRUARY 15, 1945, AT 1600

1. Coal.—During a report on the situation in the West *the C.-in-C., Navy*, asks the Fuehrer whether it would not be possible to free the left bank of the Rhine north-east of Cleves so that coal shipments along the Rhine can be resumed. *The Fuehrer* replies that this would be possible only if we undertook a sizeable offensive operation. We cannot do this at present since we do not have sufficient forces at our disposal, in view of the impending large enemy offensive.

2. On the basis of reports on enemy plans for landings in the Norway–Denmark area, the Fuehrer asks for the opinion of the C.-in-C., Navy, regarding the imminence of such landings. *The C.-in-C., Navy*, considers the immediate danger of enemy landings slight in view of the weather conditions at this time of year, and because all of the enemy forces are concentrated on the western land front—especially since the British have shown that they are neither able nor willing to attempt any daring or dangerous undertakings. The C.-in-C., Navy, still thinks the main danger lies in the Kattegat on the east coast of Jutland and the north coast of Zealand. For this reason the minefields at the western entrance to the Skagerrak are to be reinforced by more mines in the next few days. In Denmark and Norway small battle weapons have been distributed in various places as defence against landings.

3. Sea transport.—*The Fuehrer* inquires about the supply situation at the Northern Army Group and the Kurland Army Group. The figures given by Captain Assmann show that between February 1 and 13 the Kurland Army Group received about 13,000 tons, and between February 1 and 12 the Northern Army Group received about 8,000 tons of supplies, including coal and fuel. *The C.-in-C., Navy*, reports in addition that there is sufficient cargo space to send much larger shipments, since the ships carrying troops from the east to the west usually return empty. The Chief of the General Staff, Army reports that the small supply shipments are due to the lack of goods. *The Fuehrer* criticizes the fact that the Northern Army Group, which has a great number of troops and is engaged in severe combat, received fewer supplies than the Kurland Army Group, which is a third smaller, and where no attacks of any size are expected at the moment. He orders the Chief of the General Staff, Army, to investigate the supply problem of the two groups thoroughly with this in mind.

4. U-boat campaign.—In connection with the successes of the Arctic Ocean submarines against the PQ convoy, *the C.-in-C., Navy*, reports to the Fuehrer that submarine successes per submarine in operational areas amounted to 9,000 tons in December 1944, and 11,000 tons in January 1945. These figures are as high as they ever were during the most successful period of submarine warfare, but the total is considerably affected by the small number of submarines in the operational areas and

by the long periods of time required for the submarines to get to and from the operational areas. This time would be reduced considerably with the new submarine types. The number of submarines in action will increase considerably during the next few months. At present 237 submarines are being prepared for operational use: 111 of the old types, 84 of type XXI, 42 of type XXIII. Besides these, about 60 additional submarines will be committed each month. The present total of 450 commissioned submarines is the largest number Germany has ever possessed.

5. The C.-in-C., Navy, points out to the Chief, O.K.W., Operations Staff, that he can under no circumstances approve the ruling made by the Narvik Army Group, providing that as a rule the leaders of the infantry defence and not the battery commanders are to act as base commanders for the coastal batteries in the Norwegian area during enemy attacks. He will send a corresponding request to the O.K.W.

(signed) ADMIRAL ON SPECIAL DUTY.

Admiral on Special Duty with C.-in-C., Navy          February 18, 1945

## CONFERENCE OF THE C.-IN-C., NAVY, WITH THE FUEHRER ON FEBRUARY 17, 1945, AT 1600

1. Naval brigades.—*The Reichsmarschall* raised the question whether the Navy could provide emergency units to relieve the 5th Airborne Division from its sector south of Stettin. The answer of *the C.-in-C., Navy*, was a decided negative. He had on the evening of February 16 already discussed this problem with the *Reichsfuehrer S.S.*, and it was found inadvisable to use the naval emergency units from Swinemuende for such a task. These are equipped with light infantry weapons only, and are made up mostly of technicians with little military training.

2. Army support.—*The C.-in-C., Navy*, reports that the Navy will provide artillery support for the attack planned by the Northern Army Group in Samland. The Scheer or the Luetzow will support the action from Pillau and two heavy artillery carriers and the training ship Drache with six 105-mm. guns from the sea canal. He further suggests that, contrary to the plan presented, one attack group should be shifted closer to the sea canal for the assault in order to be able to take greater advantage of the artillery support to be given by the aforementioned naval vessels. The Chief of the General Staff, Army, agrees with this proposal and will transmit it to the Northern Army Group.

3. Sea transport.—*The C.-in-C., Navy*, submits to the Fuehrer a map of the Frische Haff indicating the ice conditions and the supply routes used. So far all supply shipments from Pillau went exclusively to Rosenberg. However, at the request of the Northern Army Group, a second supply line to Brandenburg, south-west of Koenigsberg, is to be established.

4. On February 16 the Admiral at Fuehrer's Headquarters transmitted to the C.-in-C., Navy, the Fuehrer's question how transport between Kurland and the Reich by sea could be increased. *The C.-in-C., Navy*, replies that all means have already been exhausted. These transports could be increased only at the expense of the Skagerrak transports. This, however, the C.-in-C., Navy, hesitates to recommend. *The Fuehrer* agrees with this opinion.

5. To the Fuehrer's second question as to how long it would take to evacuate the approximately eighteen divisions of Army Group, Kurland, *the C.-in-C., Navy*, reports that there are thirty-five transports available. One round trip would take about seven days, and each time about 25,000 men, 5,600 horses, and 3,500 vehicles could be moved. *The Fuehrer* estimates that about 300,000 men will have to be moved, including auxiliary units such as labour battalions, Organisation Todt, etc., and it would therefore take about ninety days to accomplish this. Normal delays caused by weather and blocked sea lanes are included in this estimate. Asked about possible enemy interference, *the C.-in-C., Navy*, replies that it cannot be estimated in advance. Because of their continental orientation the Russians so far have completely overlooked the effect their air force could have on our transport movements by attacking ports and convoys. At any rate they have not availed themselves of this opportunity. The first major air attack against our convoys occurred on February 16, and caused considerable damage. Should the Russians pursue such tactics energetically, they could disrupt our transport system considerably, since shipping losses cannot be replaced. With the exception of a few successful operations by Russian submarines the danger to our convoys from Russian naval forces is less serious.

6. In reply to the Fuehrer's question on how long it will take to transfer the 169th Infantry Division from Norway to Denmark, *the C.-in-C., Navy*, states that he hopes to be able to accomplish the transfer in two weeks. The transport movements in the Skagerrak will function more smoothly from now on, since two new transports and two new icebreakers were added to the naval forces there. *The Chief, Operations Division*, remarks that the trains bringing the divisions to be evacuated to the ports of embarkation will be synchronised with the sea transportation facilities.

7. U-boat campaign.—*The Fuehrer* is particularly pleased about the reports of the latest submarine successes. In this connection *the C.-in-C., Navy*, reports that seven submarines have recently returned from operations in the areas around the British Isles. These ships had to operate in narrow sea lanes and in shallow waters near the coast. They all report that the enemy defences are not very effective. This proves therefore that the superiority of enemy submarine defences has been overcome by the introduction of the *Schnorchel*. The number of submarines in operation will be increased further in the near future. Since the beginning of February, thirty-five submarines have left for the operational areas, and twenty-three more will follow before the end of the month. *The Fuehrer* asked the C.-in-C., Navy, about the use of the new submarine types, and was informed that two ships of type XXIII are already operating along the east coast of the British Isles, and that the first ship of type XXI will be ready to leave for operations along the American east coast by the end of February or the beginning of March.

8. *The C.-in-C., Navy*, explains to the Fuehrer with the aid of a map the submarine operation against the PQ convoy in the Arctic Ocean. This operation proved once again that our old types of submarines have little chance of success in mobile warfare because of their low submerged speed. Therefore it is best to station them outside enemy ports. This campaign succeeded so well because of adherence to this principle. The result of these operations provides further proof of

how futile it is to try to chase a fast carrier task force on the open sea by submarines.

9. Air raids.—In connection with the lecture given by the Chief of the Air Force Operations Staff on the protection of dams against enemy air raids, *the Fuehrer* delegates the C.-in-C., Navy, to test small surface mines or other defences in regard to their usefulness in neutralising upkeep bombs (*Rollbomben*). These are specially designed by the enemy for use against dams. These upkeep bombs float on the surface till they hit the dam. This causes them to sink, and after reaching a depth of about four metres they explode. The intended barrage is to catch the upkeep bombs on the surface and to render them harmless.

10. U-boat campaign.—At the end of the conference *the Fuehrer* emphasised the great importance which he attaches to the revival of submarine warfare for the overall war situation. *The C.-in-C., Navy*, amplifies this statement with the explanation that the ability of submarines to remain submerged has revolutionised the concepts of naval warfare. The new submarines, type XXI, can travel all the way from Germany to Japan without surfacing. All equipment at present employed in naval warfare and which determines the domination of the sea can now be circumvented and eliminated by the improvements of the submarine. These submarines can be expected to be very effective. The C.-in-C., Navy, points out that the intensification of submarine warfare depends greatly on the solution of the construction problem. There it is of greatest importance that the shipyards receive preferential treatment in matters of personnel, coal, and power. In conclusion, *the Fuehrer* especially comments on the significance of this complete revolution in submarine warfare.

(signed) ADMIRAL ON SPECIAL DUTY.

Admiral on Special Duty with C.-in-C., Navy          February 20, 1945

### CONFERENCE OF THE C.-IN-C., NAVY, WITH THE FUEHRER ON FEBRUARY 19, 1945, AT 1700

1. The Geneva Convention.—*The Fuehrer* wonders whether or not the German Reich should withdraw from the Geneva Convention. Since not only the Russians, but the enemy in the West as well, disregard International Law with their attacks against the defenceless population and the residential districts of the cities, perhaps we should take the same point of view in order to make the enemy realise that we are determined to fight for our existence with all means at our disposal. At the same time this would induce the German population to resist to the utmost. The Fuehrer asks the C.-in-C., Navy, to consider the pros and cons of this step and to report on the matter as soon as possible.

2. *The Chief of the O.K.W., Operations Staff,* reports that information has been received that an enemy army in the west is being supplied by transport gliders. *The C.-in-C., Navy,* reports in this connection that according to information sent by the submarine at Den Hoofden, no sizeable transport ships were seen along the Thames–Scheldt convoy route, merely small vessels such as LST's and coastal steamers. This may mean that the enemy has adequate supplies in that area, and that he has therefore

transferred vessels from the Thames–Scheldt route elsewhere. *The Fuehrer* asks where the C.-in-C., Navy, thinks the enemy vessels are being used. He replies that nothing definite is known about this, and requests that reconnaissance planes be sent as soon as possible to Antwerp and the ports along the British coast. *The Fuehrer* passes this request on to the *Reichsmarschall.*

(signed) ADMIRAL ON SPECIAL DUTY

Admiral on Special Duty with C.-in-C., Navy          February 21, 1945

## CONFERENCE OF THE C.-IN-C., NAVY, WITH THE FUEHRER ON FEBRUARY 20, 1945, AT 1600

1. Baltic ports.—During the discussion of further operational plans for Army warfare in the east, *the Fuehrer* asks the C.-in-C., Navy, to indicate what importance the ports of Stettin and Swinemuende have for our naval warfare. *The C.-in-C., Navy,* points out that Stettin and Swinemuende provide the backbone for our naval supply tasks in the eastern Baltic Sea. The loss of these harbours would make troop transports and supply shipments in the Baltic depend entirely on the ports in the western Baltic. With the long routes in shallow water and the great danger from mines this would mean that the time of passage is doubled, particularly since the escort forces would have to carry a greater responsibility. Besides, Swinemuende is the decisive base for naval forces in that area. Its loss would also make it considerably more difficult for us to fight the Russians in the central and western Baltic. It would become impossible to continue using the deep sea areas east of Bornholm for submarine training, and we would be forced to limit such training to the sea areas of the western Baltic, which are very shallow and thus badly suited for the purpose. The loss of the dockyards in Stettin and Swinemuende would mean that repair capacity, which is already very limited, would be decreased even further. And finally, our resources for naval warfare would be concentrated in the western Baltic and would thus become all the more vulnerable from the air. All in all, it is of the utmost importance to naval warfare to hold the Stettin area. *The Fuehrer* agrees with the statements of the C.-in-C., Navy, and decides on the operational measures of the Army with them in mind.

2. The Geneva Convention.—*The C.-in-C., Navy,* informs the Chief, O.K.W., Operations Staff, General Jodl, and the representative of the Foreign Minister at Fuehrer Headquarters, Ambassador Hewel, of his opinion concerning a possible German withdrawal from the Geneva Convention. From the military point of view, naval warfare would not profit by such an action. On the contrary, the disadvantages would outweigh the advantages. Also from a general standpoint, the C.-in-C., Navy, does not see that it could be of advantage. It would be better in any case to keep up outside appearances and carry out the measures believed necessary without announcing them beforehand. The Chief, O.K.W., Operations Staff, and Ambassador Hewel are absolutely of the same opinion.

(signed) ADMIRAL ON SPECIAL DUTY.

Admiral on Special Duty with C.-in-C., Navy  February 23, 1945

## CONFERENCE OF THE C.-IN-C., NAVY, WITH THE FUEHRER ON FEBRUARY 23, 1945, AT 1600

1. Naval commandos.—In connection with the discussion of the situation faced by Army Group Vistula *the C.-in-C., Navy,* reports that during the night from February 24 to 25 it is planned to blow up the bridges built by the Russians across the river Oder at Auras, Vogelsang, and Goeritz. This will be done by special naval units.

2. Air raids.—A report on renewed boomerang air attacks on the *Deschimag* submarine shipyards in Bremen causes *the C.-in-C., Navy,* to make the following remarks: Owing to the fact that a fog screen is ineffective and anti-aircraft affords little protection against bombs dropped from an altitude of anywhere from 9,000 to 11,000 metres, jamming stations and night fighters must be used for the defence. The Air Force High Command guarantees that two jamming stations will be set up immediately in the area west of Bremen. They will be ready to operate in about a week. It seems vitally necessary to have more mosquito fighters over the Bremen area at night. (Following the conference the C.-in-C., Navy, discussed this question in detail with the Air Force officers present, Colonel von Below, Lt.-Colonel von Greiff (General Staff), and Major Buechs. They are of the opinion that night fighting against boomerang planes approaching their target individually, is effective only when weather conditions are such that searchlights can aid the fighters. Still Lt.-Colonel von Greiff is going to suggest to the Chief of the Air Force General Staff to transfer mosquito night fighters—Me262—to Wittmund.)

3. E-boat operations.—In connection with his report on the successful E-boat operation during the night of February 21 to 22, *the C.-in-C., Navy,* summarises the experiences again in this operation in the following manner:

(*a*) Much better results are apt to be achieved if E-boats are used in large numbers. While some of the boats engage the enemy escort vessels, the others are free to attack the convoy.

(*b*) Poor visibility does not handicap the operation of the E-boats, because the disadvantages are much greater for the enemy, trying to defend himself, than for the attacking German boats.

(*c*) According to available and rather reliable information on enemy movements, the use of torpedoes by E-boats is preferable to the use of mines.

4. The Fuehrer had sent the following question to the C.-in-C., Navy: Would E-boats equipped with rocket propulsion be able to achieve high degrees of speed within a very short time, thus giving them a better chance to escape the enemy escort vessels? *The C.-in-C., Navy,* reports the result of his investigation to the Fuehrer as follows: If 10 "V.1" drives were installed, the performance of the engines would increase by 1,000 H.P. only, i.e. from 7,000 H.P. to 8,000 H.P. This represents an increase of 1 to 2 knots in the maximum speed; that would not be worth the expense involved. At the present time experiments are still being conducted with turbine drive aimed at increasing the speed of the E-boats. However, it is not possible to make any predictions as to their results at present.

(signed) ADMIRAL ON SPECIAL DUTY.

Admiral on Special Duty with C.-in-C., Navy          February 27, 1945

## CONFERENCE OF THE C.-IN-C., NAVY, WITH THE FUEHRER ON FEBRUARY 26, 1945, AT 1700

1. *Captain Assmann* reports that for the first time all troops awaiting evacuation in Oslo have been disposed of, and that at present there are not enough troops there to fill the ships available. Upon inquiry by the Fuehrer, the Deputy Chief, O.K.W., Operations Staff, Major-General Winter, confirms this statement and adds that troops cannot be brought to Oslo fast enough because of the coal shortage.

2. Since aerial reconnaissance photographs of the Thames show lively convoy traffic in the area, *the C.-in-C., Navy*, suggests attacks primarily by *Seehund* midget submarines, which now are becoming available in increasing numbers. Considering that the weather can be expected to improve at this time of the year, and that the new series has an increased operating radius, better results can be expected beginning in March. In this connection the C.-in-C., Navy, points out how important the Dutch area is to us for the use of small battle weapons.

3. Air raids.—In discussing the enemy air raid against the Weser Shipyard at Bremen the evening of February 25, *the C.-in-C., Navy*, comments that this is the fifth raid on the same shipyard since February 17, and that these attacks have already cost us five submarines of type XXI. The Air Force reports that two squadrons of night fighters are to be shifted to the Bremen area at once in order to combat the enemy boomerang attacks. It must not be forgotten that these aircraft are single-engined fighters which can operate only with searchlights, and which therefore depend to a large extent on the weather. Furthermore, two jamming stations were sent on February 25 from the Berlin area to a location near Wittmund Harbour, and two additional ones for whose transfer the Navy will also supply the fuel, will be shipped within the next few days.

4. Naval brigades.—Plans have been made to abandon the bridgehead at Schwedt in the sector of Army Group, Vistula, and to shift the 1st Naval Division from there to the sector east of Griefenhagen, Pomerania. *The C.-in-C., Navy*, reports the *Reichsfuehrer's* intention of converting the 1st Naval Division into a combat division. He agrees with the *Reichsfuehrer* that all command positions from battalion commanders on up will have to be filled by Army officers experienced in battle. However, the C.-in-C., Navy, prefers that these troops, which came from the Navy, remain a part thereof, and he asks that the Army officers assigned to the naval divisions be transferred to the Navy. The complement of special weapons and rear echelon services will have to be supplied by the Army. *The Fuehrer* agrees to this proposal.

5. In a discussion of the future operations of the Northern Army Group, the viewpoint of the Group was expressed that the sea supply lines for the East Prussian sector south of the Frische Haff cannot be maintained indefinitely, since difficulties can be expected when the ice melts. On the basis of reports received in the meantime from the Commanding Officer, Shipping and Transport, and the Naval Shore Commander, East Prussia, *the C.-in-C., Navy*, states that the passage from Pillau to Rosenberg across the Frische Haff is now almost completely free from ice. A little difficulty might be caused by shifting of the ice, but he hopes it can be

overcome with the means available to the Navy. The C.-in-C., Navy, directs that the Commanding Officer, Shipping and Transport, is to be asked for another report, first, whether supplies and reinforcements for Rosenberg can be guaranteed even when the ice melts and, second, whether and at what date a light infantry division can be transported from Rosenberg across the Haff to Pillau with the available facilities.

6. *General (S.S.) Steiner* reports to the C.-in-C., Navy, that he has orders from the *Reichsfuehrer S.S.* to organise as large a number of improvised units as possible and to equip them with numerous 2-cm. anti-aircraft guns and machine guns. They are to be utilised according to methods used in the First World War to prevent the enemy from breaking through. He requests the support of the Navy in releasing such units, including the necessary weapons. *The C.-in-C., Navy,* replies that the Navy has already, on its own initiative, given every dispensable man for land warfare, and for this reason there is not a single additional man available at the moment. However, during March 7,000 soldiers who have been at the disposal of the shipyards are to be put into active service, a fact which was ascertained only on February 24. There might be a possibility of giving some of these soldiers to General (S.S.) Steiner after April 1. No complete units can be spared, only separate men. The Navy cannot relinquish any weapons at all, since its own most urgent needs are not nearly satisfied.

7. *The C.-in-C., Navy,* requests General (S.S.) Kaltenbrunner to release the managing director of the Schnichau Shipyards at Koenigsberg, Rodin, as he is urgently needed as director of the shipyards in Norway, and it was for this reason that *Generaldirektor* Merker recalled him from Koenigsberg.

8. Asked by the C.-in-C., Navy, about the possibility of transporting *Marder* one-man torpedoes to Rhodes, the representative of the Air Force Operations Staff, Lt.-Colonel von Greiff, replies that an undertaking of this kind would be justifiable only if it is a measure of great strategic importance, since a large amount of fuel would be required, and the Fuehrer assigned the Ju290 planes in question to other operations. Since it is not a matter of prime strategic importance, the C.-in-C., Navy, abandons the project.

9. The Chief of the Army Personnel Office, *Lt.-General Burgdorff*, confirms the decision made by the Fuehrer on February 25 during the absence of the C.-in C., Navy, to appoint Vice-Admiral Hueffmeier as commander of the Channel Islands; the present commander, Lt.-General von Schmettow, has to be relieved for reasons of health. He will appoint as division commander of the divisions stationed on the Channel Islands a colonel experienced in action, one who has won the oak-leaf cluster.

(signed) ADMIRAL ON SPECIAL DUTY.

---

Admiral on Special Duty with C.-in-C., Navy      February 28, 1945

### CONFERENCE OF THE C.-IN-C., NAVY, WITH THE FUEHRER ON FEBRUARY 27, 1945, AT 1600

1. Naval brigades.—During the report on the situation at Army Group, Vistula *the Fuehrer* once more raises the question of transferring the 1st

Naval Division. The sector which the 1st Naval Division has held up to now is to be occupied by the Army troops which will become available when the Schwedt bridgehead is evacuated; the 1st Naval Division is to occupy a sector south of Stettin. The Fuehrer states that he considers it particularly important to cover Stettin and to hold northern Pomerania and West Prussia, since if this area were cut off, sea transport would be under too great a strain; the submarine training areas in the central part of the Baltic Sea could no longer be used; and the threat of the northern flank of the Russians would be eliminated. He is convinced that the naval divisions will hold their own and will succeed in this defensive assignment. *Major-General (S.S.) Fegelein* reports that the *Reichsfuehrer S.S.* has already ordered the transfer of the 1st Naval Division.

2. *The Chief of the Army General Staff* reports to the Fuehrer that he has given instructions to evacuate only the wounded whose injuries require treatment in Germany. Slightly wounded men who can be expected to recover behind the front within a short time are no longer to be evacuated in the future.

3. During the report on the situation in the Western Area mention is made of the necessity of withdrawing the 346th Infantry Division from the islands Schouwen, Goeree, and Overflakkee, at the Maas estuary, and of transferring it to the area where the Americans are attacking. Naval detachments and police forces for the Netherlands are to take its place. *The C.-in-C., Navy*, reports that the four naval detachments—about 4,000 men—which are already at the front in the Dutch area, as well as the two additional detachments stationed in the Netherlands, are available for these assignments. There are no other naval troops available in the Reich, however, which could possibly be used for land warfare; the Navy has already released all who could be spared for the Army and for the naval divisions. *The Fuehrer* emphasises the need for using camouflage measures extensively in order to keep the enemy from discovering that this front has been weakened.

4. Sea transport.—On the question of the Norway transports *the Deputy Chief, O.K.W., Operations Staff*, reports to the Fuehrer that the coal shortage is responsible for the fact that so few troops are arriving to be evacuated by sea. The Commanding General, Army, Norway, has observed the priorities established by the O.K.W. Operations Staff. An attempt is being made to make up for the present brief delay by despatching from Oslo troop units with lower priority. While at present the available shipping space is not being fully utilised for a short time, the opposite was true on various occasions in the past, and troops ready to be shipped had to wait in Oslo until enough shipping space became available. *The Fuehrer* stresses the importance of keeping a sufficient number of troops ready to utilise the ships, since it is much better to have troop units wait for transport in Oslo for several days if necessary than to waste shipping space even temporarily.

(signed) ADMIRAL ON SPECIAL DUTY.

# *March*

## U-BOAT CAMPAIGN

Principal U-boat operations were concentrated in British coastal waters, but some boats proceeded to Newfoundland and Nova Scotia, while others were also sent into the Arctic and to the eastern part of the North Atlantic. Allied air attacks were made on the U-boat training area near Bornholm Island in the Baltic, and mines were laid off U-boat bases in Oslo Fiord, and between Flensburg and the Gulf of Danzig.

Twelve Allied merchant ships, totalling 58,000 tons, were sunk for the loss of 34 U-boats, 16 of which were destroyed in air raids. A further 3 Allied ships were sunk in the English Channel by midget submarines.

## CHRONOLOGY OF IMPORTANT EVENTS—MARCH 1945

Mar. 1. U.S. 9th Army capture Muenchen-Gladbach.
Saudi Arabia declares war on Axis.
Mar. 2. U.S. 3rd Army capture Trier.
Mar. 4. Russians capture many towns east of Stettin.
Finland declares war with Germany as from September 15, 1944.
Mar. 5. German youths born in 1929 conscripted.
Mar. 6. U.S. 3rd Army reach Rhine north-west of Coblenz.
Mar. 7. U.S. 1st Army crosses Rhine at Remagen, where Germans failed to destroy bridge.
Mar. 12. Russians capture Kuestrin.
Mar. 14. 3rd Army cross Moselle south-west of Coblenz.
Mar. 16. Russians capture Griefenhagen, south of Stettin.
Mar. 17. U.S. 3rd Army enter Coblenz—Russians capture Brandenburg.
Mar. 19. 3rd Army occupy Worms, reach Mainz—Russians capture Braundsberg, with over 4,000 prisoners, 204 tanks, and 300 guns.
Mar. 20. U.S. 3rd Army occupy Ludwigshafen.
Mar. 22. Russians isolate Danzig.
Mar. 23. Major Allied assault across Lower Rhine begins.
Mar. 27. Argentina declares war on the Axis.
Mar. 28. Russians capture Gdynia—U.S. 1st Army capture Marburg.
Mar. 30. Danzig captured.
Mar. 31. General Eisenhower, in "Instructions to the *Wehrmacht*," advises German troops to surrender.

Admiral on Special Duty with C.-in-C., Navy     Berlin, March 2, 1945

### CONFERENCE OF THE C.-IN-C., NAVY, WITH THE FUEHRER ON MARCH 1, 1945, AT 1630

1. Naval brigades.—*The Fuehrer* mentions again the transfer of the 1st Naval Division. He remarks that he thinks it would be well to transfer the 2nd Naval Division by battalions as they become ready for action to the area of Angermuende, in accordance with the suggestion of the *Reichsfuehrer S.S.* However, he stresses emphatically that he insists on later committing the 2nd Naval Division in the Griefenhagen region, south of Stettin. The C.-in-C., Navy, intends to wait for the report of the Admiral at Fuehrer Headquarters, who was sent to the assembly area of the 2nd Naval Division, before he gives his opinion in this matter.

2. Sea transport.—*The C.-in-C., Navy*, declares that he cannot agree

with a notation on the map of the General Staff, Army, concerning the situation at Army Group North, which states that ice conditions are impeding supply shipments across the Haff. He explains that, generally speaking, the supplies for the 4th Army can be shipped across the Haff, although occasional interruptions must be anticipated because of ice conditions. *The Fuehrer* adds that at the present stage of the war one must expect interference with all transport; even transport on land runs the constant risk of encountering damaged railway stations and tracks.

3. U-boat campaign.—*The C.-in-C., Navy*, makes the following statements, using a submarine chart which Captain Assmann submits to the Fuehrer. It is impracticable to concentrate our submarines in the area of the British Isles, since this permits the enemy to concentrate his defensive weapons in a small area. Since, however, we cannot operate in other sea areas with the old type VII C boats, because of their low submerged speed, we will be unable to extend the operational areas, thus possibly scattering enemy defences, before the new vessels of type XXI go into action. If we still had the Biscay coast we could use the old type VII C vessels for more distant sea areas, for instance along the American coast. It seems that the enemy has not yet found any basically new means for locating and combatting submarines below the surface. In spite of that we must expect increased losses in the area around the British Isles. The enemy will do everything he possibly can to master the submarine danger in his home waters, and he will succeed more and more in doing so, considering the strength of his anti-submarine weapons. A particular difficulty for directing the submarines lies in the fact that the vessels can report their observations only on their return trip shortly before they enter port, or even not until afterwards. Thus the commanding officers cannot get an idea of the situation in the operational area and cannot draw the necessary conclusions for succeeding operations until very late.

4. *The C.-in-C., Navy*, informs the Chief, O.K.W. Operations Staff, General Staff, General Jodl, that numerous measures of the Narvik Army Group are encroaching on naval authority over coastal defence by naval forces and coastal artillery, according to a report from the Naval Command, Norway. He asks General Jodl to inform his brother (Lt.-General Jodl, in command of Narvik Army Group) that the C.-in-C., Navy, demands observance of the Fuehrer's orders dealing with this point (Fuehrer Directive No. 40 and supplements).

5. Refugees.—*The C.-in-C., Navy*, asks Colonel Zander to inform *Reichsleiter* Bormann that he cannot approve *Gauleiter* Koch's measures with respect to the refugees in Koenigsberg and Pillau. If the *Gauleiter* fears a congestion with all the simultaneous disadvantages of food shortage, danger of epidemic, and housing difficulties through the transfer of the refugees from Koenigsberg to Pillau, he should work in co-operation with the Navy to make the speed of evacuation from Koenigsberg correspond with the housing and transport facilities beforehand, instead of presenting the Navy with accomplished facts and perhaps impossible tasks. *Colonel Zander* confirms that *Reichsleiter* Bormann also does not agree with the measures of *Gauleiter* Koch, and he will do what is necessary.

(signed) ADMIRAL ON SPECIAL DUTY.

Admiral on Special Duty with C.-in-C., Navy      Berlin, March 4, 1945

### CONFERENCE OF THE C.-IN-C., NAVY, WITH THE FUEHRER ON MARCH 3, 1945, AT 1830

1. Naval brigades.—During a report on the serious situation at Army Group, Vistula, south-east of Stettin, it is mentioned that the 1st Naval Division is being transferred from its old sector to the area east of Greifenhagen. One regiment departed the evening of March 2, the second is to follow the evening of March 3. *The Fuehrer* regrets that, in spite of repeated urging on his part, the transfer has been delayed by the Army Group so long. It now appears doubtful whether the division will still have time enough to get used to the new terrain and to intrench itself there. If possible the inexperienced division should not be thrown into offensive operations right away; in purely defensive action it will no doubt do its part well.

2. *The Fuehrer* confirms his decision of March 2, that the 2nd Naval Division should have priority and be equipped with arms at once; it is then to be assigned to the area south of Stettin in order to get further training behind the front on a battalion or regimental scale. *The C.-in-C., Navy*, announces that the first units of the division can leave within ten days after receiving equipment. According to the report of the divisional commander, the division must be sent to a training area before battle, so that co-operation between Infantry and Artillery which is still unfamiliar to the troops may be practised. *The Fuehrer* declares that there is no time for this, but that there is nothing to prevent them from carrying on this training in the area behind the front, without restriction as to the use of weapons.

3. Sea transport.—The situation in the area Koeslin makes it necessary for the 2nd Army to be supplied by sea. *The C.-in-C., Navy*, points out that in the main the supplies will have to be shipped to the ports of Gdynia and Danzig, since the small east Pomeranian ports can be entered only by smaller ships. Moreover, weather conditions at this time of year often make it impossible to use them. *The Fuehrer* in this connection stresses the necessity of holding the area of Danzig and Gdynia under all circumstance, as a lifeline for the 2nd Army.

4. Holland.—In the Holland area the 346th Division which was committed on the islands of the Meuse Delta and south of Rotterdam, is being withdrawn for duty elsewhere. It is to be replaced by naval and police units. *The C.-in-C., Navy*, states once again that only the nucleus crews in the Holland area can be considered by the Navy for this task. Of these, four units of 4,000 men are already stationed at the Waal front and near Arnheim, while two more units, also about 4,000 men, are scattered in small units along the entire coast for defence purposes.

5. Coal.—The situation on the left bank of the Rhine causes *the C.-in-C., Navy*, to call attention to the importance of the Dortmund-Ems Canal for the shipment of coal and other material in the industrial area. *The Fuehrer* seizes this opportunity to stress the decisive importance of holding a wide bridgehead in the Duisburg area. In this connection *the C.-in-C., Navy*, with the aid of a map showing the inland waterways, gives the Fuehrer a summary of the Navy's plans with respect to the transport of coal through the canal; he mentions the plan to circumvent the endangered

spots along the canal with the help of field railways.   He stresses the need of providing strong anti-aircraft protection for the endangered canal areas and the sixteen hitherto unprotected locks of the Dortmund-Ems Canal.   *The Fuehrer* recognises this need.   The Navy will send further details to the O.K.W., Operations Staff, Air, immediately.

6. The problem of shipping supplies via the Frische Haff again is discussed.   Up to now the Navy has succeeded in transporting all supplies available in Pillau to Rosenberg in spite of ice conditions.

7. Baltic.—*The C.-in-C., Navy*, reports to the Fuehrer that he is worried about the mine situation in the Baltic.   The enemy is making extensive use of minesweeping interference devices such as delay clocks and period-delay mechanisms, and has begun to use deep-note firing devices. However, the C.-in-C., Navy, hopes that we shall likewise master this type of firing device, since the Mines Branch had the foresight to order mass production of anti-deep-tone mine devices (*Mandolinengeraet*) a year ago, although it was in no way certain at that time that the enemy was going to use this type of firing device.

8. U-boat campaign.—Concerning the announcement of submarine successes, *the C.-in-C., Navy*, tells the Fuehrer that it is best at present to release reports of submarine sinkings in small installments of about 50,000 tons, and not to wait until larger figures accumulate.   We should not arouse hopes prematurely that the new era in submarine warfare has begun, since we are still in a period of transition, and the new types of submarines will not become active to any extent before April.   *The Fuehrer* agrees with this opinion.   *The C.-in-C., Navy*, again points out that we must expect higher submarine losess in view of the concentration of enemy defence weapons in the area around the British Isles caused by the necessity to concentrate our submarines in that area.   The day will come when it will no longer pay to concentrate our submarines in this fashion.   We cannot expect any improvement of this situation until the new types of submarines go into action.

9. *The C.-in-C., Navy*, hands the Fuehrer a report of the Fortification Commander, La Rochelle, Vice-Admiral Schirlitz, concerning the recent sortie and the nature of the information received from the prisoners taken; general dissatisfaction with the de Gaulle government is indicated.

10. Ammunition shortage.—In view of the difficult ammunition situation of the Army, *the C.-in-C., Navy*, orders an investigation to determine whether the Navy can spare artillery ammunition for the Army.   This action is taken on the basis of a favourable report on naval ammunition supplies.

(signed) ADMIRAL ON SPECIAL DUTY.

Admiral on Special Duty with C.-in-C., Navy      Berlin, March 5, 1945

CONFERENCE OF THE C.-IN-C., NAVY, WITH THE
FUEHRER ON MARCH 4, 1945, AT 1600

1. Coal.—Due to further advances in the area of Army Group, Brno, the enemy is threatening the Duisburg harbour.   *The C.-in-C., Navy*, again points out the importance of this harbour as a port of transhipment for inland water navigation.   Only part of the coal to be shipped is handled

in Duisburg, however; most of it is transferred in the Herne and Dort-mund area. Coal shipments by the Navy on the Dortmund-Ems Canal have started. The first two barges with 500 tons of coal have arrived in Emden, while ten more barges are on the way north after having passed the section of the canal endangered by the enemy. The Chief, Air Force Operations Staff, reports that an enemy air attack caused new damage to the Dortmund-Ems Canal at Ladbergen. The extent of damage is not yet known. The construction of narrow-gauge field railways becomes even more important under the circumstances in order to make it possible to by-pass these damaged points.

2. The Fuehrer fears that enemy landings aimed at outflanking us may occur on the Italian Adriatic coast. There are no definite signs as yet substantiating such fears; nevertheless, the situation demands careful watching.

3. The question is raised that it is wrong for older men to operate the modern and very effective 8-cm. anti-tank guns, as is being done in many instances. *The Fuehrer* inquires whether the Navy could make available enough young personnel to man 200 anti-tank guns (one non-commission officer and seven men for each anti-tank gun). *The C.-in-C., Navy*, is of the opinion that it might be well to take these men from the emergency units stationed in Swinemuende, because they have many specialists in their ranks. A decision is reached first of all to send a large number of anti-tank guns to the Deivenow front where these units have been put into action.

4. *The Fuehrer* criticises the inadequate amount of ammunition available for the 8·8-cm. anti-aircraft guns of the Air Force at the Oder front. The Air Force inquires whether the Navy can provide ammunition for 8·8-cm. anti-aircraft guns, Model 36. This is to be investigated.

5. Naval brigades.—*The Chief of the Army General Staff* again raises the question of the order in which various divisions—at present either being organised or being brought up to full strength, among them the 2nd Naval Division—are to be equipped with arms. *The C.-in-C., Navy*, emphasises again that it is important to furnish the 2nd Naval Division with weapons as soon as possible. This division is composed of very good men, most of them experienced and seasoned. *The Fuehrer* decides that the 2nd Naval Division and the parachute troops be given priority in allocation of equipment.

6. Baltic ports.—During the discussion of the situation of the Northern Army Group, *the C.-in-C., Navy*, stresses the fact that it is vital to hold the area south of the Koenigsberg Sea Canal. Loss of that area could cause considerable interference with the sea traffic using the canal. Pillau could be subjected to direct fire from the Balga Peninsula.

7. *The Chief of the Army General Staff* requests that the C.-in-C., Navy, make available naval emergency units stationed in Swinemuende for transfer to the Dievenow front. *The C.-in-C., Navy*, informs him that two of the four emergency units are already in action on the Dievenow front. The two remaining emergency units at present on the western front of the defence sector, Swinemuende, are under orders to move east.

(signed) ADMIRAL ON SPECIAL DUTY.

Admiral on Special Duty with C.-in-C., Navy       Berlin, March 9, 1945

## CONFERENCE OF THE C.-IN-C., NAVY, WITH THE FUEHRER ON MARCH 8, 1945, AT 1600

1. Remagen bridge.—During the discussion of the situation on the Western Front, *the Chief, O.K.W., Operations Staff*, mentions that two Navy demolition teams were assigned to destroy the Rhine bridge at Remagen, which fell into enemy hands intact. An inquiry with the Commanding Admiral, Small Combat Units, showed that nothing was known there of such an assignment. An investigation has been ordered.

2. *The Chief, General Staff, Army*, reports on the artillery equipment on the Dievenow front. *The Fuehrer* expresses the opinion that the artillery allotted to this sector should be sufficient, especially since support can be given to the land operations by the ship artillery of the naval forces.

3. Baltic.—With reference to the loss of the passenger ship Hamburg anchored at Sassnitz, *the C.-in-C., Navy*, reports to the Fuehrer that the cause of the sinking will be investigated, and if necessary severe measures will be taken. The precarious mine situation off Sassnitz is indicative of the mine danger to which the western Baltic Sea is exposed. An intensification of enemy activity in this area would be most undesirable. This fact once more emphasises the need for holding Stettin and Swinemuende. At the same time this situation proves conclusively that shipping lanes must be closed, and was done in the past, when mines are suspected.

4. *The C.-in-C., Navy*, reports to the Fuehrer that *Gauleiter* Schwede-Koburg, in co-operation with the Navy, has taken all measures to render the harbour and the railway facilities of Sassnitz serviceable again as soon as possible.

5. In connection with the attack on the landing barge convoy in the Skagerrak on March 7 *the C.-in-C., Navy*, reports that the British Admiralty is supposed to have expressed its intention from now on to press the attacks on convoys in the Skagerrak from the air. For this reason the C.-in-C., Navy, has ordered that the most endangered stretches will in the future be travelled only at night.

(signed) ADMIRAL ON SPECIAL DUTY.


Admiral on Special Duty with C.-in-C., Navy       Berlin, March 10, 1945

## CONFERENCE OF THE C.-IN-C., NAVY, WITH THE FUEHRER ON MARCH 9, 1945, AT 1700

1. Remagen bridge.—*The C.-in-C., Navy*, reports to the Fuehrer that two detachments have been chosen for blowing up the Rhine bridge at Remagen, and that they are being sent there as fast as possible. They are to attempt to blow up each of the piers with two torpedo mines (TMC) attached to one another. It is not possible at this time to predict when the preparations will be completed; everything is being done to speed them up.

2. U-boat campaign.—Regarding the submarine situation, *the C.-in-C.*, reports that two submarines are overdue. Since all the submarines which have returned have reported successes, it can be assumed that the

missing submarines were successful, too, although we cannot find out what they accomplished. Thus we must count on the probability that the figures which we publish are really less than the actual sinkings. This has the disadvantage that the enemy might be able to draw his conclusions as to our submarine losses. Regardless of this fact the C.-in-C., Navy, thinks that we should continue the policy of publishing the exact figures of the results actually known.

3. Italy.—In a conversation with the C.-in-C., Navy, *Field Marshal Kesselring* declared that although the naval harbour Pola has been declared a fortress, he is unable to spare enough forces to hold Pola against an enemy attack for any length of time. Since it is planned to have the main battle line at the base of the Istrian Peninsula, the Field Marshal cannot send additional troops to Pola. The fortress commander of Pola, Captain Waue, who makes an excellent impression, thus faces an insoluble task. Field Marshal Kesselring agrees that Pola must remain in our hands as long as possible, in order to keep the enemy from using its harbour; still he is of the opinion that he, as Commanding General, South-west, should make the decision regarding the evacuation of Pola. He is therefore going to request that the order making Pola a defence area be cancelled. *The C.-in-C., Navy*, agrees with this point of view; his only concern is that we hold Pola as long as possible, in order to prevent the enemy from making landing preparations in a harbour close to the front. As far as our own fighting forces are concerned, Pola has no decisive importance as a point of departure.

(signed) ADMIRAL ON SPECIAL DUTY.

Admiral on Special Duty with C.-in-C., Navy      Berlin, March 11, 1945

### CONFERENCE OF THE C.-IN-C., NAVY, WITH THE FUEHRER ON MARCH 10, 1945, AT 1600

1. Italy.—The possibility of a British landing in the northern Adriatic is again discussed. *The C.-in-C., Navy*, believes that the British seem to be trying to spare their strength in view of the overall political situation. For this reason, large, independent British landing operations are not likely to be undertaken either in the Adriatic or in the German Bight. Holland is a different matter; the British must have great interest in occupying it because of the danger of the Channel traffic. *The Fuehrer* agrees with the opinion of the C.-in-C., Navy. He thinks, too, that the British inaction in Yugoslavia, where even a few troops could have caused us great difficulties, can be explained only by the fact that the British are intentionally trying to save their forces.

2. Norway.—*General Jodl* reports to the Fuehrer a request from the Commanding General, Norway, asking for permission to withdraw from the northern Norwegian area to the region south of Narvik because of lack of supplies, especially of coal and fuel. *The Fuehrer* believes that if we vacated Narvik we might be providing Sweden with an opportunity to enter the war against us, since she would then have excellent connections with the Anglo-Americans. The Lofotens are also one of the most valuable Norwegian fishing areas, and they are important for our food supply. The Fuehrer therefore does not permit an evacuation of this

area.   However, he asks for suggestions how more troops might be with-drawn from there so as to release troops for the home theatre of war.   The supply difficulties, especially in regard to coal, caused by the many troop transports in particular, must be overcome.   Of prime consideration in the Fuehrer's decision is the fact that if northern Norway were occupied by the enemy, southern Norway, which is an indispensable submarine base, would also be endangered.

3. Coal.—As for the coal situation, *the C.-in-C., Navy,* states that it is entirely a matter of inadequate transport within Germany.   If sufficient quantities of coal are brought to the German ports, he can assure their transport by sea.   According to the reports so far, 28,000 tons of coal are still to be shipped to Norway in March.   The efforts of the C.-in-C., Navy, to get additional quantities of coal to the coast via canals, by-passing the dangerous stretch near Ladbergen by means of narrow-gauge field railways, promise to be successful, and they are being continued energetically.

4. Refugees.—Concerning the transport of refugees, *the C.-in-C., Navy,* reports that he has requested the Fuehrer to give orders that the refugees be disembarked in Copenhagen, so that their evacuation will not be inter-rupted in spite of the loss of Sassnitz and in spite of the minefields in the western Baltic Sea.   Aside from the immediate evacuation of about 50,000 refugees from Kolberg, the area Danzig–Gdynia remains the main point of refugee evacuation.

5. Channel Islands.—During the report on the successful raid on the port of Granville by the forces stationed on the Channel Islands, *the C.-in-C., Navy,* states that the newly assigned commander of the Channel Islands, Vice-Admiral Hueffmeier, is the heart and soul of this vigorous action.

6. The representative of the Air Force, *Major Buchs,* reports that a gap 80 metres long was torn in the Lippe Canal near the place where it crosses the Dortmund-Ems Canal near Datteln, and the water has run out at that place.   Concerning the repair of such damage in transport facilities, the C.-in-C., Navy, says that the population must be called on to do this work just as it has been the custom for centuries, even in peace time, whenever there was a break in a dyke on the coast.   *The Fuehrer* agrees absolutely with this, and he states that he has already ordered similar measures for damages along the railways.   (About 800,000 workers are in readiness.)

7. The 2nd Army in West Prussia reports shortage of ammunition. *The C.-in-C., Navy,* states that in such situations, if necessary, even ships already at sea and carrying ammunition must be diverted and sent to the places where the need is greatest.

8. *The Chief, General Staff, Army,* reports that the Norwegian tanker Gerdmor which was intended for the eastern area has been lying in Swine-muende for several days because of sabotage by the Norwegian crew, and it still has not left port.   (It was discovered later that it was not a case of sabotage, but that the tanker was rammed twice, and that in addition the Norwegian captain had to be replaced because of drunkenness.)

9. *The Fuehrer* decides that the Naval Divisions will henceforth be known as Naval Infantry Divisions.

10. In connection with the conversation on March 9 with Field Marshal Kesselring concerning Pola, *the C.-in-C., Navy,* asks the Chief, O.K.W.,

Operations Staff, to include him when making any possible new decisions regarding the defence of Pola.

(signed) ADMIRAL ON SPECIAL DUTY.


Admiral on Special Duty with C.-in-C., Navy      Berlin, March 13, 1945

### CONFERENCE OF THE C.-IN-C., NAVY, WITH THE FUEHRER ON MARCH 12, 1945, AT 1600

1. Baltic ports.—In discussing the future operational policy of Army Group, Vistula, *the C.-in-C., Navy,* again calls attention to the fact that the loss of Stettin will result in serious consequences for our strategy. Swinemuende cannot take over the traffic from Stettin, especially since the harbour of Swinemuende, with its limited facilities makes it impossible to disperse the ships, in contrast to Stettin.   The C.-in-C., Navy, therefore regards it essential to free the lower Oder River and the eastern side of the Haff at least to the extent that traffic can get through to Stettin.   *The Fuehrer* orders the Chief of the Operations Division of the Army General Staff, Lt.-General Krebs, to make the necessary calculations for this and other operations, to be used by the Fuehrer in making future decisions. He is of the opinion, however, that judging from the information at hand a large operation such as the C.-in-C., Navy, suggest would hardly be possible.

2. Channel Islands.—*The C.-in-C., Navy,* submits to the Fuehrer the answer of the commander of the Channel Islands, Vice-Admiral Hueff-meier, to the telegram of the C.-in-C., Navy, congratulating him on the Granville sortie.   Vice-Admiral Hueffmeier expresses the hope that he will be able to hold the Channel Islands for another year.

3. U-boats.—On the basis of the final report about the operations of the first two submarines of type XXIII to go into active service, *the C.-in-C., Navy,* reports that these vessels stood the test well.   This is all the more gratifying because at the time the new submarines were put into mass production, this was done without previous trials.

4. Remagen bridge.—The British *"Atlantik-Sender"* has announced that Germany plans to use amphibious commandos from the Navy to blow up the Rhine bridge at Remagen.   *The C.-in-C., Navy,* informs the Fuehrer that he intends to carry out this plan regardless, because there is a possibility that the British made the announcement in order to mislead us.

5. *The Chief of the O.K.W.* informs the C.-in-C., Navy, that he has issued the March allotments of anti-aircraft weapons, and he asks the C.-in-C., Navy, to investigate whether the amount allotted to the Navy is large enough to take care of the needs of sea transport.   If not, he is considering special action in order to make available an adequate quantity of anti-aircraft weapons for transport and merchant ships.

6. In connection with a request by the 1st Naval Infantry Division for more ammunition and arms, *Lt.-General Buhle* reports to the C.-in-C., Navy, that requests for current ammunition requirements must be directed to the proper army; he will investigate the possibility of getting the desired arms (100 light machine guns, 30 heavy machine guns, 20 medium trench mortars).

(signed) ADMIRAL ON SPECIAL DUTY.

Admiral on Special Duty with C.-in-C., Navy      Berlin, March 14, 1945

## CONFERENCE OF THE C.-IN-C., NAVY, WITH THE FUEHRER ON MARCH 13, 1945, AT 1600

1. Baltic ports.—Future operational possibilities of Army Group, Vistula, are again discussed, although estimates and suggestions of the Army General Staff have not yet been received.   In reply to a comment made by the C.-in-C., Navy, that it is essential to open the Oder passage to Stettin, and that Swinemuende is inadequate as the only port in the central Baltic Sea, *the Fuehrer* states that he fully recognises these facts, but that for reasons of land warfare these operations will have to be postponed.

2. The Fuehrer mentions that he has given orders to renew the manufacture of ammunition for heavy naval artillery.   He is of the opinion that this would affect the armament industry only very little as far as material and labour are concerned.   The Chief of the Army Organisation Division in the O.K.W., Lt.-General Buhle (Artillery), will receive instructions to inform Speer accordingly.   The Navy is to make specific demands.

3. Refugees.—*The C.-in-C., Navy,* announces that three additional ships of the Reich Commissioner of Maritime Shipping will be used for the evacuation of refugees, and that it is necessary to continue to bring refugees in large numbers to Copenhagen.   *The Fuehrer* agrees.

4. U-boat campaign.—During a discussion of the small number of aircraft ready for action and the low effectiveness of the new types, *the C.-in-C., Navy,* seizes the opportunity to raise this subject in regard to submarines.   Of the 130 operational submarines available in February 1945 for service in the Atlantic, on an average 64 were at sea; out of this number only about 17 were in the operational zones due to the disproportion existing between time needed to reach the operational zone and time actually spent in operation.   The trip from German ports to the operational areas in the Channel and the Irish Sea takes an average of 24 days, while the trip from ports in the Bay of Biscay to the same areas required only about 4 days.

6. Sea transport.—After another talk with the Chief of the General Staff, Army, about the organisation of supply shipments to cut-off Army Groups, the C.-in-C., Navy, decides to invite all parties concerned for a discussion in order to get a clear picture of all factors involved, in order to organise matters in the most efficient manner.

(signed) ADMIRAL ON SPECIAL DUTY.


Admiral on Special Duty with C.-in-C., Navy      Berlin, March 16, 1945

## CONFERENCE OF THE C.-IN-C., NAVY, WITH THE FUEHRER ON MARCH 16, 1945, AT 1600

1. Coal.—*The Chief, O.K.W., Operations Staff,* reports to the Fuehrer on the situation in northern Norway.   While the delivery of supplies generally runs smoothly, the coal situation in Norway is constantly becoming more critical.   At the moment there are still 15,000 tons of coal in Denmark, ready to be shipped to Norway.   After that, no more coal

shipments from Germany can be counted on unless the Navy can find ways and means to provide further quantities. The railway schedule in Norway will shortly be reduced to two trains per day because of the coal shortage. This rate can be maintained even after conversion to wood fueling. In connection with the coal situation, *the C.-in-C., Navy*, states that as long as coal is available in German ports, sea transport will present no difficulties. Transport on land, however, is causing difficulties. Coal shipments on the Dortmund-Ems Canal are to be resumed as soon as possible in spite of renewed damage to the Ladbergen sector. The C.-in-C., Navy, decided with *Ministerialdirektor* Dorsch that a dump truck railway should be built to serve temporarily until an efficient narrow-gauge railway can be provided. First of all a large labour force will be needed to reload the coal. But the coal transported in this way will pro-bably be needed in the coastal areas of the homeland, since there also coal is very scarce, and our transport and escort forces never have enough.

2. Sea transport.—On March 15 *the Fuehrer* ordered the Navy to accelerate the transfer of the 169th Infantry Division from Norway to Jutland with all available means. The C.-in-C., Navy, reports that two more transports were assigned to this task, and that adequate escort forces are also available; therefore the transfer of this division will be effected as rapidly as possible. About four-fifths of the division is already in Denmark.

3. U-boat campaign.—*The C.-in-C., Navy*, reports to the Fuehrer that the first submarine, type XXI, will depart for the operational area within the next few days. Six more submarines of this type will follow in April. The C.-in-C., Navy, intends to send one group of the eight to ten boats of type IX C—to be ready for action at the end of March or beginning of April—to patrol the convoy route to America. According to reports received from our ships there is no more enemy air patrol west of 15° W. Therefore it would be to our advantage to invade this area with submarines as soon as possible in order to make successful surprise attacks on the one hand, and on the other hand to weaken the enemy's present concentration of defence weapons in the sea area around Britain. Recent happenings indicate that most of our submarine losses are due to enemy mines. The best way of overcoming this would be to operate in shallow water. The enemy will refrain from using ground mines because of the danger to his own shipping, and it is unlikely that moored mines will be laid in shallow water. At the same time the shallow water will provide for our ships the best protection against enemy radar. However, should a sub-marine be located in this area, it will have difficulty escaping enemy anti-submarine vessels.

4. Baltic ports.—*The C.-in-C., Navy*, reports to the Fuehrer that in case Danzig and Gdynia are lost, he does not plan to destroy these harbours completely, but merely to block them as effectively as possible. While the port of Danzig, being a river port, cannot be completely eliminated by mere demolition, also Gdynia would, in spite of the most thorough demoli-tion, still provide sufficient harbour space for the small requirements of the Russians. Therefore it would seem more practical to forego demolition altogether and to concentrate on blocking the ports with deep minefields. However, it is essential that the minor basins south of the main harbour of Gdynia be completely demolished. The same holds true for Pillau and

Koenigsberg. *The Fuehrer* agrees with this suggestion. In conclusion the C.-in-C., Navy, again stresses the decisive value the ports of the Bay of Danzig have for German naval as well as land warfare in this area.

5. Refugees.—*The C.-in-C., Navy*, points out to the Chief, General Staff, Army, that he cannot accept the complaints of the Fortification Commander, Kolberg, about the supposed failure of the Navy concerning the evacuation of refugees from Kolberg. He believes that the evacuation of over 60,000 refugees within twelve days by improvised means is quite exceptional and will hold its own against all criticism. The Chief, O.K.W., informs the C.-in-C., Navy, that he is of the same opinion.

6. In a conversation with Field Marshal Busch, the new Commanding General of the Operations Staff, North Coast, *the C.-in-C., Navy*, stresses the necessity of leaving the overall command authority of the immediate coastal area in the hands of the naval commanders, since experiences in the West Area proved that they are better qualified to handle the operation of weapons along the coast.

(signed) ADMIRAL ON SPECIAL DUTY.

---

Admiral on Special Duty with C.-in-C., Navy      Berlin, March 18, 1945

**CONFERENCE OF THE C.-IN-C., NAVY, WITH THE FUEHRER ON MARCH 17, 1945, AT 1600**

1. Baltic—Sea transport.—*The Chief of the General Staff, Army*, expresses to the C.-in-C., Navy, the opinion that the Fuehrer's decision to hold Kurland can partly be traced back to his concern for naval warfare. The Chief of the General Staff, Army, therefore requests that the C.-in-C., Navy, support him in his endeavour to evacuate Kurland. Though *the C.-in-C., Navy*, is convinced that problems of naval warfare did not influence the Fuehrer's decision, he nevertheless sees the necessity to clarify this problem. He reports to the Fuehrer that West Prussia is now as ever of prime importance for naval warfare, but that the Navy purely from a viewpoint of naval strategy has no interest in the defence of Kurland. The shipment of supplies to Kurland is only a strain on the Navy. *The Fuehrer* confirms the correctness of this opinion and explains at length the reasons—all based purely on considerations of land warfare—which made him decide not to abandon Kurland. In the course of the conversation the C.-in-C., Navy, states in answer to a question by the Fuehrer that it would take the Navy about five weeks to evacuate five divisions. According to rough estimates about 2,000 men, 600 horses, and 300 vehicles could be shipped every day. The Fuehrer delegates the C.-in-C., Navy, to investigate these problems again in the light of present conditions.

2. Reporting on the transport situation in Norway, *the C.-in-C., Navy*, mentions that soon three additional ships will be assigned to the transport service to make up for the loss of the transports Markobrunner and Tijunka, which were damaged by mines.

3. *The C.-in-C., Navy*, reports to the Fuehrer that the harbour patrol vessel No. 31 (a small boat about 16 metres long with one machine gun and a crew of one non-commissioned officer and five men), escaped to Sweden after the officer had been shot. One member of the crew returned

in a rubber dinghy.    It is probably the action of a madman.    The Foreign Office is requested to demand the extradition of the escaped crew.

4. On the basis of a communication from the Commanding Admiral, Eastern Baltic, transmitted via Naval Command, East, *the C.-in-C., Navy*, calls the attention of the Chief of the General Staff, Army, to the fact that the maintenance of the bridgeheads at Danzig, Gdynia, and Hela depend above all on weapons and ammunition, and he requests therefore that adequate supplies be made available.

(signed) ADMIRAL ON SPECIAL DUTY.

Admiral on Special Duty with C.-in-C., Navy      Berlin, March 19, 1945

### CONFERENCE OF THE C.-IN-C., NAVY, WITH THE FUEHRER ON MARCH 18, 1945, AT 1600

1. *The Chief of the O.K.W., Operations Staff*, reports that the main body of enemy air reconnaissance has been shifted from the Nijmegen region toward the north-east, which points to certain conclusions as to the intended direction of enemy attack.    In this connection *the C.-in-C., Navy*, reports to the Fuehrer that in the area of the German Bight and in the Skagerrak the enemy is continuing to lay mines set for two weeks, and that he has laid no mines in the Ems estuary and in the Dollart.    This points to the conclusion that the enemy wants to keep these areas open temporarily for his own movements, and that enemy landings, especially in the Ems estuary, are very possible.

2. Remagen bridge.—It was learned from American sources that the big railroad bridge at Remagen has collapsed, allegedly owing to previous damage.    *The C.-in-C., Navy*, takes this opportunity to give the Fuehrer an idea of the repeated attempts by naval detachments to destroy this bridge under the most difficult circumstances.

3. Baltic—Sea transport.—In reply to the Fuehrer's inquiry of March 17 about the transport possibilities from Kurland, *the C.-in-C., Navy*, submits the following report:

(a) The Navy can spare 28 ships with a total of 110,729 tons for the evacuation of Kurland, at the same time keeping up shipments of current supply needs, continuing with the evacuation of troops from Norway on the present scale, and evacuating the wounded and the refugees.

(b) In one round trip (about nine days) these ships can handle 23,250 men, 4,520 horses, and 3,160 vehicles.

(c) The harbours of Libau and Swinemuende will be adequate to handle these transports, provided that all transports carrying wounded and refugees are unloaded in harbours other than Swinemuende.

(d) The above figures do not take into account any exceptional intensification of enemy activity which might result in heavy losses in shipping and destruction of harbours, since this sort of thing cannot be estimated in advance.

*The Fuehrer* listens to this report without further comment.

4. *The Fuehrer* informs Minister Speer that he has decided to continue the production of ammunition for heavy ship artillery within the scope of the emergency programme.

5. U-boat campaign.—Following the report on the launching of the first submarine of type XXI, *the C.-in-C., Navy*, informs the Fuehrer of the very good results that were reported by the commander of a submarine type XXIII, Lt. Heckel.  After the attack he withdrew at a speed of 9 knots, changed over to crawling speed, and succeeded in escaping from the anti-submarine forces; they dropped their depth charges without effect far away from the submarine.  Furthermore, the C.-in-C., Navy, emphasises once more that our figures of German submarine successes as they are published are no doubt smaller than the actual results.  Assuming that the missing submarines averaged as well as those which returned, an additional 26,000 tons may have been sunk.  The submarines could do even better if we were still in the possession of the harbours in the Bay of Biscay.

6. E-boat operations.—In connection with the report on the E-boat missions during the night of March 17 *the C.-in-C., Navy*, calls attention to the great activity of the E-boats lately.  Some time ago he had been under the impression that the Commander, E-boats, had become somewhat too dogmatic in the use of his forces, although one must be very careful about establishing any set rules, considering the changing conditions and experiences.  These difficulties now seem to have been overcome.

7. During a discussion of possible enemy plans in the Mediterranean Sea, *the C.-in-C., Navy*, states that the observations of enemy ship movements through the Strait of Gibraltar are of no real value, because no one knows whether the troop ships are carrying replacements or men on leave, or whether the convoys remain in the Mediterranean or go on to East Asia.

8. Refugees.—Colonel (S.S.) Zander submits a request from *Reichsleiter* Bormann to relieve the congestion in Pillau somewhat by evacuating some 5,000 refugees, in addition to the main evacuation of refugees from West Prussia.  *The C.-in-C., Navy*, asks that the Party representative with the Naval Command, East, be given the necessary instructions; he will notify the Commanding Officer, Supply and Transports, of the measure himself.

(signed) ADMIRAL ON SPECIAL DUTY.

Admiral on Special Duty with C.-in-C., Navy     Berlin, March 21, 1945

CONFERENCE OF THE C.-IN-C., NAVY, WITH THE
FUEHRER ON MARCH 20, 1945, AT 1600

1. On the basis of reports from agents, *the Chief, O.K.W., Operations Staff*, states that the enemy will most likely make a combined air and sea landing in the area of the Ems estuary in the near future.  *The Fuehrer*, on the other hand, believes that the enemy will use his airborne troops nearer the front in direct support of an offensive by occupying bridges, crossroads, and important points rather than in an independent strategic operation.  *The C.-in-C., Navy*, states that while the Ems is the most probable goal for a possible landing, he is also of the opinion that a large independent landing operation is not likely at the moment.  It is decided that two divisions will be transferred to the area of the Ems estuary.  However, the 2nd Naval Infantry Division is to remain in its present assembly

area and after being assembled it is to be transferred to the area near the front behind Army Group, Vistula, as planned heretofore.

2. Baltic.—In answer to the Fuehrer's inquiry about participation of the task forces in the fighting around the Dohnas Mountain west of Gdynia, *the C.-in-C., Navy*, shows him the report of the Admiral, Eastern Baltic Sea, according to which the ships' artillery has been in action against targets in this area every day since March 10. On the decisive days of March 17 and 18, however, comparatively little ammunition was used. The demands of the Army, also concerning the use of ammunition, were almost entirely satisfied. *The Fuehrer* is of the opinion that the Army did not make sufficient use of the very effective ships' artillery in the decisive fighting around the Dohnas Mountain.

3. Sea transport.—The Northern Army Group reported that the transfer of the 4th Army with equipment from Rosenberg to Pillau can be accomplished in about five nights. According to the Fuehrer's statements, the 4th Army is about 150,000 men strong. In this connection *the C.-in-C., Navy*, reports that these figures reach far above the capacity of the Navy's equipment. According to latest figures, the Navy can carry only 4,000 men per night without equipment. This number could be increased to 7,000 if more ships are assigned to this task. The C.-in-C., Navy, will report the exact figures on March 21, as soon as his inquiries have been answered. The C.-in-C., Navy, orders that as a precautionary measure all naval barges available in the Baltic area are to be transferred at once to Pillau.

4. In answer to the Fuehrer's inquiry, the Chief of Staff, Army, *Lt.-General Buhle* (Artillery), reports that 450 rounds of 28-cm. ammunition (4·1 calibre lengths) from a battery of Army Group, Vistula, can be made available for the Schlesien, and that the Army can furnish 394 rounds of 28-cm. ammunition (4·1 calibre lengths) and 2,556 rounds of armour-piercing shells for the Luetzow. *The Fuehrer* orders that this ammunition be given to the Navy immediately.

5. *The C.-in-C., Navy*, reports to the Fuehrer that he is going to try to reinforce the task force in Gdynia by transferring the Luetzow from Swinemuende. (The corresponding order of the C.-in-C., Navy, effecting this transfer is telephoned to the Naval Command, Baltic, and the Naval Staff on the evening of March 20.)

6. Ammunition shortage.—*The Fuehrer* states that at the moment an adequate supply of ammunition is our most important task, even at the expense of troop transports. It would be useless to transfer more troops to the Northern Army Group before the shortage of ammunition there has been relieved. The C.-in-C., Navy, reports in this connection that according to his observations no appreciable time can be saved during the transport of ammunition to the ports, nor afterwards at sea, but only by correct assignment of the ships and accelerated turnover in the ports.

7. E-boat operations.—With the help of a map, *the Admiral on Special Duty* with the C.-in-C., Navy, explains to the Fuehrer the E-boat operations on the nights of March 17 and 18. In conclusion the C.-in-C., Navy, reports as follows:

(*a*) It was correct to continue building the offensive type of E-boat and not to give in to the numerous suggestions for constructing a defensive E-boat.

(b) The mass employment of E-boats scatters enemy defences.

(c) Torpedoes have proved more successful than mines. Therefore their use should under no circumstances be given up in favour of mines.

(d) The E-boats stand good chance of success even in poor visibility. The enemy is handicapped when he has to depend on locating devices only without being able to see, and his defences are considerably less effective.

(e) The E-boat commanders had generally made the mistake of establishing principles for the operation of E-boats which were not adequately substantiated, but to which they adhered obstinately. The C.-in-C., Navy, has intervened and has done away with such rigid conceptions. The recent successful activity of the E-boats shows that this effort has been worth while and has proved useful to E-boat operations.

8. Using a map, *the C.-in-C., Navy*, tells the Fuehrer of his plan to withdraw eight naval coastal batteries from the Kurland area for the defence of Bornholm Island, since no other batteries are available for this purpose. *The Fuehrer* agrees.

9. *The C.-in-C., Navy*, reports to the Fuehrer that he has transferred the Naval Command, West, from Bad Schwalbach to Lindau, since the front was too close to permit its proper functioning. There is at the moment no other place available. However, the C.-in-C., Navy, believes that closer connection between Naval Command, West, and the Commanding General, West, is necessary in the long run, and he intends to transfer Naval Command, West, to the vicinity of the Commanding General, West, as soon as suitable headquarters are available.

(signed) ADMIRAL ON SPECIAL DUTY.

Admiral on Special Duty with C.-in-C., Navy    Berlin, March 22, 1945

### CONFERENCE OF THE C.-IN-C., NAVY, WITH THE FUEHRER ON MARCH 21, 1945, AT 1600

1. *The Fuehrer* emphasises once more the importance of giving the Northern Army Group, and especially the 2nd Army, priority in the shipment of adequate ammunition. *The C.-in-C., Navy*, states that, according to today's report, 1,690 tons of ammunition arrived in Pillau, 454 tons in Gdynia, and an additional 233 tons are expected in Gdynia. Furthermore, the Fuehrer confirms his decision of March 20 that the 4th Army shall hold its bridgehead and will not be evacuated. However, all artillery that can be spared is to be withdrawn via Rosenberg–Pillau. In this connection the C.-in-C., Navy, comments that all available barges are being concentrated at Pillau for this purpose.

2. *The C.-in-C., Navy*, reports with the aid of a map on the seaward defences of the Ems estuary. He shows that the Ems can be considered well defended, and that a landing attempt in this coastal area is expected to cost the enemy severe losses. In reply to the Fuehrer's question, the C.-in-C., Navy, reports that he thinks an enemy landing on the West Friesian Islands very unlikely, since there is frequently surf, and the shallow tidal areas between the islands and the continent are unfavourable for landings.

(signed) ADMIRAL ON SPECIAL DUTY.

Admiral on Special Duty with C.-in-C., Navy     Berlin, March 24, 1945

## CONFERENCE OF THE C.-IN-C., NAVY, WITH THE FUEHRER ON MARCH 23, 1945, AT 1600

1. *The C.-in-C., Navy,* reports to the Fuehrer that the evacuation of the 169th Infantry Division from Norway cannot be accomplished with the desired speed at present. This is due to the fact that recently four large transports, the Isar, Markobrunner, Tijuka, and the Mar del Plata, were damaged and had to be withdrawn.

2. U-boat campaign.—*The C.-in-C., Navy,* comments on the successes of Submarine Commander Thomsen between the Bank of Newfoundland and the Channel against a convoy coming from America on the great circle. Submarine Commander Thomsen's report confirms the assumption that enemy convoys use the shortest route, i.e. the great circle, because of the present freedom of the high seas from submarine danger. The C.-in-C., Navy, on the basis of this fact, intends to comb the great circle for enemy convoys at the beginning of April with submarines of type IX C.

3. During the discussion of the situation in West Prussia, *the Fuehrer* stated that he doubts that the Army Commander used the naval artillery as much as he should have during the Russian attack on Zoppot.

4. In connection with the Fuehrer's order of March 19 in regard to the extent of destruction to be carried out in the Reich area, *the C.-in-C., Navy,* requests a decision from the Fuehrer on how the destruction of harbours and shipyards should be handled. *The Fuehrer* is of the opinion that here, too, decisions will have to be made by the authorities involved. He delegates to the C.-in-C., Navy, the power to decide the extent to which all sea ports in the Reich area are to be destroyed, and the way in which it is to be done. The O.K.W. will issue the necessary orders as suggested by the C.-in-C., Navy.

(signed) ADMIRAL ON SPECIAL DUTY.

### APPENDIX

Hitler's "scorched earth" policy is laid down in the following order which was sent to all commands on March 19, 1945:

"The battle for the existence of our people compels us to do all in our power, even within the Reich itself, to weaken the enemy's war potential and hinder his advance. Every opportunity must be utilised to the full to carry out, directly or indirectly, the most irreparable damage. It is an erroneous idea to believe that after we have won back territory which has been lost, it will be possible to put into use again installations which we now leave intact or slightly damaged. In his retreat, the enemy will leave behind him nothing but a scorched earth and will have no consideration for the people. I therefore order:

"(1) The demolition of all military services, communications, industrial and supply installations, and everything of value in the Reich, which could be of immediate or future use to the enemy.

"(2) Demolitions are to be carried out by:

Military Authorities for all military objects, including transport and communications installations.

*Gauleiters* and Reich Commissars for Defence for all industrial and supply installations as well as valuable stores.

Troops must give the necessary assistance to the *Gauleiters* and Reich Commissars for Defence in the execution of their duties.

"(3) This order is to be communicated immediately to all Commanding Officers. All directives opposing this are invalid.

(signed) ADOLF HITLER."

Admiral on Special Duty with C.-in-C., Navy     Berlin, March 26, 1945

## CONFERENCE OF THE C.-IN-C., NAVY, WITH THE FUEHRER ON MARCH 25, 1945, AT 1600

1. Baltic ports.—During the report on the situation on the sector of Army Group, Vistula, *the C.-in-C., Navy*, indicates that the Russians might attempt to break through the Dievenow position and occupy Swinemuende.   Such action would eliminate a port which is indispensible to us.   Therefore the C.-in-C., Navy, believes that it is necessary to reinforce the defences of the Dievenow sector with additional artillery and to raise the ammunition allotment which, according to reports by the local commanders, is too low.   *The Fuehrer* orders that an exact artillery chart of this sector be submitted to him by the Army General Staff on March 26 so that he can then make a decision.

2. In view of the fact that the bridgehead of the 4th Army in East Prussia has been contracted further, *the C.-in-C., Navy*, requests that the Balga Peninsula, from where Pillau is directly threatened, should be held as long as possible.   *The Fuehrer* agrees.   He has decided that first of all the supernumerary heavy equipment, especially artillery, is to be removed from Rosenberg to Pillau, and that afterwards the evacuation of the divisions can get under way.

3. During the discussion of measures to destroy the Russian Oder bridges the possibility of using "Greek fire" was brought up.   *The C.-in-C., Navy*, states in this connection that the Navy has already for some time conducted experiments along such lines, and that they will be concluded in about a week.

4. Coal.—*The C.-in-C., Navy*, again discusses with the Chief of Staff, O.K.W., the problem of coal conservation in Norway.  *The Chief of Staff, O.K.W.*, reports that a priority list for coal consumption in Norway has been set up, and that conservation of coal is being carried out wherever possible.

(signed) ADMIRAL ON SPECIAL DUTY.


Admiral on Special Duty with C.-in-C., Navy     Berlin, March 27, 1945

## CONFERENCE OF THE C.-IN-C., NAVY, WITH THE FUEHRER ON MARCH 26, 1945, AT 1600

1. Coastal fortresses.—*The Fuehrer* orders an investigation of the officers occupying the posts of fort commanders in the Western Area.   He states that these positions should be filled mainly by naval officers, since many fortresses have been given up, but no ships were ever lost without fighting to the last man.   This remark was caused by a report from the Channel Islands concerning a difference of opinion among the occupation troops in the matter of holding out to the last man.   *The C.-in-C., Navy*, informs the Fuehrer that this situation has been remedied by the recent appointment of Vice-Admiral Hueffmeier as Admiral, Channel Islands, and that in most of the other fortresses in the West (except in Lorient and St. Nazaire) naval officers have been assigned to the posts of fortress commanders.   (The C.-in-C., Navy, repeats his earlier request concerning the replacement of the fortress commander of St. Nazaire, Lt.-General Jung,

by the previous fortress commander, Lt.-General Huenten. Jung is handicapped by illness and there is no guarantee therefore that he can provide the necessary resistance.)

2. Danzig.—The developments in Danzig and Gdynia necessitate removing the wounded and refugees from these ports at once with all possible means, rather than evacuating Pillau. *The C.-in-C., Navy,* reports this matter to the Fuehrer, who agrees. The order to this effect is sent immediately to the Commanding Officer, Supply and Transports. Russian successes against the bridgeheads at Rosenberg make it necessary to transfer the troops without heavy equipment across the Haff to Pillau as soon as possible. The Navy is unable to furnish any additional vessels for the crossing, since some of the naval barges have to be used for shuttle traffic between Gdynia and Danzig.

3. *Chief of the Army General Staff* reports to the Fuehrer that altogether 118 guns of 7·5-cm. calibre and more are in use on the Dievenow front, and that 60 additional 7·5-cm. anti-tank guns are on the way. These figures coincide with those given by the Naval Shore Commander, Pomerania. The Fuehrer is of the opinion that this artillery should be adequate.

4. Norway.—The C.-in-C., Navy, and the Deputy Chief, O.K.W., Operations Staff, Major-General Winter, discuss the following matters concerning the Norwegian area on the basis of the recent report by the Commanding Admiral, Norway, Admiral Ciliax:

(*a*) The Navy needs the Class I emergency units as infantry protection for the coastal batteries, since the Commanding General, Armed Forces, Norway, did not provide adequate infantry protection.

(*b*) A decision must be reached at once concerning the problem of base commanders of the coastal batteries in Norway. *The C.-in-C., Navy,* is of the opinion that the ruling by the Commanding General of the Narvik Army Group, making the commanding officer of the infantry defence forces also the base commander in every case, is not acceptable to the Navy. *Major-General Winter* promises an early report on the decision of the O.K.W.

(*c*) As to the problem of delegating overall command authority to Army commanders below the rank of division commanders, which runs counter to Fuehrer Directive No. 40, Major-General Winter reports that due to the extensive territory in Norway such measures cannot always be avoided. The C.-in-C., Navy, agrees.

(signed) ADMIRAL ON SPECIAL DUTY.

Admiral on Special Duty with C.-in-C., Navy     Berlin, March 29, 1945

### CONFERENCE OF THE C.-IN-C., NAVY, WITH THE FUEHRER ON MARCH 28, 1945, AT 1600

1. Coal.—*The C.-in-C., Navy,* presents to the Fuehrer a general view of the coal situation on the coast, and its effects on naval operations. Due to the fact that for about a week no coal has arrived from the Ruhr area, a great coal shortage will result within the next few days. Only about 900 tons of coal will be available per day according to present estimates (400 tons from Lower Silesia and 500 tons from the mining area Ibben-

bueren), while the daily requirements for the Navy and the Reich Commissioner of Maritime Shipping in the home zone amount to 6,200 tons of coal. The 900 tons of coal are just enough to permit the shipment of supplies to Army Group, Kurland, and the Northern Army Group, and include the amount of coal required to move and safeguard the coal itself. Therefore coal-burning vessels will no longer be available for troop transports, for the evacuation of the wounded and of refugees; all this will have to be confined to the oil-burning ships at hand. It will amount to a 50 per cent. decrease in shipping space. In addition, the operation of all coal-burning escort ships in the remaining sea areas will have to be suspended. The Chief of the O.K.W. is endeavouring to increase coal deliveries to the Navy, and hopes that he can arrange for daily shipments amounting to 4,000 tons of pit coal (2,000 tons from Denmark and 1,000 tons each from Lower Silesia and Westphalia) and 4,000 tons of brown coal. (For the time being the C.-in-C., Navy, will not order convoy escorts and merchant ships to suspend operations—a move which would have serious consequences in any case. Rather he prefers to await developments, hoping that the Chief of the O.K.W. will succeed in alleviating the coal shortage.)

2. Baltic.—On March 27 *the Fuehrer* wanted to know whether submarines could be used for the purpose of sending supplies to Army Group, Kurland. In reply to this question transmitted to him by the Admiral at Fuehrer Headquarters, *the C.-in-C., Navy*, explains as follows: Submarines must limit their load to fifty tons in the Baltic Sea because of water conditions there; one round trip takes at least six days—without making allowances for possible delays. In order to move sufficient quantities of supplies, so many submarines would be required that submarine warfare would practically come to a standstill. Therefore the C.-in-C., Navy, will not approve such a plan, at least not as long as regular supply ships have a chance of reaching Kurland, and as long as they suffer only occasional losses. The Fuehrer agrees with this, but desires that in special cases submarines be used to transport items of special value (for instance tank parts).

3. Post-war German Navy.—A lengthy discussion developed between *the Fuehrer* and *the C.-in-C., Navy*, on the suitability of the various types of vessels built in the course of the expansion of the German Navy prior to the war. The C.-in-C., Navy, believes that it was a mistake to build battleships instead of concentrating on the construction of a much larger number of submarines. Our enemies had such a lead in the field of battleship construction, that it was impossible for us to overtake them. A superior submarine force would have given us a much better chance to end this war in our favour within a short time.

(signed) ADMIRAL ON SPECIAL DUTY.


Admiral on Special Duty with C.-in-C., Navy     Berlin, March 30, 1945

### CONFERENCE OF THE C.-IN-C., NAVY, WITH THE FUEHRER ON MARCH 30, 1945, AT 1630

1. Naval brigades.—*The C.-in-C., Navy*, reports to the Fuehrer that the 2nd Naval Infantry Division is expected to be fully equipped in about a week and will be ready for transfer soon thereafter. He requests

instructions to what area the division is then to be sent for continuation of training.   *The Chief of Staff, O.K.W.*, asks whether it might not be better to send the division to the Emden area contrary to present plans.   He proposes this in view of recent developments.   *The Fuehrer* remarks that he will make the decision shortly before the transfer is made.

2.  *The C.-in-C., Navy*, refers to a report given by the Chief of the Army General Staff at the Fuehrer conference on March 29 about the alleged attempt of the Norwegian tanker Gerdmoor to escape from Pillau to Sweden.   He reports to the Fuehrer that the tanker is proceeding according to schedule in a special convoy en route to Libau.   The report of the attempted escape was evidently an error.

3.  The report on the situation on the Western Front indicates that American forces have reached the Dortmund-Ems Canal and some crossed it near Ladbergen.   *The C.-in-C., Navy*, adds that the Todt Organisation has already stopped reconstructing the canal and building the narrow-gauge field railway for the circumvention of the damaged section in view of strong interference by the enemy air force.

4.  Holland.—*The Chief of Staff, O.K.W.*, reports that isolation of the Dutch redoubt must be considered a possibility, since the developments on the northern sector of the Western Front are becoming continuously more unfavourable.   He therefore recommends supplying this area with weapons and ammunition, if this is found necessary, so long as land communications remain open.   In this connection *the C.-in-C., Navy*, remarks that the shipment of supplies to the Dutch area by sea is chiefly a coal problem.   The present acuteness of the coal situation along the coast eliminates all prospects of making coal available for additional supply operations.   The C.-in-C., Navy, intends to establish a priority list covering coal distribution, in order to use the bunker coal, which is available only in limited quantities, with the greatest efficiency.   First priority will be given to the maintenance of the sea routes in the Baltic Sea, in the Skagerrak, and to the supply of Army Group, Kurland, and the Northern Army Group.   Next on the list of priorities will be the troop transports from Norway to Denmark.   All other tasks will have to be set aside in favour of the aforementioned.

5.  Russian convoys.—A strong unit of our own torpedo bombers is reported to have overshot a QP convoy which had been located several hours previously by air reconnaissance.   This evokes a discussion of the commitment of air units against targets in the open sea.   *The C.-in-C., Navy*, explains that according to the experience gained in the Bay of Biscay from co-operation with the Air Commander, Atlantic Coast, such an assignment requires crews with especially thorough training and long experience.   In order to locate an enemy convoy correctly it is necessary to have continuous air reconnaissance, which can guide our own planes to the target by constantly broadcasting the position of the convoy.   In this case the reconnaissance report was sent at 1200 and no contact was maintained; therefore the attack unit, which did not arrive till 2000 at the assumed location of the convoy, had no chance of finding the target.   *The Fuehrer* expresses the opinion that special locating planes should be provided to guide the approach of the attack unit, and that the locating devices of the Air Force still fall short of expectations.   This handicap remains despite the fact that the British locating device fell into our hands

years ago.   According to reports of the C.-in-C., Navy, the Navy has at its disposal 120 new locating devices, which are copies of the British model. These, however, are too heavy and too big for our aircraft.

6. Air raids.—*The C.-in-C., Navy*, submits to the Fuehrer a report about the bomb hits on submarine pen *Valentine*.   Two heavy high-explosive bombs (the type of the bombs has not yet been fully determined) hit and penetrated the top of the pen.   The ceiling had partly been reinforced to 7 metres, but unfortunately these bombs had struck a place of the pen which had not yet been reinforced and was only 4·5 metres thick.   However, the power of the bombs was completely spent by the penetration, so that the interior of the submarine pen remained undamaged.

7. *The Fuehrer* raises the question whether the staff of the Northern Army Group can be dispensed with after the loss of the Balga Peninsula and the isolation of the remaining bridgeheads in the area of the Gulf of Danzig.   He asks the C.-in-C., Navy, whether he thinks that this army group is needed to co-operate with the Navy in the execution of supply problems.   *The C.-in-C., Navy*, replies that it would be helpful to have an authority which would handle the supply problems in the Gulf of Danzig collectively.   However, more important to him is an authority which has full insight into the supply situation of the various defence sectors along the Gulf of Danzig, which could supervise priorities, and check the assignment of arriving ships.   The ensuing conversation shows that this task could be handled by the Quartermaster-General in the Zone of the Interior.   Therefore retention of the staff of the Northern Army Group is not necessary for regulating supplies.

(signed) ADMIRAL ON SPECIAL DUTY.

# *April—May*

U-BOAT CAMPAIGN

After a long period of trials the new U-boats were put into operation at the end of March, and the offensive was continued with vigour. On May 4, however, Doenitz ordered all U-boats at sea to cease hostilities and return to base. During the last five weeks of the war the advancing Allied armies from east and west gradually squeezed the U-boats out of the Baltic ports, and many successful attacks were made on boats escaping through the Skagerrak and Kattegat.

In April, 13 Allied merchant ships totalling 73,000 tons were sunk for the loss of 57 U-boats—the highest monthly total for the war. Of these 57 U-boats, 33 were sunk at sea, and 24 were destroyed through air raids and other causes. A further 3 Allied merchant ships, totalling 10,000 tons, were lost before hostilities ended. In the same period 25 U-boats were sunk.

CHRONOLOGY OF IMPORTANT EVENTS

April 1945

April 1. U.S. 1st and 9th Armies surround the Ruhr.

April 2. Muenster occupied—Russians gain control of main oil centre in Hungary.

April 9. Koenigsberg surrenders.
German battleship Admiral Scheer sunk.

April 12. Death of President Roosevelt.
U.S. 9th Army cross the Elbe and capture Brunswick.

April 16. Part of Ruhr pocket collapses—U.S. 7th Army reach Nuremberg.
Luetzow sunk.
Hitler sends last Order of the Day to armies on Eastern Front.

April 18. Ruhr pocket eliminated, 325,000 prisoners taken.

April 20. Russians capture many towns west of the Oder.

April 23. Russians break through northern and eastern defences of Berlin.

April 24. Himmler offers surrender to Great Britain and U.S.A. only.
British and Canadian troops enter Bremen.

April 25. Russian and American troops meet at Torgau on the Elbe.

April 26. Bremen surrenders—Stettin captured.
Goering arrested by Hitler's orders, and General Ritter von Greim appointed in command of the *Luftwaffe*.

April 28. Mussolini and 12 members of his cabinet captured and shot while attempting to cross Swiss Frontier.

April 29. Surrender of German armies in Italy signed.

April 30. Hitler commits suicide—the Reichstag building in Berlin captured by the Russians.

May 1945

May 1. Doenitz succeeds Hitler as Chancellor of the German Reich.

May 2. Surrender of Berlin.

May 3. German envoys sent to Field Marshal Montgomery's Headquarters.

May 4. German troops in Holland, north-west Germany, and Denmark surrender unconditionally.

May 7. Unconditional surrender of Germany to Western Allies and Russia, operations to cease at 2300 May 8.

Admiral on Special Duty with C.-in-C., Navy      Berlin, April 2, 1945

## CONFERENCE OF THE C.-IN-C., NAVY, WITH THE FUEHRER ON APRIL 1, 1945, AT 1630

1. Sea transport.—During the report on possible developments in the west, the problem of supplying Army Group H is brought up for discus-

sion. *Lt.-General Krebs* (Infantry), representing the Chief, General Staff, Army, mentions the statement made by a specialist on the staff of the Chief, Transport and Supply, according to which supply shipments to Holland by sea would affect shipments to the Baltic. *The C.-in-C., Navy,* criticises the fact that the utterances of a subordinate are reported to the Chief of Staff. He points out that it is at all times necessary to distribute the escort forces and means of transport adequately between the various theatres of war, and that this is being done. Supplies to Holland are shipped via the inland waterways and depend primarily on an adequate coal supply. The traffic on the inland waterways has been functioning for quite some time and is sufficient to take care of the supply demands of the Holland area so long as the inland waterways are not blocked by the enemy.

2. In the course of the report on the situation in the east, the problem of shipping ammunition to the 2nd Army in West Prussia again comes up for discussion. *Lt.-General Krebs* believes that the ammunition shortage was largely responsible for the unfavourable developments in the situation there. Among others, this shortage was caused by the long delay in shipments due to several days of bad weather. In this connection *the C.-in-C., Navy,* again points out that in his estimation the existing organisation has reacted too slowly to sudden demands for new supplies. It takes time to organise a new supply line by sea. When, therefore, such a problem arises due to the fact that an army group is cut off on land, the gap must be bridged by speedily re-routing and re-assigning the supply ships going elsewhere, until supplies can be brought up for the new service area. Until now this was generally not done in time. *The Fuehrer* agrees with the C.-in-C., Navy, and adds that mines and weather conditions must be expected to interfere with sea transport as much as enemy air raids with land operations. He believes that the generals of the Army have a strong dislike for fighting in bridgeheads with the sea at their backs; they ought to realise that the Anglo-Americans conduct practically all their warfare from bridgeheads. In addition, the generals like to concentrate their troops in a small area without considering the fact that thereby the enemy generally gets more men free than they, so that in the long run this so-called "fear of space" generally proves to be to our disadvantage.

3. Naval brigades.—Due to the difficult situation in the west, *the C.-in-C., Navy,* suggests to the Fuehrer that the 2nd Naval Infantry Division be sent to the Western Front rather than to the Eastern Front, as hitherto planned, and that the units which are comparatively fully equipped be transferred immediately. *The Fuehrer* agrees with this proposal. *The C.-in-C., Navy,* orders the Admiral at Fuehrer Headquarters to settle at once with the proper authorities all matters pertaining to a speedy transfer, so that he may then suggest to the Fuehrer the exact date for this operation.

4. Baltic.—The news was received that the Staff of the Russian Baltic Fleet has moved to Polanga, and that an advance section of the staff is located in Belgard, Pomerania. *The C.-in-C., Navy,* considers this of little importance, since Russian naval forces have on the whole played a comparatively insignificant part. He uses this opportunity to point out that the many remarks made by some generals about the increasing difficulties of sea transport are superfluous; only he is is in a position to judge this matter properly. For the time being the transport in the Baltic can

be carried out in spite of enemy interference. Should this situation change, he will report it to the Fuehrer in good time. At present sea transport could only come to a sudden halt because of no more coal and fuel deliveries.

5. Refugees.—In a telegram to the C.-in-C., Navy, *Gauleiter* Forster calls special attention to the great achievements in the evacuation of the wounded and refugees. *The C.-in-C., Navy*, states that in his opinion it is necessary to take the enormous risks involved in making these transfers with overcrowded ships and without sufficient protection, since such results cannot be achieved in any other way. *The Fuehrer* is of the same opinion and states that it is better to lose 10 per cent. en route to Germany than 90 per cent. en route to Siberia.

(signed) ADMIRAL ON SPECIAL DUTY.

Admiral on Special Duty with C.-in-C., Navy      Berlin, April 4, 1945

### CONFERENCE OF THE C.-IN-C., NAVY, WITH THE FUEHRER ON APRIL 3, 1945, AT 1630

1. Naval brigades.—During the report on the situation at the Oder front *the Fuehrer* inquires how well the 1st Naval Infantry Division is armed. *The C.-in-C., Navy*, replies that the division has not enough artillery, and that according to a recent report by the division commander, 800 of his men have no small arms except bazookas.

2. The Fuehrer then asks the C.-in-C., Navy, whether he believes that the Navy could succeed in getting supplies and replacements through to the Hel Peninsula. The C.-in-C., Navy, replies that this can probably be done so far as enemy interference is concerned, but the coal shortage is causing serious difficulties.

3. Eastern Front.—The Chief of the O.K.W., Operations Staff, informs the Fuehrer that *Gauleiter* Kaufmann requested by telephone that the Commanding General, Operations Staff, North Coast, Field Marshal Busch, be empowered to requisition soldiers of all branches of the Armed Forces to build the defences on the Vistula River. He mentioned that the Navy still has about 160,000 men in the sector of Naval Command, North, who are not included in the land defence. *The Fuehrer* refuses this request and gives the C.-in-C., Navy, full responsibility as to how naval troops are to be used.

4. Coastal fortresses.—*The Admiral on Special Duty* with the C.-in-C., Navy, discusses with the Chief of the Air Force General Staff the request of Naval Command, West, to resume the shipment of supplies by aircraft to the western fortresses, which was interrupted because of lack of fuel. *The Chief of the Air Force General Staff* promises to take up the question and to report the result as soon as possible.

(signed) ADMIRAL ON SPECIAL DUTY.

Admiral on Special Duty with C.-in-C., Navy      Berlin, April 5, 1945

### CONFERENCE OF THE C.-IN-C., NAVY, WITH THE FUEHRER ON APRIL 4, 1945, AT 1700

1. Baltic.—The Deputy Chief of the Army General Staff, *Lt.-General Krebs* (Infantry), reports that the German troops in East and West Prussia

are engaging a total of 193 Russian infantry divisions, which relieves the other fronts to a considerable degree. *The C.-in-C., Navy*, points out how necessary it therefore is to hold the Hel Peninsula in order to prevent the enemy from using the harbours in the Gulf of Danzig. Hel is also vital to German supply shipments to the bridgeheads Koenigsberg–Pillau and those east of Danzig.

2. In connection with the report on the formation of the Fleet Task Force in the Swinemuende sector under the command of the Admiral Commanding, Fleet, the *C.-in-C., Navy*, states that there is excellent co-operation between commanding officers of ships and Army command posts in the use of ships' guns against targets on land. It is his opinion, however, that the great effectiveness of the ships' guns can be increased even more by a systematic concentration on certain points. *The Fuehrer* fully agrees with this viewpoint and he explains that in order to make the most of the superior qualities of the ships' artillery it must be concentrated on definite points, and the rapid fire of the ships' guns must carefully be co-ordinated and synchronised with our land attacks. Since the use of ships' guns must be directed by the Army commanders, he asks General Krebs to instruct the Army authorities concerned accordingly.

3. Air raids.—The air raids against Kiel on April 3 and 4 prompt *the C.-in-C., Navy*, to observe that the enemy made more direct hits when he could see clearly than when he used the Rotterdam locating device in cloudy weather. This is new proof of the effectiveness of smoke cover for the protection of vital targets. He calls attention to the fact that according to information from the C.-in-C., Air, Hamburg and Bremen will no longer be protected by smoke screens owing to a scarcity of smoke acid. He requests that smoke screen protection still be used at least on the two most important targets: the submarine assembly yards, Deschimag in Bremen, and Blohm and Voss in Hamburg. *The Fuehrer* agrees and instructs the C.-in-C., Air, accordingly.

4. During the discussion of the situation at Army Group, Vistula, in a very restricted group, it becomes evident that the transfer of the 199th Infantry Division from Norway is just as important as the transfer of the 169th Infantry Division, which has just been completed. (The C.-in-C., Navy, issues the necessary directives to the naval branches concerned.)

(signed) ADMIRAL ON SPECIAL DUTY.

Admiral on Special Duty with C.-in-C., Navy       Berlin, April 8, 1945

### CONFERENCE OF THE C.-IN-C., NAVY, WITH THE FUEHRER ON APRIL 7, 1945, AT 1700

1. *The Chief, O.K.W., Operations Staff*, reports to the Fuehrer on the new organisation of command in the western theatre of war. He inquires whether the Naval Command, West, with the western fortifications subordinate to it should be put under the direct control of the Navy. *The C.-in-C., Navy*, believes that it is preferable to place it under the O.K.W., which can better control the supply shipments that are primarily dependent on air transport. *The Fuehrer* decides accordingly.

2. Sea transport.—*The Fuehrer* asks the C.-in-C., Navy, how long he thinks it will take to transfer the 199th Infantry Division from Norway to

Denmark. *The C.-in-C., Navy*, estimates that the transfer of the most important units of this division will take about two weeks. He has already ordered that this transfer be accelerated.

3. Demolition of German harbours.—*The C.-in-C., Navy*, reports to the Fuehrer the orders he has given concerning the demolition of harbours in Reich territory. He points out that he considers the destruction of the ports of Emden, Wilhelmshaven, Wesermuende, Brake, Nordenham, and Swinemuende advisable for strategic reasons, since they would be very useful to the enemy in continuing the war if they remain undamaged. This does not apply as much to the ports of Bremen and Stettin, which lie farther inland, so that the C.-in-C., Navy, will limit himself to blocking and mining these ports and destroying cranes and loading equipment without blowing up the walls of the quay. The C.-in-C., Navy, reserves his decision as to the extent of demolition of the ports from the Elbe to Greifswald. *The Fuehrer* agrees to these plans in all points. He indicates the great importance of time-fuse bombs in all demolition tasks. The Navy will investigate the possibilities of carrying out this suggestion.

4. Concerning the employment of naval forces against land targets, *the C.-in-C., Navy*, reports to the Fuehrer that some of the gun barrels of the heavy ship artillery are quite worn out. The pocket battleship Scheer is in Kiel at the moment for gun barrel replacement, while the gun barrels of the pocket battleship Luetzow indicate a decrease in muzzle velocity of about 15 per cent.

5. U-boat campaign.—Using a submarine chart, *Captain Assmann* reports on the present submarine situation. There are now 25 submarines in the operational area, 37 vessels are on the way there, 23 are returning, and 16 additional submarines are lying in Norwegian harbours ready to depart. This makes a total of 101 submarines in operation. *The C.-in-C., Navy*, reports in this connection that the fact that we have concentrated our submarines in the coastal waters around the British Isles, as has been the case for several months now, has caused the enemy also to concentrate his defences in these areas. Although enemy defence forces can no longer find our submarines by locating devices, as soon as a submarine discloses its position by attacking, such a concentrated defence action sets in that the vessel is often lost. At the moment four boats which were expected to return in the last few days are missing. Because of their low underwater speed the old types of submarine cannot escape once they are discovered, but the new types will be able to leave the danger area at high speed and thus escape the concentrated enemy defence.

To counter the above situation, the C.-in-C., Navy, intends to take the submarines out of the coastal areas for the present and to send type VII to the open ocean just west of the British Isles, and type IX in a rake formation along the great circle in the direction of America. His purpose in doing this is twofold: on the one hand he hopes that the submarines will be able to make successful surprise attacks in new regions with only slight defence opposition; on the other hand he wants to force the enemy to disperse their defence forces and thus to improve the submarine warfare conditions in the waters near the British coast. In conclusion the C.-in-C., Navy, points out how great our chances for successful submarine warfare would be now if we still had the Biscay ports.

6. *The C.-in-C., Navy*, discusses the Diesel oil situation of the Navy with the Chief, O.K.W.  He asks him to make available to the Navy 3,000 more tons of Diesel oil from the reserves of the O.K.W. for the first ten days of April, since otherwise the oil for equipping the submarines being made ready for action will not suffice.  *The Chief, O.K.W.*, promises to help as much as possible and will inform the C.-in-C., Navy, about the measures taken.

7. Coastal fortresses.—*The Chief, General Staff, Air*, reports to the Admiral on Special Duty with the C.-in-C., Navy, in answer to his inquiry, that supplies are still being shipped by air to the western fortresses. He points out, however, that this is possible only as long as the area around Stuttgart remains in our hands, and he therefore recommends that delivery of important supplies to be transported by air be expedited.

(signed) ADMIRAL ON SPECIAL DUTY.


Admiral on Special Duty with C.-in-C., Navy    Berlin, April 11, 1945

### CONFERENCE OF THE C.-IN-C., NAVY, WITH THE FUEHRER ON APRIL 10, 1945, AT 1730

1. Naval brigades.—In discussing the disarming of foreign troops attached to the German Army, *the C.-in-C., Navy*, reports that a total of 630,000 men in the Navy, including the crews of ships and vessels, have no small arms.  *The Chief of the O.K.W., Operations Staff*, states that he needs two naval battalions to replace the Georgian battalions in the Netherlands and to take over their weapons.  *The C.-in-C., Navy*, emphasises the importance of keeping the naval troops in the area of East Friesland, which lacks adequate protection, and the weapons are therefore needed there.  In view of this situation it is out of the question to transfer any naval troops to the Netherlands.  No decision is made with regard to this matter.

2. *The Fuehrer* wishes to know exactly whether on April 9, at the time of the German attack on the Hel Peninsula, the responsible Army command made the fullest possible use of the ships' artillery on the available sea forces by well co-ordinating and concentrating their fire.  *The C.-in-C., Navy*, remarks that he gave orders to comply unreservedly with all Army requests.  Due to lack of fuel the heavy ships had to withdraw to Swinemuende, and they cannot put to sea again until the fuel situation is clarified. (The investigation demanded by the Fuehrer is ordered at once.)

3. Air raids.—The enemy air raids on German harbours and submarine yards are discussed.  *The C.-in-C., Navy*, is of the opinion that they are the long-expected systematic raids against the German submarine bases. Since March 30, 24 submarines were sunk and 12 were damaged in harbours and shipyards.  Nine of those sunk were type XXI, 4 of which were to go into action in April.  *The C.-in-C., Navy*, reports, in addition, that as a result of these air raids the fleet has also suffered heavy losses: the pocket battleship Scheer capsized, cruiser Hipper was set on fire, the Emden was damaged.  This leave the pocket battleship Luetzow, the cruisers Prinz Eugen, Nuernberg, and the old battleship Schlesien for future actions.  The numerous Russian attacks on German naval forces at sea were almost entirely unsuccessful, on the other hand;

the Russians have shown themselves in general to be very inefficient in the operation of their air force against ships at sea. The Fuehrer calls attention to the fact that in the past as well, the losses suffered by the Navy were almost exclusively a result of enemy air attacks.

(signed) ADMIRAL ON SPECIAL DUTY.

Admiral on Special Duty with C.-in-C., Navy      Berlin, April 13, 1945

### CONFERENCE OF THE C.-IN-C., NAVY, WITH THE FUEHRER ON APRIL 12, 1945, AT 1700

1. Before the situation conference begins, *the C.-in-C., Navy*, has a private conference with the Fuehrer during which they discuss the following points:

(a) *The Fuehrer* agrees with the suggestion of the C.-in-C., Navy, that the latter go to North Germany near the coast in case the enemy forces evacuation of the Berlin area, since his tasks lie exclusively in that area.

(b) *The C.-in-C., Navy*, brings up the question of arming naval personnel in case the fuel shortage forces their ships out of action. All in all the Navy lacks small arms for 163,000 men. It is difficult to decide how to employ these men, for whom we can provide no arms, and to know what orders to give them. *The Fuehrer* states that he will try everything to furnish the necessary arms for the naval personnel to be employed on land.

2. Sea transport.—*The C.-in-C., Navy*, describes to the Fuehrer the transport situation in Hel and Pillau. Both places have become centres for enemy air attacks, and are also being shelled by enemy artillery. This has forced us to transfer a large part of our loading activities from the harbours to the roadsteads, making it impossible to transport tanks and vehicles of any kind out of the area of East Prussia. The C.-in-C., Navy, points out that the danger to supply shipments is in the harbours and not out at sea. He considers the reinforcement of the fighter escorts to be the only effective countermeasure. *The Chief, General Staff, Air*, reports in this connection that the airports in Samland, Bruesterort, and Neutief, are being bombarded by enemy artillery. A new airport north of Neuhaeuser, near Pillau, and an airstrip on the Hel Peninsula are therefore being constructed. Another group of fighters, Me109's, is to be transferred to Samland as soon as the airports can accommodate them. *The Fuehrer* confirms the request of the C.-in-C., Navy, and stresses the urgency of fulfilling it.

3. Fuel shortage.—Concerning the fuel situation of the Navy, *the C.-in-C., Navy*, reports that since the enemy has advanced to the Elbe, the Navy's fuel supplies coming from southern and central Germany have been cut off for the time being. This means that if we cannot re-open the traffic route soon, the Navy must depend on the supplies now at the coast. The consequences will be that submarines will be unable to operate after about April 20, and all supply traffic and all shipping will stop some time in April. The C.-in-C., Navy, asks that the bridges across the Elbe should not be blown up until the very last minute, so that this important line of transport will not be blocked for a long time. *The Fuehrer* agrees

with this request and he remarks that the Elbe must be considered a lifeline for the north German area and not as a defence line. All efforts must be made to liberate it once more.

4. U-boat campaign.—In connection with the report of a submarine which has returned from the Irish Sea, *the C.-in-C., Navy*, explains to the Fuehrer that the most important thing for the submarines operating around Great Britain is to change their positions as quickly as possible after every torpedo shot. After a submarine reveals itself by attacking, it takes about two hours for a strong defence to gather at that point; they release large numbers of depth-charges which can well prove fatal to the submarine. The submarine mentioned did not act according to this principle, was located by the defence, and damaged to such an extent that it had to break off the operation. With the new, fast type of submarine it will be easy to withdraw from the place where the torpedo was fired, and thus to escape the concentrated enemy defence.

5. *The C.-in-C., Navy*, asks the Chief, O.K.W., to order that the naval barges employed on the Elbe for coal and oil transport may under no circumstances be seized for storing ammunition, since such a procedure is very harmful to the transport of fuel for the Navy. The Chief, O.K.W., immediately issues a corresponding order.

6. *The C.-in-C., Navy*, receives a report via *Reichsleiter* Bormann concerning alleged insubordination at the 2nd Naval Infantry Division in Itzehoe. The complaint was made by the *Landrat* of Itzehoe. Upon investigation the report proved invalid. The C.-in-C., Navy, requests the *Reichsleiter* to take steps against the originator of the report.

(signed) ADMIRAL ON SPECIAL DUTY.

Admiral on Special Duty with C.-in-C., Navy     Berlin, April 15, 1945

### CONFERENCE OF THE C.-IN-C., NAVY, WITH THE FUEHRER ON APRIL 14, 1945, AT 1800

1. Baltic.—*The C.-in-C., Navy*, confirms to the Fuehrer the report made by the Admiral at Fuehrer Headquarters on April 13 that the 7th *Panzer* Division can probably be transferred from Hel to Swinemuende in five days. Whether the guns can be shipped depends on the prevailing weather conditions, and can be decided only by the responsible naval commanders on the spot.

2. Naval brigades.—During a report on the fighting of the 2nd Naval Infantry Division, *the C.-in-C., Navy*, informs the Fuehrer that the division still lacks artillery. According to the latest report, the heavy artillery section arrived at the division today. The other two sections are en route. Upon inquiry by the Fuehrer about the condition of the naval infantry divisions, the C.-in-C., Navy, states that except for the artillery at the 2nd Naval Infantry Division, which has still not all arrived, and the shortage of small arms at the 1st Naval Infantry Division, they are in good shape. He gives detailed figures on their strength. *The Fuehrer* says that because of their excellent manpower material he is considering removing at a later date the naval infantry divisions which are at the Eastern Front, since they have a purely defensive mission there, and assigning them to a task force which might be newly organised.

3. In reply to the Fuehrer's question of April 13 about whether renewed action by the Thiele task force in Samland is possible, *the C.-in-C., Navy*, states that such an assignment cannot be justified at present because of the fuel situation. For the sake of fuel it is necessary to concentrate on only one thing, in order to be able to carry out the indispensible tasks of supply and transport as long as possible. *The Fuehrer* approves this opinion.

4. Sea transport.—*The Chief of the Army General Staff* reports that the Navy was able to evacuate 157,270 wounded from the eastern theatre to the west between March 21 and April 10. He represents this as an unusual performance, which has relieved the situation of the Army High Command, East Prussia, to a very considerable degree.

5. Naval commandos.—*The C.-in-C., Navy*, reports to the Fuehrer that he probably will be in a position to make available 3,000 young men of the Navy, equipped with light packs and bazookas, to be used for fighting behind the enemy lines at the Western Front in order to harass enemy supply lines. *The Fuehrer* welcomes this offer; further details are to be clarified immediately with the proper authorities of the O.K.W.

(signed) ADMIRAL ON SPECIAL DUTY.


Admiral on Special Duty with C.-in-C., Navy      Berlin, April 17, 1945

### CONFERENCE OF THE C.-IN-C., NAVY, WITH THE FUEHRER ON APRIL 16, 1945, AT 1700

1. Eastern front.—During the discussion of the situation at Army Group, Vistula, *the C.-in-C., Navy*, reports to the Fuehrer that the Commanding General of Army Group, Vistula, General Heinrici, visited him in the afternoon of April 16. General Heinrici told him that only very few troops are holding the front at the lower Oder south of Stettin and that these troops, composed of emergency units and men who were separated from their units, are not of much value in action. The General believes that it is therefore of vital importance to withdraw one division from the southern sector of the Eastern Front, if this is at all possible, and to transfer it to the lower Oder. He asked the C.-in-C., Navy, to mention this at the Fuehrer conference. The C.-in-C., Navy, also reported that during one of his inspection trips to the front on April 15, the commanding officer of the 2nd Naval Infantry Division, Brigadier General Bleckwenn, assured him that every Russian attack will be repulsed in the sector of his division, and that he believes that the two divisions adjacent to his can also be relied upon. *The Fuehrer* replied that it is not possible to bring up another division and that it will be necessary to strengthen the Oder front by setting up a larger number of light anti-aircraft guns close to the river in order to ward off any enemy attempt to cross it. (This prompts the C.-in-C., Navy, to give orders that all light and medium anti-aircraft guns from warships and merchant vessels that are put out of commission shall be made available for land warfare at once, together with their officers and crew. If possible units are to be kept intact.)

2. Ammunition shortage.—*Gauleiter* Koch reported the existence of a serious shortage of anti-aircraft ammunition in Pillau. The Chief of the

Operations Staff, Air Force, reports that a certain amount of anti-aircraft ammunition is on the way, and that particularly in Warnemuende a considerable amount is ready for shipment. *The Fuehrer* wants to know whether the Navy can transport this ammunition to Pillau on a fast ship. *The C.-in-C., Navy*, replies that ammunition is being transported by fast vessels anyway; however, he will find out whether in this particular case special arrangements can be made in addition.

3. Man-power.—During the discussion of the situation in the area south of Uelzen *the Fuehrer* asks whether the Navy can spare personnel for our operations there. *The C.-in-C., Navy*, answers that while it is possible to make the men available, there are no weapons. It is also very difficult to find weapons for the 3,000 naval troops who are to carry on anti-tank warfare in the enemy's rear. The naval emergency units which are adequately equipped with weapons are at the front between the Weser and the Ems. Also all troops which it was possible to withdraw from the North Frisian coast and the Island of Sylt are being used to defend East Frisia. With regard to the question of attacking the enemy's supply lines, the C.-in-C., Navy, remarks that now, as in the past in France, the enemy's main problem is one of supplies. Therefore attacks on the enemy's supply lines would hit him in the most vulnerable spot.

4. *The C.-in-C., Navy*, and the Chief, O.K.W., discuss setting up the Operations Staff of Detached Command A under Major General Kinzel. This staff is to be set up as quickly as possible so that it will be in a position to direct operations when the time comes and will be able to hold the commands of the various forces in its area firmly together.

(signed) ADMIRAL ON SPECIAL DUTY.

Admiral on Special Duty with C.-in-C., Navy      Berlin, April 19, 1945

### CONFERENCE OF THE C.-IN-C., NAVY, WITH THE FUEHRER ON APRIL 18, 1945, AT 1730

1. Baltic.—During his report on the situation in Kurland, the Deputy Commanding General of the Kurland Army Group, Lt.-General Hilpert, requests reinforcement of the naval forces in this region to prevent enemy landings, which he fears may take place on the east and north coast of the Kurland peninsula. *The C.-in-C., Navy*, answers that, due to the acute fuel shortage and the lack of forces, the Navy is forced to concentrate strictly on its main tasks. These are to keep the most important routes in the Baltic and the Skagerrak open, to supply the Kurland Army Group and the Commanding General, East Prussia, and to carry out the most necessary transport of troops, refugees, and the wounded. Therefore the Navy is unable to send additional forces to the Kurland area.

2. In answer to the request of Lt.-General Hilpert also to provide a fighter escort based at Bornholm for supply convoys, *the Chief, Air Force Operations Staff*, reports that the airport of Bornholm will be ready about May 10, according to existing reports.

3. *The C.-in-C., Navy*, reports to the Fuehrer that he has ordered the establishment of an organisation which will instantly take over the crews of damaged and decommissioned ships so that they may be prepared for land fighting without delay.

4. *Defence of Berlin.*—It is reported that Minister Dr. Goebbels, in his capacity as Gauleiter of Berlin, has sent five *Volkssturm* battalions from the barracks to the Eastern Front east of Berlin. *The Fuehrer* considers it improper to send *Volkssturm* units, which are meant only for local employment, to the front lines, while large numbers of young soldiers are available in the Air Force and the Navy, and cannot be sent to the front merely because they lack arms. He orders that the Chief, Army General Staff, get in touch with the Air Force and the Navy in order to make the weapons used by the above *Volkssturm* battalions available to young soldiers.

5. Regarding the heavy air attack on Heligoland by several hundred planes at noon on April 18, *the C.-in-C., Navy*, states that in his opinion this attack was aimed against the submarine base at Heligoland; it could not very well be considered as a preparation for a landing in the German Bight, since it is unlikely that the enemy would attempt a landing there in view of the present situation on land.

6. In connection with the loss of several hundred persons in the sinking of the steamer Goya, *the C.-in-C., Navy*, points out that personnel losses in the transport in the eastern area up to this time have been extremely small, i.e. 0·49 per cent. These unfortunate losses seem large every time a ship is sunk, and it is easy to forget that at the same time a large number of ships with numerous wounded and refugees aboard reach port safely.

7. The more detailed reports on the damage done to the pocket battleship Luetzow show that here, as in the case of the Tirpitz, the special unit of British Lancaster planes with extremely heavy bombs was used. The raid occurred during the day at about 1700.

8. During the situation conference the C.-in-C., Navy, receives a request from the Commanding General, North-west, Field Marshal Busch, to bring up two naval emergency regiments from Kiel to reinforce the 2nd Naval Infantry Division. Investigation shows that these units are only inadequately supplied with Dutch rifles and have little ammunition, and are thus not suitable for front-line duty. In addition, they cannot be dispensed with as local security units in Kiel, which is overcrowded with foreign workers.

(signed) ADMIRAL ON SPECIAL DUTY.

*     *     *     *     *     *

This is the last conference of which there is a record in the German naval archives. Other documents, however, give a brief outline of the final stages of the war in Europe.

Allied troops pressed on into the centre of Germany, and the position of the *Wehrmacht* became hopeless. But Hitler, in his bunker in the *Reich* Chancellery in Berlin, hoped for a last-minute change and determined to stake everything on the defence of Berlin. To begin with, his orders and tactics still bore some relation to reality, but as the disorganisation in Germany increased and the Russians began to penetrate the outskirts of Berlin, Hitler's armies and air forces that he so diligently moved into action were nothing more than coloured pins on a map.

By April 26 Hitler's orders, even more unreal than before, had convinced Goering of his insanity, and, as second-in-command, Goering attempted to take over the leadership of the *Reich*. Hitler raged and ordered the immediate capture and execution of Goering. He was relieved of his command over the *Luftwaffe* and replaced by General Ritter von Greim.

Worse was to follow when, two days later, a press report stated that Himmler six days previously had sued for peace with Great Britain and the U.S.A. To Hitler it seemed as if he was surrounded by traitors, and early on the morning of April 29 he ordered Bormann to send the following signal to Doenitz:

To: C.-in-C., Navy                                    Time: 0325/29

Foreign Press reports a new treason. The Fuehrer expects you to take immediate and decisive action against all traitors in North Germany. Without discrimination. Schoerner, Wenck, and others must prove their loyalty to the Fuehrer by coming to the Fuehrer's aid as soon as possible.

BORMANN.

On the afternoon of the same day (April 29) the Russian encirclement of Berlin cut all the communications of the Reich Chancellery, except the radio link with the German naval headquarters. When Hitler rose (he used to sleep from 5 or 6 a.m. until noon) there was no information available for the usual afternoon situation conference. The following signal was sent:

To: C.-in-C., Navy                                    Time: 1602/29

All outside contacts with army positions cut. Urgently request over Naval W/T wave, information concerning the battle outside Berlin.

Adm. Fuehrer H.Q.

There is no record of the reply, if any was sent, but by then the Russians were drawing steadily closer to the centre of Berlin, and three hours later Hitler sent this hysterical signal via the Naval radio link:

To: *Generaloberst* Jodl                              Time: 1952/29

Inform me immediately:

    (1) Where are Wenck's spearheads?
    (2) When are they going to attack?
    (3) Where is the 9th Army?
    (4) In which direction is the 9th Army breaking through?
    (5) Where are Holste's spearheads?

ADOLF HITLER.

Nothing more was heard from Hitler. On the following day, April 30, he committed suicide with Eva Braun, and was followed by Goebbels and his family.

Doenitz at first did not know what had happened, but late that evening he received the following signal from the Admiral on Special Duty:

To: C.-in-C., Navy                          Message received at 2310, 30.4.45

*Reichsleiter* Bormann sent the following message:

(1) In the place of the former *Reichsmarschall* Goering the Fuehrer appointed you, *Herr Grossadmiral,* as his successor. Written authority is on the way. From now on, you are to order all measures arising from the present situation.

(2) Inform State Secretary Steenbracht immediately. He is to proceed to the north with a small staff.

Admiral on Special Duty.

Doenitz assumed his new position as Chancellor of the German *Reich* on May 1, and decided to make peace as rapidly as possible. He wanted to prevent as many Germans as he could from falling into the hands of the Russians, but Himmler's abortive efforts had shown clearly that a unilateral armistice with the Western Allies was out of the question. Doenitz still hoped, however, to be able to bargain with the Allies, and disposed his forces accordingly.

To: Naval Staff, *Luftwaffe,* and C.-in-C., North-west          Date: 2.5.45

The *Grossadmiral* has ordered:

(1) Hamburg is not to be defended. The troops are to be moved out of the city into the area north of Hamburg and, to avoid the threatened bombardment of the city, this fact is to be reported to the enemy by an officer with a flag of truce.

(2) In order to gain time, the battle is to be continued throughout the whole area of C.-in-C., North-west. A surprise break-through on and over the Kaiser Wilhelm Canal must be prevented, so as to give the German Government sufficient time to negotiate with Montgomery over North-west Germany. With this in view, Kaiser Wilhelm Canal is to be defended with all available forces under a unified command. The bridges are not to be destroyed. All forces withdrawing from Denmark are to be disembarked north of the canal and used in the defence of the Canal. Kiel is to be included in the defence of the Kaiser Wilhelm Canal.

JODL.

This scheme was not successful, and on May 4 negotiations were begun in earnest, while efforts were made at the same time to extricate the forces on the Eastern Front.

To: Kesselring and Winter　　　　　　　　　　　　　　　Date: 4.5.45

*General Feldmarschall* Kesselring and Lt.-General Winter:

You are authorised to conclude an armistice with the 6th American Army for the troops on the Western Front between Boehmerwald and the upper Inn. In this it must be made clear how far eastwards the Anglo-American forces intend to advance. We must thereby create the conditions for the escape of Army Groups *Loer*, *Redulic*, and *Schoerner*. Negotiations concerning latter remain in the hands of the Supreme Commander of the *Wehrmacht*.

The 7th Army is to be placed under Schoerner.

Winter's staff must escape into that area not affected by the armistice.

DOENITZ.

The Allies, however, would accept nothing except unconditional surrender, and on May 7 arrangements were made for complete capitulation.

To: All　　　　　　　　　　　　　　　　　　　　　　　Date: 7.5.45

Situation at 2000, 7.5.45.

　7.5. Provisional signing of capitulation at Rheims.
　8.5. General Keitel, General Stumpff, and Admiral Friedeburg sign the complete unconditional surrender. Thereafter, peace on all fronts as from 0000, 9.5.45.　　　　　　　　　　　　C.-IN-C., NAVY.

Two days before the surrender Doenitz, through his newly appointed Foreign Minister, Count Schwerin von Krosigk, had begun negotiations with Japan, but, as the following exchange of telegrams shows, neither country would accept responsibility for ending the Three-Power Pact, and the situation was left in mid-air.

Coded W/T message to Naval Attaché, Tokio,　　　　　　Date: 5.5.45
　for Ambassador Stahmer

Please convey my heartiest greetings to the Japanese Foreign Minister and give him this message:

Up to the last minute, the Fuehrer believed that through a military success in the decisive battle for Berlin, he could bring about the turning point in this war. For these beliefs he gave his life and died a hero's death in battle. After the adverse outcome of the battle for Berlin, the war must be considered militarily lost. Considering the complete exhaustion of the German power of resistance, it has become impossible to carry on the war and thereby continue to fulfil the obligations of our alliance with Japan.

To avoid further useless sacrifice and to maintain the substance of the German people, the German High Command considers itself compelled to enter into discussions—not yet concluded—with the Western Allies with a view to an armistice.

I ask you to inform the Foreign Minister that I deeply regret that one of my first duties as German Foreign Minister should be to have to send this communication to the Government of allied and friendly Japan. Without prejudice to the tragic outcome of this war, the German people and its Government will follow Japan's future with great interest and in the spirit of that indestructible German-Japanese friendship which is sealed by blood spilt in a common cause. We shall not give up hope that, in the interests of world peace and the welfare of all peoples, the just claim of the German and Japanese peoples to an honourable and secure future will eventually meet with success.

As far as is possible we shall keep the Japanese Government informed of the further developments in our affairs.

GRAF SCHWERIN VON KROSIGK.

Coded telegram from Tokio to German Foreign Minister      Date: 10.5.45

In accordance with instructions I contacted the Japanese Foreign Minister and gave him your message.  Foreign Minister Togo took cognisance of my statement and the compliments of the German Foreign Minister.  He said that the Japanese people had followed with great admiration the German fight to the last and the death of the Fuehrer.  The Japanese Government, however, must consider that the German Government, in commencing capitulation proceedings with the British and Americans without notifying the Japanese Government, desires to withdraw from the Military Alliance of December 11, 1941.  He asked me for written confirmation of this view.  I replied that I could not do this because, from the telegram, I only understood that we were no longer in a position to carry on the war, but that the Three-Power Pact and Military Alliance also provided for political and economical co-operation.  I also pointed out that the German Foreign Minister particularly stressed the desire of the German Government to cease hostilities with the Soviet Union.  I got the impression that the Japanese Foreign Minister wishes to release Japan from her alliance with Germany, but wants to push the responsibility and initiative for this on to Germany.  The Japanese Press confirms this impression.  In the last few days it has become very unfriendly towards Germany and has been drawing comparisons with the Badoglio regime.  In my opinion we must word our communications to Japan in such a way that we merely stress the impossibility of continuing the fight, but we must leave the Japanese to make the decision with regard to dissolution of the Three-Power Pact and Military Alliance, and possibly the breaking off of diplomatic relations.

In conclusion, it is significant that the attitude of the Japanese Army towards Germany is, so far, unaltered.  Request instructions by return.

STAHMER.

The dissolution of the Axis was the end of Germany's power.

Unlike their earlier victims, the German Government made no attempt to continue the fight from Japan or elsewhere.  The much-vaunted "*Werewolf*" organisation of Goebbels was only a bubble of opposition, easily pricked by the occupying armies, and no belligerent Nazi regime appeared in any other corner of the world.

Germany suffered total military defeat, and there was no possibility of ascribing that defeat to anything except military conquest.  The German Army, the *Luftwaffe*, and the German Navy were severally and jointly beaten by the Allies.  The revolt of July 20 was squashed long before the end, and there were, in fact, no revolutions and no mutinies to make possible any future sophistry about the "unconquerable" *Wehrmacht*.  Hitler's policy of world conquest or national suicide ensured that defeat, when it came, would be complete.  Germany paid in full the price of dictatorship.

Of the German Navy, 156 U-boats surrendered to the Allies, while a further 221 were either scuttled or destroyed by their crews.  Of the two remaining modern ships of her fleet, the Prinz Eugen was sunk during the atom bomb tests at Bikini, while the Nuernberg was given to Soviet Russia.  The auxiliaries, minesweepers, etc., were manned by German crews, and, under the orders of the British Admiralty, cleared minefields and harbours, sweeping up the litter of war.

But the final act was not staged until nearly two years after the war, when, on April 18, 1947, the fortifications of the naval base at Heligoland were destroyed and the German Navy came to an end.

# GLOSSARY

*Achse.*   Code name for the measures to be taken by the Navy in the event Italy declared a separate armistice.   See *Schwarz.*

*Alberich.*   Submarine anti-sonar rubber coatings.   The submarine hull was covered with rubber or buna foil in order to prevent detection when submerged.

*Amtsleiter.*   Functional title of certain higher officials in the administrative units of the Nazi Party.

*Aphrodite.*   Radar Decoy Balloon (RDB).   A submarine device to confuse enemy planes; it has reflective reaction similar to the conning tower of a submarine.

ARMY GROUP E.   Germany Army Group in southern Balkans and the Aegean Sea.

ARMY GROUP H.   This Army Group appeared in Western Europe in the autumn of 1944.   It controlled the armies in Holland and was subordinate to Army Group D.   It was commanded by General Kurt Student.

*ASV-Flugzeug.*   Allied aircraft which detected enemy ships and surfaced submarines by means of an "Air to Surface Vessel" radar set.

*Atlantik-Sender.*   A British radio station that specialised in German-language propaganda broadcasts.

*Attila.*   Code name for the occupation of unoccupied France.

AUROL SUBMARINE.   A turbine-driven submarine named after the fuel used. Power to operate the turbines was obtained by the decomposition of Aurol, a hydrogen peroxide fuel.

*Barbarossa.*   Code word for the invasion of the Soviet Union.

*Baurat.*   Civil servant engaged in construction engineering.   This is a high civil service rating.

*Beowulf.*   Code name for the occupation of the islands in the eastern Baltic Sea.

*Berghof.*   Name of Hitler's mountain retreat near Berchtesgaden, Bavaria.

BERLIN DEVICE (Fug 224).   The German counterpart of Allied radar gear (see "Rotterdam device").   It was an airborne radar set utilised for blind bombing and as a navigational aid.   A modified version of the Berlin device was in use on submarines.

BF109.   Same as Me109.   The *Bayerische Flugzeugwerke* was superseded by the Messerschmitt firm.

*Biber.*   A 6·2-ton one-man midget submarine, the smallest type ever built by the Germans.   It had an overall length of 28·5 feet, a diving depth of 30 metres, and was armed with two torpedoes.   Deliveries began in May 1944 and lasted until November of the same year.   The *Biber* was designed to operate from any open coast.

BLACK SUBMARINE (*schwarzes U-boot*).   Coating of rubberised or porous material on the hull of a submarine to prevent detection by anti-submarine devices.

BODY, THE.   Refers to Mussolini in connection with operation *Eiche.*

BOOMERANG ATTACKS.   German designation for an Allied method of night precision bombing.

BORMANN.   Martin Bormann performed the duties of Deputy Fuehrer, even though the office of Deputy to the Fuehrer had been abolished after Hess's flight in 1941.   He was also Chief of the Nazi Party Chancellory, and a member of the important Ministers' Council for the Defence of Germany. Towards the end of the war he became one of the most powerful men in Germany.

BROEKING SUBMARINE.   No additional information is available on this submarine. An electrical engineer engaged in submarine construction, Fritz Broeking, held the rank of Rear-Admiral in the German Navy.   Possibly the same as the Electro submarine.

CENTRAL PLANNING, COMMITTEE FOR.   An agency exercising government controls over national economy, armament, and war industries, prices, labour, construction, and utilities.   It was headed by Goering.

*Cerebus.*   Code name for the operation involving the transfer of the Scharnhorst, Gneisenau, and Prinz Eugen through the Channel in February 1942.

COCKERILL.   Shipbuilding firm, John Cockerill S.A., Hoboken-Antwerp.

*Commando Supremo.* Italian High Command.

CRUISER "L." The German cruiser Luetzow. Sold to the U.S.S.R. in an uncompleted state under the naval clause of the Russo-German Pact of 1939. Towed to Leningrad late in 1940, was to be completed there with the help of German technicians.

DANUBE MONITORS (*Donaumonitore*). Collective name for new and converted vessels of German, Hungarian, Roumanian, and Bulgarian nationality which were used on the Danube and later in the Black Sea as patrol units, anti-aircraft vessels, and minesweepers.

DEPUTY FOR THE FOUR YEARS' PLAN. Goering, who was appointed to this office, exercised control over every aspect of German economic life.

DEPUTY FOR THE GERMAN ECONOMY. This office was held by Funk, who was also Minister of Economics. In his capacity as Deputy for the German Economy he was appointed by and subordinate to Goering.

*Deschimag.* *Deschimag* stands for *Deutsche Schiff- und Maschinenbau Aktien-Gesellschaft* (German Shipyard and Machine Building Corporation). This company was one of the leading German shipbuilding firms. It owned shipyards at Bremen and Wesermuende.

DETACHED COMMAND A. A command formed for the purpose of directing operations in northern Germany in the event an Anglo-American-Russian junction severed communications between northern and southern Germany.

DM-MINE (*Druckmagnet-mine*). A mine equipped with a combined pressure unit and magnetic firing device.

*Eiche.* Code name for the operation to liberate Mussolini. The Air Forces were to be under the command of General Student who was later put in complete charge of the operation; the Naval Forces were to be under Vice-Admiral Ruge.

ELECTRO SUBMARINE (*elektro-U-Boot*). Believed to be the interim name of a type in which the electric drive was increased by additional batteries.

*Falke.* T-4 acoustic homing torpedo. Was to be used against vessels proceeding at more than 8 knots.

*Felix.* Code word for a proposed operation involving the conquest of Gibraltar, and the establishment of German naval bases on the Canary Islands, and at selected points along the Spanish coast. Spain was expected to aid in the execution of this plan.

*Feuerstein* GROUP. An alpine combat team made up of elements of the Second German Mountain Division under the command of Lieutenant-General Valentin Feuerstein. This force had orders to advance northward across roadless mountain terrain from the area of Bodo, to bring relief to the beleaguered German forces in the vicinity of Narvik.

FK WEAPONS (*Fernlenkoerper?*). Guided missile, i.e. V-1's and V-2's.

*Fliegerdivision* 7 (7th Airborne Division). This division of parachute troops was the only one of its kind attached to the Air Force. All the other parachute troops were under the command of the Army.

*FuMB* (*Funkmessbeobachtungsgeraet*). Radar interception set. Warns against enemy radar location. Also known as a radar search receiver.

*FuMG* (*Funkmessgeraet*). Radar location finding set.

G7a, G7e. Designation of German naval torpedoes, 7 metres in length and 534 millimetres (21 inches) in diameter. G7a was air driven; G7e was electrically driven.

*G7e Lut.* A G7e torpedo with a *Lut* mechanism. See *Lut.*

*Gauleiter.* Leader of one of the 42 Nazi Party administrative regions. See *Reichsstatthalter.*

GERMAN COMMITTEE. Refers to the National Free German Committee sponsored by the Russians. Field Marshal von Paulus, captured at Stalingrad, became a member of the committee in August 1944.

*Gisela.* Code name of the operation which proposed the occupation of the northern coast of Spain by German forces.

*Gotenkopf.* Rear positions to be constructed by Minister Speer's personnel on the Kuban Peninsula. The positions were designed to protect the Kerch Strait and keep open the sea routes to the Crimea as a result of the fall of Novorossisk to the Russian forces.

*Hagenuk* DEVICE.    A device that replaced the Metox.    See *Metox*.

*Hauptamtsleiter* SAUR.    Karl Otto Saur was head of the Technical Bureau (*Amt Technik*) in Speer's Ministry of Armaments and War Production.    As such he had extensive powers over the German and German-controlled heavy industries, especially the iron and steel industries.    His title of *Hauptamtsleiter* denotes a function in the Nazi Party, not in the German government service.

*Hauptdienstleiter*.    High administrative rank in the Nazi Party.

*Hornisse*.    Code name for a bomb-proof submarine sub-assembly shelter under construction at the Deschimag Shipyard in Bremen.

HYDROFOIL BOAT.    An unusually fast speedboat of revolutionary design.    Wing-like surfaces called hydrofoils permitted this boat to skim over the water, thus reducing hydrodynamic resistance to a minimum.    Only a very small number were actually built.

HYDROGENATION PLANT.    This refers to the production of motor fuels by the hydrogenation and liquefaction of coal, whereby pulverised coal is treated with hydrogen under high pressure.

*Ikarus*.    Code word for the proposed occupation of Iceland.

*J.K.H.(R) (Jagd Kanonen Haubitze, Russisch).*    A Russian or Russian-type gun used by the Germans.

*K.F.K. (Kriegsfischerkutter).*    Usually a converted vessel.    An armed converted trawler, fishing smack, or cutter used chiefly for escort and patrol duties and sometimes for minesweeping.

K.M.D., KMD-ORGANISATION.    *Organisation der Kriegsmarinedienststellen.*    The Organisation of Naval Stations was established by the Naval Staff to assure fullest use of naval and merchant transports.    Privately owned shipping firms were represented in the organisation.

*Koralle*.    Name of a Navy camp located at Bernau, a short distance north-east of Berlin.    In 1944 the C.-in-C., Navy, much of the Naval Staff, and other sections of the Naval High Command had their headquarters there.

*KT-Schiffe*.    War transports (*Kriegstransportschiffe*).    These were cargo vessels averaging about 800 tons in size and carrying a cargo of 350 to 400 tons.

KUEPFMUELLER.    Professor Kuepfmueller was head of the Scientific Staff of the German Navy (*Wissenschaftlicher Fuehrungsstab der Kriegsmarine*).

*KUJ (KriegsU-Jaeger).*    Also called *U-Jaeger*.    Anti-submarine vessels or sub-chasers.

*Kurische Nehrung*.    A long narrow tongue of land off the northern part of East Prussia separating the Kurisches Haff from the Baltic Sea.

GROUP *Landwirt*.    A group of German submarines standing by in the Bay of Biscay in June 1944 to prevent an invasion of France from that direction.

*Lut (Lageunabhaengigkeitstorpedo).*    A torpedo equipped with the Lut course-setting mechanism was constructed so as to run straight ahead for a pre-determined distance.    It would then start on a pattern run, proceeding on a previously selected mean course.    This arrangement enabled the submarine to attack from virtually any position.

*MAL (Marineartillerieleichter).*    Naval coast artillery lighter.

*Marder*.    A one-man torpedo consisting of a mother torpedo with a live torpedo underslung.    Two versions of *Marder* were in existence.    *Marder I*, a surface runner, was practically identical with *Neger* (*q.v.*), while *Marder II* was capable of submerging to a depth of 30 metres.

*Marita*.    Code name for the invasion of Greece.

*Mausi (Mausiflugzeug).*    Aircraft rigged with a device which enabled detonation of magnetic mines.    The Ju52 was the most common type of plane used for this purpose.

*M-Boot (Minensuchboot).*    Also referred to as *MS. Boot*.    A mine-searching and minesweeping vessel powered by Diesel engines.    It differed from an *R-Boote* in that the latter, a motor minesweeper, was powered by a gasoline engine.

MERCATOR SUBMARINES.    A group of ex-Italian transport submarines, their official designations being U It 21–25.    These boats, which had a carrying-capacity of 150 tons each, were engaged in commerce with the Japanese-dominated Far East. They were taken over by the Germans after the capitulation of Italy.

*Merkur.* Code name for the occupation of Crete.

*Metox.* A search receiver found to be dangerous to submarines using it because of re-radiation. Increased losses in U-boats led to the testing of all *Metox* devices. Only those found free of re-radiation were installed.

MFP (*Marinefaehrprahm*). Multi-purpose vessel similar to the American LCT. Had an average displacement of 300 tons. Used as munitions carrier (*Munitionsfaehrprahm*), landing craft, naval transport, artillery transport barge (*Artilleriefaehrprahm*), small troop transport, etc.

MINE CLEARANCE VESSELS. Various types of vesesls were used to seek, locate, sweep, and explode enemy mines. In this category fall the *M-Boote, R-Boote, Minenraeumschiffe, Sperrbrecher, MZ-Boote,* etc. They are commonly translated as minesweepers, mine-detonating or exploding vessels, mine-clearance vessels, anti-mine vessels, etc. For example, there are times when an *M-Boot* is unable to clear certain mines; a larger or more specialised vessel would then be called in to clear or sweep them.

*Ministerialdirektor.* Administrative officials holding high positions in a ministry. The *Ministerialdirektor* was immediately subordinate to an Under Secretary (*Staatssekretaer*) and was the head of a department (*Abteilung*). Subordinate to him were officials holding the rank of *Ministerialdirigent* and *Ministerialrat*.

*Ministerialdirektor* DORSCH. Xaver Dorsch was one of the most outstanding engineers of the Todt Organisation and its responsible head since 1942.

*Ministerialdirigent.* High-ranking member of the German civil service.

*Ministerialrat.* High civil service rating in Germany. The *Ministerialrat* worked under a Divisional Chief in a German ministry as a special assistant adviser, associate, or in similar capacity.

*MNL* (*Marinenachschubleichter*). Naval supply lighter, barge, small transport, etc.

*Mohr.* A small battle weapon, known to have been in the developmental stage in February–March 1944. It seems to have resembled the *Neger* and *Marder*. Information about this weapon is very scanty and no particulars are available at present. See "One-man torpedo."

*MZ-Boot.* Apparently one of the smaller mine-clearance craft.

*Nashorn* MINEFIELDS. A system of anti-submarine mine barriers, designed to keep Russian submarines from breaking out into the Baltic. It extended across the Gulf of Finland from the vicinity of the island of Nargen on the Estonian side to the area of Porkalla on the Finnish side.

*Neger.* A one-man torpedo consisting of two 21-inch electric torpedoes, one secured above the other and about 6 inches apart. The lower one was the live torpedo. The *Neger* was the first type of one-man torpedo to be used in action. See "One-man torpedo."

*NEK* (*Nachrichtenmittelerprobungskommando*). A naval unit which tests communications equipment. It should not be confused with *NVK* (*Nachrichtenmittelversuchskommando*), Communications Equipment Experimental Command.

NINA GUNS. "Nina" was the nickname (cf. "Big Bertha") given to the 30·5-cm. rapid fire gun L/40.

*Nordlicht.* Code name for the evacuation of German troops from northern Finland and northern Norway after the Finnish capitulation.

NORTHERN ROUTE. The difficult passage along the northern coast of Russia and Siberia, thence through the Bering Straits into the Pacific Ocean. Russian co-operation enabled the German auxiliary cruiser Komet (ship "45") to use this route on the way out to her operational area in the Pacific. The German code word for this operation was *Fall Gruen*.

*N-Stoff.* An igniting and incendiary agent (*Zuendstoff and Verbrennungsbeschleuniger*). The Walter firm in Kiel experimented with this substance in 1942.

*Oberregierungsrat.* High civil service administrative official, usually in charge of an administrative department.

*Obersalzberg.* Name of a mountain near Berchtesgaden, Bavaria, where Hitler had his mountain retreat, the *Berghof*.

ONE-MAN TORPEDO. The one-man torpedo consisted of an upper part, the carrier, with either one or two explosive torpedoes attached to its bottom. Originally the carrier and the explosive torpedoes were of equal size and shape, the carrier being, in fact, a converted torpedo itself. In later models the carrier was of special construction and developed into something like a midget submarine. The pilot, seated in the carrier, steered the device close enough to the target to make a hit probable. He would then release the explosive torpedo by means of an electro-magnetic mechanism. Several types, such as *Marder I* (probably identical with *Neger*), *Marder II*, *Molch*, and *Seeteufel* were developed in 1944 and 1945.

OPERATION *Gelb*. Code name for the invasion of Holland and Belgium.

ORGANISATION KALTENBRUNNER. Dr. Ernst Kaltenbrunner was in charge of Himmler's Central Reich Security Office (*Reichssicherheitshauptamt*). In mid-summer 1944 this organisation assumed control of the bulk of the intelligence organisation of the Armed Forces, the new intelligence service thus formed being known under the name of *Militaerisches Amt*.

*Pendel Peilung*. Direction finding method.

PQ. Designation of convoys proceeding eastward from the United Kingdom to northern Russia. Convoys were usually numbered, e.g. PQ 17, PQ 18, etc. See " QP," *Roesselsprung*.

PROPAGANDA COMPANY. Under the Nazi system propaganda formed an integral part of warfare. Propaganda personnel were given full military training and organised as a branch of the armed service. German propaganda companies consisted mainly of reporters and cameramen. These men were the only ones authorised to do front-line reporting, which was their main function. They also conducted propaganda addressed to the enemy as well as to the German troops. Special teams were often assigned to cover operations of news interest.

QP. Designation of convoys returning to the United Kingdom from northern Russia.

*Reichsfuehrer S.S.* Title of Heinrich Himmler in his capacity as chief of the S.S.

*Reichsleiter*. The highest rank in the Nazi Party. The individuals holding this rank formed the highest executive board of the Nazi Party. Most of them also held high positions in the *Reich* government.

*Reichsmarschall*. *Der Reichsmarschall* was a rank created especially for Goering. No other person in Germany held this military title.

*Reichsstatthalter*. Representatives of the Central Reich Authority in various German areas. Selected by the Fuehrer. In many instances identical with with Nazi Party district leaders (*Gauleiter*).

REPLACEMENT ARMY. The German Army was divided into the Field Army (*Feldheer*) and the Replacement Army (*Ersatzheer*). Each major unit in the Field Army had a counterpart of smaller size in the Replacement Army; this affiliated replacement unit was charged with training replacements for its parent unit so as to keep the latter up to regulation strength at all times. Due to the gradual depletion of German manpower, this system became more and more diluted during the war, but was never changed fundamentally. After July 1944 the Replacement Army was under the command of Heinrich Himmler.

REPLACEMENT RESERVES (*Ersatzreservisten*). Untrained reserves.

*Rheinuebung*. Code name for the Atlantic operation of Bismarck and Prinz Eugen, resulting in the sinking of the Bismarck.

*Roesselsprung*. Code name for the operation which resulted in the annihilation of convoy PQ 17. See "PQ."

ROTTERDAM DEVICE. German code name for the Allied radar gear used for high altitude bombing and as a navigational aid.

*Safari*. Code name for measures to be taken against the Danish Government if it refused to make political and economic concessions to Germany. When the Danish Government refused to declare a state of siege, impose the death sentence for strikes and sabotage, and censor its press, the Germans imposed martial law, arrested the King, cabinet members, most of the officers of the armed forces, and other leaders. When the seizure of the Danish Fleet was attempted, Danish sailors scuttled their ships or brought them into Swedish ports.

SAUCKEL. As Commissioner General for the Mobilisation of Labour, Fritz Sauckel was in charge of the allocation and mobilisation of labour in the interest of the German war effort.

*Scheer.* Operation *Scheer,* or *Wunderland,* was the code name for attacks by the pocket battleship Scheer on Russian ships and naval installations in the Arctic Ocean, August 16–30, 1942.

*Schnorchel.* An extensible intake-exhaust tube which, when upright (attached to the side of the conning tower), enabled the submarine to use its Diesel engines although almost completely submerged. The only portion of the submarines exposed was the top of the tube, and this was usually covered with an anti-radar material.

*Schwaemme.* An anti-radar material. Literal meaning: sponges.

*Schwarz.* Code name for measures to be taken by the Army in the event Italy declared a separate armistice. See *Achse.*

*SE-Aktion.* The second *SE-Aktion* was one of several special drafts for the armed forces. War workers in deferred categories were called to military service.

*Sea Lion.* See *Seeloewe.*

*Seehund.* A two-man midget submarine carrying two torpedoes. It was 38·9 feet in length, and displaced about 15 tons submerged.

*Seeloewe.* Code name of the operation for the invasion of England. The *Seeloewe* coastal sector was the strip along the Channel facing England and Wales.

*Seeloewe-Penischen.* Auxiliary vessels, probably French *peniches,* which were massed on the Channel Coast for use in connection with the invasion of Great Britain in 1940.

SIEBEL PROJECT. A project calling for the rapid development and construction of self-propelled craft to be used in the invasion of England. It was named after Colonel Siebel of the German Air Force, the officer directing it. The organisation set up for this purpose was known as Special Command Siebel (*Sonderkommando Siebel*).

*Siebelfaehre* (Siebel ferries). Multi-purpose supply and troop carriers built by the Siebel firm.

*Skl. Seekriegsleitung:* the German Naval Staff. 1/*Skl* was the Operations Division of the Naval Staff.

SMALL BATTLE UNITS. Collective term for a great variety of small attack craft such as one-man torpedoes, midget submarines, one-man and two-man assault boats, explosive motor boats, etc.

*Sperrbrecher.* Anti-mine naval unit. Mine-detonating or exploding vessel. Mine-clearance vessel. Most of the *Sperrbrecher* were converted from other types, i.e. old war vessels and merchantmen. They were of no fixed size and were considered expendable. Similar vessels were used as block ships.

*Sperrverband.* A unit formed with the specific purpose of blocking the Allied advance into Germany. Many such units were formed in the latter part of 1944.

*S.S-Verfuegungstruppen.* Original name of the *Waffen-S.S.,* the military branch of the S.S. The name indicated that they were held at the disposition of Hitler for any purpose whatever. The *Verfuegungstruppen* took part in the occupation of Austria and Czechoslovakia side by side with troops of the Army. They were subsequently formed into regular military units.

*Staatsrat* BLOHM. A member of the shipbuilding firm Blohm & Voss, Hamburg. The title of *Staatsrat* (State Councillor) was bestowed upon him in 1933 by the government of the Free City of Hamburg.

*Staatssekretaer.* An Under Secretary of a ministry. He was immediately subordinate to the minister.

*Steilheitsschaltung (A* 105 *mit Steilheitsschaltung).* Exact meaning of this term is not at present known. It is a component of the acoustic firing unit A 105. Mine experts suggest that it may be a grid plate bias switch or a rate of change firing mechanism.

*Student.* Code name for the operation to re-establish the Fascist Party in Italy following Mussolini's resignation and arrest. It tied in closely with operation *Eiche,* which Student, an Air Force General, was to command.

*Supermarina.* The Italian Admiralty.

*Tanne Ost.*   Code name for the proposed occupation of the island of Hogland in the Gulf of Finland.

TARVISIO.   Town in the Province of Venezia, Italy, near the border of Austria.

*Thetis.*   Radar decoy spar buoy (RDSB).   Submarine device to confuse enemy surface search gear by giving "false fixes."

TMC MINES.   Torpedo mines, Type C.   Torpedo mines were mines ejected through the torpedo tubes of a submarine.   Three different varieties, TMA, TMB, and TMC, are known.

TODT ORGANISATION.   A construction organisation, named after the founder, which built the German super-highways, the West Wall, and the Atlantic fortifications.   It employed domestic and foreign labour on military projects both in Germany and in the occupied countries.

TORPEDO MINES.   Torpedo mines were mines ejected through the torpedo tubes of a submarine.

*Torpedoanzeigergeraet.*   A torpedo tracking device abroad surface vessels which indicated the approach of torpedoes.

*Torpedoboot (T-Boot).*   Torpedo boat; a small destroyer type, 600 to 800 tons.

TYPE VII C.   A 500-ton sea-going submarine.   It was 67·1 metres (221·43 feet) in length, had Diesel-electric propulsion, and was armed with four bow tubes and one stern tube.

TYPE IX C.   A 740-ton ocean-going submarine.   It was 76·76 metres (237·18 feet) in length, had Diesel-electric propulsion, and was armed with four bow tubes and two stern tubes.

TYPE XXI.   A long-range ocean-going submarine.   It was 245 feet in length, prefabricated.   It had a well streamlined hull, and was capable of great underwater speed.   It had normal (Diesel-electric) submarine propulsion.   Some boats of this type served as transport submarines.

TYPE XXIII.   A short-range coastal submarine, 100 feet in length, prefabricated, and capable of great underwater speed.   It carried only two torpedoes.   Type XXIII was a smaller version of Type XXI, both types having been developed simultaneously and under the same direction.

VALUABLE OBJECT.   Reference to Mussolini in connection with operation *Eiche*.

*Wallenstein.*   *Wallenstein* was the code signal notifying the German Fleet that the Allied invasion of Europe had begun.

*Walter* or *Walther*.   Name mentioned frequently in the Fuehrer Conferences. Refers to several submarine types whose special characteristics were: (1) the addition of a turbine drive to the usual Diesel and electric propulsions; (2) the fuel (*T-stoff*) consisted of oxygen derived from the decomposition of hydrogen peroxide by the platinum technique; (3) a streamlined hull which enabled the submarine to proceed very rapidly under water.   There were *Walter* submarines proposed or in production, of varying sizes and designed for coastal, sea-going, and ocean-going use.

*Weseruebung.*   Code word for the invasion of Denmark and Norway.

WEST WALL.   A system of mine barrages in the North Sea and off the coast of Norway.   Geographically it constituted an extension of the West Wall fortifications on land.

*Wuerzburggeraet.*   A radar device which reported approaching enemy aircraft and perhaps directed fire control of anti-aircraft batteries.   These devices were used by Air Corps Signal Troops (*Luftnachrichtentruppen*).

*Wunderland.*   See *Scheer*.

*Zaunkoenig.*   T-5 (*Zaunkoenig I*) and T-11 (*Zaunkoenig II*) acoustic homing torpedoes.   Improved models of the *Falke* (T-4).   The *Zaunkoenig* was intended for use against convoy escort vessels or those proceeding at a speed between 8 and 18 knots.   The anti-destroyer torpedo (*Zerstoererknacker*) was also called *Zaunkoenig*.

Z PLAN.   Long-term ship construction programme of the German Navy, covering the period from 1939 to 1945.   It was suspended upon the outbreak of war.